INTRODUCTION TO
THE NEW TESTAMENT
IN THE ORIGINAL GREEK

INTRODUCTION TO
THE NEW TESTAMENT
IN THE ORIGINAL GREEK

WITH NOTES ON SELECTED READINGS

B. F. WESTCOTT   AND   F. J. A. HORT

HENDRICKSON
PUBLISHERS
PEABODY, MASSACHUSETTS 01961-3473

INTRODUCTION TO THE NEW TESTAMENT
IN THE ORIGINAL GREEK

Hendrickson Publishers, Inc. edition

ISBN: 0-913573-94-9

reprinted from the edition
originally published by Harper and Brothers, New York, 1882

First printing — February, 1988

Printed in the United States of America

CONTENTS OF INTRODUCTION

PART II

THE METHODS OF TEXTUAL CRITICISM   19—72

PART III

APPLICATION OF PRINCIPLES OF CRITICISM
TO THE TEXT OF THE NEW TESTAMENT 73—287

CHAPTER IV. *SUBSTANTIAL INTEGRITY OF THE PUREST TRANSMITTED TEXT* (356—374)   271—287

PART IV

NATURE AND DETAILS OF THIS EDITION 288—324

INTRODUCTION

1. THIS edition is an attempt to present exactly the original words of the New Testament, so far as they can now be determined from surviving documents. Since the testimony delivered by the several documents or witnesses is full of complex variation, the original text cannot be elicited from it without the use of criticism, that is, of a process of distinguishing and setting aside those readings which have originated at some link in the chain of transmission. This Introduction is intended to be a succinct account (I) of the reasons why criticism is still necessary for the text of the New Testament; (II) of what we hold to be the true grounds and methods of criticism generally; (III) of the leading facts in the documentary history of the New Testament which appear to us to supply the textual critic with secure guidance; and (IV) of the manner in which we have ourselves endeavoured to embody the results of criticism in the present text.

2. The office of textual criticism, it cannot be too clearly understood at the outset, is always secondary and always negative. It is always secondary, since it comes into

play only where the text transmitted by the existing documents appears to be in error, either because they differ
from each other in what they read, or for some other sufficient reason. With regard to the great bulk of the words
of the New Testament, as of most other ancient writings,
there is no variation or other ground of doubt, and therefore no room for textual criticism; and here therefore an
editor is merely a transcriber. The same may be said
with substantial truth respecting those various readings
which have never been received, and in all probability
never will be received, into any printed text. The proportion of words virtually accepted on all hands as raised
above doubt is very great, not less, on a rough computation, than seven eighths of the whole. The remaining eighth
therefore, formed in great part by changes of order and
other comparative trivialities, constitutes the whole area
of criticism. If the principles followed in the present
edition are sound, this area may be very greatly reduced.
Recognising to the full the duty of abstinence from
peremptory decision in cases where the evidence leaves
the judgement in suspense between two or more readings,
we find that, setting aside differences of orthography, the
words in our opinion still subject to doubt only make up
about one sixtieth of the whole New Testament. In this
second estimate the proportion of comparatively trivial
variations is beyond measure larger than in the former;
so that the amount of what can in any sense be called
substantial variation is but a small fraction of the whole
residuary variation, and can hardly form more than a
thousandth part of the entire text. Since there is reason to
suspect that an exaggerated impression prevails as to the
extent of possible textual corruption in the New Testament, which might seem to be confirmed by language

used here and there in the following pages, we desire to make it clearly understood beforehand how much of the New Testament stands in no need of a textual critic's labours.

3. Again, textual criticism is always negative, because its final aim is virtually nothing more than the detection and rejection of error. Its progress consists not in the growing perfection of an ideal in the future, but in approximation towards complete ascertainment of definite facts of the past, that is, towards recovering an exact copy of what was actually written on parchment or papyrus by the author of the book or his amanuensis. Had all intervening transcriptions been perfectly accurate, there could be no error and no variation in existing documents. Where there is variation, there must be error in at least all variants but one; and the primary work of textual criticism is merely to discriminate the erroneous variants from the true.

4. In the case indeed of many ill preserved ancient writings textual criticism has a further and a much more difficult task, that of detecting and removing corruptions affecting the whole of the existing documentary evidence. But in the New Testament the abundance, variety, and comparative excellence of the documents confines this task of pure 'emendation' within so narrow limits that we may leave it out of sight for the present, and confine our attention to that principal operation of textual criticism which is required whenever we have to decide between the conflicting evidence of various documents.

PART I

THE NEED OF CRITICISM FOR THE TEXT OF THE NEW TESTAMENT

5.   The answer to the question why criticism is still necessary for the text of the New Testament is contained in the history of its transmission, first by writing and then by printing, to the present time.   For our purpose it will be enough to recapitulate first in general terms the elementary phenomena of transmission by writing generally, with some of the special conditions affecting the New Testament, and then the chief incidents in the history of the New Testament as a printed book which have determined the form in which it appears in existing editions.   For fuller particulars, on this and other subjects not needing to be treated at any length here, we must refer the reader once for all to books that are professedly storehouses of information.

A. 6—14.   *Transmission by writing*

6.   No autograph of any book of the New Testament is known or believed to be still in existence.   The originals must have been early lost, for they are mentioned by no ecclesiastical writer, although there were many motives for appealing to them, had they been forthcoming, in the second and third centuries: one or two passages have sometimes been supposed to refer to them, but certainly by a misinterpretation.   The books of the New Testament have had to share the fate of other ancient writings in being copied again and again

during more than fourteen centuries down to the invention of printing and its application to Greek literature.

7. Every transcription of any kind of writing involves the chance of the introduction of some errors : and even if the transcript is revised by comparison with its ex·emplar or immediate original, there is no absolute security that all the errors will be corrected. When the transcript becomes itself the parent of other copies, one or more, its errors are for the most part reproduced. Those only are likely to be removed which at once strike the eye of a transcriber as mere blunders destructive of sense, and even in these cases he will often go astray in making what seems to him the obvious correction. In addition to inherited deviations from the original, each fresh transcript is liable to contain fresh errors, to be transmitted in like manner to its own descendants.

8. The nature and amount of the corruption of text thus generated and propagated depends to a great extent on the peculiarities of the book itself, the estimation in which it is held, and the uses to which it is applied. The rate cannot always be uniform : the professional training of scribes can rarely obliterate individual differences of accuracy and conscientiousness, and moreover the current standard of exactness will vary at different times and places and in different grades of cultivation. The number of transcriptions, and consequent opportunities of corruption, cannot be accurately measured by difference of date, for at any date a transcript might be made either from a contemporary manuscript or from one written any number of centuries before. But these inequalities do not render it less true that repeated transcription involves multiplication of error ; and the consequent presumption that a relatively late text is likely to be a relatively corrupt text

is found true on the application of all available tests in an overwhelming proportion of the extant MSS in which ancient literature has been preserved.

9. This general proposition respecting the average results of transcription requires to be at once qualified and extended by the statement of certain more limited conditions of transmission with which the New Testament is specially though by no means exclusively concerned. Their full bearing will not be apparent till they have been explained in some detail further on, but for the sake of clearness they must be mentioned here.

10. The act of transcription may under different circumstances involve different processes. In strictness it is the exact reproduction of a given series of words in a given order. Where this purpose is distinctly recognised or assumed, there can be no errors but those of workmanship, 'clerical errors', as they are called; and by sedulous cultivation, under the pressure of religious, literary, or professional motives, a high standard of immunity from even clerical errors has at times been attained. On the other hand, pure clerical errors, that is, mechanical confusions of ear or eye alone, pass imperceptibly into errors due to unconscious mental action, as any one may ascertain by registering and analysing his own mistakes in transcription; so that it is quite possible to intend nothing but faithful transcription, and yet to introduce changes due to interpretation of sense. Now, as these hidden intrusions of mental action are specially capable of being restrained by conscious vigilance, so on the other hand they are liable to multiply spontaneously where there is no distinct perception that a transcriber's duty is to transcribe and nothing more; and this perception is rarer and more dependent on

training than might be supposed. In its absence unconscious passes further into conscious mental action; and thus transcription may come to include tolerably free modification of language and even rearrangement of material. Transcription of this kind need involve no deliberate preference of sense to language; the intention is still to transcribe language : but, as there is no special concentration of regard upon the language as having an intrinsic sacredness of whatever kind, the instinctive feeling for sense cooperates largely in the result.

11. It was predominantly though not exclusively under such conditions as these last that the transcription of the New Testament was carried on during the earliest centuries, as a comparison of the texts of that period proves beyond doubt. The conception of new Scriptures standing on the same footing as the Scriptures of the Old Testament was slow and unequal in its growth, more especially while the traditions of the apostolic and immediately succeeding generations still lived ; and the reverence paid to the apostolic writings, even to the most highly and most widely venerated among them, was not of a kind that exacted a scrupulous jealousy as to their text as distinguished from their substance. As was to be expected, the language of the historical books was treated with more freedom than the rest: but even the Epistles, and still more the Apocalypse, bear abundant traces of a similar type of transcription. After a while changed feelings and changed circumstances put an end to the early textual laxity, and thenceforward its occurrence is altogether exceptional; so that the later corruptions are almost wholly those incident to transcription in the proper sense, errors arising from careless performance of a scribe's work, not from an imperfect conception of it.

While therefore the greater literalness of later transcription arrested for the most part the progress of the bolder forms of alteration, on the other hand it could perpetuate only what it received. As witnesses to the apostolic text the later texts can be valuable or otherwise only according as their parent texts had or had not passed comparatively unscathed through the earlier times.

12. Again, in books widely read transmission ceases after a while to retain exclusively the form of diverging ramification. Manuscripts are written in which there is an eclectic fusion of the texts of different exemplars, either by the simultaneous use of more than one at the time of transcription, or by the incorporation of various readings noted in the margin of a single exemplar from other copies, or by a scribe's conscious or unconscious recollections of a text differing from that which lies before him. This mixture, as it may be conveniently called, of texts previously independent has taken place on a large scale in the New Testament. Within narrow geographical areas it was doubtless at work from a very early time, and it would naturally extend itself with the increase of communication between distant churches. There is reason to suspect that its greatest activity on a large scale began in the second half of the third century, the interval of peace between Gallienus's edict of toleration and the outbreak of the last persecution. At all events it was in full operation in the fourth century, the time which from various causes exercised the chief influence over the many centuries of comparatively simple transmission that followed.

13. The gain or loss to the intrinsic purity of texts from mixture with other texts is from the nature of the

case indeterminable. In most instances there would be both gain and loss; but both would be fortuitous, and they might bear to each other every conceivable proportion. Textual purity, as far as can be judged from the extant literature, attracted hardly any interest. There is no evidence to shew that care was generally taken to choose out for transcription the exemplars having the highest claims to be regarded as authentic, if indeed the requisite knowledge and skill were forthcoming. Humanly speaking, the only influence which can have interfered to an appreciable extent with mere chance and convenience in the selection between existing readings, or in the combination of them, was supplied by the preferences of untrained popular taste, always an unsafe guide in the discrimination of relative originality of text. The complexity introduced into the transmission of ancient texts by mixture needs no comment. Where the mixture has been accompanied or preceded by such licence in transcription as we find in the New Testament, the complexity can evidently only increase the precariousness of printed texts formed without taking account of the variations of text which preceded mixture.

14. Various causes have interfered both with the preservation of ancient MSS and with their use as exemplars to any considerable extent. Multitudes of the MSS of the New Testament written in the first three centuries were destroyed at the beginning of the fourth, and there can be no doubt that multitudes of those written in the fourth and two following centuries met a similar fate in the various invasions of East and West. But violence was not the only agent of destruction. We know little about the external features of the MSS of the ages of

persecution : but what little we do know suggests that they were usually small, containing only single books or groups of books, and not seldom, there is reason to suspect, of comparatively coarse material ; altogether shewing little similarity to the stately tomes of the early Christian empire, of which we possess specimens, and likely enough to be despised in comparison in an age which exulted in outward signs of the new order of things. Another cause of neglect at a later period was doubtless obsoleteness of form. When once the separation of words had become habitual, the old continuous mode of writing would be found troublesome to the eye, and even the old 'uncial' or rounded capital letters would at length prove an obstacle to use. Had biblical manuscripts of the uncial ages been habitually treated with ordinary respect, much more invested with high authority, they could not have been so often turned into 'palimpsests', that is, had their ancient writing obliterated that the vellum might be employed for fresh writing, not always biblical. It must also be remembered that in the ordinary course of things the most recent manuscripts would at all times be the most numerous, and therefore the most generally accessible. Even if multiplication of transcripts were not always advancing, there would be a slow but continual substitution of new copies for old, partly to fill up gaps made by waste and casualties, partly by a natural impulse which could be reversed only by veneration or an archaic taste or a critical purpose. It is therefore no wonder that only a small fraction of the Greek manuscripts of the New Testament preserved to modern times were written in the uncial period, and but few of this number belong to the first five or six centuries, none being earlier than the age of Constantine. Most uncial manuscripts are more or less fragmentary ; and till lately not one was known which contained the whole New Testament unmutilated. A considerable proportion, in numbers and still more in value, have been brought to light only by the assiduous research of the last century and a half.

B. 15—18. *Transmission by printed editions*

15. These various conditions affecting the manu-script text of the New Testament must be borne in mind if we would understand what was possible to be accomplished in the early printed editions, the text of which exercises directly or indirectly a scarcely credible power to the present day. At the beginning of the sixteenth century, far more than now, the few ancient documents of the sacred text were lost in the crowd of later copies; and few even of the late MSS were em-ployed, and that only as convenience dictated, without selection or deliberate criticism. The fundamental editions were those of Erasmus (Basel, 1516), and of Stunica in Cardinal Ximenes' Complutensian (Alcala) Polyglott, printed in 1514 but apparently not published till 1522. In his haste to be the first editor, Erasmus allowed himself to be guilty of strange carelessness: but neither he nor any other scholar then living could have produced a materially better text without enor-mous labour, the need of which was not as yet apparent. The numerous editions which followed during the next three or four generations varied much from one another in petty details, and occasionally adopted fresh readings from MSS, chiefly of a common

late type: but the foundation and an overwhelming
proportion of the text remained always Erasmian, sometimes slightly modified on Complutensian authority;
except in a few editions which had a Complutensian
base. After a while this arbitrary and uncritical variation gave way to a comparative fixity equally fortuitous,
having no more trustworthy basis than the external
beauty of two editions brought out by famous printers,
a Paris folio of 1550 edited and printed by R. Estienne,
and an Elzevir (Leyden) 24mo of 1624, 1633, &c.,
repeating an unsatisfactory revision of Estienne's mainly
Erasmian text made by the reformer Beza. The reader
of the second Elzevir edition is informed that he has
before him "the text now received by all"; and thus
the name 'Received Text' arose. Reprints more or
less accurate of one or other of these two typographical
standards constitute the traditional printed text of the
New Testament even now.

16. About the middle of the seventeenth century
the preparation for effectual criticism began. The impulse proceeded from English scholars, such as Fell,
Walton, and Mill; and seems to have originated in the
gift of the Alexandrine MS to Charles I by Cyril Lucar,
the Patriarch of Constantinople, in 1628. France contributed a powerful auxiliary in Simon, whose writings
(1689—1695) had a large share in discrediting acquiescence in the accepted texts. The history of criticism
from this time could hardly be made intelligible here: it
will be briefly sketched further on, when explanations
have been given of the task that had to be performed,
and the problems that had to be solved. In the course
of the eighteenth century several imperfect and halting
attempts were made, chiefly in Germany, to apply evidence

to use by substantial correction of the text. Of these the greatest and most influential proceeded from J. A. Bengel at Tübingen in 1734. In the closing years of the century, and a little later, the process was carried many steps forward by Griesbach, on a double foundation of enriched resources and deeper study, not without important help from suggestions of Semler and finally of Hug. Yet even Griesbach was content to start from the traditional or revised Erasmian basis, rather than from the MSS in which he himself reposed most confidence.

17. A new period began in 1831, when for the first time a text was constructed directly from the ancient documents without the intervention of any printed edition, and when the first systematic attempt was made to substitute scientific method for arbitrary choice in the discrimination of various readings. In both respects the editor, Lachmann, rejoiced to declare that he was carrying out the principles and unfulfilled intentions of Bentley, as set forth in 1716 and 1720. This great advance was however marred by too narrow a selection of documents to be taken into account and too artificially rigid an employment of them, and also by too little care in obtaining precise knowledge of some of their texts: and though these defects, partly due in the first instance to the unambitious purpose of the edition, have been in different ways avoided by Lachmann's two distinguished successors, Tischendorf and Tregelles, both of whom have produced texts substantially free from the later corruptions, neither of them can be said to have dealt consistently or on the whole successfully with the difficulties presented by the variations between the most ancient texts. On the other hand, their indefatigable labours in the discovery and exhibition

of fresh evidence, aided by similar researches on the part of others, provide all who come after them with invaluable resources not available half a century ago.

18. A just appreciation of the wealth of documentary evidence now accessible as compared with that enjoyed by any previous generation, and of the comparatively late times at which much even of what is not now new became available for criticism, is indeed indispensable for any one who would understand the present position of the textual criticism of the New Testament. The gain by the knowledge of the contents of important new documents is not to be measured by the direct evidence which they themselves contribute. Evidence is valuable only so far as it can be securely interpreted; and not the least advantage conferred by new documents is the new help which they give towards the better interpretation of old documents, and of documentary relations generally. By way of supplement to the preceding brief sketch of the history of criticism, we insert the following table, which shews the dates at which the extant Greek uncials of the sixth and earlier centuries, with five others of later age but comparatively ancient text, have become available as evidence by various forms of publication. The second column marks the very imperfect publication by selections of readings; the third, tolerably full collations; the fourth, continuous texts. The manuscript known as Δ in the Gospels and as G (G_3) in St Paul's Epistles requires two separate datings, as its two parts have found their way to different libraries. In other cases a plurality of dates is given where each publication has had some distinctive importance.

(fragg. = fragments)	Select Readings	Collations	Continuous Texts
ℵ all books complete	1860		1862
B all books exc. part of Heb., Epp. Past., and Apoc.	(1580)	1788, 1799	{ (1857,) 1859, 1867, 1868
A all books		1657	1786
C fragg. of nearly all books	1710	1751, 2	1843
Q fragg. Lc. Jo.	(? 1752)		1762, 1860
T fragg. Jo. [Lc.]			1789
D Evv. Act.	1550	1657	1793, 1864
D₂ Paul	(1582)	1657	1852
N fragg. Evv.	{ (1751) + 1773 + (1830)		1846, 1876
P fragg. Evv.	(? 1752)		1762, 1869
R fragg. Lc.			1°57
Z fragg. Mt.			1801, 1880
[Σ Mt. Mc.]	(1880)		
L Evv.	1550	1751, 1785	1846
Ξ fragg. Lc.			1861
{ Δ Evv.			1836 }
{ G₃ Paul exc. Heb.		1710	+ 1791 }
E₂ Act.			1715, 1870
P₂ all books exc. Evv.			1865 + 1869

19. The foregoing outline may suffice to shew the manner in which repeated transcription tends to multiply corruption of texts, and the subsequent mixture of independent texts to confuse alike their sound and their corrupt readings; the reasons why ancient MSS in various ages have been for the most part little preserved and little copied; the disadvantages under which the Greek text of the New Testament was first printed, from late and inferior MSS; the long neglect to take serious measures for amending it; the slow process of the accumulation and study of evidence; the late date at which any considerable number of corrections on

ancient authority were admitted into the slightly modified Erasmian texts that reigned by an accidental pre-
scription, and the very late date at which ancient
authority was allowed to furnish not scattered retouch-
ings but the whole body of text from beginning to end;
and lastly the advantage enjoyed by the present. generation in the possession of a store of evidence largely
augmented in amount and still more in value, as well
as in the ample instruction afforded by previous criticism
and previous texts.

C. 20—22. *History of this edition*

20. These facts justify, we think, another attempt
to determine the original words of the Apostles and
writers of the New Testament. In the spring of 1853
we were led by the perplexities of reading encountered
in our own study of Scripture to project the construction
of a text such as is now published. At that time a
student aware of the untrustworthiness of the 'Received'
texts had no other guides than Lachmann's text and the
second of the four widely different texts of Tischendorf.
Finding it impossible to assure ourselves that either editor
placed before us such an approximation to the apostolic
words as we could accept with reasonable satisfaction,
we agreed to commence at once the formation of a
manual text for our own use, hoping at the same time
that it might be of service to others. The task proved
harder than we anticipated; and eventually many years
have been required for its fulfilment. Engrossing occu-
pations of other kinds have brought repeated delays and
interruptions: but the work has never been laid more
than partially aside, and the intervals during which it

has been intermitted have been short. We cannot on the whole regret the lapse of time before publication. Though we have not found reason to change any of the leading views with which we began to prepare for the task, they have gained much in clearness and comprehensiveness through the long interval, especially as regards the importance which we have been led to attach to the history of transmission. It would indeed be to our shame if we had failed to learn continually.

21. The mode of procedure adopted from the first was to work out our results independently of each other, and to hold no counsel together except upon results already provisionally obtained. Such differences as then appeared, usually bearing a very small proportion to the points of immediate agreement, were discussed on paper, and where necessary repeatedly discussed, till either agreement or final difference was reached. These ultimate differences have found expression among the alternative readings. No rule of precedence has been adopted: but documentary attestation has been in most cases allowed to confer the place of honour as against internal evidence, range of attestation being further taken into account as between one well attested reading and another. This combination of completely independent operations permits us to place far more confidence in the results than either of us could have presumed to cherish had they rested on his own sole responsibility. No individual mind can ever act with perfect uniformity, or free itself completely from its own idiosyncrasies: the danger of unconscious caprice is inseparable from personal judgement. We venture to hope that the present text has escaped some risks of this kind by being the production of two editors of different habits of mind, working

4

independently and to a great extent on different plans, and then giving and receiving free and full criticism wherever their first conclusions had not agreed together. For the principles, arguments, and conclusions set forth in the Introduction and Appendix both editors are alike responsible. It was however for various reasons expedient that their exposition and illustration should proceed throughout from a single hand; and the writing of this volume and the other accompaniments of the text has devolved on Dr Hort.

22. It may be well to state that the kindness of our publishers has already allowed us to place successive instalments of the Greek text privately in the hands of the members of the Company of Revisers of the English New Testament, and of a few other scholars. The Gospels, with a temporary preface of 28 pages, were thus issued in July 1871, the Acts in February 1873, the Catholic Epistles in December 1873, the Pauline Epistles in February 1875, and the Apocalypse in December 1876. The work to which this provisional issue was due has afforded opportunity for renewed consideration of many details, especially on the side of interpretation; and we have been thankful to include any fresh results thus or otherwise obtained, before printing off for publication. Accordingly many corrections dealing with punctuation or otherwise of a minute kind, together with occasional modifications of reading, have been introduced into the stereotype plates within the last few months.

PART II

THE METHODS OF TEXTUAL CRITICISM

23. Every method of textual criticism corresponds to some one class of textual facts: the best criticism is that which takes account of every class of textual facts, and assigns to each method its proper use and rank. The leading principles of textual criticism are identical for all writings whatever. Differences in application arise only from differences in the amount, variety, and quality of evidence: no method is ever inapplicable except through defectiveness of evidence. The more obvious facts naturally attract attention first; and it is only at a further stage of study that any one is likely spontaneously to grasp those more fundamental facts from which textual criticism must start if it is to reach comparative certainty. We propose to follow here this natural order, according to which the higher methods will come last into view.

SECTION I.   INTERNAL EVIDENCE OF READINGS
24—37

24. Criticism arises out of the question what is to be received where a text is extant in two or more varying documents. The most rudimentary form of criticism consists in dealing with each variation independently, and adopting at once in each case out of two or more variants that which looks most probable. The evidence here taken into account is commonly called 'Internal Evidence': as other kinds of Internal Evidence will have

to be mentioned, we prefer to call it more precisely 'Internal Evidence of Readings'. Internal Evidence of Readings is of two kinds, which cannot be too sharply distinguished from each other; appealing respectively to Intrinsic Probability, having reference to the author, and what may be called Transcriptional Probability, having reference to the copyists. In appealing to the first, we ask what an author is likely to have written : in appealing to the second, we ask what copyists are likely to have made him seem to write. Both these kinds of evidence are alike in the strictest sense internal, since they are alike derived exclusively from comparison of the testimony delivered, no account being taken of any relative antecedent credibility of the actual witnesses.

A. 25—27. *Intrinsic Probability*

25. The first impulse in dealing with a variation is usually to lean on Intrinsic Probability, that is, to consider which of two readings makes the best sense, and to decide between them accordingly. The decision may be made either by an immediate and as it were intuitive judgement, or by weighing cautiously various elements which go to make up what is called sense, such as conformity to grammar and congruity to the purport of the rest of the sentence and of the larger context; to which may rightly be added congruity to the usual style of the author and to his matter in other passages. The process may take the form either of simply comparing two or more rival readings under these heads, and giving the preference to that which appears to have the advantage, or of rejecting a reading absolutely, for violation of one or more of the congruities, or of adopting a reading absolutely, for perfection of congruity.

26. These considerations evidently afford reasonable presumptions; presumptions which in some cases may attain such force on the negative side as to demand the rejection or qualify the acceptance of readings most highly commended by other kinds of evidence. But the uncertainty of the decision in ordinary cases is shown by the great diversity of judgement which is actually found to exist. The value of the Intrinsic Evidence of Readings should of course be estimated by its best and most cultivated form, for the extemporaneous surmises of an ordinary untrained reader will differ widely from the range of probabilities present to the mind of a scholar prepared both by general training in the analysis of texts and by special study of the facts bearing on the particular case. But in dealing with this kind of evidence equally competent critics often arrive at contradictory conclusions as to the same variations.

27. Nor indeed are the assumptions involved in Intrinsic Evidence of Readings to be implicitly trusted. There is much literature, ancient no less than modern, in which it is needful to remember that authors are not always grammatical, or clear, or consistent, or felicitous; so that not seldom an ordinary reader finds it easy to replace a feeble or half-appropriate word or phrase by an effective substitute; and thus the best words to express an author's meaning need not in all cases be those which he actually employed. But, without attempting to determine the limits within which such causes have given occasion to any variants in the New Testament, it concerns our own purpose more to urge that in the highest literature, and notably in the Bible, all readers are peculiarly liable to the fallacy of supposing that they understand the author's meaning and purpose because they under-

stand some part or some aspect of it, which they take for the whole; and hence, in judging variations of text, they are led unawares to disparage any word or phrase which owes its selection by the author to those elements of the thought present to his mind which they have failed to perceive or to feel.

B. 28—37. *Transcriptional Probability*

28. The next step in criticism is the discovery of Transcriptional Probability, and is suggested by the reflexion that what attracts ourselves is not on the average unlikely to have attracted transcribers. If one various reading appears to ourselves to give much better sense or in some other way to excel another, the same apparent superiority may have led to the introduction of the reading in the first instance. Mere blunders apart, no motive can be thought of which could lead a scribe to introduce consciously a worse reading in place of a better. We might thus seem to be landed in the paradoxical result that intrinsic inferiority is evidence of originality.

29. In reality however, although this is the form in which the considerations that make up Transcriptional Probability are likely in the first instance to present themselves to a student feeling his way onwards beyond Intrinsic Probability, the true nature of Transcriptional Probability can hardly be understood till it is approached from another side. Transcriptional Probability is not directly or properly concerned with the relative excellence of rival readings, but merely with the relative fitness of each for explaining the existence of the others. Every rival reading contributes an element to

the problem which has to be solved; for every rival reading is a fact which has to be accounted for, and no acceptance of any one reading as original can be satisfactory which leaves any other variant incapable of being traced to some known cause or causes of variation. If a variation is binary, as it may be called, consisting of two variants, *a* and *b*, the problem for Transcriptional Probability to decide is whether it is easier to derive *b* from *a*, through causes of corruption known to exist elsewhere, on the hypothesis that *a* is original, or to derive *a* from *b*, through similar agencies, on the hypothesis that *b* is original. If the variants are more numerous, making a ternary or yet more composite variation, each in its turn must be assumed as a hypothetical original, and an endeavour made to deduce from it all the others, either independently or consecutively; after which the relative facilities of the several experimental deductions must be compared together.

30. Hence the basis on which Transcriptional Probability rests consists of generalisations as to the causes of corruption incident to the process of transcription. A few of the broadest generalisations of this kind, singling out observed proclivities of average copyists, make up the bulk of what are not very happily called 'canons of criticism'. Many causes of corruption are independent of age and language, and their prevalence may be easily verified by a careful observer every day; while others are largely modified, or even brought into existence, by peculiar circumstances of the writings themselves, or of the conditions of their transmission. There is always an abundance of variations in which no practised scholar can possibly doubt which is the original reading, and which must therefore be derivative;

and these clear instances supply ample materials for discovering and classifying the causes of corruption which must have been operative in all variations. The most obvious causes of corruption are clerical or mechanical, arising from mere carelessness of the transcriber, chiefly through deceptions of eye or ear. But, as we have seen (§ 10), the presence of a mental factor can often be traced in corruptions partly mechanical; and under the influence of a lax conception of the proper office of a transcriber distinctly mental causes of change may assume, and often have assumed, very large proportions. Even where the definite responsibilities of transcription were strongly felt, changes not purely clerical would arise from a more or less conscious feeling on a scribe's part that he was correcting what he deemed an obvious error due to some one of his predecessors; while, at times or places in which the offices of transcribing and editing came to be confused, other copyists would not shrink from altering the form of what lay before them for the sake of substituting what they supposed to be a clearer or better representation of the matter.

31. The value of the evidence obtained from Transcriptional Probability is incontestable. Without its aid textual criticism could rarely attain any high degree of security. Moreover, to be rightly estimated, it must be brought under consideration in the higher form to which it can be raised by care and study, when elementary guesses as to which reading scribes are likely in any particular case to have introduced have been replaced by judgements founded on previous investigation of the various general characteristics of those readings which can with moral certainty be assumed to have been introduced by scribes. But even at its

best this class of Internal Evidence, like the other, carries us but a little way towards the recovery of an ancient text, when it is employed alone. The number of variations in which it can be trusted to supply by itself a direct and immediate decision is relatively very small, when unquestionable blunders, that is, clerical errors, have been set aside. If we look behind the canons laid down by critics to the observed facts from which their authority proceeds, we find, first, that scribes were moved by a much greater variety of impulse than is usually supposed; next, that different scribes were to a certain limited extent moved by different impulses; and thirdly, that in many variations each of two or more conflicting readings might be reasonably accounted for by some impulse known to have operated elsewhere. In these last cases decision is evidently precarious, even though the evidence may seem to be stronger on the one side than the other. Not only are mental impulses unsatisfactory subjects for estimates of comparative force; but a plurality of impulses recognised by ourselves as possible in any given case by no means implies a plurality of impulses as having been actually in operation. Nor have we a right to assume that what in any particular case we judge after comparison to be the intrinsically strongest of the two or more possible impulses must as a matter of course be the one impulse which acted on a scribe if he was acted on by one only: accidental circumstances beyond our knowledge would determine which impulse would be the first to reach his mind or hand, and there would seldom be room for any element of deliberate choice. But even where there is no conflict of possible impulses, the evidence on the one side is often too slight and questionable to be implicitly trusted by any one who wishes to ascertain his author's true text, and not merely to follow a generally sound rule. Hence it is only in well marked and unambiguous cases that the unsupported verdict of Transcriptional Probability for detached readings can be safely followed.

32. But the insufficiency of Transcriptional Probability as an independent guide is most signally shown by its liability to stand in apparent antagonism to Intrinsic Probability; since the legitimate force of Intrinsic Probability, where its drift is clear and unambiguous, is not touched by the fact that in many other places it bears a divided or ambiguous testimony. The area of final antagonism, it is already evident, is very much smaller than might seem to be implied in the first crude impression that scribes are not likely to desert a better reading for a worse; but it is sufficiently large to create serious difficulty. The true nature of the difficulty will be best explained by a few words on the mutual relations of the two classes of Internal Evidence, by which it will likewise be seen what a valuable ancillary office they discharge in combination.

33. All conflicts between Intrinsic and Transcriptional Probability arise from the imperfection of our knowledge: in both fields criticism consists of inferences from more or less incomplete data. Every change not purely mechanical made by a transcriber is, in some sense, of the nature of a correction. Corrections in such external matters as orthography and the like may be passed over, since they arise merely out of the comparative familiarity of different forms, and here Intrinsic Probability has nothing to do with what can properly be called excellence or easiness. All other corrections,

that is, those which bear any relation to sense, would never be made unless in the eyes of the scribe who makes them they were improvements in sense or in the expression of sense: even when made unconsciously, it is the relative satisfaction which they give to his mental state at the time that creates or shapes them. Yet in literature of high quality it is as a rule improbable that a change made by transcribers should improve an author's sense, or express his full and exact sense better than he has done himself. It follows that, with the exception of pure blunders, readings originating with scribes must always at the time have combined the appearance of improvement with the absence of its reality. If they had not been plausible, they would not have existed: yet their excellence must have been either superficial or partial, and the balance of inward and essential excellence must lie against them. In itself therefore Transcriptional Probability not only stands in no antagonism to Intrinsic Probability, but is its sustaining complement. It is seen in its proper and normal shape when both characteristics of a scribe's correction can alike be recognised, the semblance of superiority and the latent inferiority.

34. It is only in reference to mental or semi-mental causes of corruption that the apparent conflict between Transcriptional and Intrinsic Probability has any place : and neither the extent nor the nature of the apparent conflict can be rightly understood if we forget that, in making use of this class of evidence, we have to do with readings only as they are likely to have appeared to transcribers, not as they appear to us, except in so far as our mental conditions can be accepted as truly reflecting theirs. It is especially necessary to bear

this limitation in mind with reference to one of the most comprehensive and also most widely prevalent mental impulses of transcribers, the disposition to smooth away difficulties; which is the foundation of the paradoxical precept to 'choose the harder reading', the most famous of all ' canons of criticism'. Readings having no especial attractiveness to ourselves may justly be pronounced suspicious on grounds of Transcriptional Probability, if they were likely to be attractive, or their rivals unacceptable, to ancient transcribers; and conversely, if this condition is absent, we can draw no unfavourable inferences from any intrinsic excellence which they may possess in our own eyes.

35. The rational use of Transcriptional Probability as textual evidence depends on the power of distinguishing the grounds of preference implied in an ancient scribe's substitution of one reading for another from those felt as cogent now after close and deliberate criticism. Alterations made by transcribers, so far as they are due to any movement of thought, are with rare exceptions the product of first thoughts, not second; nor again of those first thoughts, springing from a rapid and penetrating glance over a whole field of evidence, which sometimes are justified by third thoughts. This is indeed a necessary result of the extemporaneous, cursory, and one-sided form which criticism cannot but assume when it exists only as a subordinate accident of transcription. But even the best prepared textual critic has to be on his guard against hasty impressions as to the intrinsic character of readings, for experience teaches him how often the relative attractiveness of conflicting readings becomes inverted by careful study. What we should naturally expect, in accordance with what has

been said above (§ 33), is that each reading should shew some excellence of its own, apparent or real, provided that we on our part are qualified to recognise it. If any reading fails to do so, clerical errors being of course excepted, the fault must lie in our knowledge or our perception; for if it be a scribe's correction, it must have some at least apparent excellence, and if it be original, it must have the highest real excellence. Contrast of real and apparent excellence is in any given variation an indispensable criterion as to the adequacy of the evidence for justifying reliance on Transcriptional Probability.

36. Fortunately variations conforming to this normal type are of frequent occurrence; variations, that is, in which a critic is able to arrive at a strong and clear conviction that one reading is intrinsically much the most probable, and yet to see with equal clearness how the rival reading or readings could not but be attractive to average transcribers. In these cases Internal Evidence of Readings attains the highest degree of certainty which its nature admits, this relative trustworthiness being due to the coincidence of the two independent Probabilities, Intrinsic and Transcriptional. Readings thus certified are of the utmost value in the application of other methods of criticism, as we shall see hereafter.

37. But a vast proportion of variations do not fulfil these conditions. Where one reading (*a*) appears intrinsically preferable, and its excellence is of a kind that we might expect to be recognised by scribes, while its rival (*b*) shews no characteristic likely to be attractive to them, Intrinsic and Transcriptional Probability are practically in conflict. In such a case either *b* must be wrong, and therefore must, as compared with

a, have had some attractiveness not perceived by us, if the case be one in which the supposition of a mere blunder is improbable; or *b* must be right, and therefore must have expressed the author's meaning with some special fitness which escapes our notice. The antagonism would disappear if we could discover on which side we have failed to perceive or duly appreciate all the facts; but in the mean time it stands. Occasionally the Intrinsic evidence is so strong that the Transcriptional evidence may without rashness be disregarded: but such cases are too exceptional to count for much when we are estimating the general trustworthiness of a method; and the apparent contradiction which the imperfection of our knowledge often leaves us unable to reconcile remains a valid objection against habitual reliance on the sufficiency of Internal Evidence of Readings.

SECTION II.   INTERNAL EVIDENCE OF DOCUMENTS
38—48

38.   Thus far we have been considering the method which follows Internal Evidence of Readings alone, as improved to the utmost by the distinction and separate appreciation of Intrinsic and Transcriptional Probability, and as applied with every aid of scholarship and special study. The limitation to Internal Evidence of Readings follows naturally from the impulse to deal conclusively at once with each variation as it comes in its turn before a reader or commentator or editor : yet a moment's consideration of the process of transmission shews how precarious it is to attempt to judge which of two or more readings is the most likely to be right, without considering which of the attesting documents or combinations of documents

are the most likely to convey an unadulterated transcript of the original text; in other words, in dealing with matter purely traditional, to ignore the relative antecedent credibility of witnesses, and trust exclusively to our own inward power of singling out the true readings from among their counterfeits, wherever we see them. Nor is it of much avail to allow supposed or ascertained excellence of particular documents a deciding voice in cases of difficulty, or to mix evidence of this kind at random or at pleasure with Internal Evidence of Readings assumed in practice if not in theory as the primary guide. The comparative trustworthiness of documentary authorities constitutes a fresh class of facts at least as pertinent as any with which we have hitherto been dealing, and much less likely to be misinterpreted by personal surmises. The first step towards obtaining a sure foundation is a consistent application of the principle that KNOWLEDGE OF DOCUMENTS SHOULD PRECEDE FINAL JUDGEMENT UPON READINGS.

39. The most prominent fact known about a manuscript is ·its date, sometimes fixed to a year by a note from the scribe's hand, oftener determined within certain limits by palæographical or other indirect indications, sometimes learned from external facts or records. Relative date, as has been explained above (§ 8), affords a valuable presumption as to relative freedom from corruption, when appealed to on a large scale ; and this and other external facts, insufficient by themselves to solve a question of reading, may often supply essential materials to the process by which it can be solved. But the occasional preservation of comparatively ancient texts in comparatively modern MSS forbids confident reliance on priority of date unsustained by other marks of excellence.

40. The first effectual security against the uncertainties of Internal Evidence of Readings is found in what may be termed Internal Evidence of Documents, that is, the general characteristics of the texts contained in them as learned directly from themselves by continuous study of the whole or considerable parts. This and this alone supplies entirely trustworthy knowledge as to the relative value of different documents. If we compare successively the readings of two documents in all their variations, we have ample materials for ascertaining the leading merits and defects of each. Readings authenticated by the coincidence of strong Intrinsic and strong Transcriptional Probability, or it may be by one alone of these Probabilities in exceptional strength and clearness and uncontradicted by the other, are almost always to be found sufficiently numerous to supply a solid basis for inference. Moreover they can safely be supplemented by provisional judgements on similar evidence in the more numerous variations where a critic cannot but form a strong impression as to the probabilities of reading, though he dare not trust it absolutely. Where then one of the documents is found habitually to contain these morally certain or at least strongly preferred readings, and the other habitually to contain their rejected rivals, we can have no doubt, first, that the text of the first has been transmitted in comparative purity, and that the text of the second has suffered comparatively large corruption ; and next, that the superiority of the first must be as great in the variations in which Internal Evidence of Readings has furnished no decisive criterion as in those which have enabled us to form a comparative appreciation of the two texts. By this cautious advance from the known to the unknown we are enabled to deal confidently with a

great mass of those remaining variations, open variations, so to speak, the confidence being materially increased when, as usually happens, the document thus found to have the better text is also the older. Inference from the ascertained character of other readings within the identical text, transmitted, it is to be assumed, throughout under identical conditions, must have a higher order of certainty than the inferences dependent on general probabilities which in most cases make up Internal Evidence of Readings.

41. The method here followed differs, it will be observed, from that described above in involving not a single but a threefold process. In the one case we endeavour to deal with each variation separately, and to decide between its variants immediately, on the evidence presented by the variation itself in its context, aided only by general considerations. In the other case we begin with virtually performing the same operation, but only tentatively, with a view to collect materials, not final results : on some variations we can without rashness predict at this stage our ultimate conclusions; on many more we can estimate various degrees of probability; on many more again, if we are prudent, we shall be content to remain for the present in entire suspense. Next, we pass from investigating the readings to investigating the documents by means of what we have learned respecting the readings. Thirdly, we return to the readings, and go once more over the same ground as at first, but this time making a tentative choice of readings simply in accordance with documentary authority. Where the results coincide with those obtained at the first stage, a very high degree of probability is reached, resting on the coincidence of two and often three independent kinds of evidence.

Where they differ at first sight, a fresh study of the whole evidence affecting the variation in question is secured. Often the fresh facts which it brings to light will shew the discordance between the new and the old evidence to have been too hastily assumed. Sometimes on the other hand they will confirm it, and then the doubt must remain.

42.   To what extent documentary authority alone may be trusted, where the Internal Evidence of Readings is altogether uncertain, must vary in different instances. The predominantly purer text of one document may un-doubtedly contain some wrong readings from which the predominantly less pure text of another is free.   But the instances of this kind which are ultimately found to stand scrutiny are always much fewer than a critic's first impression leads him to suppose ; and in a text of any length we believe that only a plurality of strong instances confirming each other after close examination ought to disturb the presumption in favour of the document found to be habitually the better. Sometimes of course the superiority may be so slight or obscure that the documentary authority loses its normal weight.   In such cases Internal Evidence of Readings becomes of greater relative importance : but as its inherent precariousness remains undiminished, the total result is comparative uncertainty of text.

43.   Both the single and the triple processes which we have described depend ultimately on judgements upon Internal Evidence of Readings ; but the difference between isolated judgements and combined judgements is vital.   In the one case any misapprehension of the immediate evidence, that is, of a single group of individual phenomena, tells in full force upon the solitary process by which one reading is selected from the rest for adop-

tion, and there is no room for rectification. In the other case the selection is suggested by the result of a large generalisation about the documents, verified and checked by the immediate evidence belonging to the variation; and the generalisation itself rests on too broad a foundation of provisional judgements, at once confirming and correcting each other, to be materially weakened by the chance or probability that some few of them are individually unsound.

44. Nevertheless the use of Internal Evidence of Documents has uncertainties of its own, some of which can be removed or materially diminished by special care and patience in the second and third stages of the process, while others are inherent and cannot be touched without the aid of a fresh kind of evidence. They all arise from the fact that texts are, in one sense or another, not absolutely homogeneous. Internal knowledge of documents that are compared with each other should include all their chief characteristics, and these can only imperfectly be summed up under a broad statement of comparative excellence. At first sight the sole problem that presents itself is whether this document is 'better' or 'worse' than that; and this knowledge may sometimes suffice to produce a fair text, where the evidence itself is very simple. Yet it can never be satisfactory either to follow implicitly a document pronounced to be 'best', or to forsake it on the strength of internal evidence for this or that rival reading. Every document, it may be safely said, contains errors; and second only to the need of distinguishing good documents from bad is the need of leaving as little room as possible for caprice in distinguishing the occasional errors of 'good' documents from the sound parts of their text.

45. General estimates of comparative excellence are at once shown to be insufficient by the fact that excellence itself is of various kinds : a document may be 'good' in one respect and 'bad' in another.   The distinction between soundness and correctness, for instance, lies on the surface.   One MS will transmit a substantially pure text disfigured by the blunders of a careless scribe, another will reproduce a deeply adulterated text with smooth faultlessness.   It therefore becomes necessary in the case of important MSS to observe and discriminate the classes of clerical errors by which their proper texts are severally disguised ; for an authority representing a sound tradition can be used with increased confidence when its own obvious slips have been classed under definite heads, so that those of its readings which cannot be referred to any of these heads must be reasonably supposed to have belonged to the text of its exemplar.   The complexity of excellence is further increased by the unequal distribution of the mental or semi-mental causes of corruption ; while they too can be observed, classified, and taken into account, though with less precision than defects of mechanical accuracy.   Where the documentary witnesses are not exclusively MSS having continuous texts in the original language, but also, for instance, translations into other languages or quotations by later authors, similar deductions are required in order to avoid being misled as to the substantive text of their exemplars. Thus allowance has to be made for the changes of phraseology, real or apparent, which translators generally are prone to introduce, and again for those which may be due to the defects or other peculiarities of a given language, or the purpose of a given translation.   In quotations account must in like manner be taken of the modifications, in-

tentional or unconscious, which writers are apt to make
in passages which they rapidly quote, and again of the
individual habits of quotation found in this or that particular writer. In all these cases on the one hand comparative excellence is various and divided; and on the
other an exact study of documents will go a great way
towards changing vague guesses about possible errors into
positive knowledge of the limits within which undoubted
errors have been actually found to exist. The corrective
process is strictly analogous to that by which evidence
from Transcriptional Probability is acquired and reduced
to order : but in the present case there is less liability to
error in application, because we are drawing inferences
not so much from the average ways of scribes as a class
as from the definite characteristics of this or that documentary witness.

46. The true range of individuality of text cannot
moreover be exactly measured by the range of contents
of an existing document. We have no right to assume
without verification the use of the same exemplar or exemplars from the first page to the last. A document containing more books than one may have been transcribed
either from an exemplar having identical contents, or
from two or more exemplars each of which contained a
smaller number of books; and these successive exemplars
may have been of very various or unequal excellence.
As regards alterations made by the transcriber himself,
a generalisation obtained from one book would be fairly
valid for all the rest. But as regards what is usually
much more important, the antecedent text or texts
received by him, the *prima facie* presumption that a
generalisation obtained in one book will be applicable in
another cannot safely be trusted until the recurrence of

the same textual characteristics has been empirically ascertained.

47. A third and specially important loss of homogeneousness occurs wherever the transmission of a writing
has been much affected by what (§§ 5, 6) we have called
mixture, the irregular combination into a single text of
two or more texts belonging to different lines of transmission. Where books scattered in two or more copies
are transcribed continuously into a single document (§ 46),
the use of different exemplars is successive: here it is
simultaneous. In this case the individuality, so to speak,
of each mixed document is divided, and each element
has its own characteristics; so that we need to know to
which element of the document any given reading belongs,
before we can tell what authority the reading derives from
its attestation by the document. Such knowledge evidently
cannot be furnished by the document itself; but, as we
shall see presently, it may often be obtained through
combinations of documents.

48. Lastly, the practical value of the simple application of Internal Evidence of Documents diminishes as
they increase in number. It is of course in some sort
available wherever a text is preserved in more than a
single document, provided only that it is known in each
variation which readings are supported by the several
documents. Wherever it can be used at all, its use is
indispensable at every turn; and where the documents
are very few and not perceptibly connected, it is the best
resource that criticism possesses. On the other hand, its
direct utility varies with the simplicity of the documentary
evidence; and it is only through the disturbing medium of
arbitrary and untrustworthy rules that it can be made
systematically available for writings preserved in a plurality

of documents.   For such writings in fact it can be employed as the primary guide only where the better documents are in tolerably complete agreement against the worse; and the insufficiency must increase with their number and diversity.   Wherever the better documents are ranged on different sides, the decision becomes virtually dependent on the uncertainties of isolated personal judgements.   There is evidently no way through the chaos of complex attestation which thus confronts us except by going back to its causes, that is, by enquiring what antecedent circumstances of transmission will account for such combinations of agreements and differences between the several documents as we find actually existing.   In other words, we are led to the necessity of investigating not only individual documents and their characteristics, but yet more the mutual relations of documents.

SECTION III.   GENEALOGICAL EVIDENCE
49—76

A. 49—53. *Simple or divergent genealogy*

49.   The first great step in rising above the uncertainties of Internal Evidence of Readings was taken by ceasing to treat Readings independently of each other, and examining them connectedly in series, each series being furnished by one of the several Documents in which they are found.   The second great step, at which we have now arrived, consists in ceasing to treat Documents independently of each other, and examining them connectedly as parts of a single whole in virtue of their historical relationships.   In their *prima facie* character documents present themselves as so many independent and rival texts of greater or less purity.   But as a matter of fact they are not independent: by the nature of the

case they are all fragments, usually casual and scattered fragments, of a genealogical tree of transmission, sometimes of vast extent and intricacy. The more exactly we are able to trace the chief ramifications of the tree, and to determine the places of the several documents among the branches, the more secure will be the foundations laid for a criticism capable of distinguishing the original text from its successive corruptions. It may be laid down then emphatically, as a second principle, that ALL TRUSTWORTHY RESTORATION OF CORRUPTED TEXTS IS FOUNDED ON THE STUDY OF THEIR HISTORY, that is, of the relations of descent or affinity which connect the several documents. The principle here laid down has long been acted upon in all the more important restorations of classical texts : but it is still too imperfectly understood to need no explanation. A simple instance will show at once its practical bearing.

50. Let it be supposed that a treatise exists in ten MSS. If they are used without reference to genealogy by an editor having a general preference for documentary evidence, a reading found in nine of them will in most cases be taken before a rival reading found only in the tenth, which will naturally be regarded as a casual aberration. If the editor decides otherwise, he does so in reliance on his own judgement either as to the high probability of the reading or as to the high excellence of the MS. He may be right in either case, and in the latter case he is more likely to be right than not : but where an overwhelming preponderance of the only kind of documentary evidence recognised is so boldly disregarded, a wide door is opened for dangerous uncertainty.

51. Another editor begins by studying the relations of the MSS, and finds sufficient evidence, external or

internal, for believing that the first nine MSS were all copied directly or indirectly from the tenth MS, and derived nothing from any document independent of the tenth. He will then know that all their variations from the tenth can be only corruptions (successful cursory emendations of scribes being left out of account), and that for documentary evidence he has only to follow the tenth. Apart therefore from corruptions in the tenth, for the detection of which he can obviously have no documentary evidence, his text will at once be safe and true.

52. If however the result of the second supposed editor's study is to find that all the nine MSS were derived not from the tenth but from another lost MS, his ten documents resolve themselves virtually into two witnesses; the tenth MS, which he can know directly and completely, and the lost MS, which he must restore through the readings of its nine descendants, exactly and by simple transcription where they agree, approximately and by critical processes where they disagree. After these processes some few variations among the nine may doubtless be left in uncertainty, but the greater part will have been cleared away, leaving the text of the lost MS (with these definite exceptions) as certain as if it were accessible to the eyes. Where the two ultimate witnesses agree, the text will be as certain as the extant documents can make it; more certain than if the nine MSS had been derived from the tenth, because going back to an earlier link of transmission, the common source of the two witnesses. This common source may indeed be of any date not later than the earliest of the MSS, and accordingly separated from the autograph by any number of transcriptions, so that its text may vary from absolute purity to any amount of corruption: but as conjecture is the sole possible

instrument for detecting or correcting whatever errors it may contain, this common source is the only original with which any of the methods of criticism now under discussion have any concern. Where the two ultimate witnesses differ, the genealogical method ceases to be applicable, and a comparison of the intrinsic general character of the two texts becomes the only resource.

53. The relations of descent between existing documents are rarely so simple as in the case supposed. To carry the supposition only one step further, the nine MSS might have been found to fall into two sets, five descended from one lost ancestor and four from another: and then the question would have arisen whether any two of the three authorities had a common origin not shared by the third. If it were ascertained that they had, the readings in which they agreed against the third would have no greater probability than the rival readings of the third, except so far as their common ancestor was found to have higher claims to authority as a single document than the third as a single document. If on the other hand the nine could not be traced to less than two originals, a certain much diminished numerical authority would still remain to them. Since however all presumptions from numerical superiority, even among documents known to be all absolutely independent, that is, derived from the autograph each by a separate line of descent, are liable to be falsified by different lengths and different conditions of transmission, the practical value of the numerical authority of the two supposed witnesses against the third could not be estimated till it had been brought into comparison with the results yielded by the Internal Evidence of all three witnesses.

B. 54—57. *Genealogy and Number*

54. It is hardly necessary to point out the total change in the bearing of the evidence here made by the introduction of the factor of genealogy. Apart from genealogy, the one MS becomes easily overborne by the nine; and it would be trusted against their united testimony only when upheld by strong internal evidence, and then manifestly at great risk. But if it is found that the nine had a common original, they sink jointly to a numerical authority not greater than that of the one; nay rather less, for that one is known absolutely, while the lost copy is known only approximately. Where for want of sufficiently clear evidence, or for any other reason, the simplification of pedigree cannot be carried thus far, still every approximation to an exhibition of their actual historical relations presents them in a truer light for the purposes of textual criticism than their enumeration in their existing form as so many separate units. It enables us on the one hand to detect the late origin and therefore irrelevance of some part of the *prima facie* documentary evidence, and on the other to find the rest of it already classified for us by the discovered relations of the attesting documents themselves, and thus fitted to supply trustworthy presumptions, and under favourable circumstances much more than presumptions, as a basis for the consideration of other classes of evidence.

55. It would be difficult to insist too strongly on the transformation of the superficial aspects of numerical authority thus effected by recognition of Genealogy. In the crude shape in which numerical authority is often presented, it rests on no better foundation than a vague transference of associations connected with majorities of voices, this

natural confusion being aided perhaps by the application of the convenient and in itself harmless term
'authorities' to documents. No one doubts that some
documents are better than others, and that therefore a
numerical preponderance may have rightly to yield to a
qualitative preponderance. But it is often assumed that
numerical superiority, as such, among existing documents ought always to carry a certain considerable
though perhaps subordinate weight, and that this weight
ought always to be to a certain extent proportionate to
the excess of numbers. This assumption is completely
negatived by the facts adduced in the preceding pages,
which shew that, since the same numerical relations
among existing documents are compatible with the
utmost dissimilarity in the numerical relations among
their ancestors, no available presumptions whatever as to
text can be obtained from number alone, that is, from
number not as yet interpreted by descent.

56. The single exception to the truth of this
statement leaves the principle itself untouched. Where
a minority consists of one document or hardly more,
there is a valid presumption against the reading thus
attested, because any one scribe is liable to err,
whereas the fortuitous concurrence of a plurality of
scribes in the same error is in most cases improbable;
and thus in these cases the reading attested by the
majority is exempt from the suspicion of one mode
of error which has to be taken into account with respect
to the other reading. But this limited *prima facie*
presumption, itself liable to be eventually set aside on
evidence of various classes, is distinct in kind, not in
degree only, from the imaginary presumption against
a mere minority; and the essential difference is not

altered by the proportion of the majority to the minority.

57. Except where some one particular corruption was so obvious and tempting that an unusual number of scribes might fall into it independently, a few documents are not, by reason of their mere paucity, appreciably less likely to be right than a multitude opposed to them. As soon as the numbers of a minority exceed what can be explained by accidental coincidence, so that their agreement in error, if it be error, can only be explained on genealogical grounds, we have thereby passed beyond purely numerical relations, and the necessity of examining the genealogy of both minority and majority has become apparent. A theoretical presumption indeed remains that a majority of extant documents is more likely to represent a majority of ancestral documents at each stage of transmission than *vice versa*. But the presumption is too minute to weigh against the smallest tangible evidence of other kinds. Experience verifies what might have been anticipated from the incalculable and fortuitous complexity of the causes here at work. At each stage of transmission the number of copies made from each MS depends on extraneous conditions, and varies irregularly from zero upwards: and when further the infinite variability of chances of preservation to a future age is taken into account, every ground for expecting *a priori* any sort of correspondence of numerical proportion between existing documents and their less numerous ancestors in any one age falls to the ground. This is true even in the absence of mixture; and mixture, as will be shown presently (§§ 61, 76), does but multiply the uncertainty. For all practical purposes the rival probabilities represented by relative

number of attesting documents must be treated as in-commensurable.

C. 58, 59. *Manner of discovering genealogy*

58. Knowledge of the Genealogy of Documents, as of other facts respecting them, can sometimes be obtained to a certain extent from external sources, under which may be included various external indications furnished by themselves; but it is chiefly gained by study of their texts in comparison with each other. The process depends on the principle that identity of reading implies identity of origin. Strictly speaking it implies either identity of origin or accidental coincidence, no third alternative being possible. Accidental coincidences do occur, and have to be reckoned for: but except where an alteration is very plausible and tempting, the chance that two transcribers have made the same alteration independently is relatively small, in the case of three it is much smaller, and so on with rapidly increasing improbability. Hence, while a certain number of identities of reading have to be neglected as capable of either interpretation, the great bulk may at once be taken as certain evidence of a common origin. Such community of origin for a reading may of course as regards the two or more attesting documents be either complete, that is, due to a common ancestry for their whole texts, or partial, that is, due to 'mixture', which is virtually the engrafting of occasional or partial community of ancestry upon predominantly independent descent.

59. Here, as in the investigation of the comparative excellences of continuous texts, we are able to arrive at general conclusions about texts by putting together

the data furnished by a succession of variations of reading. What we have to do is to note what combinations of documents, large or small, are of frequent recurrence. Wherever we find a considerable number of variations, in which the two or more arrays of documents attesting the two or more variants are identical, we know that at least a considerable amount of the texts of the documents constituting each array must be descended from a common ancestor subsequent to the single universal original, the limitation of ancestry being fixed by the dissent of the other array or arrays. Each larger array may often in like manner be broken up into subordinate arrays, each of which separately is found repeatedly supporting a number of readings rejected by the other documents; and each such separate smaller array must have its own special ancestry. If the text is free from mixture, the larger arrays disclose the earlier divergences of transmission, the smaller arrays the later divergences : in other words, wherever transmission has been independent, the immediate relations of existing documents are exhibited by those variations which isolate the most subordinate combinations of documents, the relationships of the ultimate ancestors of existing documents by those variations in which the combinations of documents are the most comprehensive; not necessarily the most numerous individually, but the most composite.

D. 60—65. *Complications of genealogy by mixture*

60. In the texts just mentioned, in which transmission has followed exclusively the simple type of divergent ramification, cross divisions among documents are impossible, except to the limited extent within which accidental coincidence can operate. If L M are two transcripts of the original, $L^1 L^2$ of L, and $M^1 M^2$ of M, the five distributions

(i) L^1L^2 against M^1M^2, (ii) L^1 against $L^2M^1M^2$, (iii) L^2 against $L^1M^1M^2$, (iv) M^1 against $L^1L^2M^2$, and (v) M^2 against $L^1L^2M^1$ are all possible and all likely to occur: but the two distributions (vi) L^1M^1 against L^2M^2 and (vii) L^1M^2 against L^2M^1 are impossible as results of divergent genealogy. In the second distribution L^2 appears to desert its own primary array and join the array of M; but the truth is that in a text transmitted under these conditions L^1 must have introduced a corruption, while L^2 has merely remained faithful to a reading of the original which had been faithfully preserved by L and M alike. On the other hand in the sixth distribution either L^1M^1 must have the wrong reading and L^2M^2 the right, or *vice versa*: if L^1M^1 are wrong, either L and M must have both concurred in the error, which would have rendered it impossible for either L^2 or M^2 to be right, or L^1 and M^1, transcribed from different exemplars, must have each made the same change from the true reading of L and M preserved by L^2 and M^2, which is impossible except by accidental coincidence; and *mutatis mutandis* the case is the same if L^1M^1 be right and L^2M^2 wrong, and again for the two corresponding alternatives of the seventh distribution. In this fact that the sixth and seventh combinations, that is, cross combinations, cannot exist without mixture we have at once a sufficient criterion for the presence of mixture. Where we find cross combinations associated with variations so numerous and of such a character that accidental coincidence is manifestly incompetent to explain them, we know that they must be due to mixture, and it then becomes necessary to observe within what limits the effects of mixture are discernible.

61. In so far as mixture operates, it exactly inverts the results of the simpler form of transmission, its effect being to produce convergence instead of divergence. Corruptions originating in a MS belonging to one primary array may be adopted and incorporated in transcripts from other MSS of the same or of other primary arrays. An error introduced by the scribe of L^1 in one century, and unknown to $L^2M^1M^2$, may in a later century be attested by all the then extant representatives of $L^1L^2M^1$, those of M^2 alone being free from it, the reason being that, perhaps through the instrumentality of some popular text which has adopted it, it has found its way into intermediate descendants of L^2 and of M^1. It follows that, whenever mixture has intervened, we have no security

that the more complex arrays of existing documents point to the more ancient ramifications : they may just as easily be results of a wide extension given comparatively late by favourable circumstances to readings which previously had only a narrow distribution. Conversely a present narrowness of distribution need not be a mark of relatively recent divergence : it may as easily (see § 76) be the only surviving relic of an ancient supremacy of distribution now almost obliterated by the invasion of mixture. This is of course a somewhat extreme case, but it is common enough : as a matter of fact, mixture is found to operate on every scale, from the smallest to the largest.

62. Mixture being thus liable to confuse and even invert the inferences which would indubitably follow from the conditions of transmission were transmission exclusively divergent, we have next to enquire what expedients can be employed when mixture has been ascertained to exist. Evidently no resource can be so helpful, where it can be attained, as the extrication of earlier unmixed texts or portions of texts from the general mass of texts now extant. The clearest evidence for tracing the antecedent factors of mixture in texts is afforded by readings which are themselves mixed or, as they are sometimes called, 'conflate', that is, not simple substitutions of the reading of one document for that of another, but combinations of the readings of both documents into a composite whole, sometimes by mere addition with or without a conjunction, sometimes with more or less of fusion. Where we find a variation with three variants, two of them simple alternatives to each other, and the third a combination of the other two, there is usually a strong presumption that the third is the latest and due to mixture, not the third the earliest and the other two due to two independent impulses of simplification. Peculiar contexts may no doubt sometimes give rise to this paradoxical double

6

simplification: but as a rule internal evidence is decisive to the contrary. If now we note the groups of documents which support each of the three variants; and then, repeating the process with other conflate readings, find substantially the same groups of documents occupying analogous places in all cases, we gain first a verification of the presumption of mixture by the mutual corroboration of instances, and next a determination of one set of documents in which mixture certainly exists, and of two other sets of documents which still preserve some portion at least of two more ancient texts which were eventually mixed together. Sometimes the three groups are found nearly constant throughout, sometimes they have only a nucleus, so to speak, approximately constant, with a somewhat variable margin of other documents. This relative variability however, due to irregularity of mixture, does not weaken the force of the inferences to be drawn from each single instance. If a reading is conflate, every document supporting it is thereby shown to have a more or less mixed text among its ancestry; so that, in considering any other doubtful variation, we have empirical evidence that the contingency of mixture in each such document is not *a priori* unlikely. About those documents which habitually support the conflate readings we learn more, namely that mixture must have had a large share in producing their text. Similarly we learn to set an especial value on those documents which rarely or never support the conflate readings; not necessarily as witnesses to a true text, for in all these cases each true reading is paired with a simple wrong reading, but as witnesses to texts antecedent to mixture.

63. The results thus obtained supply the foundation for a further process. It is incredible that mixed texts should be mixed only where there are conflate readings. In an overwhelming proportion of cases the composition of two earlier readings would either be impossible or produce an intolerable result; and in all such cases, supposing the causes leading to mixture to be at work, the change due to mixture would consist in a simple replacement of one reading by another, such change being indifferently a substitution or an addition or an omission. Here then we should find not three variants, but two only: that is, the reading of the mixed text would be identical with one of the prior readings; and as a matter of course the documents attesting it would comprise both those that were descended from the mixed text and those that were descended from that earlier text which the mixed text has here followed. When accordingly we find variations exhibiting these phenomena, that is, having one variant supported by that set of documents which habitually attests one recurring factor of mixture in conflate readings, and another supported by all the remaining documents, there is a strong presumption that a large portion of the adverse array of documents is descended from no line of transmission independent of the remaining portion, (that is, independent of the set of documents which habitually attests the other factor of mixture in conflate readings,) but merely echoes at second hand the attestation of that remaining portion of the array: the lines of descent of the two groups which together make up the array are in short not parallel but successive. It follows that the documentary authority for the two variants respectively is virtually reduced to that of

the two groups habitually preserving the separate factors of mixture.

64.   It is true that variability in the margin of attestation, if we may for brevity repeat a phrase employed above (§ 62), may render it uncertain with which portion of the composite array certain documents should be classed, thus weakening but not destroying the force, whatever it may be, of their opposition to the reading of the single array. It is true also that the authority of the portion of documents which belongs to the mixed text does not become actually nothing : it is strictly the authority of a single lost document, one of the sources of the mixture, belonging to the same line of transmission as the earlier group of documents supporting the same reading independently of mixture, and thus adding another approximately similar member to their company. These qualifications do not however affect the substantial certainty and efficacy of the process here described, as enabling us in a large number of variations to disentangle the confusion wrought by mixture. It is independent of any external evidence as to dates, being founded solely on the analysis and comparison of the extant texts: but of course its value for purposes of criticism is much enhanced by any chronological evidence which may exist.

65.   On the other hand there is much mixture of texts for which the extant documentary evidence antecedent to mixture is too small or uncertain to be detached from the rest, and therefore to yield materials for the application of this process. In such cases we have to fall back on the principle of Internal Evidence of Groups, to be explained presently, which is applicable to mixed and unmixed texts alike.

E. 66—72. *Applications of genealogy*

66. After this brief sketch of the modes of discovering genealogical facts by means of the extant texts, which will, we hope, be made clearer by the concrete examples to be given further on, we come to the uses of the facts so obtained for the discrimination of true from false readings. One case of the examples given in § 51 shews at once that any number of documents ascertained to be all exclusively descended from another extant document may be safely put out of sight, and with them of course all readings which have no other authority. The evidence for the fact of descent may be of various kinds. Sometimes, though rarely, it is external. Sometimes it consists in the repetition of physical defects manifestly not antecedent to the supposed original, as when the loss of one or more of its leaves has caused the absence of the corresponding portions of text in all the other documents. Sometimes the evidence is strictly internal, being furnished by analysis of the texts themselves, when it is found that a fair number of mere blunders or other evidently individual peculiarities of the supposed original have been either reproduced or patched up in all the supposed derivative documents, and secondly that these documents contain few or no variations from the text of the supposed original which cannot be accounted for by natural and known causes of corruption.

67. This summary reduction of documentary evidence by the discovery of extant ancestors of other existing documents is however of rare occurrence. On the other hand, wherever a text is found in a plurality of documents, there is a strong probability that some of them are descended from a single lost original. The proof of com·

mon descent is always essentially the same, consisting
in numerous readings in which they agree among themselves and differ from all other documents, together with
the easy deducibility, direct or indirect, of all their readings from a single text. In the absence of the second
condition the result would differ only in being less
simple : we should have to infer the mixture of two or
more lost originals, independent of each other as well as
of the remaining extant documents.

68. The manner of recovering the text of a single lost
original, assuming the fact of exclusive descent from it to
have been sufficiently established, will be best explained
by a free use of symbols. Let us suppose that the extant
descendants are fourteen, denoted as *abcdefghiklmno*;
that, when their mutual relationships are examined, they
are found to fall into two sets, *abcdefghi* and *klmno*,
each having a single lost ancestor (X and Y respectively)
descended from the common original; and again that
each of these sets falls similarly into smaller sets, the first
into three, *ab*, *cdef*, and *ghi*, the second into two, *kl* and
mno, each of the five lesser sets having a single lost ancestor (αβγδε respectively) descended from the common
subordinate original, αβγ from X, δε from Y. Let us
suppose also that no cross distributions implying mutual
or internal mixture can be detected. We have then this
pedigree :

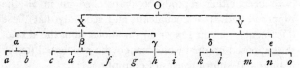

69. Readings in which all fourteen documents agree belonged indubitably to the common original O. On the other
hand the genealogical evidence now before us furnishes no
indication as to the readings of O in variations in which
all the descendants of X are opposed to all the descendants
of Y: for reasons already given (§ 57) the proportion
nine to five tells us nothing; and the greater compositeness of *abcdefghi*, as made up of three sets against two,

is equally irrelevant, since we know that each larger set has but a single ancestor, and we have no reason for preferring X singly to Y singly. These variations therefore we reserve for the present. Where however the descendants of either X or Y are divided, so that the representatives of (say) γ join those of δ and ϵ against those of a and β, and the question arises whether the reading of X is truly represented by $a\beta$ or by γ, the decision must be given for that of γ, because, mixture and accidental coincidence apart, in no other way can γ have become at once separated from $a\beta$ and joined to $\delta\epsilon$; in other words, the change must have been not on the part of γ but of $a\beta$, or rather an intermediate common ancestor of theirs. The reading thus ascertained to have been that of both X and Y must also, as in the first case, have been the reading of O. Accordingly, so far as the whole evidence now before us is concerned, that is, assuming absence of mixture with documents independent of O, all readings of $a\beta$ against $\gamma\delta\epsilon$ may be at once discarded, first as departures from the text of O, and next as departures from the text of the autograph, since the direct transmission of all the documents passes through O, and thus it is not possible, on the present conditions, for $a\beta$ to agree with the autograph against O except by conjecture or accidental coincidence. The same results follow in all the analogous cases, namely for readings of γ against $a\beta\delta\epsilon$, a against $\beta\gamma\delta\epsilon$, δ against $a\beta\gamma\epsilon$, and ϵ against $a\beta\gamma\delta$. The combinations $a\gamma$ against $\beta\delta\epsilon$ and $\beta\gamma$ against $a\delta\epsilon$ are possible only by mutual mixture among descendants of X antecedent to $a\beta\gamma$, since they form cross distributions with the assumed combination $a\beta$ against $\gamma\delta\epsilon$: but this particular mixture would not interfere with the present operation of fixing the reading of X by coincidence with the reading of Y, because there would be no more mixture with Y than in the other cases, and the force of the consent of Y with part of the descendants of X remains the same whatever that part may be.

70. It will be seen at once what a wide and helpful suppression of readings that cannot be right is thus brought about by the mere application of Genealogical method, without need of appeal to the Internal Evidence of either Texts or Readings except so far as they contribute in the first instance to the establishment of the genealogical facts. Precisely analogous processes are required where any of the five lesser sets are divided, say by opposition

of *cd* to *ef*, so that we have to decide whether the true reading of β is found in *cd* or in *ef*. The final clear result is that, when we have gone as far as the discoverable relations among our documents admit, we have on the one hand banished a considerable number of the extant variants as absolutely excluded, and on the other ascertained a considerable number of readings of O, in addition to those parts of the text of O in which all its descendants agree.

71. Two elements of uncertainty as to the text of O alone remain. First, the condition presupposed above, absence of mixture from without, does not always hold good. Where mixture from without exists, the inference given above from the concurrence of γ with $\delta\epsilon$ against $a\beta$ becomes but one of three alternatives. It is possible that mixture with a text independent of O has affected γ and Y alike, but not $a\beta$; and if so, $a\beta$ will be the true representatives of X and of O. This possibility is however too slight to be weighed seriously, unless the reading of γ and Y is found actually among existing documents independent of O, provided that they are fairly numerous and various in their texts, or unless the hypothesis of mixture is confirmed by a sufficiency of similarly attested readings which cannot be naturally derived from readings found among the descendants of O. Again, it is possible that the reading of $a\beta$ is itself due to mixture with a text independent of O: and if so, though rightly rejected from the determination of the reading of O, it may possibly be of use in determining the reading of an ancestor of O, or even of the autograph itself. But both these contingencies need be taken into account only when there is already ground for supposing mixture from without to exist.

72. The second element of uncertainty is that which always accompanies the earliest known divergence from a single original. Given only the readings of X and Y, Genealogy is by its very nature powerless to shew which were the readings of O. It regains its power only when we go on to take into account fresh documentary evidence independent of O, and work towards an older common original from which both it and O are descended. O then comes to occupy the place of X or Y, and the same process is repeated; and so on as often as the evidence will allow. It must however be reiterated (see § 52) that, when O has come to mean the autograph, we have, in reaching the earliest known divergence, arrived

at the point where Genealogical method finally ceases to be applicable, since no independent documentary evidence remains to be taken up. Whatever variations survive at this ultimate divergence must still stand as undecided variations. Here therefore we are finally restricted to the Internal Evidence of single or grouped Documents and Readings, aided by any available external knowledge not dependent on Genealogy.

F. *73—76. Variable use of genealogy according to un-equal preservation of documents*

73. The proper method of Genealogy consists, it will be seen, in the more or less complete recovery of the texts of successive ancestors by analysis and comparison of the varying texts of their respective descendants, each ancestral text so recovered being in its turn used, in conjunction with other similar texts, for the recovery of the text of a yet earlier common ancestor. The preservation of a comparatively small number of documents would probably suffice for the complete restoration of an autograph text (the determination of the earliest variations of course excepted) by genealogy alone, without the need of other kinds of evidence, provided that the documents preserved were adequately representative of different ages and different lines of transmission. This condition however is never fulfilled. Texts are not uncommonly preserved in a considerable assemblage of documents the genealogy of which can be fully worked out, but is found to conduct to one or two originals which, for all that appears to the contrary, may be separated from the autograph by many ages of transmission, involving proportionate possibilities of corruption. Here Genealogical method retains its relative value, for it reduces within narrow limits the amount of variation which need occupy an editor when he comes to the construction of his text:

but it leaves him in the dark, as all criticism dealing only with transmitted variations must do, as to the amount of correspondence between the best transmitted text and the text of his author. These cases correspond to such limited parts of the documentary evidence of more adequately attested texts as represent single stages of textual history.

74. In those rare cases, on the other hand, in which extant documentary evidence reaches up into quite ancient times the process may be carried back to a stage comparatively near the autograph: but here the evidence is as a matter of fact never abundant enough for more than rough and partial approximations to the typical process described above. Here too, as always, we have to ascertain whether the confusing influence of mixture exists, and if so, within what limits. Under such circumstances any chronological and geographical information to be obtained from without has great value in interpreting obscure genealogical phenomena, especially as marking the relative date and relative independence of the several early documents or early lost ancestors of late documents or sets of documents.

75. In proportion as we approach the time of the autograph, the weight of composite attestation as against homogeneous attestation increases; partly because the plurality of proximate originals usually implied in composite attestation carries with it the favourable presumption afforded by the improbability of a plurality of scribes arriving independently at the same alteration; partly because the more truly composite the attestation, that is, the more independent its component elements, the more divergences and stages of transmission must have preceded, and thus the earlier is likely to have been the

date for the common original of these various generations of descendants, the later of which are themselves
early. Nothing of course can exclude the possibility
that one line of transmission may have ramified more
rapidly and widely than another in the same time : yet
still the shorter the interval between the time of the
autograph and the end of the period of transmission in
question, the stronger will be the presumption that
earlier date implies greater purity of text. But the
surest ground of trusting composite attestation is attained when it combines the best documentary representatives of those lines of transmission which, as far as
our knowledge goes, were the earliest to diverge. Such
are essentially instances of ascertained concordance of
X and Y (§ 69), in spite of the dissent of some descendants of one or both.

76. The limitation to "the best documentary representatives" is necessary, because the intrusion of mixture in documents, or in lost originals of documents or
of documentary groups, may disguise the actual historical relations (see § 61), and give the appearance of
greater compositeness of attestation to readings which
have merely invaded lines of transmission that for a while
were free from them. It thus becomes specially necessary to observe which documents, or lost originals of
documents or documentary groups, are found to shew
frequent or occasional mixture with texts alien from their
own primary ancestry, and to allow for the contingency
accordingly. Many cases however of ambiguous interpretation of evidence are sure to remain, which the
existing knowledge of the history of mixture is incompetent to clear up ; and for these recourse must be had
to evidence of other kinds.

SECTION IV.   INTERNAL EVIDENCE OF GROUPS

77, 78

77. We have reserved for this place the notice of another critical resource which is in some sense intermediate between Internal Evidence of Documents and Genealogical Evidence, but which in order of discovery would naturally come last, and the value of which will have been made more apparent through the inherent and the incidental defects of Genealogical Evidence described in the preceding paragraphs. This supplementary resource is Internal Evidence of Groups. In discussing Internal Evidence of Documents, we spoke only of single documents : but the method itself is equally applicable to groups of documents. Just as we can generalise the characteristics of any given MS by noting successively what readings it supports and rejects, (each reading having previously been the subject of a tentative estimate of Internal Evidence of Readings, Intrinsic and Transcriptional,) and by classifying the results, so we can generalise the characteristics of any given group of documents by similar observations on the readings which it supports and rejects, giving special attention to those readings in which it stands absolutely or virtually alone. In texts where mixture has been various, the number of variations affording trustworthy materials for generalisations as to any one group can be only a part of the sum total of variations ; but that part will often be amply sufficient. The evidence obtained in this manner is Internal Evidence, not Genealogical. But the validity of the inferences depends on the genealogical principle that community of reading implies community of origin. If we find, for instance, in any group of documents a succession of readings

exhibiting an exceptional purity of text, that is, readings which the fullest consideration of Internal Evidence pronounces to be right in opposition to formidable arrays of Documentary Evidence, the cause must be that, as far at least as these readings are concerned, some one exceptionally pure MS was the common ancestor of all the members of the group; and that accordingly a recurrence of this consent marks a recurrence of joint derivation from that particular origin, and accordingly a strong presumption that exceptional purity is to be looked for here again. The inference holds equally good whether the transmission has been wholly divergent, or partly divergent and partly mixed; and any characteristic, favourable or unfavourable, may be the subject of it.

78. The value of Internal Evidence of Groups in cases of mixture depends, it will be seen, on the fact that by its very nature it enables us to deal separately with the different elements of a document of mixed ancestry. In drawing general conclusions from the characteristics of the text of a document for the appreciation of its individual readings successively, we assume the general homogeneousness of its text; but this assumption is legitimate only if unity of line of ancestry is presupposed. The addition of a second line of ancestry by mixture introduces a second homogeneousness, which is as likely as not to conflict with that of the first, and thus to falsify inferences drawn from the first, unless there be means of discriminating from the rest of the text the portions taken from the second original. But each well marked group of which the mixed document is a member implies at least the contingency of a distinct origin; and thus, in readings in which the document is associated with the rest of the group, its authority need not be that which

it derives in the bulk of its text from its fundamental or primary original, but is strictly that belonging to the common ancestor of its secondary original and of the other members of the group. Such readings might be truly described as forming a series of minute fragments of a copy of the lost document which was the secondary original, leaving corresponding gaps in the more or less faithfully preserved text of the primary original, except where conflate readings have wholly or partly preserved both texts. In the next Part we shall have ample opportunity of illustrating what has here been said.

SECTION V.   RECAPITULATION OF METHODS IN RELATION
TO EACH OTHER

79—84

79. To recapitulate. The method of Genealogy is an application of one part of the knowledge of Documents; and like the method founded on the Internal Evidence of Documents it involves three processes; first the analysis and comparison of the documentary evidence for a succession of individual variations ; next the investigation of the genealogical relations between the documents, and therefore between their ancestors, by means of the materials first obtained; and thirdly the application of these genealogical relations to the interpretation of the documentary evidence for each individual variation. The results of the interpretation of documentary evidence thus and thus alone made possible are various. In the first place it winnows away a multitude of readings which genealogical relations prove to be of late origin, and which therefore cannot have been derived by transmission from the autograph. Where the extant evidence suggests but

is insufficient to prove thus much, and in the case of all other variants, this method so presents and limits the possible genealogical antecedents of the existing combinations of documentary evidence as to supply presumptions in favour of one variant against another varying from what amounts under favourable circumstances to practically absolute certainty down to complete equipoise.

80. So far as genealogical relations are discovered with perfect certainty, the textual results which follow from them are perfectly certain too, being directly involved in historical facts; and any apparent presumptions against them suggested by other methods are mere guesses against knowledge. But the inequalities and occasional ambiguities in the evidence for the genealogical relations frequently admit of more than one interpretation, and this greater or less substitution of probability for certainty respecting the documentary history reduces the textual verdict to a presumption, stronger or weaker as the case may be. Genealogical presumptions ought however to take precedence of other presumptions, partly because their immediate basis is in itself historical not speculative, and the subject-matter of all textual criticism is historical, partly because the generalisations by which that historical basis is ascertained involve less chance of error than the analogous generalisations required for any kind of Internal Evidence.

81. The only safe order of procedure therefore is to start with the reading suggested by a strong genealogical presumption, if such there be; and then enquire whether the considerations suggested by other kinds of evidence agree with it, and if not, whether they are clear and strong enough to affect the *prima facie* claim of higher attestation. If they appear so to be, a

full re-examination becomes necessary; and the result, especially if similar instances recur, may be the discovery of some genealogical complication overlooked before. No definite rule can be given as to what should be done where the apparent conflict remains, more especially where the documentary evidence is scanty or obscure. For our own part, in any writing having fairly good and various documentary attestation we should think it dangerous to reject any reading clearly supported by genealogical relations, though we might sometimes feel it equally necessary to abstain from rejecting its rival.

82. Next in value to Genealogical Evidence is Internal Evidence of Documents, single or in groups. But where the documents exceed a very small number, the Internal Evidence of single Documents, as has already been explained (§ 48), is rendered for the most part practically inapplicable by the unresolved complexity. The Internal Evidence however of Groups of Documents is always applicable if there are documents enough to form groups. It is the best substitute for Genealogical Evidence proper in texts, or in any parts of texts, in which genealogical relations are too obscure for use; and it affords the most trustworthy presumptions for comparison with purely genealogical presumptions, having similar merits derived from the form of the processes by which it is obtained, while relating to a different class of phenomena. The highest certainty is that which arises from concordance of the presumptions suggested by all methods, and it is always prudent to try every variation by both kinds of Internal Evidence of Readings. The uncertainty however inherent in both, as dependent on isolated acts of individual judgement, renders them on the whole untrustworthy against a con-

currence of Genealogy and Internal Evidence of Documents; though a concurrence of clear Intrinsic with clear Transcriptional Probability ought certainly to raise at least a provisional doubt.

83. Textual criticism fulfils its task best, that is, is most likely to succeed ultimately in distinguishing true readings from false, when it is guided by a full and clear perception of all the classes of phenomena which directly or indirectly supply any kind of evidence, and when it regulates itself by such definite methods as the several classes of phenomena suggest when patiently and circumspectly studied. This conformity to rationally framed or rather discovered rules implies no disparagement of scholarship and insight, for the employment of which there is indeed full scope in various parts of the necessary processes. It does but impose salutary restraints on the arbitrary and impulsive caprice which has marred the criticism of some of those whose scholarship and insight have deservedly been held in the highest honour.

84. Nevertheless in almost all texts variations occur where personal judgement inevitably takes a large part in the final decision. In these cases there is no failure of method, which strictly speaking is an impossibility, but an imperfection or confusion of the evidence needed for the application of method. Here different minds will be impressed by different parts of the evidence as clearer than the rest, and so virtually ruling the rest: here therefore personal discernment would seem the surest ground for confidence. Yet here too, once more, the true supremacy of method is vindicated; for it is from the past exercise of method that personal discernment receives the education which tends to extinguish its illusions and

7

mature its power. All instinctive processes of criticism
which deserve confidence are rooted in experience, and
that an experience which has undergone perpetual correction and recorrection.

SECTION VI.   CRITICISM AS DEALING WITH ERRORS
ANTECEDENT TO EXISTING TEXTS
85—95

A. 85—92.   *Primitive errors*

85.   The preceding pages have dealt exclusively with
the task of discriminating between existing various readings, one variant in each case being adopted and the rest
discarded. The utmost result that can be obtained under
this condition is the discovery of what is relatively original: whether the readings thus relatively original were
also the readings of the autograph is another question,
which can never be answered in the affirmative with
absolute decision except where the autograph itself is
extant, but which admits of approximative answers varying enormously in certainty according to the nature of the
documentary evidence for the text generally. Even in a
case in which it were possible to shew that the extant documents can be traced back to two originals which diverged
from the autograph itself without any intermediate common ancestor, we could never be quite sure that where
they differed one or other must have the true reading,
since they might independently introduce different changes
in the same place, say owing to some obscurity in the
writing of a particular word. In almost all actual cases
an interval, short or long, must have divided the autograph from the earliest point or points to which genealogy
conducts us back; and any interval implies the possibility
of corruption, while every addition to the length of the
interval increases the probability of corruption. On the
other hand documentary evidence including a fair variety
of very ancient attestation may bring the meeting-point
of the extant lines of transmission so near the autograph
that freedom from antecedent corruption ceases to be
improbable, without however thereby becoming *a priori*
probable. In such cases therefore any investigation of

the ultimate integrity of the text is governed by no theoretical presumptions : its final conclusions must rest on the intrinsic verisimilitude or suspiciousness of the text itself.

86. These considerations have an important bearing on certain paradoxical conflicts of evidence respecting transmitted variations, which present themselves occasionally in most texts and frequently in many; and which are peculiarly apt to mislead editors to whom textual criticism is only a subordinate province of interpretation. The reading clearly indicated by Genealogical or other evidence obtained from whole texts, or by Transcriptional Evidence of Readings, or by both together, may be as clearly condemned by Intrinsic Evidence. We are not speaking of the numerous cases in which readings that have seemed to a critic in the first instance too strange to be true approve themselves on better knowledge, perhaps as no more than tolerable, but oftener still as having a peculiar impress of truth which once apprehended cannot easily be questioned ; or in which competent critics receive opposite impressions from the same reading, one holding it to be impossible, the other to have the stamp of originality. These differences of judgement throw no light upon readings which all competent critics feel on consideration to be impossible, and yet which are strongly attested by, it may be, every kind of evidence except Intrinsic Evidence.

87. The true solution lies in the fact that the subject matter of the different kinds of evidence is not identical. Intrinsic Evidence is concerned only with absolute originality ; it pronounces which of two or more words or phrases a given author in a given place was more likely to use, or, in extreme cases in either direction, whether either of them was what he must have used or could not possibly have used. All other kinds of evidence are concerned only or predominantly with relative originality : they pronounce, speaking roughly, which of two or more readings is more likely to have given rise to the others, or is found in the best company, or has the best pedigree. The apparent conflict therefore is dependent on the assumption, usually well founded, that the two originalities coincide. Where they do not, that is, where corruption has preceded the earliest extant documentary evidence, the most nearly original extant reading may nevertheless be wrong, simply because the reading of the autograph

has perished. What an editor ought to print in such a case, supposing he has satisfied himself that the best attested reading is really impossible, may vary according to circumstances. But it is clearly his duty in some way to notify the presumed fact of corruption, whether he can offer any suggestion for its removal or not.

88. In the cases just mentioned, while the best attested reading is found to be impossible, the other reading or readings shown by evidence not Intrinsic to be corruptions of it are or may be found quite possible, but not more : they derive their *prima facie* probability only from an assumed necessity of rejecting their better attested rival. In other cases the reading (or one of the readings) shown to be of later origin has very strong Intrinsic Evidence in its own favour; that is, we have a combination of positive clear Intrinsic Evidence for the worse attested reading with negative clear Intrinsic Evidence against the better attested reading. So complete an inversion of the ordinary and natural distributions of evidence always demands, it need hardly be said, a thorough verification before it can be accepted as certain. It does however without doubt occasionally occur, and it arises from a state of things fundamentally the same as in the former cases, with the difference that here a transcriber has happened to make that alteration which was needed to bring back the reading of the autograph, that is, has in the course of transcription made a successful Conjectural Emendation. No sharp line can in fact be drawn between the deliberate conjectural emendations of a modern scholar and many of the half or wholly unconscious changes more or less due to mental action which have arisen in the ordinary course of transcription, more especially at times when minute textual accuracy has not been specially cultivated. An overwhelming proportion of the cursory emendations thus made and silently embodied in transcribed texts are of course wrong : but it is no wonder that under favourable circumstances they should sometimes be right. It may, once more, be a matter of doubt what form of printed text it will here be most expedient under given circumstances to adopt. The essential fact remains under all circumstances, that the conjectural origin of these readings is not altered by the necessity of formally including them in the sum of attested readings ; and that an editor is bound to indicate in some manner the conjectural character of any attested reading

which he accepts as the reading intended by the author, and yet which he does not believe to have been received by continuous transmission from the autograph.

89. We have dwelt at some length on these two classes of variations because at first sight they appear to furnish grounds for distrusting the supremacy of what we have ventured to call the higher kinds of evidence. They not unnaturally suggest the thought that, whatever may be said in theory respecting the trustworthiness of evidence not Intrinsic, it breaks down in extreme cases, and must therefore contain some latent flaw which weakens its force in all. But the suspicion loses all plausibility when it is seen that it springs from a confusion as to the subject matter of attestation (see § 87), and that the attestation itself remains as secure in extreme cases as in all others. The actual uncertainties arise not from any want of cogency of method, but from inadequate quantity or quality of the concrete evidence available in this or that particular text or variation.

90. Both the classes of variations just considered imply corruption in the earliest transmitted text. The same fact of corruption antecedent to extant documentary evidence has to be recognised in other cases, some of which form a third class of variations. Besides the variations already noticed in which the evidence shews one variant to have been the parent of the rest, while yet on Intrinsic grounds it cannot be right, there are others in which the variants have every appearance of being independent of each other, while yet on Intrinsic grounds none having sufficiently good documentary attestation, or even none at all, can be regarded as right : that is to say, a convergence of phenomena points to some lost reading ás the common origin of the existing readings. Fourthly, there may be sufficient grounds for inability to accept the transmitted text even in places where the documents agree.

91. In all four cases the ground of belief that the transmitted text is wrong is Internal Evidence of Readings. In the third it is or may be a combination of Intrinsic and Transcriptional Evidence : in the first, second, and fourth it is exclusively Intrinsic Evidence, except where recognition of corruption is partly founded on perception of the lost original reading, which, as we shall see shortly, involves the use of Transcriptional Evidence. The use of Internal Evidence of Readings in detecting corruption is precisely identical with its use, or

rather one of its uses, in the discrimination of attested readings. In coming to a decision on the strength of Intrinsic Evidence, a critic makes one of three affirmations respecting two variants a and β; (1) a is more probable than β; (2) a is not only more probable than β, and is not only suitable to the place, but is so exactly and perfectly suitable that it must be right; and (3) β is not only less probable than a, but so improbable absolutely that it cannot be right, so that a as the only remaining variant must be right: (2) and (3) of course include (1), and also are compatible with each other. Now in pronouncing a text corrupt, he affirms neither more nor less than in the fundamental proposition of the third instance, in which he equally finds his whole evidence exclusively in the reading condemned, and in its own relations to the context, without reference to any other variant. In both procedures the affirmation has against it all the uncertainties which we have pointed out as inherent in the exclusive use of Intrinsic Evidence: nevertheless there are places in nearly all texts where its force is so convincing that the most cautious critic cannot refuse to make the affirmation, and in every ill preserved text they abound.

92. The first, second, and fourth cases are essentially the same. The presence of more than one variant in the first and second case does not place them on a different footing from the fourth, because all but the one are by supposition subsequent to the one, and are therefore virtually out of sight when the question of accepting the most original of attested readings as the true reading arises. A critic may doubtless feel less reluctant to pronounce a reading corrupt when he sees that it gave trouble to ancient scribes; but the encouragement is due to corroboration of personal judgement, not to any kind of evidence; it comes from the ancient scribes in the character of critics, not as witnesses to a transmitted text. On the other hand the third case has an advantage over the others by combining a certain measure of Transcriptional with Intrinsic Probability. The supposition of corruption has the strength of a double foundation when it not only accounts for our finding an impossible text but supplies a common cause for two readings, the apparent independence of which would otherwise be perplexing; and this it does even in the absence of any perception as to what conjectural reading would fulfil the various conditions of the case.

B. 93—95. *Removal of primitive errors by conjecture*

93. In discussing the corruption of texts antecedent to extant documents, the forms in which it presents itself, and the nature of the critical process by which it is affirmed, we have reserved till last a brief notice of the critical process which endeavours to remedy it, that is, Conjectural Emendation. Although in practice the two processes are often united, and a felicitous conjecture sometimes contributes strong accessory evidence of corruption, it is not the less desirable that they should be considered separately. The evidence for corruption is often irresistible, imposing on an editor the duty of indicating the presumed unsoundness of the text, although he may be wholly unable to propose any endurable way of correcting it, or have to offer only suggestions in which he cannot place full confidence.

94. The art of Conjectural Emendation depends for its success so much on personal endowments, fertility of resource in the first instance, and even more an appreciation of language too delicate to acquiesce in merely plausible corrections, that it is easy to forget its true character as a critical operation founded on knowledge and method. Like the process of detecting corruption, it can make no use of any evidence except Internal Evidence of Readings, but it depends on Intrinsic and Transcriptional Evidence alike. Where either there is no variation or one variant is the original of the rest, that is, in the fourth, first, and second of the cases mentioned above, two conditions have to be fulfilled by a successful emendation. As regards Intrinsic Evidence, it must, to attain complete certainty, be worthy of the second form of affirmation noticed above, that is, be so exactly and perfectly suitable to the place that it cannot but be right; or, to attain reasonable probability, it must be quite suitable to the place positively, and free from all incongruity negatively. As regards Transcriptional Evidence, it must be capable of explaining how the transmitted text could naturally arise out of it in accordance with the ordinary probabilities of transcription. Where there are more independent variants than one, that is, in the third case, the only difference is that the suggested correction must in like manner be capable of giving rise naturally to every such transmitted Reading. Thus in all cases the problem

involved in forming a judgement on a suggested Conjectural Emendation differs in one respect only from the ordinary problems involved in deciding between transmitted readings on the strength of Intrinsic and Transcriptional Evidence combined, and of these alone; it consists in asking whether a given reading out of two or three fulfils certain conditions well absolutely, whereas in other cases we ask which of two or three readings fulfils the same conditions best.

95. The place of Conjectural Emendation in the textual criticism of the New Testament is however so inconsiderable that we should have hesitated to say even thus much about it, did it not throw considerable light on the true nature of all textual criticism, and illustrate the vast increase of certainty which is gained when we are able to make full use of Documentary Evidence, and thus confine Internal Evidence to the subordinate functions which alone it is normally fitted to discharge.

PART III

APPLICATION OF PRINCIPLES OF CRITICISM TO THE TEXT OF THE NEW TESTAMENT

96. The principles of criticism explained in the foregoing section hold good for all ancient texts preserved in a plurality of documents. In dealing with the text of the New Testament no new principle whatever is needed or legitimate : but no other ancient text admits of so full and extensive application of all the various means of discriminating original from erroneous readings which have been suggested to scholars by study of the conditions of textual transmission. On the one hand the New Testament, as compared with the rest of ancient literature, needs peculiarly vigilant and patient handling on account of the intricacy of evidence due to the unexampled amount and antiquity of mixture of different texts, from which few even of the better documents are free. On the other it has unique advantages in the abundance, the antiquity, and above all in the variety of its documentary evidence, a characteristic specially favourable to the tracing of genealogical order.

CHAPTER I. *PRELIMINARY CHRONOLOGICAL SURVEY OF DOCUMENTS*

97—128

97. Before entering on the historical phenomena of the text itself, and the relations between its principal documents, we think it best to interpose a short general survey

of the written evidence with which all criticism has to deal, presenting it in a form somewhat different from that of the detailed catalogues which it is the office of other books to supply. The entire body of documentary evidence, with inconsiderable exceptions, consists of three parts ; extant Greek MSS, ancient translations or 'Versions' in different languages, and quotations from the New Testament made by ancient Christian writers or 'Fathers'.

A. 98—106. *Greek MSS*

98. The Greek MSS of the New Testament are divided into two classes, conventionally though somewhat incorrectly termed ' Uncials' and ' Cursives', according as they are written in capital or in minuscule characters. Since Wetstein's time (1751, 1752) it has been customary to distinguish Uncials by capital letters, and Cursives for the most part by arabic numerals. At the head of the list of Uncials stand four great MSS belonging to the fourth and fifth centuries. When complete, they all evidently contained the whole Greek Bible. At least three, and not improbably all four, had all the books of the New Testament that have been subsequently recognised as canonical, at least two containing other books in addition : as two are mutilated at the end, it is impossible to speak with greater precision. These four MSS are products of the earlier part of that second great period of Church history which begins with the reign of Constantine ; the time when the various partial Canons of Scripture were brought together and as it were codified in various ways, the first step in the process being probably the catalogue of Eusebius in his Church History (of about 325), and the most decisive step, at least for the Greek churches, the catalogue of Athanasius in his 39th Paschal Epistle, of 367. About 332 Constantine directed Eusebius to have fifty easily legible copies of the complete Scriptures executed by skilful calligraphers for the use of the churches in his newly founded capital. We learn nothing of the texts or the contents of these "sumptuously prepared volumes" (Eus. *Vit. Const.* IV 37) : but if the contained books corresponded with Eusebius's own list of a few years earlier (*H. E.* III 25), none of our present MSS can well have been of the number. The incident illustrates however a need which would arise on a smaller scale in many places, as new and splendid churches came to be built under the Christian Empire after the great persecution : and the four extant copies are doubtless casual

examples of a numerous class of MSS, derived from various origins though brought into existence in the first instance by similar circumstances. These four are the *Codex Vaticanus* (B), containing the whole New Testament except the later chapters of Hebrews, the Pastoral Epistles, Philemon, and the Apocalypse; the *Codex Sinaiticus* (א), containing all the books entire; the *Codex Alexandrinus* (A), containing all, except about the first 24 chapters of St Matthew's and two leaves of St John's Gospel and three of 2 Corinthians; and the *Codex Ephraemi* (C), containing nearly three fifths of the whole (145 out of 238 leaves), dispersed over almost every book, one or more sheets having perished out of almost every quire of four sheets. The two former appear to belong to the middle part of the fourth century: the two latter are certainly of somewhat later date, and are assigned by the best judges to the fifth century.

99. The remaining uncial MSS are all of smaller though variable size. None of them shew signs of having formed part of a complete Bible, and it is even doubtful whether any of them belonged to a complete New Testament. Six alone (including one consisting of mere fragments) are known to have contained more than one of the groups of books, if we count the Acts and the Apocalypse as though they were each a group. The Gospels are contained in fair completeness in nineteen uncial MSS (including אABC), the Acts in nine, the Catholic Epistles in seven, the Pauline Epistles in nine (besides the transcripts E_3 and F_2), and the Apocalypse in five. The numbers given for the Gospels, Acts, and Pauline Epistles do not include some more or less considerable fragments: but the line is hard to draw, and much is lost of C and Γ, which are included in the list.

100. After the four great Bibles the chronological distribution becomes remarkable. The fifth century supplies (besides AC) only Q and T, both consisting of fragments of Luke and John: the sixth century supplies for the Gospels D (all four, but incomplete), N and P (fragments of all four), Σ (Matthew and Mark, almost complete), R (fragments of Luke), and Z (fragments of Matthew); for the Acts D and E_2 (both incomplete); and for the Pauline Epistles D_2 (not quite complete): under each head some lesser fragments are not reckoned. The seventh century furnishes merely a few fragments; the eighth, besides lesser fragments, EL (Gospels), Ξ (large

fragments of Luke), and B₂ (Apocalypse). But the MSS
of the ninth and tenth centuries are about as numerous as
those of all preceding centuries together. The preceding
assignation of uncials to this or that century is founded
in most cases on no independent judgement, but on the
published estimates of the best qualified palæographers.
It is quite possible that some of the intermediate uncials
may be placed a century too high or too low, for the
absence of dated MSS before the ninth century renders
palæographical determination of the absolute chronology
as yet insecure. The approximate outlines of the relative or sequential chronology appear however to have
been laid down with reasonable certainty; so that the
total impression left by a chronological analysis of the
list of uncials can hardly be affected by possible errors of
detail.

101.   The bilingual uncial MSS have a special interest.
They are, in Greek and Latin, DΔ of the Gospels, DE₂ of
the Acts, and D₂[E₃F₂]G₃ of the Pauline Epistles; in
Greek and Thebaic (the language of Upper Egypt), the
fragmentary T of Luke and John, with some still smaller
fragments of the same kind.

102.   The Cursive MSS range from the ninth to the
sixteenth centuries. Many of them contain two or more
groups of books, and about 30 the whole New Testament.
If each MS is counted as one, irrespectively of the books
contained, the total number is between 900 and 1000.

103.   An accessory class of Greek MSS is formed by
Lectionaries or books of ecclesiastical lessons taken from
the New Testament, of which above 400 have been cata-
logued. Above four fifths contain only Gospel lessons,
most of the rest lessons from the Acts and Epistles, some
few being mixed. About 70 are uncials, and the rest
cursives. None however are believed to be older than
the eighth or possibly the seventh century, and uncial
writing continued in use for Lectionaries some time after
it had become obsolete for complete copies of the New
Testament or complete divisions of it.

104.   Such is the nominal roll of Greek MSS. If however we confine our attention to those sufficiently known
to be used regularly as direct evidence, a numerically large
deduction has to be made, the amount of which, as distinguished from its value, cannot be estimated even in
a rough manner. Comparatively few Lectionaries have as
yet been collated. Some of these have been found to con-

tain readings of sufficient value and interest to encourage further enquiry in what is as yet an almost unexplored region of textual history, but not to promise considerable assistance in the recovery of the apostolic text. Of the numerous cursive MSS of the New Testament and its parts hardly any have been printed *in extenso*. We have however complete and trustworthy collations of a select few from Tregelles, and of a large miscellaneous (English) array from Dr Scrivener, both most careful collators; and tolerably complete collations of other miscellaneous assemblages from Alter (Vienna) and Matthæi (chiefly Moscow and Dresden); with which other collations might probably be classed. On the customary mode of reckoning, by which the four traditional divisions of the New Testament (Acts and Catholic Epistles being counted as one) are taken separately, the full contents of about 150 cursives, besides Lectionaries, may be set down as practically known from these sources. A much larger number are known in various degrees of imperfection, some perhaps almost as well as those included in this first class, from the labours of a series of collators, of whom Mill, Wetstein, Griesbach, Birch, Scholz, and Muralt deserve special mention. Many others have been examined only in selected passages, by which rough presumptions, but hardly more, can be formed as to the general character of the text; and many others again are entirely unknown.

105. This large amount of present ignorance respecting the contents of cursives is much to be lamented. Valuable texts may lie hidden among them; many of them are doubtless sprinkled with relics of valuable texts now destroyed; and fresh collations always throw more or less light on the later history of the text generally, and sometimes on its earlier history. But enough is already known to enable us to judge with reasonable certainty as to the proportional amount of valuable evidence likely to be buried in the copies as yet uncollated. If we are to trust the analogy thus provided, which agrees with what might have been anticipated from the average results of continued transcription generally, nothing can well be less probable than the discovery of cursive evidence sufficiently important to affect present conclusions in more than a handful of passages, much less to alter present interpretations of the relations between the existing documents.

106. The nominal list of uncials needs hardly any appreciable deductions to make it a true representation

of the uncial evidence completely available. With the exception of the lately discovered Σ, all the older and more important uncials, some fragments excepted, have now been published in continuous texts, and the various readings of the rest are included in the *apparatus critici* of Tischendorf and (with unimportant exceptions) of Tregelles.

B. 107—122. *Versions*

107. The second class of documents consists of Versions, that is, ancient translations of the whole or parts of the New Testament, made chiefly for the service of churches in which Greek was at least not habitually spoken. Besides some outlying Versions, there are three principal classes, the LATIN, the SYRIAC, and the EGYPTIAN. The history of all is still more or less obscure.

108. The LATIN MSS are usually classified under two heads, 'Old Latin' (sometimes miscalled 'Italic') and 'Vulgate'. For some purposes the distinction is convenient and almost necessary: but it disguises the fact that there is a wider difference between the earlier and the later stages of the 'Old Latin' (in this comprehensive sense of the term) than between the later stages and the Vulgate. The statements of Tertullian leave no doubt that when he wrote, near the beginning of the third century, a Latin translation of the New Testament was already current in North Africa. How much earlier it came into existence, and in what manner, cannot be ascertained; but it may be reasonably assumed to have originated in Africa. An exact and authentic transcript of portions of the African text is conveyed to us by the early Latin patristic quotations. The rich evidence supplied by Tertullian's works is indeed difficult to disentangle, because he was fond of using his knowledge of Greek by quoting Scripture in immediate and original renderings, the proportion of which to his quotations from the existing version is indeterminate but certainly large. This disturbing element is absent however from Cyprian's quotations, which are fortunately copious and carefully made, and thus afford trustworthy standards of African Old Latin in a very early though still not the earliest stage.

109. In the fourth century we find current in Western Europe, and especially in North Italy, a second type of text, the precise relation of which to the African text of the second and third centuries has not yet been clearly ascertained. These two Latin texts have very much in

common, both in the underlying Greek text and in language; and many of the differences are fully compatible
with the supposition that the African was the parent of
the European text, having undergone revision when it
travelled northwards, and been in some measure adapted
to the needs of a more highly cultivated population. On
the other hand, other differences, not so easily accounted
for by this process, afford some justification for the
alternative view that Italy had an indigenous version of
her own, not less original than the African. The distinctively African renderings which occur not unfre-
quently in some of the best European documents may
be explained in conformity with either view; as survivors
from an earlier state, or as aliens introduced by mixture.
Recent investigations have failed to solve this difficult
problem, and it must be left for further examination:
fortunately the value of the two early forms of the Latin
text is not appreciably affected by the uncertainty. The
name 'Old Latin', in its narrower and truer sense, may
properly be retained for both, where there is no need of
distinguishing them, and for the European text, where
the African is not extant or never existed; the special
designations 'African Latin' and 'European Latin' being
employed where they bear a divided testimony.

110. After the middle of the fourth century we meet
with Latin texts which must be referred to a third type.
They are evidently due to various revisions of the
European text, made partly to bring it into accord with
such Greek MSS as chanced to be available, partly to
give the Latinity a smoother and more customary aspect.
In itself the process was analogous to that by which the
European text must have been formed, on the supposition
that it was of African parentage: but, as we shall see
presently, the fundamental text now underwent more
serious changes, owing to the character of the Greek MSS
chiefly employed. The fact that the Latin text found in
many of Augustine's writings is of this type has long been
used with good reason to shew what he meant by the
Itala which he names in a single laudatory notice (*De
doct. Chr.* ii 15). Without doubt this name was intended
to distinguish the version or text which he had in view
from the 'African' version or text with which he was
likewise familiar ('codices Afros' *Retr.* i 21 3). The only
open question is whether he had definitely before his
mind a special text due to a recent North Italian re-

vision, as has been usually assumed by those who have interpreted rightly the general bearing of his words, or was merely thinking of the text of Italy in such a comprehensive sense as would include what we have called the European text. The former view was a necessary inference from the assumption that the best known Old Latin MSS of the Gospels had a strictly African text: but much of its probability is lost when it is seen how far removed they are from a Cyprianic standard. But whatever may be the precise force of the term as used by Augustine, such revised texts as those which he himself employed constitute an important stage in the history of the Latin New Testament: and it can hardly lead to misunderstanding if we continue to denote them by the convenient name ' Italian '.

111. The endless multiplicity of text in the Latin copies at length induced Jerome, about 383, to undertake a more thorough revision of the same kind. We learn from his own account nothing about his Greek MSS except that they were "old"; or about his mode of proceeding except that he made no alterations but such as were required by the sense, and that he kept specially in view the removal of the numerous interpolated clauses by which the Gospels were often brought into factitious similarity to each other in parallel passages. Internal evidence shews that the Latin MSS which he took as a basis for his corrections contained an already revised text, chiefly if not wholly 'Italian' in character. In the Gospels his changes seem to have been comparatively numerous ; in the other books of the New Testament, which he left without any explanatory preface, but which he must have taken in hand as soon as the Gospels were finished, his changes were evidently much scantier and more perfunctory. It is worthy of notice that readings distinctly adopted in his own writings are not seldom at variance with the revised text which bears his name. These discrepancies may possibly be due to a change of view subsequent to the revision: but in any case it would be rash to assume that Jerome deliberately considered and approved every reading found in his text, even of the Gospels, and much more of the other books which passed through his hands. The name 'Vulgate' has long denoted exclusively the Latin Bible as revised by Jerome; and indeed in modern times no continuous text of any other form of the Latin version or versions was known before 1695.

112. Generations not a few had passed before the Hieronymic revision had even approximately displaced the chaos of unrevised and imperfectly revised Latin texts; and during the period of simultaneous use the Latin Vulgate, as we may now call it, suffered much in purity by the casual resumption of many readings expelled or refused by Jerome. Scribes accustomed to older forms of text corrupted by unwitting reminiscence the Vulgate which they were copying; so that an appreciable part of Jerome's work had been imperceptibly undone when the Vulgate attained its final triumph. Partly from this cause, partly from the ordinary results of transcription, the Vulgate text underwent progressive deterioration till long after the close of the Middle Ages, notwithstanding various partial attempts at correction. At length the authoritative 'Clementine' revision or recension of 1592 removed many corruptions. Many others however were left untouched, and no critically revised text of the Latin Vulgate New Testament founded systematically on more than one or two of the best MSS has yet been edited. The text of at least two of the best as yet known, and a very few others comparatively good, has however been printed at full length.

113. The existing MSS of the Old Latin Gospels, distinguished by small letters, belong for the most part to the fourth, fifth, and sixth centuries: one however (*c*), strange to say, was written as late as the eleventh century. Hardly any are quite complete, and those which contain more than inconsiderable fragments amount to about fourteen, of which on an average scarcely more than half are extant in any one passage: in this computation Ante-Hieronymic texts of all types are included. Among the few fragments not counted are two leaves which agree closely with one of the comparatively complete MSS: but with this exception all known MSS shew more or less textual individuality, and there are many traces of sporadic and casual mixture. Two of the MSS (*e k*) are substantially African, a large proportion of their texts being absolutely identical with that of Cyprian, where he differs from European MSS and Fathers; but each has also an admixture of other readings: both are unfortunately very imperfect, *e* having lost above two-fifths of its contents, chiefly in Matthew and Mark, and *k* above three-fourths, including the whole of Luke and John. Two other MSS (*f q*), and one or two fragments, must be classed as 'Italian'. The remaining ten, though

8

African readings are found to a certain extent in some of
them, and Italian readings in others, have all substantially European texts.

114.   Various modifications of late revision and mixture are represented in some Latin MSS of the Gospels,
which do not properly fall under any one of the preceding
heads.   Four of them are usually marked as Old Latin
($ff^1 g^{1.2} l$); but most of the number pass simply as copies
of the Vulgate.   With few exceptions their texts are as
yet imperfectly known; and the relations of their texts to
each other, and to the Hieronymic or any other late revisions, have still to be investigated.   They are certainly
however in most cases, and not improbably in all, monuments of the process described above (§ 112) by which
Old Latin readings, chiefly European but in a few cases
African, found their way into texts fundamentally Hieronymic.   The chief worth of these Mixed Vulgate MSS
for the criticism of the Greek text consists in the many
valuable particles of Latin texts antecedent to the Vulgate
which have thus escaped extinction by displacing Jerome's
proper readings.   Mixed texts of this class are not confined to the Gospels; but in the other books, so far as
they are yet known, their Ante-Hieronymic elements contain a much smaller proportion of valuable materials.

115.   The Gospels alone are extant in a series of tolerably
complete Old Latin MSS.   For most of the other books we
have, strictly speaking, nothing but fragments, and those
covering only a small proportion of verses.   The delusive
habit of quoting as Old Latin the Latin texts of bilingual
MSS has obscured the real poverty of evidence.   These
MSS are in Acts *Cod. Bezae* (D, *d*; as in the Gospels)
and *Cod. Laudianus* (E$_2$, *e*), and in St Paul's Epistles *Cod.
Claromontanus* (D$_2$, *d*) and *Cod. Boernerianus* (G$_3$, *g*;
without Hebrews).   The origin of the Latin text, as clearly
revealed by internal evidence, is precisely similar in all
four MSS.   A genuine (independent) Old Latin text has
been adopted as the basis, but altered throughout into
verbal conformity with the Greek text by the side of which
it was intended to stand.   Here and there the assimilation
has accidentally been incomplete, and the scattered discrepant readings thus left are the only direct Old Latin
evidence for the Greek text of the New Testament which
the bilingual MSS supply.   A large proportion of the
Latin texts of these MSS is indeed, beyond all reasonable
doubt, unaltered Old Latin: but where they exactly cor-

respond to the Greek, as they do habitually, it is impossible to tell how much of the accordance is original, and how much artificial; so that for the criticism of the Greek text the Latin reading has here no independent authority. The Latin texts of Δ of the Gospels and F_2 of St Paul's Epistles are Vulgate, with a partial adaptation to the Greek. Besides the Græco-Latin MSS there are four Gothico-Latin leaves of Romans.

116. The relics of genuine Old Latin MSS of the books after the Gospels are as follows. For Acts: a few palimpsest leaves of an African text (h); a complete European copy (g), and also the story of Stephen from a Lectionary (g_2), both agreeing closely with the quotations of Lucifer; and some palimpsest fragments of the later chapters (s), with a text of the same general type. For the Catholic Epistles: one (? European) MS of St James, and some fragments of the next three epistles in a later (? Italian) text (q): the palimpsest fragments of James and 1 Peter accompanying s of Acts are apparently Vulgate only. For the Pauline Epistles: considerable Italian fragments of eight epistles (r), with leaves from two other MSS having similar texts ($r_2 r_3$). For the Apocalypse: two palimpsest leaves of a purely African text (h), and a late European text of the whole book (g). Other portions of Ante-Hieronymic texts of different books are said to have been discovered in Italy; and doubtless others will in due time be brought to light.

117. This is the fitting place to speak of the quotations made by Latin Fathers, for they constitute a not less important province of Old Latin evidence than the extant MSS; not only furnishing landmarks for the investigation of the history of the version, but preserving numerous verses and passages in texts belonging to various ages and in various stages of modification. Even in the Gospels their aid is always welcome, often of the highest value; while in all other books they supply not only a much greater bulk of evidence than our fragmentary MSS, but also in not a few cases texts of greater antiquity. Some books and parts of books are of course much worse represented than others, more especially such books as formed no part of the original North African Canon. But in the Apocalypse Primasius, an African writer of the sixth century, has preserved to us an almost uninterrupted text, which is proved by its close similarity to the quotations of Cyprian to be African Latin of high purity. Thus, sin-

gularly enough, the Apocalypse possesses the unique advantage of having been preserved in a Latin text at once continuous and purely African. The quotations of other late African Fathers from various books exhibit an African text much altered by degeneracy and mixture, but preserving many ancient readings.

118. The SYRIAC versions are, strictly speaking, three in number. The principal is the great popular version commonly called the Peshito or *Simple.* External evidence as to its date and history is entirely wanting: but there is no reason to doubt that it is at least as old as the Latin version. Till recently it has been known only in the form which it finally received by an evidently authoritative revision, a Syriac 'Vulgate' answering to the Latin 'Vulgate'. The impossibility of treating this present form of the version as a true representation of its original text, without neglecting the clearest internal evidence, was perceived by Griesbach and Hug about the beginning of this century: it must, they saw, have undergone subsequent revision in conformity with Greek MSS. In other words, an Old Syriac must have existed as well as an Old Latin. Within the last few years the surmise has been verified. An imperfect Old Syriac copy of the Gospels, assigned to the fifth century, was found by Cureton among MSS brought to the British Museum from Egypt in 1842, and was published by him in 1858. The character of the fundamental text confirms the great antiquity of the version in its original form; while many readings suggest that, like the Latin version, it degenerated by transcription and perhaps also by irregular revision. The rapid variation which we know the Greek and Latin texts to have undergone in the earliest centuries could hardly be absent in Syria; so that a single MS cannot be expected to tell us more of the Old Syriac generally than we should learn from any one average Old Latin MS respecting Old Latin texts generally. But even this partially corrupted text is not only itself a valuable authority but renders the comparatively late and 'revised' character of the Syriac Vulgate a matter of certainty. The authoritative revision seems to have taken place either in the latter part of the third or in the fourth century. Hardly any indigenous Syriac theology older than the fourth century has been preserved, and even from that age not much available for textual criticism. Old Syriac readings have been observed as used

by Ephraim and still more by Aphraates: but at present there are no means of supplying the lack of Old Syriac MSS to any appreciable extent from patristic quotations. Of the Old Syriac Acts and Epistles nothing as yet is known. The four minor Catholic Epistles and the Apocalypse, not being included in the Canon of the Syrian Churches, form no part of the true Syriac Vulgate, but are extant in supplementary versions. None of the ,editions of the Syriac Vulgate come up to the requirements of criticism: but considerable accessions to the evidence for the Greek text are hardly to be looked for from this source.

119. A second version, closely literal in its renderings, was made by Polycarpus for Philoxenus of Mabug in 508. Little is known of it in this its original condition. We possess a revision of it made by Thomas of Harkel in 616, containing all the New Testament except the Apocalypse. The margin contains various readings taken from Greek MSS, which must either have been ancient or have had ancient texts. A third version, written in a peculiar dialect, is found almost exclusively in Gospel Lesson-books, and is commonly called the Jerusalem Syriac. The text is of ancient character: but there is no other evidence to shew when the version was made. Besides one almost complete Lesson-book known for some time, a few considerable fragments have lately come to light. They include a few verses of the Acts. Various signs render it likely that both these versions were in some sense founded on one or other of the two forms of the Peshito. But the whole subject awaits fuller investigation.

120. The third great group of Versions is the EGYPTIAN. The Coptic or Egyptian versions proper are three, very unequally preserved. The Memphitic, the version of Lower Egypt, sometimes loosely designated as the Coptic, contains the whole New Testament, though it does not follow that all the books were translated at the same period, and the Apocalypse was apparently not treated as a canonical book. The greater part of the version cannot well be later than the second century. A very small number of the known MSS have been used in the existing editions, and that on no principle of selection. A cursory examination by Dr Lightfoot has recently shown much diversity of text among the MSS; and in Egypt, as elsewhere, corruption was doubtless progressive. The version of Upper

Egypt, the Thebaic or Sahidic, was probably little if at all inferior in antiquity. It in like manner contained the whole New Testament, with the Apocalypse as an appendix. No one book is preserved complete, but the number of extant fragments, unfortunately not yet all published, is considerable. Of the third Egyptian version, the Bashmuric, about 330 verses from St John's Gospel and the Pauline Epistles alone survive. With the Egyptian versions proper it is at least convenient to associate the Æthiopic, the version of ancient Abyssinia, dating from the fourth or fifth century. Though written in a totally different language, it has strong affinities of text with its northern neighbours. The best judges maintain its direct derivation from a Greek original: but neither this question nor that of the relation of the Thebaic to the Memphitic version can be treated as definitively settled while so much of the evidence remains unpublished. The numerous MSS of the Æthiopic have been ascertained to vary considerably, and give evidence of revision: but the two editions yet printed are both unsatisfactory. No book of the New Testament is wanting.

121. Besides the three great groups two solitary versions are of considerable interest, the one from outlying Asia, the other from outlying Europe. These are the AR- MENIAN and the GOTHIC. The ARMENIAN, which is complete, was made early in the fifth century. Some modern copies, followed by the first printed edition, contain corruptions from the Latin Vulgate: but the Armenian translators certainly followed Greek MSS, probably obtained from Cappadocia, the mother of Armenian Christianity. The GOTHIC version, the work of Ulfilas the great bishop of the Goths, dates from the middle of the fourth century. He received a Greek education from his Christian parents, originally Cappadocians: and Greek MSS unquestionably supplied the original for his version. We possess the Gospels and the Pauline Epistles (Hebrews excepted), with many gaps, admirably edited from MSS of about the sixth century.

122. The other versions are of comparatively late date, and of little direct value for the Greek text, though some of them, as the Slavonic, bear traces of ancient texts. Most of them are only secondary translations from other versions, chiefly the Latin and Syriac Vulgates.

C. 123—126. *Fathers*

123. The third class of documentary evidence is supplied by the writings of the Fathers, which enable us with more or less certainty to discover the readings of the MS or MSS of the New Testament which they employed. The quotations naturally vary in form from verbal transcripts of passages, short or long, through loose citations down to slight allusions. Nay there are cases in which the absence of even an allusion allows the text read by an author to be inferred with tolerable certainty : but this negative evidence is admissible only with the utmost caution.

124. Besides the evidence as to the texts used by ancient writers which is supplied by their quotations, allusions, or silences, a few of them sometimes make direct assertions as to variations of reading within their knowledge. The form of assertion varies much, now appearing as a statement that, for instance, "some" or "many" or "the most accurate" "copies" contain this or that variant, now as an allegation that the true reading has been perversely depraved by rash or by heretical persons for some special end. This whole department of patristic evidence has a peculiar interest, as it brings vividly before the reader the actual presence of existing variations at a remote antiquity. Its true value is twofold : for the history of the whole text it certifies two or more alternative readings as simultaneously known at a definite time or locality ; and for the settlement of the text in a given passage it usually enables the reading adopted by the writer to be known with a higher degree of certainty than is attainable in a majority of cases by means of ordinary quotations. But this superior certitude must not be confounded with higher authority : the relative excellence or the historical position of the text employed by a Father has nothing to do with the relative adequacy of our means of ascertaining what his text actually was. Moreover in the statements themselves the contemporary existence of the several variants mentioned is often all that can be safely accepted : reliance on what they tell us beyond this bare fact must depend on the estimate which we are able to form of the opportunities, critical care, and impartiality of the respective writers.

125. An enumeration of the Greek Fathers would be out of place here. The names most important in textual criticism will come before us presently, when we have to

speak of the peculiar value of their evidence as enabling
us to trace the outlines of the early history of the text.
This is however the place for observing that the extent of
patristic evidence still preserved is considerably less than
might have been *a priori* anticipated.   Numerous verses
of the New Testament are rarely or never quoted by the
Fathers: the gaps in the evidence are still more striking
if we take the Ante-Nicene Fathers by themselves. A small
portion of Origen's commentaries is virtually all that remains to us of the continuous commentaries on the New
Testament belonging to this period: they include Matt. xiii
36—xxii 33 in the original Greek (perhaps in an abridged
form), and Matt. xvi 13—xxvii 66 in a condensed Latin
translation, preserving matter not found in the Greek now
extant; some verses of St Luke (a much condensed Latin
translation of Homilies on i—iv, not continuous, and on
five later passages of St Luke being also extant); John i
1—7, 19—29; ii 12—25; iv 13—54; viii 19—25 and 37—53;
xi 39—57; xiii 2—33 (little more than a sixth of the whole)
in the full original text; Romans in the much condensed
and much altered version of Rufinus; many verses of
1 Corinthians and Ephesians; and a few scattered verses
of some of the other books.   The extant commentaries
and continuous series of homilies written before the middle
of the fifth century are as follows:—Theodore of Mopsuestia on the minor Pauline Epistles in a Latin translation; Chrysostom's Homilies, which include St Matthew,
St John, Acts (ill preserved), and all the Pauline Epistles;
Theodoret on all the Pauline Epistles, his notes being
chiefly founded on the works of Theodore of Mopsuestia
and Chrysostom; and Cyril of Alexandria's Homilies on
St Luke (many fragments in Greek and large portions
in a Syriac translation) and Commentary on John i 1—x
17; xii 49—end, with fragments on the rest of the book
and on the other Gospels and several of the Pauline
Epistles; together with fragments by other writers preserved in Catenæ under various conditions, sometimes
apparently in their original integrity, but much oftener in
a condensed and partly altered shape.

126.   It is on the whole best to class with patristic
evidence a few collections of biblical extracts, with little
or no intervening matter, selected and arranged for
doctrinal or ethical purposes.   The *Ethica* of Basil of
Cæsarea (Cent. IV) and the *Parallela Sacra* of John of
Damascus (Cent. VIII) are the best known Greek ex-

amples: parts of some of Cyril of Alexandria's dogmatic writings, especially the *Thesaurus*, have nearly the same character. A Latin collection of a similar kind, the *Speculum* which wrongly bears the name of Augustine, but is of unknown authorship, has usually been placed with Old Latin MSS under the signature *m*, and contains an interesting but not early Old Latin text. Of much the same structure are the three books of *Testimonia* by Cyprian, and indeed a large part of his little treatise *De exhortatione martyrii* addressed to Fortunatus.

127, 128. *Documentary preparation for this edition*

127. It is right that we should here explain to what extent we have thought it our duty to take part ourselves in the indispensable preparatory work of collecting documentary evidence. Great services have been rendered by scholars who have been content to explore and amass texts and readings for the use of others; or again who have discussed principles and studied documents without going on to edit a text. On the other hand an editor of the New Testament cannot completely absolve himself from either of these two preliminary tasks without injury to his own text: but the amount of personal participation required is widely different for the two cases. If he has not worked out at first hand the many and various principles and generalisations which are required for solving the successive problems presented by conflicts of evidence, the resulting text is foredoomed to insecurity: but the collection of evidence is in itself by no means an indispensable apprenticeship for the study of it.

128. We have accordingly made no attempt to follow the example of those editors who, besides publishing critical texts of the New Testament, have earned the gratitude of all who come after them by collation of MSS and accumulation of registered evidence in the form of an *apparatus criticus*. As we have never proposed to do more than edit a manual text, so we have no considerable private stores to add to the common stock. The fresh evidence which we have obtained for our own use has been chiefly patristic, derived in a great measure from writings or fragments of writings first published during the last hundred years, or now edited from better MSS than were formerly known. While in this and other respects the evidence already accessible to all students has been to a

certain limited extent augmented, it has of course been frequently verified and re-examined, not only for the sake of clearing up ambiguities or doubts, but because the needful experience could hardly be otherwise acquired. The exigencies of our task demanded a personal acquaintance with the outward phenomena of MSS, with the continuous texts of individual MSS and versions, and with the varying conditions under which the New Testament is quoted and referred to by the Fathers; for no information at second hand can secure the conveyance of a correct and vivid impression of the true and complete facts by bare lists of authorities cited for a succession of detached and sharply defined various readings. But we have deliberately chosen on the whole to rely for documentary evidence on the stores accumulated by our predecessors, and to confine ourselves to our proper work of investigating and editing the text itself. Such a concentration of labour ought at least to favour an impartial survey of the entire field of evidence, and to give time and opportunity for prolonged consideration of the text and its history in various lights.

CHAPTER II. *RESULTS OF GENEALOGICAL EVIDENCE PROPER*

129—255

SECTION I.   DETERMINATION OF THE GENEALOGICAL RELATIONS OF THE CHIEF ANCIENT TEXTS

129—168

129.   After this short preliminary survey of the existing documents out of which the text of the New Testament has to be recovered, we have now to describe the chief facts respecting their ancestry and the character of their texts which have been learned by study of their contents or from any other sources, and which render it possible to deal securely with their numerous variations

in accordance with the principles of criticism explained
in the preceding section. We have already seen, first,
that decision upon readings requires previous knowledge
of documents, and secondly that the most valuable part
of the knowledge of individual documents implies a
previous knowledge of the genealogical history of the
text as a whole. The first step therefore towards fixing
the places of the existing documents relatively to each
other is to employ them conjointly as evidence for discovering the more ancient ramifications of transmission;
and for this purpose the whole mass of documents of
all dates and all kinds must at the outset be taken into
account.

A. 130, 131. *Priority of all great variations to Cent. V*

130. A glance at any tolerably complete *apparatus
criticus* of the Acts or Pauline Epistles reveals the striking
fact that an overwhelming proportion of the variants common to the great mass of cursive and late uncial Greek
MSS are identical with the readings followed by Chrysostom (ob. 407) in the composition of his Homilies.
The coincidence furnishes evidence as to place as well
as time; for the whole of Chrysostom's life, the last ten
years excepted, was spent at Antioch or in its neighbourhood. Little research is needed to shew that this
is no isolated phenomenon: the same testimony, subject
to minor qualifications unimportant for the present purpose, is borne by the scattered quotations from these and
other books of the New Testament found in his voluminous works generally, and in the fragments of his
fellow-pupil Theodorus of Antioch and Mopsuestia, and
in those of their teacher Diodorus of Antioch and Tarsus.

The fundamental text of late extant Greek MSS generally is beyond all question identical with the dominant Antiochian or Græco-Syrian text of the second half of the fourth century. The community of text implies on genealogical grounds a community of parentage : the Antiochian Fathers and the bulk of extant MSS written from about three or four to ten or eleven centuries later must have had in the greater number of extant variations a common original either contemporary with or older than our oldest extant MSS, which thus lose at once whatever presumption of exceptional purity they might have derived from their exceptional antiquity alone.

131. The application of analogous tests to other groups of documents leads to similar results. The requisite chronological criteria are to be found in the Greek patristic evidence of the second, third and fourth centuries; in the Latin patristic evidence of the third and fourth centuries; in the Old Latin version, as dated indirectly by the Latin patristic evidence ; in the Vulgate Latin, the Gothic, and virtually the Armenian versions, as dated by external evidence ; and the two (or possibly three) oldest extant Greek MSS, B, ℵ, and A; the Armenian version and probably A being however a little over the line. To this list may safely be added the Old and Vulgate Syriac, as they have some sufficient if slight patristic attestation in the early part of the fourth century, although the evidence which completely establishes their antiquity, being inferential, would not entitle them to a place here ; and also the two principal Egyptian versions, the early age of which, though destitute of the testimony which it would doubtless have received from the preservation of an early Coptic literature, is established by historical considerations independent of the character of the texts.

The list, however limited, contains a sufficient variety of strictly or approximately direct historical evidence to enable us at once to refer to the fourth century at latest the original of nearly every considerable group of extant documents which frequently recurs in the *apparatus criticus*, and indeed to carry back some to the third, and others to the second century. In each case the genealogical process here employed can of course do no more than supply an inferior limit of age: a lost original thus proved to be as old as the fourth century may, for all that we have thus far seen, be in reality as old as the other lost originals which can be positively referred to earlier times. What we have gained is the limitation of enquiry by the knowledge that all the important ramifications of transmission preceded the fifth century.

B. 132—151. *Posteriority of Syrian* (δ) *to 'Western'* (β) *and other* (*neutral*, α) *readings shown* (1) *by analysis of Conflate Readings*

132. Within this comparatively restricted field we have next to investigate the genealogical relations of the principal groups of documents, or, what is virtually the same thing, of their respective lost originals, following partly, as before, external evidence, partly the indications of sequence obtained by Internal Evidence of the Groups as wholes. The presence of early and extensive mixture betrays itself at once in the number and intricacy of cross distributions of attestation (see § 60), and thus it becomes important to ascertain at the outset whether any whole groups have been affected by it; and if such can be found, to determine the contributory groups which are thereby proved not merely to be of earlier date, but to have been the actual parents of the groups of mixed origin.

133. The clearest evidence for this purpose, as we have already seen (§ 62), is furnished by conflate readings, where they exist; and in the case of some of the primary groupings of the textual documents of the New Testament they are fortunately not wanting. Before proceeding however to examine some examples of this kind, it may be well to notice a few illustrations of the phenomenon of 'conflation' in its simpler form, as exhibited by single documents. Here and always we shall use the ordinary notation, unless there is sufficient reason for departing from it: a list of special symbols and abbreviations employed is given in the Appendix. In Acts vi 8, where the two readings πλήρης χάριτος and πλήρης πίστεως are attested each by a plurality of documents, E₂ alone combines them, by means of a conjunction, reading πλήρης χάριτος καὶ πίστεως. In Mark vi 56 the Latin MS a couples the readings ἐν ταῖς ἀγοραῖς and ἐν ταῖς πλατείαις by a conjunction, and slightly modifies them, reading in foro et in plateis. In John v 37 D makes ἐκεῖνος αὐτός out of ἐκεῖνος and αὐτός without a conjunction; and similarly John xiii 24 stands in one principal text as νεύει οὖν τούτῳ Σ. Π. καὶ λέγει αὐτῷ Εἰπὲ τίς ἐστιν περὶ οὗ λέγει, in another as νεύει οὖν τούτῳ Σ. Π. πυθέσθαι τίς ἂν εἴη περὶ οὗ λέγει, while ℵ adds one form to the other, merely changing a tense, and reads νεύει οὖν τούτῳ Σ. Π. πυθέσθαι τίς ἂν εἴη περὶ οὗ ἔλεγεν, καὶ λέγει αὐτῷ Εἰπὲ τίς ἐστιν περὶ οὗ λέγει. In 1 Cor. x 19 the readings τί οὖν φημί; ὅτι εἰδωλόθυτόν τί ἐστιν; ἢ ὅτι εἴδωλόν τί ἐστιν; and τί οὖν φημί; ὅτι εἰδωλόθυτόν ἐστίν τι· οὐχ ὅτι εἴδωλόν ἐστίν τι, or their Latin equivalents, are ingeniously interwoven by fuld. as quid ergo dico? quod idolis immolatum sit aliquid, aut quod idolum sit aliquid? non quod idolum sit aliquid. Luke xvi 30

illustrates another kind of combination, in which part of a longer reading is replaced by the whole of the shorter reading: for ἐάν τις ἐκ νεκρῶν πορευθῇ πρὸς αὐτούς or ἐάν τις ἐκ νεκρῶν ἀναστῇ (implied in the Latin reading *si quis ex mortuis resurrexerit* [v. l. *surrexerit*]) ℵ has ἐάν τις ἐκ νεκρῶν ἀναστῇ πρὸς αὐτούς, while two or three other documents retain both verbs. In 1 Cor. i 8 the Latin Vulgate effects the combination by making the one element dependent on the other, changing the Old Latin *in adventu Domini nostri* (ἐν τῇ παρουσίᾳ τοῦ κυρίου ἡμῶν) into *in die adventus Domini nostri* by incorporating the Greek reading ἐν τῇ ἡμέρᾳ τοῦ κυρίου ἡμῶν. Bold conflations, of various types, are peculiarly frequent in the Æthiopic version, at least in the extant MSS.

134. We now proceed to conflate readings involving important groups of documents, premising that we do not attempt to notice every petty variant in the passages cited, for fear of confusing the substantial evidence.

Mark vi 33 (following καὶ εἶδαν αὐτοὺς ὑπάγοντας καὶ [ἐπ]έγνωσαν πολλοί, καὶ πεζῇ ἀπὸ πάσων τῶν πολέων συνέδραμον ἐκεῖ)

(α) καὶ προῆλθον αὐτούς ℵB (LΔ 13) lt (39) 49
       lat.vg me arm (LΔ 13 lt 39 have
       προσῆλθον)
     καὶ προῆλθον αὐτὸν αὐτοῦ syr.vg

(β) καὶ συνῆλθον αὐτοῦ D 28 *b*
     καὶ ἦλθον αὐτοῦ 81 *ff i*
     καὶ ἦλθον   *a*
     om.   cu³ (*c*)

(δ) καὶ προῆλθον αὐτοὺς καὶ συνῆλθον πρὸς αὐτόν
     AEFGHKMUVΓΠ   cu.omn.exc.8
     f q syr.hl aeth

135. Here we have two short readings of three words each (α, β), differing only by the preposition compounded with the verb and by the presence or absence of the last letter, having therefore a strong *prima facie* appearance of being derived the one from the other. The documents attesting α are four uncials (two of them our two oldest), three cursives, and at least three versions in different languages, one of them made late in Cent. IV, one early in Cent. V, and the third of age treated as not yet determined, but at least not later than Cent. III. The Vulgate Syriac is on the whole a supporter of α, as it reads προῆλθον and has but one clause : its ending may be due either to modified reduplication of the last word of α or, more probably, to conflation with the last word of β. For β (and the readings evidently derived from it) we have an uncial of Cent. VI, two cursives, and three Old Latin MSS. No true Old Latin MS is in any way favourable to α or δ against β : two, *e k*, which contain other parts of this Gospel, are absent; as are also the Thebaic and Old Syriac and Jerusalem Syriac versions. The longer reading δ, which is that of the Received Text, is supported by eleven uncials, one of them of Cent. V (or possibly IV) and the rest not earlier than Cent. VIII; all cursives except five; two Latin MSS belonging approximately to the Italian revision, which cannot be younger and is probably not older than Cent. IV; and two versions unquestionably later than Cent. IV.

136. If now we compare the three readings with reference to Transcriptional Probability, it is evident that either δ is conflate from α and β, or α and β are independent simplifications of δ; for the similarity of αὐτοῦ and αὐτούς, combined with the relative dissimilarity of both to πρὸς αὐτόν, shews that δ can hardly have been a pas-

sage from α to β or from β to α; and the independent
derivation of β and δ from α, or of α and δ from β, would
be still more incredible. There is nothing in the sense
of δ that would tempt to alteration : all runs easily and
smoothly, and there is neither contradiction nor manifest
tautology. Accidental omission of one or other clause
would doubtless be easy on account of the general similarity of appearance (καὶ...ἦλθον...αυτο...), and precedents
are not wanting for the accidental omission of even both
clauses in different documents or groups of documents.
On the other hand the change from πρὸς αὐτόν of δ to
αὐτοῦ of β is improbable in itself, and doubly improbable when ἐκεῖ has preceded. Supposing however α
and β to have preceded δ, the combination of the two
phrases, at once consistent and quite distinct in meaning,
would be natural, more especially under the influence of
an impulse to omit no recorded matter ; and the change
from αὐτοῦ to πρὸς αὐτόν (involving no change of historical statement, for the place denoted by αὐτοῦ was the
place to which the Lord had gone) might commend itself
by the awkwardness of αὐτοῦ (itself a rare adverb in the
New Testament) after συνέδραμον ἐκεῖ, and by the seeming
fitness of closing this portion of narrative with a reference
to the Lord Himself, who is moreover mentioned in the
opening words of the next verse.

137. As between α and β the transcriptional probabilities are obscure. Συνῆλθον αὐτοῦ is certainly otiose
after συνέδραμον ἐκεῖ, and a sense of the tautology might
lead to change ; but the changes made by scribes hardly
ever introduce such vivid touches as this of the arrival of
the multitude before the apostles. On the other hand
προῆλθον αὐτούς might be altered on account of the un-
familiarity of the construction or the unexpectedness of

9

the sense, which harmonises with the earlier words εἶδον αὐτοὺς ὑπάγοντας but would hardly be suggested by them; and then συνέδραμον might suggest to the ear and perhaps to the mind συνῆλθον, after which αὐτούς would be inevitably read as αὐτοῦ, αὐτοῖς being in manifest contradiction to the contrast between ἐν τῷ πλοίῳ and πεζῇ: the tautology introduced might easily escape notice at first under the different phraseology, especially if συνῆλθον were taken to express the arrival subsequent to the running, though it was perceived afterwards, as we see by the omission of αὐτοῦ in *a*, and of the whole clause in *c*, where *convenerunt* stands for *cognoverunt* above.

138. As regards Intrinsic Probability, β may be dismissed at once, on grounds virtually given already. Had δ been the only extant reading, it would have roused no suspicion: but when it has to be compared with α, we cannot but notice the irrelevance of the repetition of σύν in composition with two different verbs not in immediate sequence, and the intrusiveness of καὶ προῆλθον αὐτούς between the local and the personal endings of the journey expressed by ἐκεῖ and πρὸς αὐτόν; the position of this clause can be justified only if συνέδραμον is inserted merely to account for the prior arrival, and in that case ἐκεῖ is out of place. Nor is St Mark's characteristic abundance of detail to the purpose here, for his multiplication of accessory facts is at least equalled by his economy of words. Had he wished to introduce the only fresh point in δ, that conveyed by πρὸς αὐτόν, the language natural to him would have been ἔδραμον καὶ (or better δραμόντες) προῆλθον αὐτοὺς καὶ συνῆλθον πρὸς αὐτόν. But the truth is that this fresh point simply spoils the point of ἐξελθών in v. 34; the multitude 'followed' (Matt., Luke) the Lord to the desert region (ἐκεῖ), but the

actual arrival at His presence was due to His act, not theirs, for He 'came out' of His retirement in some sequestered nook to meet them. Thus, if we look below the surface, the additional phrase in δ is found to disarrange the diction and confuse rather than enrich the sense; while according to the clear and exact language of α the fact to which the whole sentence leads up stands emphatically at its close, and there is no premature intrusion of what properly belongs to the next part of the narrative.

139. Accordingly the balance of Internal Evidence of Readings, alike from Transcriptional and from Intrinsic Probability, is decidedly in favour of the derivation of δ from α and β rather than of α and β from δ; so that, as far as can be judged without the aid of other passages, the common original of the documents attesting α and the common original of the documents attesting β must both have been older than the common original of the documents attesting δ.

140. To examine other passages equally in detail would occupy too much space. For the following similar variations it will for the most part suffice to add but brief comments to the documentary attestation.

Mark viii 26 (following καὶ ἀπέστειλεν αὐτὸν εἰς οἶκον αὐτοῦ λέγων)

(a) Μηδὲ εἰς τὴν κώμην εἰσέλθῃς (ℵ)BL 1*-209 me

(β) Ὕπαγε εἰς τὸν οἶκόν σου καὶ μηδενὶ εἴπῃς εἰς τὴν κώμην D(q)

(β₂) Ὕπαγε εἰς τὸν οἶκόν σου καὶ ἐὰν εἰς τὴν κώμην εἰσέλθῃς μηδενὶ εἴπῃς μηδὲ ἐν τῇ κώμῃ 13-69-346 28 61 81; also (omitting μηδέ) i, and (omitting μηδὲ ἐν τῇ κώμῃ) b f ff g1.2 vg
Ὕπαγε εἰς τὸν οἶκόν σου καὶ μὴ εἰς τὴν κώμην εἰσέλθῃς μηδέ τινι εἴπῃς a
Μηδὲ εἰς τὴν κώμην εἰσέλθῃς ἀλλὰ ὕπαγε εἰς τὸν οἶκόν σου καὶ ἐὰν εἰς τὴν κώμην εἰσέλθῃς μηδὲ εἴπῃς τινὶ (or μηδενὶ

εἴπῃς) [μηδὲ] ἐν τῇ κώμῃ arm ; also apparently (omitting ἀλλὰ
...σου) syr.hl.mg

Μηδενὶ εἴπῃς εἰς τὴν κώμην (or ἐν τῇ κώμῃ) (c) k

(δ) Μηδὲ εἰς τὴν κώμην εἰσέλθῃς μηδὲ εἴπῃς τινὶ ἐν τῇ
κώμῃ ACNXΔEFGHKMSUVΓΠ cu.omn.exc.8 syr.vg-hl
aeth go

Here *a* is simple and vigorous, and it is unique in the
N. T.: the peculiar initial Μηδέ has the terse force of
many sayings as given by St Mark, but the softening
into Μή by א* shews that it might trouble scribes. In β
we have *a* deprived of its novelty by the μηδενὶ εἴπῃς of
Matt. ix 6 and its parallel, and of its abruptness by the previous insertion of Ὕπαγε εἰς τὸν οἰκόν σου from Matt. viii 4
and its parallels. Then follow several different but not
all independent conflations of *a* and β. By the insertion
of *a*, a little modified, in the midst of β the Greek form of
β₂ arises; and this, with the superfluous last words removed, is the prevalent Latin reading. In one MS, *a*, a
fresh conflation supervenes, the middle clause of the Latin
β₂ being replaced by *a*, almost unaltered. Arm. (and apparently with one omission the margin of syr.hl) prefixes
a to β₂. The reading of (c) k is as short as *a*, and may be
derived directly from it; but is more probably β delivered
from its extraneous first clause by the influence of *a*.
Lastly δ combines *a* with β by substituting it for the first
clause of β; a less clumsy means of avoiding the contradiction latent in the probability that the 'house' would
be in the ' village' than the introduction of ἐάν in β₂. This
neat combination retains Μηδέ without its abruptness by
making it a conjunction, but involves a new contradiction
unless τινὶ ἐν be taken as τινὶ τῶν ἐν by a laxity ill suited
to the context. The documents attesting δ, it is to be
observed, include the early uncials CN as well as A, and
also Δ and the Syriac Vulgate.

141. Mark ix 38 (following Διδάσκαλε, εἴδαμέν τινα ἐν τῷ
ὀνόματί σου ἐκβάλλοντα δαιμόνια,)

(a)   καὶ ἐκωλύομεν αὐτόν, ὅτι οὐκ ἠκολούθει ἡμῖν אBΔ (?vv)
.   .   .   .   ἀκολουθεῖ μεθ' ἡμῶν L
καὶ ἐκωλύσαμεν αὐτόν, ὅτι οὐκ ἀκολουθεῖ ἡμῖν C cu³ f
(syr.vg-hr me aeth)

(β)   ὃς οὐκ ἀκολουθεῖ μεθ' ἡμῶν καὶ ἐκωλύομεν αὐτόν D
.   .   .   .   .   ἐκωλίσαμεν αὐτόν a k
.   .   .   .   ἡμῖν   .   ἐκωλύομεν αὐτόν 1-209

ὃς οὐκ ἀκολουθεῖ ἡμῖν καὶ ἐκωλύσαμεν αὐτόν X
13-69-346 28 al⁴ *b c ff i* vg syr.hl.mg arm

(δ) ὃς οὐκ ἀκολουθεῖ ἡμῖν, καὶ ἐκωλύσαμεν αὐτόν, ὅτι
οὐκ ἀκολουθεῖ ἡμῖν ANEFGHKMSUVΓΠ cu.omn.exc.20
syr.hl.txt go

(81 has ἠκολούθει and al¹ μεθ' ἡμῶν in the first
clause and al² μεθ' ἡμῶν in the third : 33 is defective.)

Part of the confusion of readings is due to obvious
causes, which throw little light on genealogy. From Luke ix
49 come ἀκολουθεῖ and μεθ' ἡμῶν; while in both Gospels
a general proneness to alter imperfects and the influence
of the preceding aorist have together produced ἐκωλύσομεν.
But in β, besides assimilation to St Luke, there is a bold
transposition of the last clause bringing it into proximity
to its subject, with a necessary change of ὅτι to ὅς (cf.
Matt. v 45 in similar documents); while in two modifications of β the aorist ἐκωλύσαμεν reappears, and one of
them, β₂, the most widely spread, has also ἡμῖν in conformity with *a*. The transposed clause is preserved in
both places by δ with exact similarity of ending. Here
again δ is supported by N as well as A, but not by any
early version.

142. Mark ix 49

(a) πᾶς γὰρ πυρὶ ἁλισθήσεται (ℵ)BLΔ 1-118-209 61 81
435 al⁹ me.codd the arm.codd

(β) πᾶσα γὰρ θυσία ἀλὶ ἁλισθήσεται D cu² (*a*) *b c ff i* (*k*)
tol holm gig   (*a c tol holm gig* omit ἀλί: *a* omits
γάρ: *k* has words apparently implying the Greek original
πᾶσα δὲ (or γὰρ) οὐσία ἀναλωθήσεται, ο being read for θ, and
ΑΝΑΛΩ for ΑΛΙΑΛΙC.)

(δ) πᾶς γὰρ πυρὶ ἁλισθήσεται, καὶ πᾶσα θυσία ἀλὶ
ἁλισθήσεται ACNXEFGHKMSUVΓΠ cu.omn.exc.15
f q vg syr.vg-hl me.codd aeth arm.codd go Vict   (cu¹⁰
vg.codd.opt omit ἀλί; X adds it after πυρί.)

A reminiscence of Lev. vii 13 (καὶ πᾶν δῶρον θυσίας ὑμῶν
ἀλὶ ἁλισθήσεται) has created β out of *a*, πγριαλιcθ being
read as θγciααλιαλιcθ with a natural reduplication, lost
again in some Latin copies. The change would be aided
by the words that follow here, καλὸν τὸ ἅλας κ.τ.λ. In δ the
two incongruous alternatives are simply added together,
γάρ being replaced by καί. Besides ACNX, δ has at least

the Vulgate Syriac and the Italian and Vulgate Latin, as
well as later versions.

143. Luke ix 10 (after καὶ παραλαβὼν αὐτοὺς ὑπεχώρησεν
κατ᾽ ἰδίαν)

(a) εἰς πόλιν καλουμένην Βηθσαιδά (א^cᵃ)BLXΞ 33 me the
     . κώμην . . . . D

(β) εἰς τόπον ἔρημον א* ᵉᵗ ᶜᵇ [? 13-346-] (69) 157 (syr.vt)
                              (cf. Tert)   (εἰς ἔ.τ. 13-69-346
                              syr.vt)
     εἰς τόπον ἔρημον Βηθσαιδά c ff q vg syr.vg
     εἰς τόπον ἔρημον καλούμενον Βηθσαιδά a e f

(δ) εἰς τόπον ἔρημον πόλεως καλουμένης Βηθσαιδά (A)C
     EGHKMSUVΓΔΛΠ cu.omn.exc.
     3(5) syr.hl aeth arm go
     (A cu⁴ place ἔρημον before τόπον, 1-131-209 omit it)

The change from *a* to *β* would be suggested by the
occurrence of ἔρημος τόπος in the two parallels (Matt. xiv 13;
Mark vi 31), by the words ὅτι ὧδε ἐν ἐρήμῳ τόπῳ ἐσμέν two
verses later, and by the difficulty of associating the incident with a 'city'. Two forms of *β*, in taking up the
name from *a*, still avoid this difficulty by refusing πόλιν.
In *δ* the difficulty is ingeniously overridden by keeping
both *a* and *β*, but making *β* dependent on *a*. For *δ* we
find, with AC, the four latest but no early version. In this
variation א* goes with *β*, and D virtually with *a*.

144. Luke xi 54 (after ἤρξαντο οἱ γραμματεῖς καὶ οἱ Φαρισαῖοι δεινῶς ἐνέχειν καὶ ἀποστοματίζειν αὐτὸν περὶ πλειόνων,)

(a) ἐνεδρεύοντες αὐτὸν θηρεῦσαί τι ἐκ τοῦ στόματος αὐτοῦ
     אBL me aeth Cyr.syr (om. αὐτόν א me Cyr.syr)

(β) ζητοῦντες ἀφορμήν τινα λαβεῖν αὐτοῦ ἵνα εὕρωσιν
     κατηγορῆσαι αὐτοῦ   D syr.vt
        ζητοῦντες ἀφορμήν τινα λαβεῖν αὐτοῦ ἵνα κατηγο-
     ρήσωσιν αὐτοῦ   lat.vt   (om. αὐτοῦ 1⁰ c e rhe)

(δ) ἐνεδρεύοντες αὐτόν, ζητοῦντες θηρεῦσαί τι ἐκ τοῦ στό-
     ματος αὐτοῦ, ἵνα κατηγορήσωσιν αὐτοῦ ACXEGHKMUVΓΔΛΠ
     cu.omn.exc.5   lat.vg   syr. vg-hl   (om. αὐτόν X 130
     lat.vg: καὶ ζητοῦντες cu.mu lat.vg syr.hl arm: om. ἐνε-
     δρεύοντες αὐτόν arm: om. ζητοῦντες 1-118-131-209 239)

interrogantes (? ἐπερωτῶντες) αὐτόν, ζητοῦντες θηρεῦσαί
τι ἐκ τοῦ στόματος αὐτοῦ, ἵνα ἀφορμὴν εὕρωσιν κατηγορῆσαι
αὐτοῦ f

The figurative language of *a* is replaced in *β* by a simply descriptive paraphrase, just as in the preceding sentence the chief documents that attest *β* change δεινῶς ἐνέχειν to δεινῶς ἔχειν and ἀποστοματίζειν αὐτόν to συνβάλλειν αὐτῷ : and in the second or Latin form of *β* εὔρωσιν κατηγορῆσαι becomes κατηγορήσωσιν in conformity with Matt. xii 10; Mark iii 2. In *δ* both phrases are kept, the descriptive being used to explain the figurative: the now superfluous middle part of *β* however is dropped, and ζητοῦντες is transposed to ease the infinitive θηρεῦσαι. Again the documents of *δ* include ACX, both Vulgates, and a later version. Besides the readings of some good cursives and of the Armenian, in which the influence of *a* and of *β* respectively leads to some curtailment of *δ*, *f* presents an interesting secondary conflation, the last phrase of which is derived with a neat transposition from the earliest form of *β*, whereas the *β* used in *δ* is the second form, no longer separately extant in Greek.

145. Luke xii 18 (after καθελῶ μου τὰς ἀποθήκας καὶ μείζονας οἰκοδομήσω, καὶ συνάξω ἐκεῖ πάντα)

(*a*) τὸν σῖτον καὶ τὰ ἀγαθά μου (ℵ&ᵃᶜ)BTL(X) 1-118-131-(209) (13-69-124) 157 (al) (syr.hr me the aeth) arm (the bracketed documents add μου to σῖτον)

(*β*) τὰ γενήματά μου ℵ*D 435 al²⁽³⁾ *b ff i q rhe* ⎱
       (? Iren.lat) Amb ⎰ syr.vt
τοὺς καρπούς μου lt 39 *a c d e m*

(*δ*) τὰ γενήματά μου καὶ τὰ ἀγαθά μου AQEFGHKMSU VΓΔΛΠ cu.omn.exc.12 *f* vg syr.vg-hl Bas Cyr
τὸν σῖτόν μου καὶ τὰ γενήματά μου 346

For the rather peculiar combination of τὸν σῖτον and τὰ ἀγαθά the single general term τὰ γενήματα, common in the LXX and Apocrypha, is substituted by *β*, the precise combination συνάγειν τὰ γενήματα being indeed found in Ex. xxiii 10; Lev. xxv 20; Jer. viii 13: some documents have the similar τοὺς καρπούς μου from v. 17. In *δ* the full double form of *a* is retained, but the plural τὰ γενήματα replaces τὸν σῖτον in accordance with the plural τὰ ἀγαθά. Another form of conflation of *a* and *β* appears in 346. Besides AQ and Cyril, *δ* has, as in Mark ix 49, the Vulgate Syriac and the Italian and Vulgate Latin in addition to the Harklean Syriac versions : both ℵ* and D support *β*.

146.   Luke xxiv 53 (after καὶ ἦσαν διαπαντὸς ἐν τῷ ἱερῷ)

(a)   εὐλογοῦντες τὸν θεόν ℵBC*L me syr.hr

(β)   αἰνοῦντες τὸν θεόν D *a b e ff* vg.codd Aug

(δ)   αἰνοῦντες καὶ εὐλογοῦντες τὸν θεόν AC²XFHKMSUV
ΓΔΛΠ cu.omn *c f q* vg syr.vg-hl arm
    εὐλογοῦντες καὶ αἰνοῦντες τὸν θεόν aeth

This simple instance needs no explanation. The distribution of documents is fairly typical, δ having AC²X
with the two Vulgates, the Italian Latin (and another MS
containing a similar element), and two later versions;
while the Æthiopic has an independent conflation in in-
verse order.

147.   It is worth while to note at once the distribution
of the chief MSS and versions with reference to the three
classes of readings contained in these eight ternary
variations.   Only the first hand is taken into account,
cursives differing from the main body are not noticed, and
slightly aberrant readings are classed with those from which
they deviate least.   Several MSS and versions are too fragmentary to give more than faint indications of the origin
of their texts within these narrow limits, and indeed for
the rest of them the results can be only provisional.

	α	β	δ	Total		α	β	δ	Total
ℵ	6	2	o	8	Lat.vt	o	8	o	8
A	o	o	8	8	it	1	2	5	8
B	8	o	o	8	vg	1	3	4	8
C	2	o	4	6	Syr.vt	o	3	o	3
D	1	7	o	8	vg	2	1	5	8
L	8	o	o	8	hl	o	o	8	8
N	o	o	2	2	hr	3	o	o	3
Q	o	o	1	1	Memph	8	o	(1 codd)	8
T	1	o	o	1	Theb	3	o	o	3
X	2	1	4	7	Aeth	3	o	5	8
Δ(Mc)	3	o	1	4	Arm	3 (or 2)	2	3 (or 4)	8
(Lc)	o	o	4	4	Goth	o	o	4	4
Ξ	1	o	o	1					
Late uncials and Cursives						o	o	8	8

148.   Comparison of these eight variations strongly
confirms the conclusion to which the independent evi-

dence respecting each has provisionally led, that the
longer readings marked δ are conflate each from two
earlier readings. The fundamental grouping of documents also remains the same throughout, notwithstanding
the partial fluctuation. The conflate readings marked δ
are found in AC(N) of the earlier and in all later uncials
except L, not invariably however in C, X, or Δ; as also
in the great mass of cursives, and in the Gothic and
Harklean Syriac, two versions known to be late. On
the other hand no δ or conflate readings are found in
אBDL lat.vt syr.vt me (the), these four versions being
also the most ancient. The most constant witnesses
for the readings marked β are D and most or all of the
Old Latin MSS, though they do not always support the
same modification of β: and in the three places in which
it is extant the Old Syriac is with them. The most
typical group attesting the readings marked α, which in
these passages we have found reason to believe to be
the original readings, consists of אBL and the Egyptian
versions, with the Jerusalem Syriac in its three places;
though א twice passes over to the ranks of β, even in
Luke ix 10, where D is virtually with α. The five remaining comparatively late versions or forms of versions
contain either readings of all three classes in different
proportions, or (Æthiopic) both δ readings and α readings: and CX have a similar variable character.

149. Speaking roughly then we may assign the attestation of Greek MSS thus: to α a small handful of
uncials, including the two oldest, and a few varying
cursives, sometimes wanting; to β D and sometimes a
few varying cursives, with the rare accession of א or
another uncial; to δ nearly all the later uncials, with
two or three of the older, especially A, and nearly all

the cursives. The like rough distribution of the three great families of versions which date from early times will be as follows : to α the Egyptian, and to β the Old Latin and Old Syriac; while the later versions, dating from the fourth and following centuries (one perhaps a little earlier), with one limited exception include δ readings, and two here exhibit δ readings alone.

150. To the best of our belief the relations thus provisionally traced are never inverted. We do not know of any places where the α group of documents supports readings apparently conflate from the readings of the β and δ groups respectively, or where the β group of documents supports readings apparently conflate from the readings of the α and δ groups respectively. Hence it is certain not only that the δ readings were always posterior in date to the α and the β readings in variations illustrating the relation between these three groups by means of conflation, but also that the scribes or editors who originated these δ readings made use in one way or another of one or more documents containing these α readings, and one or more documents containing these β readings ; that is, they either wrote with documents of both classes before them, or wrote from documents of one class which had readings from the other class written in the margin, or wrote from documents of one class while carrying in their own minds reminiscences from documents of the other class of which they had had knowledge at some previous time.

151. Now it is morally impossible that their use of documents of either or both classes should have been confined to those places in which conflation enables us to detect it in actual operation. The facts observed thus far do not forbid the hypothesis that the originators

of the δ readings made use likewise of documents belong·
ing to some additional class, conceivably purer than the
documents which furnished them with α and with β
readings respectively, and that these additional documents may have been followed by them in a greater or
less part of the rest of their text. But the proved actual
use of documents of the α and β classes in the conflate
readings renders their use elsewhere a *vera causa* in the
Newtonian sense. With every allowance for the provisional possibility of some use of other hypothetical
documents, it may be safely taken for granted that those
documents which we know to have been either literally
or virtually in the hands of the δ scribes were freely
employed by them in other parts of their text.

C. 152—162. *Posteriority of 'Syrian' to 'Western' and
     other (neutral and 'Alexandrian') readings shown
     (2) by Ante-Nicene Patristic evidence*

152. The next step accordingly is to discover
whether traces of such employment can be found. The
variations in the Gospels afford innumerable opportunities
for recognising singly the three principal groups of documents, detached from the rest. Oppositions of each of
the three groups in turn to all or nearly all the other
extant documents abound everywhere, presenting a succession of Distinctive readings of each group, that is,
readings having no other attestation : ternary variations
in which each of the three groups approximately attests
a different variant occur also, but much more rarely. The
large field of documentary evidence over which we are
now able to range enlarges at the same time our knowledge of the groups themselves. Other Greek MSS and
other MSS of versions become available : but above

all we obtain some valuable geographical and historical data from the patristic quotations which in many cases give clear additional attestation to the several groups.

153. It will be convenient from this point to designate two of the primary groups of documents no longer by Greek letters but by names. We shall call the β group 'Western', an appellation which has for more than a century been applied to its leading members. It was given at a time when the patristic evidence was very imperfectly known, and its bearing ill understood; and was suggested by the fact that the prominent representatives of the group were Græco-Latin MSS, certainly written in the West, and the Old Latin version, which throughout its range from Carthage to Britain is obviously Western. The fitness is more open to question since it has become evident that readings of this class were current in ancient times in the East as well as the West, and probably to a great extent originated there. On the whole we are disposed to suspect that the 'Western' text took its rise in North-western Syria or Asia Minor, and that it was soon carried to Rome, and thence spread in different directions to North Africa and most of the countries of Europe. From North-western Syria it would easily pass through Palestine and Egypt to Ethiopia. But this is at present hardly more than a speculation; nor do any critical results depend upon it. Whatever may have been the original home of the 'Western' text, a change of designation would now cause more confusion than it would remove, and it remains true that the only continuous and approximately pure monuments of the 'Western' texts now surviving have every right to the name. The δ group we propose to call 'Syrian', for

reasons which have partly been noticed already, and which will appear more clearly further on. To these must here be added another group, which would be fitly marked γ, for, as we shall see, its originals must have preceded those of the Syrian group. The local relations of those of its habitual representatives which can be geographically fixed prescribe for it the name 'Alexandrian'.

154. We have hitherto spoken of the primary groups and the ancient texts attested by them with reference to the Gospels alone, where the evidence is at once most copious and most confused. For a full knowledge of their characteristics however it is necessary to pursue them through other books of the New Testament. St Paul's Epistles stand next to the Gospels in the instructiveness of their variations, and fortunately tolerably unmixed Western texts of them are preserved in two independent Greek uncials and in a large body of quotations from Latin Fathers. The Western attestation of the Acts is much less full, and suffers grievously in parts by the loss of leaves in the *Codex Bezae* (D); but still it can be fairly made out; while the Alexandrian text stands out in much prominence, far more so than in the Pauline Epistles. In the Catholic Epistles the Western text is much obscured by the want of the requisite documents, either Greek or Latin, and probably also by the limited distribution of some of the books in early times; so that it can rarely be relied on for the interpretation of evidence: on the other hand the Alexandrian text is as conspicuous as in the Acts. In the Apocalypse the difficulty of recognising the ancient texts is still greater, owing to the great relative paucity of documents, and especially the absence or loss of this book from the Vatican MS (B) which is available for nearly all the rest

of the New Testament; and thus the power of using a directly genealogical method is much limited.

155. The variations here mentioned between different parts of the New Testament are, it will be noticed, of two kinds, being due partly to the varying amount and distribution of documentary evidence which happens to be extant at the present day, partly to the facts of ancient textual history disclosed by the evidence. It is important to observe that, wherever the evidence is copious and varied enough to allow the historical facts to be ascertained, the prevalent characteristics of the ancient texts, as regards both their readings and their documentary attestation, are identical or at least analogous throughout, the diversities which exist being almost wholly confined to proportion.

156. Patristic evidence, which we have now to examine for indications of the ancient texts, needs at all times to be handled with much circumspection, for it includes data of every degree of trustworthiness. The uncertainty which affects many apparent patristic attestations, that is, the difficulty of knowing how far they can safely be taken as conveying to us the readings of the MSS used by the Fathers, arises from two causes. First, what a Father actually wrote is very liable to be falsified by the proneness of both scribes and modern editors to alter the text before them into conformity with the written or printed text most familiar to themselves; and since a text substantially identical with that of δ was unquestionably the only text likely to be known to transcribers generally throughout the centuries to which existing Greek patristic MSS with the rarest exceptions belong, as also to the authors of nearly all the

current editions of the Greek Fathers till quite lately, it is no wonder that those Greek corruptions which can on sufficient evidence be determined as such are almost invariably found to consist in the introduction, not in the removal, of δ readings; and nearly the same may be said as to Vulgate readings in the texts of Latin Fathers. This kind of corruption is hardly ever systematic or thorough, but it is common enough; it is usually abundant in those passages of Christian writers which owe their preservation to Catenæ, especially where, as frequently happens, they have been evidently condensed by the compiler. It may often be detected by recourse to better MSS, by comparison with other quotations of the same passage by the same writer, or, best of all, by close examination of the context: but in many cases a greater or less degree of doubt remains as to the words actually written by a Father.

157. The second possible cause of error in dealing with patristic evidence is laxity of quotation by the writers themselves, more especially when they quote indirectly or allusively. The laxity may arise either from conscious or semi-conscious modification for the sake of grammar or convenience, or from error of memory, a frequent cause of error being confusion with other similar passages. Here too there is a considerable residuum of more or less doubtful cases, though comparison with other quotations of the same passage and above all experience will remove many *prima facie* ambiguities. Allusive references are sometimes as decisive as full and direct quotations, and they have the advantage of being much less liable to corruption by scribes and editors. But whatever imperfections of verification of patristic evidence may cling to particular passages, they do not to

any appreciable extent affect the generalisations as to the patristic attestation of particular groups of documents obtained by taking a large number of passages together. The broad facts come out clearly : where there is doubt, it for the most part relates to the presence or absence of rare exceptions.

158. When we examine the remains of the Ante-Nicene Christian literature with a view to collect evidence respecting the ancient texts which the groupings of the extant documents shew to have existed, we are for some time after the apostolic age hampered both by the paucity of the writings preserved and by the scantiness and comparative vagueness of the textual materials contained in them. The only period for which we have anything like a sufficiency of representative knowledge consists roughly of three quarters of a century from about 175 to 250 : but the remains of four eminent Greek Fathers, which range through this period, cast a strong light on textual history backward and forward. They are Irenæus, of Asia Minor, Rome, and Lyons; his disciple Hippolytus, of Rome ; Clement, of Athens and Alexandria ; and his disciple Origen, of Alexandria and Palestine. To the same period belong the Latin representatives of North Africa, Tertullian and Cyprian, as also Cyprian's Roman contemporary Novatian. Towards the close of the third century we have somewhat considerable remains of Methodius, of Lycia and Tyre, an enemy of the Origenian school; and in the first third of the fourth century several writings of Eusebius of Cæsarea in Palestine, the most learned of its disciples. For the second half of the third century we have other fragments, but they are few in number.

159. The most striking phenomenon of the evidence belonging to the time before 250 is the number of places in which the quotations exhibit at least two series of readings, Western and what may be called Non-Western. The first clear evidence of any kind that we possess, that obtained from recorded readings of Marcion (Pontus and Rome) and from the writings of Justin Martyr (Samaria and Rome), is distinguished by readings undoubtedly Western, and thus shews that texts of this character were in existence before the middle of the second century. The same character of text is found in Irenæus and Hippolytus, and again in Methodius and predominantly in Eusebius. Thus the text used by all those Ante-Nicene Greek writers, not being connected with Alexandria, who have left considerable remains is substantially Western. Even in Clement of Alexandria and in Origen, especially in some of his writings, Western quotations hold a prominent place.

160. On the other hand the many Non-Western readings supplied by Clement of Alexandria prove that great divergencies were in existence at latest by the end of the second century. Any possible doubts on this head that could be suggested by his free mode of citation would be entirely swept away by what we find in Origen's extant writings. Many of the verses which he quotes in different places shew discrepancies of text that cannot be accounted for either by looseness of citation or by corruption of the MSS of his writings; and in most instances the discrepant readings are those of the primary extant groups, including the 'Alexandrian' group, of which we shall presently have to speak in detail. It is even possible, as Griesbach shewed long ago, to trace to a certain extent his use of different MSS

10

when writing different treatises; and moreover he now
and then refers in express words to variations between
MSS, as indeed Irenæus had at least once done. Many
of his readings in variations in which Western documents
stand opposed to all other documents are distinctly
Western, many more are distinctly Non-Western. On
the other hand his quotations to the best of our
belief exhibit no clear and tangible traces of the Syrian
text.

161. That these characteristics, positive and negative, of the quotations found in Origen's writings are due
to accident is in the highest degree improbable. A long
and laborious life devoted chiefly to original biblical
studies, combined with a special interest in texts, and
the twofold opportunities supplied by the widely different circumstances of Alexandria and Palestine, to say
nothing of varied intercourse with other lands, could
hardly fail to acquaint him with all leading types of
Greek text current in the Churches, and especially in the
Eastern Churches: and as a matter of fact we find all
other known great types of text represented in his
writings except the one; that one moreover, had it
then existed, being more likely to have come to the
notice of a dweller in Palestine than any other.

162. Nor is the testimony that of a single Father,
however well placed and well fitted for reflecting the lost
testimony of all contemporary Churches on such a
matter. The whole body of patristic evidence down to
his death, or later, tells the same tale. Before the middle
of the third century, at the very earliest, we have no
historical signs of the existence of readings, conflate or
other, that are marked as distinctively Syrian by the
want of attestation from groups of documents which have

preserved the other ancient forms of text. This is a fact of great significance, ascertained as it is exclusively by external evidence, and therefore supplying an absolutely independent verification and extension of the result already obtained by comparison of the internal character of readings as classified by conflation.

D.   163—168.   *Posteriority of Syrian to Western, Alexandrian, and other (neutral) readings shewn (3) by Internal Evidence of Syrian readings*

163.   The Syrian conflate readings have shown the Syrian text to be posterior to at least two ancient forms of text still extant, one of them being 'Western', and also to have been, at least in part, constructed out of both. Patristic evidence has shewn that these two ancient texts, and also a third, must have already existed early in the third century, and suggested very strong grounds for believing that in the middle of the century the Syrian text had not yet been formed.   Another step is gained by a close examination of all readings distinctively Syrian in the sense explained above, comparing them on grounds of Internal Evidence, Transcriptional and Intrinsic, with the other readings of the same passages.   The result is entirely unfavourable to the hypothesis which was mentioned as not excluded by the phenomena of the conflate readings, namely that in other cases, where the Syrian text differs from all other extant ancient texts, its authors may have copied some other equally ancient and perhaps purer text now otherwise lost.   In themselves Syrian readings hardly ever offend at first.   With rare exceptions they run smoothly and easily in form, and yield at once to even a careless reader a passable sense,

free from surprises and seemingly transparent. But when distinctively Syrian readings are minutely compared one after the other with the rival variants, their claim to be regarded as the original readings is found gradually to diminish, and at last to disappear. Often either the transcriptional or the intrinsic evidence is neutral or divided, and occasionally the two kinds of evidence appear to be in conflict. But there are, we believe, no instances where both are clearly in favour of the Syrian reading, and innumerable where both are clearly adverse to it.

164. The testimony of the simpler variations in which the other ancient texts are united against the Syrian reading is remarkably confirmed by that of many of those variations in which they are divided among themselves. Here one of the readings has to approve itself on transcriptional grounds by its fitness to give rise not to one but to two or more other readings, that is either to each independently or to one which will in like manner account naturally for the third (or the rest); and the failure of the Syrian reading to fulfil this condition is usually manifest. The clearest cases are those in which the immediate parent of the Syrian reading is seen to be itself in turn derived from another, so that the two steps of the process illustrate each other: not a few distinctively Syrian readings are in reality Western or Alexandrian readings, somewhat trimmed and modified.

165. To state in few words the results of examination of the whole body of Syrian readings, distinctive and non-distinctive, the authors of the Syrian text had before them documents representing at least three earlier forms of text, Western, Alexandrian, and a third. Where they found variation, they followed different procedures

in different places. Sometimes they transcribed unchanged the reading of one of the earlier texts, now of this, now of that. Sometimes they in like manner adopted exclusively one of the readings, but modified its form. Sometimes they combined the readings of more than one text in various ways, pruning or modifying them if necessary. Lastly, they introduced many changes of their own where, so far as appears, there was no previous variation. When the circumstances are fully considered, all these processes must be recognised as natural.

166. Thus not only do the relations disclosed by the conflate Syrian readings reappear conspicuously in the much larger field of distinctively Syrian readings generally, but no fresh phenomenon claims to be taken into account, unless it be the existence of the Alexandrian text, which has its own extant attestation apart from the Syrian text. Taking these facts in conjunction with the absence of distinctively Syrian readings from the patristic evidence of the Origenian and Ante-Origenian periods, while nevertheless distinctive readings of all the texts known to have been used in the production of distinctively Syrian readings abound in the Origenian period, as also, with the possible exception of distinctively Alexandrian readings, in the Ante-Origenian period, we are led to conclude that the hypothesis provisionally allowed must now be definitively rejected, and to regard the Syrian text as not only partly but wholly derived from the other known ancient texts. It follows that all distinctively Syrian readings may be set aside at once as certainly originating after the middle of the third century, and therefore, as far as transmission is concerned, corruptions of the apostolic text.

167. The same facts lead to another conclusion of equal or even greater importance respecting non-distinctive Syrian readings, which hold a conspicuous place by their number and often by their intrinsic interest. Since the Syrian text is only a modified eclectic combination of earlier texts independently attested, existing documents descended from it can attest nothing but itself: the only authority which they can give to readings having other documentary attestation, that is to readings Syrian but not distinctively Syrian, is the authority of the Syrian text itself, which resolves itself into that of a lost ancient MS of one or possibly more of those older texts from which the Syrian text was in any given variation derived. Accordingly a reading supported both by the documents belonging to the Syrian group and by those belonging to *e.g.* the Western group has no appreciably greater presumption in its favour than if it were supported by the Western group alone: the only accession is that of a lost Western MS not later in date than the time when the Syrian text was formed; and in almost all cases this fact would add nothing to our knowledge of the ancestry of the reading as furnished by the Non-Syrian documents attesting it.

168. If our documents were free from all mixture except that contained in the Syrian text, that is, if no document of later origin itself combined elements from different texts, the application of this principle would be always clear and certain. Since however most of the more important documents are as a matter of fact affected by later mixture, the origin of any given reading in them can only be determined by grouping; and since grouping is sometimes obscure, a greater or less degree of doubt about the antecedents of a non-distinctive Syrian reading

may in such cases remain. Thus it may be ·clear that a reading was first Western and then Syrian, while yet there may be a doubt whether certain of the attesting documents derived it from a Syrian or from an earlier source. If from the former, the reading must be held to be in effect distinctively Western : if from the latter, the possibility or probability of its having existed not only in the Western but in a Non-Western Pre-Syrian text has to be taken into account. These occasional ambiguities of evidence do not however affect the force or the ordinary applicability of the principle itself: and in practice the doubt is in most cases removed by Internal Evidence of Groups.

SECTION II. CHARACTERISTICS OF THE

CHIEF ANCIENT TEXTS

169—187

169. Leaving for the present the Syrian text and its own history, we must now go back to the earlier periods within which the primary ramifications of the genealogical tree have been shown to lie. It follows from what has been said above that all readings in which the Pre-Syrian texts concur must be accepted at once as the apostolic readings, or to speak more exactly, as the most original of recorded readings. Indeed this is only repeating in other words that all distinctively Syrian readings must be at once rejected. The variations between Pre-Syrian texts raise much more difficult questions, which can be answered only by careful examination of the special characteristics of the several texts.

A. 170—176. *Western characteristics*

170. On all accounts the Western text claims our attention first. The earliest readings which can be fixed chronologically belong to it. As far as we can judge from extant evidence, it was the most widely spread text of Ante-Nicene times ; and sooner or later every version directly or indirectly felt its influence. But any prepossessions in its favour that might be created by this imposing early ascendancy are for the most part soon dissipated by continuous study of its internal character. The eccentric Whiston's translation of the Gospels and Acts from the *Codex Bezae*, and of the Pauline Epistles from the *Codex Claromontanus*, and Bornemann's edition of the Acts, in which the *Codex Bezae* was taken as the standard authority, are probably the only attempts which have ever been made in modern times to set up an exclusively or even predominantly Western Greek text as the purest reproduction of what the apostles wrote. This all but universal rejection is doubtless partly owing to the persistent influence of a whimsical theory of the last century, which, ignoring all Non-Latin Western documentary evidence except the handful of extant bilingual uncials, maintained that the Western Greek text owed its peculiarities to translation from the Latin ; partly to an imperfect apprehension of the antiquity and extension of the Western text as revealed by patristic quotations and by versions. Yet, even with the aid of a true perception of the facts of Ante-Nicene textual history, it would have been strange if this text as a whole had found much favour. A few scattered Western readings have long been approved by good textual critics

on transcriptional and to a great extent insufficient grounds; and in Tischendorf's last edition their number has been augmented, owing to the misinterpreted accession of the Sinai MS to the attesting documents. To one small and peculiar class of Western readings, exclusively omissions, we shall ourselves have to call attention as having exceptional claims to adoption. But when the Western readings are confronted with their ancient rivals in order to obtain a broad comparative view of the two texts, few scholars could long hesitate to pronounce the Western not merely to be the less pure text, but also to owe its differences in a great measure to a perilous confusion between transcription and reproduction, and even between the preservation of a record and its supposed improvement; and the distrust thus generated is only increased by further acquaintance.

171. What has been here said is equally true whether we confine ourselves to Western readings having only a Western attestation or include with them those Western readings which, having been adopted into the Syrian text, have a combination of Western and Syrian attestation. When once the historical relations of the texts have been ascertained, it would be arbitrary to refuse the evidence of the latter class in studying the general character of Western readings apart from attestation, for the accident of their appropriation by the Syrian text when the other Western readings were neglected can have no bearing on the antecedent relations of the whole class to the apostolic originals. But as a matter of fact the general conclusions would be the same in either case: throughout both classes of Western readings there is no diversity of salient characteristics.

172. To what extent the earliest MSS of the distinctively Western ancestry already contained distinctive
Western readings, cannot now be known. However they
may have differed from the apostolic autographs, there
was at all events no little subsequent and homogeneously
progressive change. It is not uncommon to find one,
two, or three of the most independent and most au-
thentically Western documents in agreement with the
best representatives of Non-Western Pre-Syrian texts
against the bulk of Western authorities under circumstances which render it highly difficult to account for
the concurrence by mixture : and in such cases these
detached documents must attest a state of the Western
text when some of its characteristic corruptions had not
yet arisen, and others had. On the other hand it is
probable that even the relatively latest Western readings
found in distinct provinces of Western documents, for
instance in different languages, were already in existence
at a very early date of Church history, it may be before
the end of the second century.

173. The chief and most constant characteristic of
the Western readings is a love of paraphrase. Words,
clauses, and even whole sentences were changed, omitted,
and inserted with astonishing freedom, wherever it seemed
that the meaning could be brought out with greater force
and definiteness. They often exhibit a certain rapid
vigour and fluency which can hardly be called a re-
bellion against the calm and reticent strength of the
apostolic speech, for it is deeply influenced by it, but
which, not less than a tamer spirit of textual correction,
is apt to ignore pregnancy and balance of sense, and
especially those meanings which are conveyed by exceptional choice or collocation of words. An extreme

form of the paraphrastic tendency is shown in the interpolation of phrases extending by some kind of parallelism the language of the true text; as καὶ τῆς νύμφης after εἰς ὑπάντησιν τοῦ νυμφίου in Matt. xxv 1; γεννῶνται καὶ γεννῶσιν between οἱ υἱοὶ τοῦ αἰῶνος τούτου and γαμοῦσιν καὶ γαμίσκονται in Luke xx 34; and ἐκ τῆς σαρκὸς αὐτοῦ καὶ ἐκ τῶν ὀστέων αὐτοῦ after μέλη ἐσμὲν τοῦ σώματος αὐτοῦ in Eph. v 30. Another equally important characteristic is a disposition to enrich the text at the cost of its purity by alterations or additions taken from traditional and perhaps from apocryphal or other non-biblical sources; as Σὺ εἶ ὁ υἱός μου ὁ ἀγαπητός, ἐν σοὶ εὐδόκησα (originating of course in Ps. ii 7) given as the words spoken from heaven at the Baptism in Luke iii 22; and a long interpolation (printed in the Appendix) beginning Ὑμεῖς δὲ ζητεῖτε after Matt. xx 28. The two famous interpolations in John v and viii, which belong to this class, will need special notice in another place. Under the present head also should perhaps be placed some of the many curious Western interpolations in the Acts, a certain number of which, having been taken up capriciously by the Syrian text, are still current as part of the Received text: but these again will require separate mention.

174. Besides these two marked characteristics, the Western readings exhibit the ordinary tendencies of scribes whose changes are not limited to wholly or partially mechanical corruptions. We shall accordingly find these tendencies, some of them virtually incipient forms of paraphrase, in other texts of the New Testament: but in the Western text their action has been more powerful than elsewhere. As illustrations may be mentioned the insertion and multiplication of genitive pronouns, but

occasionally their suppression where they appeared cum-brous; the insertion of objects, genitive, dative, or ac-cusative, after verbs used absolutely; the insertion of conjunctions in sentences which had none, but occa-sionally their excision where their force was not perceived and the form of the sentence or context seemed to com-mend abruptness; free interchange of conjunctions; free interchange of the formulæ introductory to spoken words; free interchange of participle and finite verb with two finite verbs connected by a conjunction; substitution of compound verbs for simple as a rule, but conversely where the compound verb of the true text was difficult or unusual; and substitution of aorists for imperfects as a rule, but with a few examples of the converse, in which either a misunderstanding of the context or an outbreak of untimely vigour has introduced the imperfect. A bolder form of correction is the insertion of a negative particle, as in Matt. xxi 32 (οὐ being favoured, it is true, by the preceding τοῦ), Luke xi 48, and Rom. iv 19; or its omission, as in Rom. v 14; Gal. ii 5; v 8.

175. Another impulse of scribes abundantly exem-plified in Western readings is the fondness for assimi-lation. In its most obvious form it is merely local, abolishing diversities of diction where the same subject matter recurs as part of two or more neighbouring clauses or verses, or correcting apparent defects of symmetry. But its most dangerous work is 'harmonistic' corruption, that is, the partial or total obliteration of differences in passages otherwise more or less resembling each other. Sometimes the assimilation is between single sentences that happen to have some matter in common; more usually however between parallel passages of greater length, such especially as have in some sense a common

origin. To this head belong not only quotations from the Old Testament, but parts of Ephesians and Colossians, and again of Jude and 2 Peter, and, above all, the parallel records in the first three Gospels, and to a certain extent in all four. It is difficult to exaggerate the injury thus inflicted upon the resources for a right understanding of the Gospel history by the destruction of many of the most characteristic and instructive touches contributed by the several narratives, whether in the form of things otherwise said, or of additional things said, or of things left unsaid. A sense of the havoc wrought by harmonistic corruption in the Old Latin texts, in their origin Western texts, has been already mentioned as one of the primary motives alleged by Jerome for his revision ; and though his effort had only a limited success, the Vulgate contrasts favourably with prior Latin texts of the Gospels in this respect. It should be observed that the harmonistic changes in the Western as in all other texts were irregular and unsystematic. Nor is it rare to find Western changes proceeding in an opposite direction ; that is, to find paraphrastic or other impulses followed in the text of one Gospel in unconsciousness or disregard of the creation of new differences from the language of a parallel narrative.

176. It must not be supposed that the liberties taken by the authors of the Western readings, though far exceeding what we find appearing for the first time in other texts of the New Testament, are unknown in other literature transmitted under not unlike circumstances. Several books of the Apocrypha of the Old Testament exist in two forms of text, of which one is evidently an amplified and interpolated modification of the other. Analogous phenomena in various manners

and degrees occur in the texts of some of the earliest post-apostolic Christian writings, as the Epistle of Barnabas and the *Shepherd* of Hermas; and even the interpolations of the Ignatian Epistles are to a certain extent of the same kind. In the Christian 'apocryphal' or legendary literature, some of which, in its elements if not in its present shape, is undoubtedly as old as the second century, much of the extraordinary diversity in different MSS can only be explained by a hardly credible laxity of idea and practice in the transmission of texts. Some at least of the writings here mentioned, if not all of them, had a large popular currency: and it is probably to similar conditions of use and multiplication, prevailing during the time of the slow process by which the books of the New Testament at last came to be placed on the same footing as those of the Old, that we must look for a natural explanation of the characteristics of their Western texts. In surveying a long succession of Western readings by the side of others, we seem to be in the presence of a vigorous and popular ecclesiastical life, little scrupulous as to the letter of venerated writings, or as to their permanent function in the future, in comparison with supposed fitness for immediate and obvious edification.

B.　177—180.　*The neutral text and its preservation*

177. We now proceed to other Pre-Syrian texts. If it be true, as we have found reason to believe, first, that during that part of the Ante-Nicene period of which we have any direct knowledge 'Western' texts were at least dominant in most churches of both East and West, and secondly, that, whatever may be the merits of individual

Western readings, the Western texts generally are due to a corruption of the apostolic texts, it is natural to ask where comparatively pure texts were preserved. The only extant patristic writings which to any considerable extent support extant Pre-Syrian readings at variance with Western readings are connected with Alexandria, that is, the remains of Clement and Origen, as mentioned above (§ 159), together with the fragments of Dionysius and Peter of Alexandria from the second half of the third century, and in a certain measure the works of Eusebius of Cæsarea, who was deeply versed in the theological literature of Alexandria. In like manner, of the three great versions or families of versions which must date from the earliest centuries, two in their Old or unrevised form must be classed as Western, the Latin clearly and almost entirely, the very imperfectly preserved Syriac more obscurely: but it is only the two versions of Lower and of Upper Egypt, and the latter, which is the further from Alexandria, less than the former, that can be pronounced extensively Non-Western. That a purer text should be preserved at Alexandria than in any other church would not in itself be surprising. There, if anywhere, it was to be anticipated that, owing to the proximity of an exact grammatical school, a more than usual watchfulness over the transcription of the writings of apostles and apostolic men would be suggested and kept alive. But the rapid total extinction of comparatively pure texts in all other places would undeniably be a riddle hard of solution.

178. No such enigmatic history however demands acceptance. The early traces of a text free from Western corruption in churches remote from Alexandria, though relatively few in number, are indubitable and significant.

They are the same facts that were mentioned above
(§ 172) in speaking of the progressiveness of Western
changes, only seen from the other side. When we find
that those very Western documents or witnesses which
attest some of the most widely spread and therefore
ancient Western corruptions attest likewise ancient Non-
Western readings in opposition to most Western documents, we know that they must represent a text in
process of transition from such a text as we find at Alexandria to a more highly developed Western text, and
consequently presuppose a relatively pure Non-Western
text. This early evidence is sometimes at once Greek,
Latin, and Syriac, sometimes confined to one or two of
the languages. It shews that at least in remote antiquity the Non-Western text was by no means confined to
Alexandria.

179. As regards the other facts of the Ante-Nicene
period, the negative evidence is not of a trustworthy
kind. If we deduct from the extant Ante-Nicene Greek
patristic quotations those of the Alexandrian Fathers, the
remainder, though sufficient to shew the wide range of
the Western text, is by no means sufficient by itself to
disprove the existence of other texts. What we have
urged in a former page (§ 162) respecting the absence of
patristic evidence for the Syrian text before the middle of
the third century at earliest was founded on the whole
evidence, including that of Clement and Origen, Origen's
evidence being in amount more than equal to all the rest
put together, and in probable variety of sources and
actual variety of texts exceptionally comprehensive : and
moreover this negative argument was confirmed by the
internal phenomena of the Syrian text itself. But further,
much positive evidence for the persistence of Non-West·

ern texts in various regions throughout the Ante-Nicene period is contained in the varied texts of Fathers and versions of the fourth and fifth centuries. It is true that the only considerable text of a Father or version of this later period which closely approximates to a Non-Western Pre-Syrian text, that of the younger Cyril, has again Alexandria for its locality. It is true also that it is not absolutely impossible for the large Non-Western Pre-Syrian elements which enter into many mixed texts of the later period to have all radiated from Alexandria in the third century. Nevertheless the preservation of early Non-Western texts in varying degrees of purity in different regions would account for the facts much more naturally than such a hypothesis. On the one hand there is no reason to think the prominence of Alexandria in the extant evidence accidental: nowhere probably was the perpetuation of an incorrupt text so much an object of conscious desire and care, and the local influence of Origen's school for some generations after his death was likely to establish a tradition of exceptional jealousy for the very words of Scripture. On the other hand our documentary evidence, taken as a whole, equally suggests, what historical probability would have led us to anticipate, that in various and perhaps many other places the primitive text in varying degrees of purity survived the early Western inundation which appeared to submerge it.

180. Such being the facts, we have not thought it advisable to designate Non-Western Pre-Syrian readings generally as 'Alexandrian', although this, or something like this, is the sense in which the term 'Alexandrian' is commonly used, when it is not extended to all ancient readings alike that are not found in the later Greek MSS.

11

Not only were these readings not confined to Alexandria, but a local name suggests erroneous associations when applied to a text which owes its comparative isolation to the degeneracy of its neighbours. On the laxity with which existing MSS are themselves often called Alexandrian we shall have occasion to remark hereafter.

C. 181—184. *Alexandrian characteristics*

181.   There is moreover, as we have already intimated, a class of ancient readings to which the name 'Alexandrian' of right belongs.   They are brought to light by a considerable number of variations among those documents which have chiefly preserved a Non-Western Pre-Syrian text, and which are shown by the whole distribution of documentary evidence to have nothing to do with variations between Western and Non-Western texts. They enter largely, as we shall see presently, into the texts of various extant uncial MSS, and with the help thus afforded to the recognition of documentary grouping it is usually easy to see which variants in successive variations have the distinctively 'Alexandrian' attestation, and thus to arrive at a comparative view of the general internal characteristics of the two series of readings.

182.   The differences of type are by no means so salient here as in the previous comparison of Western with Non-Western texts; but on due consideration the case becomes clear.   On grounds of Intrinsic and Transcriptional Probability alike, the readings which we call Alexandrian are certainly as a rule derived from the other Non-Western Pre-Syrian readings, and not *vice-versa*. The only documentary authorities attesting them with any approach to constancy, and capable of being assigned

to a definite locality, are quotations by Origen, Cyril of Alexandria, and occasionally other Alexandrian Fathers, and the two principal Egyptian Versions, especially that of Lower Egypt.   These facts, taken together, shew that the readings in question belong to a partially degenerate form of the Non-Western Pre-Syrian text, apparently limited in its early range, and apparently originating in Alexandria.   It cannot be later in date than the opening years of the third century, and may possibly be much earlier.   Some of its readings at one time attracted the attention of critics, owing to certain peculiarities in their secondary attestation : but the greater number have been confused with other Non-Western readings, doubtless owing to the accidental loss of all Greek MSS having an approximately unmixed Alexandrian text.   Had D of the Gospels and Acts and $D_2E_3F_2G_3$ of the Pauline Epistles all in like manner perished, it would have been in like manner far harder than now to form a clear conception of the Western text, and consequently of early textual history.

183.   The more startling characteristics of Western corruption are almost wholly absent from the Alexandrian readings.   There is no incorporation of matter extraneous to the canonical texts of the Bible, and no habitual or extreme licence of paraphrase; though a certain amount of paraphrase and what may be called inventive interpolation finds place in the less read books, that is, the Acts and Catholic Epistles (especially 1 Peter), and probably the Apocalypse.   The changes made have usually more to do with language than matter, and are marked by an effort after correctness of phrase.   They are evidently the work of careful and leisurely hands, and not seldom display a delicate philological tact which

unavoidably lends them at first sight a deceptive appearance of originality. Some of the modes of change described above as belonging to incipient paraphrase occur as distinctly here as in the Western texts, though as a rule much more sparingly ; and the various forms of assimilation, especially harmonistic alteration and interpolation in the Gospels, recur likewise, and at times are carried out in a very skilful manner.

184. Alexandrian changes sometimes occur in places where Western changes exist likewise, sometimes where they do not; and again the Syrian text sometimes follows one, sometimes another, of the three antecedent texts in the former case, of the two in the latter. Considerable variety of distribution, irrespective of Non-Syrian mixture, accordingly arises in the documentary attestation. We often find the Alexandrian group opposed to all other documents, often the Alexandrian and Syrian groups combined in opposition to the others, implying an adoption of an Alexandrian reading by the Syrian text. But the most instructive distributions, as exhibiting distinctly the residual Pre-Syrian text which is neither Western nor Alexandrian, are those produced by the simultaneous aberration of the Western and Alexandrian texts, especially when they severally exhibit independent modes of easing an apparent difficulty in the text antecedent to both.

D. 185—187. *Syrian characteristics*

185. The Syrian text, to which the order of time now brings us back, is the chief monument of a new period of textual history. Whatever petty and local mixture may have previously taken place within limited

areas, the great lines of transmission had been to all appearance exclusively divergent. Now however the three great lines were brought together, and made to contribute to the formation of a new text different from all. As we have seen, the reading now of one, now of another was adopted, such adoption being sometimes a mere transcription but often accompanied by a varying amount of modification not rarely resulting in an entirely new reading. Occasionally also the readings of two of the antecedent texts were combined by simple or complex adaptations. The total process to which these operations belonged was essentially different from the preceding processes of change. In itself the mixture of independent texts might easily be, and perhaps usually was, fortuitous or even unconscious. But the complexity of the Syrian text as derived from three distinct sources simultaneously, the elaborate manner in which they are laid under contribution, and the interfusion of adjustments of existing materials with a distinctly innovative process, shown partly in verbal transformation of adopted readings, partly in assimilative or other interpolations of fresh matter, belong to a manner of change differing as widely from change of either the Western or the Alexandrian type as even Western change from ordinary careless transcription. The Syrian text must in fact be the result of a 'recension' in the proper sense of the word, a work of attempted criticism, performed deliberately by editors and not merely by scribes.

186. The guiding motives of their criticism are transparently displayed in its effects. It was probably initiated by the distracting and inconvenient currency of at least three conflicting texts in the same region. The alternate borrowing from all implies that no selection of

one was made,—indeed it is difficult to see how under the circumstances it could have been made,—as entitled to supremacy by manifest superiority of pedigree. Each text may perhaps have found a patron in some leading personage or see, and thus have seemed to call for a conciliation of rival claims: but at all events, if a new measure was to be adopted for promoting unity of text, no course was so natural and convenient as the acceptance of the traditional authority of each text already accredited by honour and use, at least in an age when any really critical perception of the problem involved in the revision of a written text would have been an anachronism. It would have been no less an anachronism at each variation to find reasons for the preference to be given to this or that text in specialities of documentary attestation or again in consideration of Transcriptional Probability. The only grounds of selection, affording any true means of advancing towards textual purity, that could find place in the conditions of the time, or that can now be discerned in the resulting text, depend on a rough and superficial kind of Intrinsic Probability. But the governing impulses, just as in the case of nearly all licentious as distinguished from inaccurate transcription, unquestionably arose from a very natural failure to distinguish between the purity of a text and its present acceptability or usefulness.

187. The qualities which the authors of the Syrian text seem to have most desired to impress on it are lucidity and completeness. They were evidently anxious to remove all stumbling-blocks out of the way of the ordinary reader, so far as this could be done without recourse to violent measures. They were apparently equally desirous that he should have the benefit of in-

structive matter contained in all the existing texts, provided it did not confuse the context or introduce seeming
contradictions. New omissions accordingly are rare, and
where they occur are usually found to contribute to
apparent simplicity. New interpolations on the other
hand are abundant, most of them being due to harmonistic or other assimilation, fortunately capricious and
incomplete. Both in matter and in diction the Syrian
text is conspicuously a full text. It delights in pronouns, conjunctions, and expletives and supplied links
of all kinds, as well as in more considerable additions.
As distinguished from the bold vigour of the 'Western'
scribes, and the refined scholarship of the Alexandrians,
the spirit of its own corrections is at once sensible and
feeble. Entirely blameless on either literary or religious
grounds as regards vulgarised or unworthy diction, yet
shewing no marks of either critical or spiritual insight,
it presents the New Testament in a form smooth and
attractive, but appreciably impoverished in sense and
force, more fitted for cursory perusal or recitation than
for repeated and diligent study.

SECTION III.   SKETCH OF POST-NICENE
TEXTUAL HISTORY

188—198

A.   188—190.   *The two stages of the Syrian text*

188. We have thus far found it conducive to clearness to speak of the Syrian text in the singular number.
Two stages of it however can be traced, which may have
been separated by an interval of some length. At an

early period of modern textual criticism it was perceived
that the Vulgate Syriac version differed from early versions generally, and from other important early documentary authorities, in the support which it frequently
gave to the common late Greek text: and as the version
enjoyed a great traditional reputation of venerable antiquity, the coincidence attracted much interest. Eventually, as has been already noticed (§ 118), it was pointed
out that the only way of explaining the whole body of
facts was to suppose that the Syriac version, like the
Latin version, underwent revision long after its origin,
and that our ordinary Syriac MSS represented not the
primitive but the altered Syriac text: and this explanation has been signally confirmed in our own day by the
discovery of part of a copy of the Gospels in which the
national version is preserved approximately in its Old
or unrevised state. Two facts render it highly probable
that the Syriac revision was instituted or sanctioned by
high authority, personal or ecclesiastical; the almost
total extinction of Old Syriac MSS, contrasted with the
great number of extant Vulgate Syriac MSS; and the
narrow range of variation found in Vulgate Syriac
MSS, so far as they have yet been examined. Historical antecedents render it tolerably certain that the
locality of such an authoritative revision, accepted by
Syriac Christendom, would be either Edessa or Nisibis,
great centres of life and culture to the churches whose
language was Syriac, but intimately connected with Antioch, or else Antioch itself, which, though properly
Greek, was the acknowledged capital of the whole Syrian
population of both tongues. When therefore we find
large and peculiar coincidences between the revised Syriac text and the text of the Antiochian Fathers of the

latter part of the fourth century, and strong indications that the revision was deliberate and in some way authoritative in both cases, it becomes natural to suppose that the two operations had some historical connexion.

189. Nevertheless the two texts are not identical. In a considerable number of variations the Vulgate Syriac sides with one or other of the Pre-Syrian texts against the Antiochian Fathers and the late Greek text, or else, as we have already found (§§ 134, 143), has a transitional reading, which has often, though not always, some Greek documentary attestation. These lesser irregularities shew that the Greek Syrian revision in its ultimate form, the only form adequately known to us, and the Syriac revision, though closely connected in origin, cannot both be due to a single critical process performed once for all. The facts would, we believe, be explained by the supposition, natural enough in itself, that (1) the growing diversity and confusion of Greek texts led to an authoritative revision at Antioch, which (2) was then taken as a standard for a similar authoritative revision of the Syriac text, and (3) was itself at a later time subjected to a second authoritative revision, carrying out more completely the purposes of the first; but that the Vulgate Syriac text did not undergo any corresponding second revision. The revision apparently embodied in the Harklean Syriac will be noticed further on.

190. The final process was apparently completed by 350 or thereabouts. At what date between 250 and 350 the first process took place, it is impossible to say with confidence; and even for conjecture the materials are scanty. There can be little doubt that during the long respite from persecution enjoyed by the Church in the latter half of the third century multiplication of copies

would be promoted by the increase of converts and new security of religious use, and confusion of texts by more frequent intercourse of churches. Such a state of things would at least render textual revision desirable; and a desire for it might easily arise in a place where a critical spirit was alive. The harmony between the characteristics of the Syrian revision and the well known temper of the Antiochian school of critical theology in the fourth century, at least on its weaker side, is obvious; and Lucianus the reputed founder of the school, himself educated at Edessa, lived in the latter part of the third century, and suffered martyrdom in 312. Of known names his has a better claim than any other to be associated with the early Syrian revision; and the conjecture derives some little support from a passage of Jerome, which is not itself discredited by the precariousness of modern theories which have been suggested by it. When he says in his preface to the Gospels "Praetermitto eos codices quos a Luciano et Hesychio nuncupatos paucorum hominum adserit perversa contentio", he must have had in view some definite text or texts of the Gospels or the New Testament generally, appealed to by some definite set or sets of men as deriving authority from names honoured by them. Jerome's antagonism to Antiochian theology would readily explain his language, if some Antiochian Father had quoted in controversy a passage of the New Testament according to the text familiar to him, had been accused of falsifying Scripture, and had then claimed for his text the sanction of Lucianus. Whether however Lucianus took a leading part in the earlier stage of the Syrian revision or not, it may be assigned with more probability either to his generation or to that which immediately followed than to any other;

and no critical results are affected by the presence or absence of his name.

B. 191—193. *Mixture in the fourth century*

191. Two successive external events which mark the opening years of the fourth century, the terrible persecution under Diocletian and his colleagues and the reaction under Constantine, doubtless affected the text not less powerfully than the Canon of the New Testament. The long and serious effort of the imperial government to annihilate the Scriptures could not be otherwise than unequally successful in different places; and thus while throughout whole regions all or nearly all existing MSS would perish without leaving their text transmitted through fresh copies, the vacant places would presently be filled, and more than filled, by transcripts which would import the texts current in more fortunate lands. Thus whatever irregularities in the geographical distribution of texts had grown up in the earlier centuries would be suddenly and variously multiplied. Moreover the tendency of the changes brought about in that century of rapid innovation by the new relations between the Church and the empire, and by the overwhelming influence of theological controversies, was unfavourable to the preservation of local peculiarities of any kind. It is therefore no wonder that the ancient types of text now lose themselves in a general medley, not indeed vanishing entirely from view, but discernible only in fragments intermingled with other texts. Whatever may be the causes, mixture prevails everywhere in the fourth century: almost all its texts, so far as they can be seen through the quotations of the Fathers, are more or less chaotic.

192.   The confusion was naturally most extensive in
the Greek texts; but the versions did not altogether
escape it.   Enough is already known of the Latin texts
to enable us to see what kind of processes were at work.
Along with the old Western licence as to diction, in
which Latin scribes must have long continued to indulge,
we find not only indigenous mixture, the combination of
diverging or possibly of independent Latin types, but
also mixture with Greek texts.   Combinations of this
latter kind were in fact more or less rude revisions, not
differing in essential character from the Hieronymic
revision to which the Vulgate is due.   As in that better
known case, they proceeded from a true feeling that a
Greek MS as such was more authentic than a Latin MS
as such, uncontrolled by any adequate sense of the difference between one Greek MS and another.   As was
to be expected, the new Greek elements of these revised
Latin MSS came from various sources, now Pre-Syrian
with or without the specially Alexandrian corruptions,
now distinctly Syrian, Greek readings of this last type
being however almost confined to the Italian and Hieronymic revisions.   How far the mixture perceptible in
Egyptian texts should be referred to this time, it is not
as yet possible to say.

193.   Exact knowledge of the patristic texts of the
fourth century is much impeded by the uncritical manner
in which the works of most of the Greek Fathers have
been edited.   But wherever firm ground can be reached,
we find essentially the same characteristics; almost total
absence of all the ancient texts in approximate integrity,
and infinitely varying combinations of them, together
with an increasing infusion of the later Syrian readings.
The most remarkable fact, standing out in striking con-

trast to the previous state of things, is the sudden collapse of the Western text after Eusebius: a few writers offer rare traces of the expiring tradition in occasional purely Western readings which subsequently vanish; but even this slight and sporadic testimony is exceptional. On the other hand elements derived from Western texts entered largely into most of the mixtures which encounter us on every side. A similar diffusion of large elements derived from the Alexandrian text, discernible in the patristic evidence, is still better attested by versions or revisions of versions in this and the next following period, and apparently by the phenomena of subsequent Greek MSS. At Alexandria itself the Alexandrian tradition lives on through the fourth century, more or less disguised with foreign accretions, and then in the early part of the fifth century reappears comparatively pure in Cyril. On the growing influence of the Syrian texts throughout this time enough has already been said.

C. 194, 195. *Final supremacy of the Syrian text*

194. The history of the text of the New Testament in the following centuries is obscure in details; but the facts which stand out clearly are sufficient for the purposes of criticism. The multiplicity of texts bequeathed by the fourth century was of long continuance. If, passing over the four great early Bibles אBAC, and also the Græco-Latin and Græco-Egyptian MSS, we fix our attention on what remains to us of purely Greek MSS down to the seventh or eighth century, we cannot but be struck by the considerable though unequal and on the whole decreasing proportion in which Pre-Syrian readings

of all types are mingled with Syrian. On the other hand before the close of the fourth century, as we have said, a Greek text not materially differing from the almost universal text of the ninth century and the Middle Ages was dominant, probably by authority, at Antioch, and exercised much influence elsewhere. It follows that, however great and long continued may have been the blending of texts, the text which finally emerged triumphant in the East was not a result of any such process, in which the Antiochian text would have been but one factor, however considerable. With one memorable exception, that of the Story of the Woman taken in Adultery, there is evidence of but few and unimportant modifications of the Antiochian text by the influence of other ancient texts before it became the current text of the East generally.

195.   Two classes of causes were at work to produce this singular result. On the one hand Greek Christendom became more and more contracted in extent. The West became exclusively Latin, as well as estranged from the East: with local exceptions, interesting in themselves and valuable to us but devoid of all extensive influence, the use and knowledge of the Greek language died out in Western Europe. Destruction of books, which had played so considerable a part in textual history at the threshold of the Constantinian age, was repeated again and again on a larger scale, with the important difference that now no reaction followed. The ravages of the barbarians and Mahometans annihilated the MSS of vast regions, and narrowly limited the area within which transcription was carried on. Thus an immense number of the MSS representing texts furthest removed in locality from Antiochian (or Constantinopolitan) influence

perished entirely, leaving no successors to contribute readings to other living texts or to transmit their own texts to
the present day. On the other hand Greek Christendom
became centralised, and the centre, looked up to increasingly as such while time went on, was Constantinople. Now Antioch is the true ecclesiastical parent
of Constantinople; so that it is no wonder that the
traditional Constantinopolitan text, whether formally
official or not, was the Antiochian text of the fourth
century. It was equally natural that the text recognised
at Constantinople should eventually become in practice
the standard New Testament of the East.

D. 196, 197. *Relics of Pre-Syrian texts in cursives*

196. We have hitherto treated the Greek text of the
Middle Ages as a single text. This mode of representation, strictly true in itself, does not convey the whole
truth. An overwhelming proportion of the text in all
known cursive MSS except a few is as a matter of fact
identical, more especially in the Gospels and Pauline
Epistles, however we may account for the identity. Further, the identity of readings implies identity of origin;
the evidence already given has shown many of the characteristic readings to have originated about 250—350,
assigning them at the same time a definite single origin,
for we need not here distinguish stages in the Syrian revision; and there are no reasons whatever for assigning
a different origin to the rest. If an editor were for any
purpose to make it his aim to restore by itself as completely as possible the New Testament of Antioch in
350, he could not help taking the approximate consent
of the cursives as equivalent to a primary documentary

witness; and he would not be the less justified in so doing for being unable to say precisely by what historical agencies the one Antiochian original was multiplied into the cursive hosts of the later ages. But it is no less true that the consent is only approximate. Although numerous important variations between the Antiochian and other more ancient texts have left no trace in known cursive texts, hardly a verse is free from deviations from the presumed Constantinopolitan standard, sometimes found in a few cursives or one, sometimes even in a large array; and there are not wanting cursives which suggest a doubt whether such a standard forms any part of their ancestry. These diversities of cursive texts, perceptible enough even in Mill's pages, and brought into clearer relief by the collations made or employed by Griesbach and Scholz, can now be studied as to all their characteristic phenomena by means of Dr Scrivener's exhaustive collations.

197. Variations of cursives from the prevalent late text are of two kinds, differing in origin, though not always capable of being distinguished. They are due either to mixture with other texts, or to ordinary degeneracy of transmission. In the latter case they must of course have originated in an age which deprives them at once of all critical value and of all but the most subordinate historical interest: in the former case they not only often supply important documentary evidence for the restoration of the apostolic text, in which light we shall have to consider them presently, but form a remarkable link historically between the ninth and following centuries and the preceding periods, being in fact analogous to the Old Latin readings often preserved in Vulgate Latin MSS. They are virtually copies of minute frag-

ments of lost MSS, belonging doubtless in most instances to the middle or late uncial times, but sometimes of an earlier date, and in either case derived directly or indirectly, wholly or partially, from ancient texts. They shew that the final victory of the Antiochian text did not carry with it a total suppression of MSS of other texts; while the fact that the cursives with distinctly mixed texts are not only proportionally but absolutely much more numerous in the tenth and eleventh than in the twelfth and later centuries shews equally that the MSS of other texts fell more and more into neglect. The cursives mentioned above as probably or possibly independent of any Constantinopolitan origin are doubtless on this supposition copies, more or less pure, of MSS similar to those which, immediately or remotely, furnished detached ancient readings to the mixed cursives. They might be compared to the Old Latin *c*, written several centuries not only after the formation of the Latin Vulgate, but even after its general adoption.

E. 198. *Recapitulation of history of text*

198. The continuity, it will be seen, is complete. Early in the second century we find the Western text already wandering into greater and greater adulteration of the apostolic text, which, while doubtless holding its ground in different places, has its securest refuge at Alexandria; but there in turn it suffers from another but slighter series of changes: and all this before the middle of the third century. At no long time after we find an attempt made, apparently at Antioch, to remedy the growing confusion of texts by the editing of an eclectic text combining readings from the three principal texts, itself

12

further revised on like principles, and in that form used
by great Antiochian theologians not long after the middle
of the fourth century. From that date, and indeed
earlier, we find a chaos of varying mixed texts, in which
as time advances the elder texts recede, and the Antiochian text now established at Constantinople increasingly
prevails. Then even the later types with mixed base
disappear, and with the rarest exceptions the Constantinopolitan text alone is copied, often at first with relics of
its vanquished rivals included, till at last these too dwindle,
and in the copies written shortly before the invention of
printing its victory is all but complete. At each stage
there are irregularities and obscurities: but we believe
the above to be a true sketch of the leading incidents in
the history of the text of the New Testament; and, if it
be true, its significance as a key to the complexities of
documentary evidence is patent without explanation.

SECTION IV.   RELATIONS OF THE PRINCIPAL EXTANT
DOCUMENTS TO THE CHIEF ANCIENT TEXTS

199—223

A.   199, 200.   *Nature of the process of determination*

199.   In the preceding pages we have been tracing
the history of ancient lines of transmission, divergent and
convergent, by means of evidence chiefly furnished by
the existing documents. In order to use the knowledge
thus obtained for the restoration of the text, we have next
to follow the converse process, and ascertain which
ancient text or texts are represented by each important
document or set of documents. Up to a certain point

this exploration of the ancestry of documents has been performed already at an earlier stage of the investigation, for we could have made little progress if we had not been able to recognise certain more or less defined groups of documents as habitually attesting analogous ancient readings, and thus as being comparatively faithful representatives of particular ancient texts. But we are now enabled both to verify with increased exactness the earlier classifications, and to extend them to other documents the texts of which were too ambiguous at first sight to allow them to be classified without the aid of standards external to themselves.

200. The evidence is supplied by the numerous variations in which each variant can at once be assigned with moral certainty to some one of the ancient texts, to the exclusion of those variations in which the grouping of documents is at this stage obscure. At each variation we observe which ancient text is attested by the document under examination. The sum of these observations contains the required result. Neglecting petty exceptions as probably due to some unnoticed ambiguity, unless they happen to be of special clearness, we find that the document habitually follows some one ancient text; or that it sometimes follows one, sometimes another, but has no characteristic readings of the rest; or again that it follows all in turn. Thus we learn that it has transmitted one ancient type of text in approximate purity; or that it is directly or indirectly derived by mixture from two originals of different defined types; or that it has arisen from a more comprehensive mixture. The mixture may of course have taken place in any proportions, and the same observations which bring to light the various elements will supply also a fair estimate of the

proportions between them: most commonly there is no
difficulty in recognising one text as the base on which
readings of one or more other types have been inserted
in greater or less number. From the component elements of the text of a document as thus empirically
ascertained to be present in the illustrative variations
taken into account, and also, more roughly, from their
proportions, the component elements of its text generally,
and their proportions, become approximately known.
This knowledge supplies a key to other less simple variations, by shewing either to which ancient text a given
reading must be referred, so far as its attestation by each
such document is concerned, or at least to which ancient
text or texts each such document gives little or no warrant
for referring it. The uses of the information thus obtained, and their limitation, will appear in due time.

B. 201—212. *Texts found in Greek MSS*

201. We have next to give a brief account of the
relations of the principal extant documents to ancient texts
as ascertained in the manner described above.   Greek
Uncial MSS are arranged here in the order that seems
most convenient for exhibiting their textual composition,
without reference to any supposed order of excellence.
Some repetitions have been found unavoidable.

202.   Western texts virtually unmixed survive exclusively in Græco-Latin MSS written in Western Europe.
They are well represented in the Gospels and Acts by D,
some leaves in different places and some whole chapters
at the end of Acts being however lost.   Though the MS
was written in Cent. VI, the text gives no clear signs of
having undergone recent degeneracy: it is, to the best of
our belief, substantially a Western text of Cent. II, with
occasional readings probably due to Cent. IV.   Much
more numerous are readings belonging to a very early
stage of the Western text, free as yet from corruptions
early enough to be found in the European or even in the

African form of the Old Latin version, and indeed else-where. In spite of the prodigious amount of error which D contains, these readings, in which it sustains and is sustained by other documents derived from very ancient texts of other types, render it often invaluable for the secure recovery of the true text: and, apart from this direct applicability, no other single source of evidence except the quotations of Origen surpasses it in value on the equally important ground of historical or indirect instructiveness. To what extent its unique readings are due to licence on the part of the scribe rather than to faithful reproduction of an antecedent text now otherwise lost, it is impossible to say: but it is remarkable how frequently the discovery of fresh evidence, especially Old Latin evidence, supplies a second authority for readings in which D had hitherto stood alone. At all events, when every allowance has been made for possible individual licence, the text of D presents a truer image of the form in which the Gospels and Acts were most widely read in the third and probably a great part of the second century than any other extant Greek MS.

203. Western texts of the Pauline Epistles are preserved in two independent uncials, D_2 and G_3, in G_3 to the exclusion of Hebrews. What has been said of D of the Gospels may be applied with little deduction to the Pauline D_2, allowance being made for the inferior interest of all Western texts of St Paul. The text of G_3, to a great extent coincident, apparently represents a later type, but still probably not later than Cent. IV. It is to be observed that though many readings of D_2 in opposition to G_3 are supported by other very ancient texts, others receive no such confirmation, and are shown by Latin evidence to be no less Western than those of G_3. But this is merely an example of the variety of Western texts. Since G_3 was apparently written late in Cent. IX, probably at St Gallen by an Irish scribe (though it may possibly have been brought to St Gallen from Ireland), the nature of its text may be due either to the preservative power of the seclusion of Greek learning in the West or to direct transcription from a very much older copy. The text of the Gospels in what was originally part of the same MS is, we shall see, entirely different. Two of the uncial Græco-Latin copies of the Pauline Epistles, E_3 and F_2, cannot count as independent sources of evidence: E_3 has long been recognised as a transcript of D_2, and we believe

F_2 to be as certainly in its Greek text a transcript of G_3; if not, it is an inferior copy of the same immediate exemplar. Not a single Greek MS of any age, as we have already (§ 171) had occasion to notice, has transmitted to us an Alexandrian text of any part of the New Testament free from large mixture with other texts.

204. Tried by the same tests as those just applied, B is found to hold a unique position. Its text is throughout Pre-Syrian, perhaps purely Pre-Syrian, at all events with hardly any, if any, quite clear exceptions, of which the least doubtful is the curious interpolation in Rom. xi 6. From distinctively Western readings it seems to be all but entirely free in the Gospels, Acts, and Catholic Epistles : in the Pauline Epistles there is an unquestionable intermingling of readings derived from a Western text nearly related to that of G_3; and the facility with which they can generally be here recognised throws into clearer relief the almost total absence of definite Western influence in the other books. Here and there indeed may be found readings which are perhaps in some sense Western, having some slight Old Latin or similar attestation : but they are few and not clearly marked, so that their existence does not sensibly render less significant the absence of distinctively Western readings manifestly such. Respecting Alexandrian readings negative statements as to a document containing a Non-Western Pre-Syrian text can never be made without hesitation, on account of the narrow limitation of the difference of documentary attestation characteristic of the two forms of this text respectively. But we have not been able to recognise as Alexandrian any readings of B in any book of the New Testament which it contains; so that, with the exceptions already noticed, to the best of our belief neither of the early streams of innovation has touched it to any appreciable extent. This peculiar character is exhibited to the eye in the documentary evidence of those variations in which both a Western and an Alexandrian corruption is present, and one of these corruptions is adopted in the Syrian text, B being then conspicuous in the usually slender array supporting the reading from which both have diverged. It must not of course be assumed to follow that B has remained unaffected by sporadic corruption independent of the three great lines, Western, Alexandrian, and Syrian. In the Gospel of St Matthew for instance it has occasionally admitted widely spread readings of very

doubtful genuineness. But the influence of these three lines upon almost all extant documents has been so enormous that the highest interest must already be seen to belong to a document of which thus far we know only that its text is not only Pre-Syrian but substantially free from Western and Alexandrian adulteration.

205. The relations to ancient texts which disclose themselves on analysis of the text of ℵ are peculiarly interesting. As in its contemporary B, the text seems to be entirely, or all but entirely, Pre-Syrian: and further a very large part of the text is in like manner free from Western or Alexandrian elements. On the other hand this fundamental text has undergone extensive mixture either with another text itself already mixed or, more probably, with two separate texts, one Western, one Alexandrian. Thus, widely different as is ℵ from the Syrian text, as well as independent of it, it is analogous in composition, except that it shews no trace of deliberate adjustment and critical modification. The mixture is unequally distributed, being most abundant in the Gospels and apparently in the Apocalypse, and least abundant in the Pauline Epistles; but it is never absent for many verses together. The Western readings are specially numerous in St John's Gospel, and in parts of St Luke's: they belong to an early and important type, though apparently not quite so early as the fundamental text of D, and some of them are the only Greek authority for Western readings which, previous to the discovery of ℵ, had been known only from versions.

206. Every other known Greek MS has either a mixed or a Syrian text, mixture becoming rarer as we approach the time when the Syrian text no longer reigned supreme, but virtually reigned alone. Moreover every known Greek MS except those already mentioned contains a Syrian element, which is in almost all cases large, but is very variable. The differences in respect of mixture fall under three chief heads;—difference in the proportion of Syrian to Pre-Syrian readings; difference in the proportion of Pre-Syrian readings neither Western nor Alexandrian to those of both these classes; and difference in the proportion of Western to Alexandrian readings. It is to be observed that the Non-Syrian element of these mixed Greek MSS is hardly ever, if ever, exclusively Western or exclusively Alexandrian. Sometimes the one type predominates, sometimes the other, but neither appears quite alone. This state of things would naturally arise if, as

was to be anticipated from the phenomena of the fourth century, the Pre-Syrian texts in their purer forms quickly died out, and were replaced by a multitude of mixed texts. In like manner it is no wonder that the Pre-Syrian text neither Western nor Alexandrian, which already by the fourth century was apparently less popular than that of either the Western or the Alexandrian type, is afterwards found less conspicuously represented in mixed texts than its rivals.

207. The text of A stands in broad contrast to those of either B or ℵ, though the interval of years is probably small. The contrast is greatest in the Gospels, where A has a fundamentally Syrian text, mixed occasionally with Pre-Syrian readings, chiefly Western. In the other books the Syrian base disappears, though a Syrian occurs among the other elements. In the Acts and Epistles the Alexandrian outnumber the Western readings. All books except the Gospels, and especially the Apocalypse, have many Pre-Syrian readings not belonging to either of the aberrant types : in the Gospels these readings are of rare occurrence. By a curious and apparently unnoticed coincidence the text of A in several books agrees with the Latin Vulgate in so many peculiar readings devoid of Old Latin attestation as to leave little doubt that a Greek MS largely employed by Jerome in his revision of the Latin version must have had to a great extent a common original with A. Apart from this individual affinity, A both in the Gospels and elsewhere may serve as a fair example of the MSS that, to judge by patristic quotations, were commonest in the fourth century. Even the difference of text in the Gospels, though very possibly due only to accidental use of different exemplars for different groups of books, corresponds to a difference existing on a larger scale; for the Syrian text of the Gospels appears to have become popular before that of the rest of the New Testament.

208. In C the Syrian and all three forms of Pre-Syrian text are combined in varying proportions; distinctively Syrian readings and such distinctively Western readings as were not much adopted into eclectic texts being however comparatively infrequent.

209. With respect to the texts of extant uncial MSS of the Gospels later than the four great Bibles, a few words on some of the more important must suffice. The Greek text of the Græco-Thebaic fragments of St Luke

and St John (T, Cent. V) is entirely Pre-Syrian and almost entirely Non-Western. That of the considerable fragments of St Luke called Ξ has a similar foundation, with a larger share of Alexandrian corrections, and also a sprinkling of Western and Syrian readings: this character is the more remarkable as the date seems to be Cent. VIII. Of greater general importance is L of about the same date, which contains the Gospels in approximate completeness. The foundation of the text is Non-Western Pre-Syrian. No extant MS has preserved so many Alexandrian readings in the Gospels, but the early readings neither Western nor Alexandrian are also very numerous. On the other hand the fundamental text has been largely mixed with late Western and with Syrian elements. The composition, it will be seen, has analogies with that of ℵ, though the actual texts are entirely independent, and the much smaller proportion of Alexandrian corrections in ℵ, the great dissimilarity of its Western element, and the absence of a Syrian element, constitute important differences. In three Gospels the St Gallen MS Δ (see above on G₃ of the Pauline Epistles, § 203) has an ordinary Syrian text sprinkled thinly with Alexandrian and a few Western readings. But in St Mark this fundamental text is for the most part displaced by mixture with a Non-Western Pre-Syrian text of the same type as the fundamental text of L and Ξ, and thus full of Alexandrian corrections as well as other early Non-Western readings: traces of the process remain in conflate or intermediate readings. The numerous fragments of PQRZ of the Gospels (see § 100) are variously mixed, but all have a large proportion of Pre-Syrian readings; in such MSS as NXΓ(?Σ), and still more as KM, Pre-Syrian readings are very much fewer. The smaller fragments we must pass over, with one exception : too few lines of Wᵈ (St Mark) survive to enable us to form a trustworthy conception of its text generally; but it includes a large Western element of a very curious type.

210. The *Codex Laudianus* (E₂) of Acts is interesting on more accounts than one. It was apparently the identical Greek MS used by Bede. As it is Græco-Latin in form, its text might be expected to be Western. A Western text it does contain, very distinctly such, though evidently later than that of D; but mixed on apparently equal terms, though in varying proportions, with a no less distinctly Alexandrian text: there are also Syrian readings, but they are fewer in number. P₂ is all but purely

Syrian in the Acts and 1 Peter, while in the other Epistles and the Apocalypse a similar base is variously mixed with another text predominantly but not exclusively Alexandrian, often agreeing with A where A has readings of this class. The Pauline fragments M_2 and H_3 have mixed texts, that of M_2 being of more ancient character and more interesting. The historical antecedents of B_2, and indeed of all MSS of the Apocalypse, are still obscure.

211. A few words must suffice here on Greek Cursives. By far the most free from Syrian readings is 61 of the Acts, which contains a very ancient text, often Alexandrian, rarely Western, with a trifling Syrian element, probably of late introduction. The cursive which comes nearest to 61 of Acts in antiquity of text, though at a long interval, is 33 of the Gospels; which has indeed a very large Syrian element, but has also an unusual proportion of Pre-Syrian readings, chiefly Non-Western of both kinds though also Western: the same type of text runs through the whole MS, which is called 13 in the Acts and Catholic Epistles, and 17 in the Pauline Epistles. Most cursives of the Gospels which contain many ancient readings owe more to Western than to Alexandrian sources. Among these may be named four, 13, 69, 124, and 346, which have recently been shown by Professors Ferrar and T. K. Abbott to be variously descended from a single not very remote original, probably uncial: its Non-Syrian readings belong to very ancient types, but their proportion to the fundamentally Syrian text as a whole is not great. Nearly the same may be said of 1 and 209 of the Gospels, which contain a large common element of ancient origin, partly shared by 118, as also by 131. The most valuable cursive for the preservation of Western readings in the Gospels is 81, a St Petersburg MS called 2^{pe} by Tischendorf as standing second in a list of documents collated by Muralt. It has a large ancient element, in great measure Western, and in St Mark its ancient readings are numerous enough to be of real importance. Another more than usually interesting text, somewhat of the same type but much more largely Syrian, is that of lt 39, the British Museum Gospel Lectionary called y by its collator Dr Scrivener. In 157 of the Gospels we have the best example of the few cursives which more nearly resemble 33 in the composition of their Pre-Syrian element, though not connected with 33 by any near affinity.

212. The proportion of cursives of the Acts and

Catholic Epistles containing an appreciable amount of Pre-Syrian readings is much larger than in the Gospels or even in the Pauline Epistles, and the Alexandrian readings thus attested are greatly in excess of the Western, without taking into account 61 or 13. Fortunately however Western texts are not altogether ill represented, though only by scattered readings, chiefly in 137, 180, and 44, this last being a MS belonging to the Baroness Burdett-Coutts (iii 37), for the loan of a collation of which we have to thank Dr Scrivener's kindness; and to these MSS should be added 31 (the Leicester MS called 69 in the Gospels), which has many Non-Alexandrian Pre-Syrian readings of both kinds. The chief characteristics of the ancient elements in the cursive texts of St Paul are the extreme irregularity with which they appear in different parts of his epistles, and the small proportion of Western readings to others. Certain corrections in the margin of 67 (66 of the Acts and Catholic Epistles) stand apart by their inclusion of a relatively large number of very ancient readings, which have no other cursive attestation, some distinctively Western, others not so: these marginal readings must have been derived from a MS having a text nearly akin to that of the fragmentary MS called M_2, though not from M_2 itself. Besides 17, mentioned above, no other MSS of St Paul require special notice. Much ancient evidence is assuredly preserved in not a few cursive texts of the Apocalypse: but they have not as yet been traced with any clearness to their sources.

C. 213—219. *Texts found in Versions*

213. Analogous phenomena of mixture to those observed in most Greek MSS recur in the later Versions and states of versions: but the want of adequate knowledge of individual MSS of all versions except the Old Latin leaves much uncertain that will doubtless hereafter be cleared up. The African and European Latin, as has been already intimated, represent Western texts of different antiquity: but most of the aberrant readings found in single MSS are probably due to independent mixture with other Greek texts. In the Italian and Vulgate revisions mixture with Greek texts of various types played a large part : in the Italian Latin the Syrian contingent is especially conspicuous. We have already spoken of the

various forms of Latin mixture which are perceptible in
'Mixed Vulgate' MSS (§ 114): it is likewise possible that
some of their Non-Western readings may have come
directly from Greek MSS.

214. The textual character of the Old state of the
national or Peshito Syriac version is to a certain extent
ambiguous, as being known only through a solitary and
imperfect MS. We cannot always distinguish original
readings of the version, antecedent to the bulk of Western readings, from readings in no sense Western introduced into it by mixture in the later generations
before our MS was written. In many cases however
the discrimination is rendered morally certain by the
grouping of documents: and at all events the widest
examination of all classes of documents only confirms the
general conclusions on the history of the Syriac version set
forth above (§ 118) as suggested by the *prima facie* relations of early grouping. In its origin the version was at
least predominantly Western of an early type, such few
Alexandrian readings as occur having probably come in
at a later though still early time. At the revision, whether
independent or conforming to a Greek Syrian revision,
changes having the Syrian characteristics already described
were introduced into the fundamental text. The revised
or Vulgate Syriac text differs from the final form of the
Greek Syrian text chiefly in retaining many Non-Western
readings (some few of them apparently Alexandrian) which
afterwards gave way to Western or to new (distinctively
Syrian) readings.

215. The Harklean Syriac, which the thorough recasting of diction constitutes rather a new version founded on
the Vulgate Syriac than a revision of it in the ordinary
sense, receives its predominant character from the multitudes of ordinary Antiochian readings introduced; but
readings of more ancient Greek types likewise make their
appearance. Taken altogether, this is one of the most
confused texts preserved: but it may be rendered more
intelligible by fresh collations and better editing, even if
they should fail to distinguish the work of Thomas of
Harkel from that of his predecessor Polycarpus. It would
not be surprising to find that Polycarpus simply converted
the Vulgate Syriac into an exact imitation of the Greek
Antiochian text, and that the more ancient readings were
introduced by Thomas from the "three (*v. l.* two) approved
and accurate Greek copies in the Enaton of the great city

of Alexandria, in the holy monastery of the Enatonians", with which he states that he carefully compared his predecessor's version. In this case the readings noted in the margin might well be those which he did not see fit to adopt, but thought it best to place on record in a secondary place. The Non-Antiochian readings in the text, with or without an asterisk, have the same general character as the marginal readings, and can mostly claim a very high antiquity: many of them are distinctively Western, and they include a large proportion of the peculiar Western variations and interpolations in the Acts. In the Catholic Epistles the readings of the Harklean Syriac have a more mixed character than in the other books.

216. The Jerusalem Syriac Lectionary has an entirely different text, probably not altogether unaffected by the Syriac Vulgate, but more closely related to the Old Syriac. Mixture with one or more Greek texts containing elements of every great type, but especially the more ancient, has however given the whole a strikingly composite character. Variations occur to a certain extent between repetitions of the same passages in different parts of the Lectionary, and also between the several MSS in the few places where the new fragments contain the same portions with each other or with the principal MS. These differences are probably caused by mixture with late Greek MSS; which is indeed likely to have affected this Syriac text in all the extant copies: but for the most part the same peculiar text presents itself throughout.

217. The Egyptian versions are substantially true to their *prima facie* character. The main body of both versions is founded on a very ancient Non-Western text, sometimes affected by the Alexandrian corrections, sometimes free from them. Neither of them however has escaped mixture. Syrian readings are rare, even in the printed editions, and it is probable that they belong only to a late and degenerate state of the versions: the variation which Dr Lightfoot has found as to the presence or absence of some conspicuous interpolations, Syrian by either origin or adoption, in different Memphitic MSS, and the appearance of a series of them in the margins but not the text of the leading Oxford MS, suggest that this element may have been wholly wanting in the first few centuries. The Western influence is more deeply seated, but is probably of two kinds. The Memphitic no less than the Thebaic has Western readings, but they are

with comparatively few exceptions, readings much current in the fourth century, and possibly owe their place to comparatively late mixture. The Thebaic on the other hand has a large proportion of distinctively Western readings of an older type. Whatever may be the real origin of the Æthiopic, it is on the one hand strongly Syrian, on the other in strong affinity with its Egyptian neighbours, and especially its nearer neighbour the Thebaic : both ancient Western and ancient Non-Western readings, Alexandrian and other, are conspicuous in its unsettled but certainly composite text.

218. The two solitary outlying versions bear marks of their late date, but not less of the valuable texts which were still current when they were made. The Armenian includes at least three large elements, Syrian, early Western, and early Non-Western, including some Alexandrian modifications. The coincidence of many of the Western readings in the Armenian with the Latin Vulgate, in conjunction with the real adulteration of the first printed edition from the Latin Vulgate, as mentioned above (§ 121), has brought this version under a vague suspicion of having been at some period subjected to Latinising corruption. The coincidences however with the Old Latin in peculiar readings against the Vulgate Latin are likewise numerous, and can only be explained by descent from a Greek Western original. The Gothic has very much the same combination as the Italian revision of the Old Latin, being largely Syrian and largely Western, with a small admixture of ancient Non-Western readings. Whether the copies which furnished the Western element were obtained by Ulfilas in Europe or brought by his parents from Cappadocia, cannot be determined : in either case they were Greek, not Latin.

219. It will be seen that, extensive and intricate as have been the results of mixture upon Versions, the broad historical relations of their texts correspond to the relations found among other documentary authorities. The only readings, belonging to distinctive types, that can with any certainty claim the authority of either of the three great independent families of versions originating in the earliest period are either Western or Alexandrian. Apparent exceptions to this statement may be found in occasional Syrian readings, or what appear to be such, attested by the Old Syriac or the Memphitic : but the evident presence of a late or extraneous element in the solitary

MS of the one and in the printed editions, founded on late MSS, of the other, together with the prevailing character of both texts, renders it highly improbable that these exceptions existed in the versions in their earlier days. The Revised Syriac is the first version to betray clearly the existence of the Greek Syrian revision, exhibiting a large proportion of the characteristically Syrian new readings and combinations of old readings. Various Latin revised texts follow, with analogous but different combinations, two alone deriving a very large share of their complexion from the Syrian text. The Egyptian texts, and especially the Memphitic, likewise sooner or later became adulterated, as we have said, with extraneous elements; but at what dates is uncertain. The only versions, besides the Italian and Vulgate Latin, in which the completed Syrian text is clearly and widely represented are definitely known to be of the fourth or later centuries, that is, the Gothic, Æthiopic, Armenian, and Harklean Syriac: the date of the Jerusalem Syriac is unknown.

D. 220—223. *Texts found in Greek Fathers*

220. Enough has already been said (§§ 158—162) on the texts which can be recognised in the extant remains of the several Ante-Nicene Greek Fathers. A few supplementary remarks must however be inserted here on the peculiar nature of the textual evidence furnished by Greek works preserved, wholly or in great part, only in ancient translations. In the quotations found in these works the texts of Versions and Fathers are variously blended together, so that their testimony needs to be examined with special care, while it is often too valuable to be neglected. Irenæus furnishes the most prominent example. Of his great treatise against heresies, which is extant in a Latin translation, no Greek MS is known to exist. Epiphanius however, writing about 375, has transcribed into his own principal work the greater part of the first of the five books. Other Greek writers and compilers, from Eusebius onwards, have preserved many short fragments, a few being likewise extant in a Syriac or Armenian dress. Secure knowledge of the character of the text of the New Testament used by Irenæus himself can of course be obtained only from the Greek extracts and from such readings extant only in Latin as are distinctly fixed by the

context; and it is solely from these materials that we have described his text as definitely Western. In the use of the Greek extracts the age and other circumstances of the several sources from which they are derived have to be considered. The Greek transmission is independent of the Latin transmission, but not always purer. Greek corruptions absent from the Latin version, due either to the use of degenerate MSS of Irenæus by late writers or to degenerate transmission of the works of these writers themselves, can often be detected in the language of Irenæus himself, and might therefore be anticipated in his quotations. But these individual ambiguities do not disturb the general results. The passages subject to no reasonable doubt render it certain that the translator largely modified biblical quotations in conformity with an Old Latin text familiar to him, but perhaps unconsciously, certainly irregularly and very imperfectly. We thus learn what antecedents to the Latin readings we have to take into account as possible where the Greek has perished, aided by the fact that passages quoted several times exhibit a text sometimes identical, sometimes modified in various degrees. Occasionally, with the help afforded by the other Old Latin evidence, we can arrive at moral certainty that the translator has faithfully reproduced his author's reading: but more commonly the two alternatives have to be regarded as equally possible. Both texts are Western; and the evidence is valuable, whether it be that of Irenæus or virtually of a fresh Old Latin MS, though in the former case it is much more valuable. Were indeed Massuet's commonly accepted theory true, that the Latin version of Irenæus was used by Tertullian, the biblical text followed by the translator would take precedence of all other Old Latin texts in age. We are convinced however, not only by the internal character of this biblical text but by comparison of all the passages of Irenæus borrowed in substance by Tertullian, that the Greek text alone of Irenæus was known to him, and that the true date of the translation is the fourth century. The inferior limit is fixed by the quotations made from it by Augustine about 421.

221. Several important works of Origen are likewise, wholly or in part, extant only in Latin, and need similar allowance for two alternatives in the employment of their evidence as to biblical texts. Caution is especially needed where Rufinus is the translator, as in the early treatise

De Principiis, the commentaries on Canticles and Romans, and the Homilies on several early books of the Old Testament and on three Psalms: for his well known licence in manipulating Origen's own language undoubtedly extended to the quotations; and at least in the commentaries the depravation of text has apparently been increased by the condensation of the voluminous original. Yet even here numerous readings can be determined with certainty as Origen's. More reliance can be placed, though still with some reserve, on Jerome's translations, that is, those of the Homilies on St Luke, (Isaiah?), Jeremiah (mostly also extant in Greek), and Ezekiel, and of two on Canticles. For part of the commentary on St Matthew we have an interesting anonymous translation, the portion for xvii 34—xxvii 66 being preserved in no other shape. For xvi 13—xxii 33 it overlaps an extant section of the Greek text; and comparison suggests that they are both independent condensations of a fuller original, so that neither can be safely neglected, though the Latin has the disadvantages of Old Latin modification as well as greater brevity. It has however occasionally preserved matter omitted altogether by the Greek abbreviator. Other Greek patristic writings extant in Latin may be passed over.

222. The Syriac MSS brought to England within the present century have contributed some valuable patristic texts. The *Theophania* of Eusebius, edited and translated by Dr Lee, presents phenomena analogous to those of the Latin Irenæus. Some of the readings are undoubtedly of Old Syriac parentage, and introduced by the translator; others as certainly belong to Eusebius; and many may have either origin. Moreover the predominant colour of both texts is Western, though the influence of a Non-Western text over Eusebius is also perceptible. The help of Greek fragments is available both here and in the other Syriac patristic translation most useful to the textual critic, that of a large part of the younger Cyril's Homilies on St Luke, edited and translated by Dr Payne Smith. In this instance the disturbing element is the Vulgate Syriac: but the great bulk of the text of the biblical quotations is unaffected by it, and takes high rank as a documentary authority for a Non-Western Pre-Syrian text of the verses which it covers.

223. Respecting Post-Nicene Greek patristic writings generally it will suffice here to refer to what has been said already (§ 193) on the extremely mixed character of their

13

texts, shewing a growing preponderance of Syrian readings even where the text of Antioch was not adopted almost or altogether without modification. With the works of Cyril of Alexandria may be named an obscure exposition of faith (Κατὰ μέρος πίστις), formerly called a work of Gregory of Neocæsarea (Cent. III), and now attributed with much probability to Apollinaris, which has a remarkable Pre-Syrian and chiefly Non-Western text. A more than average proportion of similar elements presents itself in the quotations of Epiphanius; and even so late a writer as John of Damascus (Cent. VIII) makes considerable use of an ancient text.

SECTION V. IDENTIFICATION AND ESTIMATION OF READINGS AS BELONGING TO THE CHIEF ANCIENT TEXTS

224—243

A. 224. *Nature of the process of identification*

224. The constituent elements of each principal extant document, so far as they have been contributed by the several great ancient types of text, having thus been approximately determined, we are now in a position to determine by their aid the ancient distribution of a much larger number of separate readings than was possible when only the comparatively unmixed representatives of each type were taken into account. Here then at last genealogical evidence becomes extensively applicable to use in the discrimination of false readings from true. As each variation comes before us with its two or more variants, each attested by a group of documents, we are now enabled in a large proportion of cases to assign at once each variant to one of the ancient texts on the strength of the grouping of documents which makes up its attestation, and thereby to obtain (to say the least) a presumption of the highest value as to its genuineness or spuriousness.

B. 225, 226. *Identification and rejection of Syrian readings*

225. The first point to decide with respect to each reading is whether it is Pre-Syrian or not. If it is attested by the bulk of the later Greek MSS, but not by any of the uncials אBCDLPQRTZ (Δ in St Mark) Ξ (also 33) in the Gospels (the smaller fragments we pass over here), אABCDE₂ (also 13 61) in Acts, אABC (also 13) in the Catholic Epistles, or אABCD₂G₃ (also 17 67**) in the Pauline Epistles, and not by any Latin authority (except the latest forms of Old Latin), the Old or the Jerusalem Syriac, or either Egyptian version, and not by any certain quotation of a Father earlier than 250, there is the strongest possible presumption that it is distinctively Syrian, and therefore, on the grounds already explained (§ 158), to be rejected at once as proved to have a relatively late origin. It is true that many documents not included in these privileged lists contain Pre-Syrian elements; but only in such small proportion that the chance of a Pre-Syrian reading finding attestation in these late relics of vanishing or vanished texts, *and none in the extant documents wholly or mainly of Pre-Syrian ancestry*, is infinitesimal; and, when this hypothetical possibility is set against the *vera causa* supplied by the Syrian revision, becomes yet more shadowy. The special need of strictly limiting early patristic authority for the present purpose to what is ' certain' will be explained further on.

226. The Syrian or Post-Syrian origin of a reading is not much less certain if one or two of the above Greek MSS, as CLPQR 33 in the Gospels, AC[E₂] 13 in the Acts and Catholic Epistles, and AC 17 in the Pauline

Epistles, are found on the side of the later MSS, or even if similar testimony is *prima facie* borne by such a version as the Memphitic, the MSS of which have not yet been subjected to a critical sifting. It would be useless to attempt to lay down absolute rules of discrimination; the essential prerequisites for striking the balance are familiarity with the documents, and a habit of observing their various groupings: but the fundamental materials of judgement must be such facts and combination of facts, slightly sketched in the preceding pages, as are implied in the rough arrangement of documents just given. The doubt that must sometimes remain is not often whether a given reading is Syrian, but whether it is distinctively Syrian, that is, whether it originated with the Syrian revision, or was an older reading, of whatever type, adopted by the Syrian revisers. In the final decision, as will be seen, this doubt is very rarely of practical moment.

C.   227—232.   *Identification of Western and of Alexandrian readings*

227.   Distinctively Syrian and Post-Syrian readings being set aside, there remain only such readings as the nature of their documentary attestations marks out, often with certainty, often with high probability, as older than 250.   Such readings may with substantial truth be called 'Ante-Nicene'; but the term 'Pre-Syrian', if less familiar, is not less convenient, and certainly more correct. The account which we have already given of the early history of the text must have dispelled any anticipation that textual criticism, in reaching back to the middle of the third century, would have nearly ful-

filled its task. In truth not only the harder but the
larger part remains. We have to begin with simply
endeavouring to range under the three principal types
or lines of text all readings evidently worthy of attention
as possibly right, at the same time making full use of
the instruction to be gained by observing the attestations
of all Pre-Syrian readings whatever, whether they have
any appearance of being possibly right or not. Of the
variations in which the endeavour is baffled we shall
speak presently. Multitudes of variations present no
difficulty at all, and as many need only a little consideration to interpret them.

228. Such Western readings as have acquired no
accessory attestation by adoption into the Syrian or other
mixed texts catch the eye at once in books or parts of
books in which we have one or more Greek MSS with a
tolerably unmixed Western text and in which Old Latin
evidence is not wanting. In the Gospels such readings
are attested by D, the chief Old Latin MSS and Fathers,
the Old Syriac, and the Greek Ante-Nicene Fathers,
those of Alexandria partially excepted. They are not
materially less conspicuous if in the Gospels they are
likewise supported by a stray uncial as $\aleph$ or X or Γ,
or by a few cursives, as 81 (especially), or 1 and its
kindred, 13 and its kindred, 22, 28, 157, &c., or by the
Latin or Syriac Vulgate (indeed any Syrian text), or the
Thebaic, Æthiopic, Armenian, or Gothic. In Acts D
and the Old Latin fragments and Fathers, with the Greek
patristic evidence as above, are the primary attestation:
$\aleph$, E_2, 31, 44, 61, 137, 180, &c., or any of the above versions except the Gothic, especially the Harklean Syriac
or Thebaic, may be the secondary; the numerous quotations by Irenæus taking a prominent place. In the

Pauline Epistles the primary documents are D_2G_3 (E_3 and F_2 need no further mention), the Old Latin fragments and Fathers, and Greek patristic quotations as above: in the second place may stand ℵ or B, 31, 37, 46, 80, 137, 221, &c., or any of the above versions, the Gothic in particular. The secondary documents here named are only those whose sporadic attestation of Western readings not afterwards Syrian is most frequent: from readings of this class few if any uncials having a large Pre-Syrian element are entirely free.

229. The analogous Alexandrian readings need more attention to detect them. Since it has so happened that every MS containing an approximately unmixed Alexandrian text has perished, the Alexandrian readings can have no strictly primary attestation among extant documents, and are therefore known only through documents containing large other elements. In the Gospels they are chiefly marked by the combination ℵCLX 33, and also Z in St Matthew, Δ in St Mark, Ξ and sometimes R in St Luke, with one or both of the Egyptian versions, and sometimes another version or two, especially the Armenian or the Vulgate or another revised Latin text; and of course Alexandrian Fathers. The least inconstant members of this group are CL and the Memphitic. In the Acts the chief representatives are ℵACE₂ 13, 61, and other cursives, as 27 29 36 40 68 69 102 110 112; and the same in the Catholic Epistles, with the loss of E_2 and 61, and the partial accession of P_2; and in the Pauline Epistles ℵACP₂ 5 6 17 23 39 47 73 137 &c.; with the same versions, so far as they are extant, and Fathers as in the Gospels. As however all these documents abound in neutral readings, and most of them in Western readings, the identification of Alexandrian

readings can be effected only by careful observation and comparison of contrasted groupings in successive variations. The process is a delicate one, and cannot be reduced to rule : but, though many cases must remain doubtful, we believe that the identification can usually be made with safety.

230. In each of the two classes of variations just noticed the array opposed to the group representing the aberrant text, that is, the Western or the Alexandrian text, as the case may be, owes much of its apparent variety, and more of its apparent numbers, to the presence of the irrelevant Syrian contingent. Two other classes of variations, differing from these in nothing but in the transposition of the habitually Syrian documents to the aberrant side, must evidently be interpreted in precisely the same way. Readings having only characteristic Western and characteristic Syrian attestation must have belonged to the Western text: readings having only characteristic Alexandrian and characteristic Syrian attestation must have belonged to the Alexandrian text.

231. On the other hand the rival readings cannot be exactly described except in negative terms. Against a Western stands a Non-Western Pre-Syrian reading: against an Alexandrian stands a Non-Alexandrian Pre-Syrian reading. The attestation of these readings is simply residual; that is, each of them must have been the reading of all extant Pre-Syrian texts, whatever they may be, except the Western in the one case, the Alexandrian in the other. It follows that, unless reason has been found for believing that all attestation of texts neither Western nor Alexandrian has perished, it must be presumed that the rival reading to a Western reading is not exclusively Alexandrian, and that the rival

reading to an Alexandrian reading is not exclusively Western.

232. A large proportion of variations still remains in which the assignation of the readings to different types of ancient text is in various degrees difficult or uncertain. The difficulty arises chiefly from two causes, the mixed composition of some of the principal extant documents, especially Greek uncials, and the not infrequent opposition of documents habitually agreeing as witnesses for one of the aberrant types, resulting in apparent cross distribution. Owing to the former cause Western readings, for instance, which were saved from the extinction which befel their parent texts in the Greek East in the fourth century by their reception into eclectic texts of that period, must naturally be often found attested by documents lying outside the properly Western group. Almost all our better uncials occur singly in their turn as supporters of very distinctly Western readings, and therefore it would be surprising if two or three of them were never to hold the same position together; so that a reading which two or three of them concur in supporting may quite possibly have had a Western origin. But where there is no clear inequality of number and also of predominant character in the attestation which documents of this kind give to the two rival readings of a variation, it may be difficult or impossible to say whether the opposition is between a Western and a Non-Western, or between a Non-Alexandrian and an Alexandrian reading. The cases of apparent cross distribution, of which the Old Latin evidence furnishes the most conspicuous examples, are of course equally due to mixture, and especially to the mixture produced by revision of versions after Greek MSS. Latin MSS known to contain revised texts may

naturally be taken to follow a Non-Western source where they stand in opposition to MSS of purer Old Latin pedigree; and in many similar instances a complete survey of the documentary evidence suffices to bring to light the essential features of the grouping in spite of partial confusion. But among these cases likewise there remain ambiguities which can be cleared up only by other kinds of evidence, or which cannot be cleared up at all.

D. 233—235. *Identification of neutral readings*

233. Besides all the various classes of binary variations examined in the preceding paragraphs, and besides those ternary variations in which the third variant is distinctively Syrian, there are, as we have already seen (§ 184), many other ternary variations in which one reading has a characteristic Western attestation, another has a characteristic Alexandrian attestation, the Syrian evidence being in support of either the first or the second, while the third is attested by documents ascertained to be of wholly or chiefly Pre-Syrian origin: in other words, both the principal aberrant texts stand clearly side by side, each clearly distinguished from a third text. Such third reading may doubtless be, and often manifestly is, nothing but a secondary modification of one of the other readings; for, as has been already intimated, it is not unusual to find together less and more developed Western readings, or less and more developed Alexandrian readings, or both together: nor are mixtures of the two lines unknown. But there are many other third readings which cannot without great difficulty be assigned on either external or internal grounds to such an origin, and

which must stand on at least an equal rank with the other two, as having to all appearance an independent ancestry.

234. If then a Pre-Syrian text exists which is neutral, that is, neither Western nor Alexandrian, the phenomena of attestation provide two resources for learning in what documents we may expect to find such a text preserved, comparison of the two fundamental types of binary variations, and direct inspection of the ternary or yet more complex variations last mentioned. In order to avoid needless repetition, the information thus obtained has been to a certain extent employed already in the account of the constituent elements of different documents (§§ 199—223): but, strictly speaking, it is only at the present stage of the investigation that the large body of evidence supplied by the binary variations becomes available. By comparison of binary variations we find what documents recur oftenest in the attestations of Non-Western and the attestations of Non-Alexandrian readings, taken together; in other words, what documents are oftenest found joining others in opposition to either of the aberrant texts singly. By inspection of ternary variations we find what documents oftenest stand out in clear detachment from all others by patent opposition to a Western and an Alexandrian text simultaneously.

235. As might be expected, the results of both processes are accordant as to the documents which they designate as most free at once from Western and from Alexandrian peculiarities. We learn first that, notwithstanding the lateness of our earliest Greek MSS as compared with some of the versions, and the high absolute antiquity of the fundamental texts which the older ver-

sions represent, the constituent texts of our better Greek MSS must be in the main of at least equal antiquity, and that the best of them are, even as they stand, more free from Western and Alexandrian peculiarities than any version in its present state. We learn next that B very far exceeds all other documents in neutrality of text as measured by the above tests, being in fact always or nearly always neutral, with the exception of the Western element already mentioned (§ 204) as virtually confined to the Pauline Epistles. At a long interval after B, but hardly a less interval before all other MSS, stands ℵ. Then come, approximately in the following order, smaller fragments being neglected, T of St Luke and St John, Ξ of St Luke, L, 33, Δ (in St Mark), C, Z of St Matthew, R of St Luke, Q, and P. It may be said in general terms that those documents, B and ℵ excepted, which have most Alexandrian readings have usually also most neutral readings. Thus among versions by far the largest amount of attestation comes from the Memphitic and Thebaic; but much also from the Old and the Jerusalem Syriac, and from the African Latin ; and more or less from every version. After the Gospels the number of documents shrinks greatly; but there is no marked change in the relations of the leading uncials to the neutral text, except that A now stands throughout near C. In Acts 61 comes not far below ℵ, 13 being also prominent, though in a much less degree, here and in the Catholic Epistles. The considerable Pre-Syrian element already noticed (§ 212) as distinguishing a proportionally large number of cursives in this group of books includes many neutral readings: for examples of these cursives it will suffice to refer to the two lists given above (§§ 228, 229), which include the more important MSS. In some of the

Catholic Epistles, as also in the subsequent books, an appreciable but varying element of the text of P_2 has the same character.   For the Pauline Epistles there is little that can be definitely added to אBAC except 17 and P_2: the best marked neutral readings are due to the second hand of 67.

E.   236—239.   *Suspiciousness of Western and of Alexandrian readings*

236.   Nearly all that has been said in the preceding pages respecting the documentary attestation of the three leading types of Pre-Syrian text remains equally true whatever be the historical relation of these types to each other.   On the other hand, it was necessary at an earlier stage (§§ 173 ff., 183), in describing the characteristics of the Western and Alexandrian texts, to state at once the general conclusions on this head to which we are irresistibly led by Internal Evidence of Texts, alike on that more restricted study of Western and Alexandrian readings which is limited to variations in which their characteristic attestation is least disguised by extraneous evidence, and on the more comprehensive study of all readings that can be ultimately recognised as Western or Alexandrian.   In a vast majority of instances the result is identical: in binary variations the Non-Western reading approves itself more original than the Western, the Non-Alexandrian than the Alexandrian: in ternary variations the neutral reading, if supported by such documents as stand most frequently on the Non-Western and Non-Alexandrian sides in binary variations, approves itself more original than the Western and also more original than the Alexandrian.   The Western and Alex-

andrian texts as wholes are therefore in the strictest sense, as we have called them partly by anticipation, aberrant texts.

237. It does not follow however that none of their distinctive readings are original. If it could be shown with reasonable certainty that the three lines diverged simultaneously from the apostolic autographs, or from a common original derived almost immediately from the autographs, the chance that one line alone has preserved true readings where the two others agree, that is, that two transcribers have independently made the same changes, would be infinitesimal (see § 75), except as regards changes of a very obvious and tempting kind. No such presupposition is however imposed by the actual evidence: we have no right to affirm that the two great divergences were simultaneous, not successive. Both are indeed of such extreme antiquity that a strong presumption must always lie against an exclusively Western or exclusively Alexandrian reading; since, apart from accidental coincidence, its genuineness would presuppose as a necessary condition, not only that the two divergences were not simultaneous, but that the rival reading came into existence either at the first divergence or between the first and the second.

238. Of the unfavourable presumptions arising out of the internal character of distinctive Western and distinctive Alexandrian readings generally we have said enough already (§§ 170 ff., 181 ff.). A certain number might on purely internal grounds be received or rejected with equally or almost equally good reason: it is however, we believe, quite safe to dismiss them along with their much more numerous associates that are condemned by individual internal evidence no less than by the pre-

vailing character of the text to which they belong: it
may be added that they are seldom intrinsically of
much interest. Others remain which by strong internal probability of some kind plead against summary
rejection. The plea can never with prudence be set
entirely aside: but the number of such readings which
eventually make good a claim to a possible place in
the apostolic text is, in our judgement, exceedingly
small.

239. There are indeed some Western readings in
the Gospels, and perhaps in the Acts, which cannot be
explained by accidental error of transcription, or by any
of the ordinary causes of textual corruption, such as
paraphrase, or assimilation to other passages of the
New or Old Testament; and in such cases an incau-
tious student may be easily tempted by the freshness of
the matter to assume that it must have come from the
hand of the writer of the book before him. The assumption would be legitimate enough were the Western texts
of late origin: but it loses all its force when we remember (see § 173) that in the second century oral
traditions of the apostolic age were still alive; that at
least one written Gospel closely related to one or more of
the four primary Gospels, together with various forms of
legendary Christian literature concerning our Lord and
the Apostles, was then current in some churches; and
that neither definition of the Canon of the New Testament nor veneration for the letter as distinguished from
the substance of its sacred records had advanced far
enough to forbid what might well seem their temperate
enrichment from such sources as these. Transcriptional
probability is likewise of no little weight here: the absence of Western readings of this kind from the Non-

Western texts is inexplicable on the supposition that they formed part of the apostolic text.

F.   240— 242.   *Exceptional Western non-interpolations*

240.   On the other hand there remain, as has been before intimated (§ 170), a few other Western readings of similar form, which we cannot doubt to be genuine in spite of the exclusively Western character of their attestation.   They are all omissions, or, to speak more correctly, non-interpolations, of various length: that is to say, the original record has here, to the best of our belief, suffered interpolation in all the extant Non-Western texts.   The almost universal tendency of transcribers to make their text as full as possible, and to eschew omissions, is amply exemplified in the New Testament.   Omissions of genuine words and clauses in the Alexandrian and Syrian texts are very rare, and always easy to explain.   In the Western text, with which we are here concerned, they are bolder and more numerous, but still almost always capable of being traced to a desire of giving a clearer and more vigorous presentation of the sense.   But hardly any of the omissions now in question can be so explained, none in a satisfactory manner.   On the other hand the doubtful words are superfluous, and in some cases intrinsically suspicious, to say the least; while the motive for their insertion is usually obvious.   With a single peculiar exception (Matt. xxvii 49), in which the extraneous words are omitted by the Syrian as well as by the Western text, the Western non-interpolations are confined to the last three chapters of St Luke.   In various parts of the Gospels other Western omissions are to be found, which

it would be rash to condemn absolutely, the attestations being precisely similar to those of the non-interpolations which we accept, and the internal evidence, intrinsic and transcriptional, being open to some doubt; in other words, an intermediate class of Western omissions that may perhaps be non-interpolations must be admitted. Examples will be found in Matt. (vi 15, 25;) ix 34; (xiii 33;) xxi 44; (xxiii 26;) Mark ii 22; (x 2;) xiv 39; Luke v 39; x 41 f.; xii 19, 21, 39; xxii 62; (xxiv 9;) John iii 32; iv 9. With the difficult question of notation here involved we are not for the moment concerned: it is enough here to repeat that we find ourselves wholly unable to believe some of the clauses and sentences omitted by Western documents to be genuine, while in other not obviously dissimilar cases our judgement remains suspended.

241. These exceptional instances of the preservation of the original text in exclusively Western readings are likely to have had an exceptional origin. They are easily reconciled with the other phenomena if we suppose, first, that the text which became fixed at Alexandria, and in due time was partially adulterated by Alexandrian corruptions, was an offshoot from the text which we have called the neutral text, and which had parted company from the earliest special ancestry of the Western text at a yet earlier date; and secondly, that the interpolations which give rise to the appearance of Western omissions took place in the interval, if not at the actual divergence, and thus stand in all Non-Western texts, whether derived through Alexandria or not. These interpolations are for the most part quite unlike Alexandrian interpolations, and have much more of a 'Western' character; so that the hypothesis which might at first

sight suggest itself, of their having originated at Alexandria, and thence spread by mixture to Non-Western texts elsewhere, is set aside by internal evidence as well as by the want of other corroborative instances. The purely documentary phenomena are compatible with the supposition that the Western and the Non-Western texts started respectively from a first and a second edition of the Gospels, both conceivably apostolic: but internally none of the Non-Western interpolations certainly justify this claim to a true though a secondary kind of originality, and some of them, it is not too much to say, shew a misunderstanding which renders it impossible to assign to them any worthier origin than to ordinary Western interpolations.

242. Nothing analogous to the Western non-interpolations presents itself among distinctively Alexandrian readings of any form, omissions, additions, or substitutions. Now and then, though fortunately but rarely, the attestation of what seems to be an Alexandrian reading, unusually well attested, approaches too near the attestation of some neutral readings to exclude doubt as to the true origin, while internal evidence is likewise indecisive. But this occasional ambiguity of external evidence is not to be confounded with incongruities of internal character in readings of clearly defined external type. No variations are known to us in which a distinctively Alexandrian reading, indubitably such, approves itself as genuine against Western and neutral texts combined, or even against the neutral text alone. Of the numerous variations which at first sight appear to involve conflicts between the neutral text and the Western and Alexandrian texts combined it will be more opportune to speak further on.

14

G. 243. *Recapitulation of genealogical evidence proper*

243. To sum up what has been said on the results of genealogical evidence proper, as affecting the text of the New Testament, we regard the following propositions as absolutely certain. (I) The great ancient texts did actually exist as we have described them in Sections II and III. The main line of neutral and comparatively pure text was from an early time surrounded and over-shadowed by two powerful lines containing much aber-ration, the 'Western' being by far the most licentious and the most widely spread, and the Alexandrian being formed by skilful but mostly petty corrections which left the neutral text untouched, at all events in the Gospels and Pauline Epistles, except in a very small proportion of its words. Late in the third century, or soon after, MSS came to be written in which the three main texts were mixed in various proportions, and the process went for-ward on a large scale in the following century, when all the unmixed texts began to die out. The Western, hitherto the most influential of all texts, now disappeared rapidly, lingering however, it would seem, in the West. One of the mixed texts was formed in Syria with care and contrivance, modifying as well as combining the earlier texts, and by the middle of the fourth cen-tury was established in influence. For some centuries after the fourth there was in the East a joint currency of the Syrian and other texts, nearly all mixed, but at last the Syrian text, the text of Constantinople, almost wholly displaced the rest. (II) In the Gospels and Pauline Epistles, and to a less extent in the Acts, all the four principal forms of text are fairly represented in extant documents; in other books the representation of

one or more of the texts is seriously incomplete or doubtful. (III) The extant documents contain no readings (unless the peculiar Western non-interpolations noticed above are counted as exceptions), which suggest the existence of important textual events unknown to us, a knowledge of which could materially alter the interpretation of evidence as determined by the above history. (IV) In a large proportion of variations the assignation of the several readings to the several ancient texts by means of extant documents is clear and certain, and thus affords a sure clue to the original reading. (V) In many other ancient variations the distribution of documentary evidence must as a matter of fact be due to ancient distribution among the several texts, with or without subsequent mixture, although the extant documentary evidence is too scanty or too confused to allow confident decision between two or more possible views of the historical antecedents of the several readings. This last proposition implies that we have to do with many variations in which the tests supplied by the general history of the text of the New Testament are not available for direct use, and other critical resources are needed. To these we must presently turn.

SECTION VI. REVIEW OF PREVIOUS CRITICISM WITH RE-
FERENCE TO ANCIENT TEXTS

244—255

A. 244—246. *Foundation of historical criticism by
Mill, Bentley, and Bengel*

244. Before however we pass from the great ancient texts, it will be right to interpose a few words of comment on previous criticism dealing with the same subject. Al-

though the series of editions which can be said to approximate to a true text of the New Testament begins in 1831, the preliminary studies of the eighteenth century, unduly neglected since the earlier part of the present century, form the necessary introduction to all secure progress hereafter. It will be sufficient to mark the most salient points in the progress of criticism.

245. Mill led the way in 1707 not only by his ample collection of documentary evidence but by his comprehensive examination of individual documents, seldom rising above the wilderness of multitudinous details, yet full of sagacious observations. He incidentally noticed the value of the concurrence of Latin evidence with A, the most conspicuous and the only complete representative of an ancient Non-Western Greek text then sufficiently known; and this glimpse of genealogical method was not lost upon Bentley, who with clear and deliberate purpose made Greek and Latin consent the guiding principle of his own project for a restoration of the text. The actual project fell to the ground until it was revived and carried out in Lachmann's edition of 1831, the starting point of the later period; in which however it assumed a somewhat different shape through the substitution of the Old Latin for the Vulgate Latin, and the ranging of the Greek Western uncials on the Latin or, as it was more properly called, the 'Western' side. But the principle itself was received at once into fruitful soil, and contributed more than any other antecedent to the criticism of the intervening period.

246. How deeply the value of the principle, as set forth in Bentley's *Proposals* of 1720, impressed Bengel, although he accepted it only in part, is evident from many pages of his Introduction of 1734. Bengel himself pointed out the deceptiveness of numerical superiority detached from variety of origin, prepared for sifting the confused mass of Greek MSS by casting upon it, as he said, the Versions and Fathers as an additional heap, and endeavoured to classify the documents known to him according to their presumed derivation from ancient texts. He divided them into two great 'nations' or 'families', the 'Asiatic' and the 'African', answering roughly to what we have called Syrian and Pre-Syrian; and further, less distinctly, subdivided the latter into two subordinate 'nations' or 'families', represented typically by A and by the Old Latin. At the same time he laid great stress on internal evidence, in this as in other respects making large use of

materials scattered through Mill's notes; and it is chiefly to his earnest if somewhat crude advocacy that Transcriptional Probabilities under the name of 'the harder reading' owe their subsequent full recognition.

B. 247—249. *Development of historical criticism by Griesbach, in contrast with Hug's theory of recensions*

247. Bengel was succeeded in Germany by Semler, and under his influence by a group of acute and diligent textual critics, stimulated to fresh researches both by Bengel's writings and by the rich accession of new materials from Wetstein's edition of 1751-2, and from the various explorations and collations which were vigorously carried on in the later years of the century. What Bengel had sketched tentatively was verified and worked out with admirable patience, sagacity, and candour by Griesbach, who was equally great in independent investigation and in his power of estimating the results arrived at by others. Bengel's 'Asiatic' text he called 'Constantinopolitan': the two more ancient texts, which he clearly defined, he called 'Western' and 'Alexandrian'. Unfortunately he often followed Semler in designating the ancient texts by the term 'recension', and thus gave occasion to a not yet extinct confusion between his historical analysis of the text of existing documents and the conjectural theory of his contemporary Hug, a biblical scholar of considerable merit, but wanting in sobriety of judgement.

248. Hug started from what was in itself on the whole a true conception of the Western text and its manifold licence. He called it the κοινὴ ἔκδοσις, or 'Vulgate Edition', taking the name from the text of the LXX as it was in its confusion before the reform attempted by Origen in his Hexapla. But further he conjectured that the disorderly state of this popular text led to its being formally revised in three different lands, the product of each revision being a 'recension' in the strict sense of the word. The alleged evidence consists in two well known passages of Jerome. In the first he speaks of the diversity of copies of the LXX in different regions; Alexandria and Egypt appeal, he says, to the authority of Hesychius; Constantinople and Antioch approve of the copies of Lucian the Martyr; the intermediate provinces read the Palestinian volumes, wrought out by Origen and published by Eusebius and

Pamphilus ; and the whole world is set at discord by this
threefold difference. In the second passage, already cited
(§ 190), he is stating vaguely to what Greek sources he proposes to have recourse in correcting the Latin Gospels.
"I pass by", he says, "those volumes which bear the
names of Lucianus and Hesychius, and are upheld by the
perverse contentiousness of a few men": he adds in obscure language that 'they had neither been allowed to
make corrections (*emendare*) after the Seventy in the Old
Testament, nor profited by making corrections in the New
Testament'. The latter quotation, enigmatic as it is, distinctly implies the existence of copies of the New Testament or the Gospels bearing in some way the names of Lucianus and Hesychius, and supposed to have in some way
undergone correction; and likewise associates the same
names with some analogous treatment of the LXX. As
they appear in company with Origen's name in a similar
connexion in the first quotation, Hug supposed that Hesychius had made a recension of both Testaments for Alexandria, Lucianus for Antioch, and Origen for Palestine.
He had next to discover descendants of the supposed
recensions in existing groups of documents, and had no
difficulty in assigning the Constantinopolitan text to Lucianus : but since Hesychius plausibly claimed the 'Alexandrian' text, he could find no better representation of
Origen's supposed work than an ill defined and for the
most part obscure assemblage headed by AKM.

249. Origen's quotations prove conclusively that no
such text as these documents present can ever have proceeded from him : and it is hardly less certain, as Griesbach
shewed by the implicit testimony of various passages, that
he never made anything like a recension of the New Testament. It does not follow that the same can be said of
Lucianus and Hesychius. As we have already observed
(§§ 185, 190), the Syrian text must have been due to a revision which was in fact a recension, and which may with
fair probability be assigned to the time when Lucianus
taught at Antioch. Of the Alexandrian corrections more
than one stage can certainly be traced : whether the primary corrections were due to a distinct revision cannot,
we think, be determined, and it would be little gain to
know. That Hesychius had no hand in any revision
which can have produced them is proved by the occurrence
of many of them in Origen's writings, at a much earlier
date. But it is quite conceivable that Hesychius made or

adopted some eclectic text too short-lived to have left recognisable traces of itself in extant evidence, though it may be a hidden factor in the process of mixture to which some of our texts are partly due. Thus much it is but just to Hug to say, though the point is of no practical consequence. But neither the deserved discredit into which Hug's theory of recensions as a whole has fallen, nor the uncertainty as to the precise nature of the facts referred to in Jerome's second passage, create any doubt as to the soundness of Griesbach's fundamental classification of texts, which rests entirely on the independent base furnished by the observed phenomena of existing documents.

C. 250—253. *Defects of Griesbach's criticism*

250. There are indeed some defects in Griesbach's view which he could hardly have failed to correct if all the evidence now accessible had been in his hands. Perhaps the most important of these is a confusion between the classification of ancient texts and the classification of documents derived from them. He was aware indeed that no existing MS preserves any 'recension' or leading ancient text in absolute purity, and that one source of corruption was the intrusion of readings out of another 'recension' (Preface to Gospels of 1796, p. lxxviii; cf. *Meletemata*, pp. xxxviii f.). But still in effect he treated our documents as capable of being each on the whole identified with some one ancient text. In other words, he failed to apprehend in its true magnitude the part played by mixture in the history of the text during the fourth and following centuries, or to appreciate the value of the observation of groupings as a critical instrument by which a composite text can be to a great extent analysed into its constituent elements.

251. Hardly if at all less important was his confusion of Alexandrian readings with readings preserved wholly or chiefly at Alexandria. His discrimination of the internal character of Western and Alexandrian corrections (ib. p. lxxvii) is excellent as far as it goes, and may supply useful guidance in some cases of obscure attestation. But his mode of using the two great texts can be justified only on the impossible assumption that the Alexandrian text, with its bulk of pure readings and its distinctive corruptions alike, was, so to speak, full-blown from the beginning.

The very fact that these corruptions originated at Alexandria implies that MSS free from them, as well as from Western corruptions, existed previously at Alexandria; and there is no apparent reason why this earlier form of text should not have been propagated in greater or less purity at Alexandria by the side of the altered text or texts. If it was, and if any existing documents represent it, their text, whatever its value may be, has not the defects of a distinctive Alexandrian text. But further there is no apparent reason why documents should not exist derived from sister MSS to those which originally came to Alexandria, and which thus were the parents of later MSS current at Alexandria, including those in which the Alexandrian corrections originated; and if so, no ordinary internal evidence can enable us to decide whether the ancestry of any given existing documents having this character of text was altogether independent of Alexandria, or had its home at Alexandria but was unaffected by any distinctive Alexandrian corruption. Griesbach seems however to have tacitly assumed both that Alexandria had but one Non-Western text, and that no early Non-Western text survived except at Alexandria; and accordingly in most variations the critical problem which virtually presented itself to him was merely whether it was more likely on internal grounds that the (assumed) Western reading was a corruption of the (assumed) Alexandrian or the Alexandrian of the Western, the characteristics of each 'recension' and the special probabilities of the immediate context being considered together.

252. Thus owing to an imperfect conception of the process of transmission, leading to a misinterpretation of quite the most important evidence, unchecked by attention to grouping, Griesbach was driven to give a dangerously disproportionate weight to internal evidence, and especially to transcriptional probability, on which indeed for its own sake he placed excessive reliance : and this, not his wise anxiety to discriminate the ancient sources of readings before counting or weighing authorities, is the chief cause of the inferiority of his own text of the New Testament, which stands in singular contrast to the high qualities of his criticism. The other great cause of its insufficiency we have already mentioned (§§ 16, 17), his use of the Received Text as a basis for correction. To have taken as his basis those ancient texts in which he himself placed most confidence would have increased

the difficulties of his task as an editor, since they frequently did not offer him the same reading; but, as Lachmann triumphantly shewed, in no other way was it possible to avoid the errors that must often find acceptance
when numberless variations are approached from the
wrong side.

253. The limitations of view in Griesbach and his
predecessors were the natural result of the slenderness of
their materials. Bentley and Bengel wrote when A was
for practical purposes the one ancient purely Greek uncial;
and the peculiarities of its text, used as a standard, coloured
their criticism, and to a certain extent even that of Griesbach. He learned much from his study of C and L : but
the very large distinctively Alexandrian element which
they contain had probably a considerable share in leading
him implicitly to assume that any extant ancient text not
Western must be Alexandrian, and that in the most exclusive sense. A later generation has less excuse for over-
looking the preservation of a neutral text, in approximate
integrity in B, and in greater or less proportions in many
other documents; or for questioning the vast increase of
certainty introduced by its recognition in weighing the
claims of rival Pre-Syrian readings.

D. 254, 255. *Permanent value of Griesbach's criticism*

254. In dwelling on Griesbach's errors at some length,
notwithstanding the neglect into which his writings have
unhappily fallen, we should be grieved even to seem re-
gardless of a name which we venerate above that of every
other textual critic of the New Testament. It was essential to our purpose to explain clearly in what sense
it is true, and in what sense it is not true, that we
are attempting to revive a theory which is popularly
supposed to have been long since exploded. No valid
objection can, we believe, be brought against the
greater part of Griesbach's historical view. It is commonly met by vague sceptical assertions which make no
attempt to deal with the actual phenomena. Criticisms
which merely shewed that he had been led into too broad
and unqualified assertions as to this or that document
have left untouched or even unawares strengthened his
main positions. The most plausible allegation, that his
latest discoveries as to Origen's readings compelled him

to abandon his attempt to distinguish between his 'Western' and his 'Alexandrian' readings, and thus destroyed the basis of what is called his theory, depends on a double misconception.   The recognition of the fact that Origen sometimes used a MS either 'Western' or containing a large 'Western' element did indeed render it impossible to affirm that a reading found in Origen must needs be 'Alexandrian', that is, it prescribed special care in the interpretation of one single source of evidence; but it made no change in other respects: and the *Meletemata* of 1811, in which the recognition is conveyed, reiterate Griesbach's familiar statements in precise language, while they shew a growing perception of mixture which might have led him to further results if he had not died in the following spring.

255.   It is not necessary to our purpose to pass under review the principles and texts of Griesbach's three great successors, all of whom have published texts of a substantially ancient type, and from each of whom, from Tregelles in particular, we have learned much.   But we are bound to express our conviction that the virtual abandonment of Griesbach's endeavour to obtain for the text of the New Testament a secure historical foundation in the genealogical relations of the whole extant documentary evidence has rendered the work of all appreciably more imperfect in itself, and less defensible on rational grounds. Such corrections of Griesbach's leading results as have been indicated above (§§ 250—252) would have removed the difficulties which have unquestionably been felt by dispassionate judges, though they have also been distorted and exaggerated by partisans.   In taking up his investigations afresh, we have, we trust, found a way not only to make a somewhat nearer approximation to the apostolic text than our immediate predecessors, but also to strengthen the critical bases on which their own texts are for the most part founded.

CHAPTER III. *RESULTS OF INTERNAL EVI-DENCE OF GROUPS AND DOCUMENTS*

256—355

A. 256—260. *General considerations on Documentary Groups*

256. In attempting to give an account of the manner in which the historical relations of the great ancient texts of the New Testament can be safely used for decision between rival readings, we have of necessity (see § 72) transgressed the limits of purely genealogical evidence, in so far as we have dwelt on the general internal character of the Western and Alexandrian texts as a ground for distrusting readings apparently Western only, or Western and Syrian only, or Alexandrian only, or Alexandrian and Syrian only. The evidence which has been thus appealed to is in effect Internal Evidence of Groups (§§ 77, 78), in principle identical with Internal Evidence of Documents in virtue of the genealogical axiom that, accidental coincidences apart, identity of reading implies ultimate identity of origin. Thus, to take the simplest case, finding a frequent recurrence of D, the Old Latin, and the Old Syriac in isolated combination, we knew that in each such reading they must be all lineally descended from a single common ancestor. Having found reason to think that readings attested by

this particular group of documents are of great antiquity, we examined them successively in order to ascertain their prevailing internal character by means of variations in which the internal evidence is morally free from doubt.

257. Now a moment's consideration shews that the essentials of this process are independent of the historical adjuncts here attached to it, and remain the same for every possible combination of documents; and that therefore its power of employing easy variations as a key to difficult variations is of universal range. So applied, it is essentially a particular mode of using Internal Evidence of Documents; only not continuous extant documents but, as it were, fragmentary lost documents. Whenever a particular detached combination of documents is of sufficiently frequent occurrence to give room for generalisations, and those of its readings which admit of being provisionally accepted or rejected on Internal Evidence of Readings, Intrinsic and Transcriptional, are found to be all or nearly all apparently right, we are justified in anticipating that its other readings, as to which our judgement has thus far been suspended, or even on the whole adverse, are right too, and in requiring on re-examination very strong local internal evidence to rebut the favourable presumption. A similar recurrence of numerous apparently wrong readings will throw suspicion on the other or doubtful readings of the same group, provided that it remains in all cases literally or practically detached: we say practically, because the accession of a group containing no document outside the habitual attestation of such a text as the Syrian violates detachment in appearance alone. Either the favourable or the unfavourable presumption may also

be further defined according to particular classes of readings.

258. Since in all cases the inference depends on assumed homogeneousness of text, its basis may appear to be subject to uncertainty; for homogeneousness is interrupted by the intrusion of mixture, and it is theoretically possible that lost originals of groups might be mixed, as well as extant MSS. But the originals from which most groups which it is in practice worth while to keep in mind must have diverged can with difficulty be referred to so late a date as the times of general mixture, and no clear evidence of antecedent mixture has come to our own notice. The homogeneousness of the fundamental texts of all important groups may therefore, we believe, be safely trusted.

259. The limitation, more or less strict, to detached combination is necessary because otherwise the characteristics of the special common ancestor will be mixed up with the characteristics of a remoter and for present purposes less important ancestor. In all places where there is no variation D and the two associated versions are likewise found in combination, not the less truly because all other documents have the same reading; and this combination points with equal certainty to a single common ancestor: but here the single common ancestor was the apostolic autograph, followed perhaps by an indefinite number of immediate descendants; whereas what we want to know is the character of the special ancestor, as displayed either in departure from the original text or in fidelity shewn to it where others have departed from it. Similarly, where we find D and its associates agreeing with, for instance, ℵBCL and the Memphitic against all other documents, if we have ascer-

tained that this second group often stands in opposition
to the first, we know that the reading must have existed
in a common ancestor of the two special ancestors, and
that therefore it can tell us nothing about the special
characteristics of either.

260. The most delicate and difficult part of the
use of groupings in criticism consists in judging how far
a group loses its virtual identity by slight losses or slight
accessions of constituent members. The least important
losses and accessions from this point of view are evidently
those which accompany fragmentariness of text, so that
the change is not, for instance, from concurrence to
opposition, but from concurrence to total absence, or *vice
versa:* in such cases much depends on the number and
variety of the remaining members. Others again, which
look as if they ought to be important, are found in experience to be of little or no account: that is, if we treat
separately the groupings with and without the varying
member, the characteristics are found to be identical; so
that the same results would have been reached by treating
both forms of combination as a single group. An excellent example is supplied by many of the Alexandrian
corrections in St Mark, where we have every binary and
ternary combination of אCLΔ besides the full quaternion. But the accession or loss of any primary document
should always be treated as constituting a new group
until observation has shown that no real difference can
be detected in the results. How easily readings having
the same origin might come to have an attestation per-
petually varying within certain limits may be readily
understood, for instance in such an example as that
just cited, as soon as we apprehend clearly the manner
in which ordinary casual mixture came to pass. Whether

two or more MSS were deliberately compared for simultaneous use, or variations were noted in a margin and then at the next stage taken up into the text, or reminiscences of a text formerly heard or read became intermingled with the immediate impressions of eye and ear in transcription,—in all these cases a transcriber was making a conscious or unconscious selection of readings to insert into his fundamental text; and no two transcribers would make exactly the same selection. However great may be the superficial complexities of existing attestation, the primitive relations of text from which they are derived must have been simple; as otherwise each variation must have exhibited a much greater number of variants : and thus it is no wonder that after a while we find ourselves enabled to ascribe practical identity to groups not identical as to all their members.

B. 261—264. *Progressive limitation of Groups with reference to Primary Greek MSS*

261. It might perhaps be imagined that the possible combinations of our numerous documents would constitute an intractable multitude of groups: but no such difficulty exists in practice. Genealogical possibilities make up the merest fraction of arithmetical possibilities; and of the combinations that actually occur only a small proportion deserve more than momentary attention. The Syrian text as a whole must, we believe, be condemned by Internal Evidence of Groups almost as surely as by the evidence connected with the history of texts; and texts supported by only a portion of the Syrian phalanx have still less claim to consideration. Greek manuscripts containing a large amount of Pre-Syrian text, early Ver-

sions, and early Fathers are not numerous, and to a great extent are fragmentary or discontinuous; and combinations into which none of them enter may evidently in most cases be safely neglected. A student soon becomes aware that the groupings which can by any possibility affect his judgement in doubtful variations are sure to contain one or more of a very small number of primary documents. If at any time in the examination of a specially difficult case his attention is attracted by a reading supported by a group hitherto neglected by him, he will naturally take fresh opportunities of observing its characteristics. But the whole operation is simpler than it seems on paper.

262. No one, we believe, who agrees explicitly or implicitly with the account which we have given of the Syrian text and its attestation would hesitate, after studying the Internal Evidence of Groups, to take אBCDL 33 in the Gospels, אABCDE₂ 13 61 in Acts, אABC 13 in the Catholic Epistles, and אABCD₂G₃ 17 in the Pauline Epistles, as the primary documents in the sense just mentioned. This is of course entirely consistent with the assignation of substantial weight to numerous other documents in different degrees in the decision between rival readings. What is meant is that all groups containing none of these primary documents are found so habitually to support the obviously wrong variants where internal evidence is tolerably clear, that they must lie under the strongest suspicion in doubtful variations. Some few other Greek MSS, mostly fragmentary, might to a certain extent claim to be placed in the same class (see § 225): but it is safer to keep to these conspicuously preeminent and approximately complete copies. In strictness the African and European Latin,

the Old Syriac, the Egyptian versions, and the Ante-Nicene Fathers should be added to the list: we venture however to omit them here for the sake of simplicity, the practical effect of omitting them being extremely small, as will be explained further on.

263. Now if each of the Greek MSS singled out as primary is individually entitled to this exceptional distinction as a representative of Pre-Syrian texts, we should naturally expect the complete combinations of them to attest a specially pure text; the text thus attested being certified by the concurrence of all the great lines of transmission known to have existed in the earliest times, since undoubtedly all known Pre-Syrian forms of text are sufficiently represented among the primary MSS except the Western texts of the Catholic Epistles (in so far as they have a Western text) and of part of the Acts, and these exceptions are shown by the analogies of other books to affect little beyond degrees of certainty. And this is precisely what we do find: the groups formed by the complete combinations of these primary documents attest clearly the purity of their ancestry by the prevailing internal excellence of their readings. The number of their readings which can with any show of reason be pronounced to be apparently corruptions of other existing readings is exceedingly small; and in our opinion the claim is in all these cases unfounded.

264. When these groups lose their most distinctively Western members, D in the Gospels and Acts and D_2G_3 in the Pauline Epistles, and with them, as usually happens, one or more of the predominantly Western versions, totally different because less comprehensive groups come into view, ℵBCL 33 in the Gospels, ℵABC and the one or two cursives in the other books; but

15

these also, when tried by internal evidence, are found not less constantly to bear the marks of incorrupt transmission. Thus far we have been dealing with essentially the same distributions as in former pages, though from a different point of view : the last result is nearly equivalent to the former conclusion that, certain peculiar omissions excepted, the Western text is probably always corrupt as compared with the Non-Western text.

C. 265—267. *Relation of Primary Greek MSS to other documentary evidence*

265. Before we proceed to examine the character of the more narrowly limited groups, it is necessary to consider in some little detail the bearing of the evidence of Greek MSS not singled out for primary authority, and of all versions and patristic quotations. Texts in all the languages supply a greater or less amount of various Pre-Syrian evidence having a strong *prima facie* claim to authority, the true force of which manifestly cannot be left undetermined. It is needless to discuss variations in which the secondary Pre-Syrian evidence (the Syrian evidence may be passed over here and elsewhere) is predominantly on the side of the primary group, or in which it divides itself with anything like equality: the apparent difficulty begins with the numerous cases in which the reduced band of primary MSS is sustained by only a small proportion of the secondary evidence; and then the question arises whether any and if so what amount or weight of secondary evidence, in conjunction with outlying primary MSS, ought to balance or outweigh the strong antecedent authority of the primary band of primary MSS. The question here is not, as it was above

(§ 262), whether this or that document should be included among primary documents, but whether the documents accepted as primary, whichever they may be, can safely be allowed an absolutely paramount authority. Taking for granted that all the documentary evidence contributes, more or less appreciably, to the formation of a right judgement as to the merits of all rival readings, and further that in many variations documents not classed as primary contribute materially to a right decision, either directly or as aiding the interpretation of the whole evidence, we have still to ask how far primary documents can be implicitly trusted where they have little or no support from other documents. The doubt presents itself most strongly in readings attested by a very small number of primary MSS exceptionally commended by Internal Evidence of Groups and Documents: but the principle is not affected by the number.

266. The strongest presumption against the legitimacy of any such separate authority of the primary MSS is derived from the *prima facie* superiority of composite to homogeneous attestation (see § 75); while on the other hand (see § 76) it is checked by the contingency, varying in probability according to the ascertained elements of the secondary documents that may be in question, that apparent compositeness of attestation may really be due to mixture and therefore delusive. A satisfactory answer to the question can however be obtained from two sources only, Internal Evidence of such groups as consist wholly or almost wholly of primary MSS, and consideration of the nature of the texts of the secondary documents as bearing on the point at issue. On the Internal Evidence of the more important groups of this class enough will be said in the following sections. We are

for the present concerned with the preliminary enquiry whether any class of secondary documents has such a textual character that their total or almost total absence from the attestation of a reading otherwise sufficiently attested by primary MSS should throw doubt on its genuineness.

267. To conduct the enquiry with due circumspection, it is necessary to pay special attention to those variations in which the extant evidence includes important secondary documents preserved only in fragments, and especially documents which would merit a place on the primary list but for their imperfect preservation. If in such cases the result were often unfavourable to the primary MSS, it would evidently in variations where they are absent be requisite to take into account the twofold contingency of their hypothetical presence on this or on that side. If however, on careful consideration of every kind of evidence, their actual presence is not found to justify doubts as to the antecedent authority of the primary MSS, we can with the more confidence trust the primary MSS in those more numerous variations where, with perhaps no accession to the number of their allies, they are confronted by a less imposing array.

D.   268. *Absence of Secondary Greek MSS from Groups containing Primary Greek MSS*

268. The first class of secondary documents, according to the usual order, is formed by the secondary Greek MSS; in which we do not include those whose texts are wholly or almost wholly of Syrian origin. Nothing can be clearer than the mixed character of all these MSS; so that, in supposing them to have derived

a given reading from, for instance, a Western origin,
ultimate or immediate, we are not contradicting the
known fact that they have numerous ancient Non-Western readings, when it is equally known that they contain
numerous Western readings. If in some places their
aggregation in opposition to the primary MSS appears
too great to be explained by accidental coincidence of
several separate mixtures with Western or other sources,
we have to remember, first, that none or almost none
of them are without a large Syrian element, and secondly,
that there is no reason to suppose the Syrian to have
been the only eclectic text which had a wide influence
about the fourth century.

E. 269—273. *Absence of Versions from Groups containing Primary Greek MSS*

269. Respecting Versions, it is to be observed at the
outset that the large extent to which they have either
from the first or at some later time participated in
Western corruption must lead us to expect from them
but scanty support to the true reading in a large proportion of Pre-Syrian variations. Of the versions more
ancient than the times of general mixture, the Old Latin
being wholly Western, and the Old Syriac, as now extant
for not quite half of the Gospels and for no other books,
being almost wholly Western, there remain only the two
closely related Egyptian versions, of which the Thebaic,
itself preserved only in fragments, contains so large a
Western element that earlier critics reckoned it as wholly
Western. It is certain, on evidence already given (§§ 120,
217), that the original Memphitic version became ultimately corrupted from common Greek sources, and the

printed editions to a great extent represent this debased
form of Memphitic text; so that till the best MSS have
been completely collated, we have no security that Memphitic readings at variance with the general character of
the version belong to its primitive state.   Moreover, as
we have seen, even in its earlier days it was probably
touched by the Western influence.   There remain the
later versions and the revised forms of the Latin and
Syriac versions; and though they all contain Non-Western Pre-Syrian elements in various proportions, and accordingly have all a certain number of readings in
common with the primary Greek MSS against most versions, we have no right to regard their predominant or
even concordant opposition as outweighing an otherwise
trustworthy attestation.

270.   This distribution of Western and Non-Western
texts among versions is reflected in the range of support
which the primary Greek MSS (in opposition to D in
the Gospels and Acts, D_2G_3 in the Pauline Epistles)
most usually receive from the several versions.   Their
most constant allies are, as we should expect, one or
both of the Egyptian versions.   Next to them probably
come documents essentially Western, but preserving
much of the earlier state of text which existed when
many of the Western readings had not yet arisen, such
as the Old Syriac and the African Latin.   But, as we
have said, the primary Greek MSS likewise receive in
turn the support of every other version, sometimes of
several at once, not seldom even where all or nearly
all other Greek MSS stand in opposition.

271.   On the other hand the support of versions
is sometimes wholly wanting.   Before however this distribution can be rightly judged, a very large majority

of the variations *prima facie* belonging to it must be cleared away. The causes of the irrelevance fall under two principal heads, inability to express Greek distinctions, and freedom of rendering. Where the variation lies between two approximately synonymous words, it is often impossible to say which it was that the author of a given version had before him. Such version cannot therefore be cited for either variant, and the necessary absence of a version from the side of the primary Greek MSS in an *apparatus criticus* leaves it undecided whether the Greek original of the version had or had not their reading. A similar uncertainty attends grammatical forms partially identical in meaning, such as the aorist and perfect of verbs; and also, though not in all cases, the presence or absence of the article. The ambiguity caused by freedom of rendering is sometimes not essentially different from the preceding cases, namely, where the genius of the translator's language would have rendered literal translation of one of the Greek readings unendurably stiff, or even impossible, and the most obvious rendering of it coincides with what would be a literal representation of the other Greek reading.

272. But, apart from this involuntary licence, most translators are liable to deviate from their original by slight verbal paraphrase in just the same way as transcribers of the fundamental text: in other words, many associations of versions with Greek evidence in support of changes of diction are due to accidental coincidence. Every paraphrastic impulse which affects a transcriber is not less likely to affect a translator, who has a strong additional temptation to indulge the impulse in the fact that he is creating a new set of words, not copying words set one after another before him. One of the commonest

forms of paraphrase is a change of order; and a large
proportion of the readings in which the primary Greek
MSS stand alone differ from the rival readings in order
only. How little reliance can be placed on the adverse
testimony of versions in such a matter is indeed proved
by the absence of Greek or any other authority for numberless scattered inversions of order, to be found in MSS
of so literal a version as the Old Latin. Other changes
of a paraphrastic kind, in which versions may have the
appearance of supplying attestation in another language
to similar Greek readings, but which doubtless were often
in fact made by the translators and the Greek scribes
independently, are the insertion of expletives, more especially pronouns (very liberally added as suffixes by
Syriac translators), καί after οὕτως, and the like; the
resolution or introduction of participial constructions;
and permutations of conjunctions, and introductory language generally. In some of these cases a peculiarity
of form in one Greek reading renders it probable that
versions which attest it are faithfully reproducing their
original, while it remains uncertain which original un-
derlies any or all of the versions on the opposite side:
in other cases either Greek reading might so easily be
paraphrased by the other, either in Greek or in any
other language, that no single version can be safely taken
to represent exactly its original; though it is usually
probable that some only of the versions have disguised
their fundamental reading.

273. But, when allowance has been made for all
these cases in which the apparent isolation of the primary
Greek MSS is possibly or probably delusive, a certain
number of variations remain in which the isolation must
in the present state of our evidence be counted as

unambiguous. For the reasons given above, the supposition that readings thus unattested by any version may yet be original is consistent with the known facts of transmission; and continuous examination of the readings attested by the primary Greek MSS without a version fails to detect any difference of internal character between them and readings in which the primary Greek MSS are sustained by versions. While therefore so narrow a range of attestation renders special caution imperative with respect to these readings, and some of them cannot be held certain enough to render all recognition of their rivals superfluous, we have found no sufficient reasons either for distrusting them generally or for rejecting any of them absolutely.

F. 274—279. *Absence of Fathers from Groups containing Primary Greek MSS*

274. The presence or absence of Fathers as allies of the primary Greek MSS is evidently to a great extent fortuitous, depending as it does so much on the nature of the passage, as causing it to be quoted often, seldom, or not at all. Except therefore in the comparatively few cases in which it is morally certain that a passage must have been quoted by one or more given Fathers in given contexts, had it stood with a particular reading in the text used by him or them, negative patristic evidence is of no force at all.

275. This universal rule is completely applicable to the variations which we are now considering, where neither variant is attested by any Father who does not habitually follow a Syrian text: it is applicable in principle, but subject to more or less qualification, where

the reading opposed to that of the primary Greek MSS has patristic attestation not obviously Syrian, and their reading has none. The extent of its applicability must be affected by the usual character of the text of the Fathers who cite the passage. Almost all Greek Fathers after Eusebius have texts so deeply affected by mixture that their dissent, however clearly established, cannot at most count for more than the dissent of so many secondary Greek uncial MSS, inferior in most cases to the better sort of secondary uncial MSS now existing. The patristic evidence which can appreciably come into account must thus be limited to that of Ante-Nicene Fathers, and those very few later Fathers who used approximately Ante-Nicene texts.

276. But further, the apparent patristic evidence literally or virtually Ante-Nicene requires in its turn critical sifting. All the possible sources of error explained in former pages (§§ 156, 157) have to be kept constantly in mind; with the additional consideration that here we are dealing with detached variations, in which, except in the way of observation of analogies, we can obtain no corrective help from other variations. Positive grounds for distrusting the faithful transmission of a patristic attestation concordant with the Syrian text may very often be found, for instance in a recorded variation of MSS or in the clear implication of the context. Where this is the case, there is nothing arbitrary in ignoring the printed testimony, or even, if the evidence is strong enough, in reckoning it as favourable to the rival reading. Wherever a transcriber of a patristic treatise was copying a quotation differing from the text to which he was accustomed, he had virtually two originals before him, one present to his eyes, the other to his

mind; and, if the difference struck him, he was not unlikely to treat the written exemplar as having blundered. But since the text familiar to nearly all transcribers after the earlier ages, to say nothing of editors, was assuredly the Syrian text, this doubleness of original could arise only where the true patristic reading was Non-Syrian. For the converse supposition there is no similar justification: for the only known causes that can be assigned for the appearance of a Non-Syrian reading in a patristic quotation are faithful transmission and accidental error; and where the reading is independently known to be of high antiquity, the chance of accidental coincidence in error is in an immense preponderance of cases too minute to come into account.

277. Even where there is no obvious positive internal ground for doubting whether the words written by a Father have been faithfully preserved, some slight uncertainty must always rest on a patristic attestation of a variant adopted by the Syrian text, since the supposed doubleness of original remains equally possible, and equally likely, whether the circumstances of the individual quotation do or do not happen to contain suspicious indications. This uncertainty ceases to be slight when the apparent position of the patristic testimony creates a grouping unlike any of the groupings into which it habitually enters, and when if transferred to the other side it would find itself in accustomed company.

278. Again, there is often reason to doubt whether what a Father wrote was identical with what he read: positive grounds may be found for distrusting a free quotation as faithfully representing the biblical text used, provided that the difference between one variant and another is such as might readily be reproduced accident-

ally by the free manner or the special purpose of the citation. Patristic quotations in short, like versions, may easily seem to make up a composite attestation, when it is really nothing more than an accidental coincidence. Such deceptive attestations might conceivably arise in either direction: but in a large majority of cases they would be due to a paraphrastic impulse such as that which we find working in scribes; that is, for either process the original peculiarities of order or diction which tempt to modification would be the same. In like manner the intermingling of unconscious reminiscences of parallel or similar passages, a specially fruitful cause of corruption in patristic quotations, may easily result in readings identical with readings due in MSS to harmonistic or other assimilation, and thus produce a deceptive semblance of joint attestation. Accordingly quotations apparently opposed to the primary Greek MSS are oftener found to be for these reasons questionable representatives of the texts used by the patristic writers than those which seem to support the primary Greek MSS. Suspicions as to fidelity of quotation, unsustained by other evidence, by the nature of the case can never transpose attestation from one side to the other; they can only create uncertainty: but uncertainty suffices to destroy the force of the *prima facie* contrast between the presence of patristic attestation on the one side and its absence on the other.

279. Lastly, even the presence of tried and verified Pre-Syrian patristic evidence in opposition to the primary Greek MSS, in conjunction with its absence from their side, loses much of the weight to which it would otherwise be entitled, when the actual texts employed in the extant writings of the Ante-Nicene Fathers are

taken into consideration. Western readings, it will be remembered, are abundant in Clement and Origen, much more in Eusebius; and these are the only Ante-Nicene Fathers, represented to us by more than petty fragments, whose texts are not approximately Western. Now the readings of primary Greek MSS with which we are here concerned have opposed to them D in the Gospels and Acts, D_2G_3 in the Pauline Epistles and almost always other Western documents as well, making up a clear Western element in the attestation, whether the origin be 'Western' or not. If therefore even Clement or Origen swell the array, the source of their readings in these passages, as in many others where no doubt is possible, may be Western; and if so, they contribute nothing towards shewing that these readings were only preserved by the Western text, not originated by it. Nevertheless, since the greater part of the texts of the Alexandrian Fathers is Non-Western (see § 159), their certified opposition to a reading of the primary Greek MSS ought to forbid its unqualified acceptance except after the fullest consideration.

G. 280. *Absence of Versions and Fathers from Groups containing Primary Greek MSS*

280. We have spoken separately of the absence of Versions and of Fathers from the company of the primary Greek MSS: it remains to consider the rare and extreme cases in which Versions and Fathers are absent together. Independently of the special utility of versions and patristic quotations in supplying the landmarks of textual history their certified testimony has a high corroborative worth. The unknown Greek MSS

from which they all derive their authority preceded our earliest extant MSS in several cases by long periods eventful in textual history, and thus at least rescue any reading of our MSS which they undoubtedly attest from the suspicion of having come into existence at any recent stage of transcription, in the century, we may say, preceding 350. This ancillary aid of Versions and Fathers in individual variations is invaluable, notwithstanding their unfitness to supply a primary and continuous standard of text as compared with our best Greek MSS. But, though the security of verification is withdrawn where Versions and Fathers are both absent, it by no means follows that a positive insecurity takes its place. Every version, so far as it is at present known to us, contains so many readings which it is morally impossible to believe to be right, and a certain proportion of these readings are scattered in such apparent irregularity, that we have no right to assume either that the deficiencies of one version, as the Memphitic, would in every case be made up by some other version, or that deficiencies of all versions and deficiencies of all extant patristic evidence would never happen to coincide. Moreover the transition to total absence of Versions and Fathers is bridged over by the many places in which a secondary version, as the Æthiopic or Armenian, supplies the only accessory authority. The whole number of cases where the primary Greek MSS stand alone is extremely small, when the deceptive variations mentioned above (§§ 271, 272), have been set aside: and neither in their internal character nor in their external relations to other documents have we found reason to deny to such readings the favourable presumption which their attestation by the better of the extant Greek MSS would confer.

A.   281—283.   *Relation of variations between Primary
Greek MSS to the chief ancient texts*

281.   After this examination of the relation of the
evidence of Versions and Fathers to that of the primary
Greek MSS in respect of the final process of determining the text, we must now resume the consideration
of the numerous variations in which the primary Greek
MSS differ widely among themselves.   Here, in investigating Internal Evidence of Groups for each individual
group or class of groups, we lose clear and obvious
parallelism with the great ancient texts.   But the distribution of attestation for most of the groups must as
a matter of fact have in most cases been determined
by the great ancient texts, with or without subsequent
mixture, whether it be in our power to assign each document to a definite text or not (see § 243 V); and therefore that cannot well be the right reading which would
render the documentary distribution incompatible with
known genealogies.   It is not indeed requisite that we
should be able to decide between two or more possible
histories of a variation; but an important confirmation
is wanting when we are unable to suggest at least
one such history consistent alike with the composition
of documents as known through the simpler and more
normal distributions of attestation, and with the genuineness of the reading commended by Internal Evidence of
Groups and other considerations.   Before therefore **we**

proceed to enquire into the character of special groups in detail, it will be right to examine a little more closely the probable relation of the primary ancient lines of transmission to many important variations now to be considered.

282. The principal difficulty with which we have to deal arises from an apparent combination of Western and Alexandrian attestations in opposition to a group of documents which bears no clear and obvious marks of compositeness of attestation, but which is commended by Internal Evidence of Groups; so that the preference accorded to this group seems to involve the paradox of a preference of a single line of descent to two concordant lines of descent. Given the independence of the Western and Alexandrian texts, the supposed preference is genealogically untenable as regards readings which could not owe their place in both texts to accidental coincidence in error. Now, though no contradiction is involved in the hypothesis of the adoption of early Alexandrian readings into a late Western text or of early Western readings into a late Alexandrian text, the actual evidence contains comparatively few traces of any such relation of dependence; while the definite original parallelism of the two texts is evinced by the many places in which they smooth away difficulties of language by entirely different devices. Either therefore (1) the readings of which we are now speaking as found only in the better of the primary Greek MSS must be of Alexandrian origin; or (2) they must have originated in some indeterminate equally aberrant text, assignation of them to a Western origin being in most cases clearly impossible; or (3) the opposed attestation cannot rightly be said to combine the two primary aberrant texts.

283. The two former suppositions stand in so flagrant opposition to the suggestions of internal evidence, howsoever obtained, and harmonise so ill with the results furnished by other groupings, that nothing but the proved inadmissibility of the third supposition could justify their acceptance. The third supposition is however natural enough, as soon as we recognise on the one hand the wide and early prevalence of Western readings, and on the other the mixed composition of the Greek MSS which are the chief extant representatives of the Alexandrian text (compare § 269). The Alexandrian text of the Gospels for instance would have been hopelessly obscure but for the very large Alexandrian elements which אCL(Δ) 33 contain in various places and proportions: yet the presence of a Western element in these MSS is equally indubitable, and it furnishes what must be in most cases the true key to the paradox. The readings attested by the best of the primary Greek MSS are as a rule simply Non-Western readings which are extant in an exceptionally small number of existing documents because the Western corruptions of them obtained an exceptionally early and wide popularity in one or other of the eclectic texts of the third and fourth centuries. That one of these eclectic texts arose at Alexandria, the text of Hesychius (see § 249) being indeed probably of this character, is likely enough; and, if so, it might be called a late Alexandrian text: but such a fact would only serve to illustrate the conclusion just stated. This conclusion harmonises in every respect with all known facts; and we are unable to think of any other interpretation which can be consistently applied without startling incongruities alike of external and of internal evidence.

16

B. 284—286. *General relations of* B *and* ℵ *to other documents*

284. When the various subordinate groupings which arise by the defection of one or another member of the leading groups of primary Greek MSS described as mainly Non-Western are tested by the prevalent character of their readings, the results thus obtained are for most of them as well marked as in the cases where the primary Greek MSS agree together. Two striking facts here successively come out with especial clearness. Every group containing both ℵ and B is found, where Internal Evidence is tolerably unambiguous, to have an apparently more original text than every opposed group containing neither; and every group containing B, with the exception of such Western groups as include B in the Pauline Epistles, is found in a large preponderance of cases, though by no means universally, to have an apparently more original text than every opposed group containing ℵ.

285. Thus Internal Evidence of Groups conducts us to conclusions respecting these two MSS analogous to, and confirmatory of, the conclusions obtained independently by ascertaining to what extent the principal extant documents severally represent the several ancient lines of text. We found ℵ and B to stand alone in their almost complete immunity from distinctive Syrian readings; ℵ to stand far above all documents except B in the proportion which the part of its text neither Western nor Alexandrian bears to the rest; and B to stand far above ℵ in its apparent freedom from either Western or Alexandrian readings with the partial exception in the Pauline Epistles already mentioned more than once (§§ 204 ff.).

286. The two processes deal with distinct classes
of phenomena, the one with distributions of external
attestation, the other with internal characteristics. The
former simply registers in what company a given document is or is not found, with reference to certain well
marked assemblages constantly recurring and having a
conspicuously ancient origin: the latter deduces from
those variations which on internal grounds afford clear
presumptions the quality of the texts attested by the
various groups into which a given document enters, and
thus ultimately the quality of the document itself as
a whole. The results of the former process are brought
into comparison with those of the latter by a similar
but independent deduction of the texts of the observed
assemblages of documents. To a certain limited extent the materials in this case are identical with those
employed in the latter process, for the various Syrian,
Western, and Alexandrian assemblages are included
among the numerous groups. But this partial coincidence does not materially impair the independence of
the two processes, at least as regards any mixed or any
approximately neutral document; for among the variations from which the character of, let us say, the Western
text is deduced there will be found many in which
each of the mixed documents now in question stands
in opposition to the Western reading; and again many
groupings, which by the ascertained quality of their
texts go to shew the quality of a given document included
in them all, are of too ambiguous composition to be
used as evidence of the character of the Western or
other assemblages. Thus the correspondence between
the results of the two modes of investigating the groups
containing א and B, and again those containing B with-

out א, is not created, as might be incautiously surmised, by a twofold presentation of inferences essentially the same, but amounts to a real verification. On the other hand the ascertainment of the quality of any single document by bringing together the ascertained qualities of the texts of the different groups of which it is a member is not essentially different from the direct ascertainment of its quality on internal grounds without intermediate reference to groups, except in its omission to take into account those variations in which the document stands absolutely alone.

C. 287—304. *Relation of* B *to* א *and characteristics of Groups containing both* B *and* א

287. It now becomes necessary to scrutinise more closely the trustworthiness of the propositions laid down above respecting the preeminent excellence of the Vatican and Sinaitic MSS, which happen likewise to be the oldest extant Greek MSS of the New Testament. It is at the outset essential to distinguish carefully the readings and the groups of documents in which they stand side by side from those in which one of them stands alone. Following the gradual narrowing of groups, we come first to the combination אB, which is, as we have intimated, wherever it occurs, the constant element of those variable groups that are found to have habitually the best readings. The statement remains true, we believe, not less when the groups dwindle so as to leave אB comparatively or absolutely alone than when they are of larger compass. The cases in which אB have no support of Greek MSS, or no support at all, are connected by every gradation with the cases in which they stand at the head

of a considerable group; and the principle is not affected by the size of the groups. But when the number of members is nearly or quite reduced to two, it is of consequence to find out what can be known respecting the antecedents of each, and especially respecting their mutual relations.

288. The first point that arises for examination is the independence of their testimony. The numerous readings in which they stand alone against all or nearly all extant Greek MSS suggests at once the enquiry whether they had separate ancestries or were, to a greater or less extent, copies of a single exemplar. The enquiry is the more necessary because the two MSS are really brought together as to their transcription in a singular manner by the fact observed by Tischendorf, that six leaves of the New Testament in ℵ, together with the opening verses of the Apocalypse, besides corrections, headings, and in two cases subscriptions, to other parts, are from the hand of the same scribe that wrote the New Testament in B. The fact appears to be sufficiently established by concurrent peculiarities in the form of one letter, punctuation, avoidance of contractions, and some points of orthography. As the six leaves are found on computation to form three pairs of conjugate leaves, holding different places in three distant quires, it seems probable that they are new or clean copies of corresponding leaves executed by the scribe who wrote the rest of the New Testament, but so disfigured, either by an unusual number of corrections of clerical errors or from some unknown cause, that they appeared unworthy to be retained, and were therefore cancelled and transcribed by the 'corrector'. However this may be, their internal character of text differs in no respect from that of their neighbours.

The fact that the scribe of B was a 'corrector' of ℵ shews that the two MSS were written in the same generation, probably in the same place: but as regards the text it has no independent force, though it would have to be taken into account if the internal evidence were to point to the use of a common exemplar.   On the other hand a strong presumption to the contrary is created by remarkable differences in the order of the books, the divisions into sections, and other externals.

289.   Turning then to the internal evidence afforded by the texts themselves, we are at once confronted by the question,—How can we know that any two MSS are both derived from a common parent or near ancestor?   Certainly not, as is often assumed, from the bare fact that they have many readings in common, with or without the support of other documents.   What is absolutely certain in these cases is that those readings have some common ancestor, coincidences in independent error being always excepted; and it is morally certain that the same ancestor supplied more or less of the rest of the text.   But this ancestor may have been at any distance from the MSS, near or remote, back to the autograph itself inclusive. That this is no exaggeration will be seen at once by following the course of transmission downwards instead of upwards.   Whenever an original reading has disappeared from all representatives of all originally independent lines of transmission except two, and each of these two lines has either but a single extant representative or has itself lost the true reading in all its extant representatives but one, the resulting distribution is precisely as supposed, two MSS against the rest: and this is a common case in many texts.   To what stage in the transmission the common ancestor implied by the identical

readings belonged, can in fact, so far as it can be determined at all, be determined only by the internal character of these readings, and by the genealogical relationships to other documents disclosed by these and the
other readings.

290. As soon as the test furnished by the most elementary analysis of attestations, and consequently of
genealogies, is applied, the supposition that the texts of
‫א‬ and B as wholes are in any one book or chapter of the
Testament derived from a single near ancestor falls to
the ground. It is negatived at the first glance by the
multitude of variations in which they are divided, while
each is associated with a variety of attestation. Apart
from the associated attestations the diversities of reading would be inconclusive: they might have been produced
by the independent carelessness or licence of two transcribers of the same exemplar. But where each discrepant
reading has other witnesses, and there is no room for
accidental coincidence, the discrepancies in two transcripts of the same exemplar can have no other origin
than mixture; that is, at least one of the transcripts
must be virtually a transcript of two different originals.
In this restricted sense alone is the hypothesis of a proximate common origin of ‫א‬ and B worthy of being seriously
examined; that is, in the sense that a single proximate
original has supplied a large common element in their
texts.

291. To examine the hypothesis in this shape, we
must put out of sight all the elements of each MS which
it owes to undoubted mixture with texts capable of being
recognised through a long succession of variations, and
which may therefore easily have come in together; that
is, every clearly Western and every clearly Alexandrian

reading of ℵ in such books as are preserved in B, and every clearly Western reading of B in the Pauline Epistles. The residue would then approximately represent each text reduced to the form which it must have had just before the great final independent mixture, upon the hypothesis that antecedent to this mixture the two texts had a common proximate origin. To make comparison clearer, we may further leave out of account every reading of either MS singly which has no other attestation whatever.

292. The resulting text however would still entirely fail to shew the imagined agreement. Multitudes of discrepancies between ℵ and B would remain, in which each MS would have some very early documentary evidence supporting it. Doubtless the hypothesis might still be rendered possible by supposing all the readings in which ℵ and B differ to have been taken simultaneously in one of these MSS from a single accessory original, or each MS to have its own accessory original. But the same conjectural mode of composition might be imagined with equal propriety for any other pair of MSS having at least an equal number of coincidences peculiar to themselves and no greater number of discrepancies. It is only one among an almost infinite number of at least equally probable contingencies, and has therefore no *a priori* probability of its own, though it would have no inherent improbability if other textual phenomena pointed to it. The problem cannot possibly be solved on the ground of attestation alone: but, so far as the phenomena of attestation contribute to its solution, they do not suggest a near common origin for even the residuary portions of ℵ and B.

293. We now come to the indications furnished by

the internal character of identical readings. If some of the identical readings are manifestly wrong, and if they further are of such a nature that accidental coincidence will not naturally account for their having the double attestation, they must have had a common original later than the autograph; and it becomes probable that some at least of those other identical readings which afford no clear internal evidence of the intrinsic kind had likewise only that later MS than the autograph for their common original. But this negative fact is all that we learn; and it is compatible with even the extreme supposition that the common source of the identical readings was the original of all extant documents, though itself but imperfectly representing the autograph, and thus that these readings, wrong though they be, were the ancestors of all other existing variants of the same variations (see §§ 86, 87). If on the other hand some of the wrong identical readings are manifestly derived from other existing readings, the common original must of course have been later than the common original of the other readings; but the question of its remoteness or proximateness to the two extant MSS remains undecided.

294. The only quite trustworthy evidence from internal character for derivation from a common proximate original consists in the presence of such erroneous identical readings as are evidently due to mere carelessness or caprice of individual scribes, and could not easily have escaped correction in passing through two or three transcriptions. To carry weight, they must of course be too many to be naturally accounted for by accidental coincidence of error in two independent scribes. Now, to the best of our belief, ℵ and B have in common but one such reading, if we set aside the itacisms, or permutations of

vowels, current in uncial times, as between o and ω, η
and ει; including the confusion between ἡμεῖς and ὑμεῖς.
This solitary blunder is παραλλαγὴ ἢ τροπῆς ἀποσκιάσματος
for π. ἢ τ. ἀποσκίασμα in James i 17. The final -ατος
might possibly be derived from an αὐτός which stands at
the head of the next verse in a good cursive (40) and in
two Syriac texts, and which has much intrinsic force: on
this supposition the reading of א and B, though erroneous,
would be nearer to the true reading than the common
reading. But the evidence as a whole does not point to
so deeply seated a corruption; and it may be fairly assumed that the reading -ατος is due either to thoughtless
assimilation to the preceding genitive or to a mental
separation of ἀπό from σκίασμα and consequent correction of the supposed solecism. But, though a series
of such coincidences would imply community of proximate origin, a single instance does not, nor would two or
three. Our extant MSS afford examples of more startling
coincidences, unquestionably accidental, as σειροῖς ζόφοις
(אA) for σειροῖς ζόφου in 2 Pet. ii 4, φθορᾶς φθαρτῆς
(אAC) for σπορᾶς φθαρτῆς in 1 Pet. i 23, and ἐξίσταντο
(א*C*D*) for ἐξίστατο, followed by Ἀκούσαντες δὲ οἱ
ἀπόστολοι, in Acts viii 13, the subject of the verb being
ὁ Σίμων. The coincident readings of א and B likewise
include one or two peculiar spellings having a somewhat problematical appearance : they occur however
in peculiar words, in which it is difficult to find a
trustworthy criterion of intrinsic certainty or even probability. They include likewise a few substantive readings which are capable of being accounted for as
blunders, but which may as reasonably be admitted as
genuine, and in most cases are sustained by internal
evidence.

295. Thus far we have obtained only negative results. We have found readings that are explicable by the supposition of a common proximate original: we have found none that it is difficult to explain without it. We must now turn to such positive indications of the relative antiquity of the common original as can be obtained by taking genealogical relations into account. These are of two kinds, arising from comparisons in which the two MSS are taken together, and from those in which they are taken separately.

296. Under the former head we have to compare the readings in which ℵ and B together stand unsupported with those in which they have the concurrence of one or two important MSS or of ancient versions and quotations without extant MSS. Here we are merely reconsidering from a special point of view the evidence from which the enquiry started (§ 287), the Internal Evidence of Groups. Having found ℵB the constant element in various groups of every size, distinguished by internal excellence of readings, we found no less excellence in the readings in which they concur without other attestations of Greek MSS, or even of Versions or Fathers. The two sets of groupings, containing no reading in common, illustrate and confirm each other. The general character of the readings of both is the same, so that there is no internal evidence against the natural presumption that they come from the same source. But the readings of ℵB in which they are associated with other and various witnesses for very early texts cannot by the nature of the case have originated with the scribe of a proximate common source; so that, if the common source was proximate, they must have been received and transmitted from an earlier source: and accordingly there is no reason, in the absence

of constraint from internal evidence, to imagine a different origin for those readings of אB which have no other attestation. It might indeed be suggested that both sets of readings were obtained from a single proximate common source, but that the one set originated there, while the other was transmitted. But against this contingent possibility must be set the comparative inconstancy of the members of the smaller groups containing אB, and the consequent probability that occasionally they would all be found ranged against readings having the same parentage as those which they elsewhere concur with אB in supporting (see § 280).

297. These considerations shew that the common original of אB for by far the greater part of their identical readings, whatever may have been its own date, had a very ancient and very pure text, and that there is no sufficient reason for surmising that the rest of their identical readings came from any other source. They prove that one of three alternatives must be true: either the respective ancestries of א and B must have diverged from a common parent extremely near the apostolic autographs; or, if their concordant readings were really derived from a single not remote MS, that MS must itself have been of the very highest antiquity; or, lastly, such single not remote MS must have inherited its text from an ancestry which at each of its stages had enjoyed a singular immunity from corruption. For practical purposes it is of little moment which alternative is true. The second and third alternatives would leave open the possibility that single readings of אB, otherwise unsupported, may have originated with the common proximate source here implied: but there is no difference between the three alternatives as regards the general character and

date of the readings taken together, and the consequent presumption in favour of any one of them.

298.   When however we go on, secondly, to compare the identical readings of ℵB with the readings of ℵ unsupported by B and of B unsupported by ℵ, the first alternative obtains so much positive corroboration that the second and third may be safely dismissed. For the present purpose we must neglect the numerous readings in which ℵ or B forms part of a large group, and attend to those readings only in which they stand respectively in opposition to all or almost all other Greek MSS, but with some other support : with the places where they stand absolutely alone we are not for the present concerned. It is then seen that a large proportion of the small groups containing one or other of the two MSS contain also other documents (versions or quotations) attesting a high antiquity of text.   Many of the readings of B having this accessory attestation are doubtless wrong, and, as we shall see presently, a much greater number of the readings of ℵ : what we are now concerned with however is not genuineness but antiquity.   Each of the two MSS is proved by these readings to be at least in part derived from an original preserving an extremely ancient text, for the most part not represented by our other extant MSS : and these two texts are by the nature of the case different from each other.

299.   The distinct existence of these two independent texts is further illustrated by places where they emerge into view simultaneously ; that is, in a certain number of those ternary or yet more composite variations in which the readings of ℵ and of B are different from each other, but are closely connected together in opposition to the reading or readings of the great bulk of docu-

ments, and in which each of the two MSS is supported by a small number of documents having a largely Pre-Syrian text. In these cases, allowance being made for the possibility of an occasional accidental coincidence, the reading of neither ℵ nor B can have originated in the process of transcription from a proximate common source, and the two MSS confront each other with exclusively early texts of different ancestry.

300. It follows from the binary and the ternary variations alike that the hypothesis of a proximate common original for the identical readings of ℵB involves the necessity of postulating at least three independent sources of exceptionally ancient character of text for the two MSS, independently of sources akin to documents still largely extant. It is at once obvious that the same phenomena are accounted for with much greater probability by the simple explanation that the identical readings do not represent a third and proximate common original, containing a single pure text preserved with extraordinary fidelity, but are merely those portions of text in which two primitive and entirely separate lines of transmission had not come to differ from each other through independent corruption in the one or the other.

301. The importance of this conclusion is so great that we venture to repeat in other and fewer words the principal steps which lead to it. Whatever be the mutual relation of ℵ and B, each of them separately, ℵ in the Apocalypse excepted, is found on comparison of its characteristic readings with those of other documentary authorities of approximately determinate date to have a text more ancient by a long interval than that of any other extant Non-Western MS containing more than a few verses; to be in fact essentially a text of the second

or early third century. This fact, which is independent of coincidences of אB, so that it would remain true of א if B were unknown, and of B if א were unknown, suggests the most natural explanation of their coincidences. They are due, that is, to the extreme and as it were primordial antiquity of the common original from which the ancestries of the two MSS have diverged, the date of which cannot be later than the early part of the second century, and may well be yet earlier. So high an antiquity would of course be impossible if it were necessary to suppose that the 'common original' was a single archetypal MS comprising all the books as they now stand in either existing MS. But, as has been noticed elsewhere (§ 14 : see also § 352), there is reason to suspect that the great MSS of the Christian empire were directly or indirectly transcribed from smaller exemplars which contained only portions of the New Testament; so that the general term 'common original', which we have used for the sake of simplicity, must in strictness be understood to denote the several common originals of the different books or groups of books. There is however no clear difference of character in the fundamental text common to B and א in any part of the New Testament in which B is not defective. The textual phenomena which we find when we compare them singly and jointly with other documents are throughout precisely those which would present themselves in representatives of two separate lines diverging from a point near the autographs, and not coming into contact subsequently. Other relations of pedigree are doubtless theoretically possible, but involve improbable combinations.

302. An answer, in our opinion a true and sufficient answer, is thus found to the question how far the testimo-

nies of א and B are independent of each other. Their independence can be carried back so far that their concordant testimony may be treated as equivalent to that of a MS older than א and B themselves by at least two centuries, probably by a generation or two more. Here, as always, high relative and absolute antiquity supplies a strong presumption of purity, but cannot guarantee it: on the one hand the writings of the New Testament were liable to textual change in the earliest generations of their existence as well as a little later; on the other the close approach to the time of the autographs raises the presumption of purity to an unusual strength. It must be remembered however that part of the evidence with which we have been dealing relates to quality as well as to antiquity: Internal Evidence of Groups, independently of the aid which it gives towards ascertaining the proximity or distance of the common original of א and B, retains its own direct value. As was pointed out above (§ 296), even if it were credible that they were divided from their common ancestor by no more than two or three transcriptions, we should have on this ground to ascribe to the ancestry of the common ancestor an extraordinary freedom from corruption.

303. That absolute purity cannot be ascribed to all readings attested by אB is implied in the existence of the Western non-interpolations (§ 240). We shall presently have to notice the possibility of a concurrence of א and B in support of wrong Western readings in St Paul's Epistles, implying a departure in the ancestries of both from their common fundamental text; and this is perhaps the most natural explanation of the attestation of the unquestionably wrong reading ἦλθεν for ἦλθον by אBD₂G₃ cu² Orig in Gal. ii 12. Account must likewise be taken of

the places in which, without difference of reading between
א and B, the true text appears to be lost in all existing
documents, or in all but one or two of a subsidiary
character.   Besides these clear or possible errors in אB
there are some few variations in which their joint reading, though supported by some other testimony, is subject
to more or less of doubt.   But we have not found reason
to make any further deduction from their united authority.
In this as in all similar cases no account of course can be
taken of coincidences that might be easily due to the
independent origination of the same error by two different
scribes.   Under this head preeminently fall identical
changes of an itacistic kind, as the confusion between
imperatives in -ε and infinitives in -αι, and also between ἡμεῖς and ὑμεῖς : it seldom happens that both MSS
go unquestionably astray together in such points, for
their laxity is but comparative, but examples do occur.
When these indecisive coincidences have been set aside,
no readings of אB remain which we could venture to pronounce certainly or probably wrong as against other
existing readings.   This general immunity from substantive errors that can without room for doubt be recognised
as errors in the common original of אB, in conjunction
with its very high antiquity, provides in a multitude of
places a safe criterion of genuineness, not to be distrusted
except on very clear internal evidence.   Accordingly, with
the exceptions mentioned above, it is our belief (1) that
readings of אB should be accepted as the true readings
until strong internal evidence is found to the contrary,
and (2) that no readings of אB can safely be rejected
absolutely, though it is sometimes right to place them
only on an alternative footing, especially where they
receive no support from Versions or Fathers.

17

304. Sufficient examples of important or interesting readings attested by אB, but lost from the texts of all other extant uncials, will be found in the Appendix, as in the notes on Matt. v 22; x 3; xi 19; xvi 21; xvii 20; xxviii 6; Mark ix 29; xvi 9—20; Acts xx. 5, 28; 1 Pet. v 2; Eph. i 1. Two or three additional places may be noticed here, in which there is reason to think that the bearing of the internal evidence is liable to be misunderstood.

Mark iv 8 καὶ ἄλλα ἔπεσεν κ. τ. λ., καὶ ἐδίδου καρπὸν ἀναβαίνοντα καὶ αὐξανόμενα אB (αὐξανόμενον ADLΔ cu¹, αὐξάνοντα C and most documents). Here the true force of the parable requires that not the fruit, but the plants into which the seeds have expanded, be said to mount up and grow. The temptations to corruption were peculiarly strong; ἀναβαίνοντα, immediately following καρπόν, had an ambiguous termination readily assumed to belong to the masculine accusative, and thus drew after it the other participle, one text adopting the middle form, which involved least change, the other the neuter form, which coincided with ἀναβαίνοντα: an additional motive for alteration would be the apparent paradox of seeds being said to 'mount up', a paradox which St Mark apparently intended to soften by means of the order of words. Finally the Western and Syrian texts completed the corruption by changing ἄλλα to the ἄλλο of vv. 5, 7.

John iv 15 ἵνα μὴ διψῶ μηδὲ διέρχωμαι (or -ομαι) ἐνθάδε ἀντλεῖν א*B Orig⁵ (ἔρχωμαι most documents). Διέρχομαι is here used in its idiomatic sense 'come all the way', which expresses the woman's sense of her often repeated toil. Being commonly used in other senses, the word was easily misunderstood and assumed to be inappropriate; and the change would be helped by the facility with which one of two similar consecutive syllables drops out.

Acts xxviii 13 καταχθέντες εἰς Συρακούσας ἐπεμείναμεν ἡμέρας τρεῖς ὅθεν περιελόντες κατηντήσαμεν εἰς Ῥήγιον א*B g (*tulimus et* [= '*weighed anchor*', as vg *cum sustulissent de Asso* for ἄραντες ἆσσον in xxvii 13]) memph ('*going forth*'); where most documents have περιελθόντες. Περιελόντες here is explained by the use of the same verb in xxvii 40, καὶ τὰς ἀγκύρας περιελόντες εἴων εἰς τὴν θάλασσαν, where it clearly means the casting loose (literally 'stripping off') of the anchors (with their cables) in order to set the vessel free to drive, though it is otherwise unknown as a nautical term. By analogy it must here mean the casting loose of the cables which attached the vessel to the shore in harbour (called in ampler phrase τὰ ἀπόγεια λύσασθαι, λῦσαι, ἀποκόψαι &c.), the elliptic employment of transitive verbs being common in Greek nautical language as in English (compare ἄραντες in xxvii 13, cited above). The general sense then is merely 'and loosing from thence', that is, from Syracuse, where there had been a stay of three days. On the other hand the run from Syracuse to Rhegium could never be described as circuitous (περιελθόντες), unless the ship were thrown out of her course by contrary winds, a circumstance not likely to be noticed by means of an obscure implication (cf. xxvii 4, 7, 8); while scribes, to whom this geographical difficulty was not likely to suggest itself, would be tempted by the superficial smoothness of περιελθόντες.

D. 305—307. *Binary uncial combinations containing* B *and* ℵ *respectively*

305. We come next to the variations in which ℵ and B stand on different sides. The first step towards dealing successfully with the problems which here arise is to examine the internal character of the readings attested by the two series of binary groups formed by ℵ and by B combined with each other primary Greek MS. Now every such binary group containing B is found by this process to offer a large proportion of readings which on the closest scrutiny have the ring of genuineness, while it is difficult to find any readings so attested which look suspicious after full consideration. Such groups are in the Gospels BL, BC, BT, BΞ, BD, AB, BZ, B 33, in St Mark BΔ ; in the Acts AB, BC, BD, BE₂, B 61; in the Catholic Epistles AB, BC, BP₂; in the Pauline Epistles AB, BC, BM₂, (BP₂,) B 17, B 67**. These readings are in fact for most of the groups, especially those belonging to the Gospels, hardly of less uniformly good character than the readings of ℵB. Once more, their character is not found appreciably different whether

they do or do not receive the support of Versions or Fathers.

306. One binary group containing B requires separate mention, namely BD_2 of the Pauline Epistles. From what has been already said (§§ 204, 228) on the Western element of B in these Epistles it will be evident that the combinations BD_2G_3 and BG_3, when they are unsustained by clear Non-Western Pre-Syrian attestation, may be taken to imply a Western reading. The question thus arises whether the same is to be said of BD_2. On the one hand D represents on the whole an earlier and purer form of the Western text than G_3, so that, were not B known to contain a Western element in these epistles, the combination BD_2 would, like the BD of the Gospels and Acts, have a strong presumption in its favour; and the presumption, though weakened, is by no means destroyed by the contingency which has thus to be taken into account. On the other hand D_2 has some clearly Western corruptions from which G_3 is free; and the analogy of BD_2G_3 and BG_3 preclude any assumption that BD_2 could not have this character. The decision must accordingly rest with Internal Evidence, which is on the whole definitely favourable to the BD_2 readings, while some of them are not free from doubt. They cannot as a class be condemned with the readings of BD_2G_3 and BG_3; but neither is it certain that none of them are of the same origin and quality. Since the inferior quality of BG_3 and the ambiguity as to BD_2 are explained by the exceptional intrusion of an alien element into the Pauline text of B, the existence of which alien element is ascertained independently of the quality of its readings, the character of the fundamental text of B, as shown

by the other binary combinations, evidently remains unaffected.

307. When ℵ is tested in like manner, the results are quite different. None of its binary combinations, if their readings are examined consecutively, are found to be habitually of good character, though here and there readings occur which are not to be hastily dismissed. The readings of ℵD in the Gospels and Acts are often interesting, but they are shown by the Versions and Fathers which usually support them to be simply Western: the character of ℵD with the Old Latin, of ℵ with the Old Latin, and of D with the Old Latin is identical. Except in the peculiar Western non-interpolations we have never found reason to trust ℵD. It is worth mention here that much the most considerable deduction to be made from the superiority of text in Tischendorf's *editio octava* to his earlier editions is due to the indiscriminate vagueness of his estimate of ℵ: a large proportion of those readings adopted by him which we have been obliged to reject are ordinary Western readings which are attested by ℵ in consequence of the Western element which it contains. With ℵD of the Gospels may be classed ℵG$_3$ of the Pauline Epistles; while the rarer combination ℵD$_2$ of the Pauline Epistles contains both bad and good readings, the latter being apparently confined to the parts where B is defective, and elsewhere to those variations in which the reading of B is that of its Western element peculiar to these books, so that in the absence of this element we might have expected ℵBD$_2$ in place of ℵD$_2$. Trial by Internal Evidence is likewise unfavourable to such groups as in the Gospels ℵL, ℵC, ℵT, ℵΞ, ℵZ, ℵ 33, in St Mark ℵΔ; in the Acts ℵA, ℵC, ℵE$_2$, ℵ 61; in the Catholic Epistles ℵA, ℵC, ℵP$_2$; in the

Pauline Epistles אA, אC, (אP₂,) א 17; though they contain
a few readings which may perhaps be genuine. Their
pedigree is usually, we believe, perhaps almost always,
Alexandrian. The character is here, as elsewhere, ascertained independently of the origin : but it is instructive to see how completely the results of the comparison
of binary groups containing א and B respectively are
explained by the presence of large Western and Alexandrian elements in א. The character of what remains
of the text of א after their subtraction must be largely
excellent, as the character of אB shews; an estimate of
the degree of excellence cannot however be formed till
we have taken another step.

E. 308—325. *Singular and subsingular readings of* B

308. The readings of B and of א respectively have
now to be compared in those variations in which they
stand unsustained by any other Greek uncial MS. Such
readings are of two kinds, 'singular readings', as they
are usually called, which have no other direct attestation
whatever, and what may be called 'subsingular readings', which have only secondary support, namely, that
of inferior Greek MSS, of Versions, or of Fathers, or of
combinations of documentary authorities of these kinds.
Subsingular readings of B, which are in fact the readings of a particular class of groups containing B, will
require consideration presently. What we have to say
on the singular readings of B may be made clearer by
a few remarks on singular readings generally.

309. The attention *prima facie* due to singular readings of any one document is evidently variable, ac-

cording to the number and genealogical relations of
the whole body of extant documents. If a text is
preserved in but two documents, every reading of each
where they differ is a singular reading, one or other of
which must be right; unless indeed both are wrong, and
the true reading has perished. If the documents are
more numerous, the singular readings of one document
have no less *prima facie* authority than the rival readings
found in all other documents alike, provided that the
other documents have had a common original (see § 52),
making the readings common to them to be virtually,
though not in appearance, as 'singular' as the others.
The same principle holds good whatever be the total
number of documents, unless they have all only one
common ancestor; that is, the *prima facie* authority of
the singular readings of any document cannot be estimated by the bare numerical relation (see §§ 54—57),
but varies partly with the independence of ancestry of
the one document in relation to all the rest, partly with
the affinities of ancestry among the rest. Where the
whole pedigree is very complex, as in the New Testament, any documents which frequently stand in very
small groups attesting evidently genuine readings, against
the bulk of documents of various ages, must evidently
contain so large elements having an independent ancestry that the *a priori* presumption against their singular readings cannot be much greater than against
singular readings at their best, that is, in texts preserved
in two documents only.

310. On the other hand (see §§ 56, 58) the singular readings of a document may always be due either
to inheritance from a more or less remote ancestry, which
may be of any degree of purity, or to quite recent

corruption, or, which is much the commonest case, partly to the one, partly to the other. Whatever a document has inherited of the autograph text is of necessity included in its proper or ancestral text; and in order to ascertain the character of those of its singular readings which belong to its ancestral text, we must sift away as far as possible those other singular readings which are mere individualisms, so to speak, originating with the scribe or one of his immediate predecessors. Complete discrimination is of course impossible in the absence of the exemplar or exemplars; but every approximation to it is a gain. Except by conjecture, which does not concern us here, no scribe can make a text better than he found it; his highest merit is to leave it no worse. The inherited text of a document must therefore have been usually better, never worse, than the text which it actually presents to the eye; and the character of the inherited text is inevitably disguised for the worse by every ' individualism' which remains undetected.

311. Individualisms may obviously belong to various types, from purely clerical errors to alterations of purely mental origin. Sufficient clerical errors betray themselves, beyond the possibility of doubt, to enable us with a little care to form an estimate of the degree of general accuracy attained by the scribe of a given document, and also of the kinds of mistakes to which he was prone (see § 45). The mere subtraction of a large number of irrelevant readings from the gross list of singular readings gives, as we have seen, greater exactness to the appreciation of the character of the ancestral text. But moreover the further knowledge gained respecting the habits of the scribe becomes of use both positively and negatively in dealing at a later stage with individual

variations. Singular readings which make good sense and therefore need imply no clerical error, but which might also be easily explained as due to a kind of clerical error already fixed upon the scribe by undoubted examples, are rendered by the presence of possible clerical error as a *vera causa* more doubtful than they would otherwise be. Singular readings which make good sense, and which cannot be explained by clerical error except such as lies outside the known proclivities of the scribe, acquire a better title to consideration. Again, those singular readings which are evidently errors, but are not clerical errors, can likewise be classified, and the results of classification used in the same manner : for instance, in the New Testament an appreciable number of the singular readings of A consist in the permutation of synonyms, and it can hardly be doubted that these readings are true individualisms. Whether however such singular readings are individualisms or of older date, is often not easy to tell : but it is always useful to remember that the text of a document as it stands is partly ancestral, partly due to transcriptional error in the last stage or stages of transmission, though definite indications of the one or the other origin may be wanting for each indi-vidual variation.

312. When the singular readings of B are examined for the purpose here explained, it is found that on the one hand the scribe reached by no means a high standard of accuracy, and on the other his slips are not proportionally numerous or bad. Like most transcribers, he occasionally omits necessary portions of text because his eye returned to the exemplar at the wrong place. As the longer portions of text so omitted consist usually either

of 12 to 14 letters or of multiples of the same, his exemplar was doubtless written in lines of this length. Often, but not always, an obvious cause of omission may be found in *homoeoteleuton*, the beginning or ending of consecutive portions of text with the same combinations of letters or of words. Reduplications due to the same cause likewise occur, but more rarely. More characteristic than these commonest of lapses is a tendency to double a single short word, syllable, or letter, or to drop one of two similar consecutive short words, syllables, or letters. The following are examples : Mark ix 25 εгωεгωεπιτασσω for εгωεπιτασσω ; Acts xviii 17 τογτωντωντω for τογτωντω ; Mark xiii 13 εισστελος for ειστελος ; John xiv 10 λεгω for λεгωλεгω ; Luke. vii 24 сαλεγομεν for сαλεγομενον ; Mark iii 5 λει for λεгει ; vi 22 ειελθογσησ for εισελθογσησ ; vii 21 διλογισμοι for διαλογισμοι ; also without similarity of form, Mark vi 1 εξηθεν for εξηλθεν ; vii 18 ασγντοι for ασγνετοι. Occasionally we find assimilations of ending, as Mark v 38 αλαλαζοντας πολλας (for πολλα) ; Rom. xiv 18 δοκιμοις τοις ανθρωποις (for δοκιμος) ; or even, but very rarely, such verbal assimilations as κήρυγμα ὃ ἐκήρυξεν in Acts x 37 for βάπτισμα ὃ ἐκήρυξεν.

313. The singular readings of B which cannot strictly be called clerical errors, and yet which appear to be individualisms of the scribe, are confined within still narrower limits. A current supposition, to which frequent repetition has given a kind of authority, that the scribe of B was peculiarly addicted to arbitrary omissions, we believe to be entirely unfounded, except possibly in the very limited sense explained below, while the facts which have given it plausibility are everywhere conspicuous.

In the New Testament, as in almost all prose writings which have been much copied, corruptions by interpolation are many times more numerous than corruptions by omission. When therefore a text of late and degenerate type, such as is the Received Text of the New Testament, is consciously or unconsciously taken as a standard, any document belonging to a purer stage of the text must by the nature of the case have the appearance of being guilty of omissions; and the nearer the document stands to the autograph, the more numerous must be the omissions laid to its charge. If B is preeminently free from interpolations, Western, Alexandrian, or Syrian, it cannot but be preeminently full of what may relatively to the Received Text be called omissions. Strictly speaking, these facts have no bearing on either the merits or the demerits of the scribe of B, except as regards the absolutely singular readings of B, together with those nearly singular readings in which the other attestation may easily be due to accidental coincidence : multitudes of the so called omissions of B are found in other good documents, few or many, and therefore, if not genuine, must at least have originated at a point in the line of transmission antecedent to B. It has seemed best however to speak of the supposed omissions of B here once for all, both those which concern the character of B individually and those which concern the character of the older text or texts from which it was derived.

314. The great mass of omissions, or rather for the most part non-interpolations, which B shares with other primary documents being set aside as irrelevant, it remains to be considered whether its singular readings, which alone are relevant, include such and so many

omissions as to indicate a characteristic habit of the scribe. It is a conceivable hypothesis that the scribe of B, besides inheriting a text unusually free from interpolations, was one of the very few transcribers addicted to curtailment, and thus corrupted the inherited text in a direction opposite to the usual course of transcription : the question is whether such a hypothesis is borne out by a comprehensive examination of the facts. What has been said above (§ 312) as to omissions due to purely clerical error need not be repeated. The only readings of B which can with any plausibility be urged on behalf of the hypothesis are the instances in which it omits slight and apparently non-essential words found in all other documents, such as pronouns and articles. It is on the one hand to be remembered that such words are peculiarly liable to be inserted, especially in Versions and quotations by Fathers; and still more that we find numerous similar omissions in good groups containing B, with every gradation in the amount of support which it receives, so that these omissions in B alone might be taken as genuine non-interpolations without incongruity as to the attestation, as well as consistently with the general character of the text of B. In our opinion this is the most probable account of the matter in some cases, and possibly in all : but it is on the whole safer for the present to allow for a proneness on the part of the scribe of B to drop petty words not evidently required by the sense, and therefore to neglect this class of omissions in B alone, where good confirmatory external or internal evidence is wanting. If however a like scrutiny is applied to important words or clauses, such as are sometimes dropped in the Western texts for the sake of apparent directness or simplicity, we find no traces whatever of a similar tendency in B. Omissions due to clerical error, and especially to *homoeoteleuton*, naturally take place sometimes without destruction of sense : and all the analogies suggest that this is the real cause of the very few substantial omissions in B which could possibly be referred to a love of abbreviation. As far as readings of any interest are concerned, we believe the text of B to be as free from curtailment as that of any other important document.

315. The chief feature of the few remaining individualisms of B, so far as they can be recognised with fair certainty as such, is their simple and inartificial character. Nearly all of them are due to easy assimilation, chiefly between neighbouring clauses or verses, occasionally between parallel passages. Consecutive words are perhaps occasionally transposed : but here on the other hand account has to be taken of the peculiar habitual purity of the text of B in respect of the order of words ; a purity which is specially exhibited in numerous ternary or more composite variations, in which B is the sole or almost the sole authority for the one collocation which will account for the other variants. Of paraphrastic change there is little or nothing. The final impression produced by a review of all the trustworthy signs is of a patient and rather dull or mechanical type of transcription, subject now and then to the ordinary lapses which come from flagging watchfulness, but happily guiltless of ingenuity or other untimely activity of brain, and indeed unaffected by mental influences except of the most limited and unconscious kind.

316. This examination of the tolerably certain individualisms of B, of all kinds, prepares the way for an

examination of the character of its remaining singular
readings. We must first however consider the readings
of a set of groups intermediate between those last considered (§§ 281—304) and B, that is, what we have called
the subsingular readings of B. When the groups formed
by B with one or more secondary Greek MSS and with
one or more Versions or Fathers are tried by Internal
Evidence, the proportional number of readings which
are to all appearance genuine is very large indeed. Readings so attested cannot in fact be well distinguished in
character from readings of אB. When B stands supported by only a single version, the results are by
no means so uniform. When it is followed only by
the Old Latin, or one or more Old Latin MSS or
Fathers, the readings seldom commend themselves as
worthy of unreserved confidence, though it is no less true
that they are seldom manifestly wrong (see § 204) : they
may as a rule be strictly called doubtful readings. On the
other hand when the associated version is the Memphitic,
Thebaic, or Old Syriac, the presumption of genuineness
raised by the habitual character of the readings is much
greater, and not a few of them are almost certainly right.
With other versions the combinations are various in
quality, as might be expected from the mixed origin of
the versions themselves and their present condition as
edited.

317. These diminutions of attestation lead us continuously to the singular readings proper. Here too so
many readings of B by itself commend themselves on
their own merits that it would be rash to reject any
hastily, though undoubtedly not a few have to be rejected
at last. Occasionally too some stray quotation of a
Father shews that readings of B which might have been

thought to be individualisms were really at least several generations older than the age when B was written. Thus in 1 Cor. xiii 5 it has τὸ μὴ ἑαυτῆς with Clem. *Paed.* 252 for τὰ ἑαυτῆς, retained by Clem. *Strom.* 956; both readings being shown by the respective contexts to have been actually used by Clement, and both making excellent sense. But, wherever there is no such accessory authority, clear internal evidence is needed to justify the acceptance of singular readings of B, since the possibility that they are no more than individualisms is constantly present.

318. The special excellence of B displays itself best perhaps in ternary or more than ternary variations. This has been already noticed (§ 315) in reference to collocations of words; but the statement is equally true as regards readings of all kinds. Where the documents fall into more than two arrays, the readings of B are usually found to be such as will account for the rival readings, and such as cannot easily be derived from any one of them, or any combination of them. Not the least instructive are what may be termed composite ternary variations, which easily escape notice in the cursory use of an ordinary *apparatus criticus.* They arise when two independent aberrant texts have removed a stumbling-block due to the original form of a phrase or sentence by altering different parts of the phrase, not by altering the whole or the same part in a different manner. If, as is usual, the evidence affecting each alteration is presented separately, we have in form not a single ternary variation but two or more successive binary variations. Now in such cases it is of frequent occurrence to find B nearly or even quite alone in supporting what is evidently the genuine variant

in each binary variation, while most of the other documents, representing ancient as well as later texts, divide
themselves into those which are right in one place and
those which are right in another.

319. If it is suggested that these phenomena might
be due to a skilful selection and combination of readings
from two sources by the scribe of B, the hypothesis is
decisively negatived by several considerations. If it
were true for composite variations, it should fit also
the ternary variations of the more obvious type, in which
B similarly supports the neutral reading; whereas in
most of them it would be peculiarly difficult to derive
the neutral reading from any kind of coalescence of the
aberrant readings. Secondly, the process hypothetically
attributed to the scribe of B is incongruous with all that
is known of his manner of transcription and capacity
of criticism. Thirdly, the ternary variations in which B
stands absolutely alone are not separable in character
from those in which its readings are 'subsingular', having
the support of, for instance, one or two early versions;
and thus the operation would have to be attributed to
one or more scribes of the first or early second century,
while it would demand a degree of skill of which we have
no example in extant records. Fourthly, the hypothesis
is distinctly condemned by transcriptional evidence,
which has an exceptional force in ternary variations (see
§ 29).

320. It should be noticed that some few variations
in the Pauline Epistles, in which the local Western element of B has affected the text, present a deceptive
appearance of exceptions to what has been stated. Thus
the accessory Western text, which makes itself felt in
simple conflations (Col. i 12 καλέσαντι καὶ ἱκανώσαντι B

from ἱκανώσαντι and the Western καλέσαντι, 2 Thess.
iii 4 καὶ ἐποιήσατε καὶ ποιεῖτε καὶ ποιήσετε B from [καὶ]
ποιεῖτε καὶ ποιήσετε and the Western καὶ ἐποιήσατε καὶ
ποιεῖτε), is but partially followed in the composite ternary
variation of Rom. x 5. Here the scribe of B adopted
two out of three closely connected Western (and subsequently Syrian) changes, the transposition of ὅτι and
the insertion of αὐτά after ποιήσας, but in the third place
negligently left αὐτῇ untouched, doubtless the reading
of his primary exemplar, and thus produced an impossible combination. Combinations like these imply imperfect workmanship, not skilful choice. Nor is it
material to know whether the scribe of B himself took
the Western readings from a second exemplar, or, as
seems more likely, merely copied a single exemplar with
marginal or interlinear corrections which he incorporated
into the text (see §§ 335 ff.): the essential nature of the
process is not changed by its being carried a single step
back. Except in so far as even the slightest mixture may
be said to involve some kind of selection, we hold it
to be certain that the readings of B are never the result
of any eclectic process. Its occasional individual aberra-
tions of course sometimes take place where there is
variation already, and therefore sometimes go to make up
ternary variations. But it remains true that the readings
of B in ternary variations, simple or composite, are
habitually those of the original text, and the readings of
the other texts divergent attempts to amend it.

321. What has been said on the excellence usually
shown by the readings of B in ternary variations will be
made more intelligible by two or three examples of different
types.

James v 7 ἰδοὺ ὁ γεωργὸς ἐκδέχεται τὸν τίμιον καρπὸν
τῆς γῆς, μακροθυμῶν ἐπ' αὐτῷ ἕως λάβῃ πρόϊμον καὶ ὄψιμον

18

B (? 31) lat.vg the (? aeth) arm.   One text supplies the
concluding adjectives with καρπόν (from the first clause) as
a substantive (‫ א‬9 ƒ me syr.hl.mg pp, with slight variations), another, the Syrian, with ὑετόν (AK₂L₂P₂ cuᵖˡ syr.
vg-hl.txt ppˢᵉʳ).   Here the elliptic expression has manifestly
given rise to two different corrections; and B is the only
certain Greek authority for the true text.   This is an example of the simplest and most fundamental form of ternary readings, with the neutral text clearly exhibited.

322.   Mark vi 43 καὶ ἦραν κλάσματα δώδεκα κοφίνων
πληρώματα B.   The easier κλασμάτων of viii 20 (πόσων
σφυρίδων πληρώματα κλασμάτων ἤρατε, where the necessary
order enforces the genitive) is adopted by ‫ א‬13-69-124-
346 209 (1 omits).   The Western (and Syrian) text, starting
from this last reading, borrows κοφίνους πλήρεις, to replace
the last two words, from viii 19 ; Matt. xiv 20 (AD unc¹¹
cuᵖˡ latt syrr me); most Latins, with 33 and some secondary Greek MSS, introducing further assimilations to Matt.
There are also two remarkable conflations : LΔ vary from
B only by adopting κοφίνους from the Western reading (or
the antecedent parallel passages) ; 28, which has many
relics of a very ancient text hereabouts, retains the κλάσματα of B, but for the rest follows the Western and Syrian
text.   Here the choice clearly lies between three readings,
those of B, of ‫ א‬and the lost early originals of two texts now
partially preserved in cursives, and of LΔ ; and the difficulty
of accounting for the well attested κλάσματα is unfavourable
to the second.   The reading of LΔ, κλάσματα δώδεκα κοφίνους πληρώματα, which has no intrinsic probability, may be
due to accidental mixture (in v. 31 they, and they alone,
have the impossible εὐκαίρου): the reading of B, which
has much intrinsic probability, was likely to be changed
on account of the double accusative, even apart from the
influence of parallel passages, and might easily give rise
to all the other variants with the help of harmonistic
assimilation.   If we take the three parts of the composite
variation separately, a good group is found supporting
each of the three readings of B; κλάσματα being attested
by BLΔ 28, κοφίνων by ‫ א‬B 1-209 13-69-124-346, and
πληρώματα by ‫ א‬BLΔ 1-209 13-69-124-346.   This last
specially certain attestation marks the virtual authority for
the entire fundamental text from which the Western correction departed, the peculiar word πληρώματα being the
turning-point of change; and evidently the common ancestor of ‫ א‬&c. altered one of the three preceding words,

and the common ancestor of LΔ another, while B alone
held fast the true text throughout.

323. Once more, the unique character of B in a series
of separate but mutually related variations, making up as it
were an extended composite variation, is illustrated by
St Mark's account of the denials of St Peter. Alone of
the evangelists St Mark notices two crowings of a cock.
According to the true text he follows the same lines as
St Matthew and St Luke, while he makes the requisite
additions in three places: that is, he inserts the word
'twice' (δίς) in both the prediction (xiv 30) and St Peter's
recollection of the prediction (xiv 72 *b*), and the phrase 'a
second time' (ἐκ δευτέρου) in the statement that 'a cock
crew' immediately after the third denial (xiv 72 *a*). Thus
all the points are tersely but sufficiently given. The text
however, as it thus stood, presented more than one temptation to correction. At the first of the four places (v. 30)
the direct harmonistic influence from the other Gospels
was naturally strong and unchecked, and thus the first δίς
is largely omitted (by ℵC* aeth arm as well as the Westerns,
D cu² lat.afr-eur). When v. 72 *a* was reached, ἐκ δευτέρου
was as naturally a stumbling-block for a different reason,
because there had been no mention of a previous cock-
crowing. The supposed difficulty was met in two ways:
a text now represented by a small group (ℵL *c* vg.cod),
doubtless Alexandrian, assimilated v. 72 to v. 68 and the
parallel narratives by striking out ἐκ δευτέρου; while the
Western text boldly adapted v. 68 to v. 72 by inserting καὶ
ἀλέκτωρ ἐφώνησεν after προαύλιον. Lastly v. 72 *b* was
affected by the various texts both of the preceding words
and of the original prediction (v. 30), here expressly repeated and thereby brought into strict parallelism, and
accordingly δίς is omitted by more documents than ἐκ
δευτέρου. The Syrian text makes the whole uniformly
symmetrical and complete by accepting the Western interpolation in v. 68, while it retains δίς in both places.
The confusion of attestation introduced by these several
cross currents of change is so great that of the seven principal MSS ℵABCDLΔ no two have the same text in all
four places. Neither of the two extreme arrangements,
the Syrian (with A), which recognises the double cock-
crowing in all four places, and that of ℵ *c*, which recognises
it nowhere but simply follows the other Gospels, could have
given rise to the other readings. The chief cause of dis-
turbance is manifestly the attempt to supply an explicit

record of the first cock-crowing; and the original absence of καὶ ἀλέκτωρ ἐφώνησεν in v. 68 is sufficiently attested by אBL lt 17 *c* me. Half however of this group, as we have seen, followed the alternative expedient of omitting ἐκ δευτέρου, two of the number going on to omit the following δίς : and thus it appears that the only consistent authorities for the true text in this series of variations are B, a lectionary, and the Memphitic.

324. Such being the results of an examination of ternary variations, it is no wonder that binary variations likewise supply us with multitudes of readings of B, slenderly supported or even alone, which have every appearance of being genuine, and thus exemplify the peculiar habitual purity of its text. Readings like these are striking illustrations of the danger of trusting absolutely to even an overwhelming plurality of early and good authorities (see § 282 f.), and the need of bearing in mind the distorting effects of mixture. For instance it is morally certain that in Gal. vi 15 B, with two good cursives and some Versions and Fathers, is right in reading οὔτε γάρ for ἐν γὰρ Χριστῷ Ἰησοῦ οὔτε, which is borrowed from v 6 ; and yet the array sustaining the interpolation includes אACD₂G₃P₂ with Versions and Fathers. Such a distribution could never have arisen except by a wide early adoption of a yet earlier aberration of some influential text, which here was evidently Western. On the other hand there are many subsingular readings of B that cannot claim more than the secondary rank of alternative readings which may possibly be genuine, and there are many others that may be safely rejected. The claims of absolutely singular readings of B in binary variations are naturally found to be usually of no great strength, though some among them appear to be very possibly genuine, and their genuineness would not be out of harmony with the known textual relations of B.

325. The existence of numerous genuine subsingular readings of B in binary variations gives the key to the origin of another class of variations, fundamentally the same but different in appearance, which, though rare in the Gospels, are not uncommon in the other books preserved in B. The peculiarity of these variations consists in the agreement of B with the Syrian text against the great mass of documents representing the more ancient texts. How is this distribution to be explained? Are these readings of B corruptions of its fundamental text from a Syrian source, or do they belong to its fundamental text, so that they must have stood in the purest of the texts out of which the Syrian text was constructed? Internal evidence is decisively favourable to the second answer for at least the larger number of passages, and thus affords a strong presumption for the rest. Perhaps the most striking example is the well known variation in 1 Cor. xv 51, where there can be no doubt that the peculiar form of St Paul's words, together with forgetfulness of the language of the apostolic age (1 Thess. iv 15, 17), led to a transposition of the negative from the first clause to the second, and the introduction of a seemingly easy but fallacious antithesis. Here the wrong position of the negative is supported by $\aleph$(A)CG$_3$ 17 with some Versions and Fathers, and also with a verbal change, which probably formed part of the corruption in its earliest shape, by D$_2$ with other Versions and Fathers. Thus B alone of primary uncials, sustained however by the Memphitic and apparently by Origen and other good Fathers, as also by lost MSS mentioned by Fathers, upholds the true position in company with the Syrian text. The only difference of distribution between such cases and those noticed in the last paragraph is the

shifting of the Syrian documents from the one side to
the other ; and such a shifting is the natural result of the
eclecticism of the Syrian revisers (see §§ 185 f.).   Two
causes have doubtless contributed to the unequal occurrence of the readings here described, genuine readings
attested by B almost alone in addition to the Syrian
documents, so that if the Syrian attestation were removed
they would be subsingular readings of B; their greater
abundance in the Acts and Epistles than in the Gospels
being partly due to the more rapid and more widely
current corruption of the Gospels, and partly to the
relative paucity of extant uncials containing the Acts and
Epistles.   The former cause belongs to the actual history
of the text; the latter is a mere accident in the preservation of documents to this day.

F.   326—329.   *Singular and subsingular readings of ℵ and other MSS*

326.   Turning from B to ℵ, we find ourselves dealing
with the handiwork of a scribe of different character.
The omissions and repetitions of small groups of letters
are rarely to be seen; but on the other hand all the
ordinary lapses due to rapid and careless transcription
are more numerous, including substitutions of one word
for another, as when γινώσκει αὐτούς replaces σκηνώσει
ἐπ' αὐτούς in Apoc. vii 15.   Some of these substitutions
have a kind of sense of their own which is out of all
relation to the context, as εἰς τὴν Ἀντιπατρίδα (from Acts
xxiii 31) for εἰς τὴν πατρίδα in Matt. xiii 54 ; and
ἀγαπήσας τοὺς Ἰουδαίους (for ἰδίους) τοὺς ἐν τῷ κόσμῳ in
John xiii 1.   The singular readings are very numerous,
especially in the Apocalypse, and scarcely ever com-

mend themselves on internal grounds. It can hardly be doubted that many of them are individualisms of the scribe himself, when his bold and rough manner of transcription is considered; but some doubtless are older. Little encouragement however to look favourably upon them is given by an examination of the subsingular readings. Many of these, as has been already noticed (§ 205), are clearly Western corruptions, of which οἶνον οὐκ εἶχον ὅτι συνετελέσθη ὁ οἶνος τοῦ γάμου in John ii 3 is an example; and many others are probably of Alexandrian origin: but, whatever may be the sources, the prevalent internal character where it can be known is such as to raise a strong presumptive suspicion where it is obscure. There are however a few subsingular readings of ℵ which recall the predominant character of subsingular readings of B, and are possibly or even probably genuine. Such are the omission of υἱοῦ θεοῦ in Mark i 1, and of ἡ πύλη in Matt. vii 13; the insertion of Ἡσαίου in Matt. xiii 35; μηδένα (for μηδὲν) ἀπελπίζοντες in Luke vi 35; ᾔτησαν τὸν (for ᾐτήσαντο) Πειλᾶτον in Acts xiii 28; ἔδωκα for ἔδωκαν in Matt. xxvii 10. The fact that Origen's name occasionally stands among the accessory authorities is a warning against hasty rejection; and though subsingular readings of ℵ attested by Origen are doubtless often only Alexandrian, this is probably not always the case.

327. These various characteristics of the singular and subsingular readings of ℵ are easily explained in connexion with the relation between the texts of B and of ℵ described above, and at the same time enable this relation to be ascertained with somewhat greater precision. The ancestries of both MSS having started from a common source not much later than the autographs,

they came respectively under different sets of influences, and each in the course of time lost more or less of its original purity. With certain limited exceptions already noticed, the concordance of B and ℵ marks that residual portion of the text of their primitive archetype in which neither of the two ancestries had at any point adopted or originated a wrong reading. Where their readings differ, at least one of the ancestries must have departed from the archetypal text. The possibility that both have gone astray in different ways must remain open, for it would be only natural that there should be an occasional coincidence of place between corruptions admitted into the one line of transmission and corruptions admitted into the other; and as a matter of fact there are a few passages where it is difficult to think that either B or ℵ has preserved the reading of the common original. But these coincidences are likely to be only exceptional; and all that has been observed up to this point respecting the character of our two MSS justifies a strong initial presumption in each particular case that the text of their archetype is preserved in one or other of them.

328. It follows that any subsingular, or even singular, reading of either B or ℵ may owe the limitation of its attestation to either of two totally different sets of antecedents. A subsingular reading of B (or ℵ) may be, first, equivalent to a subsingular reading of ℵB combined, which has lost part of its attestation by the accidental defection of ℵ (or B); it may be, secondly, an early corruption limited in range of acceptance. Both explanations being in all cases possible, the antecedent probabilities differ widely according as the one or the other MS is in question. The ancestry of B posterior to the common archetype was probably a chain of very few

links indeed; certainly the various transcribers who had
a hand in making it must either have been in a position
which kept them ignorant of the great popular textual
corruptions of the second and third centuries or must
have for the most part preferred to follow their own inherited exemplars. It was not so in all cases, as is shown
by such examples as those which have been cited above
(§ 326); and an exceptional adulteration of the fundamental text of B must be recognised as having occasionally left ℵ alone where ℵB ought, so to speak, to
have stood together. On the other hand the certainty
that the ancestry of ℵ posterior to the common archetype
must, at one or more points in its history, have been
exposed to contact with at least two early aberrant texts,
since it accepted a considerable number of their readings
(§ 205), enables us to account at once for the good internal character of most subsingular readings of B, and
for the questionable internal character of most subsingular readings of ℵ. Where the corrupt readings
adopted by the ancestors of ℵ happened to be widely
adopted in current texts likewise, B would be left with
little or no support from Greek MSS; that is, the true
text of the common archetype would be preserved in
subsingular readings of B. Where the corrupt readings
adopted by the ancestors of ℵ happened to find little or
no reception in eclectic texts, B and mixed Greek texts
generally would be found alike attesting the true text
of the common archetype, and subsingular readings of
ℵ would be nothing more than examples of early aberration early extinguished. The erroneous subsingular readings of B, proportionally as well as absolutely much less
numerous than those of ℵ, may be described in the same
general terms with respect to their genealogical cha-

racter, subject to the difference that the sources of corruption in B are for the most part of a sporadic and indeterminate character (§ 204). Finally, the absence of any external criterion for referring the various singular and subsingular readings of either MS to one or other of the two possible origins, combined with the exceptional antiquity and purity of the fundamental text which they both preserve intact in very large though unequal proportions, demands a specially vigilant consideration for every such reading of both before it is definitely rejected.

329. It may be added explicitly here that, except for the Apocalypse, and the peculiar Western non-interpolations of the Gospels, a similar examination of the singular and subsingular readings of every extant MS except B and ℵ leads to entirely unfavourable results. There are a few, a very few, cases in which the genuineness of such a singular or subsingular reading must be admitted as possible : but all such readings occur, we believe, in ternary or more composite variations, and differ from the readings of B or ℵ merely by the absence of some slight erroneous modification. The same general statement may likewise be made respecting the trial of individual MSS by means of binary combinations into which ℵ and B do not enter (as in the Gospels CD, CL, CZ, CΔ, DL, DZ, LΔ, LΞ, AC, AD &c.), or indeed respecting any other application of Internal Evidence of Groups to the testing of their internal character.

G. 330—339. *Determination of text where* B *and* ℵ *differ*

330. It will be evident from the foregoing pages that B must be regarded as having preserved not only

a very ancient text, but a very pure line of very ancient
text, and that with comparatively small depravation either
by scattered ancient corruptions otherwise attested or by
individualisms of the scribe himself.   On the other hand
to take it as the sole authority except where it contains
self-betraying errors, as some have done, is an unwar-
rantable abandonment of criticism, and in our opinion
inevitably leads to erroneous results.   A text so formed
would be incomparably nearer the truth than a text
similarly taken from any other Greek MS or other single
document: but it would contain many errors by no
means obvious, which could with more or less certainty
have been avoided by the free use of all existing evidence.

331.   Enough has already been said on the determination of the text where B is supported by א.   A few
words must be added here on the mode of dealing with
the numerous variations in which these two preeminent
MSS differ from each other.   Setting aside ternary variations, most of the distributions in which the conflict of
א and B requires notice belong to one or other of the
three following types: (1) B with a small group against
the rest; (2) א and B each with a large group dividing
the array; and (3), much less important, א with a small
group against the rest.   The characteristics and twofold
genealogical antecedents of the first and third have been
already considered (§§ 324, 326 ff.).   In the first two
cases, and also to a limited extent in the third, Genealogy
and Internal Evidence of Groups have brought us to the
point of having two readings before us, with so real a
conflict of authority that, notwithstanding the habitually
greater integrity of text in B than in א, the normal relations between the different kinds of evidence are to

a certain extent disturbed. Two classes of evidence rise
into unusual importance here, Secondary documentary
evidence and Internal evidence. The effects of both
under these circumstances are the same; first to rescue
a slenderly attested reading from being entirely set aside,
and next, if the two classes of evidence sustain each
other, or either is of exceptional strength, to render
superfluous the retention of the other reading as an
alternative. The bearing of Internal evidence, which
here can be only Internal Evidence of Readings, requires no special comment. The change in the relative
importance of Secondary documentary evidence will need
a little explanation.

332. All Secondary documentary evidence has its
value for these variations, in so far as it shews a given
reading attested by a primary MS not to be an individualism; provided of course that the coincidence is such
as cannot well be accidental. By supplying diversity of
attestation, it has at the least the effect of proving that
the reading had some sort of pedigree; and, considering
the absence of very close and immediate relations of
affinity between most extant documents, the pedigree
must usually have been of some length. Little would be
gained by this were the uncial itself secondary : but if
its readings are habitually good in an exceptional proportion, the relative probability of the given reading is at
once much increased.

333. There is however a much greater increase
of authority when the secondary evidence is that of a
peculiarly good element in a mixed document, being
then equivalent to fragments of a document which if continuously preserved would have been of primary or not
much lower rank. Such elements are found, for instance,

in some Mixed Latin MSS, and also in some cursive
Greek MSS. If a given cursive is observed to concur
several times with the very best documents against not
only all or almost all other cursives but almost all
uncials in favour of a manifestly right reading, we know
that it must contain an element of exceptional purity,
and reasonably infer that the same element is the parent
of other less certain readings in supporting which it
joins with perhaps a single primary uncial only.   Under
these conditions the uncial may receive weighty documentary support from an apparently insignificant document.

334.   On a superficial view it might seem arbitrary to
assign a given cursive or other mixed document high
authority in those variations which differ from the common text, and refuse it any authority where it agrees
with the common text.   As however has been implicitly
shown in former pages (§ 197), this view derives its
plausibility from neglect of the conditions on which
criticism allows authority to a document on the ground
that it is 'good', that is, gives it relative confidence in
doubtful cases because it has been found on the right
side in clear cases in which most documents are on the
wrong side.   If the homogeneousness of a cursive text
is found to be broken by sporadic ancient readings, we
know that we have virtually two distinct texts to deal
with under the same name; that is, the readings discrepant from the common text proclaim themselves as
derived from a second ancestor which had an ancient
text.   It can never indeed be positively affirmed that
all the readings agreeing with the common text came
distinctively from the principal or Syrian ancestor of the
supposed cursive, for in regard of any one such reading

it is always speculatively possible that it may have had a place in the virtually Pre-Syrian as well as in the Syrian ancestor: but in the face of the certainty that it must have existed in the Syrian ancestor this speculative possibility has no appreciable force for the purposes of criticism.

335. It so happens that the relation between two extant uncial MSS of St Paul's Epistles illustrates vividly the composite origin of many texts, including the texts of some at least of such cursives as have been noticed above. The St Germain MS E_3, apparently written in Cent. X or late in Cent. IX, has long been recognised as a copy of the Clermont MS D_2, executed after D_2 had suffered much revision by correcting hands: all possible doubt as to the direct derivation of the one from the other is taken away by the senseless readings which the scribe of E_3 has constructed out of a combination of what was written by the original scribe of D_2 and what was written by its correctors;—an interesting illustration, it may be observed in passing, of the manner in which the strange Βεωορσόρ of ℵ* in 2 Pet. ii 15 must have resulted from a fusion of the two readings Βεώρ and Βοσόρ. D_2, it will be remembered (§§ 100 f., 203), was written in Cent. VI, and has a Western text. The readings introduced by the two chief correctors, referred to Cent. VII ($D_2{}^a$) and Cent. IX ($D_2{}^b$) respectively, and especially the readings due to the later of the two, are for the most part Syrian: on the other hand, while the later corrector alters many Pre-Syrian readings which his predecessor had passed over, he fails to make his own assimilative revision complete.

336. A short passage from D_2 (Rom. xv 31—33) will sufficiently exhibit the chief phenomena of the corrections and transcription, the readings of the correctors being set between the lines: ἵνα ῥυσθῶ ἀπὸ τῶν ἀπιθούντων ἐν τῇ
ἵνα ἡ διακονία εἰς
Ἰουδαίᾳ καὶ ἡ δωροφορία μου ἡ ἐν Ιη̄μ̄ εὐπρόσδεκτος γένηται
θῡ
τοῖς ἁγίοις, ἵνα ἐν χαρᾷ ἔλθω πρὸς ὑμᾶς διὰ θελήματος Χῡ Ἰῡ
dots
καὶ ἀναψύξω μεθ᾽ ὑμῶν· ὁ δὲ θεὸς τῆς εἰρήνης ἤτω μετὰ πάντων ὑμῶν᾽ ἀμήν. This passage contains five distinctively Western readings, of which the first four, ἡ δωροφορία, ἐν (before Ἰερουσαλήμ), Χριστοῦ Ἰησοῦ, and the interpolation of ἤτω, are brought by the correctors into conformity with

the true and the Syrian texts alike; the fifth, ἀναψύξω
μεθ' ὑμῶν for συναναπαύσωμαι ὑμῖν, remains untouched. The
two Western readings which are also Syrian, γένηται τοῖς
ἁγίοις for τ. ἁ. γ. and ἔλθω...καί for ἐλθών, are likewise left as
they were. Lastly, the second ἵνα, omitted by all Pre-
Syrian authorities, is inserted in agreement with the Syrian
text. Of the five changes here made E_3 adopts the first
three, substituting them for the original readings of D_2.
The last two it neglects, retaining the original readings:
the correctors' omission of ἤτω was apparently expressed
by cancelling dots, which might easily escape the eye; the
disregard of θεοῦ is probably due merely to carelessness,
of which the scribe gives abundant signs. It will be seen
at once that, if both the later corrector of D_2 and the scribe
of E_3 had done effectually that which they evidently proposed to do, E_3 would in this place have simply represented
the Syrian text; and that the combined negligence was
the cause of the survival of three Western readings.

337. These instructive phenomena naturally receive
little consideration now, because the exact knowledge that
we possess of the original D_2 renders attention to the copy
E_3 superfluous. Supposing however that D_2 had been lost,
the complex antecedents of the text of E_3 would have been
unknown: it would have presented itself merely as a Syrian
document sprinkled with Western readings. When then
we find other late MSS having a Syrian text sprinkled
with Western or other Pre-Syrian readings, we may reasonably take D_2 and E_3 as exhibiting the manner in which
the mixture has probably arisen, and indirectly illustrating
other possible modes of mixture. Evidently the textual value
of E_3 is virtually confined to the fragments which it preserved of the original writing of D_2, while in the absence of
D_2 there would be no way of distinguishing these fragments
from the rest of the text except by their discrepance from
the Syrian text: and in like manner discrepance from the
Syrian text is the only safe test for the readings of the
ancient element in any late mixed document, because in
late times the texts which would be virtually taken as
standards for assimilative correction were naturally Syrian,
no others being current.

338. It is true that by attending to the discrepant
readings alone we should be neglecting some readings
which as a matter of fact were in the original writing of
D_2, namely the Western readings that became Syrian (in
the passage cited these are the change of order and the

resolved construction) : but if D_2 had been lost there would have been no means of knowing this. Two courses alone would have been open; to attend exclusively to the readings discrepant from the Syrian text, as being almost certainly derived from the Non-Syrian element in the ancestry of E_3; or to allow to all the readings of E_3 whatever authority the discrepant readings might claim. In the former case there would be a negative disadvantage; a necessary loss of evidence, but no falsification of it : the composite text of E_3 would be virtually ignored outside the definite limits, but the risk of attributing to the better element of its ancestry readings due in fact to the worse would be avoided. In the latter case there would be a certainty of extensive positive error, since E_3 obviously abounds in purely Syrian readings, and yet, for want of a discriminative test, they would be included with the rest in the general attribution of the authority belonging properly to the more ancient element alone. Here again D_2 and E_3 elucidate the necessity of limiting the separate authority of cursives containing ancient elements of text to their Non-Syrian readings (see the end of § 334).

339. Some weight might doubtless be consistently given to the cumulative negative evidence against a reading supplied by the absence of any cursive attestation whatever; because it might be anticipated that the fortuitous irregularity with which the ancient readings are scattered over any one mixed text would be neutralised by the juxtaposition of all mixed texts, so that a genuine reading would be likely to obtain attestation from at least one or other of the number. But the anticipation is not verified by experience, for numerous absolutely certain readings have no cursive or other similar attestation; and this fact has to be taken into account in doubtful cases. Here, as in all cases where textual character is in question, what is said of cursives applies equally to late uncials : the outward and formal difference between the two classes of MSS involves no corresponding difference of texts.

H. 340—346. *Determination of text where* B *is absent*

340. The comparative certainty afforded by the peculiar character of B is felt at once when we pass to parts of the text where it is wanting. As regards the ancient

texts, we lose the one approximately constant Greek neutral document: as regards Internal Evidence of Groups, we lose all the groups into which B enters. This state of evidence occurs under three different conditions; first, in detached variations in the Pauline Epistles, where the Western element of B has displaced its fundamental or neutral element, the absence of which is virtually equivalent to the absence of B; secondly, in those parts of the Pauline Epistles which were contained in the lost leaves of B, but in which the relations of the other documents are to a considerable extent illustrated by facts of grouping observed in those parts of the same series of books for which B is extant; and thirdly, in the Apocalypse, where analogies of grouping are to say the least imperfect, and the few important documents common to the rest of the New Testament present themselves in novel relations.

341. First both in order of books and in gradation come the isolated W.estern readings of B in the Pauline Epistles. Where BD₂G₃ or BG₃ with other chiefly Western documents stand alone among Pre-Syrian documents, there is no difficulty. Distinctively Western substitutions or additions attested by B are with a few doubtful exceptions, as κημώσεις 1 Cor. ix 9, ἑρμηνευτής xiv 28, ἐνδεικνύμενοι 2 Cor. viii 24, ὑμεῖς...ἐστέ Gal. iv 28, which it is prudent to retain as alternatives, of no better character than similar distinctively Western readings not supported by B. Such readings therefore as πληροφορῆσαι for πληρῶσαι Rom. xv 13 (cf. v. 29 *v.l.*), φιλοτιμοῦμαι xv 20, δωροφορία for διακονία xv 31, Ἀριστοβόλου xvi 10, οὐδὲ ἀπῆλθον Gal. i 17, and the transposition of τῇ οὔσῃ ἐν Κορίνθῳ and ἡγιασμένοις ἐν Χριστῷ Ἰησοῦ (ancient lines) in 1 Cor. i 2 we have had no hesitation in rejecting.

19

The internal evidence is not so clear with respect to distinctively Western omissions, and for the present at least it is safest to indicate doubt about words omitted by this group. But where other documents not clearly Western form part of the attestation, interpretation of the evidence is often difficult, if the rival reading is well attested. We can have no security in these cases that B derived its reading from its neutral element : and, if it derived it from its Western element, then two alternatives are possible : either the accessory documents are really Non-Western, in which case the rival reading is often Alexandrian; or they are mixed (usually Syrian) and have adopted a Western reading, in which case the rival reading is more likely to be simply Non-Western, although its attestation is consistent with its being Alexandrian. In these cases we have exactly the state of things, as far as regards extant attestation, which Griesbach assumed to have from early times existed everywhere (see § 251), an attestation which might easily be only Western opposed to an attestation which might easily be only Alexandrian. If however these variations are examined together, Internal Evidence is generally favourable to the apparently Non-Western readings : but in not a few cases the other reading must be retained as an alternative, or even appears to be the more probable of the two.

342. Since in the Pauline Epistles B (as well as $\aleph$, A, and C) sometimes supports distinctively Western readings, so that they gain, for instance, the attestation BD_2G_3 as well as $\aleph D_2G_3$, AD_2G_3, and (more rarely) CD_2G_3 and even ACD_2G_3 and occasionally $\aleph ACD_2G_3$, it might be asked what security we have that $\aleph BD_2G_3$, or even the same group with other uncials added, do not make a Western combination. As a matter of attestation

the contingency contains no improbability; and the recognition of it prescribes special watchfulness where there is no sufficient accessory Non-Western attestation, this being in fact another of the cases in which secondary documentary evidence of the better sort acquires a high interpretative value. But Internal Evidence is so favourable to the group אBD₂G₃ that except in a very few cases, as οὖ Rom. iv 8, αἰχμαλωτίζοντά με ἐν τῷ νόμῳ vii 23, ἡ omitted after τοῦ θεοῦ 1 Cor. xv 10, ἁγίοις omitted 1 Thes. v 27, and καὶ τῆς ἁγνότητος added 2 Cor. xi 3, we have not found reason to treat their readings as doubtful.

343. We come next to the analogous difficulties which arise where B totally fails us as regards direct evidence, but still affords some indirect aid in the interpretation of groupings, namely in the latter part (ix 14—end) of the Epistle to the Hebrews, in the Pastoral Epistles, and in the Epistle to Philemon. Here too the main distinctive problem is how to distinguish oppositions of Western and Non-Western from oppositions of Non-Alexandrian and Alexandrian readings; and it has to be dealt with in the same manner as in the former case. Another uncertainty is suggested by a recollection of the excellence of subsingular readings of B in those parts of the Pauline Epistles which are preserved in it, and of the similar excellence of readings differing in attestation from these by the mere addition of the Syrian documents (§§ 324 f.). Evidently the only resource here is to allow an alternative place to readings slenderly supported, or supported chiefly by Syrian documents, provided that the attestation includes such documents as are often associated with B in its subsingular readings, and that the local internal evidence is favourable. It would be con-

venient to an editor in this part of the New Testament
to assign to ℵ such an authority as a consideration of
the whole evidence has up to this point constrained us
to assign to B.   But the absolute excellence of ℵ is
neither lessened nor increased by the loss of a purer MS :
the comparative excellence of its fundamental text and
the deterioration of that text by mixture alike remain
unchanged, while the discrimination of the different elements through grouping is deprived of one important
resource.   Such being the case, the text of these eighteen
or nineteen chapters of the Pauline Epistles is undeniably
less certain than that of the rest, though, as far as we can
judge, the uncertainty is small in amount and of no real
moment.

344.   When at last we reach the Apocalypse, new
and troublesome conditions of evidence are encountered.
Not only is B absent, but historical landmarks are obscure, and familiar documents assume a new position.
Probable traces of a Western and perhaps an Alexandrian
text may be discerned, with analogous relations to the
extant uncials which contain other books : but they are
not distinct enough to give much help, and for the most
part Internal Evidence of Groups is the highest available guide of criticism.   As before, ℵ has a large neutral
element; but in addition to mixture, probably Western
and Alexandrian, evident individualisms of the scribe, or
of one of his immediate predecessors, come forth in
much greater luxuriance than before, as also they do in
the Epistle of Barnabas which follows the Apocalypse
in the same handwriting ; this less scrupulous treatment
of the text being perhaps connected with the ambiguous
authority of the Apocalypse in the canonical lists of
Cent. IV.   Nor is internal evidence as a rule here

favourable to ℵ unsupported by other uncials : indeed a large proportion of the readings of the binary combinations ℵA, ℵC, ℵP₂ are questionable or clearly wrong. C preserves nearly the same character as in the Acts and Epistles. The elements of A apparently remain unchanged ; but the ancient or neutral element is larger. Both these MSS however acquire a high relative eminence through the want of compeers, or documents approximately such. Their consent is well supported by internal evidence, even where it has no documentary confirmation ; and A stands quite alone, or unsustained by any other Greek MS, in some manifestly right readings, such as κατήγωρ in xii 10, and εἴ τις εἰς αἰχμαλω-σίαν εἰς αἰχμαλωσίαν ὑπάγει in xiii 10. On the other hand the absolute proportion of wrong readings is great in each of them singly. As in most of the Epistles, P₂ contains, in the midst of a somewhat degenerate text, so many good readings that it is entitled to an appreciable authority in doubtful cases ; while the comparatively few readings of B₂ which rise above its generally low level of character are such as imply a source of no distinctive value. Cursives containing not a few ancient readings are fairly numerous, and yield valuable help ; as do the Latin versions, and in a less degree the rest, which seem to be all of comparatively late date, and certainly have texts of an extremely mixed character. Careful study of grouping goes far towards shewing which readings may safely be neglected; and Internal Evidence of Read-ings is often sufficiently decisive in this book to allow a clear decision to be made between those that remain. Yet the state of the documentary evidence renders it necessary to leave a considerable number of alternative readings. With the fullest allowance for the peculiarities of the rough Palestinian Greek, which indeed for the most part may be classified under a very small number of grammatical heads, several places remain where no document seems to have preserved the true text, and it is quite possible that the discovery of new and better documents might bring to light other unsuspected corruptions. Nothing however in the extant evidence suggests the probability that they would be of any importance.

345. We are by no means sure that we have done all for the text of the Apocalypse that might be done with existing materials. But we are convinced that the only way to remove such relative insecurity as belongs to it would be by a more minute and complete examination of the genealogical relations of the documents than we have been able to accomplish, nor have we reason to suspect that the result would make any considerable change.

346. The relation of the 'Received Text' to the ancient texts in the Apocalypse requires separate notice. In all other books it follows with rare exceptions the text of the great bulk of cursives. In all the books in which there was an undoubted Syrian text the text of the great bulk of cursives is essentially Syrian, with a certain number of later ('Constantinopolitan') modifications; in other books the text is, if not Syrian, at least such as must have been associated with the original Syrian books at Constantinople. The exceptional readings of the 'Received Text', in which it abandons the majority of the cursives, are hardly ever distinctively Alexandrian; in almost all cases they are Western readings, sometimes very slenderly attested, which evidently owe their place to coincidence with the Latin Vulgate,

having been adopted by Erasmus in the first instance, and never afterwards removed. The foundation of the 'Received Text' of the Apocalypse on the other hand was a transcript of the single cursive numbered 1 : Erasmus had in his earlier editions no other Greek MS to follow, though eventually he introduced almost at random a certain number of corrections from the Complutensian text. Now 1 is by no means an average cursive of the common sort. On the one hand it has many individualisms and readings with small and evidently unimportant attestation : on the other it has a large and good ancient element, chiefly it would seem of Western origin, and ought certainly (with the somewhat similar 38) to stand high among secondary documents. While therefore the text of 1 differs very widely from the true text by its Western readings, its individualisms, and the large late or Constantinopolitan element which it possesses in common with other cursives, a text formed in the way that the 'Received Text' is formed in other books would probably have differed from the true text on the whole much more. Thus the 'Received Text' of the Apocalypse has a curiously anomalous position. Besides containing a small portion of text which, like some single words in other books with less excuse, was fabricated from the Latin by Erasmus without any Greek authority to supply a defect in his one MS, it abounds in readings which cannot be justified on any possible view of documentary evidence, and are as a matter of fact abandoned by all textual critics : and yet the proportion of cases in which it has adopted the readings most current in the degenerate popular Greek texts of the Middle Ages, though large, is probably smaller than in any other book of the New Testament.

I. 347—355. *Supplementary details on the birthplace and the composition of leading MSS*

347. In all that we have hitherto said we have taken no account of the supposed locality in which MSS were written, except in certain definite cases. The reason is because we do not believe anything certain to be as yet known. Up to a certain point the bilingual MSS (Græco-Latin and Græco-Thebaic) tell their own tale: about no other important early MS is it as yet possible to make any geographical assertion with confidence. It is indeed usually taken for granted that the chief uncials of the New Testament were written at Alexandria. This floating impression appears to be founded on vague associations derived from two undoubted facts; (1) that the translations of the Old Testament which form the LXX were made at Alexandria, while the chief uncials of the New Testament agree in some prominent points of orthography and grammatical form (by no means in all) with the chief uncials of the LXX, the four oldest being moreover parts of the same manuscript Bibles, and (2) that A was at some unknown time, not necessarily earlier than the eleventh century, preserved at Alexandria, and is hence called the *Codex Alexandrinus*. The supposition cannot be pronounced incredible; but it is at present hardly more than a blind and on the whole improbable conjecture. An Alexandrian origin, much more an exclusively Alexandrian or Egyptian use, cannot be reasonably maintained for most of the unclassical orthographies and grammatical forms found in MSS of the New Testament, as we shall have to explain more at length in Part IV. The character of the substantive

texts affords only the most uncertain indications; for (1) there is no reason to suppose that more than a small fraction of the readings often called Alexandrian had any special connexion with Alexandria, and (2) the clearest phenomena of Versions of the fourth and fifth centuries shew how widely spread at that time were Greek MSS containing a large proportion of those readings which did really originate at Alexandria.

348. Possibly hereafter some of the external accompaniments of the text may be found to contain trustworthy evidence. At present we know of almost nothing to appeal to except such orthographies as are shown by their isolated distribution to be due to scribes, not to the autographs. This evidence at best points only to the home or school of the scribe himself, and cannot take account of migration on his part. Such as it is, it suggests that A and C were connected with Alexandria. Orthographies apparently Alexandrian occur also in א, but chiefly or wholly in words for which A or C have them likewise. On the other hand some Western or Latin influence is very clearly marked in the usual or occasional spelling of some proper names, such as Ισακ and Ιστραηλ[ειτης] or Ισδραηλ[ειτης]. In B the Alexandrian indications are to the best of our belief wholly wanting. Western indications are fainter than in א, but not absent. The superfluous euphonic τ is sometimes inserted in Ισραηλ-[ειτης] but only in Acts, apparently implying the presence of Western or Latin influence in the scribe of that manuscript of Acts which was copied by the scribe of B. The substitution of Χριστὸς Ἰησοῦς for Ἰησοῦς Χριστός in places where it is almost certainly not right is mainly confined to Western documents, and it is also in St Paul's Epistles a favourite individualism of B.

349. Again it is remarkable that the principal Latin system of divisions of the Acts, found in the *Codex Amiatinus* and, slightly modified, in other Vulgate MSS, is indicated by Greek numerals both in ℵ (with large irregular omissions) and in B, but is otherwise unknown in Greek MSS and literature. The numerals were apparently inserted in both MSS, certainly in ℵ, by very ancient scribes, though not by the writers of the text itself, B indeed having antecedently a wholly different set of numerals. The differences in detail are sufficient to shew that the two scribes followed different originals: the differences of both from the existing Latin arrangement are still greater, but too slight to allow any doubt as to identity of ultimate origin. The coincidence suggests a presumption that the early home, and therefore not improbably the birthplace, of both MSS was in the West.

350. The other systems of divisions marked in B and ℵ have not hitherto yielded any trustworthy indications; and, what is more surprising, the same must be said of the structure and contents of the MSS themselves. It might have been anticipated that in order to ascertain the regions in which they were written it would suffice to observe what books they do or do not include, and in what manner the books are arranged, account being taken of the Old as well as the New Testament. But the attempt is baffled by the scantiness of our information. Comparison with the few extant catalogues and other evidence of local use in the fourth century leads only to ambiguous results; and the difficulty of decision is increased by the wide differences of structure and arrangement between B and ℵ, and again between both and A.

351. Taking all kinds of indications together, we are inclined to surmise that B and ℵ were both written in the West, probably at Rome; that the ancestors of B were wholly Western (in the geographical, not the textual sense) up to a very early time indeed; and that the ancestors of ℵ were in great part Alexandrian, again in the geographical, not the textual sense. We do not forget such facts as the protracted unwillingness of the Roman church to accept the Epistle to the Hebrews, commended though it was by the large use made of it in the Epistle of Clement to the Corinthians: but the complex life of Christian Rome in the fourth century cannot safely be measured by its official usage; and it would be strange if the widely current History of Eusebius led no Roman readers to welcome the full Eusebian Canon, with the natural addition of the Apocalypse, a book always accepted in the West. The supposition here made would account for all ascertained facts and contradict none. Yet we are well aware that other suppositions may be possibly true; and we must repeat that the view which we have here ventured to put forward as best explaining the sum total of the phenomena is only a surmise, on which we build nothing.

352. The fundamental similarity of text throughout the whole of B, and again throughout the whole of ℵ with the exception of the Apocalypse, deserves special notice, because it is more probable that the exemplars from which they were taken contained each only a single book or group of books than that they were large enough to contain the whole series of books (see §§ 14, 301). Even among cursives it is not uncommon to find one or more groups of books written in a different age from the rest, with which they are bound up; so that a transcript

of the whole volume would really represent two different
exemplars (see § 46) : and for a different reason a similar
diversity of sources must often have been disguised by
transcription in the fourth and fifth centuries. The transition from small portable MSS of limited contents is
strikingly illustrated by a fortunate accident in the transcription of one of the four great comprehensive MSS
which are the earliest now extant. In the MS of the
Apocalypse from which C was taken some leaves had
been displaced, and the scribe of C did not discover the
displacement. It thus becomes easy to compute that
each leaf of the exemplar contained only about as much
as 10 lines of the text of the present edition ; so that
this one book must have made up nearly 120 small
leaves of parchment, and accordingly formed a volume
either to itself or without considerable additions. The
distinctive character of text exhibited by A in the Gospels,
by Δ in St Mark, and by B in the Pauline Epistles, as
also the orthography of B (Ιστρ.) peculiar to the Acts, are
instances of indications which equally shew the precariousness of assuming with respect to any one MS of the
New Testament that all the books in it were copied from
a single volume. In some cases, as we have suggested
above (§ 320) with reference to B in the Pauline Epistles,
the discrepant character of text in particular books or
groups of books was doubtless introduced not by the
immediate exemplar but by previous interlinear or marginal corrections made in its predecessor : but in most
cases the range of the corrections would be limited by
the contents of the accessory copy which furnished them ;
so that the cause of the discrepancy of text would be
ultimately the same. It is indeed quite uncertain to
what extent the whole New Testament was ever included

in a single volume in Ante-Nicene times. On the other
hand the average conditions to which different volumes
of the sacred writings would be exposed in the same
place were not likely to differ much, in so far as they
were likely to affect the text. It is therefore not surprising that we find great fundamental similarity of text
throughout MSS which probably derived different groups
of books from different exemplars, and that definite evidence of separate origins is sometimes present, sometimes
wanting.

353. A word may be added here respecting the different
'hands' of MSS. It sometimes happened that the original
scribe ('first hand') of a MS discovered that he had begun
to transcribe wrongly, and accordingly corrected himself
before going further : in such cases what he first wrote
may have been either a mere blunder or the unconsciously
remembered reading of another copy. After the completion of a MS it was often revised by a 'corrector' with a
view to the removal of clerical errors. The thoroughness
with which this laborious process was carried out must
however have varied to a singular extent : and moreover
the revision appears sometimes to have included the occasional introduction of readings from a different exemplar.
Changes made by a hand apparently contemporary with
the original hand may usually be set down to the 'corrector'. Additional changes might be made subsequently
at any date on account of observed difference of reading
from another MS simultaneously read or another current
text. Sometimes these changes were confined to a small
portion of text, or were sprinkled very thinly over the
whole, sometimes they were comparatively systematic :
but it is hardly ever safe to assume that a reading left unchanged is to be taken as ratified by the copy or text
from which neighbouring changes were derived. Since
corrections in previously written MSS, as distinguished
from corrections made in the process of transcription, are
not likely to be conjectures, they may be treated as virtually particles of other lost MSS at least as early as the
time of correction : the textual value of the lost MSS can
of course be ascertained only by successive examination

of their successive particles, and therefore often but imperfectly.

354. For some six centuries after it was written B appears to have undergone no changes in its text except from the hand of the 'corrector', the 'second hand'. Among his corrections of clerical errors are scattered some textual changes, clearly marked as such by the existence of very early authority for both readings : the readings which he thus introduces imply the use of a second exemplar, having a text less pure than that of the primary exemplar, but free from clear traces of Syrian influence. The occurrence of these definite diversities of text renders it unsafe to assume that all singular readings which he alters were individualisms of the first hand, though doubtless many of them had no other origin. The scale of alteration was however very limited : hardly any of the corrections affect more than two or three letters, except the insertions of rightly or wrongly omitted words. Some few of the early corrections perceptible in the MS appear to have been made by the original scribe himself ; and to his hand Tischendorf refers seven alternative readings placed in the margin of Matt. xiii 52 ; xiv 5 ; xvi 4 ; xxii 10 ; xxvii 4 ; Luke iii 1 (*bis*). In the tenth or eleventh century, according to Tischendorf's apparently well founded judgement, the faded characters of the fourth century were retraced in darker ink. The readings adopted for renewal were almost always those of the second hand ; and words or longer portions of text wrongly repeated by the original scribe were left untouched. There was no systematic attempt to correct the text itself, except as regards the orthography, which was for the most part assimilated to the common literary standard ; but Syrian readings were introduced here and there, though rarely, if ever, in cases where there would be more than a trifling difference in the space occupied by the old and the new readings respectively. We have passed over the readings of this third hand of B in the Appendix because they not only were inserted at a very late period, but exhibit no distinctive internal character. Confusion between the second and third hands of B has led to much error ; and it is only of late that the true history of the changes undergone by the MS has been fully understood.

355. The original writing of ℵ has escaped retracement, but it has been altered much at different times. The three principal hands alone need mention here. The 'cor-

rector' proper (א*) made use of an excellent exemplar, and the readings which he occasionally introduces take high rank as authorities. Those of another hand (א^b) of somewhat similar appearance but ill determined date (? Cent. VI) are likewise for the most part distinctly ancient, but include many of later origin. The much more numerous readings introduced by א^c (? Cent. VII) are for the most part Syrian; but scattered among them are readings handed down from a high antiquity: the exemplar employed by this writer had apparently some such mixed character as we find in X of the Gospels. These examples will suffice to illustrate the phenomena of correction generally. The manner in which it produces mixture of texts in transcripts from corrected MSS has been already explained by the example of D_2 and E_3 (§§ 335—339). In some instances, as often in A and C, an erasure preceding correction has completely obliterated the original writing: but, as the amount of space which it occupied can almost always be ascertained, a comparison of the lengths of the existing variants is usually sufficient to determine the reading with tolerable certainty.

CHAPTER IV. *SUBSTANTIAL INTEGRITY OF THE PUREST TRANSMITTED TEXT*

356—374

356. Having now described the nature of the evidence available for settling the text of the New Testament, and explained the modes of applying it which leave least room for error, it is right that we should give some answer to the reasonable enquiry whether there is good ground for confidence that the purest text transmitted by existing documents is strictly or at least substantially identical with the text of the autographs. This enquiry will however be best approached through another, which is closely connected with the subject of the preceding chapter; namely, whether there is or is not reason to

think that, notwithstanding the peculiar authority conferred on the best uncials by the clear results of Genealogical Evidence proper and of Internal Evidence of
Groups, the true reading is sometimes one that is attested
by inferior documents alone.   This antecedent enquiry
is complementary to a question discussed in another
place (§§ 265—283), how far Primary Greek MSS may
safely be trusted where accessory attestation is more or less
completely wanting.   From the nature of the case there
is no room for absolute and unqualified answers : but
we trust that the following considerations, taken along
with what has been said already, will meet all such
doubts as can be raised with a fair show of reason.

357—360. *Approximate non-existence of genuine readings unattested by any of the best Greek uncials*

357.   The vague but necessary term 'inferior documents' covers two classes of evidence which demand
attention on wholly different grounds; first, Greek uncials
which in external character, as in conventional designation, have no generic difference from the best Greek
uncials, and secondly, the earlier Versions and Fathers.
First then it may be asked,—Given the relative supremacy which we have been led to ascribe under normal
conditions to B and א in most books, and to some
extent to A and C in the Apocalypse, is there or is
there not good ground to expect that the true reading
should sometimes exist not in them but in less good or
in secondary Greek uncials?   There is no theoretical
improbability in the supposition here made.   This is
obviously true in cases where א and B are at variance, that
is, where the positive evidence afforded by the coinci-

dence of two extremely ancient independent lines is absent: for, where they differ from each other, the true reading may differ from that of either, and may have survived in an independent line to a somewhat later time, and so have found its way into other uncials. But the theoretical possibility holds good likewise where B and ℵ agree, though reduced within much narrower limits. Near as the divergence of the respective ancestries of B and ℵ must have been to the autographs, there must have been an appreciable interval of transcription (§§ 241, 301 ff.); and it is *a priori* conceivable that relics of a line of transmission starting from a yet earlier point should find their way into one or another uncial of the fifth or following centuries, and further that such relics should include genuine readings which disappeared in the writing of an intermediate ancestor of B and ℵ.

358. When however the readings of secondary or even primary uncials in opposition to B and ℵ are consecutively examined, they present no such phenomena, whether of accessory attestation or of internal character, as might have been expected were the supposition true. The singular readings with rare and unimportant exceptions have all the appearance of being individualisms. The scanty subsingular readings having some attestation by early Versions or Fathers will be noticed under the next head. The readings attested by two or more of these uncials, which make up by far the greater part of the whole number of these readings, can be recognised at once as distinctively Syrian or Alexandrian or Western, or as obvious modifications of extant readings having one or other such attestation and character. Among all the endless varieties of mixture there is a striking sameness in the elements mixed. The imme-

diate sources of all our uncials not purely Syrian, except B and א, were evidently for the most part the popular eclectic texts of about the fourth century, Syrian or other, and not the various earlier and simpler Ante-Nicene texts from which the eclectic texts were compounded, and which the eclectic texts soon drove out of currency. Lastly, the verdict of internal evidence is almost always unfavourable where it is not neutral.

359. Passing backwards to Ante-Nicene times, we have to deal with the second question,—May we or may we not reasonably expect to find true readings in very limited but very ancient groups of documents in opposition to B and א? There are many Pre-Syrian readings the antiquity of which is vouched for by Versions or Fathers, but which nevertheless are supported by no Greek MS but a stray uncial or two, or only by a few cursives, (such cursives naturally as are otherwise known to contain ancient elements of text,) or even in many cases by no Greek MS at all. The attestation of these readings, or at least of the second and third classes of them, resembles the accessory attestation of the subsingular readings of B, which we have already learned to judge on the whole favourably: it resembles also the accessory attestation of the subsingular readings of א, which we have rarely found to have the stamp of genuineness. All such readings shew how plentiful a crop of variation existed in the early centuries and was swept out of sight by the eclectic texts.

360. Readings thus attested by Versions and Fathers almost without support from existing Greek MSS have as yet received from critics no attention proportionate to their historical interest. The accident of their neglect by the Greek editors of the fourth century,

and their consequent approximate or complete extinction
in Greek copies of the New Testament, can have no
bearing on the character of their pedigree in the earlier
ages. It is therefore but right to enquire whether the
accidental preservation of B and ℵ does or does not give
their texts an undeserved preeminence, which they would
have lost had continuous uncials existed containing such
texts as these stray readings represent. A scrutiny of
the readings themselves dispels the suspicion. We have
for our own part been quite prepared to find among
these relics of ancient variation many readings highly
commended by Internal Evidence : but experience has
not justified any such anticipation. A very few readings
absent from all existing Greek MSS we have thought it
safest to retain as alternative readings ; for instance in
Matt. iv 17 Ἤγγικεν (for Μετανοεῖτε, ἤγγικεν γάρ), attested
by syr.vt Orig(as represented by schol Procop.*Es.*144
Hier.*Es.*128) Vict.ant.*Mc.*273(expressly) ; and in 1 John
iv 3 λύει (for μὴ ὁμολογεῖ), attested by 'ancient copies'
mentioned by Socrates, and also by lat.vg Iren.lat(with
context) Orig.*Mt.*lat;(?schol) Tert Lucif Aug Fulg. There
are a few others supported by yet slighter authority,
which have an appearance of intrinsic probability in places
where the better attested readings seem to be specially
difficult ; and these we have not attempted to separate
from purely conjectural readings. Readings belonging
to either of these classes are however in the highest
degree exceptional, and do not disturb the general impression produced by examination of the whole number.
Most indeed of the readings of great antiquity which
stand in no extant Greek uncial are seen at a glance to
be ordinary Western readings ; so that doubtless the
reason why those of them which occur in the Gospels

and Acts are deprived of the support of D is simply the comparative purity of its early Western text. While then it cannot be confidently affirmed that no relics of lines of transmission independent of the ancestries of B and ℵ now exist in one or more secondary documents of one kind or another (compare § 357), the utmost number of such relics is too petty, even with the inclusion of doubtful instances, to affect appreciably the conclusions already obtained. It is of course only with such evidence as actually exists that the primary uncials can be brought into comparison: but the fullest comparison does but increase the conviction that their preeminent relative purity is likewise approximately absolute, a true approximate reproduction of the text of the autographs, not an accidental and deceptive result of the loss of better Greek MSS.

361—370. *Approximate sufficiency of existing documents for the recovery of the genuine text, notwithstanding the existence of some primitive corruptions*

361. The way has now been cleared for the final question,—Is it or is it not reasonable to expect that in any considerable number of cases the true reading has now perished? Have we a right to assume that the true reading always exists somewhere among existing documents? The question is often foreclosed on one or both of two grounds which in our judgement are quite irrelevant. First, some think it incredible that any true words of Scripture should have perished. In reply it is a sufficient *argumentum ad hominem* to point to the existence of various readings, forming part of various texts accepted for long ages, and the frequent difficulty of

deciding between them, even though we say nothing of difficulties of interpretation: on any view many important churches for long ages have had only an approximately pure New Testament, so that we have no right to treat it as antecedently incredible that only an approximately pure New Testament should be attainable now, or even in all future time.   For ourselves we dare not introduce considerations which could not reasonably be applied to other ancient texts, supposing them to have documentary attestation of equal amount, variety, and antiquity. Secondly, the folly and frivolity of once popular conjectures have led to a wholesome reaction against looking beyond documentary tradition.   Some of them are attempts to deal textually with what are really difficulties of interpretation only; the authors of others, though they propose remedies which cannot possibly avail, are not thereby shown to have been wrong in the supposition that remedies were needed; and a few have been perhaps too quickly forgotten.   Though it cannot be said that recent attempts in Holland to revive conjectural criticism for the New Testament have shown much felicity of suggestion, they cannot be justly condemned on the ground of principle.   The caution imposed by the numerous failures of the earlier critics has on the whole worked well; but it has no bearing on the question at issue.

362.   On the other hand a strong presumption in favour of the immunity of the text of the New Testament from errors antecedent to existing documents is afforded by the facts mentioned under the last head (§§ 357—360). If among the very ancient evidence now extant, collected from various quarters, so little can be found that approves itself as true in opposition both to B and ℵ,

there is good reason at the outset to doubt whether **any**
better readings have perished with the multitudes of
documents that have been lost.

363.   The question however needs more careful consideration on account of the apparent ease and simplicity
with which many ancient texts are edited, which might be
thought, on a hasty view, to imply that the New Testament cannot be restored with equal certainty.   But this
ease and simplicity is in fact the mark of evidence too
scanty to be tested; whereas in the variety and fullness
of the evidence on which it rests the text of the New
Testament stands absolutely and unapproachably alone
among prose writings.   For all other works of antiquity,
the Old Testament (in translations) and some of the
Latin poets excepted, MSS earlier than the ninth or
even tenth century are of extreme rarity.   Many are
preserved to us in a single MS or hardly more; and
so there is little chance of detecting corruption wherever
the sense is good.   Those only which are extant in
many copies of different ages present so much as a
distant analogy with the New Testament: and, if through
the multitude of various readings, and the consequent
diversities of printed editions, they lose the fallacious
uniformity of text which is the usual result of extreme
paucity of documents, there is always a nearer approximation to perfect restoration.   Doubtful points are out
of sight even in critical editions of classical authors
merely because in ordinary literature it is seldom worth
while to trouble the clearness of a page.   The one
disadvantage on the side of the New Testament, the
early mixture of independent lines of transmission, is
more than neutralised, as soon as it is distinctly perceived, by the antiquity and variety of the evidence;

and the expression of doubt wherever doubt is really felt is owing to the paramount necessity for fidelity as to the exact words of Scripture.

364. But it will be seen from the preceding pages that we possess evidence much more precisely certified than by the simple and general titles of antiquity, excellence, and variety. Two or three of our best documents might have been lost, and yet those titles might still be justly claimed; while without those documents both the history of the text and its application would be so imperfectly understood that the results in that case would be both different and more uncertain. It is the minute study of the whole evidence in relation to the best documents which brings out their absolute and not merely their relative excellence. The external evidence is therefore such that on the one hand perfect purity is not *a priori* improbable, and a singularly high degree of purity is highly probable; and yet the conditions are not such—it is difficult to see how they could ever be such—as to exclude the possibility of textual errors.

365. These general probabilities however are but preparatory to the definite question,—Are there as a matter of fact places in which we are constrained by overwhelming evidence to recognise the existence of textual error in all extant documents? To this question we have no hesitation in replying in the affirmative. For instance in 2 Pet. iii 10 אBK₂P₂ with three of the best cursives and two Versions read στοιχεῖα δὲ καυσούμενα λυθήσεται καὶ γῆ καὶ τὰ ἐν αὐτῇ ἔργα εὑρεθήσεται. Before εὑρεθήσεται two other Versions insert a negative. C replaces εὑρεθήσεται by ἀφανισθήσονται, for which we find κατακαήσεται in AL₂ and most cursives and

several Versions and Fathers; while one representative of the Old Latin omits it altogether. External evidence is here strongly favourable to εὑρεθήσεται, as must be felt even by those who do not see any special significance in the concordance of ℵ and B. Internal evidence of transcription is absolutely certain on the same side, for εὑρεθήσεται fully accounts for all four other readings, two of them being conjectural substitutes, two less audacious manipulations; while no other reading will account for the rest. Yet it is hardly less certain by intrinsic probability that εὑρεθήσεται cannot be right: in other words, it is the most original of recorded readings, the parent of the rest, and yet itself corrupt. Conditions of reading essentially the same, in a less striking form, occur here and there in other places.

366. But there is no adequate justification for assuming that primitive corruption must be confined to passages where it was obvious enough to catch the eye of ancient scribes, and would naturally thus lead to variation. Especially where the grammar runs with deceptive smoothness, and a wrong construction yields a sense plausible enough to cause no misgivings to an ordinary reader, there is nothing surprising if the kind of scrutiny required for deliberate criticism detects impossible readings accepted without suspicion by all transcribers. On the various kinds of primitive errors, and the nature of the evidence on which in each case their existence can be affirmed, we have said enough in the Second Part (§§ 85—92).

367. Little is gained by speculating as to the precise point at which such corruptions came in. They may be due to the original writer, or to his amanuensis if he wrote from dictation, or they may be due to one of the

earliest transcribers. Except from extraneous sources, which here have no existence, it is never possible to know how many transcriptions intervened between the autograph and the latest common ancestor of all the elements in all extant documents ; and a corruption affecting them all may evidently have originated at any link of that initial chain. Moreover the line of demarcation between primitive and other corruptions is less easy to draw than might be supposed. As was intimated above (§ 360), account has to be taken of a few places in which what appears to be the true reading is found exclusively in one or two secondary or hardly even secondary documents ; perhaps transmitted from the autograph, and preserved by some rare accident of mixture notwithstanding the otherwise complete extinction of the line of transmission by which it had been conveyed, perhaps due only to a casual and unconscious emendation of an erroneous current reading. But these gradations of primitiveness in corruption have no practical moment. The only fact that really concerns us is that certain places have to be recognised and marked as insecure.

368. The number of such places which we have been able to recognise with sufficient confidence to justify the definite expression of doubt is not great. If we exclude books in which the documentary attestation of text is manifestly incomplete, as the Apocalypse, some of the Catholic Epistles, and the latter part of Hebrews, it is relatively extremely small. There may be and probably are other places containing corruption which we have failed to discover : but judging by analogy we should expect the differences to be of no real interest. We cannot too strongly express our disbelief in the existence of undetected interpolations of any moment. This

is of course, strictly speaking, a speculative opinion, not a result of criticism. But we venture to think that the processes of criticism which it has been our duty to consider and work out have given us some qualifications for forming an opinion as to the probabilities of the matter. There are, it ought to be said, a few passages of St Matthew's Gospel (xii 40 ; [xiii 35 ;] xxiii 35 ; xxvii 9) in which it is difficult to believe that all the words as they stand have apostolic authority : the second part of xxvii 49 would have to be added to the list, if sufficient reasons should be found for accepting the possible but doubtful view that it is not a Non-Western interpolation, but an original reading omitted without authority by the Western text. But the question which these passages raise is rather literary than textual, for we see no reason to doubt that, as regards the extant form or edition of the first Gospel, their text as it stood in the autograph has been exactly preserved.

369. It will not be out of place to add here a distinct expression of our belief that even among the numerous unquestionably spurious readings of the New Testament there are no signs of deliberate falsification of the text for dogmatic purposes. The licence of paraphrase occasionally assumes the appearance of wilful corruption, where scribes allowed themselves to change language which they thought capable of dangerous misconstruction ; or attempted to correct apparent errors which they doubtless assumed to be due to previous transcription ; or embodied in explicit words a meaning which they supposed to be implied. But readings answering to this description cannot be judged rightly without taking into account the general characteristics of other readings exhibited by the same or allied docu-

ments. The comparison leaves little room for doubt
that they merely belong to an extreme type of paraphrastic alteration, and are not essentially different from
readings which betray an equally lax conception of
transcription, and yet are transparently guiltless of any
fraudulent intention. In a word, they bear witness to
rashness, not to bad faith.

370. It is true that dogmatic preferences to a great
extent determined theologians, and probably scribes, in
their choice between rival readings already in existence :
scientific criticism was virtually unknown, and in its
absence the temptation was strong to believe and assert
that a reading used by theological opponents had also
been invented by them. Accusations of wilful tampering
with the text are accordingly not unfrequent in Christian
antiquity : but, with a single exception, wherever they
can be verified they prove to be groundless, being in
fact hasty and unjust inferences from mere diversities of
inherited text. The one known exception is in the case
of Marcion's dogmatic mutilation of the books accepted
by him : and this was, strictly speaking, an adaptation for the use of his followers ; nor had it apparently
any influence outside the sect. Other readings of his,
which he was equally accused of introducing, belonged
manifestly to the texts of the copies which came into his
hands, and had no exceptional character or origin. The
evidence which has recently come to light as to his disciple Tatian's Diatessaron has shown that Tatian habitually abridged the language of the passages which he
combined; so that the very few known omissions which
might be referred to a dogmatic purpose can as easily
receive another explanation. The absence of perceptible
fraud in the origination of any of the various readings

now extant may, we believe, be maintained with equal confidence for the text antecedent to the earliest extant variations, in other words, for the purest transmitted text, though here internal evidence is the only available criterion; and, as we have intimated above, any undetected discrepancies from the autographs which it may contain, due to other or ordinary causes, may safely on the same evidence be treated as insignificant. The books of the New Testament as preserved in extant documents assuredly speak to us in every important respect in language identical with that in which they spoke to those for whom they were originally written.

C. 371—374. *Conditions of further improvement of the text*

371. The text of this edition of course makes no pretension to be more than an approximation to the purest text that might be formed from existing materials. Much, we doubt not, remains to be done for the perfecting of the results obtained thus far. Even in respect of the discovery of new documents, and fuller acquaintance with the contents of some that have in a manner been long known, useful contributions to the better understanding of obscure variations may fairly be expected. It is difficult to relinquish the hope that even yet Lagarde may be able to accomplish at least a part of his long projected edition of the testimonies of the oriental versions, so that the New Testament may be allowed to enjoy some considerable fruits of his rare gifts and acquirements : a complete and critically sifted exhibition of the evidence of the Egyptian versions would be

a specially acceptable boon. But it would be an illusion to anticipate important changes of text from any acquisition of new evidence. Greater possibilities of improvement lie in a more exact study of the relations between the documents that we already possess. The effect of future criticism, as of future discovery, we suspect, will not be to import many fresh readings; but there is reason to hope that the doubts between alternative readings will be greatly reduced.

372. We must not hesitate however to express the conviction that no trustworthy improvement can be effected except in accordance with the leading principles of method which we have endeavoured to explain, and on the basis of the primary applications of them which have been here made to the interpretation of the documentary phenomena of the New Testament. It is impossible to entertain an equal degree of confidence in the numerous decisions which we have felt ourselves justified in making in comparatively obscure or difficult variations ; because in these cases a greater liability to error was involved in the proportionally larger part inevitably played by individual personal judgements. Even where a text is certain enough to make the exhibition of alternative readings superfluous, gradation of certainty is a necessary consequence of the manifold gradations of evidence. But, while we dare not implicitly trust our own judgement in details, the principles of criticism here followed rest on an incomparably broader foundation, and in an overwhelming proportion of cases their application is free from difficulty. As was said at the outset, the best textual criticism is that which takes account of every class of textual facts, and assigns to the subordinate method corresponding to each class of textual

facts its proper use and rank. All that has been said in the intervening pages has been an attempt to translate into language the experience which we have gradually gained in endeavouring to fulfil that aim.

373. There is no royal road to the ascertainment of the true texts of ancient writings. Investigation of the history and character of documentary ancestries would indeed be out of place for the text of the New Testament if the documentary evidence were so hopelessly chaotic that no difference of authority could carry much weight as between readings all having some clearly ancient attestation. The consequent necessity of always judging chiefly by Internal Evidence of Readings would undeniably save much labour. But it would introduce a corresponding amount of latent uncertainty. The summary decisions inspired by an unhesitating instinct as to what an author must needs have written, or dictated by the supposed authority of 'canons of criticism' as to what transcribers must needs have introduced, are in reality in a large proportion of cases attempts to dispense with the solution of problems that depend on genealogical data. Nor would there be a material increase of security by the assignment of some substantial weight to documentary evidence, so long as it were found or thought necessary to deal with each passage separately, and to estimate the balance of documentary evidence by some modification of numerical authority, without regard either to genealogical affinities as governing the distribution of attestation or to the standard of purity which this or that document or group of documents habitually attains. Under all these circumstances the absence or neglect of the most essential kinds of textual evidence would leave a real precariousness of text which could be avoided only

by an enormously increased exhibition of alternative readings.

374. For scepticism as to the possibility of obtaining a trustworthy genealogical interpretation of documentary phenomena in the New Testament there is, we are persuaded, no justification either in antecedent probability or in experience; and, if this be so, the range of uncertainty is brought at once within narrow limits. When it is clearly understood that coincidence of reading infallibly implies identity of ancestry wherever accidental coincidence is out of the question, all documents assume their proper character as sources of historical evidence, first respecting the antecedent lines of textual transmission, and then respecting the relation of each reading to these antecedent texts. Nearly a century and a half ago the more important ancient texts were clearly recognised, and the great subsequent accession of materials has but added certainty to this first generalisation, while it has opened the way for further generalisations of the same kind. Again, when it is seen that the variations in which decision is free from difficulty supply a trustworthy basis for ascertaining the prevalent character of documents and groups of documents, and thus for estimating rightly the value of their testimony in other places, little room is left for difference of estimate. Whatever may be the ambiguity of the whole evidence in particular passages, the general course of future criticism must be shaped by the happy circumstance that the fourth century has bequeathed to us two MSS of which even the less incorrupt must have been of exceptional purity among its own contemporaries, and which rise into greater preeminence of character the better the early history of the text becomes known.

PART IV

NATURE AND DETAILS OF THIS EDITION

A. 375—377. *Aim and limitations of this edition*

375. The common purpose of all critical editions of ancient books, to present their text in comparative purity, is subject to various subordinate modifications. Our own aim, like that of Tischendorf and Tregelles, has been to obtain at once the closest possible approximation to the apostolic text itself. The facts of textual history already recounted, as testified by versions and patristic quotations, shew that it is no longer possible to speak of "the text of the fourth century", since most of the important variations were in existence before the middle of the fourth century, and many can be traced back to the second century. Nor again, in dealing with so various and complex a body of documentary attestation, is there any real advantage in attempting, with Lachmann, to allow the distributions of a very small number of the most ancient existing documents to construct for themselves a provisional text by the application of uniform rules, and in deferring to a separate and later process the use of critical judgement upon readings. What is thus gained in facility of execution is lost in insecurity of result: and while we have been led to a much slower and more complex mode of procedure by the need of obtaining impersonal and, if the word may be forgiven,

inductive criteria of texts, documents, and readings, we
have at the same time found it alike undesirable and impossible to take any intermediate text, rather than that
of the autographs themselves, as the pattern to be reproduced with the utmost exactness which the evidence
permits.

376. Two qualifications of this primary aim have
however been imposed upon us, the one by the imperfection of the evidence, the other by the nature of the
edition. Numerous variations occur in which the evidence has not appeared to us decisive in favour of one
reading against the other or the others ; and accordingly
we have felt bound to sacrifice the simplicity of a single
text to the duty of giving expression to all definite doubt.
In this respect we have followed Griesbach, Lachmann,
and Tregelles : and it is a satisfaction to observe that
Tischendorf's latest edition, by a few scattered brackets
in the text and occasional expressions of hesitation in
the notes, shewed signs of a willingness to allow the
present impossibility of arriving every where at uniformly
certain conclusions. Secondly, it did not on the whole
seem expedient, in a manual text of the New Testament
intended for popular use, to give admission to any readings unattested by documentary evidence, or to give the
place of honour to any readings which receive no direct
support from primary documents. Since then the insertion of any modern conjectures would have been
incompatible with our purpose, we have been content
to affix a special mark to places where doubts were
felt as to the genuineness of the transmitted readings,
reserving all further suggestions for the Appendix : and
again, by an obvious extension of the same principle,
the very few and unimportant readings which have both

21

an inferior attestation and some specially strong internal probability have not been elevated above a secondary place, but treated as ordinary alternative readings. Thus the text of this edition, in that larger sense of the word 'text' which includes the margin, rests exclusively on direct ancient authority, and its primary text rests exclusively on direct ancient authority of the highest kind.

377. Alternative readings are given wherever we do not believe the text to be certain, if the doubt affects only the choice between variations found in existing documents. It is impossible to decide that any probable variation, verbal or real, is too trivial for notice; while it would be improper to admit any variation to a place among alternative readings except on the ground of its probability. Nothing therefore is retained among alternatives which in our judgement, or on final consideration in the judgement of one of us, has no reasonable chance of being right. But no attempt is made to indicate different shades of probability beyond the assignment to the principal and the secondary places respectively: and all probable variations not in some sense orthographical are given alike, without regard to their relative importance. Nor would it be strictly true to say that the secondary or alternative readings are always less probable than the rival primary readings; for sometimes the probabilities have appeared equal or incommensurable, or the estimates which we have severally formed have not been identical. In these cases (compare § 21) precedence has been given to documentary authority as against internal evidence, and also on the whole, though not without many exceptions, to great numerical preponderance of primary documentary authority as against high but narrowly limited attestation.

B. 378—392. *Textual notation*

378. The notation employed for expressing these diversities of probability or authority will need a little explanation in detail. We have been anxious to avoid excessive refinement and complexity of notation: but, as variations or readings of which we felt bound to take notice are of three classes, which must on no account be confounded, we have been obliged to use corresponding means of distinction. Moreover every various reading belonging to any of these classes must by the nature of the case be either an *omission* of a word or words which stand in the rival text, or an *insertion* of a word or words absent from the rival text, or a *substitution* of a word or words for another word or other words employed in the rival text, or of an order of words for another order found in the rival text; and clearness requires that each of these three forms of variation should as a rule have its own mode of expression.

379. The first class consists of variations giving rise to alternative readings in the proper sense; that is, variations in which both readings have some good ancient authority, and each has a reasonable probability of being the true reading of the autograph. To these the fundamental and simplest notation belongs. A secondary reading consisting in the omission of words retained in the primary reading is marked by simple brackets [ ] in the text, enclosing the omitted word or words. A secondary reading consisting in the insertion of a word or words omitted in the primary reading is printed in the margin without any accompanying marks, the place of insertion being indicated by the symbol ᵀ in the text.

A secondary reading consisting in the substitution of other words for the words of the primary reading is printed in the margin without any accompanying marks, the words of the primary reading being enclosed between the symbols ⌐ ⌐ in the text. Where there are two or more secondary readings, they are separated by *v.* in the margin ; unless they differ from each other merely by the omission or addition of words, in which case they are distinguished from each other by brackets in the margin, enclosing part or the whole of the longer reading. Occasionally one of two secondary readings differs from the primary reading by omission only, so that it can be expressed by simple brackets in the text, while the other stands as a substitution in the margin. Changes of punctuation have sometimes rendered it necessary to express a possible omission by a marginal reading rather than by brackets (Luke x 41, 42; John iii 31, 32 ; Rom. iii 12). Changes of accent have sometimes been likewise allowed to affect the form of alternative readings ; but only when this could be done without inconvenience. A few alternative readings and punctuations are examined in the Appendix : they are indicated by *Ap.* attached to the marginal readings. Where there is likely to be any confusion of marginal readings answering to different but closely adjoining places in the text, they are divided by a short vertical line.

380. The second class of notation is required for places in which there is some reason to suspect corruption in the transmitted text, if there is no variation, or in all the transmitted texts, if there is more than one reading (§§ 365—368). Under this head it has been found convenient to include a few places in which the reading

that appears to be genuine is not absolutely unattested, but has only insignificant authority (§§ 360, 367). Such suspicion of primitive corruption is universally indicated by an *obelus* (†) in the margin or small *obeli* (††) in the text, and further explained by a note in the Appendix. The typical notation consists of *Ap.*† in the margin, the extreme limits of the doubtful words in the text being marked by ⌐ ¬. In a single instance (Apoc. xiii 16) the reading suspected to be genuine has been prefixed to *Ap.*† on account of the peculiar nature of the evidence. We have not however thought it necessary to banish to the Appendix, or even the margin, a few unquestionably genuine readings which are shown by documentary and transcriptional evidence to have been in all probability successful ancient emendations made in the process of transcription, and not to have been transmitted continuously from the autograph (§ 88). Such true readings, being at once conjectural and traditional, have been placed in the text between small *obeli* (††), the best attested reading being however retained in the margin with *Ap.* added, and an account of the evidence being given in the Appendix.

381. Both the preceding classes of notation refer exclusively to places in which in our opinion there is substantial ground for doubting which of two or more extant readings is genuine, or in which no extant reading —in a few cases no adequately attested extant reading— can be confidently accepted as genuine. The third class of notation on the other hand deals exclusively with readings which we believe to be certainly foreign to the original text of the New Testament in the strictest sense, and therefore to have no title to rank as alternative

readings, but which have in various degrees sufficient interest to deserve some sort of notice.

382. For ordinary readings of this kind the Appendix is the fitting repository. In the Gospels and Acts however there are a considerable number of readings that have no strict claim to a place except in the Appendix, and yet plead strongly for a more immediate association with the true text. To have allowed them to be confounded with true alternative readings would have practically been a deliberate adulteration of the New Testament : but we have thought that on the whole historical truth would be best served by allowing them some kind of accessory recognition, and thus we have been forced to adopt additional modes of notation with peculiar symbols. None can feel more strongly than ourselves that it might at first sight appear the duty of faithful critics to remove completely from the text any words or passages which they believe not to have originally formed part of the work in which they occur. But there are circumstances connected with the text of the New Testament which have withheld us from adopting this obvious mode of proceeding.

383. The first difficulty arises from the absence of any sure criterion for distinguishing Western omissions due to incorrupt transmission, that is, Western non-interpolations, from Western omissions proper, that is, due only to capricious simplification (§ 240): whoever honestly makes the attempt will find his own judgement vacillate from time to time. On the whole it has seemed best that nothing should at present be omitted from the text itself on Western authority exclusively. Those Western omissions therefore which we can confidently accept as, properly speaking, non-interpolations are

marked by double brackets ⟦ ⟧ ; while those about which there is a reasonable doubt are marked by simple brackets [ ], that is, they are not distinguished from ordinary cases of ambiguous evidence. Western omissions evidently arbitrary are of course neglected. The omission of the singular addition to Matt. xxvii 49 has been treated as a Western non-interpolation, as its early attestation was Western, though its adoption by the Syrian text has given it a wide range of apparent documentary authority. The last three chapters of St Luke's Gospel (xxii 19 f. ; xxiv 3, 6, 12, 36, 40, 51, 52) supply all the other examples.

384. The second consideration which has led to the adoption of an accessory notation for certain noteworthy rejected readings is of a different kind. It has been already pointed out (§§ 173, 239) that some of the early Western interpolations must have been introduced at a period when various forms of evangelic tradition, written or oral, were still current. There is accordingly no improbability in the supposition that early interpolations have sometimes preserved a record of words or facts not otherwise known to us. From a literary point of view such fragmentary and, as it were, casual records are entirely extraneous to the Gospels, considered as individual writings of individual authors. From a historical, and, it may be added, from a theological point of view their authority, by its very nature variable and indefinite, must always be inferior to that of the true texts of the known and canonical books ; but as embodiments of ancient tradition they have a secondary value of their own which, in some cases at least, would render their unqualified exclusion from the Bible a serious loss. A rule that would for instance banish altogether from the printed

Gospels such a sentence as the first part of Luke xxiii 34 condemns itself, though the concurrence of the best texts, Latin and Egyptian as well as Greek, shews the sentence to be a later insertion. Yet single sayings or details cannot be effectually preserved for use except as parts of a continuous text : and there is no serious violation of the integrity of the proper evangelic texts in allowing them to yield a lodgement to these stray relics surviving from the apostolic or subapostolic age, provided that the accessory character of the insertions is clearly marked. Double brackets ⟦ ⟧ have therefore been adopted not only for the eight interpolations omitted by Western documents and by no other extant Pre-Syrian evidence, but also for five interpolations omitted on authority other than Western, where the omitted words appeared to be derived from an external written or unwritten source, and had likewise exceptional claims to retention in the body of the text (Matt. xvi 2 f.; Luke xxii 43 f. ; xxiii 34), or as separate portions of it (Mark xvi 9—20; John vii 53—viii 11).

385.   In addition to the specially important interpolations thus printed in the same type as the true text but with double brackets, there are many Western additions and substitutions which stand on a somewhat different footing from ordinary rejected readings ; not to speak of the very few which, being possibly genuine, there was no need to separate from ordinary alternative readings. It was not so easy to decide whether any notice should be taken of any others. The influence of extraneous records or traditions of one kind or another is clearly perceptible in some cases, and its presence may with more or less probability be suspected in others. On the other hand the great mass of these readings can have no other source

than paraphrastic or assimilative impulses of an ordinary kind. On the whole it seemed advisable to place in the margin between peculiar marks ⊣ ⊢ a certain number of Western interpolations and substitutions containing some apparently fresh or distinctive matter, such as might probably or possibly come from an extraneous source or which is otherwise of more than average interest, but having no sufficient intrinsic claim to any form of incorporation with the New Testament. We wish it accordingly to be distinctly understood that readings so marked are in our judgement outside the pale of probability as regards the original texts, and that it is only necessities of space which compel us unwillingly to intermix them with true alternative readings. Except in so far as they are all Western, they form an indefinite class, connected on the one side by intermediate examples (as Luke ix 54f.; xxiv 42) with the doubly bracketed readings, and on the other including readings which might with equal propriety have been noticed only in the Appendix (see § 386), or even passed over altogether. From the nature of the case the line was hard to draw, and perhaps some inconsistencies may be found, too much, rather than too little, having doubtless been here and there included; but for the present a provisional course has much to recommend it. Ultimately the readings enclosed within ⊣ ⊢ may probably be omitted with advantage. The Epistles and Apocalypse contain no Western readings which have any distinct title to be so marked. The paraphrastic change to which such books are liable differs much from the variation in the record of facts and sayings which easily invades books historical in form, more especially if other somewhat similar writings or traditions are current by their side.

386. There remain, lastly, a considerable number of readings which had no sufficient claim to stand on the Greek page, but which for one reason or another are interesting enough to deserve mention. They are accordingly noticed in the Appendix, as well as the other readings having some peculiar notation. It did not appear necessary to define by marks their precise place in the text: but the line to which each belongs is indicated in the margin by *Ap.* unaccompanied by any other word or symbol. This class of rejected readings, which includes many Western readings along with many others of various origin, is of course, like the preceding, limited only by selection, and might without impropriety have been either enlarged or diminished.

387. The examination of individual readings in detail is reserved for the Appendix. In a few cases however a short explanation of the course adopted seems to be required here. First in importance is the very early supplement by which the mutilated or unfinished close of St Mark's Gospel was completed. This remarkable passage on the one hand may be classed among the interpolations mentioned at the end of § 384 as deserving of preservation for their own sake in spite of their omission by Non-Western documents. On the other it is placed on a peculiar footing by the existence of a second ancient supplement, preserved in five languages, sometimes appearing as a substitute, sometimes as a duplicate. This less known alternative supplement, which is very short, contains no distinctive matter, and was doubtless composed merely to round off the abrupt ending of the Gospel as it stood with ἐφοβοῦντο γάρ for its last words. In style it is unlike the ordinary narratives of the Evangelists, but comparable to the four introductory

verses of St Luke's Gospel. The current supplement (xvi 9–20) was evidently an independently written succinct narrative beginning with the Resurrection and ending with the Ascension, probably forming part of some lost evangelic record, and appropriated entire, as supplying at once a needed close to St Mark's words and a striking addition to the history, although the first line started from the same point as the beginning of the sixteenth chapter. The two supplements are thus of very unequal interest; but as independent attempts to fill up a gap they stand on equal terms, and may easily be of equal antiquity as regards introduction into copies of St Mark's Gospel; so that we have felt bound to print them both within ⟦ ⟧ in the same type. Moreover, as we cannot believe that, whatever may be the cause of the present abrupt termination of the Gospel at v. 8, it was intended by the Evangelist to end at this point, we have judged it right to mark the presumed defect by asterisks, and to suggest the probability that not the book and paragraph only but also the last sentence is incomplete.

388. The Section on the Woman taken in Adultery (John vii 53–viii 11) likewise required an exceptional treatment. No interpolation is more clearly Western, though it is not Western of the earliest type. Not only is it passed over in silence in every Greek commentary of which we have any knowledge, down to that of Theophylact inclusive (Cent. xi–xii); but with the exception of a reference in the Apostolic Constitutions (? Cent. iv), and a statement by an obscure Nicon (Cent. x or later) that it was expunged by the Armenians, not the slightest allusion to it has yet been discovered in the whole of Greek theology before the twelfth century. The

earliest Greek MSS containing it, except the Western *Codex Bezae*, are of the eighth century. It is absent from the better MSS of all the Oriental versions except the Æthiopic, and apparently from the earliest form of the Old Latin. In the West it was well known in the fourth century, and doubtless long before. It has no right to a place in the text of the Four Gospels: yet it is evidently from an ancient source, and it could not now without serious loss be entirely banished from the New Testament. No accompanying marks would prevent it from fatally interrupting the course of St John's Gospel if it were retained in the text. As it forms an independent narrative, it seems to stand best alone at the end of the Gospels with double brackets to shew its inferior authority, and a marginal reference within ⊣ ⊢ at John vii 52. As there is no evidence for its existence in ancient times except in Western texts, we have printed it as nearly as possible in accordance with Western documents, using the text of D as the primary authority, but taking account likewise of the Latin evidence and of such later Greek MSS as appear to have preserved some readings of cognate origin. The text thus obtained is perhaps not pure, but it is at least purer than any which can be formed on a basis supplied chiefly by the MSS of the Greek East.

389.   The short Section on the Man working on the Sabbath bears a curious analogy to the preceding, and is not unlikely to come from the same source. As however it is at present known only from the *Codex Bezae*, in which it replaces Luke vi 5, transposed to the end of the next incident, we have with some hesitation relegated it to the Appendix.

390.   The double interpolation in John v 3, 4 has been for other reasons consigned to the same receptacle.

Both its elements, the clause ἐκδεχομένων τὴν τῶν ὑδάτων κίνησιν and the scholium or explanatory note respecting the angel, are unquestionably very ancient : but no good Greek document contains both, while each of them separately is condemned by decisive evidence. In internal character it bears little resemblance to any of the readings which have been allowed to stand in the margin between the symbols ⊣ ⊢; and it has no claim to any kind of association with the true text.

391. In some of the best documents a modified form of St John's statement (xix 34) about the piercing of our Lord's side is inserted in St Matthew's text after xxvii 49, although our Lord's death follows in the next verse. If the words are an interpolation, as seems on the whole most probable, their attestation involves no special anomaly, not being essentially different from that of the interpolations in Luke xxii and xxiv which are found in the best documents but omitted by the Western (§§ 240 f., 383). The superficial difference of attestation would seem to be chiefly if not wholly due to the accident that here the Syrian revisers preferred the shorter Western text. On this supposition the fortunate circumstance that their habitual love of completeness met with some counteraction, probably from a sense of the confusion arising out of the misplacement of the incident, has saved the texts of later times from a corruption which they might easily have inherited, and would doubtless have held fast. Apart however from the possibility that the words did belong to the genuine text of the first Gospel in its present form (see § 368), we should not have been justified in excluding them entirely from our text so long as we retained similar interpolations; and we have therefore inserted them, like the rest, in double brackets.

392. Besides the three classes of notation already explained, a peculiar type has been found necessary for the words ἐν Ἐφέσῳ in Eph. i 1. If there were here, as usual, a simple issue of genuineness or spuriousness, the words would have to be condemned. But the very probable view that the epistle traditionally entitled ΠΡΟΣ ΕΦΕΣΙΟΥΣ was addressed to a plurality of churches has naturally given rise to a supposition that the words are not so much spurious as local, filling up an intentional gap in the text rightly for Ephesian readers, but intended to be replaced by ἐν and another name for readers belonging to other churches addressed. In expression of this view we have retained the words with a change of type in preference to leaving a blank space; as we see no reason to doubt that at least one primary recipient of the epistle was Ephesus, from which great centre it would naturally be forwarded to the churches of other cities of Western Asia Minor. We have thought it safer however to enclose ἐν Ἐφέσῳ in ordinary brackets, as Origen is perhaps right, notwithstanding the fanciful interpretation with which he encumbers his construction, in taking the words τοῖς ἁγίοις τοῖς οὖσιν καὶ πιστοῖς ἐν Χριστῷ Ἰησοῦ to run on continuously, so that no place would be left for a local address.

C. 393—404. *Orthography*

393. A short explanation remains to be given respecting the Orthography adopted, and also the various typographical details or other external arrangements, some purely formal, some closely related to sense, by which the contents of ancient MSS are presented in a shape adapted for ready use and understanding. An editor of the New Testament is often driven to wish that it were possible to evade the necessity of choosing between one mode of spelling and another. Much time would be saved by

adopting a conventional spelling, such as stands in the Received Text; and the many points of orthography in which there is little hope of arriving at approximate certainty in the present state of knowledge throw some serious discouragement on the attempt to reproduce the autographs in this as well as in more important respects. Yet it is not seemly, when the text of the New Testament is being scrupulously elaborated word by word, that it should be disfigured many times in every page by a slovenly neglect of philological truth. The abandonment of all restoration of the original forms of words is also liable to obliterate interesting and perhaps important facts, affinities of authorship and the like being sometimes indicated by marks trivial in themselves. No strictly middle course is satisfactory: for, though not a few ancient spellings are placed above doubt by the consent of all or nearly all the better uncials, there is every gradation of attestation between these and spellings of highly questionable authority. We have therefore thought it best to aim at approximating as nearly as we could to the spelling of the autographs by means of documentary evidence; with this qualification, that we have acquiesced in the common orthography in two or three points, not perhaps quite free from doubt, in which the better attested forms would by their prominence cause excessive strangeness in a popular text. Under the head of spelling it is convenient to include most variations of inflexion.

394. Much of the spelling in the current editions of Greek classical authors is really arbitrary, depending at least as much on modern critical tradition as on ancient evidence, whether of MSS of the book edited or of MSS of other books or of statements of Greek grammarians. Indeed to a great extent this artificiality of spelling is inevitable for want of MSS of any considerable antiquity. In the Greek Bible however, and especially in most books of the New Testament, there is a tolerable supply of available resources, so that criticism can occupy a position not unlike that which it holds with respect to Latin writings preserved in fairly ancient MSS.

395. The spellings found in good MSS of the New Testament at variance with the MSS of the middle ages and of the Received Text are probably in a few cases the true literary spellings of the time, though not found in printed editions of other books: but for the most part they

belong to the 'vulgar' or popular form of the Greek language. There has been as yet so little intelligent or accurate study of the later varieties of Greek that we must speak with some reserve: but we believe it is not too much to say that no undoubted peculiarities of a local or strictly dialectic nature are at present known in the New Testament. The often used term 'Alexandrine' is, thus applied, a misnomer. The erroneous usage apparently originated partly in the mere name *Codex Alexandrinus,* the MS so called having been for a long time the chief accessible document exhibiting these forms, partly in the Alexandrian origin of the Septuagint version, assumed to have supplied the writers of the New Testament with their orthography: the imagined corroboration from the existence of the same forms in Egypt is set aside by their equally certain existence elsewhere. The term 'Hellenistic' is less misleading, but still of doubtful propriety. It was coined to denote the language of Greek-speaking Jews: but, though the only extant books exhibiting in large number these modes of language were written either by Greek-speaking Jews or by Christians who might have derived them from this source, the same modes of language were certainly used freely by heathens in various parts of the Greek world. Another objection to the term 'Hellenistic' is the danger of confusion with the 'Hellenic' or 'Common Dialect', that is, the mixed and variable literary language which prevailed from the time of Alexander except where Attic purity was artificially cultivated; a confusion exemplified in the practice of calling Philo a 'Hellenistic' writer, though he has hardly a better title to the name than Polybius.

396. A large proportion of the peculiar spellings of the New Testament are simply spellings of common life. In most cases either identical or analogous spellings occur frequently in inscriptions written in different countries, by no means always of the more illiterate sort. The Jewish and Christian writings which contain them are of popular character: naturally they shew themselves least where literary ambition or cultivation are most prominent. Many found in inscriptions, in the LXX, and in some Christian apocryphal books are absent from the New Testament. Within the New Testament there is a considerable general uniformity: but differences as to books and writers are likewise discernible, and worthy of being noted; thus these spellings are least frequent with St Paul and the author of

the Epistle to the Hebrews, who are in other respects the most cultivated writers.

397, A question might here be raised whether there is sufficient ground for assuming that the spellings found in the oldest MSS of the New Testament were also, generally speaking, the spellings of the autographs; whether in short the oldest extant orthography may not have been introduced in the fourth or some earlier century. Versions afford no help towards answering the question; and Fathers not much more, owing to the lateness of the MSS in which nearly all their writings have been preserved; though it is instructive to observe that the better MSS of some patristic writings shew occasional unclassical forms or spellings as used by the authors in their own persons as well as in quotations, while they disappear in inferior MSS. Although however there is a lack of direct evidence, the probabilities of the case are unfavourable to the hypothesis of the introduction of such forms by transcribers of the New Testament. In the fourth and following centuries, and even during a great part of the third, a natural result of the social position of Christians would be a tendency of scribes to root out supposed vulgarisms, as is known to have been the case in the revisions of the Old Latin as regards grammatical forms as well as vocabulary. In this matter the orthography of late MSS has no textual authority. Like their substantive text, it is a degenerate descendant from the orthography of the early Christian empire, and cannot have survived independently from primitive times; so that its testimony to classical spellings is without value, being derived from the literary habits of scribes, not from their fidelity in transmission. Hence, be the spellings of our best MSS right or wrong, they are the most trustworthy within our reach. Even if it be taken as a possible alternative that they originated with the scribes of the second century, we must still either follow our best MSS or rewrite the orthography by blind conjecture. The simpler supposition that in the main they were transmitted from the autographs need not however be questioned. The unclassical forms or spellings of our MSS were certainly current in the apostolic age, as is proved by inscriptions; and they are not out of keeping with the prevalent characteristics of the diction of the New Testament: so that no tangible reason can be given why the apostles and other writers should not have employed them.

22

398. Accordingly in orthographical variations we have followed essentially the same principles as in the rest of the text; allowance being made in their application for the much smaller amount of documentary evidence, and for the facility with which all experience shews that accustomed spellings flow from the pens of otherwise careful transcribers. Possibly we may here and there have erred in adopting an unclassical form or spelling. It is still more probable that the writers of the New Testament employed unclassical forms or spellings in many places where no trace of them now exists, and where therefore their present use could not be justified. Yet we have taken much pains as to individual details, and given perhaps only too much time to what are after all trifles, though in not a few cases there was little hope of arriving at more than provisional results without a disproportionate extension of the field of labour. Fortunately in this matter the individual details are of less consequence than the general colouring which they collectively produce, and about the truth of the general colouring here given we have no misgiving. Even in details a liberal indication of alternative readings (see § 403) goes far towards suggesting the probable limits of uncertainty.

399. The course of orthographical change during the centuries known to us from extant MSS coincided approximately with that of verbal or substantive change. But ancient spellings died out much more quickly than ancient substantive readings; so that the proportion of MSS containing them is considerably smaller. The evidence as to some of these spellings is complicated by coincidence with the range of itacism : that is, some of the rival forms differ from each other only by permutation of such vowels, including diphthongs, as are also liable to be exchanged for each other in mere error. Throughout the uncial period, of which alone it is necessary to speak here, some licence as to itacism is always present, and in a few late uncials the licence is gross and extensive : yet the confusion of vowels, especially in the more ancient copies, is found to lie within constant limits, which are rarely transgressed. Thus ℵ shews a remarkable inclination to change ει into ι, and B to change ι into ει, alike in places where either form is possible and in places where the form actually employed in the MS is completely discredited by the want of any other sufficient evidence or analogy; the converse confusions being very rare in both, and particu-

larly in B. Hence B has to be left virtually out of account as an authority against unclassical forms with ι, and ℵ against unclassical forms with ει; while in the converse cases the value of their evidence remains unimpaired, or rather is enhanced, allowance being made for the possible contingency of irregular permutations here and there. Till the unsifted mass of orthographical peculiarities of a MS has been cleared from the large irrelevant element thus contributed by what are probably mere itacisms, no true estimate can be formed of its proper orthographical character. When this rectification has been made, it becomes clear that the unclassical forms and spellings abound most in the MSS having the most ancient text, and that their occurrence in cursives is almost entirely limited to cursives in which relics of a specially ancient text are independently known to exist.

400. To accept however every ancient spelling differing from the late spellings would be as rash as to accept every Western reading because it is very ancient. Curiously enough, but quite naturally, the Western documents are rich in forms and spellings not found in other documents, and some few are also confined to documents in which the Alexandrian text is very prominent. Here again B holds a neutral place, having many spellings in common with each class of text. We have as a rule taken only such unclassical spellings as had the support of both classes, or of either alone with B. Even where B stands alone, we have usually followed it for the text, unless forbidden by some tolerably strong internal or analogical reason to the contrary. But in many cases there is no room for hesitation about the reading, all the best uncials being concordant.

401. The irregularity of the extant orthographical evidence is so great that it would have often been unsatisfactory to decide on the form to be given to a word in any one place without previous comparison of the evidence in all or nearly all places where the same or similar words occur. Most orthographical variations have been carefully tabulated, and the readings decided on consecutively as they stood in the tables, not as they occur scattered among substantive readings. Many of the particulars required were not to be found in the published *apparatus critici* : but the labour involved in collecting them has not been fruitless. Examination of the columnar tables of attestation, by bringing to light approximate uniformi-

ties affecting particular books or writers, or collocations of letters or words, and the like, has often shown that an exceptional smallness or largeness of evidence has been probably due to accident. On the other hand it would be unreasonable to assume that the same writer, even in the same book, always spells a word in the same way. Absolute uniformity belongs only to artificial times; and, after full allowance has been made for anomalies of evidence, the verdict of MSS is decisive against the supposition. Absolute uniformity therefore we have made no attempt to carry out, even within narrow limits; while we have assumed the existence of such a moderate or habitual uniformity in the usage of the writers as would enable us to come to a decision for the text in difficult cases. Many ancient spellings are therefore adopted in individual places on evidence which might be perilously small if they were taken alone, and if substantive readings were in question ; but we have printed absolutely nothing without some good documentary authority.

402. In some departments of orthography the evidence is so unsatisfactory that the rejected spellings are but little less probable than those adopted; and thus they should in strictness be accounted alternative readings. But to have printed them in the margin along with the substantive alternatives would have crowded and confused the pages of our text beyond measure, without any corresponding gain. They are therefore reserved for the Appendix, in which a few additional remarks on some special points of orthography, especially on some forms of proper names, may fitly find a place. The alternative readings thus relegated to the Appendix under the head of orthography include not only forms of inflexion, but forms of particles, as ἄν or ἐάν, and variations in the elision or retention of the last vowel of ἀλλά and of such prepositions as end with a vowel. We have ventured to treat in the same manner variations of the indicative or subjunctive after such particles as ἵνα, ἐάν, and ὅταν, and after relatives with ἄν or ἐάν.

403. A word may be interposed here on a topic which in strictness belongs to Part III (compare § 303), but which it is more convenient to notice in connexion with orthography. Attention was called above (§ 399) to the necessity of making allowance for purely itacistic error in considering the properly orthographical testimony of MSS. But there is another more important question con-

cerning itacistic error, namely how far its early prevalence invalidates the authority of the better MSS as between substantive readings which differ only by vowels apt to be interchanged. The question cannot be answered with any confidence except by careful comparison of the various places in the New Testament which are affected by it. The results thus obtained are twofold. It becomes clear that in early times scribes were much more prone to make changes which affected vowels only than to make any other changes; and that every extant early document falls in this respect below its habitual standard of trustworthiness. Readings intrinsically improbable have often a surprising amount of attestation; and thus internal evidence attains unusual relative importance. It is no less clear that the several documents retain on the whole their relative character as compared with each other, and that readings unsupported by any high documentary authority have little probability. Where the testimony of early Versions and Fathers is free from uncertainty, it has a special value in variations of this kind by virtue of mere priority of date, as the chances of corruption through such interchange of vowels as is not obviously destructive of sense are considerably more increased by repetition of transcription than the chances of corruption of any other type: but MSS of Versions are in many cases liable to corresponding errors of precisely the same kind, and the interpretations of Fathers are open to other special ambiguities.

404. Probably the commonest permutation is that of *o* and *ω*, chiefly exemplified in the endings -ομεν and -ωμεν, -ύμεθα and -ώμεθα. Instances will be found in 1 Cor. xv 49, where we have not ventured to reject either φορέσωμεν or φορέσομεν; and in Rom. v 1, where the imperative εἰρή-νην ἔχωμεν, standing as it does after a pause in the epistle, yields a probable sense, virtually inclusive of the sense of εἰρήνην ἔχομεν, which has no certain attestation of good quality but that of the 'corrector' of ℵ. Another frequent permutation is that of ε and αι; likewise exemplified in forms of the verb, especially in the infinitive and the second person plural of the imperative. Thus in Luke xiv 17 it is difficult to decide between *Ἔρχεσθε* and *ἔρχεσθαι*, or in xix 13 between πραγματεύσασθαι and Πραγματεύσασθε, the infinitive in the latter place being justified by St Luke's manner of passing from *oratio obliqua* to *oratio recta*. Gal. iv 18 furnishes one of the few instances in which B and ℵ have happened to fall into

the same itacistic error, both reading ζηλοῦσθε where ζηλοῦσθαι alone has any real probability. Examples of another type are the Western καινοφωνίας for κενοφωνίας in 1 Tim. vi 20 ; 2 Tim. ii 16 ; and the more perverse confusion by which in Matt. xi 16 the idiomatic τοῖς ἑτέροις, the other 'side' or party in the game played by the children sitting in the marketplace, appears in the Syrian text as τοῖς ἑταίροις with αὐτῶν added. The interchange of ε and η may be illustrated by ἦμεν and ἤμην in Acts xi 11, where the best uncials are opposed to the versions ; and of ει with η by εἰ and ᾖ in 2 Cor. ii 9 : less frequent forms of itacism may be passed over. Lastly, itacism plays at least some part in the common confusion of ἡμεῖς and ὑμεῖς. The prevailing tendency is to introduce ἡμεῖς wrongly, doubtless owing to the natural substitution of a practical for a historical point of view, as is seen to a remarkable extent in 1 Peter : but there are many per-mutations which cannot be traced to this cause. The peculiarly subtle complexity of the personal relations between St Paul and his converts as set forth in 2 Corin-thians has proved a special snare to scribes, the scribes of the best MSS not excepted. Occasionally the varia-tion between ἡμεῖς and ὑμεῖς is of much interest. Thus, though the limited range of attestation has withheld us from placing τινὲς τῶν καθ᾽ ἡμᾶς ποιητῶν in the text proper of Acts xvii 28, there would be a striking fitness in a claim thus made by St Paul to take his stand as a Greek among Greeks ; as he elsewhere vindicates his position as a Roman (xvi 37 ; xxii 25, 28), and as a Pharisee (xxiii 6).

D. 405—416. *Breathings, Accents, and other accessories of printing*

405. Orthography deals with elements of text trans-mitted uninterruptedly, with more or less of purity, from the autographs to the extant MSS. In passing next from the letters to the various marks which custom and conveni-ence require to be affixed to them, we leave, with one partial exception, the domain of the written tradition. Whether the autographs contained Breathings, Accents, and the like, it is impossible to know. None exist in the earlier uncials of the New Testament, and it is morally certain that they were not included in transcription during a succession of centuries ; so that, if any existed in the first instance, the record of them must have speedily

perished. The earliest MSS of the New Testament that exhibit breathings and accents are in any case too degenerate
in orthography and in substantive text alike to be followed
with any confidence, even were it possible to regard them
as having inherited these marks from an unbroken succes
sion of ancestral MSS. But in truth they have no authority derived from ancestral transmission at all, the
accessory marks having been doubtless chosen or placed,
when they were first inserted, in conformity with the pronunciation or grammatical doctrine of the time. They are
the expression of a tradition, but not of a tradition handed
down through transcription, nor a tradition belonging to
the New Testament more than to any other book containing any of the same words. The one exception to this
statement is made by the conversion of a preceding hard
consonant, κ, π, or τ, into an aspirate consonant, which
thus carries in itself the impress of the rough breathing.
The opportunity for such conversion of course arises only
in ἀντί, ἀπό, ἐπί, κατά, μετά, ὑπό, where the final vowel
suffers elision, in verbs compounded with these prepositions, and in the particle οὐκ.

406. The problem therefore, as limited by the evidence, is to discover not what the apostles wrote, but what
it is likely that they would have written, had they employed
the same marks as are now in use, mostly of very ancient
origin: and the only safe way to do this is to ascertain,
first, what was the general Greek usage, and next, whether
any special usage of time, place, or other circumstances
has to be further taken into account. The evidence at the
command of modern grammarians for this purpose consists partly of the statements or precepts of ancient grammarians, partly of the records of ancient grammatical
practice, that is, the marks found in such MSS as contain
marks. To this second class of evidence the later uncials
and earlier cursives of the New Testament make an
appreciable contribution, which has not yet received due
attention from grammarians: but their testimony respecting ancient Greek usage, though it has thus its use, in
combination with other evidence, when marks have to be
affixed to the text of the New Testament, must not be
confounded with a direct transmission of affixed marks
from primitive times.

407. Some few unusual Breathings indicated by aspiration of the preceding consonant occur in good MSS of
the New Testament; but their attestation is so irregular

that it is difficult to know what to do with them. They are assuredly not clerical errors, but genuine records of pronunciation, whether of the apostolic age or some other early time, and have to a certain extent the support of inscriptions, even of inscriptions from Attica. They seem to be chiefly relics of the digamma, and are interesting as signs of the variety of spoken language which often lies concealed under the artificial uniformity of a literary standard. The range of good MSS supporting them in one place or another is remarkable, and in some few places they can claim a large aggregation of good MSS: yet in others they receive but little attestation, and usually they receive none at all. In two or three cases we have admitted them to the text, content elsewhere to leave them for the present as alternatives in the Appendix, where any needful details as to these or other accessory marks will be found. The amply attested reading οὐκ ἔστηκεν in John viii 44 does not come under the present head, ἔστηκεν being merely the imperfect of στήκω, as it appears also to be in Apoc. xii 4. The sense of an imperfect rather than a present is required by the context, which must refer to the primal apostasy as representing the Jews' abandonment of the truth into which they were born ; and there is a fitness in the virtually intensive force ('stand fast') which belongs by prevalent though not constant usage to στήκω. The imperfect of this somewhat rare verb is not on record : but imperfects are too closely connected with presents to need separate authority, and multitudes of unique forms of verbs are known only from single passages. The aspiration of αυτοῦ used reflexively is discussed in the Appendix.

408. The breathings of proper names possess a semblance of documentary evidence in the Latin version and its presentation of names with or without H. Yet, however early the first link in the Latin chain may be, it is evidently disconnected from the Palestinian pronunciation of Greek, the true object of search. The serious inconsistencies and improbabilities contained in the Latin usage condemn it equally on internal grounds: it is obviously due rather to unconscious submission to deceptive analogies and associations of sound than to any actual tradition. The breathings of Greek and Latin proper names can usually be fixed by the etymology: where this fails, it is seldom difficult to find direct or indirect authority in coins, inscriptions, or even early MSS of Latin authors. The well

attested aspirate of the African *Hadrumetum* prescribes πλοίῳ Ἀδραμυντηνῷ, as the name of the obscurer Asiatic city must have had the same origin. In proper names transliterated from the Hebrew or Aramaic we have in like manner exactly followed the Hebrew or Aramaic spelling, expressing א and ע by the smooth breathing, and ה and ח by the rough breathing. This principle, manifestly the only safe guide in the absence of evidence, sanctions Ἄβελ, Ἄγαρ, Ἀκελδαμάχ, Ἀλφαῖος, Ἀνανίας, Ἄννα, Ἄννας, Ἀρέτας, Ἀριμαθαία, Ἐμμώρ, Ἐνώχ, Ἐσρώμ, Εὔα, Ὡσηέ; also Ἀλληλουιά as well as Ὡσαννά. In Ἀρ Μαγεδών, *Mount Megiddo*, the common identification of Ἀρ with הַר is accepted. It is true that the rare form עָר, denoting a 'city', is represented in the *Ar-Moab* of Num. xxi 28; (cf. xxii 36;) Is. xv 1, (transliterated by Theodotion in Isaiah, but by no other Greek authority in either place,) and in the Ἀρσαμόσατα of classical authors, the name of a city near the sources of the Tigris. But better parallels on Jewish soil are supplied by Ἀρ Γαριζείν, *Mount Gerizim*, from two Greek Samaritan sources (Ps. Eupolem. ap. Eus. *P.E.* ix 419 A; Damasc.*Vit.Marin.* ap. Phot.*Bibl.*345 b 20 [τῷ Ἀργαρίζῳ]: cf. Freudenthal *Alex.Polyhist.* 86 ff.), and by Ἀρ Σαφάρ, *Mount Shapher*, from the LXX of Num. xxxiii 23 f. in A and most MSS. The context points to a 'mount' rather than a 'city'; and the name *Mount Megiddo* is not difficult to explain, though it does not occur elsewhere. In Ἀλφαῖος we follow the Vulgate Syriac (the Old Syriac is lost in the four places where the name occurs), which agrees with what the best modern authorities consider to be the Aramaic original. We have also in the text accepted the authority of the Syriac for Ἄγαβος (from עָגַב): but Ἄγαβος (from חָגָב) is supported by the existence of a *Hagab* in Ezr. ii 45 f.; Neh. vii 48. In like manner Ἐβέρ, Ἐβραῖος, Ἐβραΐς, Ἐβραϊστί have every claim to be received: indeed the complete displacement of *Ebraeus* and *Ebrew* by *Hebraeus* and *Hebrew* is comparatively modern. All names beginning with י have received the smooth breathing. No better reason than the false association with ἱερός can be given for hesitating to write Ἰερεμίας, Ἰερειχώ, Ἰεροσόλυμα (-μείτης), Ἰερουσαλήμ.

409. On the other hand an interesting question is raised by the concurrence of several of the best MSS in Gal. ii 14 in favour of οὐχ Ἰουδαϊκῶς, the only other well attested reading οὐχὶ Ἰουδαϊκῶς being probably a correction: nowhere else in the New Testament is any

similar proper name preceded by a hard consonant, so as to give opportunity for aspiration. The improbability of a clerical error is shown by the reading οὐχ Ιούδα in Susan. 56, attested by at least three out of the four extant uncials (ABQ), the reading of the fourth (V) being unknown; combined with the fact that this is the only other place in the Greek Bible where an opportunity for aspiration occurs before a similar proper name. It seems to follow that, where יְהוֹ at the beginning of proper names was transliterated by Ιου- (and by analogy יְהוֹ by Ιω-), the aspirate sound coalesced in pronunciation with the semi-vowel. On this view Ιουδαῖος and all derivatives of Ιούδας, together with Ιωράμ and Ιωσαφάτ, should always carry the rough breathing. We have however refrained from abandoning the common usage in the present text.

410. The Iota adscript is found in no early MSS of the New Testament. As the best MSS make the infinitive of verbs in -όω to end in -οῖν (κατασκηνοῖν Matt. xiii 32 and Mark iv 32; φιμοῖν 1 Pet. ii 15; ἀποδεκατοῖν Heb. vii 5), analogy is distinctly in favour of allowing the Iota subscript of ζῆν and infinitives in -ᾷν. Indeed even in ordinary Greek the practice of withholding it, which Wolf brought into fashion, has been questioned by some high authorities. Ἡρῴδης is well supported by inscriptions, and manifestly right: of course its derivatives follow it. It seems morally certain that the Greeks wrote not only πρῷρα, ὑπερῷον, but ἀθῷος, ᾠόν, ζῷον; and we had good precedents for accepting these forms. Almost as much may be said for σῴζω (see K.H.A.Lipsius *Gramm. Unters.* 9; Curtius *Das Verb. d. griech. Spr.* ed. 2. ii 401): but it had found no favour with modern editors when our text was printed, and we did not care to innovate on its behalf then, or to alter the plates in more than a hundred passages on its behalf now. Once more, authority has seemed to prescribe εἰκῇ, κρυφῇ, πανταχῇ, πάντῃ, λάθρᾳ.

411. Details of Accents need not be discussed here. The prevalent tendency of most modern grammarians, with some notable exceptions, has been to work out a consistent system of accentuation on paper rather than to recover the record of ancient Greek intonations of voice, with all their inevitable anomalies: but we have not ventured on any wide departures from custom. With some recent editors we have taken account of the well attested fact that certain vowels which were originally long became short in the less deliberate speech of later

times, and have affixed the accents accordingly (see
Lobeck *Paralip.* Diss. vi; Mehlhorn *Gr. Gr.* 26, 31, 158;
Cobet *N.T.Praef.* li; K.H.A.Lipsius 31 ff.). The example
of C.E.C.Schneider, who usually shews good judgement
in these matters, has encouraged us to drop the unnecessary mark or space distinguishing the pronoun ὅτι from
the particle.

412. In the division of words at the end and beginning
of lines we have faithfully observed the Greek rules, of
which on the whole the best account is in Kühner's Grammar, i 273 ff. (ed. 2). It has been urged that the scribe
of ℵ copied an Egyptian papyrus, on the ground that
some of the lines begin with θμ, a combination of letters
which may begin a word in Coptic, but cannot in Greek.
The truth is that θμ, following the analogy of τμ, is a
recognised Greek beginning for lines. It was a Greek
instinct, first doubtless of pronunciation and thence of
writing, to make syllables end upon a vowel, if it was in
any way possible; and the only universally accepted
divisions between consonants occur where they are double,
where a hard consonant precedes an aspirate, or where the
first consonant is a liquid except in the combination μν.
Among the points on which both precept and practice
differed was the treatment of prepositions in composition
as integral parts of a word, in the two cases of their being
followed by a consonant or by a vowel: in allowing division after πρός and εἰς, but joining the final consonant
of the preposition to the next syllable in other cases, even
after σύν, we have been guided by the predominant though
not uniform usage of ℵABC. In most particulars of the
division of syllables these MSS habitually follow the
stricter of the various rules laid down by grammarians,
more closely indeed than such papyrus MSS as we have
compared with them by means of facsimile editions,
though miscellaneous deviations may occasionally be
found. The rarest of such lapses are violations of the
rule that a line must on no account end with οὐκ, οὐχ,
or a consonant preceding an elided vowel, as in ἀπ', οὐδ',
ἀλλ'; in which cases the consonant must begin the next
line, unless of course the separation of the two adjacent
syllables can easily be altogether avoided. In the case
of compound Hebrew proper names, as Βηθλεέμ, we have
ventured for the present purpose to treat each element as
a separate word.

413. Quotations from the Old Testament are printed

in 'uncial' type. Under this head are included not only
passages or sentences expressly cited in the context as
quotations, but sentences adopted from the Old Testament
without any such indication, and also all phrases apparently
borrowed from some one passage or limited number of
passages, and in a few places characteristic single words.
The line has been extremely difficult to draw, and may
perhaps have wavered occasionally. Words or forms of
speech occurring in either the Massoretic Hebrew alone or
the Septuagint alone have been treated as belonging to the
Old Testament, as well as those which stand in both texts ;
and the various readings belonging to different states of the
LXX, as preserved in its extant MSS, have likewise been
taken into account. On the other hand words occurring
in the midst of quotations, and not clearly capable of being
referred to an Old Testament original, have been left in ordinary type. A list of references to the passages, phrases,
and words marked as taken from the Old Testament is
given in the Appendix. Hebrew and Aramaic words transliterated in Greek, not being proper names, are marked by
spaced type ; inscribed titles and the peculiar formulæ
quoted in Rom. x 9, 1 Cor. xii 3, and Phil. ii 11, are
printed entirely in ordinary capitals.

414. The use of capital initials for the most part tells
its own tale ; but some explanation is required as to the
exceptional employment of Κύριος and Χριστός. Wherever
κύριος is preceded by an article, it is manifestly a pure
appellative, and needs no capital. When the article is
wanting, apart from such phrases as ἀπὸ θεοῦ πατρὸς ἡμῶν
καὶ κυρίου Ἰησοῦ Χριστοῦ and ἐν κυρίῳ ['Ιησοῦ], in a considerable number of cases the form is evidently taken from
the LXX, where it usually represents *Jehovah* (*Jahveh*),
Adonai, or some other name of God. Direct and in this
respect exact quotations from the LXX, which evidently
throw no light on the usage of the writer who quotes
them, similar direct quotations in which Κύριος is not the
word employed in at least one existing texts of the LXX,
reminiscences of one or more passages in the LXX, and
detached phrases of frequent occurrence in it (as ἄγγελος
Κυρίου) make up the greater number of these cases. The
only writers who in our judgement employ the anarthrous
Κύριος as a name after the manner of the LXX, but quite
independently, are St James, St Peter, and (in the Apocalypse) St John ; and even in reminiscences of the LXX,
or short phrases taken from it, the distribution of this use

of Κύριος is strikingly limited. In all these five classes of passages, which shade into each other, the capital has been used, because here Κύριος is the equivalent of a proper name, though it may sometimes contain a secondary allusion to the Greek signification. On the other hand after careful examination we can find no instance in which the omission of the article need be referred to the Greek idiom by which, for instance, ἥλιος and κόσμος are often used anarthrously, that is, in which κύριος seems to be used convertibly with ὁ κύριος. In other words, where the God of Israel is not intended, the absence of the article is always accompanied by a directly or indirectly predicative force in κύριος, and a capital initial would certainly be wrong. Such passages are numerous in St Paul's epistles, very rare elsewhere.

415. The grounds of distinction for χριστός and Χριστός are different. Here the Greek word exactly translates an appellative of the Old Testament which was in popular speech becoming or become a proper name, and in like manner it becomes at last a proper name itself. We doubt whether the appellative force, with its various associations and implications, is ever entirely lost in the New Testament, and are convinced that the number of passages is small in which Messiahship, of course in the enlarged apostolic sense, is not the principal intention of the word. The presence or absence of the article is only an imperfect criterion, as its absence is compatible with the meaning "a Christ", and its presence with limitation to a single definite person. Adequate representation of the gradation of use is beyond the power of notation: yet we could not willingly give support to the perverse interpretation which makes [ὁ] χριστός a merely individual name, as we should have done had we used the capital initial always. In using it where the article is absent (the forms Ἰησοῦς Χριστός, Χριστὸς Ἰησοῦς being included), and avoiding it where the article is present (ὁ χριστὸς Ἰησοῦς being included) and in the vocative of Matt. xxvi 68, we have, we hope, obtained fair approximations to the predominant force of the word. In 1 Peter alone it seemed best to retain the capital both with and without the article, for fear of obscuring the apparently complex usage of this epistle. Fortunately both forms throughout the New Testament are bound together by the common accent, the oxytone Χριστός never having been exchanged for the Χρίστος appropriate to a true proper name.

416. An initial capital has likewise been used for ῞Υψιστος in the four places, all in St Luke's Gospel, in which it stands in the singular without an article. In this shape it exactly represents the anarthrous *Elion*, a very ancient name not confined to the Jews, and is virtually itself a proper name. In the LXX the article is usually inserted: but in Ecclesiasticus, doubtless a better authority for Palestinian custom, ῞Υψιστος occurs frequently, and has the article but once, except in combination with another title.

E. 417--423. *Punctuation, Divisions of text, and Titles of books*

417. Punctuation properly includes not stops only, but spaces at the beginning, middle, or end of lines, and indeed any notation having a similar effect, that is, the distribution of words into clauses, and of clauses into sentences of greater or less complexity. In this sense probably no MSS are without punctuation, though in the earlier biblical MSS it is vague and comparatively infrequent. Comparison of the punctuation of extant MSS leads to the conclusion that, though in some places breaks or stops occur with fair constancy, there has been no transmission of punctuation of any kind from the autographs; so that whatever punctuation is found is merely a record of ancient interpretations of unknown authority. Punctuations presupposed in the renderings of Versions may often be older, but they have essentially the same character; and those which are involved in the renderings or interpretations of Fathers differ only as having usually the authority, whatever it may be, of known expositors or theologians. Many interpretations embodying punctuations naturally became traditional within a wider or narrower sphere: but the starting-point of each tradition must have been an individual act of judgement upon an inherited text, not a continuously transmitted reproduction of an original punctuation as part of a text. Modern editors have therefore no option but to punctuate in accordance with the best interpretation that they are themselves able to arrive at, with ancient and modern aids; and no unwillingness to encumber a text with needless comments can dispense them from the necessity of deciding a multitude of subtle and difficult points of interpretation, to be expressed only by stops.

418. In arranging the punctuation, on which we have bestowed especial pains, we have followed the example first set by Lachmann in aiming at the greatest simplicity compatible with clearness. We fear that we may not always have succeeded in preserving a strictly uniform scale of punctuation; but some of the deviations have been intentional, being made with a view to help the reader through confusions or ambiguities. In some cases of doubt, or of division of judgement, an alternative punctuation has been placed in the margin.

419. Punctuation passes insensibly into the larger arrangements denoted by paragraphs and sections. The course which we have followed has been to begin by examining carefully the primary structure of each book as a whole, and then to divide it gradually up into sections of higher or lower rank, separated by spaces, and headed if necessary by whole words in capitals. In the subdivision of sections we have found great convenience in adopting the French plan of breaking up the paragraphs into subparagraphs by means of a space of some length. In this manner we have been able to keep together in combination a single series of connected topics, and yet to hold them visibly apart. The advantage is especially great where a distinct digression is interposed between two closely connected portions of text. We have been glad at the same time to retain another grade of division in the familiar difference between capitals and small letters following a full stop. Groups of sentences introduced by a capital thus bear the same relation to subparagraphs as subparagraphs to paragraphs. The transitions of living speech are often however too gradual or too complex to be duly represented by punctuation or any arrangement of type. The utmost that can then be done is to mark those articulations of a book, paragraph, or sentence which apparently dominate the rest, and to preserve the subordination of accessory points of view to the main course of a narrative or argument.

420. Passages apparently metrical in rhythm have been printed in a metrical form, whether taken from the Old Testament or not; and in the former case fresh words substituted or added in the same strain have been dealt with in the same way. We have not thought it necessary to follow the Massoretic arrangements of passages from the poetical books of the Old Testament, even in passages transcribed without modification. In many places

indeed it would have been impossible, owing to the changes of form or language introduced in the process of quotation. We have merely tried to indicate probable or possible lines of Hebraic metrical structure clothed in a Greek dress, first by assigning a separate line to each member, and then by expressing the most salient parallelisms through an artificial ordering of lines. Doubtful cases however have not been rare; and we are far from supposing that the divisions and distributions here employed are exclusively right.

421. The hymns of the Apocalypse shew, strange to say, no metrical arrangement of diction, so that they could be marked only by a narrower column of type; and in Luke ii 14 the diversities of possible construction led to the adoption of the same course. On the other hand the example of Eph. v 14, which seems to be taken from a Christian source, has emboldened us to give a metrical form to the latter part of 1 Tim. iii 16, the difficulties of which are certainly somewhat lightened by the supposition that it is part of a hymn. But we are unable to recognise in the Pastoral Epistles any other quotations, metrical or not, such as are supposed by some to be introduced or concluded by the phrase πιστὸς ὁ λόγος. We have been especially glad to mark the essentially metrical structure of the Lord's Prayer in St Matthew's Gospel, with its invocation, its first triplet of single clauses with one common burden, expressed after the third but implied after all, and its second triplet of double clauses, variously antithetical in form and sense. Other typographical arrangements speak for themselves.

422. In the order of the different books we have for various reasons not thought it advisable to depart from traditional arrangements. We should have defeated our own purpose had we needlessly mixed up such disputable matter as the chronology and authorship of the apostolic writings with the results of textual criticism, obtained by different methods from evidence of an entirely different kind. We have however followed recent editors in abandoning the Hieronymic order, familiar in modern Europe through the influence of the Latin Vulgate, in favour of the order most highly commended by various Greek authority of the fourth century, the earliest time when we have distinct evidence of the completed Canon as it now stands. It differs from the Hieronymic order in two respects. First, the Acts are immediately followed by the Catholic

Epistles. The connexion between these two portions, commended by its intrinsic appropriateness, is preserved in a large proportion of Greek MSS of all ages, and corresponds to marked affinities of textual history. This connexion is not sacrificed in the arrangement found in the Sinai MS and elsewhere, by which the Pauline Epistles are placed next to the Gospels. The Sinaitic order has the undoubted advantage of keeping together those books of the New Testament which were most decisively invested with a scriptural character in the earlier ages. But there is a manifest incongruity in placing the Acts in the midst of the Epistles; and moreover, since the choice lies between what are after all only rival traditions, strong reasons would be needed to justify us in forsaking the highest ancient Greek authority, in accordance with which the Pauline Epistles stand after the Catholic Epistles. Secondly, the Epistle to the Hebrews stands before the Pastoral Epistles. It is certainly not satisfactory to ourselves personally to separate what we believe to be genuine writings of St Paul from the bulk of his works by an epistle in which we cannot recognise his authorship. But no violence has, we trust, been here done to truth in deferring throughout to the most eminent precedent, since the Epistle to the Hebrews is on all hands acknowledged as in some sense Pauline, and St Paul's epistles addressed to single persons may very well be placed by themselves. We have therefore been content to indicate the existence of three groups in the table prefixed to the whole Pauline collection.

423. The titles of the books of the New Testament are no part of the text of the books themselves. Their ultimate authority is traditional, not documentary. In employing them according to universal custom, we neither affirm nor question their accuracy in respect of authorship or destination. In length and elaboration they vary much in different documents: we have adopted the concise and extremely ancient form preserved in אB and some other documents, which is apparently the foundation of the fuller titles. In prefixing the name ΕΥΑΓΓΕΛΙΟΝ in the singular to the quaternion of 'Gospels', we have wished to supply the antecedent which alone gives an adequate sense to the preposition ΚΑΤΑ in the several titles. The idea, if not the name, of a collective 'Gospel' is implied throughout the well known passage in the third book of Irenæus, who doubtless received it from earlier genera-

23

tions. It evidently preceded and produced the commoner usage by which the term 'Gospel' denotes a single written representation of the one fundamental Gospel. There are apparent references to "the Gospel" in a collective sense in Justin Martyr, while he also refers to 'the memoirs of the apostles' as 'called Gospels'. The difference in orthography between the title ΠΡΟΣ ΚΟΛΑΣΣΑΕΙΣ and St Paul's words ἐν Κολοσσαῖς has too strong documentary attestation to be rejected: the evidence is fully set forth by Dr Lightfoot (*Col.* p. 17), who has arrived independently at the same conclusion. The spelling *Colassae* was in use at a time subsequent to the apostolic age; and a current pronunciation might easily fix the form of name for the epistle, while St Paul's way of writing was faithfully retained by most transcribers in the text itself.

F. 423, 424. *Conclusion*

424. In conclusion we desire to express sincere acknowledgements to our publishers for the patience with which they have endured the protraction of this edition through many long years, and for the considerate kindness with which they have forwarded our wishes in various ways. No less acknowledgements are due to the officers and workmen of the Cambridge University Press for the equal patience with which they have carried out a work troublesome in itself, and rendered doubly troublesome by intermissions and revisions. To Dr Tregelles, had he been still living, it would have been to us a special pleasure to express our sense of the generous encouragement always received from him. Many friends have earned our gratitude by help rendered in various ways. Among them we must especially single out Mr A. A. VanSittart and the Rev. Hilton Bothamley, to whose minute care in the examination of the proof sheets the text owes much in the way of typographical accuracy, and who have contributed invaluable assistance of other

kinds. A certain number of misprints, chiefly in accents and breathings, which had escaped notice in the first or private issue, owe their rectification to notes kindly furnished by correspondents in England, Germany, and America. Any further corrections of overlooked errors of the press will be sincerely welcomed: with the utmost desire to secure accuracy, we have learned increasingly to distrust our own power of attaining it in the degree to which an edition of the New Testament should aspire.

425. It only remains to express an earnest hope that whatever labour we have been allowed to contribute towards the ascertainment of the truth of the letter may also be allowed, in ways which must for the most part be invisible to ourselves, to contribute towards strengthening, correcting, and extending human apprehension of the larger truth of the spirit. Others assuredly in due time will prosecute the task with better resources of knowledge and skill, and amend the faults and defects of our processes and results. To be faithful to such light as could be enjoyed in our own day was the utmost that we could desire. How far we have fallen short of this standard, we are well aware: yet we are bold to say that none of the shortcomings are due to lack of anxious and watchful sincerity. An implicit confidence in all truth, a keen sense of its variety, and a deliberate dread of shutting out truth as yet unknown are no security against some of the wandering lights that are apt to beguile a critic: but, in so far as they are obeyed, they at least quench every inclination to guide criticism into delivering such testimony as may be to the supposed advantage of truth already inherited or ac-

quired. Critics of the Bible, if they have been taught by the Bible, are unable to forget that the duty of guile-less workmanship is never superseded by any other. From Him who is at once the supreme Fountain of truth and the all-wise Lord of its uses they have received both the materials of knowledge and the means by which they are wrought into knowledge: into His hands, and His alone, when the working is over, must they render back that which they have first and last received.

ΕΞ ΑΥΤΟΥ ΚΑΙ ΔΙ ΑΥΤΟΥ ΚΑΙ ΕΙС ΑΥΤΟΝ ΤΑ ΠΑΝΤΑ.

ΑΥΤΩ Η ΔΟΞΑ ΕΙС ΤΟΥС ΑΙΩΝΑС.

ΑΜΗΝ.

APPENDIX

I. NOTES ON SELECT READINGS

THE subjects of the following notes may be classified under four heads. First, the few peculiar clauses or passages, partly Western interpolations, partly Non-Western interpolations, which are printed between ⟦ ⟧ either within the text itself or appended to it (*Introd.* § 240 f., 383, 384), and the Western additions and substitutions printed in the margin of the text between ⊣⊢ in the Gospels and Acts (*Introd.* § 385). Secondly, miscellaneous rejected readings sufficiently interesting to deserve special notice (*Introd.* § 386). The places where they occur are indicated by *Ap.* in the margin. Thirdly, a few variations, also marked by *Ap.*, in which there has been reason for discussing alternative readings or punctuations retained in the text and margin. Fourthly, words or passages, marked with *Ap.*† in the margin, in which one or both of us have been unable to acquiesce in any well attested extant reading as right, and accordingly believe or suspect some 'primitive error' or corruption to be present, whether a probable suggestion as to the true reading can be offered or not (*Introd.* § 361—368, 380, 88).

These notes do not form a critical commentary, though some of them, taken singly, might properly be so described in reference to particular passages. As regards the great bulk of the readings simply indicated by *Ap.*, and to a certain extent the readings enclosed between ⊣⊢ in the margin, the list might without any serious difference of purpose have been made much longer. Perhaps less uniformity of standard in selection has been maintained than might have been desired: but the list was not intended to have any completeness except in respect of the more important or interesting readings, and those of less moment which we have noticed have been taken in great measure for their illustrative and as it were representative character.

Again, as compared one with another, the notes are written on a great variety of scale, ranging from a bare classification of documents to long and minute discussion of every kind of evidence. These deliberate irregularities, though doubtless sometimes affected by accidental circumstances, have been guided by a practical purpose: that is, in reciting documentary evidence, we have assumed that our readers would have access to the *apparatus critici* of Tischendorf and Tregelles ; and we have rarely thought it necessary to discuss the claims of rival readings except where there is still difference of opinion among competent persons, and the true bearing of the evidence appears to be as yet but imperfectly understood. The frequent indications and occasional fuller statements of Internal Evidence, Intrinsic and Transcriptional, will shew, we trust, that the constancy of our eventual adhesion to documentary authority has been preceded by careful consideration of the interpretation of each particular context, and by attention to the various influences that might affect transcription. In this and other respects the Appendix may be taken as an illustrative supplement to the Introduction.

In the short statements of documentary evidence our chief aim has been to reduce the confused catalogues of 'authorities' to some degree of order by means of classification. Readings which could safely be referred to one or other of the early lines of transmission are simply described as 'Western ', 'Alexandrian ', 'Syrian', 'Western and Syrian' (that is, originally Western and then adopted into the Syrian text), and so on. After each of these designations follows in brackets a list of the languages in which the reading is extant, the several Latin, Syriac, and properly Egyptian versions being taken together under these three heads, and languages for which the evidence is uncertain or suspicious being usually enclosed in square brackets : where 'Gr.' is followed by square brackets containing the symbol for one or two documents (as D in many

Western readings), it is to be understood that there is no other Greek authority for the reading. The enumeration of languages is often followed by specification ('incl.') of documents having an exceptional claim to be mentioned ; such as primary MSS not habitually found supporting readings of the ancient text or texts to which the reading in question belongs, but especially Greek or Latin Ante-Nicene Fathers, or occasionally Fathers of later date but exceptional text, as Cyril of Alexandria. On the other hand the dissent of documents which do often attest readings of somewhat similar ancestry is frequently noticed (as 'not *c ff* syr. vt '), especially if such attestation occurs in the immediate neighbourhood.

A full enumeration of documents attesting readings referred definitely to ancient texts is given only where the adverse testimony of documents of the same class is considerable, or there is some other special reason for completeness. A full enumeration is likewise given for readings not referred to an ancient text ; for readings adopted in the text itself where the reading rejected is both Pre-Syrian (of any type) and Syrian ; for variations in which the documents are split by diversity of reading into several small groups ; and for a few important variations treated more fully than the rest. These documentary statements are intended to be in one sense complete ; no tangible item of evidence within our knowledge has been absolutely passed over : but we have not cared to waste space, and distract attention from the weightier evidence, by an exhaustive enumeration of every petty 'authority', for instance of all late Fathers ; and have usually preferred to gather up a handful of such virtually irrelevant names under a single designation, such as pp^{ser}. With cursives we have dealt in the same manner, usually citing by their numbers those only which have a considerable proportion of Pre-Syrian readings, and briefly indicating the existence of others. Suspicious evidence, such as that of the inferior MSS of Versions and uncertified and questionable quotations of Fathers, is often enclosed in [ ]. Mere indirectness of evidence, usually though not always involving some little uncertainty, is marked with ( ), a ? being added where there is a more appreciable degree of uncertainty. But variations and gradations of trustworthiness can be only imperfectly expressed by any notation.

The amount of detail given in patristic references has varied according to circumstances. Standard pages (or, in certain cases, chapters) have been systematically specified for citations loosely or incorrectly recorded by others, or now first recorded; and also, less consistently, in many other cases, especially for the Ante-Nicene Fathers. In the absence of a reference to pages or chapters, the book containing a quotation has been specified wherever it could affect the character or the certainty of the attestation. For instance the text followed by Origen in his Comm. on St Matthew (Orig. *Mt*) has a much more Western character than the text followed in his Comm. on St John (Orig. *Jo*). Similarly the quotations of Cyril of Alexandria can be less relied on when they occur in books not edited since Aubert's time, as the *Thesaurus*, *Glaphyra*, and *De Adoratione*, the Epistles, and the Commentary on Isaiah, than when they occur in the books edited by the lamented Mr P. E. Pusey, as the Commentaries on the Minor

Prophets and St John and some of the minor dogmatic treatises; and these again differ in authority according to the MSS extant. We have of course been careful to mark distinctly the quotations of Greek writers which are extant only in Latin or Syriac, and which may thus come from either of two sources (*Introd.* § 220), and also to distinguish, when possible, the work of different translators. But it must suffice to notice once for all the complexity of the testimony obtained from the Armenian translation of Ephrem's Syriac commentary (or parts of it) on Tatian's Diatessaron, now made accessible by Moesinger's Latin rendering. It is often difficult to distinguish Ephrem's own (Syriac) readings from those which he found in the Syriac Diatessaron; and hardly ever possible to distinguish Tatian's own Greek readings from Old Syriac readings introduced by his translator.

The following are the chief abbreviations used in reference to MSS and in some cases to other documents :—'unc' uncials; 'cu' cursives; 'al' (after specified cursives) other (cursives); 'al⁶' six others (most of these enumerations are only approximative); 'al^p' a few others; 'al^{mu}' many others; 'al^{pm}' very many others; 'al^{pl}' nearly all others; 'al^{bo}' others having good texts or textual elements; 'al^{opt}' others having exceptionally good texts or textual elements. Hyphens are used for linking together the cursives (of the Gospels) 13-69-124-346 and 1-118-131-209 (see *Introd.* § 211), as their joint authority where they agree is only the authority of a single common original.

The notation of Greek MSS here adopted is that which is now everywhere current, with various slight modifications. Where however the same capital letter denotes different MSS in different parts of the New Testament, we have distinguished the MSS containing a second or a third group of books by the corresponding ('inferior') numerals, placed at the foot of the letter on the right side (see *Dict. of Bible* ii 513). Thus D is the *Cod. Bezae*, of the Gospels and Acts; D$_2$ the *Cod. Claromontanus*, of the Pauline Epistles; G one of the *Codd. Wolfii*, of the Gospels, G$_2$ a St Petersburg fragment of the Acts; G$_3$ the *Cod. Boernerianus*, of St Paul's Epistles; B the *Cod. Vaticanus* (1209) of most of the N.T.; B$_2$ the much later and in all respects inferior *Cod. Vaticanus* (2066) of the Apocalypse; L the *Cod. Regius* (62) of the Gospels; L$_2$ the late and inferior *Cod. Passionei*, of the Acts, Catholic, and Pauline Epistles: and so with others. For distinguishing the 'hands' of the different correctors of uncials we have followed the notation introduced by Tischendorf for ℵ, using [abc] for the first, second, or third correctors, in preference to multiplying asterisks; the hand of the original scribe being, as usual, marked with a single asterisk. For the determination of 'hands' we are of course dependent on the judgement of editors, which must occasionally rest on somewhat ambiguous grounds. Having occasion to cite the fourth of the seven fragmentary MSS combined by Tischendorf under the single letter I (see the clear enumeration in Dr Scrivener's *Introd.*[2] 122 f.), we have distinguished it as I$_d$: the portions of the other MSS should be called I$_a$ I$_b$ I$_c$ I$_e$ I$_f$ I$_g$ respectively.

Some important cursives, hitherto identified by an irregular and inconvenient notation, we have ventured to designate by numerals which have been recently set free. In the

following list the possessors, reputed dates, and collators of these cursives are mentioned after the two forms of notation.

Gospels

81 2^{pe} of Tisch.: St Petersburg: Cent. X: Muralt
82 Venice: XII: [Burgon in *Guardian*, 1874, p. 49: specimen only]
102 w^{scr} of Tisch.: Trin. Coll., Cambridge: A.D. 1316: Scrivener

Acts and Catholic Epistles

44 Burdett Coutts (iii 37): XII: Scrivener MS
102 k^{scr} of Tisch. (= 102 of the Gospels: see above)
110 a^{scr} of Tisch.: Lambeth: XII or XIII: Scrivener
112 c^{scr} of Tisch.: Lambeth: XV: Scrivener, from Sanderson

Pauline Epistles

27 k^{scr} of Tisch. (= 102 of the Gospels: see above)

Lectionaries (*of the Gospels*)

38 x^{scr} of Tisch.: Arundel, Brit. Mus.: IX: Scrivener
39 y^{scr} of Tisch.: Burney, Brit. Mus.: ? XII: Scrivener
59 z^{scr} of Tisch.: Christ's Coll., Cambridge: XI or XII: Scrivener

In the notation of Old Latin MSS we have done little more than attach letters to new documents. These are, with their reputed dates and the names of their editors,

Gospels (*European*)

j Saretianus (fragg. Lc; Jo.): IV or V: [Amelli, specimen only]
r Dublinensis (fragg.): [Gilbert, and Bradshaw MS, specimens only]
a$_2$ Fragmenta Curiensia (Lc): V: Ranke

Acts (*African*)

h Fragmenta Regia: V or VI: VanSittart

Acts (*European*)

g Gigas Holmiensis: ? XIII: Belsheim

g₂ Fragmentum Ambrosianum: X or XI: Ceriani

Catholic Epistles (? *Italian*)

q Freisingensis (fragg. 1 2 Pet; 1 Jo): VI: Ziegler

Pauline Epistles (*Italian*)

(*r* Freisingensis (fragg.): V or VI: Ziegler

r₂ Freisingensis alter (frag. Phi; 1 Th): VII: Ziegler

r₃ Gottvicensis (fragg. Ro; Ga): VI or VII: Rönsch

Apocalypse (*African*)

h Fragmenta Regia: V or VI: VanSittart

Apocalypse (*Late European or Italian*)

g Gigas Holmiensis: ? XIII: Belsheim.

On *m* see *Introd.* § 126: by *sess* is meant the *Cod. Sessorianus* (A) of the *Testimonia* of Cyprian, cited separately for readings differing from those of Cyprian and of the Vulgate. We have assimilated the notation of the following MSS of the Gospels to the usual Vulgate form, since, though usually classed as Old Latin, they appear rather to have a Vulgate text with different Old Latin admixtures (see *Introd.* § 114):- *corb*(=*ff¹*); *rhe* (=*l*); *ger₁* (=*g¹*); *ger₂* (=*g²*). The simple notation *ff* is thus set free for the important MS usually called *ff²*, which has no affinity to the MS called *ff¹*: the *ff* of Martianay's

MS of St James may also with advantage be reduced to *f*.

Latin Vulgate MSS are designated in the usual manner. In all books but the Acts and Apocalypse (the text being there Old Latin), *gig* denotes the Bohemian *Gigas* of Stockholm as collated by Belsheim, and in the Gospels *holm* the *Cod. aureus Holmiensis* as published by him; also *rushw* the Rushworth Gospels as collated by Stevenson and Skeat, and *cant* the Cambridge Gospels (Kk 1 24, Lc Jo only, ?Cent. VIII), both good specimens of the 'British' type of Mixed texts (see B. F. Westcott in *Dict. of Bible* iii 1694). Similarly in Acts *seld* denotes the Selden MS (Bodl. 3418), for which Mr J. Wordsworth has kindly allowed us to use his collation; and in the Pauline Epistles *nev* the Neville MS in Trinity College, Cambridge (B 10 5, ?Cent. IX). In most cases however we have not specified individual MSS in referring to variations among Vulgate texts

The Old (Curetonian) Syriac is denoted by 'syr.vt'; the Revised or Vulgate Syriac by 'syr.vg'; the Harklean Syriac by 'syr.hl', or where it has accessory readings or marks (*Introd.* §§ 119, 215) by 'syr. hl.txt', 'syr.hl.mg', 'syr.hl.*', which explain themselves; and the Jerusalem Syriac by 'syr.hr', with indication of differences between the London and St Petersburg fragments published by Land and the Vatican MS.

Where more than one Latin or Syriac version has the same reading, 'lat' or 'syr' is not repeated for each, but a hyphen is inserted, as 'lat.it-vg' 'syr.vt-vg-hr': but where all Latin or Syriac versions agree, they are represented collectively as 'latt' or 'syrr'. For brevity the version of Lower Egypt is usually called 'me', that of Upper Egypt 'the', and the Gothic 'go'. The better of the known MSS of versions are occasionally distinguished as 'codd.opt'. Uscan's Armenian readings are rarely cited where they appear to be derived from the Latin Vulgate (see *Introd.* §§ 121, 218).

The patristic notation for the most part explains itself. Some of the abbreviations noticed above for Greek MSS are applied *mutatis mutandis* to Versions and Fathers : thus 'al' is occasionally used after the names of Fathers to denote unimportant patristic testimonies, especially those of doubtful but not early authorship. A 'superior' numeral affixed to the name of a Father (as Clem³) denotes the existence of so many quotations to the same effect in his extant works, or in some one work of his if the numeral is affixed to the name of the work : but in reference to modern writers and editors (as Matthaei²) a 'superior' numeral is used to distinguish the first second or later editions. In some of the many cases in which an ancient author or work supports, or seems to support, different readings in different places it has been thought worth while to carry numerical precision a step further, and indicate the proportion of the several testimonies : thus 'Hil 3/5' denotes that the reading in question is attested by Hilary three times, the whole number of places in which he has either this or a different reading being five.

The mark + denotes the addition of the words following: < the omission of the words following: || indicates a parallel passage, ||| more

parallel passages than one. The abbreviations 'ap.' 'cf.' are treated as pure symbols, not as governing a case. The readings which stand at the head of each note, and the other variants contrasted with them, retain the accentuation which they have, or would have, as parts of the text itself : thus in the note on Mc i 41 σπλαγχνισθείς and ὀργισθείς have the grave accent, because here they are not independent or strictly final oxytones, being treated as fragments of a clause which runs on continuously to the pause at αὐτῷ. Places where a 'primitive error' is suspected are marked with (†). Criticisms for which one of the editors alone is responsible are enclosed in [ ] with an initial.

We are much indebted to Dr Wright for the pains which he has taken in furnishing us with the readings of selected Æthiopic MSS in an ample list of passages, and for other similar help ; and also to Mr VanSittart for the loan of his collation of some cursives in several of the Pauline Epistles, and to Dr Scrivener for the loan of his collation of 44 of the Acts and Catholic Epistles.

These explanations will, we trust, suffice to render the contents of the following notes intelligible by themselves to any careful reader. We must repeat however that the primary purposes of the notes are explanation and illustration ; and that, though they silently correct many erroneous statements of fact, they are not intended as substitutes for the more detailed exhibitions of documentary evidence attached to the larger critical editions.

i 8 Ἰωρὰμ δὲ ἐγέννησεν] + τὸν Ὀχοζίαν, Ὀχοζίας δὲ ἐγέννησεν τὸν Ἰωάς, Ἰωὰς δὲ ἐγέννησεν τὸν Ἀμασίαν, Ἀμασίας δὲ ἐγέννησεν some Syriac MSS and writers, and at least one MS of aeth: D, defective here, interpolates the same names in Lc iii, where it replaces the names of the genealogy between David and Joseph by the names given in Mt. The absence of these three names is expressly attested by Jul.afr(Cat.Cram.*Mt*.9). From i Chr iii 11 f.

i 11 Ἰωσείας δὲ ἐγέννησεν] + τὸν Ἰωακείμ, Ἰωακεὶμ δὲ ἐγέννησεν some Greek (Cent. x and later) and Syriac MSS, and apparently Iren. 218 by implication, and Epiph. i 21 f., whose language about a reading "of the accurate copies" removed by "certain ignorant persons" was probably intended to refer to these words rather than to part of v. 12: D, defective here, interpolates τοῦ Ἰωακείμ in Lc iii. From i Chr iii 15 f.

i 18 τοῦ δὲ [Ἰησοῦ] Χριστοῦ] (marg.) τοῦ δὲ χριστοῦ Ἰησοῦ B Orig. *Lc*.lat. Hier; and perhaps *Jo*. 15 (ἡ εὐαγγελισθεῖσα ἡμῖν διὰ τῆς γενέσεως Χριστοῦ Ἰησοῦ χαρά); but Orig.*Lc*.gr and again *ad loc.* (Galland xiv b 73 = Migne vii 289) has text, as has Tat.*Diat*.arm.20.

< Ἰησοῦ *d* (D.gr being defective) latt.omn syr.vt Iren.lat. 191,204 expressly (though the Greek of 191 as imperfectly preserved by Germanus has τοῦ δὲ Ἰ. Χ.) *Vita S. Syncleticae* ascribed to Ath.*Opp*. ii. 700 Theod.mops.*Incarn*.syr.(p. 52 Sachau, ? from syr.vt) Thphl.cod pp[lat]: it may be accidental that Clem. 401 has the phrase τὴν γένεσιν τοῦ χριστοῦ.

A peculiar and difficult variation. Text, which is much the best attested reading, is intrinsically improbable, the article being nowhere in the N. T. prefixed to Ἰ. Χ. in any good MS: indeed its presence in this position could hardly be reconciled with the appellative force which χριστός assuredly must retain in St Matthew, and which is not lost in the partial assimilation to a proper name. Moreover the occurrence of the phrase γενέσεως Ἰησοῦ Χριστοῦ in i 1 could hardly fail to lead to the introduction of Ἰησοῦ Χριστοῦ by scribes in connexion with ἡ γένεσις here. The clearly Western τοῦ δὲ χριστοῦ on the other hand is intrinsically free from objection. [Yet it cannot be confidently accepted. The attestation is unsatisfactory, for no other Western omission of a solitary word in the Gospels has any high probability;

nor was τοῦ δὲ χριστοῦ in itself a phrase likely to provoke alteration ; while on the other hand it might easily arise from assimilation to the preceding ἕως τοῦ χριστοῦ. Nor is the presence of the name Ἰησοῦ improbable, as v. 16 shews. The phenomena can hardly be accounted for except by a phrase sufficiently uncommon to provoke alteration, and containing both Ἰησοῦς and ὁ χριστός. These conditions are fulfilled by τοῦ δὲ χριστοῦ Ἰησοῦ, the reading of at least B, though here the authority of B is weakened by its proneness to substitute X. Ἰ. for Ἰ. X. in the Pauline Epistles. They would be fulfilled equally by τοῦ δὲ Ἰησοῦ τοῦ χριστοῦ : but there is no authority for the second τοῦ. H.]

ibid. γένεσις] γέννησις Pre-Syrian (? Alexandrian) and Syrian (Gr. : vv ambiguous) ; incl. L and Orig. *loc.* expressly (Galland *l. c.*). Probably suggested by ἐγεννήθη in v. 16 : compare also the parallel corruption of γενέσει into γεννήσει in Lc i 14.

i 25 υἱόν] τὸν υἱὸν [αὐτῆς] τὸν πρωτότοκον Syrian (Gr. Lat.[it-vg] Syr. Æth. Arm.) ; incl. Ath.*Apoll* Epiph : τὸν πρωτότοκον Tat.*Diat.* arm.25. From Lc ii 7.

ii 11 τοὺς θησαυροὺς] τὰς πήρας Epiph. i 430, 1085, who calls text a reading of ' some copies '. Perhaps a confusion of the canonical Gospel with the apocryphal *Book of James* xxi 3. See on Lc ii 7.

iii 15 *fin.*] + *et cum baptizaretur* (+ *Jesus*), *lumen ingens circumfulsit* (*magnum fulgebat*) *de aqua, ita ut timerent omnes qui advenerant* (*congregati erant*) *a* (*ger₁*) and apparently Juvencus : *k* is defective. Probably from an apocryphal source : according to the ' Ebionite ' Gospel cited by Epiph. i 129 c, immediately after the voice from heaven, περιέλαμψε τὸν τόπον φῶς μέγα. So Justin *Dial.*88

κατελθόντος τοῦ Ἰησοῦ ἐπὶ τὸ ὕδωρ καὶ πῦρ ἀνήφθη ἐν τῷ Ἰορδάνῃ ; a lost *Praedicatio Paulli* (auct. *Rebapt.* 17) stated *cum baptizaretur ignem super aquam esse visum* ; Ephr.*Diat.* arm.43 refers to the light ; and the tradition has left other traces.

iv 10 ὕπαγε]+ὀπίσω [μου] Western and Syrian (Gr. Lat. Syr. Æth. Arm.) ; not *k* Iren.lat Tert. From xvi 23.

v 4, 5] ꓙ μακάριοι οἱ πραεῖς κ.τ.λ. μακάριοι οἱ πενθοῦντες κ.τ.λ. ꓾ Western (Gr.[D 33] Lat. Syr. ; not *b* Tert) ; incl. (Clem,) Orig.*Mt*, and probably Ephr.*Diat.*arm.62.

v 22 πᾶς ὁ ὀργιζόμενος τῷ ἀδελφῷ αὐτοῦ] + εἰκῇ Western and Syrian (Gr. Lat. Syr. Eg. Arm. Goth.) ; incl Iren.lat³; Eus.*D.E.*; Cyp. Text אB Greek MSS known to Aug cu¹ lat.vg aeth pp ; so apparently Just Ptolem (? Iren. 242*fin.*) Tert ; and certainly Orig on Eph iv 31, noticing both readings, and similarly Hier *loc,* who probably follows Orig; .also Ath. *Pasch.* syr. 11 ; Ps.Ath. *Cast.* ii 4 (" so the accurate copies ") ; and others. Δ⁵ is wrongly cited for omission : the marks taken for cancelling dots are corrections of two slips of the pen, and due to the original scribe.

v 37 ναὶ ναί, οὒ οὔ] τὸ Ναί ναὶ καὶ τό Οὔ οὔ lt 59 and some early and late Greek Fathers. Nearly as Ja v 12. Perhaps from an extraneous source, written or oral.

vi 13 *fin.*] + ὅτι σοῦ ἐστὶν ἡ βασιλεία καὶ ἡ δύναμις καὶ ἡ δόξα εἰς τοὺς αἰῶνας. ἀμήν. Syrian (Gr. Lat. [*f q ger₁*] Syr. Æth. Arm. Goth.). Similar but shorter doxologies are added in *k* (om. ἡ βασ. and ἡ δόξα) theb(the same, but + ἡ ἰσχύς) syr.vt(om. ἡ δύν.). Text אBDZ 1-118-209 17 130 lat.vt.pl-vg me pp ; incl. all Greek commentators on the Lord's Prayer (Orig Cyr.hr Greg.nys Max) except Chrys and his followers (Isid.pel

Thphl Euthym); and all Latin commentators (Tert Cyp Hil Chrom Juv Aug &c.), the *Op.imperf.* being probably a translation. The Doxology stands in full in the Lord's Prayer as prescribed in *Const.Ap.* III 18 2, and apparently also in VII 24 1 (see Lagarde 207 f.), though in the common texts founded on the *ed. princeps* ἡ βασιλεία is followed immediately by ἀμήν.

There can be little doubt that the Doxology originated in liturgical use in Syria, and was thence adopted into the Greek and Syriac Syrian texts of the N. T. It was probably derived ultimately from 1 Chr xxix 11 (Heb.), but, it may be, through the medium of some contemporary Jewish usage : the people's response to prayers in the temple is said to have been " Blessed be the name of the glory of his kingdom for ever and ever". In the extant Greek liturgy bearing St James's name, the base of which was certainly Syrian, the *embolism*, or expanded last double petition of the L. P., ends with ὅτι σοῦ ἐστιν ἡ βασιλεία καὶ ἡ δύναμις καὶ ἡ δόξα, τοῦ πατρὸς καὶ τοῦ υἱοῦ καὶ τοῦ ἁγίου πνεύματος, νῦν καὶ ἀεί, that is, the Doxology with a doctrinal expansion; and three late writers cite the liturgical ascription approximately in this form : one of them, Euthymius, elsewhere distinctly describes it as " the concluding acclamation which was added by the divine luminaries and masters of the Church". The Doxology can be traced in other liturgies believed on other grounds to be derived from that ascribed to St James, or to have come under Constantinopolitan (=Antiochian) influence ; but apparently in these alone ; and the language of Cyr.hr (*Catech.* xxiii 18) leaves no doubt that in his time (about 349) it was absent from the liturgy of Jerusalem ; as it certainly

is from all extant Latin liturgies. The natural impulse to close the prayer in actual use with a doxology (cf. Orig. *Orat.* 271 f.) is illustrated by the parallel Latin doxology noticed by 'Ambr.' *Sacr.* v: 25, *per dominum nostrum J. C., in quo tibi est, cum quo tibi est, honor, laus, gloria, magnificentia, potestas cum spiritu sancto a saeculis et nunc et semper et in omnia saecula saeculorum : Amen* : and various embolisms include other ascriptions of praise. It may possibly be owing to a reminiscence of liturgical use of the Syrian or some other doxology that the elaborate ascription with which Greg.nys concludes his last Oration on the L. P. contains ἡ δύναμις καὶ ἡ δόξα instead of the more usual ἡ δόξα καὶ τὸ κράτος; though he certainly treats no such words as parts of the L. P. itself, as he must have done had he read them in the text of Mt. His ascription has indeed much more in common with the developed doxology of the existing Greek liturgies, as cited above. The ecclesiastical currency of similar language in Cent. IV is further attested by Epiph (*Haer.* 786: cf. *Anc.* 42 ; Did. *Trin.* iii 21 p. 402 ; Caesar. i 29), ὁμολογοῦντες αὐτοῦ τὸ τῆς εὐλογίας κράτος καὶ διὰ λεπτολογίας ἐροῦμεν Σή ἐστιν ἡ δύναμις, σὸν τὸ κράτος, σή ἐστιν ἡ τιμή, σή ἐστιν ἡ δόξα, σή ἐστιν ἡ εὐλογία, σή ἐστιν ἡ ἰσχύς, σή ἐστιν ἡ δύναμις [sic]. There is thus no improbability in the supposition that the doxologies in *k* and theb are of independent origin rather than mutilations of the Syrian text. The *Amen* added by some late Latin documents which omit the Doxology proper is certainly independent, and its insertion analogous to that of the Doxology.

Another apparently liturgical interpolation occurs in several Latin

Fathers, the addition of *quam ferre* (*sufferre*) *non possumus* to *temptationem*: it is not known to exist in any Latin MS of the Gospel itself.

vi 33 τὴν βασιλείαν] + τοῦ θεοῦ most documents. Others (early Fathers) add τῶν οὐρανῶν; others (as *k* Cyp³), omitting here, replace αὐτοῦ by τοῦ θεοῦ; me aeth read αὐτοῦ in both places; Eus omits in both places. Text א(B) *m ger₂ am rhe harl*: B transposes βασιλείαν and δικαιοσύνην.

vii 13 πλατεῖα] (marg.) + ἡ πύλη most documents. Text א* lat.vt (not lat.ser) and many Greek and Latin Fathers, early and late: D is defective. In 14 ἡ πύλη is likewise omitted by cu³ lat.vt.codd and a very similar array of Fathers; not by א* *b c for* and probably Orig (see below).

A peculiar variation, the patristic evidence being unusually discordant with that of MSS and versions, and both the patristic evidence and the *prima facie* balance of the evidence of MSS and versions being at variance with internal evidence. Transcriptional considerations give high probability to the composite reading formed by the omission of the first ἡ πύλη and the retention of the second: unlikely itself to arise from either the double insertion or the double omission, it will fully account for both. The best attested of the three readings, the double insertion, is the furthest removed of all from the whole of the somewhat copious stream of patristic attestation prior to Chrys among Greeks and to Amb among Latins. Till the latter part of the fourth century the first ἡ πύλη has no Greek or Latin patristic evidence in its favour, much against it; while the second ἡ πύλη differs only by having in its favour one or two quotations of Orig, and against it an ampler list, including some fourteen quotations or clear allusions of Orig. The modification which a written phrase sometimes undergoes in becoming proverbial might account for part of this distribution, but not for its approximate exclusiveness.

The first ἡ πύλη being then regarded as probably not genuine, it is not necessary to decide whether it should be interpreted as a 'West ern non-interpolation', or, as we rather suspect, as one of those rare readings in which the true text has been preserved by א without extant uncial support, owing to the exceptional intrusion of a late element into B (of which some examples occur further on in this Gospel) or perhaps to accidental coincidence in independent assimilation of the two verses. Under all the circumstances we have thought it right to retain ἡ πύλη in the margin, though there is little probability of its being genuine. It was natural to scribes to set v. 13 in precisely antithetic contrast to v. 14: but the sense gains in force if there is no mention of two gates, and if the contrast in v. 13 is between the narrow gate and the broad and spacious way.

vii 21 *fin.*] +⊢ οὗτος εἰσελεύσεται εἰς τὴν βασιλείαν τῶν οὐρανῶν ⊢ Western (Gr.[Cᵃ 33] Lat. Syr.): D is defective.

vii 22 Κύριε κύριε] + οὐ τῷ ὀνόματί σου ἐφάγομεν καὶ [τῷ ὀνόματί σου] ἐπίομεν syr.vt Just Orig³ Hier Aug². Perhaps from an extraneous source, written or oral: but cf. Lc xiii 26.

vii 29 *fin.*] +⊢ καὶ οἱ Φαρισαῖοι ⊢ Western (Gr. Lat. Syr.); incl. Cᵃ 17 33 al Eus. 1/2: D is defective. Probably from Lc v 30.

viii 11 μετὰ 'Αβραὰμ] ἐν τοῖς κόλποις [τοῦ] 'Α. (also εἰς τοὺς κόλπους 'Α. and ἐν κόλπῳ 'Α.), mostly with omission of καὶ 'Ισαὰκ...οὐρανῶν, cuᵖ

Hom.Cl and several Greek Fathers, most of whom have text elsewhere. Perhaps from an extraneous source, written or oral: but cf. Lc xvi 23. Similarly in Jo i 18 (εἰς τὸν κόλπον) there is some slight evidence for ἐν [τοῖς] κόλποις, and Erigena *ad l.* (p. 502 Floss) has the curious statement '*qui est in sinu Patris*', *vel ut in Graeco scribitur* '*qui est in sinum Patris*' *vel* '*in sinibus Patris*': *in quibusdam codicibus Graecorum singulariter sinus Patris dicitur, in quibusdam pluraliter, quasi sinus multos Pater habeat.*

viii 12 ἐκβληθήσονται] ⊣ ἐξελεύσονται ⊢ Western (Gr. Lat.[afr] Syr.) incl. ℵ* Heracl Eus. *Theoph.*syr Cyp. 1/3 : D is defective : *ibunt* lat.eur-it Iren.lat Cyp.1/3.

viii 28 Γαδαρηνῶν] Γερασηνῶν Western (?Gr. Lat. Syr. Eg.); Γεργεσηνῶν Alexandrian and Syrian (Gr. Eg. Æth. Arm. Goth.). In Mc v 1 Γερασηνῶν is changed to Γεργεσηνῶν, Alexandrian (Gr. Syr. Eg. Æth. Arm.), and Γαδαρηνῶν, Syrian (Gr. Syr. Goth.); and in Lc viii 26, 37 Γερασηνῶν to Γεργεσηνῶν, Alexandrian (Gr. Syr. Eg. Æth. Arm.), and Γαδαρηνῶν, Syrian (Gr. Syr. Goth.). Orig. *Jo.* 140, incidentally discussing the three names on geographical grounds and without reference to difference between the Gospels, rejects Gadara (found by him 'in a few' copies) and Gerasa in favour of Gergesa. Epiph (*Haer.* 650 BC) assigns Γεργεσηνῶν to Mc and Lc (the form of sentence suggesting however that Γερασηνῶν was meant in one Gospel); and Γαδαρηνῶν, with Γεργεσηνῶν in 'some copies', to Mt.

There is no need to assume that all three forms must have found a place originally in one or other Gospel. Documentary evidence shews clearly Γαδαρηνῶν as the true reading in Mt, Γερασηνῶν in Mc

and Lc. The Western text simply assimilates all three variations by introducing Γερασηνῶν in Mt. The Alexandrian text likewise assimilates all three, but substitutes for both the original names a name supposed to be more correct geographically, and also resembling the Γεργεσαῖοι of the LXX. Thirdly, the Syrian text in the earlier form represented by syr.vg inverts the Western process by reading Γαδαρηνῶν in all three places; though again the Greek Constantinopolitan form of it adopts in Mt the Alexandrian Γεργεσηνῶν : Chrys, strange to say, avoids using any name in discussing the narrative, but in the next Homily (342 c) speaks retrospectively of τῶν ἐν Γαδάροις. In Lc Γεργεσηνῶν has an exceptionally good attestation, though of a distinctly Alexandrian colour, and might claim a place as an alternative if v. 26 stood alone : the fuller evidence however preserved in v. 37 is decisive for Γερασηνῶν.

ix 15 νυμφῶνος] ⊣ νυμφίου ⊢ Western (Gr.[D] Lat. Eg. Æth. Goth.). From the following ὁ νυμφίος, through failure to understand the Jewish phrase.

x 3 Θαδδαῖος] ⊣ Λεββαῖος ⊢ (also spelt Λεβαῖος) Western (Gr.[Dcu¹] Lat. Syr.[hr. cod]) : the Latin authority seems to be African only, *k* codd.ap.Aug. Text ℵB 17 124 *c corb* vg me the Hier. *loc*(apparently). In Mc iii 18 Λεββαῖος is likewise a Western (Gr.[D] Lat.) corruption of Θαδδαῖος, these being the only two places where either name occurs. The clearly defined attestation is unfavourable to the genuineness of Λεββαῖος in either Gospel. This name is apparently due to an early attempt to bring Levi (Λευείς) the publican (Lc v 27) within the Twelve, it being assumed that his call was to apostleship; just as in

Mc ii 14 Λευείς is changed in Western texts to Ἰάκωβος because τὸν τοῦ Ἀλφαίου follows, and it was assumed that the son of Halphæus elsewhere named as one of the Twelve must be meant. The difference between the two forms of the name would be inconsiderable in Aramaic, *Lewi* and *Levi* or *Lebi* or *Lebbi;* and Λεββαῖος might as easily represent *Lebbi* as Θαδδαῖος *Thaddi.* Indeed the identity of Levi and Lebbæus, evidently resting on the presumed identity of the names in Greek, is implied in a remark of Orig quoted on Mc iii 18, and in a scholium (best given by Matthaei[1] on Mc ii 14) which may be ultimately derived from a lost comment of his.

Another Western substitute for Θαδδαῖος is *Judas Zelotes*, a well supported Old Latin reading (*a b h* and Mixed MSS), found also in the list in the Roman Chronography of 354, p. 640 Mommsen. Jude is evidently introduced for assimilation to the list in Lc (vi 16). The addition of *Zelotes* is probably due to a punctuation of Lc's text which might not seem unnatural if no connexion of sense were recognised between Καναναῖος and ζηλωτής, τὸν καλούμενον Ζηλωτήν being detached from Σίμωνα and prefixed to καὶ Ἰούδαν Ἰακώβου, 'him who bore the names *Zelotes* and *Judas Jacobi'.* Conflation of this reading with lat.vg produced the curious *Thatheus Zelotis* of *rushw.*

The Syrian reading Λεββαῖος ὁ ἐπικληθεὶς Θαδδαῖος (Gr. Syr. Æth. Arm.) is a conflation of the true and the chief Western texts. The two names having been preserved and applied to the same apostle in Mt, it was apparently thought superfluous to repeat the process in Mc. By a further conflation Ἰούδας ὁ καὶ is prefixed in 243. The two

principal names change places by another conflation in 13-346.

x 23 φεύγετε εἰς τὴν ἑτέραν] + + κἂν ἐκ ταύτης διώκωσιν ὑμᾶς, φεύγετε εἰς τὴν ἄλλην ⊢ Western (Gr. Lat. Arm.), with much variation; incl.Orig.*Cels*; *Mart*; *Jos*.lat.ruf; Tat.*Diat*.arm. 94. A natural continuation, probably suggested by ἑτέραν, which in many documents, whether independently or under the influence of the interpolation, is altered into ἄλλην.

x 42 ἀπολέσῃ τὸν μισθὸν] + ἀπόληται ὁ μισθὸς ⊢ Western (Gr.[D] Lat. Eg. Æth.). Cf. Sir ii 8, οὐ μὴ πταίσῃ ὁ μισθὸς αὐτῶν.

xi 19 ἔργων] τέκνων Western and Syrian (Gr. Lat. Syr. ? Arm. Goth.). Text ℵB* MSS known to Hier 124 syr.vg-hl.txt me aeth arm. codd Hier. From Lc vii 35, where conversely ℵ introduces ἔργων from this place.

xiii 35 τοῦ προφήτου] (marg.) Ἡσαίου τοῦ προφήτου ℵ* 1 13-124-346 33 253 *rushw* aeth.cod. Hom. Cl Porph (ap. *Brev. Psalt.* in Hier. *Opp.* vii 270 Vall.). According to Eus.*Ps*.lxxviii.*tit.* 'some, not understanding' that the 'prophet' intended by Mt was Asaph, "added in the Gospel διὰ Ἡσαίου τοῦ προφήτου: but in the accurate copies", he proceeds, "it stands without the addition διὰ Ἡσαίου [*sic*], simply thus &c.": a loose condensation of Eus in Cord. Cat. *Ps.* ii 631 substitutes 'ancient' for 'accurate'. Hier. *loc.* says that he had read 'Ἡσαίου 'in some MSS', and supposes that afterwards, since the passage was not found in Isaiah, the name *a prudentibus viris esse sublatum.* He further conjectures that Ἀσάφ was the original reading, unintelligently corrected into Ἡσαίου. The *Brev. in Ps.* states definitely that Ἀσάφ was found 'in all old MSS', but was removed (*tulerunt,*

? sustulerunt) 'by ignorant men'; that by an error of scribes 'Hσαίου was written for 'Aσάφ; and that at the time of writing (*usque hodie*) many copies of the Gospel still had 'Hσαίου. This is perhaps only an exaggerated reproduction of Jerome's account; but the unknown author or compiler must have had some other authority for at least the reference to Porphyry and for some remarks which follow. Possibly both he and Jerome may have used some lost passage of Eus written in reply to Porphyry. No extant document is known to have 'Aσάφ.

[It is difficult not to think 'Hσαίου genuine. There was a strong temptation to omit it (cf. xxvii 9; Mc i 2); and, though its insertion might be accounted for by an impulse to supply the name of the best known prophet, the evidence of the actual operation of such an impulse is much more trifling than might have been anticipated. Out of the 5 (6) other places where the true text has simply τοῦ προφήτου, in two (Mt ii 15 [Hosea]; Acts vii 48 [Isaiah]), besides the early interpolation in Mt xxvii 35 [Psalms], no name is inserted; in two a name is inserted on trivial evidence (Mt ii 5, *Micah* rightly, and *Isaiah* [by *a*] wrongly; xxi 4, *Isaiah* and *Zechariah* both rightly [Zech by lat.vt]); and once (Mt i 22) *Isaiah* is rightly inserted on varied Western evidence. Also for the perplexing 'Iερεμίου of xxvii 9, omitted by many documents, *rhe* has 'Hσαίου. Thus the erroneous introduction of Isaiah's name is limited to two passages, and in each case to a single Latin MS. On the other hand the authority of *rushw* and aeth is lessened by the (right) insertion of 'Hσαίου by one in Mt i 22, and by both in xxi 4. The adverse testimony of B is not decisive, as it

24

has a few widely spread wrong readings in this Gospel. H.]

xiii 55 'Iωσήφ] 'Iωσῆς Syrian (Gr. Syr. Arm.); also '*k q***', but *?Josef* (f for ſ), the form elsewhere used by *k*. Probably from common use, supported (in the gen. 'Iωσῆτος) by Mc vi 3; xv 40, 47. Another ancient reading here is 'Iωάννης, probably from the familiar combination of James and John: some Latin MSS combine this with text. For both the brother of the Lord and the brother of James the Less Mt here (and probably xxvii 56) uses 'Iωσήφ, Mc (*ubi sup.*) the Græcised form 'Iωσῆς. The Syrian tendency, apparently shown also in Acts iv 36 (cf. i 23), was to introduce 'Iωσῆς, the Western to introduce 'Iωσήφ.

xv 30(†) χωλούς, κυλλούς, τυφλούς, κωφούς] The documents shew great diversity of order among the words, partly due to the influence of v. 31. No single order is supported by more than a small amount of evidence. Not being able to arrive at any safe conclusion, we have printed the order of B, and prefer marking the reading as uncertain to affixing a series of alternatives. Possibly one of the words should be omitted.

xvi 2, 3 [['Oψίας — δύνασθε]] < אBVXΓ 'most MSS' known to Jerome 13-124 157 all[11] syr.vt me. cod arm Orig.*loc.* Text Western and Syrian (Gr. Lat. Syr. Eg. Æth.). Both documentary evidence and the impossibility of accounting for omission prove these words to be no part of the text of Mt. They can hardly have been an altered repetition of the ‖ Lc xii 54, 55, but were apparently derived from an extraneous source, written or oral, and inserted in the Western text at a very early time.

xvi 21 'Iησοῦς Xριστὸς] ο 'Iησοῦς most documents, including Orig.

loc[2]; Ἰησοῦς D ; omitted by אᶜ and some Fathers. Text א*B me. The high though limited attestation of text is sustained, and the *prima facie* presumption against it as at variance with the usual language of the Gospel narratives is removed, by the absence of erroneous introductions of Ἰ. Χ. elsewhere in the Gospels (see on i 18), by the want of apparent motive for introducing it here and the facility with which it would be changed to the commoner form, and above all by the special fitness of Ἰ. Χ. to mark the beginning of the second half of the Ministry. The introductory phrase Ἀπὸ τότε ἤρξατο is used in like manner in iv 17 to introduce the first half of the Ministry, and occurs nowhere else in the Gospel; while the double name could not well be used in narrative till the climax of the Ministry had been reached, as it is in xvi 13—20.

xvii 12,13 οὕτως—αὐτῶν. τότε— αὐτοῖς.] τότε—αὐτοῖς. οὕτως—αὐτῶν. Western (Gr. Lat.): the omission of οὕτως — αὐτῶν by Just.*Dial.*49 is doubtless owing to the context. Probably due to a wish to bring together the sentences relating to John the Baptist.

xvii 20 *fin.*]+(v. 21) τοῦτο δὲ τὸ γένος οὐκ ἐκπορεύεται εἰ μὴ ἐν προσευχῇ καὶ νηστείᾳ Western and Syrian (Gr. Lat. Syr. [Eg.] Arm.); incl. Orig.*loc.* Text א*B 33 *e corb* syr.vt-hr[2] me cod the aeth Eus.*Can.* Though earlier than Origen's (mainly Western) MS, this interpolation from ‖ Mc ix 29 can hardly belong to the earliest Western text, being absent from the African *e* and from syr.vt, and being subsequent to the interpolation of καὶ νηστείᾳ into Mc's text. It occurs with much variation: *daemonii* is a well attested Latin addition to γένος; the verb is

ἐκβάλλεται in א* latt.omn Ps.Ath (not D syr.vg Orig.*loc*); προσευχῇ and νηστείᾳ are inverted in vv and Orig.*loc.*lat; &c.

xviii 10 *fin.*]+(v. 11) ἦλθεν γὰρ ὁ υἱὸς τοῦ ἀνθρώπου σῶσαι τὸ ἀπολωλός. Western and Syrian (Gr. Lat. Syr. [Eg.] Arm. [Æth.]). Text אBL* 1* 13 33 *e corb* syr.hr.vat me the aeth.cod Orig.*loc*(almost certainly, if the Latin is taken into account) Eus.*Can.* Interpolated either from Lc xix 10 (a different context) or from an independent source, written or oral. Various secondary documents insert ζητῆσαι καί from Lc.

xviii 20 appears in D as οὐκ εἰσὶν γὰρ δύο ἢ τρεῖς συνηγμένοι εἰς τὸ ἐμὸν ὄνομα παρ᾽ οἷς οὐκ εἰμὶ (ειμει) ἐν μέσῳ αὐτῶν.: *ger*₁ adds to text an abridged form of the same. Western. Probably due to a misreading of the initial ΟΥ as οὐ.

xix 16. Διδάσκαλε] + ἀγαθέ Pre-Syrian and Syrian (Gr. Lat. Syr. Eg. Arm.). Text אBDL 1 22 al[2] *a e corb* aeth Orig.*loc* Hil.*loc.* From ‖ Mc x 17; Lc xviii 18. With this variation may be taken the following

17 Τί με ἐρωτᾷς περὶ τοῦ ἀγαθοῦ] Τί με λέγεις ἀγαθόν Syrian (Gr. Lat. Syr. Eg.). From ‖ Mc x 18; Lc xviii 19.

εἷς ἐστιν ὁ ἀγαθός] οὐδεὶς ἀγαθὸς εἰ μὴ εἷς Syrian (Gr. Lat. Syr. Eg. Æth.). From ‖ Mc x 18; Lc xviii 19.

Also + ὁ θεός Western and Syrian (Gr. Lat. Syr. Eg. Æth.). Text אBDL 1 22 *a* (*e*) syr.hr arm Orig.*loc.* From ‖ Mc x 18; Lc xviii 19. Also + ὁ πατήρ [μου ὁ ἐν τοῖς οὐρανοῖς], variously modified, *e* and, without reference to any particular Gospel, several ancient writers (Just Hom.Cl Ptolem Marcos Naass Clem Orig Tat.*Diat.* 169, 173 &c.). Similarly ὁ πατήρ is found in arm.codd in Mc and

Lc, and in *d* and Marcion in Lc. Probably from an independent source, written or oral. The earliest of these corruptions are the additions of ἀγαθέ and ὁ θεός, which are supported by most, not the best, lat.vt.codd and by syr.vt and me (these last omitting ἀγαθόν, so as to retain ἀγ. once only), not however by any good uncial except C: even here text is sustained by the best Greek and (*a e corb* Hil and *a* [*e*]) Latin evidence, as also by aeth in v. 16 and syr.hr arm in v. 17. The other more important changes apparently date only from the Syrian revision. Orig.*loc* has text throughout, and expressly vouches for Τί με ἐρωτᾷς περὶ τοῦ ἀγαθοῦ (and perhaps what follows) against the reading of Mc and Lc. The other early quotations (as Just Marcos) may come from any Gospel or from more than one.

xix 19 καὶ ἀγαπήσεις...ὡς σεαυτόν < syr.hr.vat (not lond). Orig.*loc* expresses a strong doubt whether this clause is genuine, appealing to its absence in Mc and Lc, and regarding it as inconsistent with v. 21. Apparently the doubt was not supported by any manuscript authority. The reading of syr.hr might easily arise from the omission in ||| Mc x 19; Lc xviii 20.

xx 16 *fin.*]+ ┤ πολλοὶ γάρ εἰσιν κλητοὶ ὀλίγοι δὲ ἐκλεκτοί. ├ Western and Syrian (Gr. Lat. Syr. [Æth.] Arm.); incl. Orig.*loc*. Text אBLZ cu¹ me the aeth.cod. From xxii 14, the close of a similar parable.

xx 28 *fin.*]+ὑμεῖς δὲ ζητεῖτε ἐκ μικροῦ (μεικρου) αὐξῆσαι καὶ ἐκ μείζονος ἐλαττον εἶναι. εἰσερχόμενοι δὲ καὶ παρακληθέντες δειπνῆσαι μὴ ἀνακλίνεσθε (-εινεσθαι) εἰς τοὺς ἐξέχοντας τόπους, μή ποτε ἐνδοξότερός σου ἐπέλθῃ καὶ προσελθὼν ὁ δειπνοκλήτωρ εἴπῃ σοι Ἔτι κάτω χώρει, καὶ καταισχυνθήσῃ. ἐὰν δὲ ἀναπέσῃς εἰς τὸν

ἥττονα τόπον καὶ ἐπέλθῃ σου ἥττων, ἐρεῖ σοι ὁ δειπνοκλήτωρ Σύναγε ἔτι ἄνω, καὶ ἔσται σοι τοῦτο χρήσιμον. Western (Gr.[D] Lat. Syr.). The first part only, ὑμεῖς—εἶναι, is preserved in *m ger₁* and apparently Leo (he quotes no more); the second part only, εἰσερχόμενοι to χρήσιμον, in *ger₂* and apparently Hil.*Mt*. The first part must come from an independent source, written or oral; the second probably comes from the same, but it is in substance nearly identical with Lc xiv 8—10.

xx 33 *fin.*]+ *Quibus dixit Jesus Creditis posse me hoc facere?* qui responderunt ei Ita, Domine *c*, from ix 28. + 'and we may see Thee' syr.vt.

xxi 12 τὸ ἱερόν] + ┤ τοῦ θεοῦ ├ Western and Syrian (Gr. Lat. Syr.); incl. Orig.*loc*. Text Orig.13 33 al *b* syr.hr me the arm aeth Orig.*Jo* (giving the whole context in each Gospel) Chr (?Hil). Probably suggested by Mal iii 1 in connexion with the context, though the word there in the LXX is ναόν: ἱερόν is hardly at all used in the LXX proper, but 2 Esd (Apocr.) v 43,54 has τὸ ἱερὸν τοῦ θεοῦ, which cannot have been a rare phrase: ὁ ναὸς τοῦ θεοῦ occurs in several places of the N.T., including Mt xxvi 61, whence a wide range of Western (not Greek) documents imports τοῦ θεοῦ after τὸν ναόν into xxvii 40. The absence of τ. θ. from ||| Mc xi 15; Lc xix 45 (cf. Jo ii 14) at all events cannot weigh against the overwhelming documentary authority for omission.

xxi 17 *fin.*] + *et (ibique) docebat eos de regno Dei* some Mixed Latin MSS. Cf. Lc xi 11.

xxi 28—31. Combinations of two principal simple variations, the placing of the recusant but at length obedient son first or last, and the reading of 'first' or 'last' in v. 31, here make up a ternary variation consisting of the three following readings:

α (text), this son last, with ὕστερος; so B 13-69-124-346 al³ latt.ser syr.hr me aeth.codd arm Ps.Ath and apparently Isid.pel and Dam:

β (Western), this son first, with (ὕστερος or) ἔσχατος; so D lat.vt-vg Hil:

γ (Pre-Syrian [?Alexandrian] and Syrian), this son first, with πρῶτος; so אCLX cett lat.codd syr.vt-vg-hl [aeth] Eus Chr (apparently Cyr.al) Hier:

also Hipp has ἔσχατος (α or β); Orig.*loc* has this son first (? β or γ).

It will be seen that both α and γ are easy and harmonious; while the intermediate arrangement β, agreeing with γ in order and virtually with α in the final word, involves a patent contradiction. Transcriptional evidence, if taken alone, would thus suggest the originality of β, both as the only difficult reading and as easily explaining the existence of α and γ as divergent corrections: but the intrinsic difficulty is excessive and the documentary evidence unsatisfactory. It remains that β must owe its intermediate character to its having formed a middle step either from α to γ or from γ to α. Both α and γ are well attested: but the group supporting α is of far the higher authority, and moreover the best documents supporting γ incur distrust in this passage by supporting also the manifest correction οὐ for οὐδέ in v. 32.

The Western alteration of α to β is strange at first sight, but, on the assumption that there is no interpolation in v. 31, a remark of Hier furnishes a clue to it: *si autem novissimum voluerimus legere, manifesta est interpretatio, ut dicamus intelligere quidem veritatem Judaeos, sed tergiversari et nolle dicere quod sentiunt, sicut et baptismum Joannis scientes esse de caelo dicere noluerunt;* referring to what he had said on v. 27, *illi in eo quod nescire se responderant mentiti sunt: ... ex quo ostendit et illos scire, sed respondere nolle, et se nosse, et ideo non dicere quia illi quod sciunt taceant, et statim infert parabolam, &c.* The interpretation of v. 31 suggested by Hier may well have been taken for granted by others before him: by a not unnatural misunderstanding Christ's words Ἀμὴν λέγω ὑμῖν κ.τ.λ. might be assumed to have been said in contradiction and rebuke of the preceding answer of the Jews, which would accordingly be taken as a wilful denial of the truth, and thus appear to necessitate an inversion in vv. 28—30: considerable transpositions occur elsewhere in Western texts, and the order introduced here might seem to be borne out by the order of the second and third clauses of v. 32, assumed to be together an expansion of the first clause. The same somewhat obscure verse illustrates the Western licence, for οὐ is inserted by lat.vt.omn between τοῦ and πιστεῦσαι, and οὐδέ is omitted by D *c e*, both changes being due to the misinterpretation of τοῦ (lat.vt.omn) *quod [non] credidistis.* Ἔσχατος, naturally opposed to πρῶτος, is apparently a Western correction of ὕστερος (B), which is used but twice in the LXX, being replaced by ἔσχατος even in such contexts as Deut xxiv 3: the fact that *novissimus* in both places and in 1 Ti iv 1 represents ὕστερος shews that versions must on this point be treated as neutral.

The subsequent alteration of β to γ by the simple substitution of πρῶτος would easily arise from a sense of the contradiction which β presents on the assumption that the Jews' answer was meant to express the truth, provided that a happened not to be known to those who made the alteration. Thus the third reading would in effect be equivalent to the first, with the difference that against all biblical analogy it would make the call of the Jews on the larger scale, and of the chief priests and elders on the smaller, to follow after that of the Gentiles and of the publicans and harlots respectively.

Lachmann in the preface to his vol. ii (p.v) treats the Jews' answer as an early interpolation, together with the following words λέγει αὐτοῖς ὁ Ἰησοῦς. He was doubtless moved by the difficulty which it occasions in conjunction with the Western order, which he had adopted : but he points out that Origen's commentary (pp. 770 f.) contains no reference to anything said by the Jews. [Considering the difficulty of the Western combination of readings it seems not unlikely that Lachmann is substantially right; in which case the Western change of order would probably be due to a retrospective and mechanical application of προάγουσιν. W.] Lachmann weakens his suggestion however by including λέγει αὐτοῖς ὁ Ἰησοῦς in the supposed interpolation : this phrase might easily seem otiose if it followed immediately on words of Christ, and might thus be thought to imply the intervention of words spoken by others.

xxii 12 Ἑταῖρε] < Orig.*loc*. A scholium preserved in a few cursives, and probably derived from some lost passage of Orig, states that Ἑταῖρε was found "in a few copies".

xxiii 14 *fin.*]+(v. 13) Οὐαὶ ὑμῖν, γραμματεῖς καὶ Φαρισαῖοι ὑποκριταί, ὅτι κατεσθίετε τὰς οἰκίας τῶν χηρῶν καὶ προφάσει μακρὰ προσευχόμενοι· διὰ τοῦτο λήμψεσθε περισσότερον κρίμα. Western (Gr. Lat. Syr.).

Adapted from Mc xii 40; Lc xx 47. Retained by the Syrian text (Gr. Lat. [*f*] Syr. [Eg.] Æth.) before v. 14, with a transference of the δέ from v. 14. Text אBDLZ 1-118-209 28 33 (? 346) *a e corb* vg me. cod the arm Orig.*Jo*; *loc*.lat Eus. *Can* Hier.*loc*.

xxiii 27 οἵτινες ἔξωθεν μὲν φαίνονται ὡραῖοι ἔσωθεν δὲ γέμουσιν] ἔξωθεν ὁ τάφος φαίνεται (-τε) ὡραῖος ἔσωθεν δὲ γέμει (-μι) Western, D Clem Julian Iren.lat. Probably from an extraneous source, written or oral. א* omits οἵτινες.

xxiii 35 υἱοῦ Βαραχίου] < א* and at least 4 cursives, three of them lectionaries. Eus cannot be cited for this reading, though he three times omits the words; *D. E.* 385, where he throughout combines the texts of Mt and Lc, taking most from Lc; *ib*.445; and *Theoph*.gr. (Mai *N. P. B.* iv 125); both the quotations in these last places being condensed and allusive, and each of them containing a characteristic reading of Lc: in neither of the three places does he refer expressly or implicitly to either Gospel in particular. The last passage, which seems genuine, is not found in the Syriac *Theophania* (iv 14): but in another place of the Syriac version (iv 17), where xxiii 33--36 are quoted at length, the words are retained. They are found also in Orig.*loc*; *Afric* and Iren.lat. Omitted in ‖ Lc xi 51. Jerome states that in the Gospel used by the Nazarenes the words were replaced by *filium Joiadae*.

xxiv 36 οὐδὲ ὁ υἱός]<(? Alexandrian and) Syrian (Gr. Lat. Syr. Eg.). Text א*.ᶜBD 13-124-346 28 86 lat.vt-vg.codd syr.hr aeth arm Orig.*loc*.lat(distinctly by context) Chrys Hil.*loc* Op.imp.*loc*. Jerome states the words to be present in "certain Latin MSS" but absent from "Greek copies, and especially those of Adamantius and Pierius", and then comments on them as occurring " in some ", *i.e.* apparently some Greek MSS. Ambrose (*De fide* v 193), evidently referring to Mt, though he seems to include Mc (in whose text the words stand in all documents except X vg.cod), says that " the old Greek MSS " omit the words. Bas, Did, and some later Greek Fathers notice the words as absent from Mt though present in Mc. Several Fathers, from Iren onward, refer to οὐδὲ ὁ υἱός without shewing whether they had in view both Gospels or one only : this is the case in most of the places where Cyr.al discusses the words ; but one of them is said to come from his Comm. on Mt (Mai *N. P. B.* ii 482), and two others follow closely upon comments on v. 29 of this chapter (*Zech.* 800 D; *Hom.* in Mai *l. c.* 481 = Pusey v 469).

The words must have been absent from many of the current texts of Mt by the middle of Cent. IV; but the documentary evidence in their favour is overwhelming. Although assimilation to Mc would account for their presence if the attestation were unsatisfactory, their omission can be no less easily explained by the doctrinal difficulty which they seemed to contain. The corruption was more likely to arise in the most freely used Gospel than in Mc, and having once arisen it could not fail to be readily welcomed.

xxv 1 τοῦ νυμφίου] + ┥ καὶ τῆς νύμφης ┝ Western (Gr. Lat. Syr. Arm.).

xxv 41 τὸ πῦρ τὸ αἰώνιον] τὸ σκότος τὸ ἐξώτερον Just Hom.Cl and several Syrian and other late Fathers (Dr E. Abbot), by a confusion with v. 30; vi 23; viii 12 : also 40* Chr[1] al (Dr E. Abbot) combine the phrases in the form τὸ πῦρ τὸ ἐξώτερον. In v. 46 κόλασιν is variously altered in lat.vt, becoming *ignem* (*a b c ff h corb* al) by confusion with v. 41, *ambustionem* (Cyp Aug), and *combustionem* (Aug Fulg Prom); but it is preserved in (*d* with D) ger₁ Junil (*poenam*) and *f* vg (*supplicium*).

ibid. τὸ ἡτοιμασμένον] + ὃ ἡτοίμασεν ὁ πατήρ μου ┝ Western (Gr. Lat.) ; incl. Just Hom.Cl Iren.lat[5] Orig.lat.Ruf[3];*Mt*.lat.885(but not *loc*) (Hipp) Cyp[3] (some of these writers omitting μου); while others, as Clem Orig.lat.Ruf[6] Tert.1/2 substitute ὁ κύριος or *Deus* for ὁ πατήρ μου; not Tert.1/2 Aug Ephr.*Diat*.arm.75, nor Orig.*Jo* Eus[4] Cyr.al.*Jo*. Probably from an extraneous source, written or oral.

xxvi 15 ἀργύρια] + στατῆρας ┝ Western (Gr. Lat.). The conflate reading στατῆρας ἀργυρίου also occurs (Gr. Lat.).

xxvi 73 δῆλόν σε ποιεῖ] + ὁμοιάζει ┝ Western (Gr. Lat.).

xxvii 2 Πειλάτῳ] + Ποντίῳ ┝ Πειλάτῳ Western and Syrian (Gr. Lat. Syr. Æth. Arm. Goth.); incl. Orig. *loc*.lat.(clearly). Text אBL 33 syr.vg me the aeth.cod Orig.*Jo*. (Petr.al). From Lc iii 1; Act iv 27; 1 Ti vi 13, the insertion being naturally made at the first place where Pilate's name occurs in the Gospels.

xxvii 9 Ἱερεμίου] om. 33 157 *a b* vg.codd (and [Latin] MSS mentioned by Aug) syr.vg. Ζαχαρίου is substituted by 22 syr.hl.mg, and *Esaiam* by *rhe*. The two chief corrections are due to the absence of this passage from the existing texts of Jeremiah, and the occurrence of nearly the same words in the book of Zechariah. Orig.*loc*.lat, followed by Eus.*D. E.*481, suggests as one solution of the difficulty an error of copyists by which Ἱερεμίου was substituted for Ζαχαρίου. Such is also the view taken in the *Brev. in Ps.* p. 271 (see above on xiii 35), and probably also by Hier, who however *ad l.* contents himself with expressing an opinion that the quotation was from Zechariah, not from an apocryphal Hebrew book professing to be a prophecy of Jeremiah, in which he had seen the identical words. Aug. *De cons. evv.* iii 29 ff. states that "not all [Latin] MSS of the Gospels" have Jeremiah's name, and refers to the suppositions that it was either corrupted from Zechariah or spurious: but he rejects these expedients on the grounds that "Jeremiah's name stands in a larger number of manuscripts, that those who have examined the Gospel with special care in Greek copies declare themselves to have found it in the more ancient Greek [MSS]", and that there was no motive for adding the name, whereas the difficulty might easily lead rash persons (*audax imperitia*) to omit it.

xxvii 16 f. Βαραββᾶν...[τὸν] Βαραββᾶν ἢ 'Ιησοῦν τὸν λεγόμενον Χριστόν] 'Ιησοῦν Βαραββᾶν...'Ιησοῦν Βαραββᾶν ἢ 'Ιησοῦν κ. τ. λ. 1*-118-209* 299** syr.hr.²(cod.vat, not cod.petrop) arm Orig.lat.txt(in v. 17, not v. 16). Orig.lat on xxiv 7 (p. 853) expresses an opinion that "in like manner as, according to some, Barabbas was also called *Jesus*, and yet was a robber, having nothing of Jesus but the name, so there are many Christs, but only in name". The comment on the passage itself (p. 918) begins thus, "In many copies it is not stated (*non continetur*) that Barabbas was also called *Jesus*, and perhaps [the omission is] right" &c. The whole paragraph is manifestly authentic, though doubtless abbreviated by the translator. In S and various cursives occurs the following scholium, "In many ancient copies which I have met with (or 'read', ἐντυχών)

I found Barabbas himself likewise called *Jesus* ; that is, the question of Pilate stood there as follows, Τίνα θέλετε ἀπὸ τῶν δύο ἀπολύσω ὑμῖν, 'Ιησοῦν τὸν Βαραββᾶν ἢ 'Ιησοῦν τὸν λεγόμενον Χριστόν ; for apparently the paternal name (πατρωνυμία) of the robber was *Barabbas*, which is interpreted *Son of the teacher*". The scholium is usually assigned in the MSS either to "Anastasius Bishop of Antioch" (? latter part of Cent. vi) or to Chrysostom, who is certainly not the author. In a Venice MS however (Galland *B. P.* xiv 2 81 = Migne vii 308) it is attributed to Origen, and followed immediately by a few lines having a distinctly Origenian character "By this composition therefore (??, Συντιθέμενον οὖν) the name of Βαραμβᾶν [*sic*] signifies *Son of our teacher ;* and of what teacher must we deem the 'notable robber' to be a son but of the man of blood, the murderer from the beginning " &c.? On the whole it seems probable that the two scholia are distinct, and that Origen's name belongs to the second alone ; while it is no less probable that the matter of the first scholium was obtained from Origen's commentary by a late writer, who may be Anastasius. It is in any case certain that the reading 'Ιησοῦν [τὸν] Βαραββᾶν was known to Origen, and not absolutely rejected by him, though the general tenour of his extant remarks is unfavourable to it.

Abulfaraj *ad l.* in his Syriac *Storehouse of Mysteries* states that Barabbas was called Jesus, being so named after his father to avoid confusion, and that this reading was still (Cent. xiii) found in Greek copies (Nestle in *Theol. LZ.* 1880 p. 206): a statement that Barabbas bore the name *Jesus* occurs likewise in the *Bee* of Solomon of Bassora (Assemani *B. O.* iii 2, cited by Nestle), another Syriac writer of the same century, in the midst of a number of additions to the Gospel narrative from apocryphal sources.

Jerome *ad l.*, after transcribing 16—18, adds "This man in the Gospel entitled 'according to the Hebrews' is called by interpretation *Son of their teacher*, [even he] who had been condemned for sedition and murder" (*Iste* ...filius magistri *eorum interpretatur, qui propter &c.*). It is morally certain that (1) the last clause (virtually taken from Lc xxiii 19) is added by Jerome himself to mark the character of the 'son of their teacher', St Matthew having merely called him *vinctum insignem;* and (2) that *eorum* is part of the cited interpretation, not due to Jerome himself, though possibly thrown by him into the third person by *oratio obliqua*. But it is quite uncertain whether the 'interpretation', evidently in Greek, was substituted for the name Βαραββᾶν or only added to it. On the former supposition, which is usually taken for granted, it is likely that a personal name would precede, and this might be ʼΙησοῦν. But Jerome's language would be equally appropriate if the Gospel according to the Hebrews had no more than Βαρ[ρ]αββᾶν, ὁ ἑρμηνεύεται ʽΙὸν τοῦ διδασκάλου αὐτῶν (or ἡμῶν); and in that case there would be no evidence for connecting ʼΙησοῦν Βαραββᾶν with the Gospel according to the Hebrews, from which otherwise it would be natural to derive the reading as found in a text of St Matthew.

This remarkable reading is attractive by the new and interesting fact which it seems to attest, and by the antithetic force which it seems to add to the question in v. 17 : but it cannot be right. It is against all analogy that a true reading should be preserved in no better Greek MS than the common original of 1-118-209, and in none of the more ancient versions; and the intrinsic difficulty of accounting for a change in the antithetic names in vv. 20, 26 is very great. The most probable explanation is a repetition of ĪN in v. 17 from ΥΜΙΝ (Tregelles), or an accidental overleaping of Βαραββᾶν ἤ, speedily detected and corrected by cancelling ĪN with dots which the next transcriber failed to notice (Griesbach): on either supposition the intercalated ʼΙησοῦν must subsequently have been inserted for clearness in v. 16. Either of these explanations would be amply satisfactory if the text of Orig.lat (the commentary being ambiguous) were not the only document which inserts ʼΙησοῦν in v. 17 alone; though again the whole number of documents which insert [τὸν] ʼΙησοῦν in v. 16 is virtually but five. Derivation from the Gospel according to the Hebrews (see above) is also possible, and receives some little support from the approximate coincidence between the 'interpretation' reported by Jerome and that which is given in one of the manifestly imperfect extracts from Origen, who refers to that Gospel once elsewhere in the same commentary (p. 671 lat).

xxvii 32 Κυρηναῖον] + ┤ εἰς ἀπάντησιν αὐτοῦ ├ Western (Gr. Lat.).

xxvii 34 οἶνον] ὄξος Syrian (Gr. Lat. Syr.): also Orig.*loc.*lat in text and once in comm.; but οἶνον is implied in what follows. Probably from Ps lxix 21: in Mc and Lc there is no mention of χολή, the Psalm having both χολή and ὄξος.

xxvii 35 *fin.*] + ἵνα πληρωθῇ τὸ ῥηθὲν ὑπὸ τοῦ προφήτου Διεμερίσαντο τὰ ἱμάτιά μου ἑαυτοῖς, καὶ ἐπὶ τὸν ἱματισμόν μου ἔβαλεν κλῆρον Western

(Gr. Lat. Syr. Arm.); incl. Eus. *D.E.*: but omitted by D, most of the Mixed Latin texts, probably syr.vg (MSS differ), and Orig.*loc*.lat Hil.*loc*. Abulfaraj notices the insertion, but did not find it in 'three ancient MSS'. From Jo xix 24. This is one of the Non-Syrian readings adopted by Erasmus, doubtless from the Latin Vulgate, and retained in the 'Received Text'.

xxvii 38 after δεξιῶν *c* adds *nomine Zoatham* and after εὐωνύμων *nomine Camma;* in Mc xv 27 the same additions are made by *c* with the names spelt as *Zoathan* and *Chammatha*. From some unknown apocryphal source. The apocryphal *Gesta Pilati* c. 9 (10) give the names as Δυσμᾶς and Γεστᾶς. Other names from late traditions are collected by Thilo *Cod. Apocr. N. T.* 143, 580 f.

xxvii 45 ἐπὶ πᾶσαν τὴν γῆν] < ℵ* 248 *rhe*; also Lact, but only in a loose paraphrase. Possibly omitted to remove one of the difficulties which Origen's comment (922 ff.) shews to have been felt in his time; but more probably by accident.

xxvii 46 Ἐλωί ἐλωί λεμὰ σαβαχθανεί] + Ἠλεί ἠλεί λαμὰ ζαφθανεί + Western (Gr. Lat.); ἠλεί (ἠλί) being also Syrian. Probably an attempt to reproduce the Hebrew as distinguished from the Aramaic forms, ζαφθανεί standing roughly for *azavthani* (Hier. *c. Ruf.* ii 34 [expressly *in ipsa cruce*] has *azabathani*). In Mc xv 34 ἠλεί and ζαφθανεί are again Western readings (Gr. Lat.), but there the Syrian text retains ἐλωί: B (*i*) have the curious form ζαβαφθανεί (*zapapthani*). In both places the Syrian text has λιμά, which the 'Received Text' deserts for the Western λαμά, changed in Mc apparently without Greek authority into λαμμά (*lamma* lat.vg.codd).

xxvii 49 ⟦ἄλλος δὲ λαβὼν λόγχην

—αἷμα.⟧ < Western and Syrian (Gr. Lat. Syr. Eg. Arm. Goth.); incl. Orig.*loc*.lat(also by implication *Cels*) Eus. *Can* Mac.magn.32(and the heathen writer cited by him, 22) Sev pp^lat. Text ℵBCL(U)Γ, 5 unimportant cursives, several Mixed Latin MSS (chiefly of the British type), syr.hr.vat(omitted in another lesson, and in a London fragment), aeth, Chrys and also, it is said, 'Tatian' 'Diod' Cyr.al.

An anonymous scholium in 72 attests the presence of this sentence "in the 'historical' Gospel (τοῦ καθ' ἱστορίαν εὐαγγελίου) of Diodorus and Tatianus and divers other holy Fathers". Another scholium which follows, probably extracted from a book on the differences of the Gospels, illustrates the statement by quoting 1 Cor v 7 (ἐτύθη), and then reconciles it with St John's account by supposing St Matthew to have inserted the incident by anticipation. This second scholium is preceded by words that seem to attribute it to Chrysostom (τοῦτο λέγει καὶ ὁ Χρυσόστομος); but they are probably only a misplaced marginal note calling attention to the similar interpretation implied in Chrysostom's Homily *ad l.* p. 825 c. What is in at least its latter part the same scholium, but apparently beginning at an earlier point, is attributed in another cursive (238) to Severus (Matthaei[1] *ad loc.*). The authorship is however rendered doubtful by a more authentic fragment of Severus. In a letter partially preserved in Syriac (ap.Petr. jun. in Assemani *B. Q.* ii 81) he mentions the reading as having been vigorously debated at Constantinople in connexion with the matter of the patriarch Macedonius, when the magnificently written copy of St Matthew's Gospel said to have been discovered in Cyprus with the body of St Barnabas in the reign of Zeno (? 477) was consulted and found not to contain the sentence in question : he adds that none of the old expositors mentioned it except Chrys and Cyr.al (*i.e.* probably in his lost commentary *ad l.*). The 'magnificent' copy of St Matthew, though said to have been written by Barnabas himself (Alex.mon. *Laud. in Ap. Barn.* 30 in Migne lxxxvii p. 4103), was doubtless of quite recent origin, the discovery having been opportunely made by Anthemius bishop of Salamis when he was vindicating the independence of Cyprus against the patriarch of Antioch, Peter the Fuller. The opposite view as to the reading is implied in a sarcastic statement of the Chronicle of Victor Tununensis(inCanis.-Basn.*Lect.Ant.* i 326) that "at Constantinople the holy Gospels were by command of the emperor Anastasius censured and corrected, as having been composed by unlettered (*idiotis*) evangelists". At least one other textual variation (1 Ti iii 16) was a subject for dispute in the same bitter controversy of 510, 1 between the Monophysite Severus and the Chalcedonian Macedonius, which ended in the expulsion of Macedonius by the emperor Anastasius. Liberat. *Brev* speaks of Macedonius as having been expelled *tamquam evangelia falsasset, et maxime illud apostoli dictum* Qui apparuit &c.

Nothing is known of the work of ' Diodorus ' mentioned by the scholium: the commentary of Diodorus of Tarsus "on the four Gospels" (Theodorus. Lector ap. Suid. *s.v.*) can hardly be meant. The work of 'Tatianus' has naturally been identified with the Diatessaron of Justin's disciple Tatian, which cannot have been much later than the middle of Cent. II : but, strange to say, Ephrem's Comm. on the Diatessaron shews no trace of the words in this place, while it contains an exposition of them (or of the corresponding words) at the proper place in St John's Gospel (p. 259).

Even if the words ἄλλος δὲ κ.τ.λ. had a place here in Tatian's Diatessaron, the hypothesis that they originated in its harmonistic arrangement is practically excluded by their remarkable documentary attestation, pointing to the highest antiquity. There is moreover no evidence that this obscure work was known out of Syria, where Tatian founded his sect; and the evil repute attached to his name renders the adoption of a startling reading from such a source highly improbable.

Two suppositions alone are compatible with the whole evidence. First, the words ἄλλος δὲ κ.τ.λ. may belong to the genuine text of the extant form of Mt, and have been early omitted (originally by the Western text) on account of the obvious difficulty. Or, secondly, they may be a very early interpolation, absent in the first instance from the Western text only, and thus resembling the Non-Western interpolations in Luke xxii xxiv except in its failure to obtain admission into the prevalent texts of the third and fourth centuries. The *prima facie* difficulty of the second supposition is lightened by the absence of the words from all the earlier versions, though the defectiveness of African Latin, Old Syriac, and Thebaic evidence somewhat weakens the force of this consideration. We have thought it on the whole right to give expression to this view by including the words within double brackets, though we did not feel justified in removing them from the text, and are not prepared to reject altogether the alternative supposition.

xxvii 56 Μαρία ἡ τοῦ Ἰακώβου

καὶ Ἰωσὴφ μήτηρ καὶ ἡ μήτηρ τῶν
υἱῶν Ζεβεδαίου] M. ἡ τοῦ Ἰακώβου
καὶ ἡ Μαρία ἡ Ἰωσὴφ καὶ ἡ Μαρία ἡ
τῶν υἱῶν Ζεβεδαίου ℵ* : the correction in ℵᶜ leaves the second ἡ untouched, perhaps by accident, yet
in accordance with 131; and B 131
have the same reading καὶ ἡ Ἰωσ.
μήτηρ in Mc xv 40. In aeth (Wright)
both Ἰακώβου and Ἰωσὴφ have
μήτηρ : on the other hand the μήτηρ
after Ἰωσὴφ is omitted by Old and
Mixed Latin documents.

xxviii 6 ἔκειτο] + ⊣ ὁ κύριος ⊢ Western and Syrian (Gr. Lat. Syr.).
Never applied to Christ in Mt except
in reported sayings.

xxviii 7 (†) ἰδοὺ εἶπον] καθὼς εἶπεν
ὑμῖν cu²ƒ. [Comparison with Mc xvi
7 gives much probability to the suggestion of Maldonat and others that
εἶπον is a primitive corruption of
εἶπεν, O for ε. The essential identity
of the two records in this place
renders it improbable that the corresponding clauses would hide total
difference of sense under similarity
of language; while ἰδού might easily
mislead a scribe.   As recalling
sharply an earlier prediction or
command, ἰδοὺ εἶπεν is the more
forcible though less obvious reading.
H.]

ST MARK

i 1 Ἰησοῦ Χριστοῦ] + (margin) υἱοῦ
θεοῦ Pre-Syrian and, with τοῦ prefixed
to θεοῦ, Syrian (Gr. and all vv). Text
ℵ* 28 255 lat.vg.cod. Athelst(Bentl.)
Iren¹ Orig.*Jo³*; *Cels; Rom.*lat.Ruf
Bas ["Serap" *s.q.*] Ps.Tit 'Victo-
rin.petab'(in Apoc iv 7) Hier². Iren
has both readings, υἱοῦ [τοῦ] θεοῦ 187,
205 (lat only, but confirmed by context 205), and omission 191 (gr
lat): the peculiar passage containing
the quotation without *v̇. θ.* was probably derived from an earlier author.
Severianus (*De sigillis*, Chrys. *Opp.*
xii 412), dwelling on the reticence of
Mt Mc Lc as to the Divine Sonship,
says that Mc speaks of υἱὸν θεοῦ "but
immediately contracts his language
and cuts short his conception", quoting in proof vv. 1, 2 without *v̇. θ.* :
if the text is sound, his MS must
have had a separate heading ΑΡΧΗ
ΕΥΑΓΓΕΛΙΟΥ ΙΗΣΟΥ ΧΡΙΣΤΟΥ
ΥΙΟΥ ΘΕΟΥ, followed by a fresh
beginning of the text without *v̇. θ.*,
and such a reduplication of the open-

ing words in the form of a heading
might in this place easily arise from
conflation; the alternative possibility that he refers only to the absence of such language as that of Mt
i 20—23; Lc i 32—35, and that
v̇. θ. has been lost from his text in
transcription, does not agree well
with the context.

Omission, possibly Alexandrian,
is certainly of very high antiquity.
On the whole it seems to deserve
the preference: but neither reading
can be safely rejected.

Several Fathers connect v. 1 with
v. 4 (Ἀρχὴ τ. εὐ....ἐγένετο Ἰωάνης),
treating vv. 2, 3 as a parenthesis.
But Hos i 2 sufficiently justifies the
separateness of v. 1.

i 41 σπλαγχνισθείς] ⊣ ὀργισθείς ⊢
Western (Gr.[D] Lat.).   A singular
reading, perhaps suggested by v. 43,
perhaps derived from an extraneous
source.

ii 14 Λευείν] ⊣Ἰάκωβον ⊢ Western
(Gr. Lat. ?Syr.); incl. (Ephr.*Diat.*

arm. 58); found 'in some' copies according to a confused scholium (printed by Matthaei[1] *ad l.*), not improbably derived from some comment of Origen. His extant remark on the publican *Lebes* (see on iii 18; Mt x 4) shews only that he himself read Λευείν here : his notice of a textual variation can refer only to iii 18. The following words τὸν τοῦ Ἀλφαίου doubtless suggested the Western reading here.

iii 18 Θαδδαῖον] ᚻ Λεββαῖον ⊦ Western (Gr.[D] Lat.). See on Mt x 4. Here lat.vt (except *c*) is concordant in supporting Λεββαῖον. In reply to a taunt of Celsus that Christ chose for His apostles " publicans and sailors", Orig.*Cels.* 376 first allows no publican but Matthew, and then refers concessively to " Lebes [Λεβής, but ? Λευείς] a publican who followed Jesus": " but ", he adds, " he was in no wise of the number of the apostles except according to some copies of the Gospel according to Mark". The reference here is evidently first to Mc ii 14 and then, for the apostleship, to iii 18. There is no ground for altering *Mark* to *Matthew*, or for supposing any textual error on the part of Orig beyond failure to observe that in Mt, as well as in Mc, Θαδδαῖον was not the only reading.

iii 29 ἁμαρτήματος] κρίσεως Syrian (Gr. Lat. Syr. Æth.); not Ephr. *Diat*.111. Another early, probably Western, correction is ἁμαρτίας.

iii 32 οἱ ἀδελφοί σου] + ᚻ καὶ αἱ ἀδελφαί σου⊦ Western and probably Syrian (Gr. Lat. Syr[hl.mg] Goth.); not *e* syr.vg. Neglected by Erasmus, doubtless as unsupported by lat.vg, and hence absent from the 'Received Text'. Probably suggested by v. 35, but possibly derived from an extraneous source (cf. vi 3 ‖ Mt xiii 56).

iv 9 ἀκουέτω] + ᚻ καὶ ὁ συνίων συνι-

ἐτω (-ειων -ειετω) ⊦ Western (Gr.[D] Lat. [Syr.]).

iv 21 ἐπὶ] ὑπὸ (אB* 13·69·346 33) is evidently an error, due to mechanical repetition. But the concurrence of four such documentary authorities, all independent, implies the highest antiquity, the number rendering accidental coincidence very unlikely. In all probability ὑπό was a primitive corruption, rightly corrected to ἐπί by a very early conjecture: the error could hardly fail to strike most transcribers, and the remedy was obvious, even without the help of Mt v 15; Lc xi 33.

iv 28 πλήρη σῖτον] πληρες σειτος B ; πληρης ο σειτος D ; πληρης σιτον C*(vdtr) cu²; πληρες σιτον cu¹; πλήρη τὸν σῖτον 81 ; πληροῖ σῖτον cu⁵ (?me.codd); text אAC^aLΔ un^pl cu^pl. [This strange confusion is easily explained if the original reading was πλήρης σῖτον, as in C* (apparently) and 2 good lectionaries. Πλήρης is similarly used as an indeclinable in the accusative in all good MSS of Acts vi 5 except B, and has good authority in the LXX. H.]

v 33 τρέμουσα] + ᚻ διὸ πεποιήκει λάθρᾳ ⊦ Western (Gr. Lat. Arm.).

vi 3 ὁ τέκτων, ὁ υἱὸς] ὁ τοῦ τέκτονος υἱὸς καὶ Western (Gr. Lat. Æth. Arm.); not D: syr.hr simply omits ὁ τέκτων. From Mt xiii 55.

In reply to a scoff of Celsus, Origen says (vi 36) that "Jesus Himself has nowhere been described as a carpenter in the Gospels current in the churches". The natural inference is not that the reading of text was unknown to Origen or rejected by him, but that he either forgot this passage or, perhaps more probably, did not hold Mc responsible for the words of the Galileans. His concluding phrase shews that he had in mind the explicit account given in apocryphal narratives (see Just. *Dial*. 88 and the authorities collected by Thilo on the Latin *Infancy* c. 10).

ibid. καὶ Ἰωσῆτος] καὶ Ἰωσὴφ Western (Gr. Lat. Æth.); incl. ℵ, but not D : καὶ Ἰωσῆ Syrian (Gr. Syr. Arm. Goth.): om. *cffi*, three MSS which have a special common element. See on Mt xiii 55, whence Ἰωσήφ is derived.

vi 20 ἠπόρει] ἐποίει Western and Syrian (Gr. and all vv but memph): Δ omits with the following καί. Text ℵBL me; also anon. in Pouss.cat. *loc.*

vi 33 καὶ προῆλθον αὐτούς] καὶ συνῆλθον αὐτοῦ ⊦Western (Gr. Lat.). For other variants, including a Syrian conflate reading, see *Introd.* §§ 134—8.

vi 36 κύκλῳ] ἔγγιστα ⊦ Western (Gr.[D] Lat.).

vi 47 ἦν] ⊣ πάλαι ⊦ Western (Gr. ? Lat.): it is not clear whether the variously transposed *jam* of Old and Mixed Latin MSS represents πάλαι or the not otherwise attested ἤδη.

vi 56 ἀγοραῖς] ⊣ πλατείαις ⊦ Western (Gr. Lat. Syr. Goth.).

vii 3 πυγμῇ, owing to its obscurity, is variously altered and translated, the chief substitute being πυκνά (*subinde, crebro* Latt) ℵ and some vv (cf. Lc v 33): Δ omits.

vii 4 χαλκίων] ⊣ καὶ κλινῶν ⊦ Western and Syrian (Gr. and all vv but memph); also Orig.*Mt.* Text ℵBLΔ lt. 48 62 me. Probably from an extraneous source, written or oral: cf. J. Lightfoot *ad l.*

vii 6 τιμᾷ] ⊣ ἀγαπᾷ ⊦ Western (Gr.[D] Lat. Æth.[conflate]); (?incl. Clem). Probably from a lost reading of LXX Is xxix 13 : Tert *Marc.* iii 6; iv 12, 17, 41 (not so Cyp) has *diligit* (-*unt*), chiefly if not wholly quoting Isaiah. Clement's φιλοῦσι (206) and ἀγαπῶν (583) seem on comparison with 143,461,577 to be derived from Mc.

vii 9 τηρήσητε] ⊣ στήσητε ⊦ Wes-

tern (Gr. Lat. Syr. Arm.).

vii 13 τῇ παραδόσει ὑμῶν] ⊣ τῇ μωρᾷ ⊦ Western (Gr.[D] Lat. Syr. [hl. mg]).

vii 19 ἀφεδρῶνα] ⊣ ὀχετὸν ⊦ Western (Gr.[D] Lat.).

vii 28 Ναί, κύριε] ⊣ Κύριε, ἀλλὰ ⊦ Western (Gr.[D] Lat.); also without ἀλλά (Gr. Arm.).

viii 22 Βηθσαιδάν] ⊣ Βηθανίαν ⊦ Western (Gr. Lat. Goth.).

viii 26 Μηδὲ εἰς τὴν κώμην εἰσέλθῃς] ⊣ Μηδενὶ εἴπῃς εἰς τὴν κώμην ⊦, with or without the addition of Ὕπαγε εἰς τὸν οἶκόν σου, Western (Gr. Lat. Syr.[hl.mg] Arm.). For other variants, including a Syrian conflate reading, see *Introd.* § 140.

ix 24 παιδίου] ⊣ ⊣ μετὰ δακρύων ⊦ Western and Syrian (Gr. Lat. Syr. Goth.). Text ℵA*BC*LΔ 28 *k* me the arm aeth.

ix 29 προσευχῇ] ⊣ καὶ νηστείᾳ ⊦ Western and Syrian (Gr. and, in one order or another, all vv but *k*); νηστ. καὶ προσευχ. syr.vg-hr aeth arm. Text ℵ*B *k* and apparently Clem. 993, τῆς πίστεως τὴν εὐχὴν ἰσχυροτέραν ἀπέφηνεν ὁ σωτὴρ τοῖς πιστοῖς ἀποστόλοις ἐπί τινος δαιμονιῶντος ὃν οὐκ ἴσχυσαν καθαρίσαι, εἰπών Τὰ τοιαῦτα εὐχῇ κατορθοῦται.

ix 38 καὶ ἐκωλύομεν αὐτόν, ὅτι οὐκ ἠκολούθει ἡμῖν] ⊣ ὃς οὐκ ἀκολουθεῖ μεθ' ἡμῶν, καὶ ἐκωλύομεν αὐτόν ⊦, so or with ἐκωλύσαμεν, Western (Gr. Lat. Syr.[hl.mg] Arm.). For other variants, including a Syrian conflate reading, see *Introd.* § 141.

ix 49 πᾶς γὰρ πυρὶ ἁλισθήσεται] ⊣ πᾶσα γὰρ θυσία ἀλὶ ἁλισθήσεται ⊦ Western (Gr. Lat.). From Lev vii 13. For a Syrian conflate reading see *Introd.* § 142. A few cursives add ἄρτος after πᾶς (cf. LXX Job vi 6).

x 19 Μὴ φονεύσῃς, Μὴ μοιχεύσῃς] ⊣ Μὴ μοιχεύσῃς, Μὴ πορνεύσῃς ⊦ Western (Gr.[D] Lat.). Μὴ μοιχεύσῃς, Μὴ φονεύσῃς (likewise Western and)

Syrian (Gr. Lat. Syr. Æth. Arm. Goth.). Other variations occur. The third or ultimately Syrian reading, of which the second is perhaps a corruption, comes from Lc xviii 20; Rom xiii 9; the same order occurs in Philo *De decal.* 24 f. and elsewhere (cf. Ex xx 13 ff. LXX cod. B): in Lc xviii 20 the order is conversely corrupted from Mt or Mc in latt syrr.

x 24 δύσκολόν ἐστιν] + τοὺς πεποιθότας ἐπὶ [τοῖς] χρήμασιν Western and Syrian (Gr. Lat. Syr. [Eg.] Arm. Goth.); incl. Clem.al; Ephr. *Diat.*170. Text אBΔ k me.cod. Evidently inserted to bring the verse into closer connexion with the context by limiting its generality: compare also Job xxxi 24 ; Ps. lii (li) 7; lxii (lxi) 10; 1 Ti vi 17. Similar supplements are *divitem* (*c ff*) and τοὺς τὰ χρήματα ἔχοντας from v. 23 (aeth): *a* has a conflation of these last words with the common reading.

x 27 ἀδύνατον ἀλλ' οὐ παρὰ θεῷ, πάντα γὰρ δυνατὰ παρὰ [τῷ] θεῷ] + ἀδύνατόν ἐστιν παρὰ δὲ τῷ θεῷ δυνατόν ⊢ Western (Gr. Lat. Æth.).

x 30 οἰκίας καὶ ἀδελφοὺς καὶ ἀδελφὰς καὶ μητέρας καὶ τέκνα καὶ ἀγροὺς μετὰ διωγμῶν, καὶ ἐν τῷ αἰῶνι τῷ ἐρχομένῳ ζωὴν αἰώνιον] + ὃς δὲ ἀφῆκεν οἰκίαν καὶ ἀδελφὰς καὶ ἀδελφοὺς καὶ μητέρα καὶ τέκνα καὶ ἀγροὺς μετὰ διωγμοῦ ἐν τῷ αἰῶνι τῷ ἐρχομένῳ ζωὴν αἰώνιον λήμψεται ⊢ Western (Gr.[D] Lat.) ; διωγμοῦ (D) seems however to have no Latin attestation.

x 51 'Ραββουνεί] + Κύριε ραββεί ⊢ Western (Gr.[D] Lat.); also 'Ραββεί (Lat. Syr.), from which by conflation with the Κύριε of Mt Lc (cu¹ here) the double reading has probably arisen.

xi 32 εἴχον] + ᾔδεισαν ⊢ Western (Gr. Lat. Arm.).

xii 14 κῆνσον] + ἐπικεφάλαιον ⊢ Western (Gr. Lat. Syr.).

xii 23 ἐν τῇ ἀναστάσει] + ὅταν ἀνα-

στῶσιν late Western and Syrian (Gr. Lat. Syr. Arm. Goth.); not D *b c k* syr.vg; ὅταν οὖν ἀναστῶσιν ἐν τῇ ἀναστάσει 13-69-346; ἐὰν οὖν ἀναστῶσιν [? ἐκ νεκρῶν] aeth. Though not now extant separately except in aeth, ὅταν ἀναστῶσιν (from v. 25) was probably first substituted for text, and afterwards conflate with it. With transpositions, *k* inserts here *si mulier mortua est et mulier sine filis, cui remanet mulier munda ?* and *c* similarly *et mulier relicta est sine filiis: cui enim manebit uxor munda?*

xii 40 χηρῶν] + ⊣ καὶ ὀρφανῶν ⊢ Western (Gr. Lat.); not *e k.*

xiii 2 *fin.*] + ⊣ καὶ διὰ τριῶν ἡμερῶν ἄλλος ἀναστήσεται ἄνευ χειρῶν ⊢ Western (Gr.[D] Lat.): some Latin documents (chiefly African) for ἀναστήσεται have ἐγερθήσεται (*excitabitur, resuscitetur* [*sic*]); *c* has ἐγερῶ αὐτόν. From xiv 58; Jo ii 19.

xiii 8 λιμοί] + ⊣ καὶ ταραχαί Pre-Syrian (? Alexandrian) and Syrian (Gr. Lat.[*a*] Syr. Eg. Arm.); incl. Orig.*Mt*.lat (expressly). Text אBDL lat.afr-eur-vg me aeth. Inserted probably either for the sake of rhythm, a similar effect being produced by the Western (Gr. Lat.) substitution of καί for the second ἔσονται ; or from an extraneous source, written or oral (cf. vii 4 καὶ κλινῶν). In the ‖ Lc xxi 11 a Western text inserts καὶ χειμῶνες.

xiv 4 ἦσαν δέ τινες ἀγανακτοῦντες πρὸς ἑαυτούς] + ⊣ οἱ δὲ μαθηταὶ αὐτοῦ διεπονοῦντο καὶ ἔλεγον ⊢ Western (Gr. Lat. Arm.), with slight variations.

xiv 41 ἀπέχει] + τὸ τέλος Western (Gr. Lat. Syr. Arm.); D *c q* further read καί for ἦλθεν, and the versions (except *a q*) ἐπέχει (with one cursive) for ἀπέχει : ccnjunctions are also added. These variations and others, as the substitution of ἅπαξ by aeth, all arise from the difficulty presented by the very rare impersonal ἀπέχει, unknown elsewhere (the gloss in Hesychius being doubtless founded on this passage) except in Ps.Anacr. xv 33. The addition of τὸ τέλος comes from the ‖ Lc xxii 37 καὶ γὰρ τὸ περὶ ἐμοῦ τέλος ἔχει : so a scholium in Pouss. cat. p. 321, ἀπέχει, τουτέστι πεπλήρωται, τέλος ἔχει τὸ κατ' ἐμέ ; and Euthym on Mt xxvi 45 (nearly as a scholium in a Venice MS of Theophylact on Mc), Μάρκος δέ φησιν εἰπεῖν αὐτὸν ... ὅτι Ἀπέχει, τουτέστιν Ἔλαβε τὴν κατ' ἐμοῦ ἐξουσίαν ὁ διάβολος, ἢ Ἀπέχει τὰ κατ' ἐμέ, ἤγουν Πέρας ἔχει, καὶ γὰρ καὶ παρὰ τῷ Λουκᾷ εἴρηκεν ὅτι Τὰ περὶ ἐμοῦ τέλος ἔχει.

xiv 51 καὶ κρατοῦσιν αὐτόν] + οἱ νεανίσκοι Syrian (Gr. Lat.[a] Syr. Æth. Arm. Goth.), perhaps modified from an earlier form of the reading, exhibited by good cursives and apparently theb, οἱ δὲ νεανίσκοι κρατοῦσιν αὐτόν. Probably supplied to give the verb a subject.

xiv 58 ἀχειροποίητον οἰκοδομήσω] ╫ ἀναστήσω ἀχειροποίητον ├ Western (Gr.[D] Lat.). Cf. Jo ii 20 (ἐγερεῖς).

xiv 68 *fin.*] + καὶ ἀλέκτωρ ἐφώνησεν. Western and Syrian (Gr. and most vv). Text אBL lt 17 *c* me: in Woide's MS of theb the insertion precedes καὶ ἐξῆλθεν. The interpolation was evidently made to justify the subsequent ἐκ δευτέρου in v. 72. Conversely in v. 72 there is an (?Alexandrian) omission of ἐκ δευτέρου itself in אL *c* vg.cod, and a corresponding (partly Alexandrian) omission of δίς in אC*Δ 251 *c ff q ger, rhe* aeth, both changes producing assimilation to the other Gospels; while the earlier and more isolated δίς of v. 30 disappears for the same reason in a considerable assemblage of documents, אC*D 238 lt 150 *a c ff i k* vg.codd aeth arm. Accordingly B (?lt 17) and memph alone

preserve the neutral or true reading throughout. See *Introd.* § 323.

xv 25 τρίτη] ἕκτη syr.hl.mg aeth ; also written in the margin of B.M. Add. 11300 (Dr Scrivener's k), but by 'a recent hand'. From Jo xix 14, where the converse corruption occurs. The *Brev. in Psalt.* p. 271 (see on Mt xiii 35), inverting a supposition of Eus, calls text a clerical error arising from the similarity of Γ (3) to F (6).

ibid. ἐσταύρωσαν] ╫ ἐφύλασσον ├ Western (Gr.[D] Lat.). Probably introduced to avoid the seeming anticipation of v. 27 (σταυροῦσιν), the Hebraistic use of ἦν...καί not being understood.

xv 27 *fin.*] + (v. 28) καὶ ἐπληρώθη ἡ γραφὴ ἡ λέγουσα Καὶ μετὰ ἀνόμων ἐλογίσθη Western and Syrian (Gr. Lat. Syr. [Eg.] Æth. Arm. Goth.), incl. Hier. *Is.* 624. The balance of probability is in favour of a reference to this reading in Orig. *Cels.* ii 44, though the reference may be (as apparently in viii 54) to Lc xxii 37 alone; and also of its inclusion in Eus.*Can,* when the various perturbations of the sectional numbers are taken into account, though the canonical numbers in A, the oldest authority, would suggest rather the absence of v. 28 and the treatment of v. 30 as a section distinct from v. 29. Text אABCDX 157 and many inferior cursives, chiefly lectionaries, *k* me.cod.txt the ; thus including D *k*, representatives of the earlier Western text. The quotation from Is liii 12 occurs, though in a different context, in Lc xxii 37: the condemnation of v. 28 by documentary evidence is confirmed by the absence of quotations from the O. T. in this Gospel except at the opening and in reported sayings.

'Vig.thaps'.*Eut.* iv 6 attributes to Eutyches (or a contemporary Eutychian?) the curious reading νεκρῶν for ἀνόμων, of which there is no other clear trace, though the phrase ἐν νεκροῖς κατελογίσθη happens to occur in Hipp.*Ant.* 26.

xv 34 ἐγκατέλιπες] ┤ ὠνείδισας ├ Western (Gr. Lat.); also the heathen writer cited by Macar.magn. 21.

xv 47 Ἰωσῆτος] Ἰακώβου Western (Gr. Lat.), from xvi 1; text being also modified to Ἰωσήφ (Gr. Lat. Æth.), on which see on Mt xiii 55; Mc vi 3; and to Ἰωσῆ, Syrian (Gr. Syr. Goth.). Some Latin MSS combine Ἰακώβου and Ἰωσήφ, either simply by *et* or in the form *Maria Jacobi et Maria Joseph.*

xvi 3 ἐκ τῆς θύρας τοῦ μνημείου; καὶ] *k* has *ab osteo? Subito autem ad horam tertiam tenebrae diei* [l. *die*] *factae sunt per totum orbem terrae, et descenderunt de caelis angeli et surgent* [l. *surgentes*] *in claritate vivi Dei simul ascenderunt cum eo, et continuo lux facta est. Tunc illae accesserunt ad monimentum, et.* Doubtless from an apocryphal or other extraneous source: cf. Mt xxviii 2.

xvi 9—20. We have thought it right to state and discuss the evidence affecting the end of St Mark's Gospel at a length disproportionate to the usual scale of these notes. Much of the evidence is of so intricate and in a manner disputable a nature that a bare recital of its items, ranged according to our judgement on one side or another, would have done injustice both to the merits of the case and to the eminent critics who have treated of this at first sight difficult variation. The variation itself is moreover almost unrivalled in interest and importance, and no other that approaches it in interest and importance stands any longer seriously in need of full discussion. A preliminary table will make the contents of the following note more readily intelligible.

xvi 9—20 [['Αναστὰς — σημεί-
ων.]] and [[Πάντα—σωτηρίας]] < אB,
most of the MSS known to Eus
and probably Hier, some of the
older MSS of arm, and, by clear
implication, Vict.ant and the author
of a ὑπόθεσις to the Gospel: on the
negative evidence of various Fathers,
Greek and Latin, and on the patristic evidence generally, see below.

In B the scribe, after ending the
Gospel with v. 8 in the second
column of a page, has contrary to
his custom left the third or remaining column blank; evidently because one or other of the two subsequent endings was known to him
personally, while he found neither
of them in the exemplar which he
was copying. The same use of
blank spaces is found in L at Jo
vii 53—viii 11, and also, very in-
structively, in Δ + G₃, in which the
absence of familiar words from the
exemplar must in different places
have been due to several different
causes, accidental loss of leaves of
the exemplar (Ro ii 16—25; 1 Co
iii 8—16; vi 7—14; Col ii 1—8),
mere carelessness of its writer (2 Ti
ii 12 f.), and, as here in B, difference of inherited text (Mc iii 31;
Jo vii 53—viii 11; Ro viii 1; xiv 23
[xvi 25—27]; xvi 16). In all such

cases the attestation given to the omitted words is simply chronological and, under favourable circumstances, indirectly geographical; amounting to a proof that they were in existence at the date when the extant MS was written, and were known to its scribe: while on the other hand the omission of the words has in addition a qualitative attestation, determined by the habitual internal character of the text of the extant MS, and varying in authority accordingly. Here therefore the authority for the omission is the authority of the habitual character of B.

In L v. 8 comes to an end in the middle of the last line but one of a column, and a termination of the Gospel in some sense at this point is implied by the ornamental marks which make up the last line of the column. In the next column we find, first, the note "These also are in a manner [or 'somewhere', *i.e.* in some authorities] current" (φερετε που και ταυτα), surrounded by ornamental lines, and introducing the Shorter Conclusion (Πάντα—σωτηρίας); and then another note, similarly decorated, "And there are these also current (εστην δε και ταυτα φερομενα) after ἐφοβοῦντο γάρ", introducing the Longer Conclusion (vv. 9—20, Ἀναστὰς—μετ' αὐτῶν. ἀμήν.). Last comes the colophon, ευαγγελιον κατα μαρκον, decorated like the preceding notes (not so the colophon of Lc: the last leaves of Mt and Jo are lost), and immediately followed by the chapter-headings of Lc. It seems tolerably certain that the exemplar contained only the Shorter Conclusion, and that the Longer Conclusion, which probably was alone current when L was written, was added at the end from another copy.

In 22, as Dr Burgon (*Last Twelve*

Verses of S. Mark, p. 230) was the first to point out, the word τέλος is inserted after both v. 8 and v. 20, while no such word is placed at the end of the other Gospels. The last twelve verses are moreover separated from the rest of the chapter by a clear break, and preceded by a note, written in shorter lines than those of the text, "In some of the copies the Gospel is completed at this point, but in many these also are current" (ἔως ὧδε πληροῦται ὁ εὐαγγελιστής, ἐν πολλοῖς δὲ καὶ ταῦτα φέρεται). The two insertions explain each other, and distinctly imply that this Gospel was considered in some sense to end at v. 8, in some sense at v. 20: for the other Gospels there was but a single and obvious end, and thus no monitory τέλος was needed. This evidently ancient notation, having in the course of time doubtless ceased to be understood, has apparently left traces of itself in other cursives, becoming confused however with the liturgical τέλος which from about the eighth or ninth century is often found marking the end of ecclesiastical lections, and which ultimately became common: as v. 8 forms the close of a lection, the confusion is inevitable. On the other hand it is impossible to explain the phenomena of such a MS as 22 by the liturgical use alone. The true origin of the double τέλος which it presents is illustrated by the exact and independent parallel of a double colophon in some of the more ancient Armenian MSS, which have εὐαγγέλιον κατὰ Μάρκον after both v. 8 and v. 20. In each case the peculiar notation implies an antecedent text which terminated at v. 8.

The direct patristic testimony begins with Eusebius, whose treatment of the question is known from three independent sources. Considerable extracts from his work *On the discrepance of the Gospels*, in three books of answers to queries, are extant in a condensed form (Mai *N. P. B.* iv 255 ff.). In the first query of the third book Eusebius's correspondent Marinus asks " How it is that in Matthew the Saviour appears as having been raised up ὀψὲ σαββάτων [xxviii 1], but in Mark πρωὶ τῇ μιᾷ τῶν σαββάτων" [xvi 9, incorrectly combined with xvi 2]. Eusebius replies: " The solution will be twofold (διττὴ ἂν εἴη). For one man, rejecting the passage itself (τὸ κεφάλαιον αὐτό), the section which makes this statement, will say that it is not current in all the copies of the Gospel according to Mark. That is, the accurate copies determine the end of the narrative according to Mark (τὰ γοῦν ἀκριβῆ τῶν ἀντιγράφων τὸ τέλος περιγράφει τῆς κ.τ.λ.) at the words of the young man" &c., ending ἐφοβοῦντο γάρ. " For at this point the end of the Gospel according to Mark is determined in nearly all the copies of the Gospel according to Mark ('Εν τούτῳ γὰρ σχεδὸν ἐν ἅπασι τοῖς ἀντιγράφοις τοῦ κατὰ Μ. εὐαγγελίου περιγέγραπται τὸ τέλος); whereas what follows, being but scantily current, in some but not in all [copies], will be redundant [i.e. such as should be discarded: τὰ δὲ ἐξῆς, σπανίως ἔν τισιν ἀλλ' οὐκ ἐν πᾶσι φερόμενα, περιττὰ ἂν εἴη], and especially if it should contain a contradiction to the testimony of the other evangelists. This is what will be said by one who declines and entirely gets rid of [what seems to him] a superfluous question (παραιτούμενος καὶ πάντῃ ἀναιρῶν περιττὸν ἐρώτημα). While another, not daring to reject anything whatever that is in any way (ὁπωσοῦν) current in the Scripture of the Gospels, will say [reading φήσει for

φησί] that the reading (ἀνάγνωσιν) is double, as in many other cases, and that each [reading] must be received, on the ground that this [reading] finds no more acceptance (ἐγκρίνεσθαι) than that, nor that than this, with faithful and discreet persons. Accordingly, on the assumption that this view is true, it is needful to interpret the sense of the passage (ἀναγνώσματος)." Eusebius then proposes to reconcile the two statements by changing the punctuation of v. 9.

Some slight roughnesses in the Greek of this passage are evidently due to condensation. Thus the duplicate phrases in apposition, τὸ κεφάλαιον αὐτό and τὴν τοῦτο φάσκουσαν περικοπὴν and again περὶ ως and ἔν τισιν ἀλλ' οὐκ ἐν πᾶσι, may very possibly have been brought together from different similar sentences. The only point which presents any real difficulty is the unique compound phrase τὸ τέλος περιγράφει (περιγέγραπται), literally to 'limit (or determine) the end'. This might mean to mark off the end, as by a colophon, ornamental line, or other notation. But it is probably only a pleonastic way of expressing more emphatically the sense of the common elliptic περιγράφω (to 'end' a book or statement), used by various writers and by Eusebius himself, as *P. E. sub fin.* τὰ μὲν τῆς Εὐαγγελικῆς Προπαρασκευῆς ἐν τούτοις ἡμῖν περιγεγράφθω. Compare τὸν τοῦ ἡλίου περίδρομον εἶναι περιγραφὴν τοῦ πέρατος τοῦ κόσμου in the *Placita Philos*. ii 1 (Diels *Doxogr.* p. 328). The Greek words cannot possibly mean the inscription of the formula [τὸ] τέλος, either followed (as in 22) or not followed by vv. 9—20; so that Eusebius is not likely to have had the formula in view when he was employing the common word τέλος in its natural sense.

Strangely enough, the answer given by Eusebius to the next question, relating to a supposed contradiction between Mt xxviii 1 and Jo xx 1, is, taken by itself, inconsistent with his former answer: it implicitly excludes that interpretation of ὀψὲ σαββάτων in Mt which had been there assumed as a standard for correcting the construction of Mc xvi 9. This second answer, evidently founded on the Epistle of Dionysius of Alexandria to Basilides, is however in effect, though not in form, a third alternative solution of the first difficulty. It thus merely affords an additional illustration of the indecision often displayed by Eusebius, especially in presence of a conflict of traditional authorities. In the textual question likewise he shews indecision; but of a kind which marks plainly at what point the Gospel ended, as used and adopted by him. His second supposed critic accepts the presence and absence of vv. 9—20 as alike to be received, simply because it would be rash to reject from Scripture a passage sanctioned by any sort of ecclesiastical usage. Yet this balanced view, by which the omission of these verses is placed on a level with their prudential reservation, is itself placed on a level with their unqualified rejection. Thus, while Eusebius himself to a certain extent exemplifies the instinctive hankering after inclusiveness of text which has led to the facile retention of so many interpolations, he allows it to be transparent that he did not seriously regard the disputed verses as part of the Gospel. And this interpretation of his language is strikingly confirmed by the total absence of any allusion to their contents in another answer to Marinus (296 ff.), in which he carefully compares the appearances recorded in the Gospels

with the list in 1 Cor xv 5 ff. Moreover the order which he adopts, placing the final narrative of Mt (xxviii 16—20) before some of the appearances mentioned by St Paul, virtually excludes parallelism with the final narrative of Mc (xvi 14—20), which runs on to the Ascension.

Whatever may have been his own judgement, the textual facts stated by Eusebius at the outset have an independent value, and require to be carefully noted. In two places he says vaguely that vv. 9—20 are " not current in all copies of the Gospel", " current in some but not in all". But, wherever he takes clear account of quality or quantity, the testimony borne by his language is distinctly unfavourable to these verses: " the accurate copies " end the Gospel at the preceding verse; this is the case " in almost all the copies of the Gospel"; the disputed verses " are current to a scanty extent, in some " copies, though not in all. Whether the statement is original or, as Matthaei and Dr Burgon suggest, reproduced from the lost comment of an earlier writer, as Origen, cannot be decided. If it was borrowed from Origen, as we strongly suspect that it was, the testimony as to MSS gains in importance by being carried back to a much earlier date and a much higher authority. Whoever was the author, he must of course be understood to speak only of the copies which had come directly or indirectly within his own knowledge, not of all copies then existing in his time.

Secondly, either rejection or ignorance of vv. 9—20 is clearly implied in a remarkable scholium bearing the name of Eusebius, preserved in 255, a Moscow cursive (Matthaei[1] *Mc.* 269; Burgon 319 ff.). Enumerating in a summary and almost tabular manner the appearances of Christ after the Resurrection, it states that "according to Mark He is not said to have appeared to the disciples after the Resurrection"; and thus it implies the rejection of at least vv. 14 ff. This scholium is indeed, as Dr Burgon points out, an abridgement of an anonymous scholium forming a continuous comment on Jo xxi 14, which, as published by Matthaei[1] (2 *Thess.* 228 f.) from 3 Moscow MSS, 237, 239, 259, makes no reference to Mc. It is difficult however to believe that the original writer ignored Mc altogether, as assuming xvi 12 f. and 14 ff. to be sufficiently covered by his explicit references to Lc (xxiv 13 ff.) and Mt (xxviii 16 ff.) ; and still more that the abbreviator, totally disregarding these two passages of xvi, invented his definite negative statement because he noticed the absence of S. Mark's name. There can be little doubt that he had before him some such text as this, κατὰ μὲν γὰρ τὸν [Μάρκον οὐ λέγεται ὤφθαι τοῖς μαθη-ταῖς· κατὰ δὲ τὸν] Ματθαῖον ὤφθη αὐτοῖς ἐν τῇ Γαλιλαίᾳ μόνον, and that the bracketed words were omitted by *homoeoteleuton* in a common source of the Moscow MSS. The Eusebian authorship of the scholium is not affected by a slight coincidence (οὐ...συνεχῶς) of phrase with Chrys on Jo xxi 14; for the idea literally expressed by it, the 'discontinuity' of the appearances, is at least as old as Origen (*Cels.* ii 65 f.). This second direct testimony as to the text used by Eusebius is closely related to the negative evidence supplied by the answer noticed above (Mai 296 ff.); and both extracts may well have come from the same work.

The third testimony is that of the Eusebian Canons, which according to the more ancient and trustworthy

documents omitted vv. 9—20. The best evidence from Greek MSS, supported by the Latin Vulgate and the statement of a scholium in 1 and 209 (which have a common ancient source), ἕως οὗ καὶ Εὐσέβιος ὁ Παμ-φίλου ἐκανόνισεν, shews conclusively that v. 8 either formed or commenced the last section (numbered 233), though in some MSS its numeral naturally slipped down to the larger break at v. 9, after these verses had become part of the accepted text ; and further, since section 233 belongs to Canon 2, which consists of passages common to all of the first three Gospels, it must have ended as well as commenced with v. 8. It was equally natural that the supposed neglect on the part of Eusebius should in due time be systematically rectified; so that many MSS divide vv. 9—20 into supplementary sections, and alter the canons accordingly. His own text is but placed in clearer relief by these changes.

The principal statement of Eusebius was reproduced without acknowledgement by later writers in various forms. The epistle of Jerome to Hedibia (120 Vall.) contains answers to 12 queries on biblical difficulties. In several cases even the queries are free translations of those which stand under the name of Marinus, and therefore probably owe their wording to Jerome himself; while the answers are condensations of the answers of Eusebius. On the third query Jerome says "*Hujus quaestionis duplex solutio est: aut enim non recipimus Marci testimonium, quod in raris fertur evangeliis, omnibus Graeciae libris pene hoc capitulum non habentibus, prae-sertim quum diversa atque contraria evangelistis ceteris narrare videa-tur ; aut hoc respondendum*" &c. This is certainly not an independent statement: yet it is not likely that a man so conversant with biblical texts as Jerome would have been content to repeat it unmodified, considering the number and importance of the verses in question, had it found no degree of support in the Greek MSS which had come under his own observations. The *Epistle to Hedibia* was written at Bethlehem in 406 or 407, when he was about 66 or 67 years old.

An Oration on the Resurrection, variously attributed to Gregory of Nyssa, who cannot be the author, to Hesychius of Jerusalem, and to Severus of Antioch, contains a remark that "in the more accurate copies" the Gospel ended at ἐφοβοῦντο γάρ, "but in some is added" Ἀναστὰς δὲ κ.τ.λ. Both the immediate context and other parts of the Oration abound in matter taken from Eusebius, and the textual statement is evidently nothing more than a brief paraphrase of his words, entitled to no independent authority. Near the end of the Oration the writer himself quotes xvi 19 as τὸ παρὰ τῷ Μάρκῳ γεγραμμένον; so that, in borrowing from Eusebius the solution of a difficulty, he must have overlooked the inconsistency of the introductory words with his own text of the Gospel.

Another work attributed to Hesychius (*Quaest.* lii in Cotel. *M.E.G.* iii 45) has been supposed to imply the absence of vv. 9—20, by saying that Mc "ended his narrative when "he had told in a summary manner "the particulars down to the men-"tion of the one angel". But the context shews that the writer is speaking exclusively of the appearances to the women, and has specially in view the absence of the additional incident supplied by Lc xxiv 24: moreover in *Quaest.* l, p. 40, he uses a phrase founded on xvi 9.

A third reproduction of the Eusebian statement occurs in the commentary on St Mark's Gospel which in most MSS is attributed to Victor of Antioch, a writer known only by the occurrence of his name in Catenæ and compiled commentaries. This work of his quotes Cyr.al, and thus cannot be earlier than the middle of Cent. V: it probably belongs to Cent. V or VI, but there is no clear evidence to fix the date. In commenting on xvi 1 (not 9), Victor refers to Ἀναστὰς δὲ κ.τ.λ. as added "in some copies" of the Gospel, and to the apparent discrepance with Mt thus arising: "we might have said", he proceeds, "that the passage which is current as standing last in some [copies] of Mc. is spurious"; but, for fear of "seeming to take refuge in too easy an expedient" (ἐπὶ τὸ ἔτοιμον πεφυγέναι), he prefers to meet the difficulty by punctuation. In this passage, and still more in the adjoining context, Eusebian materials abound, and Eusebius is named in the next paragraph. Thus far therefore no conclusion either as to Victor's own text or as to the text of MSS within his knowledge can safely be drawn from his words.

This however is but a part of his evidence. The paragraph containing the reference to the textual variation is followed by another paragraph which the MSS place as a note on v. 9 (or 9 ff.), but which actually deals with vv. 6—8 alone. On all the weighty matter contained in vv. 9—20 Victor is entirely silent. This silence is the manifest cause of the displacement of his last paragraph in the MSS of the Gospel which contain his commentary, and it can have but one interpretation: vv. 9—20 must have been absent from his copy of the Gospel.

Though Victor's own work ends

at v. 8, each of the two principal editions, by Poussin and Cramer respectively, has a subsequent note or scholium. A short anonymous commentary (from a Vatican MS) which Poussin intersperses with that of Victor and with a third, has 8 lines on v. 9; and here Eusebius is cited by name, the subject being Mary Magdalene, with reference to the appearance to her and the other women narrated in vv. 1 ff. But there is no evidence for connecting this note directly or indirectly with Victor.

The other scholium, which concludes Cramer's edition and is found in many MSS, deserves more attention. "Although", it says, "the "words 'Αναστὰς δὲ κ.τ.λ., and "those which next follow in the "Gospel according to Mark, are "absent from very many copies, "as some supposed them to be as "it were spurious, yet we, from "accurate copies, as having found "them in very many, in accordance "with the Palestinian Gospel of "Mark, as the truth is, have put "together" &c.: what follows is corrupt, but must in substance mean the insertion or retention of vv. 9—20. This scholium evidently presupposes the critical remark which Victor borrowed from Eusebius, and must be intended to refer back to it. Victor himself cannot possibly be its author. It is chiefly found in anonymous MSS, with a few in which another name is prefixed to the commentary, very rarely in those which bear his name; and this fact is the more important because the variations in the MSS shew the commentary to have undergone much bold rehandling. The scholium does not qualify Victor's own words but contradicts them : nor could the two passages have stood thus far apart and out of visible connexion, had

they proceeded from a single author, with whom the first was but intended to prepare the way for the second. These considerations are independent of the cessation of Victor's comments at v. 8, and the combined evidence leaves no room for doubt. The scholium must have been added at the end of the book by some Greek editor who was modifying or abridging the Victorian commentary, possibly the unknown Peter of Laodicea whose name appears in some of the MSS, and who cannot be a fictitious personage. His evident purpose was to undo the impression which might be left by Victor's words, and with this view he appealed to MSS extant in his own time. What was the value of the "accurate copies" and "the Palestinian Gospel of Mark" appealed to by an unknown editor in the sixth or some later, perhaps much later, century, in defence of the current text of his time against an ancient criticism, it is neither possible nor important to know.

The third commentary printed by Poussin comes likewise to an end at v. 8 in the Toulouse MS employed by him. But it is not yet known whether other MSS attest a similar text; and at all events the Toulouse scholia are here almost identical with those that are attributed to Theophylact, which certainly cover vv. 9—20.

On the other hand the short anonymous Argument (ὑπόθεσις) prefixed to the Gospel in Poussin's edition (p. 1) must have been written by some one who used a copy from which vv. 9—20 were absent. After a very brief account of the evangelist he gives the substance of i 1—20, and then passes almost at once to the Last Supper, the Betrayal, the Crucifixion, the parting of the garments, the Burial, and the Resurrection; ending with the words καὶ τοῦτο ταῖς γυναιξὶν ὁ καταβὰς ἄγγελος ἀπήγγειλεν, ἵνα καὶ αὗται ἀπαγγείλωσι τοῖς μαθηταῖς (xvi 7). Thus he is silent, not only as to the appearances in vv. 9—13, but as to the last charge, and even the Ascension. The author cannot be Victor, whose own Preface (πρόλογος) is extant, and contains likewise an account of the evangelist.

On the relics of the Eusebian tradition of a discrepance of reading which survive into the middle ages a few words will suffice. Whatever may have been the currency of the original work of Eusebius, or of extracts from it, the *Oration on the Resurrection* and the scholium appended to the Victorian commentary were evidently well known. Euthymius, followed by a Venice MS of Theophylact, refers distinctly to "some of the interpreters". The writers of the several scholia (four forms are known) which appear in a few cursives were content to preserve a record of the absence of vv. 9—20 from "some of the copies", while they variously described the opposing authorities as "some" or "many" or "the more ancient" copies: but doubtless these variations were arbitrary, the discrepance of reading having vanished some centuries earlier. In three MSS derived from a common original, 20 215 300, the scholium strangely stands within the text between vv. 15 and 16, as though the omitted verses were 16—20: the obvious explanation that it was originally a footnote, referred to at v. 9 by a marginal asterisk which the scribe of the common original overlooked, is singularly confirmed by its present position as the last words of a page of text in all three MSS. These MSS, as also Λ and a few cursives, profess in subscriptions to

the Gospels to have been written with collation of "the ancient copies at Jerusalem" (some add "which are laid up in the Holy Mountain"), much in the same way as the Pseudo-Victorian scholium (above, p. 35) appeals to "the accurate copies" and "the Palestinian Gospel of Mark".

For many details of fact respecting the MSS of the Victorian commentary, and also of the scholia generally, we are indebted to Dr Burgon's indefatigable researches, the results of which are given in his book already named, and in his supplementary letters to the *Guardian* newspaper of 1873-4.

The positive patristic evidence for the omission of vv. 9—20, it will have been seen, is supplied by Eusebius and his various followers, among whom Victor and probably Jerome alone carry additional weight as independent witnesses, and by the unknown author of the ὑπόθεσις. The negative evidence cannot however be passed over, as the peculiar contents of these verses confer on it an unusual degree of validity. They contain (1) a distinctive narrative, one out of four, of the events after the day of the Resurrection; (2) one of the (at most) three narratives of the Ascension; (3) the only statement in the Gospels historical in form as to the Session at the Right Hand; (4) one of the most emphatic statements in the N. T. as to the necessity of faith or belief; and (5) the most emphatic statement in the N. T. as to the importance of baptism; besides other matter likely to be quoted. The silence of writers who discuss with any fulness such topics as these is evidently much more significant than the mere absence of quotations of passages which it was equally natural to quote or not to quote; and, even where there are no such express discussions, the chances that one or other of these verses would have been casually quoted in voluminous writings, if it had been known and received, are unusually high.

In the whole Greek Ante-Nicene literature there are at most but two traces of vv. 9—20, and in the extant writings of Clem.al and Origen they are wholly wanting. Unfortunately no commentary of Origen on any Gospel narrative of the Resurrection and the subsequent events has been preserved; and the evidence from the silence of both these writers is of the casual rather than the special kind.

On the other hand the negative evidence of Cyril of Jerusalem (about 349) is peculiarly cogent. Lecturing the candidates for baptism on the Creed of Jerusalem, he illustrates copiously from Scripture the clause καὶ καθίσαντα ἐκ δεξιῶν τοῦ πατρός without referring to xvi 19 (*Catech.* xiv 27—30). It is true that a little earlier (c. 24), in speaking of the preceding clause on the Ascension itself (καὶ ἀνελθόντα εἰς τοὺς οὐρανούς), he reminds his hearers of a public sermon on the Ascension which he had preached in their presence the day before; and, though he recapitulates in a cursory way some points he had expounded at length, he quotes no passage from the N.T. But with the clause on the Session, which peculiarly interested him on account of his aversion to the doctrine of Marcellus, he pursues a different plan. His whole list of illustrative passages had evidently included a considerable number from the O.T.: but, after citing Is vi 1 and Ps xciii 2, he now (cc. 27 f.) stops short, proposes to cite "a few only out of many" texts, contents himself with one more "clear" testimony from the Psalms (cx 1), and

then proceeds to the N.T., from which he quotes no less than eleven passages. For the topic which alone here engaged him (καθ. ἐκ δεξιῶν) the list is virtually exhaustive: the only omissions are the parallels in Mc and Lc to Mt xxii 43, which evidently did not need repetition; Heb viii 1, which adds nothing to i 3; and Act vii 55, which relates to 'standing' (ἑστῶτα ἐκ δεξ.). Such a list could not have omitted what would have been to Cyril the most pertinent and fundamental passage of all if he had found it in his Gospels. Again his lectures on Baptism (iii: see especially c. 4) and on Faith (v: see especially c. 10) are no less destitute of any reference to xvi 16, though he is especially fond of quoting terse and trenchant sentences. It would be strange indeed if all three omissions were accidental.

With respect to slighter evidence, it is at least worthy of notice that vv. 9—20 have apparently left no trace in the voluminous writings of Athanasius, Basil, Gregory of Nazianzus, Gregory of Nyssa, Cyril of Alexandria, and Theodoret. With some of these authors the silence may well be accidental, and especially with Theodoret, but hardly with all. It may be added that the *prima facie* significance of Cyril's silence is not materially lessened by the fact that he transcribes without remark Nestorius's quotation of v. 20; for, unlike the other quotations in the extract from Nestorius, it does not affect Cyril's argument: see also the case of Macarius below, p. 40.

Passing to the Latin Fathers, we find strong negative evidence that vv. 9—20 were unknown to Tertullian and Cyprian. Tertullian's book *De baptismo*, in 20 chapters, is a defence of baptism and its necessity against one Quintilla, dealing specially with the relation of baptism to faith. To those who said *Baptismus non est necessarius quibus fides satis est* he replies that after faith had come to include the Nativity, Passion, and Resurrection, *lex tinguendi imposita est et forma praescripta ; Ite, inquit, docete nationes, tinguentes eas in nomine Patris et Filii et Spiritus Sancti ; huic legi collata definitio illa* Nisi quis renatus fuerit ex aqua et spiritu non intrabit in regnum caelorum *obstrinxit fidem ad baptismi necessitatem* (c. 13) : yet neither here nor elsewhere does he refer to the verse which would have supplied him with the desired authority in five words. Some imaginary references to these verses by Tertullian in other books hardly deserve a passing notice : for *Apol.* 21 see Mt xxviii 19; Lc xxiv 47; Act xi 19; Col i 23 &c.; for *Apol.* 51 Mc xii 36 &c.; for *Anim.* 25 Lc viii 2.

The baptismal controversies in which Cyprian was engaged afforded no such stringent motive for adducing Mc xvi 16, though it might have been expected to be cited somewhere in the epistles bearing on this subject : but there can be only one reason for its absence from the third book of his collection of *Testimonies* from Scripture, which includes such heads as these, *Ad regnum Dei nisi baptizatus et renatus quis fuerit pervenire non posse* (25), *Eum qui non crediderit jam judicatum esse* (31), *Fidem totum prode esse et tantum nos posse quantum credimus* (42), *Posse eum statim consequi [baptismum] qui vere crediderit* (43). This evidence of the earlier Fathers of North Africa is specially important on account of the local and genealogical remoteness of their text from the texts which supply nearly all the other evidence to the same effect.

It may be added that Lucifer and Hilary, who have purer texts than

any other Latin Fathers of Cent. IV, leave vv. 9—20 unnoticed : but their silence may be due to the absence of sufficient motives for quotation. Jerome, in condensing the remarks of Eusebius, seems studiously to avoid coming to a decision, *aut enim non recipimus &c., aut hoc respondendum &c.*

The Shorter Conclusion Πάντα δὲ —σωτηρίας is found (with unimportant variations) in L as an alternative to vv. 9—20 and preceding them (see above, p. 30); in 274 in a footnote without introductory formula (Burgon in *Guardian*, 1873, p. 112) ; in *k* continuously with v. 8, (which takes the form *illae autem cum exirent a monumento fugerunt tenebat enim illas tremor et pavor propter timorem,*) and without notice of vv. 9—20 ; in syr.hl in the margin with the note "These also are in a manner [or 'somewhere', *i.e.* in some authorities : cf. p. 30] added," and followed by ἀμήν, the text having vv. 9—20 ; in the margin of the best Oxford Memphitic MS (Hunt. 17 : see Lightfoot in Scrivener's *Introduction*[2] p. 332) ; and in at least several Æthiopic MSS continuously with v. 8, and followed continuously by vv. 9—20, without note or mark of any kind (Dr Wright). No mention or trace of the Shorter Conclusion has been found in any Father.

The Longer Conclusion, vv. 9—20, is found in ACDXΓΔΣ and all late uncials, (in L, as the secondary reading,) in MSS known to Eus and probably Hier, MSS known to the scribe of B, all cursives, *c ff n o q* lat.vg syr.(vt)-vg-(hr)-hl.txt memph (aeth, as the secondary reading) [the later MSS of arm] and goth : on Fathers, Greek, Latin, and Syriac, see below.

The only extant fragment of Mc in syr.vt contains vv. 17—20; so that it cannot be known whether vv. 9—20 were continuous with v. 8, or divided from it by the Shorter Conclusion or in any other way. Syr.hr is not in this instance an independent witness: it is known only from Melkite lectionaries, which reproduce the Greek lectionary of Antioch and Constantinople, and naturally would not omit a whole lesson. The Thebaic version is lost from xv 32 to the end of the Gospel: what is sometimes cited as a loose rendering of xvi 20, on which verse (perhaps in combination with the Shorter Conclusion) it is doubtless founded, is not a biblical but a quasi-patristic text: it is a detached fragment of a translation of some apocryphal Acts of Apostles (for illustrations see Lipsius in Smith and Wace's *Dict. Chr. Biogr.* i 19 ff.), preserved by adhesion to the Askew MS of the *Pistis Sophia* (Woide in Ford *Cod. Alex. App.* 45, 19); and the age of the unknown original work is of course uncertain.

The Greek patristic evidence for vv. 9—20 perhaps begins with Justin (*Ap.* i 45), who interprets ʽΡαβδὸν δυνάμεως ἐξαποστελεῖ σοι ἐξ Ἰερουσαλήμ (Ps cx 3) as predictive τοῦ λόγου τοῦ ἰσχυροῦ ὃν ἀπὸ Ἰερουσαλὴμ οἱ ἀπόστολοι αὐτοῦ ἐξελθόντες πανταχοῦ ἐκήρυξαν. On the one hand it may be said that the combination of the same four words recurs in v. 20; on the other, that they were natural and obvious words to use and to combine, and that v. 20 does not contain the point specially urged by Justin, ἀπὸ Ἰερουσαλὴμ... ἐξελθόντες (cf. *Ap.* i 39, 49), which is furnished by Lc xxiv 47 ff.; Act i 4, 8. On both sides the evidence is slight, and decision seems impossible. It should be added however that the affinity be-

tween Justin's text and that of Irenæus (see below) leaves the supposition of a reference to v. 20 free from antecedent improbability as regards textual history.

Irenæus (188) clearly cites xvi 19 as St Mark's own (*In fine autem evangelii ait Marcus*, corresponding to *Marcus interpres et sectator Petri initium evangelicae conscriptionis fecit sic*); and the fidelity of the Latin text is supported by a Greek scholium.

Irenæus and possibly Justin are the only Greek Ante-Nicene Fathers whose extant works shew traces of vv. 9—20. The name of Hippolytus has been wrongly attached to an undoubted quotation of vv. 17, 18 in the first paragraph of the Eighth Book of the Apostolic Constitutions. His name is indeed connected indirectly by a slight and suspicious tradition (see Lagarde *Rell. jur. ecc. ant.* p. viii; Caspari *Quellen z. Gesch. d. Taufsymb.* iii 387 ff.) with an extract from a somewhat later part of the same Eighth Book; and he is recorded to have written a treatise entitled Περὶ χαρισμάτων ἀποστολικὴ παράδοσις, while an extract including the quotation bears the title Διδασκαλία τῶν ἁγίων ἀποστόλων περὶ χαρισμάτων. But, even on the precarious hypothesis that the early chapters of the Eighth Book were founded to some extent on the lost work, the quotation is untouched by it, being introduced in direct reference to the fictitious claim to apostolic authorship which pervades the Constitutions themselves (τούτων τῶν χαρισμάτων προτέρον μὲν ἡμῖν δοθέντων τοῖς ἀποστόλοις μέλλουσι τὸ εὐαγγέλιον καταγγέλλειν πάσῃ τῇ κτίσει κ.τ.λ.). Moreover the χαρίσματα about which Hippolytus wrote can hardly have been anything but the prophetic gifts of the Church, which he would naturally defend, as his master Irenæus (p. 192) had done, against both the disparagement of his antagonists the Alogi and the perversion of the Montanists; while the χαρίσματα of the passage of Const. Ap. are miscellaneous and vague, and what is said about them bears no trace of the age and circumstances of Hippolytus.

In the fourth and early part of the fifth centuries vv. 9—20 were used by Marinus the correspondent of Eusebius, the anonymous heathen writer cited by Macarius Magnes (96; and ? Macarius himself, 108), the Apostolic Constitutions (Books VI and VIII), Epiphanius (*Haer.* 386, 517), Didymus (*Trin.* ii 12), (? Chrysostom), and Nestorius (ap. Cyr. *Adv. Nest.* p. 46); and also the apocryphal *Gesta Pilati* (c. 14, εἴδομεν τὸν Ἰησοῦν καὶ τοὺς μαθητὰς αὐτοῦ καθεζόμενον εἰς τὸ ὄρος τὸ καλούμενον †Μαμβήχ†, καὶ ἔλεγεν τοῖς μαθηταῖς αὐτοῦ Πορευθέντες— ἔξουσιν· ἔτι τοῦ Ἰησοῦ λαλοῦντος πρὸς τοὺς μαθητὰς αὐτοῦ εἴδομεν αὐτὸν ἀναληφθέντα εἰς τὸν οὐρανόν). The Dialogues of a 'Cæsarius' and the *Synopsis Scripturae Sanctae* of an 'Athanasius' belong to later times, when the verses were doubtless universally received; and the same may be said of the scholia of Pseudo-Victor. Whether Chrysostom should be included in the list, is less easy to decide. The ultimate authorship of a passage containing a very clear recital of vv. 19 f. is attributed to him (*Opp.* iii 765) by Montfaucon, though it is extant only as part of an anonymous Homily on the Ascension, preached at an unknown date on the Mount of Olives. The supposition is a mere conjecture (*ib.* 757), resting on the somewhat precarious ground that the contents agree with the known subject of a lost Homily of Chrysostom, but is

not improbably true. Another supposed reference in Chrys. *Hom. in* 1 *Cor.* 355 B may be either taken directly from Mc xvi 9 or deduced from Jo xx 1—18. Chrysostom's text might reasonably be expected to contain vv. 9—20; and it is strange that his voluminous works have supplied to one so well acquainted with them as Matthæi these two doubtful examples only. A doubt of another kind hangs about the apparent ratification by Macarius Magnes of his heathen predecessor's quotation. It is highly improbable that they used precisely the same text, and yet Macarius invariably takes the successive quotations as they were offered to him, with all their details, including some peculiar readings.

The only Ante-Nicene Latin evidence that can in any way be cited in favour of vv. 9—20 is derived from the opinion officially delivered by one of the 87 North African bishops at the Council of Carthage under Cyprian (*Sent. episc.* 37) in 256. Vincentius of Thibaris is said to have referred to the rule of truth "*quam Dominus praecepto divino mandavit apostolis dicens* Ite in nomine meo manum inponite, daemonia expellite, *et alio loco* Ite et docete* &c. (Mt xxviii 19): *ergo primo per manus inpositionem in exorcismo, secundo per baptismi regenerationem,*" &c. It is not easy to determine the origin of the words first put forward as a quotation. If they were founded on vv. 17, 18, χεῖρας ἐπιθήσουσιν must have been detached from ἐπὶ ἀρρώστους, shifted back two lines, and intercalated between ἐν τ. ὀνόματί μου and δαιμόνια ἐκβαλοῦσιν, to make up an authority for exorcism as a rite preceding baptism. The argument in favour of this possible though difficult supposition is the absence of any other passage in which the laying on of hands is spoken of with reference to the future. On the other hand vv. 17, 18 contain not a command to the apostles, but a promise of powers to those who should believe. Other sources can likewise be found for the seeming quotation. Its first and last words, *Ite* and *daemonia expellite*, are copied from the charge to the apostles in Mt x 6—8; the association of *in nomine meo* with exorcism is a natural adaptation of Mt vii 22; Mc ix 38 f.; Lc ix 49; x 17; and the introduction of the imposition of hands might be suggested by the various passages in which it is mentioned as accompanying Christ's own acts of healing. Neither in vv. 17 f. nor anywhere else in the New Testament is the imposition of hands coupled with exorcism. On the whole the balance of the somewhat ambiguous evidence is against any reference to vv. 17 f. in the words of Vincentius. It should be added that the few biblical quotations in the opinions delivered by other bishops contain some distinct differences of text, Greek and Latin, from the quotations in Cyprian's writings.

In the fourth century vv. 9—20 are quoted freely by Ambrose and Augustine, and thenceforward by Latin writers generally. Jerome, who (about 383) had allowed them a place in the Vulgate, adopted, as we have seen (p. 33 f.), the language of Eusebius some 24 years later. In two other places he shews acquaintance with them; once (*Contra Pelag.* ii 15) in noticing a remarkable interpolation (see note on v. 14), and once in referring to Mary Magdalene's delivery from possession, recorded also, but with a different verb, in Lc viii 2. Whatever may have been his own judgement, the phrase quoted above, *in*

raris fertur evangeliis, omnibus Graeciae libris pene hoc capitulum non habentibus, implies by the insertion of *Graeciae* that, as far as his knowledge went, the verses were proportionally of commoner occurrence in Latin than in Greek MSS.

The testimony of the Old Syriac in favour of vv. 9—20 is confirmed by quotations in Aphraates, who lived early in Cent. iv.

The Lection-systems of the churches constitute in this instance a fourth class of documentary evidence, which would be of great value if records of the practice of the earlier ages had been preserved. Unfortunately this is not the case. Beyond a few slight indications, nothing has survived of the lection-systems anterior to the middle of Cent. iv, apparently a time of great liturgical change. All analogies from the early history of ecclesiastical antiquities render it morally certain that wide diversity of local use prevailed for a while, and then gradually passed away, or became nearly conterminous with the range of isolated communions, as wider and wider spheres came under the control of centralisation. Moreover the diversity found in all or nearly all the extant lection-systems excludes the hypothesis of their having proceeded from a single or almost single common origin in earlier times, except to a certain extent the Latin systems. The only coincidence worthy of attention is in the practice of reading the Acts between Easter and Whitsuntide, attested by Chrysostom from Antioch and Augustine from N. Africa, and found to some extent elsewhere : but so natural a sequel to the last chapters of the Gospels, which were read as a matter of course at the Paschal season, and so appropriate an accompaniment to the 'Pentecostal' period, might easily be adopted in many regions independently.

The existing lection-systems of great churches may often have to some extent preserved local arrangements of the earliest centuries; but to what extent is quite uncertain: there is indeed reason to doubt how far it was in accordance with early custom to assign chapters to days as well as books to seasons. The large prevalence of 'discontinuous' lections (that is, lections chosen out in some such manner as the 'Gospels' and 'Epistles' of the West, as distinguished from consecutive portions of a book of the Bible,) throws great difficulties in the way of discriminating later accretions by means of internal evidence: and from the continuous reading of the Gospels the last chapters in particular seem to be always excepted. It was at Eastertide and on Ascension Day that Mc xvi 9—20 was chiefly read; and this circumstance would render it impossible to assume a high antiquity for the reading of lessons taken from these verses, even if a high antiquity could be assumed for the main framework of any of the extant lection-systems in which they occur. It could rarely happen that a church would fail to read them publicly at one or both of these seasons, so soon as it possessed them in the current copies of the Gospel itself: an accepted change in the biblical text, bestowing on it a new narrative which touched the Resurrection in its first verse and the Ascension in its last, would usually be soon followed by a corresponding change in public reading. Now, whatever may have been the earlier history of these verses, they were very widely current in the biblical text at the time for which any lection-system is known in its

details, and thus would naturally by that time enjoy an almost equal range of liturgical use, either by recent acquisition or by ancient custom: whether they had been read publicly for one half-century or for five, the phenomena now accessible to us would be the same.

For the sake of completeness, the extant evidence from lections may be briefly noticed, though for the reasons just given it is without critical value. Some incidental references in Chrysostom's Homilies sufficiently shew the substantial identity of the system which was in use at Antioch in the closing years of Cent. IV, and at Constantinople a little later, with at least a large part of the Greek lection-system of the eighth and all following centuries, as recorded in Lectionaries and in Gospels provided with tables or marginal indications of lections. In other words, the local use of Antioch, and probably of N.W. Syria, became first the local use of the imperial city, and then grew into the universal use of the Greek Church and Empire, that is, of so much of them as remained after the Saracen conquests of Cent. VII (compare *Introduction* § 195); as also of those members of the same (Melkite) communion whose language was Syriac, including the Melkites of Palestine, to whom we owe the 'Jerusalem Syriac' Lectionaries.

Nothing is known of this lection-system before Chrysostom, or outside of Antioch and Constantinople in his days. Its Palm Sunday lections contain no reference to the Ascension and Session at the Right Hand, which the elder Cyril (xiv 24) states that he had been led by the lections read to make the subject of his sermon on that day at Jerusalem. It fails to exhibit a combination of lections for the use of which at an intermediate time, doubtless in Cappadocia, we have the authority of Basil (*Hom.* viii p. 114). Its supposed attestation by the Epiphanius of Cent. IV is found only in a homily which the editor Petau, with the general assent of later critics, assigns to one or other of the Epiphanii of a later age. Chrysostom alleges "the law of the fathers" (*Hom. in Act.* ix, *Opp.* iii 102 B) as the authority for the arrangement of lessons; which cannot therefore have been introduced in his own memory, that is, later than about 360 : of more definite historical knowledge the vague phrase has no trace.

In the extant Constantinopolitan Lectionaries and other records, and therefore probably in the Antiochian system, Mc xvi 9—20 is read on Ascension Day, and forms one of the 11 'Morning Gospels of the Resurrection' into which Mt xxviii (except 1—15), Mc xvi, Lc xxiv, and Jo xx xxi are divided, and which have various liturgical uses. There is no sufficient authority for the addition of 9—20 to the preceding verses in the Matins lection for the 3rd Paschal Sunday (see Matthaei *Ev. Gr. Goth.* 16 ; Scholz i 456 ; Scrivener *Introd.*[2] 75 ; as against Matthaei[2] i 731) ; and the reading of them on St Mary Magdalene's day was apparently occasional and late.

A fragment of the (late) Alexandrian Greek lection-table (Zacagni *Coll. Mon.* xci ff. ; 712 ff.), preserved in a single cursive of Cent. XI, does not contain the Gospel lections. The Jacobite Copts read vv. 9—20 on Ascension Day (Malan *Orig. Doc. of Copt. Ch.* iv 63 ; Lagarde *Orientalia* i 9) ; the Jacobite Syrians on Tuesday in Easter-week (Adler *Verss. Syr.* 71 ; Payne Smith *Cat. Bodl.* 146 ; both

cited by Dr Burgon) ; and the Armenians on Ascension Day (Petermann in Alt *Kirchenjahr* 234). The lection-systems of the Nestorian Syrians (Mesopotamia) and of Ethiopia are as yet difficult of access.

Three of Augustine's sermons (ccxxxi 1, ccxxxiii *passim*, ccxxxix 2) shew that in his time, early in Cent. V, the narratives of all four evangelists were read at Easter in N. Africa, and that vv. 9—20 was included. The tabulation of the Capuan lections in the *Codex Fuldensis* (Cent. VI) does not include the Gospels. The better preserved lection-systems of Latin Europe, namely the Roman, which ultimately more or less completely superseded the rest, the Ambrosian (Milan), the Mozarabic (Spain), and the two Gallican, from the Luxeuil Lectionary and the Bobio Sacramentary respectively, are preserved only in a comparatively late shape. With one or two ambiguous exceptions they all read vv. 9—20 for Easter-tide or Ascension-day. Careful investigations of the Roman and (Luxeuil) Gallican systems have been published in separate works by E. Ranke : and his article *Perikopen* in Herzog's *Real-Encyklopädie* as yet stands alone, brief though it be, as a comparatively critical and systematic account of the ancient lection-systems generally.

To recapitulate what has been said as to the evidence of lections. All or nearly all the various extant systems, Eastern and Western, so far as they are known, contain vv. 9—20: many or all of them probably, the Constantinopolitan certainly, represent with more or less of modification the systems of Cent. V or even in part Cent. IV ; and these in their turn were probably in most cases founded on earlier local systems. On the other hand N. Africa is the only region in which vv. 9—20 can be certainly shown to have been read at the beginning of Cent. V: in all the other cases these verses might or might not be an adventitious supplement inserted in some late century without giving any sign of extraneousness; while their manifest appropriateness to two great festivals would naturally bring them into liturgical use so soon as they became part of the current biblical text, on the hypothesis that they were absent from it before. Thus the only tangible testimony which the extant systems render to vv. 9—20 belongs to a time at which all testimony on behalf of these verses has become superfluous. Lastly, any early lection-systems that may in some sense be preserved in extant systems are but the survivors of a multitude that have perished. Even if all regions from which a single local system has apparently risen into wide jurisdiction are set aside, there remain Asia Minor, Greece and Macedonia, Greek Italy, and Palestine, as homes of numerous Greek churches whose native arrangements of Scripture lections are entirely unknown.

The nature of the documentary evidence affecting this important variation has necessitated a lengthened exposition. It remains to arrange and interpret the scattered testimonies.

The Shorter Conclusion has no claim to be considered part of St Mark's true text. Its attestation proves its high antiquity, but is not favourable to its genuineness. Its language and contents have no internal characteristics that make up for the weakness of the documentary authority: the vagueness and generality of the last sentence finds no parallel in the Gospel narratives, and the last phrase is slightly rhe-torical. Nor, secondly, is it credible that the Shorter Conclusion originated with a scribe or editor who had vv. 9—20 in the text which lay before him. The petty historical difficulty mentioned by Marinus as to the first line of v. 9 could never have suggested the substitution of 4 colourless lines for 12 verses rich in interesting matter; and no other reason can be found for so wholesale a change. It remains then, thirdly, certain that the Shorter Conclusion was appended by a scribe or editor who knew no other ending to the Gospel than v. 8, was offended with its abruptness, and completed the broken sentence by a summary of the contents of Lc xxiv 9—12, and the Gospel by a comprehensive sentence suggested probably by Mt xxviii 19; Lc xxiv 47; Jo xx 21.

Hence the documentary evidence for the Shorter Conclusion resolves itself into additional evidence (indirect, it is true, in form, but specially certified by the nature of the indirectness) for the omission of vv. 9—20. The early date at which the Shorter Conclusion was originally composed and appended is shown by the variety of its distribution, Greek (including syr.hl, which is virtually Greek: see *Introd.* §§ 119, 215), Latin, Memphitic, and Æthiopic; the various lines of which must have diverged from a common original, itself presupposing a yet earlier MS or MSS which ended with v. 8. It may be assumed that the exemplars from which L (according to the interpretation of the double ending suggested above, p. 30) and the Æthiopic took their primary text, antecedent to the addition of vv. 9—20 from the text current around them, were descendants of this original; and that the marginal records in 274 syr.hl memph were taken from three other descendants of it.

These several lost exemplars must have simply concluded the Gospel with πάντα δὲ—σωτηρίας, following continuously on ἐφοβοῦντο γάρ, and this is precisely the form of text which *k* presents : but, curiously enough, the text of *k* in this place must have had a less simple origin. The habitual fundamental text of *k* is pure early African or Cyprianic (§§ 113); so that either the early African text must itself have had the Shorter Conclusion, which is possible but hardly likely, or the fundamental text must here, as is found occasionally, have been supplemented from another source ; and in that case, since the Shorter would never have been substituted for the Longer Conclusion, the fundamental text must have had neither. The two alternatives alone are possible : either the Shorter Conclusion stood in the early African text, and is thus carried visibly back to a high antiquity ; or the early African text closed the Gospel with vv. 9—20, and the addition in *k* represents only a sixth descendant of the original above mentioned, and has nothing to do with the early African text, which must on this supposition have closed the Gospel with v. 8. In the one case the absence of any supplement after v. 8 is attested by the African text itself, in the other for a text which preceded it.

It is now evident that the documentary authority for the Shorter Conclusion is, when reduced to its elements, *a fortiori* documentary authority for the omission of both Conclusions, and that the original list (p. 29) must be enlarged accordingly. The following statement of it includes, within [ ], the principal negative evidence, to the exclusion of inconsiderable names ; capitals being used for those writers whose silence cannot with reasonable pro-

bability be regarded as accidental, as well as for Eusebius, Victor, and the author of the ὑπόθεσις.

ℵB

A MS or MSS antecedent to the Shorter Conclusion (which is attested by the primary texts of L aeth, by *k* as it now stands, and by the margins of 274 syr.hl me.cod)

Most of the MSS known to Eus and probably Hier

MSS antecedent to 22.

Lat.afr (as latent in *k* : and see [TERT CYP] below)

Arm.codd.opt

[Clem Orig] EUS [CYR.HR Ath Bas Greg.naz Greg-nys Cyr.al Thdt] VICT.ANT AVCT.HYPOTH [TERT CYP Lucif Hil] (HIER neutral)

The list of documents supporting vv. 9—20 may be repeated here in the same form for comparison.

ACDXΓΔΣ, all late uncials, and all cursives

MSS known to the scribe of B

(The secondary reading of L and of 22)

MSS known to Eus and probably Hier

c ff n o q lat.vg and Latin MSS known to Hier

Syr.(vt)-vg-(hr)-hl.txt

Memph (and the secondary reading of aeth)

Goth

(? JUST) IREN MARIN AVCTETHN (?? MAC.MAGN) CONST. AP EPIPH DID (?? CHRYS) NEST GEST.PIL Ps-VICT expressly (appealing to MSS) and other late writers

(?? VINCENT.THIB) AMB (HIER neutral) AUG and later Latin writers

APHRAATES

Lection-system of N. Africa early in Cent. v, and later Lection-systems generally.

The genealogical relations of this variation cannot be made out with certainty from the extant evidence: there is good reason to think that vv. 9—20 are Western and the Shorter Conclusion probably Alexandrian; but it would be unsafe to treat this supposition as clearly established. Yet Internal Evidence of Groups affords safe grounds for a decision. The unique criterion supplied by the concord of the independent attestations of ℵ and B is supported by three independent indications as to lost ancient Greek MSS (including a strong statement by Eusebius, or perhaps Origen, as to the MSS known to him); by two independent versions (one of them being the earliest extant Latin); and by three independent writers (one in the middle of Cent. IV, the two others probably in Cent. V), without taking into account any one whose silence can reasonably be misinterpreted. Omission was accordingly at least very ancient; it was widely spread; and its attestation includes a group (ℵ + B + lat.afr) on which the habitual character of its readings confers a specially high authority. The testimony of Old Latin MSS is unfortunately very defective here: we have neither the (predominantly) African *e*, nor the two best of the European class, *a b*, nor the middle European *i*: all the extant MSS are either Italian, or else European of a comparatively late and Italianising type. But the phrase employed by Jerome (above, p. 33), and the reading of D render it likely enough that vv. 9—20 were current in the European Latin texts generally. More important testimony is borne to these vv. by the Memphitic. In the case of a passage so likely to steal in from Greek texts, it is difficult to suppress a suspicion as to the incorruptness of the existing MSS.

If the text of the extant MSS, none being older than Cent. XII or possibly X, is incorrupt, as it well may be, still the number of early interpolations which found a place in the Memphitic is not small. The Syriac evidence adds no important fresh element to the other attestation of vv. 9—20: of the three other Oriental versions one is defective, and two adverse. The Greek patristic evidence proves, if proof were needed, the great antiquity of these verses; but it is all of one colour, and belongs to the least pure line of Ante-Nicene transmission. When every item has been taken into account, the conclusion to be drawn from the Documentary evidence alone is that vv. 9—20 are a very early interpolation, early and widely diffused and welcomed; though not so widely as to be known at the place at which the Shorter Conclusion was inserted, or at the several places at which it was accepted; and not so widely as to prevent the perpetuation of copies wanting both Conclusions, in Palestine or elsewhere, on into the fourth and fifth centuries.

This provisional conclusion is however at once encountered by a strong show of Intrinsic evidence. It is incredible that the evangelist deliberately concluded either a paragraph with ἐφοβοῦντο γάρ, or the Gospel with a petty detail of a secondary event, leaving his narrative hanging in the air. Each of the two points of intrinsic evidence is of very great weight: but the first admits, as we shall see, a two-sided application; and such support as either of them lends to the genuineness of vv. 9—20 is dependent on the assumption that nothing but a deliberate intention of the evangelist to close the Gospel at v. 8 could have caused its termination at that point in the most original text transmitted to us. The assumption fails however, for two other contingencies have to be taken into account: either the Gospel may never have been finished, or it may have lost its last leaf before it was multiplied by transcription. Both contingencies are startling when first presented to the mind: but their possibility is included in the fact of human agency. The least difficult explanation of the omission of vv. 9—20 on the hypothesis that they are genuine is by the loss of a leaf in a MS of some later but still very early date; and an external incident possible in the second century cannot safely be pronounced impossible in the first.

These considerations are of course negative only: they remove a *prima facie* difficulty in the way of rejecting the genuineness of vv. 9—20, but they contain no argument against the genuineness. On the other hand, though the presence of these verses furnishes a sufficient conclusion to the Gospel, it furnishes none to the equally mutilated sentence and paragraph. The author of the Shorter Conclusion perceived and supplied both wants: his first sentence is just such a final clause as v. 8 craves, and craves in vain. Once more, the verbal abruptness is accompanied by a jarring moral discontinuity. When it is seen how Mt xxviii 1—7 is completed by 8—10, and Lc xxiv 1—7 by 8,9, it becomes incredible not merely that St Mark should have closed a paragraph with a γάρ, but that his one detailed account of an appearance of the Lord on the morning of the Resurrection should end upon a note of unassuaged terror. To escape this result by treating the terror

as due to unbelief, and thus associating it with the thrice recounted unbelief of the Eleven in vv. 11, 13, 14, only introduces fresh difficulties: for (1) the women receive no reassurance in vv. 9—20, vv. 15 ff. being addressed to the Eleven alone; and (2) the discord between v. 8, as the intended close of a group of verses, and the other Gospels becomes aggravated. Mt relates that the women "departed quickly from the tomb with fear *and great joy* to tell the disciples", Lc that they did actually tell the tale "to the Eleven and all the rest". If v. 8 of Mc was only a circumstantial account of the immediate terror of the women, and their consequent silence on their way to the Eleven, and was followed (or was intended to be followed) by the telling of the tale to the Eleven, as recorded by Lc and implied by Mt, with or without the interposed meeting with Christ recorded in Mt, the verse is congruous with its own position and with the parallel narratives. But, if the story was meant to end with v. 8, (or only to be taken up after a fresh start by vv. 10, 11, which speak of Mary Magdalene alone,) the fear and the silence implicitly obtain from their position a different character, at variance with the spirit as well as the letter of Mt and Lc; and the difference is but emphasised by the accession of the idea of unbelief.

A second considerable item of Intrinsic evidence *prima facie* favourable to the genuineness of vv. 9—20 is derived from their general character. Whether they are historically trustworthy or not, their contents are not such as could have been invented by any scribe or editor of the Gospel in his desire to supply the observed defect by a substantial and dignified ending.

They have every appearance of being founded on definite written or oral traditions. But, though this characteristic distinguishes them broadly from the Shorter Conclusion, and shews that they do not owe their original existence to any ordinary incident of transcription, it does not thereby identify their authorship with that of the preceding verses. A third alternative remains, to which we shall return presently, that they were adopted by a scribe or editor from some other source.

We do not think it necessary to examine in detail the Intrinsic evidence supposed to be furnished by comparison of the vocabulary and style of vv. 9—20 with the unquestioned parts of the Gospel. Much of what has been urged on both sides is in our judgement trivial and intangible. There remain a certain number of differences which, taken cumulatively, produce an impression unfavourable to identity of authorship. Had these verses been found in all good documents, or been open to suspicion on no other internal evidence, the differences would reasonably have been neglected. But, when the question is merely whether they confirm or contravene an adverse judgement formed on other grounds, we can only state our belief that they do to an appreciable extent confirm it. On the other hand the supposed indications of identical authorship break down completely on examination. The vocabulary and style of vv. 9—20 not being generically different from that of the first three Gospels, it is naturally easy to discover many coincidences with Mc as with the others. But we have failed to recognise any coincidences which point to identity of parentage with Mc in a trustworthy and significant manner; and we believe the

supposed harmonies with the general purpose or structure of Mc to be in like manner illusory.

These various internal relations of vv. 9—20 to the whole of Mc afford however much less important Intrinsic evidence than the structure of the section itself in relation to the preceding verses of c. xvi. The transition from v. 8 to v. 9 is, when carefully examined, not less surprising on the one side than on the other: the abrupt close of v. 8 is matched by a strangely retrospective leap at the beginning of v. 9. In vv. 1—8 it is told how Mary Magdalene and the other two women prepared spices, came to the tomb λίαν πρωὶ [τῇ] μιᾷ τῶν σαββάτων... ἀνατείλαντος τοῦ ἡλίου, found the stone rolled away, saw within the tomb a young man robed in white, received from his lips a message from the Lord to the disciples, and then fled away in fear. If vv. 9 ff. are genuine, they must correspond to Mt xxviii 9 f. There however the narrative proceeds naturally; the women ran to tell the disciples, "and behold Jesus met them". Here on the other hand we encounter a succession of incongruities: (1) there is no indication to mark the appearance as an incident of the flight just mentioned;—(2) Mary Magdalene alone of the three is mentioned, though nothing is said of her being in advance of or detached from the rest;—(3) her former unhappy state is noticed (παρ᾽ ἧς κ.τ.λ.), opportunely if the writer were here first mentioning her, and if he knew the incident in a form corresponding to Jo xx 1-18, inopportunely if he had mentioned her a few lines before, and if, in accordance with Mt xxviii 9 (αὐταῖς), he believed her to have still had the companions named in v. 1;— (4) the position of πρῶτον, whe·

ther absolutely or in relation to vv. 12,14, suits the beginning of a narrative, whereas in a continuation of vv. 1—8 it would naturally be inserted in a more accessory manner;—(5) ἀναστὰς δέ reads excellently as the beginning of a comprehensive narrative, but, as a statement of antecedent fact not witnessed by human eyes, it is out of place in the midst of an account of the things actually seen and heard by the women;—(6) πρωὶ πρώτῃ σαββάτου is without force as a slightly varied repetition from v. 2, though almost necessary to an initial record of the Resurrection;—and (7) the absence of ὁ Ἰησοῦς in v. 9 (wrongly inserted in many documents) agrees ill with the exclusively indirect references to Christ in vv. 1—8, and contrasts remarkably with the emphatic phrases used in the analogous places of the other Gospels (Mt xxviii 9 καὶ ἰδοὺ Ἰησοῦς; Lc xxiv 15 [καὶ] αὐτὸς Ἰησοῦς; Jo xx 14 θεωρεῖ τὸν Ἰησοῦν ἑστῶτα); while, if vv. 9—20 belonged originally to a different context, the name might easily have stood at the head of preceding sentences on the Death and Burial. Separately and collectively, these various peculiarities of language are inconsistent with an original continuity between vv. 1—8 and what follows, and, with the qualified exception of the last, mark v. 9 as the initial sentence of a narrative which starts from the Resurrection.

It remains to consider the Transcriptional Probabilities of the two readings; that is, to enquire how far it is possible to account for the introduction of vv. 9—20 on the hypothesis that they are an interpolation, or for their omission on the hypothesis that they are genuine. If they are genuine, the cause of omission

must have been of some unusual kind. Neither the slight historical difficulty mentioned by Marinus, nor the strangeness of the transition from v. 8 to v. 9, nor any other strictly internal ground of offence can have led to so violent a remedy as the excision of the last twelve verses of a Gospel, leaving a sentence incomplete: remedial omissions on this scale, and having such results, are unknown.

Nor again can omission be explained by misunderstanding of the word τέλος which often stands after v. 8 in cursives, as it does in other places of the N.T., few in some MSS, many in others. Wherever the word is a remnant of the significant double τέλος found in 22 (see above, p. 30), it was probably handed down from an early copy, but a copy the form of which already presupposes the existence of both readings. For the common liturgical use of τέλος, as denoting the end of a (Constantinopolitan) lection, there is no evidence earlier than Cent. VIII: the addition of τὸ τέλος [καὶ ἡ ὥρα] to ἀπέχει by D cu^bo lat.vt syrr in Mc xiv 41 cannot possibly have had this origin (see note *ad l.*). But, even on the hypothesis that τέλος was so used in MSS of Cent. II, it is incredible that any scribe should be beguiled by it into omitting the subsequent verses which according to the very hypothesis he must have been accustomed to read and hear.

There remains only the supposition of accidental loss. The last leaf of a MS of Cent. II might easily be filled with vv. 9—20, and might easily be lost; and thus the MS would naturally become the parent of transcripts having a mutilated text. It is not so easy to understand how a defect of this magnitude in so conspicuous a part of the Gospels could be widely propagated and adopted, notwithstanding the supposed existence of a fuller text in the copies current all around. Nevertheless the loss of a leaf in Cent. II does afford a tenable mode of explaining omission, and would deserve attention were the Documentary and the Intrinsic evidence ambiguous.

On the other hand the question whether the insertion of vv. 9—20 can be readily accounted for, on the hypothesis that they are not genuine, at once answers itself in part; that is, as regards the probability that some addition would be made after v. 8. The abruptness of termination could escape no one, and would inevitably sooner or later find a transcriber or editor bold enough to apply a remedy. What was here antecedently probable is confirmed by the actual existence of the Shorter Conclusion, the manifest product of some such editorial audacity: and its testimony to this effect remains unchanged, whether the antecedent text which lacked vv. 9—20 was itself preceded or not by a fuller text which contained them.

It is not however an addition in the abstract that has to be accounted for, but the definite and remarkable addition of vv. 9—20. Here the Intrinsic evidence already adduced against the genuineness of these verses (pp. 46—49) is from another side a *prima facie* difficulty in explaining how they could be inserted. A scribe or editor, finding the Gospel manifestly incomplete, and proceeding to conclude it in language of his own, would never have begun with the words which now stand in v. 9. If he noticed the abruptness of v. 8 as a sentence and as the end of a paragraph, he must have at least added some such words as the first sentence of the Shorter Conclusion. If he noticed

only the abruptness of v. 8 as the end of the Gospel, and was provided with fresh materials from traditional or other sources, still he must have expressed some kind of sequence between the old part of the narrative and the new, instead of turning suddenly back to the Resurrection and its day and hour, and bringing Mary Magdalene freshly and alone upon the scene, as though she had not been one of three whom the preceding verse had left fleeing from the tomb in speechless terror.

This consideration, equally with the intrinsic character of the contents of vv. 9—20 (see pp. 47 f.), excludes the supposition that these verses originated in a desire of a scribe or editor to round off the imperfect end of the Gospel. It is in like manner fatal to an intermediate view which has found favour with some critics, that vv. 9—20 are a supplement added by the evangelist at a later time to the work previously left for some reason unfinished. This mode of attempting to solve the problem is not altogether inconsistent with the documentary evidence: but it leaves v. 9, both in itself and in relation to v. 8, more hopelessly enigmatic than it stands on any other view. On the other hand the language of v. 9 presents no difficulty if it is the beginning of a narrative taken from another source.

When the various lines of Internal Evidence, Intrinsic and Transcriptional, are brought together, they converge to results completely accordant with the testimony of the documents, but involving limitations to which ordinary documentary evidence, taken by itself, has no means of giving expression. If the transition from v. 8 to v. 9 were natural, omission might be explained by a very early accidental loss of a leaf: but both sides of the juncture alike cry out against the possibility of an original continuity. The case is hardly less strong (1) against an intended conclusion of the Gospel with v. 8; and (2) against the invention of vv. 9—20 by a scribe or editor. But neither of these two suppositions is a necessary element in the result suggested by the Documentary attestation, that vv. 9—20 and the Shorter Conclusion were alike absent from the earliest and purest transmitted text, and alike added at a later time owing to a sense of incompleteness. There is however no difficulty in supposing on the contrary (1) that the true intended continuation of vv. 1—8 either was very early lost by the detachment of a leaf or was never written down; and (2) that a scribe or editor, unwilling to change the words of the text before him or to add words of his own, was willing to furnish the Gospel with what seemed a worthy conclusion by incorporating with it unchanged a narrative of Christ's appearances after the Resurrection which he found in some secondary record then surviving from a preceding generation. If these suppositions are made, the whole tenour of the evidence becomes clear and harmonious. Every other view is, we believe, untenable.

The opening words of v. 9 Ἀναστὰς δὲ πρωΐ, without ὁ Ἰησοῦς or any other name, imply a previous context, and mark vv. 9—20 as only the conclusion of a longer record: but to what length the record extended, it is idle to speculate. On the other hand it is shown by its language and structure to be complete in itself, beginning with the Resurrection and ending with the Ascension. It thus constitutes a condensed fifth narrative of the Forty Days. Its authorship and its precise date must remain unknown: it is however apparently older than the time when the Canonical Gospels were generally received; for, though it has points of contact with them all, it contains no attempt to harmonise their various representations of the course of events. It manifestly cannot claim any apostolic authority; but it is doubtless founded on some tradition of the apostolic age.

xvi. 14 *fin.*] + *Et illi satisfaciebant dicentes Saeculum istud iniquitatis et incredulitatis substantia* [al. *sub Satana*] *est, quae non sinit per immundos spiritus veram Dei apprehendi virtutem : idcirco jamnunc revela justitiam tuam* "some copies and especially Greek MSS...in the end of the Gospel according to Mark" according to Hier. *Dial. c. Pelag.* ii 15, who begins with quoting the whole verse (*Postea... non crediderunt*). "If you dispute this authority (*Cui si contradicitis*)", he continues, "at least you will not dare to repudiate the saying *Mundus in maligno positus est* (1 Jo v 19) and Satan's audacious temptation of his Lord" &c. Compare Tert. *De res. carn.* 59, *Sed futurum, inquis, aevum alterius est dispositionis et aeternae : igitur* hujus aevi substantiam *non aeternam diversa possidere non posse.*

ST LUKE

i 28 *fin.*] +ἐ εὐλογημένη σὺ ἐν
γυναιξίν. ⊢ Western and Syrian (Gr.
Lat. Syr. Æth. Goth.); incl. Eus.
D.E. Tert.*Virg.vel.* Ephr.*Diat.*
arm. 49. Text ℵBL 1-131 81** al
syr.hr me the arm pp^ser; also probably Petr.al.47Routh Ps.Tit.*Man.*
82 Lag Sever.*Jo.*Cram.30auct.*Prom.*
172, who quote no further.

From v. 42, perhaps through
the medium of the apocryphal Book
of James 11 f. (according to most
MSS), where v. 42 is omitted at its
proper place.

i 35 γεννώμενον] +ἐκ σοῦ Western
(Gr. Lat. Syr. Æth. [Arm.]);
incl. Just Valentinian.ap.Hipp Iren.
lat Greg.thaum Ath Tert.*Prax.*26;
not D *b ff f q* vg Eus.*D.E.* Tert.
*Prax.*27 Cyp: Tert.*Marc.*iv 7 has
in te nascetur.

Supplied from a desire of symmetry after the two preceding
clauses; and suggested by the context.

i 46 Μαριάμ] *Elisabet a b rhe*
Iren.lat.235 (codd.opt) and copies
known to Orig(or Hier his translator)
Hom. Lc. vii p. 940: Mary's name is
said to be here "in some copies"
while "according to other MSS" it
is Elizabeth that prophesies; other
passages of this and the following
Homily (*e.g.* viii p. 940 *fin. Ante
Johannem prophetat Elisabeth, ante
ortum Domini salvatoris prophetat
Maria*) shew that text was assumed
to be right. All the evidence is
probably Western, but of limited
range; text being found in D *c e*
(*ff*?) *f q* vg Tert Iren.lat.[235
codd.]; 185 Amb Aug.

Probably due partly to an assumption that the hymn was included in the subject of v. 41

(ἐπλήσθη πνεύματος ἁγίου), partly
to the use of αὐτῇ in v. 56.

ii 2   αὕτη ἀπογραφὴ πρώτη ἐγέ-
νετο] αὕτη ἡ ἀπογραφὴ πρώτη ἐγένετο Pre-Syrian (? Alexandrian) and
Syrian (Gr.; vv ambiguous); incl.
ℵ°ACLR Eus.*Ps.*²; *D.E.* (cod.opt.).
Also αὕτη ἀπογραφὴ ἐγένετο πρώτη
probably Western (ℵ*D [?Just] Orig.
*Mt.*lat): the early correction producing this reading in ℵ was probably, as Tischendorf thinks possible, made by the original scribe, who
at first wrote ΔΥΤΗΝΔΠΟΓΡΔΦΗΝ,
doubtless rather by mechanical assimilation of αὕτη ἀπογραφή to the
preceding πᾶσαν τὴν οἰκουμένην than
by misreading of ΔΥΤΗΗΔΠΟΓΡΔΦΗ.
Text B 81 131 203.

The peculiarity of the language
was thus removed or diminished in
two different and independent ways,
by inserting ἡ (a mere repetition
of the last preceding letter) between
αὕτη and ἀπογραφή, and by placing
the verb before πρώτη.

ii 7 φάτνῃ] σπηλαίῳ repeatedly Epiph. i 431 A, C, D; 47D (his
double phrase ἐν φάτνῃ καὶ [ἐν]
σπηλαίῳ in one place seems to be
partly from v. 12), but doubtless by
a confusion with the apocryphal
Book of James (18 ff.): cf. Ephr.
*Diat.*266. See on Mt ii 11.

ii 14 εὐδοκίας] (margin) εὐδοκία
Pre-Syrian (perhaps Alexandrian)
and Syrian (Gr. Syr. Eg. Æth. Arm.);
incl. Orig³ (*Cels.* i 60; *Ps.* xlvi 9
[Cord.]; *Jo.* 15) *[Ps.]Meth Eus²
(*D.E.*163,342) Cyr.hr.xii 32 Epiph.
*Haer.*i 354 Greg.naz.*Or.* xlv 1 Did³
([?*]*Ps.* lxxi.18; lxxxv 1; *Trin.*i 27
p.84) Cyr.al⁹ (*loc.* [gr syr, and again
syr]; xv 28 [gr syr]; *Is.* xliv 23;

Fid. 6 [=*Inc.unig.* 681]; 154; *Hom. in Opp.* v 459 Pusey; *Dial. ad Herm.* ap. Pitra *Spic.Sol.* i 341; **Anthropomorph.*28); but the contexts are neutral in all the places not marked with *, and the supposed quotation from Meth is taken from a work of very doubtful authenticity, the *Or. in Sym. et Annam*: to the evidence must be added the *Gloria in excelsis* in Greek, on which see below. Text ℵ*ABD latt.omn go Iren.lat.186 Orig.lat. Hier.*Hom.Lc.* xiii p.946(and context) Orig.*Mt.*lat.537 Ps.Ath.*Synt. ad polit.* p. 587 pp.lat.omn; also the Latin *Gloria in excelsis*.

The only assured Ante-Nicene patristic testimony for either variant is the passage from Origen's Homily translated by Jerome, the reading *in hominibus bonae voluntatis* of the actual quotation being confirmed by what follows: "*Si scriptum esset super terram pax et hucusque esset finita sententia, recte quaestio nasceretur* [sc. as to discrepance with Mt x 34]: *nunc vero in eo quod additum est, hoc est quod post pacem dicitur*, in hominibus bonae voluntatis, *solvit quaestionem,* pax *enim quam non dat Dominus* super terram *non est* pax bonae voluntatis: *neque enim ait simpliciter* Non veni pacem mittere, *sed cum additamento*, super terram; *neque e contrario dixit* Non veni pacem mittere super terram hominibus bonae voluntatis." Here Orig, whose style can be recognised throughout, especially in the clause beginning *pax enim*, manifestly reads εὐδοκίας, combining it in construction with εἰρήνη, not with ἀνθρώποις.

The reading of Iren must remain uncertain. The actual quotation may be due either to himself or to the Latin translator; and Origen's interpretation shews the ambiguity of a sentence on the next page: "*In eo*

enim quod dicunt Gloria in altissimis Deo et in terra pax, *eum qui sit* altissimorum *hoc est supercaelestium factor, et eorum quae* super terram *omnium conditor, his sermonibus glorificaverunt, qui suo plasmati, hoc est* hominibus, *suam benignitatem salutis de caelo misit.*" The pause at the outset in εἰρήνη recurs in Origen, and *benignitas salutis* may be a paraphrase either of εἰρήνη εὐδοκίας or of εὐδοκία alone.

It is no less uncertain, though on different grounds, whether Origen used a different text of this verse in different writings, or whether the three places in which his extant works exhibit εὐδοκία have been altered in transcription or printing. No stress can be laid on the quotation in *Mt.*lat, as it may have been modified by the translator, and the corresponding Greek text has suffered condensation. But, as regards the Greek quotations, few changes could arise more easily than the dropping of a single letter, where its removal produced assimilation to two previous nominatives; and in this case the usual influence of the current Constantinopolitan text of the Gospel would be powerfully reinforced by the influence of the text of the yet more familiar *Gloria in excelsis*.

The same remark applies to most of the other patristic quotations indicated above. It is probable enough that εὐδοκία was the original reading of many among them; while no less probably it is in some cases due to transcribers or editors: in such a variation as this the need of verifying quotations by contexts (see *Introd.* §§ 156, 276 f.) is at its highest. Some uncertainty likewise attaches to the solitary Post-Nicene patristic testimony in favour of εὐδοκίας, that of a little treatise wrongly ascribed to Athanasius;

since here too the context is neutral and a modern editor might follow the Latin Vulgate : but in any case the evidence is late and unimportant.

In the *Codex Alexandrinus* the Psalter is followed by various hymns, including the *Gloria in excelsis* or Morning Hymn, which begins with Δόξα—εὐδοκ. ; and there the reading is εὐδοκία, while in Lc it is εὐδοκίας. There is however no real inconsistency : in matters of text the *Gloria in excelsis* stands in the same relation towards the New Testament as the Epistle of Athanasius to Marcellinus, which is in like manner prefixed to the Psalter in the same MS ; and no one would expect the quotations in the Epistle to be conformed in text to the biblical books from which they are taken, or *vice versa*. The true bearing of the reading of A in the hymn is twofold ; it is an important testimony as to the text of the hymn, which is itself one of the documentary authorities for the text of Lc ; and on the other hand, by shewing that the scribe was likely to be familiar with the reading εὐδοκία, it increases the probability that when he wrote εὐδοκίας he was faithfully reproducing what he found in his exemplar of the Gospels. The other early Greek Bibles furnish no similar evidence : B and ℵ add nothing at the end of the Psalms, and in C the Psalter is one of the books that have perished.

The *Gloria in excelsis* is extant in three forms. First, as appended to Greek Psalters. Greek Psalters have as yet been little examined ; but εὐδοκία will probably be found a constant reading : it is certainly the reading of the Zurich Psalter (Cent. VII) as well as of A. Second, as contained in the Apostolic Constitutions (vii 47), where some varia-

tions are evidently due to the author of the work, but others seem to be original differences of text : here too εὐδοκία is the reading. Third, as included in Latin Liturgies, with differences which in like manner appear to be original : here the reading is always εὐδοκίας (*bonae voluntatis*). Whatever may be thought of Bunsen's attempted restoration of the original form (*Hippolytus*[2] ii 99 f.), he is probably right in his view that none of the three extant forms (compared in *Anal. Antenic.* iii 86 f.) exhibit the hymn in a pure and unaltered state ; and, if so, the Greek reading εὐδοκία cannot stand above all doubt. On the one hand the Latin reading may easily come from a Latin version of Lc (not the Vulgate,—which has *altissimis* for *excelsis* and prefixes *in* to *hominibus*,—unless it be in a 'Mixed' form): on the other hand the Psalters might easily follow the current biblical texts of their time, which certainly had εὐδοκία; and no composition taken up into the Apostolic Constitutions was likely to escape assimilation to their habitually Syrian text. Thus the *Gloria in excelsis* is on the whole favourable to εὐδοκία; but its testimony is not unaffected by the uncertainty which rests in such a case on all unverified patristic evidence.

The agreement not only of ℵ with B but of D and all the Latins with both, and of A with them all, supported by Origen in at least one work, and that in a certified text, affords a peculiarly strong presumption in favour of εὐδοκίας. If this reading is wrong, it must be Western ; and no other reading in the New Testament open to suspicion as Western is so comprehensively attested by the earliest and best uncials. The best documents supporting εὐδοκία are LPΞ 33 memph

(C and theb are defective); and the distribution of evidence presents no anomaly if εὐδοκία was an Alexandrian correction, adopted in the Syrian text. The only question that can arise is whether internal evidence enforces an interpretation of the historical relations of the two readings different from that which the documentary distribution suggests.

As regards Transcriptional Probability, εὐδοκίας might conceivably arise by mechanical assimilation to the preceding ἀνθρώποις in the final letter, or by an instinctive casting of the second of two consecutive substantives into the genitive case: but either impulse would be liable to restraint from the greater apparent difficulty of εὐδοκίας. On the other hand the seeming parallelism of ἐπὶ γῆς εἰρήνη with ἐν ἀνθρώποις εὐδοκ. would strongly suggest assimilation of case for the two final substantives; and the change would be aided by an apparent gain in simplicity of sense.

Consideration of Intrinsic Probabilities is complicated by the variety of possible arrangements and constructions. With εὐδοκία the passage falls into three clauses. If these are strictly coordinate, as is usually assumed, two or three serious difficulties present themselves. The second clause is introduced by a conjunction, while the third is not (some versions shew a sense of the incongruity by inserting a second conjunction before ἐν ἀνθρώποις); 'men' are not naturally coordinated with 'the highest' and with the 'earth', while 'the highest' and the 'earth' stand in the clearest antithesis; and, to regard these terms from another point of view, 'men' and the 'earth' do not constitute two distinct spheres. If therefore εὐδοκία is right, the second and third clauses

must together stand in antithesis to the first.

Other difficulties however emerge here. The words of the third clause may be taken in two different senses. If, according to the analogy of εὐδοκεῖν ἐν (iii 22 ‖ Mt iii 17 ‖ Mc i 11; Mt xvii 5; 1 Co x 5; He x 38 from LXX), they are taken to refer to God as 'well pleased in' mankind, the order is unaccountable, as we should expect ἐν ἀνθρώποις to come last; and the absence of any intended parallelism between ἐπὶ γῆς and ἐν ἀνθρώποις renders an apparent parallelism peculiarly improbable. Nothing is gained by mentally supplying ἐν αὐτοῖς and thus keeping ἐν ἀνθρώποις in true parallelism to ἐπὶ γῆς by changing its sense. Not to speak of the harshness of phrase, God's good pleasure in mankind cannot be said to have its seat in mankind. Similarly, in whichever way ἐν ἀνθρώποις be understood, εὐδοκία in the nominative is implicitly represented as 'on earth', and a εὐδοκία which is 'on earth' can hardly be God's εὐδοκία in mankind.

These difficulties may be avoided if we change the reference of εὐδοκία, and understand it as the universal satisfaction of mankind, the fulfilment of their wants and hopes (cf. Ps cxlv 16 ἀνοίγεις σὺ τὰς χεῖράς σου καὶ ἐμπιπλᾷς πᾶν ζῷον εὐδοκίας). Yet, though the words will bear this sense, and the sense itself is not out of place, they are not a natural expression of it; and their obscurity is at least sufficient, in conjunction with the still more serious difficulties attending the other interpretation of εὐδοκία, to leave the current Greek reading destitute of any claim to be accepted as preeminently satisfactory for its own sake.

The difficulties of the reading εὐδοκίας are two, the apparent obscurity of εὐδοκίας and the inequality of the two clauses if the first ends with θεῷ. Origen's combination of εὐδοκίας with εἰρήνη would deserve serious attention if no better interpretation were available: the trajection would be similar to that in Heb xii 11, ὕστερον δὲ καρπὸν εἰρηνικὸν τοῖς δι᾽ αὐτῆς γεγυμνασμένοις ἀποδίδωσιν δικαιοσύνης, and would be perfectly legitimate and natural in the sense "peace in men, [even the peace that comes] of [God's] favour": the unquestionable trajection of ἐν ὀνόματι Κυρίου in the similar passage xix 38 is no easier. But it is simpler to take ἐν ἀνθρώποις εὐδοκίας as nearly equivalent to ἐν ἀνθρώποις εὐδοκητοῖς, εὐδοκητός being an extremely rare word, not used even in the LXX, in which εὐδοκέω and εὐδοκία are comparatively common. Mill (*Prol.* 675) supplied the true key to the expression by calling it a Hebraism; and the Greek of Lc i ii, especially in the hymns, has a marked Hebraistic character. The sense corresponds closely to the use of εὐδοκέω, -ία, in the Old Testament, and of their Hebrew originals רָצוֹן, רָצָה, sometimes rendered by other Greek words. There is no need to take εὐδοκίας as distinguishing certain men from the rest: the phrase admits likewise the more probable sense " in (among and within) accepted mankind": the Divine 'favour' (Ps xxx 5,7; lxxxv 1; lxxxix 17; cvi 4) or 'good pleasure', declared for the Head of the race at the Baptism (iii 22), was already contemplated by the angels as resting on the race itself in virtue of His birth.

The difficulty arising from unequal division, Δόξα ἐν ὑψίστοις θεῷ being overbalanced by καὶ ἐπὶ γῆς εἰρήνην ἐν ἀνθρώποις εὐδοκίας, is of little moment. Parallelisms of clauses not less unequal abound in the Psalms; and the difference of subject will explain the greater fulness of the second clause.

[Moreover the words admit of a more equal division, which has considerable probability on other grounds :—

Δόξα ἐν ὑψίστοις θεῷ καὶ ἐπὶ γῆς,
εἰρήνη ἐν ἀνθρώποις εὐδοκίας.

The position of καὶ ἐπὶ γῆς would of course be unnatural if it were simply coordinate with ἐν ὑψίστοις, but not if it were intended to have an ascensive force, so as to represent the accustomed rendering of glory to God ἐν ὑψίστοις as now in a special sense extended to the earth. Other examples of similarly ascensive trajections are Lc vii 17 καὶ ἐξῆλθεν ὁ λόγος οὗτος ἐν ὅλῃ τῇ Ἰουδαίᾳ περὶ αὐτοῦ καὶ πάσῃ τῇ περιχώρῳ; Act xxvi 23 οὐδὲν ἐκτὸς λέγων ὧν τε οἱ προφῆται ἐλάλησαν μελλόντων γίνεσθαι καὶ Μωυσῆς. The sense recalls the first and last verses of Ps viii, the Psalm of the visitation of man by God. In this arrangement "glory" and "peace" stand severally at the head of the two clauses as twin fruits of the Incarnation, that which redounds to "God" and that which enters into "men". H.]

Εὐδοκίας cannot therefore be pronounced improbable, to say the least, on Intrinsic grounds, and Documentary evidence is strongly in its favour. [As however ἀνθρώποις εὐδοκίας is undoubtedly a difficult phrase, and the antithesis of γῆς and ἀνθρώποις agrees with Ro viii 22f., εὐδοκία claims a place in the margin. W.]

ii 33 ὁ πατὴρ αὐτοῦ καὶ ἡ μήτηρ] Ἰωσὴφ καὶ ἡ μήτηρ αὐτοῦ Western and Syrian (Gr. Lat. Syr. Goth.); but not D. Both readings are combined by 157 *cant* aeth; and various documents supporting text add a

second αὐτοῦ at the end. The substitution of the name evidently proceeded from an unwillingness to call
Joseph ὁ πατὴρ αὐτοῦ. In like
manner in v. 41 οἱ γονεῖς αὐτοῦ becomes in lat.eur (not *e* nor lat.it-vg)
Joseph et Maria [*mater ejus*]: in v.
48 ἰδοὺ ὁ πατήρ σου κἀγώ is wholly
or partly omitted by lat.vt syr.vt
and the apocryphal Book of Thomas,
c.19 : and in v. 43, by a more widely
spread corruption, ἔγνωσαν οἱ γονεῖς
αὐτοῦ becomes ἔγνω Ἰωσὴφ καὶ ἡ
μήτηρ αὐτοῦ, Western and Syrian
(Gr. Lat. Syr. Æth. Goth.); but
not D *a e* vg Aug. It may be noticed
here that in Mt i 16 a similar cause
has led to the change of τὸν Ἰωσὴφ
τὸν ἄνδρα Μαρίας ἐξ ἧς ἐγεννήθη
Ἰησοῦς ὁ λεγόμενος Χριστός to τὸν
Ἰωσὴφ ᾧ μνηστευθεῖσα παρθένος
Μαριὰμ ἐγέννησεν Ἰησοῦν τὸν λεγόμενον Χριστόν in 346 *d* (D is defective)
lat.vt syr.vt pp.lat, Western.

iii 1 ἡγεμονεύοντος] ⊣ ἐπιτροπεύ-
οντος ⊢ Western (Gr.[D Eus Chron.
Pasch] Lat.).

iii 16 ἁγίῳ] < 63 64 Clem.995
(or possibly Heracleon quoted by
him) Tert.*Bapt*(apparently) Aug
(very expressly). A remarkable
reading, apparently Western : if
better attested, it would be highly
probable. See also on iv 1.

iii 22 Σὺ εἶ ὁ υἱός μου ὁ ἀγαπητός, ἐν σοὶ εὐδόκησα] ⊣ Υἱός μου
εἶ σύ, ἐγὼ σήμερον γεγέννηκά σε ⊢
Western (Gr. Lat.); incl. MSS (evidently Greek as well as Latin) mentioned by Aug, and Just.*Dial.*88,103
Clem.113 Meth.*Symp*; but not *e*
nor lat.it-vg nor Eus.*Steph*. Aug
speaks of this version of the words
spoken from heaven as the reading
of "some MSS", "though it is
stated" (*perhibeatur*), he says, "not
to be found in the more ancient
Greek MSS". The 'Ebionite' Gospel read by Epiph.*Haer*.138 combined both representations of the

voice from heaven, inserting Ἐγὼ σήμερον γεγέννηκά σε between text and
Mt iii 17, very slightly modified.

Doubtless from a traditional source,
written or oral, and founded on Ps
ii 7.

iii 24 τοῦ Ματθάτ τοῦ Λευεί] <
Africanus ap.Eus (Iren apparently,
for he counts only 72 generations)
Eus.*Steph* Amb. According to
Sabatier *c* reads merely *Levi*,
omitting *qui fuit Mat. qui fuit*.

iii 33 τοῦ Ἀδμεὶν τοῦ Ἀρνεί] τοῦ
Ἀμιναδάβ(-άμ) τοῦ Ἀράμ Western
and Syrian (Gr. Lat. Syr. Goth.:
cf. Æth.); evidently from Mt i 4,
itself founded on Ruth iv 19 f.; 1
Chr ii 10. Text B (?131 ?157) (apparently syr.hl.mg): also τοῦ Ἀδάμ
τοῦ Ἀδμὶν τοῦ Ἀρνεί א*, τοῦ Ἀδάμ
being likewise prefixed to the Western
reading by aeth. Text is moreover a
factor in the other conflations. With or
without addition of other names or
forms of names, Ἀδμείν (-ὶν) and
Ἀρνεί (-νί) are attested by אBLXΓ
13-69-124-346 131 157 al^p syr.
hl.mg arm : and they will account
for all the other readings except
perhaps τοῦ Ἀδάμ of א aeth, which
may however be only the latter half
of Ἀμιναδάμ, a form of Ἀμιναδάβ
found in various documents. *Amin-
adab* and *Admin*, *Aram* and *Arni*,
are evidently duplicate forms of the
same pair of names, preserved in
different family records, as is the
case with many names in the Old
Testament. Many late Greek MSS
and some versions add τοῦ Ἰωράμ
after τοῦ Ἀράμ.

iv 1 ἁγίου] < Ath.*Ep.Serap.* i 4
expressly. No other evidence is
known; and it seems not unlikely
that Ath wrote with a confused
recollection of iii 16.

iv 44 Ἰουδαίας] ⊣ Γαλιλαίας ⊢
Western and Syrian (Gr. Lat. Syr.
Æth. Arm. Goth.). Text אBCLQR
1·131·209 22 157 al^11 lt 59 al^5 me

syr.hl.txt. Two lectionaries have
αὐτῶν. From Mc i 39; cf. Mt iv
23.

v 10 f. stand as ἦσαν δὲ κοινωνοὶ
αὐτοῦ Ἰάκωβος καὶ Ἰωάνης υἱοὶ Ζεβε-
δαίου· ὁ δὲ εἶπεν αὐτοῖς Δεῦτε καὶ μὴ
γείνεσθε ἁλιεῖς ἰχθύων, ποιήσω γὰρ
ὑμᾶς ἁλιεῖς ἀνθρώπων· οἱ δὲ ἀκούσαντες πάντα κατέλειψαν ἐπὶ τῆς γῆς
καὶ ἠκολούθησαν αὐτῷ. in D e (but
e has Qui [sic] ait ad Simonem Ihs
Nolite esse for ὁ δὲ...γείνεσθε).

v 14 εἰς μαρτύριον αὐτοῖς] ┤ ἵνα
εἰς μαρτύριον ᾖ [ἦν D*] ὑμεῖν τοῦτο ┝
Western (Gr.[D Marcion] Lat.);
incl. Tert, but not e lat.it-vg.

vi 1 ἐν σαββάτῳ] ┼ ┤ δευτεροπρώτῳ ┝ Western and Syrian (Gr.
Lat.[a ff f* vg] Syr. Arm. Goth.);
incl. Greg.naz (see below) Epiph²
Amb² Hier: e has (sabbato) mane,
which cannot be meant to render
δευτεροπρώτῳ: it may either stand
for πρώτῳ (see further on) or be
an independent interpolation. Text
ℵBL 1·118·209 22·69 33 157 (lectionaries) b c f ** q rhe syr.vg-hl.mg-
(hr) me aeth.

The excellence and comprehensiveness of the attestation of text
is decisive against this curious
reading, which has no other clearly
Pre-Syrian authority than that of
D a ff (syr.vt is defective), and is
commended by Transcriptional evidence alone. It certainly could
not have been introduced in its integrity through any of the ordinary
impulses that affect transcribers, and
its patent difficulty might have led
to omission: but all known cases of
probable omission on account of
difficulty are limited to single documents or groups of restricted ancestry, bearing no resemblance to
the attestation of text in either variety or excellence. No evidence is
extant from any source that δευτερό-
πρωτος, or any similar word in
Greek or Hebrew, was a term of

the Jewish calendar; nor, to judge
by the usual practice of the evangelists, was a technical term of this
kind likely to be employed in this
manner, without article or introductory formula. All purely numerical renderings, of which the
least untenable is ‘second in a first
pair of sabbaths’, break down by
the want not merely of sufficient
etymological analogies but of justification in the narrative: the Intrinsic difficulty of the reading lies
in the context as well as in the
word itself.

If a reasonable sense could have
been established for δευτεροπρώτῳ,
it might have been supposed to
come from an extraneous source.
But a more probable explanation
has been suggested by Meyer. The
occurrence of ἐν ἑτέρῳ σαββάτῳ in
v. 6 might naturally suggest the
insertion of πρώτῳ, which then
might be changed to δευτέρῳ on
consideration of iv 31 ff. Supposing the dots intended to cancel
πρώτῳ to have been negligently
omitted, or to have been overlooked by the next transcriber, as
experience shews similar dots to
have been often omitted or overlooked, he would naturally combine the two words in one. A few
Greek MSS even now read δευτέρῳ
πρώτῳ, but perhaps only by corruption of δευτεροπρώτῳ.

*Attrita frons interpretatur saepe
quod nescit; et quum aliis persua-
serit sibi quoque usurpat scientiam.
Praeceptor quondam meus Gregorius
Nazianzenus, rogatus a me* [doubt-
less at Constantinople in the year
380 or 381] *ut exponeret quid sibi
vellet in Luca* sabbatum δευτερό-
πρωτον, *id est* secundo-primum, *ele-
ganter lusit, Docebo te, inquiens,
super hac re in ecclesia, in qua
mihi omni populo acclamante cogeris
invitus scire quod nescis, aut certe,*

si solus tacueris, solus ab omnibus stultitiae condemnaberis. Hier. *Ep.* 52 p. 263.

vi 5 is transposed by D to the end of the next sabbatical miracle, after v. 10, the following being substituted here : Τῇ αὐτῇ ἡμέρᾳ θεασάμενός τινα ἐργαζόμενον τῷ σαββάτῳ εἶπεν αὐτῷ Ἄνθρωπε, εἰ μὲν οἶδας τί ποιεῖς, μακάριος εἶ· εἰ δὲ μὴ οἶδας, ἐπικατάρατος καὶ παραβάτης εἶ τοῦ νόμου. Possibly from the same source as the Section on the woman taken in adultery ([Jo] vii 53—viii 11).

vi 17 Ἰερουσαλήμ] + καὶ Πιραίας אֵ*; *et trans fretum a b c ff q ger*₁ *rhe cant ;* probably also *e,* which has *et de transmarinis,* omitting the following καὶ τῆς παραλίου, rendered *et maritima* by most Latins. The Latin reading probably represents καὶ Περαίας (of which καὶ Πιραίας must be a corruption), which must thus be regarded as Western : Perea is not named in the New Testament. Perhaps from an extraneous source, written or oral. For καὶ Ἰερουσαλήμ—Σιδῶνος D has only καὶ ἄλλων πολέων, which is inserted by conflation after Σιδῶνος in *c e* go.

vii 14 Νεανίσκε] + † νεανίσκε ⊦ Western, D *a ff (cant).*

viii 26, 37 Γερασηνῶν] Γεργεσηνῶν Alexandrian (Gr. Syr.[hr] Eg. Æth. Arm.) ; incl. Cyr.al.*loc.*gr. (Mai) in v.26. Γαδαρηνῶν Syrian (Gr. Syr. Goth.). Text in v. 26 BD latt syr.hl.mg Cyr.*loc.*syr. (text and comm.*bis*); in v. 37 BC*D latt the. See on Mt viii 28.

viii 51 καὶ Ἰωάνην] < Iren. 151 expressly. Arguing against heretics who ascribed special sacredness to certain numbers on the ground of Scriptural examples, and for this purpose gathering together numerous similar examples of the number five of which they took no account, he says "*Quintus autem ingressus*

Dominus ad mortuam puellam sus-citavit eam, nullum enim, *inquit,* permisit intrare nisi Petrum et Jacobum et patrem et matrem puellae ". No other authority is known for the omission.

ix 27 τὴν βασιλείαν τοῦ θεοῦ] τὸν υἱὸν τοῦ ἀνθρώπου ἐρχόμενον ἐν τῇ δόξῃ αὐτοῦ D Orig.*Jo.*366, quoting verbally the reports of Mt Mc Lc. From Mt xvi 28 combined with Mt xxv 31. Orig.*loc.* (Galland xiv b 95 ff. = Migne vii 340 ff.) confuses the readings, giving first τὸν υἱὸν τοῦ ἀνθρώπου ἐλθόντα ἐν τῇ βασιλείᾳ αὐτοῦ, almost as Mt xvi 28 (cf. Lc xxiii 42), and then the same with καὶ ἐν τῇ δόξῃ αὐτοῦ added. The reading of syr.vt seems to be conflate, "the kingdom of God coming in glory ".

ix 37 τῇ ἑξῆς ἡμέρᾳ] + διὰ τῆς ἡμέρας ⊦ Western (Gr.[D] Lat.). Evidently due to a desire to keep the two incidents connected in time, no interval being expressed in Mt Mc. The same motive has given rise to the renderings of some vv, *illa die f,* 'on that day again' syr.vt, 'on the same day' theb.

ix 54 ἀναλῶσαι αὐτούς] + + ὡς καὶ Ἡλείας ἐποίησεν ⊦ Western and Syrian (Gr. Lat. Syr. [Eg.] Æth. Goth.); incl. a clear allusion in 'Clem.' 1019 f. (see below). Text אBLΞ 71 157 *e* vg syr.vt me.codd arm Cyr.*Jo;loc.*syr;(?Ephr.*Diat.*95).

ix 55 ἐπετίμησεν αὐτοῖς] + + καὶ εἶπεν Οὐκ οἴδατε ποίου πνεύματός ἐστε ⊦ Western and (with οἵου for ποίου, and ὑμεῖς added after ἐστε) Syrian (Gr. Lat. Syr. [Eg.] [Æth.] Arm. Goth.); incl. 'Clem.' 1019 f. (in a fragment the last words of which, containing the reference to this passage, are somewhat more likely to be Clement's own than to have been added by the catenist Macarius Chrysocephalus, since they give Οὐκ...ἐστε according to the

Western form, not the Syrian) Epiph (Did). Text אABCLXΞ un⁶ 28 33 71 ?81 157 al^mu lat. vg.codd me.codd aeth.codd Cyr. *Jo*; *loc.*syr.

Also + ⊣ [ὁ υἱὸς τοῦ ἀνθρώπου οὐκ ἦλθεν ψυχὰς [ἀνθρώπων] ἀπολέσαι ἀλλὰ σῶσαι.] ⊢ Western and, with γάρ inserted after ὁ, Syrian (Gr. Lat. Syr. [Eg.] [Æth.] Arm. Goth.): several vv omit ἀνθρώπων, and some Greek MSS read ἀποκτεῖναι for ἀπολέσαι. D, which retains καὶ εἶπεν... ἐστε, omits this third clause : in other respects the distribution of documents is virtually the same in both cases.

In v. 54, it will be seen, the distribution differs considerably in both directions. There *e* syr.vt arm support omission, while ACX un⁶ (as well as D), nearly all cursives, and aeth retain the inserted clause. The documents which omit all three clauses are אBLΞ 71 157 lat.vg. codd me.codd Cyr: those which retain all are uncials of Cent. IX, a large majority of cursives, the European and Italian Latin, the Vulgate and later Syriac versions, and the Gothic; with some Memphitic and Æthiopic MSS. It thus appears that the two latter clauses were inserted first, and then the addition to v. 54; but that a common source of ACX &c., probably an eclectic text antecedent to the Syrian revision, stopped short without adopting the earlier and bolder interpolations: D may in like manner have refrained from adopting the last, though we have thought it safer to mark the defection of the one early Greek testimony by [ ]. There can be little doubt. that the second and third clauses, if not also the first, were derived from some extraneous source, written or oral: for the third cf. xix 10; Jo iii 17.

ix 62 ἐπιβαλὼν...ὀπίσω] ⊣ εἰς τὰ ὀπίσω βλέπων καὶ ἐπιβάλλων τὴν χεῖρα αὐτοῦ ἐπ' ἄροτρον ⊢ Western (Gr.[D Clem] Lat.).

xi 2 ἐλθάτω ἡ βασιλεία σου] ἐλθέτω τὸ ἅγιον πνεῦμά σου ἐφ' ἡμᾶς καὶ καθαρισάτω ἡμᾶς Greg.nys.*Prec.*738 very expressly twice over, as given by Lc, not Mt: at least two MSS, as cited by Krabinger p. 141, have τὸ πνεῦμά σου τὸ ἅγιον. A similar statement by Maximus Confessor is doubtless borrowed from Gregory. In commenting rapidly on the successive clauses of the Lord's Prayer in Lc,—whether according to his own text, or Marcion's, or both, is as usual uncertain,—Tert(*Marc.* iv 26) places first after *Pater* a petition for the Holy Spirit, followed by a petition for God's kingdom. An early Western text (Marcion's or Tertullian's) must therefore have had either the clause noticed by Gregory or at least the first part of it ; but it must have stood in the place of ἁγιασθήτω τὸ ὄνομά σου. In D ἁγιασθήτω ὄνομά σου (*sic*) is followed by ἐφ' ἡμᾶς, which, as Dr Sanday suggests, may be a trace of ἐλθέτω τὸ ἅγιον πνεῦμά σου ἐφ' ἡμᾶ s [κ.τ.λ.]. No other record of this singular reading is extant: it is passed over by Orig.*Orat*² as well as by later writers : unfortunately only four lines have been preserved of Orig.*loc*, and nothing of Orig on Mt vi 9 ff. Possibly suggested by v. 13.

xi 13 πνεῦμα ἅγιον] ⊣ ἀγαθὸν δόμα ⊢ Western (Gr.[D] Lat.): Orig(*Mt.*650 ; *Orat.*213) refers probably to this reading, though perhaps he is but loosely combining the two clauses ; but on Mt vii 11 (Galland xiv b 75 = Migne vii 292: also, under Cyril's name, Mai *N. P. B.* iii 130) he expressly ascribes πνεῦμα ἅγιον to Lc, ἀγαθά to Mt: so also Amb. Evidently derived from δόματα ἀγαθά in the former clause of the verse. Various forms of conflation present themselves, L cu^P (chiefly lectionaries) lat.vg syr.hl. mg Cyr.*loc.*syr (text and comm. distinctly) having πνεῦμα ἀγαθόν, mm *spiritum bonum datum*, and aeth ἀγαθὸν δόμα πνεύματος ἁγίου.

xi 35, 36 (†) (v. 35) σκόπει...ἐστίν] εἰ οὖν τὸ φῶς τὸ ἐν σοὶ σκότος, τὸ σκότος πόσον Western (Gr. Lat. : cf. Syr.), most of the Latins adding *ipsae* or *tuae* to the second *tenebrae* and inserting *sunt :* syr.vt adds this sentence after text. From Mt vi 23.

(v. 36) εἰ οὖν...φωτίζῃ σε]<Western (Gr. Lat. Syr.). The omission is probably in like manner due to the absence of any similar sentence in Mt.

ὡς ὅταν..φωτίζῃ] καὶ ὡς [ὁ] λύχνος [τῆς] ἀστραπῆς φωτίσει *c f* vg (me) aeth (<καί. A curious recasting of the verse is substituted in *q* and, with some variations, added at the end in *f*: its original, to judge by comparison of the two forms, which are both corrupt, was probably εἰ οὖν τὸ σῶμα τὸν ἐν σοὶ λύχνον μὴ ἔχον φωτινὸν σκοτινόν ἐστιν, πόσῳ μᾶλλον ὅταν ὁ λύχνος [σου] ἀστράπτῃ φωτίζει σε (or φωτίσει σε). Before τῇ ἀστραπῇ +ἐν B me Orig.*loc*² (Galland xiv b 102 f. = Migne vii 356): Cyr.*Lc* is defective here in Syriac as well as Greek.

All the extant variations are probably due to the extreme difficulty of the verse. The passage probably contains a primitive corruption somewhere, though no conjecture that has yet been made has any claim to be accepted.

xi 42 κρίσιν] κλῆσιν Marcion according to Epiph. i 313, 332 and Tert.*Marc.* iv 27. Perhaps only due to an itacism and an easy interchange of liquids, though κρίσιν might possibly be distasteful to Marcion.

27

xi 44 ὡς τὰ μνημεῖα τὰ]+ μνημεῖα + Western (Gr.[D] Lat. Syr.).

xi 48 καὶ συνευδοκεῖτε]+ μὴ συνευδοκεῖν + Western(Gr.[D] Lat.).

xi 52 ἤρατε]+ ἐκρύψατε + Western (Gr.[D 157] Lat. Syr.: cf. Æth. Arm.) : aeth arm combine both readings.

xi 53 f. Κἀκεῖθεν ... στόματος αὐτοῦ]+ Λέγοντος δὲ αὐτοῦ ταῦτα πρὸς αὐτοὺς ἐνώπιον παντὸς τοῦ λαοῦ ἤρξαντο οἱ φαρισαῖοι καὶ οἱ νομικοὶ δεινῶς ἔχειν καὶ συνβάλλειν αὐτῷ περὶ πλειόνων, ζητοῦντες ἀφορμήν τινα λαβεῖν αὐτοῦ ἵνα εὕρωσιν κατηγορῆσαι αὐτοῦ + Western (Gr. Lat. throughout: Syr. in parts). For a Syrian conflation and other variations in v. 54 see *Introd.* § 144.

xii 18 τὸν σῖτον καὶ τὰ ἀγαθά μου]+τὰ γενήματά μου + Western (Gr. Lat. Syr.): also τοὺς καρποὺς μcυ (Gr. Lat.). For a Syrian conflation see *Introd.* § 145.

xii 26 εἰ οὖν...λοιπῶν] + καὶ περὶ τῶν λοιπῶν τί + Western (Gr.[D] Lat.).

xii 27 αὐξάνει· οὐ κοπιᾷ οὐδὲ νήθει] + οὔτε νήθει οὔτε ὑφαίνει + Western (Gr.[D Clem] Lat. Syr.) ; partially adopted by other Latins.

xii 38 κἂν ἐν τῇ δευτέρᾳ...οὕτως,] + καὶ ἐὰν ἔλθῃ τῇ ἑσπερινῇ φυλακῇ καὶ εὑρήσει, οὕτως ποιήσει, καὶ ἐὰν ἐν τῇ δευτέρᾳ καὶ τῇ τρίτῃ· + Western (D throughout): parts of the reading are also attested as follows :— τ. ἑσπερινῇ φ. Gr. Lat. Syr. ; incl. Marcion (ap.Epiph) Iren.lat Meth : postponement of κ. ἐν τῇ δευτέρᾳ κ. [ἐν] τῇ τρίτῃ Gr. Lat. Syr.; incl. Iren.lat Meth : ποιήσει Gr.[D] Lat.[*e*]. After οὕτως and some vv add ποιοῦντας instead of ποιήσει; and 1-118-209 lat.vt.codd ; ser.codd syr.vt Iren.lat further add [μακάριοι εἰσιν] ὅτι ἀνακλινεῖ αὐτοὺς καὶ διακονήσει αὐτοῖς, partly from the end of the verse, partly from v. 37. The Syrian reading is the same as text, slightly modified by one form of the Western reading.

xiii 8 κόπρια] ┤ κόφινον κοπρίων ├ Western (Gr.[D] Lat.); incl. Orig. *Lev*.lat. Ruf. 190 (apparently ⸱ with context).

xiv 5 υἱὸς] ὄνος Pre-Syrian (? Alexandrian) (Gr. Lat.[eur-vg] Syr. Eg. [Æth.] Arm.), from xiii 15 : syr.vt aeth.cod add ἢ ὄνος to text. Πρόβατον D aeth.cod, from Mt xii 11. Text (also Syrian) AB un[10] cu[pl] lat. afr-it syr.(vt)-vg-hl the (aeth.cod) Cyr.*loc*.gr.syr. Authority is remarkably divided, B *e* syr.vt the Cyr being opposed to אLX, the best cursives, and some early vv. There is no intrinsic difficulty in either reading: the falling of children into wells must have been a common occurrence, and Wetstein quotes from the Mishna (Bava Kamma v 6) *Si in puteum incidat bos aut asinus, ... filius aut filia, servus aut ancilla*. The obvious temptation to change υἱός to the easier word, supported by parallelism, and the difficulty of accounting for the converse change constitute strong Transcriptional evidence, which agrees with the specially high excellence of the group attesting υἱός. In adopting ὄνος, Erasmus, and after him the 'Received Text', abandoned Syrian authority to follow the Latin Vulgate.

xv 16 χορτασθῆναι] ┤ γεμίσαι τὴν κοιλίαν αὐτοῦ ├ Western (late) and Syrian (Gr. Lat. Syr. Eg. Arm.); incl. Cyr.*loc*.syr.txt. Text אBD LR 1·131 13-69-124-346 al[2] *e f* syr.(vt?)-hr the aeth (go) (Orig. iii 982 κορεσθῆναι) 'Chrys'(ap.Wetst.) anon.Cram.(? Tit)*loc* Cyr.frag.gr (Mai *P.N.B* ii 346, not on Lc). Both readings are combined by *a*. The combination ἐπιθυμῶν χορτασθῆναι in xvi 21 might give rise to text, though the contexts are altogether different. But the Western reading may as easily be a para-

phrastic exposition of the supposed meaning of χορτασθῆναι. It misses the true point however, for the Prodigal Son could easily 'fill his belly' with the 'husks', though he could not 'be satisfied' with them. The documentary evidence here is in any case decisive.

xvi 22 f. καὶ ἐτάφη. καὶ ἐν τῷ ᾅδῃ ἐπάρας] καὶ ἐτάφη ἐν τῷ ᾅδῃ ἐπάρας א *q* aeth (lat.vt-vg syr.hr Adamant), the words allowing a full stop after either ἐτάφη or ᾅδῃ. The latter punctuation is assumed in lat.vt-vg syr.hr Adamant(in Orig. *Opp.* i 827), which prefix or add a conjunction to ἐπάρας, some documents further adding *in* (or *de*) *inferno*. With the other punctuation the reading would deserve consideration if it were better attested. In its origin however it was probably combined with the division assumed by the translators, being apparently an early Western attempt to amend the brief ending of v. 22 by joining καὶ ἐτάφη to words answering to εἰς τὸν κόλπον Ἀβραάμ.

xvii 11 καὶ Γαλιλαίας] + *et Jericho* (*Hiericho*) Western (Lat. Syr.); not D : syr.vt has εἰς for καί. A singular addition, perhaps derived from an extraneous source, written or oral.

xviii 30 πολλαπλασίονα] ┤ ἑπταπλασίονα ├ Western (Gr.[D] Lat. Syr.[hl.mg.]). Perhaps from an extraneous source, written or oral.

xx 20 παρατηρήσαντες] ┤ ἀποχωρήσαντες ├ Western (Gr.[D] Lat. Æth. Goth.): syr.vt substitutes 'afterwards', and syr.vg omits altogether. The absolute use of παρατηρήσαντες was evidently a stumbling block.

xx 34 Οἱ υἱοὶ τοῦ αἰῶνος τούτου] +┤ γεννῶνται καὶ γεννῶσιν, ├ (some γεννῶσιν καὶ γεννῶνται) Western (Gr. Lat. Syr.: cf. Æth.); incl. (probably Clem. 551 Iren. 168 gr.lat.) Orig.*Mt* (probablyMethod. 79   Mac.magn. 214, 221). The insertion in aeth is after γαμίσκονται: lat.vt (exc. *a*) omits γαμοῦσιν καὶ γαμίσκονται. Probably from an extraneous source, written or oral.

xx 36 δύνανται] + μέλλουσιν ⊢ Western, (Gr.[D] Lat. Syr.[hl.mg.]); incl. Marcion or Tert.

ibid. ἰσάγγελοι γάρ εἰσιν, καὶ υἱοί εἰσιν θεοῦ] ἰσάγγελοι γάρ εἰσιν + τῷ θεῷ ⊢ Western (Gr.[D] and virtually Lat.); not Orig.1 *Cor.* 250 Cram.: lat.vt has *aequales enim sunt angelis Dei* or similar words, perhaps implying θεοῦ: ἀλλὰ ὡς ἄγγελοί εἰσι θεοῦ καὶ 157.

xxi 11 *fin.*] + (? καὶ χειμῶνες) *et hiemes* (*tempestates*) Western (Lat. Syr. Æth.); incl. Orig.*Mt.*lat.355 (apparently from the Greek, which is defective here); but not D *e*. Probably from an extraneous source, written or oral. In the ‖ Mc xiii 8 καὶ ταραχαί is similarly inserted.

xxi 18] < syr.vt Marcion ap. Epiph ; not Orig.*Mart.* Probably due to absence from the ‖‖‖, especially Mc xiii 13.

xxi 38 *fin.*] The common source of 13-69-124-364 here inserted the Section on the woman taken in adultery ([Jo] vii 53—viii 11). The Section was probably known to the scribe exclusively as a church lesson, recently come into use ; and placed by him here on account of the close resemblance between vv. 37, 38 and [Jo] vii 53; viii. 1, 2. Had he known it as part of a continuous text of St John's Gospel, he was not likely to transpose it.

xxii 19, 20 ⟦τὸ ὑπὲρ ὑμῶν διδόμε-νον· τοῦτο..ἐκχυννόμενον⟧ < Western (Gr.[D] Lat.: cf. Syr.): D *a ff i rhe* simply omit ; *b e* likewise transpose vv. 17, 18 to the end of v. 19, after τὸ σῶμά μου: syr.vt differs from them by inserting τὸ ὑπὲρ ὑμῶν· τοῦτο ποιεῖτε εἰς τὴν ἐμὴν ἀνάμνησιν

between τὸ σῶμά μου and vv. 17, 18. The Latins which omit and trans-pose nothing are *c f q* vg, *f q* being Italian, and *c* having many Italian readings. Lt 32 and some MSS of syr.vg omit vv. 17, 18, but probably only by *homoeoteleuton*. Text is sup-ported by Marcion or Tert (iv 40) Eus.*Can* Cyr.*loc.*syr.txt : the refe-rence in Orig.*Mt.*823 is uncertain.

The only motive that could appa-rently in any way account for the omission as a corruption would be a perception of the double reference to the Cup. But this explanation involves the extreme improbability that the most familiar form of the Words of Institution, agreeing with St Paul's record, should be selected for omission; while the vaguer, less sacred, and less familiar words, in great part peculiar to Lc, were re-tained. In the case of D *a ff i rhe* the selection would be improbable likewise as seeming to identify the Cup of v. 17, preceding the Bread, with the Cup of the other records, following the Bread. A sense of this discrepance is presupposed by the transposition in *b e* syr.vt; and again their reading adds a second difficulty to the supposed selection by involving a gratuitously double process, omission and transposition.

On the other hand, if the words were originally absent, the order of vv. 17—19 being as in the common text, the two other readings at once explain themselves as two inde-pendent attempts to get rid of the apparent inversion of order. In *b e* (syr.vt) this is effected by a simple transposition ; in most documents by an adaptation of St Paul's familiar language. When the apostle's account of the Cup was being borrowed, it was natural to introduce with it, for the enrichment of the Gospel narra-tive, the immediately preceding line concerning the Bread. The only substantive element not derived from St Paul, the last clause τὸ ὑπὲρ ὑμῶν ἐκχυννόμενον, causes no difficulty : St Paul's corresponding sentence being implicitly contained in his τοῦτο ποιεῖτε εἰς τὴν ἐμὴν ἀνάμνησιν, already appropriated, a neater ending was obtained by taking a phrase from Mc (cf. Mt) with the substitution of ὑμῶν for πολλῶν in accordance with St Paul's ὑπὲρ ὑμῶν in the former verse. Some trifling variations from his diction are only such as are commonly found to accompany the adoption of additional matter from parallel places. The insertion of τὸ ὑπὲρ ὑμῶν...ἀνάμνησιν (without διδόμενον) in syr.vt was probably independent, and due merely to the desire of making the account more complete.

Intrinsically both readings are difficult, but in unequal degrees. The difficulty of the shorter reading consists exclusively in the change of order as to the Bread and the Cup, which is illustrated by many phenomena of the relation between the narratives of the third and of the first two Gospels, and which finds an exact parallel in the change of order in St Luke's account of the Temptation (iv 5—8 ; 9—12), corrected in like manner in accordance with Mt in some Old Latin MSS and in Amb. The difficulty of the longer reading is that it divides the institution of the Cup into two parts, between which the institution of the Bread is interposed. It has long been a favourite expedient to identify the cup of v. 17 with the first (or second) of the four cups which accompanied the Paschal supper according to the Mishna. The identification involves however a startling displacement both of the only command to drink or receive recorded by Lc in connexion with a cup, and of the declaration λέγω ὑμῖν, οὐ μὴ

πίω κ.τ.λ. attached to the Institution of the Cup by Mt and Mc ; divorcing them from the Institution itself, and transferring them to the time of the rites preparatory to the Supper. The supposition that vv. 17, 18 contain an anticipatory reference to the Institution of the Cup, as recorded in v. 20, is no less improbable.

These difficulties, added to the suspicious coincidence with 1 Co xi 24 f., and the Transcriptional evidence given. above, leave no moral doubt (see *Introd.* § 240) that the words in question were absent from the original text of Lc, notwithstanding the purely Western ancestry of the documents which omit them.

xxii 42 εἰ βούλει...γινέσθω.] + μὴ τὸ θέλημά μου ἀλλὰ τὸ σὸν γενέσθω· εἰ βούλει παρένεγκε τοῦτο τὸ ποτήριον ἀπ᾽ ἐμοῦ.+ Western (Gr.[D] Lat.). Compare the inversion in ix 62.

xxii 43, 44 [[ὤφθη δὲ αὐτῷ ἄγγελος —ἐπὶ τὴν γῆν.]] <ℵªABRT MSS known to Epiph 'very many MSS' known to Hil (? many) MSS known to Hier MSS known to Anast. sin (13-69-124, see below) *f* (?very many) Latin MSS known to Hil (? many) Latin MSS known to Hier syr.hl.mg me.codd.opt(cf. Lightfoot in Scrivener's *Introd.*[2] 332 ff.) the.cod arm Cyr.*loc*.syr (text and comm.) Dam.*Par.*(probably) Amb.*loc.* The suitability of these verses for quotation in the controversies against Docetic and Apollinarist doctrine gives some weight to their apparent absence from the extant writings of Clem Orig (? Ath, see below) Cyr.hr Greg.nys. Their controversial use led to gratuitous accusations of wilful excision ; as by (timid) "orthodox persons" according to Epiph, by "some of the Syrians" according to Photius, and by the Armenians according to late writers ; while an

Armenian writer cited by Wetstein retaliated by urging that the verses were inserted by Saturnilus the Syrian 'Gnostic' (Cent. II). Anast. sin (*Hodeg.* p. 338 Gretser = lxxxix 289 Migne) speaks of the attempt of 'some' to remove them as having failed owing to the testimony of translations : "the passage stands", he says, "in all the foreign [ἐθνικοῖς] Gospels, and in most [πλείστοις] of the Greek". Their absence from 'some copies' is noticed in a scholium in the cursive 34.

In a few late uncials, a few cursives, and syr.hl.cod.mg they are marked with asterisks or obeli. In ℵ the passage is cancelled by curved marks at the beginning and end and by dots, and the marks and dots have been subsequently expunged. In Tischendorf's judgement they were inserted by the corrector A and expunged by the corrector C. His identification of the hands in respect of mere marks may be precarious, though he had no bias against the passage, which he retains : but it is in the highest degree improbable that it would be marked for deletion by a corrector of late times. His decision is therefore probably right : but the point is of little consequence. The testimony of A is not affected by the presence of Eusebian numerals, of necessity misplaced, which manifestly presuppose the inclusion of vv. 43 f. : the discrepance merely shews that the biblical text and the Eusebian notation were taken by the scribe from different sources, as they doubtless were throughout.

In the Greek lectionaries and in syr.hr (which like them follows the lection-system of Constantinople, see p. 42) vv. 43, 44 are omitted in the lection which would naturally include them, but inserted after Mt xxvi 39 in the long Gospel for the Liturgy on

Thursday in Holy Week, which likewise in a manner includes part of Jo xiii imbedded in the text of Mt (see below) : in syr.hr they displace Mt xxvi 40,41 except a few words. In most lectionaries the opening phrase of v. 45 is attached to them : but in M and others (cf. Matthaei[2] on v. 45) the inserted portion ends with γῆν. As one among the many liturgical notes added to the margin of C by the second corrector (= third hand, Cent. IX?), they stand opposite to Mt xxvi 40. In 13·69·124 likewise they are found (without the clause from v. 45) in Mt xxvi, and there alone. Their presence in that position is doubtless owing to ecclesiastical use : whether the same may be said of their absence from Lc is doubtful, as xxi 38 *fin.* affords an example of a large analogous interpolation made by the scribe of the original of these cursives, due apparently not to transposition but to fresh insertion from a liturgical source. The compositeness of text in 13 is illustrated by the presence of the words ὤφθη δέ, after which the scribe broke off and followed that exemplar of his which omitted the verses. In commenting on Mt xxvi 39—41, which he quotes continuously, Chrys refers incidentally to points contained in vv. 43 f.; and it is quite possible that he wrote under the influence of the liturgical connexion, as the Constantinopolitan lections for Holy Week may well have been used at Antioch in his time (see p. 42) : but a mere comparison of the parallel narratives of the evangelists would suffice to suggest to him the reference.

Text ℵ*·ᶜDLQX un[13]   MSS known to Epiph (see below) to Hil to Hier 'most MSS' known to Anast.sin cu[pl] lat.vt-vg syr.vt·vg-hl [me.codd] the.cod aeth [arm.codd]   Just Iren.gr.lat Hipp Dion.

al.*Mart* Eus. *Can* Arius 'Ath.'(?)*Ps.*
1121 (this fragment appears in a
condensed shape under the yet more
improbable name of Cyr.al in Mai
N. P. B. iii 389) Epiph("in the un-
corrected copies") Greg.naz Did[3]
anon. Cram(? Tit) Syrian and later
pp Hil(see above) Hier(see above)
Aug pp[lat] Ephr.*Diat.*arm. 235.

The documentary evidence clearly
designates text as an early Western
interpolation, adopted in eclectic
texts. With the apparent exception
of Dion. al, which it is not difficult to
account for, the early patristic evidence on its behalf is purely Western:
on the unfavourable side, the silence
of Clem might be accidental, but
hardly so the silence of Orig (or, later,
of Cyr.hr, [Ath,] and Greg.nys); and
unfavourable evidence other than
negative, if not furnished by an express statement, could exist only in
the form of a continuous quotation
or comment including the preceding
and following verses, whereas no
such comprehensive quotation or
comment is extant in Greek before
Cyr.al.   Setting aside the mixed
MSS LQX and good cursives with
similar texts, the non-patristic Pre-
Syrian evidence for text consists of
א*D latt syrr, a frequent Western
combination.

Notwithstanding the random suggestions of rash or dishonest handling thrown out by controversialists
there is no tangible evidence for the
excision of a substantial portion of
narrative for doctrinal reasons at any
period of textual history. Moreover,
except to heretical sects, which exercised no influence over the transmitted text, the language of vv. 43 f.
would be no stumbling-block in the
first and second centuries; and to a
later time than this it would be impossible to refer the common original
of the documents which attest omission.

The supposition that these verses
were omitted in the biblical text
because they were intercalated in
Mt xxvi in a Constantinopolitan
lection is equally untenable. It is
true that they are dropped in the
Constantinopolitan lection for the
Tuesday after the Sunday answering
to the Western Sexagesima, consisting of xxii 39—xxiii 1, and their
absence from that lection may be
explained by their occurrence in the
Holy Thursday lection. But several
considerations deprive this fact of
relevance to the question as to the
biblical reading. First, direct influence of the gap in the lection
xxii 39—xxiii 1 is excluded by the
at least relatively late date of the
ordinary (not special) week-day lection-system, to which this lesson
belongs, and which is absent from
the earliest lectionaries, and moreover betrays by its structure its adventitious and supplementary character (see E. Ranke in Herzog *R. E.*
xi 376—380). Next, other similar
transpositions occur elsewhere in the
Constantinopolitan system : yet the
resulting omissions in lections have
not affected the biblical text. Thirdly,
as has been already stated (p. 42),
the Constantinopolitan system is
either only the local system of Antioch or a descendant of it, and the
Antiochian or Syrian system cannot
be traced back beyond the latter
part of Cent. IV. Fourthly, vv. 43 f.
are retained in St Luke's Gospel not
merely by the Syrian Greek text but
by all Syriac versions from syr.vt onwards, that is, by the only documents
that could be affected by proximity
to the Antiochian lection-system;
while most, perhaps all, of the
documents which omit these verses
must have been in their origin
remote from any such influence
of neighbourhood. With respect
to the Homilies of Cyr.al, which

clearly omit vv. 43, 44 in the midst of a cited portion of text, vv. 39—46, it may be added that, if they are founded on fixed ecclesiastical lections, which is doubtful, the distribution does not harmonise with the Constantinopolitan system. Lastly, it is in the highest degree improbable either that a passage long enough to fill 11 lines in ℵ should be unconsciously dropped under the spell of the Sexagesima week-day lection, or that a recollection of both lections should persuade a scribe to exclude from St Luke's Gospel three important sentences which lay before him in his exemplar.

On the other hand it would be impossible to regard these verses as a product of the inventiveness of scribes. They can only be a fragment from the traditions, written or oral, which were, for a while at least, locally current beside the canonical Gospels, and which doubtless included matter of every degree of authenticity and intrinsic value. These verses and the first sentence of xxiii 34 may be safely called the most precious among the remains of this evangelic tradition which were rescued from oblivion by the scribes of the second century.

xxii 68 οὐ μὴ ἀποκριθῆτε] + ἢ ἢ ἀπολύσητε ⊦ Western and Syrian (Gr. Lat. Syr. Æth.). Text ℵBLT 1-131-209 22 157 *for* me the Cyr.*Fid.*91;*loc.*syr (not added by Vict.*Mc.*430Cr.[=331Pous.] Amb): some of these documents subjoin μοι. Added apparently to bring out more clearly the assumed sense.

xxiii 2 διαστρέφοντα τὸ ἔθνος ἡμῶν] + καὶ καταλύοντα τὸν νόμον καὶ τοὺς προφήτας Western (Gr.[Marcion ap. Epiph] Lat.): some of the later Latins add *nostram* to *legem*. After the next words καὶ... διδόναι (given by Epiph as κελεύοντα

φόρους μὴ διδόναι, but probably only through his loose manner of reference) Marcion's text had καὶ ἀποστρέφοντα τὰς γυναῖκας καὶ τὰ τέκνα (see on v. 5).

xxiii 5 *fin.*] + *et filios nostros et uxores avertit a nobis, non enim baptizantur* [*-atur c*] *sicut* [*et*] *nos* [*nec se mundant*] (*c*) *e* : see Marcion under v. 3. Doubtless Western, though of limited range.

xxiii 34 ⟦ὁ δὲ Ἰησοῦς—ποιοῦσιν.⟧ < ℵ*BD* 38 82 435 *a b* me.codd. opt(cf. Lightfoot in Scrivener's *Introd.*² 332 ff.) the Cyr.*loc.*syr ; *Julian.* ap. Areth. *Apoc.* 287 Cram. (περὶ ὧν καὶ ὁ χριστὸς ἔλεγε Πάτερ, ...ποιοῦσιν, εἰ καὶ Κυρίλλῳ τῷ Ἀλεξανδρεῖ ἐν ιγ [no longer extant] τῶν κατὰ Ἰουλιανοῦ ⊦ ἐλέγχῳ πρὸς ⊦ (? ἐλέγχοντι ὡς) νόθον τοῦτο τὸ ῥητὸν ἔδοξεν ἀποσκυβαλίσαι· ἀλλ' εἰ ἐκεῖνος οὕτως, ἡμῖν οὐ τοῦτο δοκεῖ. Text Western and Syrian (Gr. Lat. Syr. [Eg.] Æth. Arm.); incl. ℵ*·ᶜACDᶜᵒʳLQX *e* Iren.lat.210(cf.198,207) Hom.Cl Orig.*Lev.*lat.Ruf Eus.*Can* Const. Ap² *Gest.Pilat.*10 'Cyr.'*Lc.* gr. 196 anon.Cram(? Tit) Chr Thdt Dam. *Par* Ephr.*Diat.*arm.117, 256, 265. The fragment (on Lc vi 27) ascribed to Cyr.al bears his name in the three MSS in which Mai found it and in Cramer's MS (p. 52), and there is nothing in its language inconsistent with Cyr's authorship : yet it is difficult not to suspect some confusion of names in the face of the distinct and forcible testimony of Arethas as well as the reading of the text prefixed to the (Syriac) Homily on vv. 32—43, which itself unfortunately breaks off in the only extant MS before v. 34 is properly reached. The Greek fragment omits Πάτερ, as do A and one MS of the *Gesta Pilati*. According to Hegesippus (Eus. *H. E.* ii 23 16) James the Lord's brother at his martyrdom by stoning στραφεὶς ἔθηκε τὰ γόνατα λέγων Παρακαλῶ

κ⁴ριε θεὲ πάτερ, ἄφες αὐτοῖς, οὐ γὰρ
οἴδασι τί ποιοῦσιν.

The curved marks denoting deletion in ℵ are referred by Tischendorf to the corrector A somewhat
less confidently in this verse than in
xxii 43 f., where see the note. Here
too they have been expunged, and
must therefore be due to a corrector
who was not the last; and here,
even more strongly than in the
former case, the early extinction of
the reading points to at least an
early date for the marks. The
corrector who introduced the sentence into D is pronounced by Dr
Scrivener to be not earlier than
Cent. IX.

The documentary distribution suggests that text was a Western interpolation, of limited range in early
times (being absent from D *a* ʓ
though read by *e* syr.vt Iren Hom.
Cl Eus.*Can*), adopted in eclectic
texts, and then naturally received
into general currency.

Its omission, on the hypothesis of its
genuineness, cannot be explained in
any reasonable manner. Wilful excision, on account of the love and
forgiveness shown to the Lord's own
murderers, is absolutely incredible:
no various reading in the New Testament gives evidence of having
arisen from any such cause. Nor
again can it be traced to a break in
the Constantinopolitan lection for
the Thursday before the Sunday answering to the Latin Quinqua-
gesima. The break does not occur
immediately before ὁ δὲ Ἰησοῦς, but
after ἐκεῖ ἐσταύρωσαν αὐτόν in the
middle of v. 33; and the lection
does not begin again before v. 44:
so that only a small fraction of the
gap in the lection, 3 lines out of 59
in ℵ, is taken up with ὁ δὲ Ἰησοῦς...
ποιοῦσιν, and this fraction and the
gap have different beginnings and
different endings. This long gap is

moreover the second in the lection,
for v. 32 is likewise omitted, the intention probably being to shorten
the chapter by dropping all that is
said about the two robbers, together
with the intervening matter except
part of v. 33, which was indispensable to the coherence of the narrative. Further, this lection belongs
to the apparently later portions of
the lection-system (see p. 66), whereas there is no gap in two probably
earlier lections which likewise cover
the same ground, the eighth Gospel
of the Passion, and the sixth Gospel
of the Vigil of Good Friday. On
the fundamental irrelevance of the
Constantinopolitan lection-system to
all questions as to the origin of early
readings, especially in the case of
readings attested by no Syrian authority, enough has been said already (pp. 42 ff., 66).

Few verses of the Gospels bear in
themselves a surer witness to the
truth of what they record than this
first of the Words from the Cross:
but it need not therefore have belonged originally to the book in
which it is now included. We cannot doubt that it comes from an extraneous source. Nevertheless, like
xxii 43 f.· Mt xvi 2 f., it has exceptional claims to be permanently retained, with the necessary safe-
guards, in its accustomed place.

xxiii 43] Marcion according to
Epiph omitted σήμερον...παραδείσῳ,
i. e. doubtless the whole verse. Orig.
𝒥o states that 'some' were so trou-
bled by the apparent discordance
with Mt xii 40 as to suspect that
σήμερον κ.τ.λ. was a spurious addition to the Gospel. Taken literally,
this would imply that the words
were absent from other texts than
that of Marcion, as he did not recognise St Matthew's Gospel. But it is
more likely that Orig had Marcion
in mind, and conjecturally attributed

to him a sense of the apparent discrepance which he himself thought it necessary to subject to a careful examination. In that case the omission was probably one of Marcion's arbitrary tamperings with the text.

In D vv. 42, 43 stand thus :—καὶ στραφεὶς πρὸς τὸν κύριον εἶπεν αὐτῷ Μνήσθητί μου ἐν τῇ ἡμέρᾳ τῆς ἐλεύσεώς σου. ἀποκριθεὶς δὲ ὁ Ἰησοῦς εἶπεν αὐτῷ τῷ ἐπλησοντι [l. ἐπιπλήσσοντι] Θάρσει, σήμερον κ.τ.λ.

xxiii 45 ἐνάτης τοῦ ἡλίου ἐκλείποντος] ┤ἐνάτης, [καὶ] ἐσκοτίσθη ὁ ἥλιος ├ Western and Syrian (Gr. Lat. Syr. Arm.: cf. Æth.); incl. 'most copies' known to Orig(*Mt.*) (? Marcion ap. Epiph) (Jul.Afr) Orig.*Mt.*lat. 293 (Chr) (?? Cyr.*loc*.gr) (scholia) : ἐσκοτίσθη δὲ ὁ ἥ. D: <καὶ *a b c e* arm : 251 aeth combine both readings, aeth substituting κόσμος for ἥλιος : syr.hr and the *Gesta Pilati* (see below) have τοῦ ἡλίου σκοτισθέντος : syr.vt is defective. Also < καὶ ἐσκοτίσθη ὁ ἥλιος Cᵃ 33, as ||| Mt Mc. Text ℵBC*⁽ᵛⁱᵈ⁾L 'most copies' known to Orig.*Mt.*lat.82 some lectionaries in one lection(see below) me the (cf. aeth) syr.hl. mg (?? Iren.lat) Orig.*Cels*⁴; *Lc* ; *Cant.*lat.Ruf. (Cyr-hr²ᵛˑ³) Cyr.al. *Mt* (anon.Pous.) (Ps.Dion) Max : ℵL ltᵖ Orig¹ have ἐκλιπόντος. A liturgical note cited by Matthaei² states that some lectionaries read τοῦ ἡλίου ἐκλείποντος in the lection for the Thursday before Quinquagesima (εἰς τὴν ε̄ τῆς τυροφάγου) instead of καὶ ἐσκοτίσθη...ἐσχίσθη [*sic*, but evidently meaning ἥλιος], but that in the two other lections (see above, p. 68) they agree completely with the other copies.

The words καὶ ἐσκοτίσθη ὁ ἥλιος close a very brief summary of three lines, answering to vv. 33—44, which Epiph.*Haer.*317 in his loose manner sets down as a foundation for accusing Marcion of inconsistency in not omitting the Crucifixion. His comment (347) dwells only on ἐσταύρωσαν : but he probably took the last words of his abridged quotation from Marcion's text of Lc, not merely from his own. An allusion of Iren. 275 suggests τ. ἡλ. ἐκλ., though not conclusively (*sol medio die* occidit). Jul.Afric (Routh *Rell. Sac.* ii 297 f.) shews that he must have read ἐσκοτίσθη by arguing that the darkness was not an eclipse without referring to the word which was interpreted in this sense. Besides the well known passages of Orig, a scholium attributed to him in at least two sources (Matthaei¹ on Mt xxvii45; Galland xiv b 82 = Migne vii 308 Περὶ ταύτης...ἐκρεμάσθη), and, to judge by internal evidence, with good reason (notwithstanding the ascription of the first few lines to Greg.nys in Nicet.*Mt.*798 Pous.), speaks of the darkness as ταύτης τῆς ἐκλείψεως. Chrys.*Mt* on the other hand repudiates the idea of an eclipse, and is followed by one or two late scholiasts. An anonymous scholium printed by Poussin (*Mc.* 350) has the remarkable words Σκότος ἐγένετο ὥσπερ τοῦ ἡλίου ὑποχωρήσαντος τῇ κατὰ τοῦ δεσπότου παροινίᾳ, καὶ οὐκ ἀνεσχομένου δοῦναι τὴν οἰκείαν φωταγωγίαν τοῖς θεοκτόνοις, wrongly attributing them to Gregory [Naz.] ἐν τοῖς πρὸς Κληδόνιον: their author is possibly Cyr.al (see below), whose Homilies are defective here. The words ὁ μὲν γὰρ ἥλιος ἐσκοτίζετο occur in a Greek fragment bearing his name in a MS elsewhere too liberal in what it assigns to him (Mai *N. P. B.* ii 436): it may be his, but it is more likely to be by Tit.bost. On the other hand part of the verse is quoted with τ. ἡλ. ἐκλ. in another fragment likewise bearing his name (Nicet.*Mt.*797 Pous.), which has points of connexion with the fragment attributed to Greg.naz. In the *Gesta Pilati* (11) the reading is τοῦ ἡλίου σκοτισθέντος, due either to conflation of the two principal readings or to an independent attempt to obviate the misinterpretation of ἐκλείποντος: the same purpose is carried out further, after a few lines, by putting the words ἐ- κλειψις ἡλίου γέγονεν κατὰ τὸ εἰωθός into the mouth of the unbelieving Jews.

Transcriptional evidence fully confirms the clear testimony of documents. The genitive absolute of text might easily be changed to a finite verb with a conjunction, answering to the finite verbs on either side; the converse change would be improbable. The familiar σκοτίζομαι applied to the sun (as Mt xxiv 29 ‖ Mc xiii 24; Ap ix 2; Eccl xii 2; cf. Is xiii 10) could never be a stumblingblock: the less common ἐκλείπω, nowhere else applied to the sun in the Greek Bible, might easily provoke paraphrase, even if it did not give more serious offence by suggesting the in this place impossible sense of eclipse. We learn from Orig (for his in substance, not the Latin translator's, the long and elaborate discussion certainly is) that already in his day attacks were made on the Gospel not only on the ground of the silence of historians about the darkness, but also on account of the impossibility of an eclipse at full moon. He notices and warmly repudiates the answer of some Christians, that there was the special miracle of an eclipse under unwonted conditions; and himself meets the difficulty by accepting the reading καὶ ἐσκοτίσθη ὁ ἥλιος. To account for the existence of the other reading he first suggests that it may have arisen from a desire of greater explicitness, with an assumption that the dark-

ness could not be due to anything but an eclipse; but he thinks it more likely that the change was insidiously made by enemies of the Church, that they might use it as a point of attack on the Gospels. A little further on he strangely asserts that "the evangelists made no mention at all of the sun in this place", and argues that the darkness was probably due to clouds of extreme murkiness, as though he omitted both readings with C^a 33. In the earlier Comm. on Canticles, and even in the contemporary (Eus. *H.E.* vi 36) books against Celsus (ii 33, 35), Orig follows the reading of text, for he assumes the occurrence of an eclipse (33 *s. fin.*), apparently a miraculous eclipse (35); so that he seems in his Comm. on Mt to have written under the influence of the Western MS or MSS which have so largely affected the text of this work elsewhere. A writer in Cent.VI, who personates Dionysius the Areopagite (*Ep.* vii p. 775), describes the circumstances of a miraculous eclipse as witnessed by himself at Heliopolis at the time of the Crucifixion, εἰπὲ δὲ αὐτῷ Τί λέγεις περὶ τῆς ἐν τῷ σωτηρίῳ σταυρῷ γεγονυίας ἐκλείψεως; ἀμφοτέρω γὰρ τότε κατὰ Ἡλίου Πόλιν ἅμα παρόντε τε καὶ συνεστῶτε παραδόξως τῷ ἡλίῳ τὴν σελήνην ἐμπίπτουσαν ἑωρῶμεν, οὐ γὰρ ἦν συνόδου [a conjunction of sun and moon] καιρός· κ.τ.λ. In commenting on this passage (ii 311 Cord.) Maximus Confessor says "Note here the solution of the difficulty (ἀπορήματος) in the evangelist Luke. Now no one has explained the strangeness of the manner [*om.* and] of the marvel save he [Dion] alone: for, the divine Luke having said ἀπὸ Ϛ ὥρας σκότος ἐν τῷ σταυρῷ τοῦ κυρίου γενέσθαι τοῦ ἡλίου ἐκλείποντος, it was a matter of debate (ἀμφεβάλλετο) among all how he described as an ἔκλειψις &c. Nearly all the commentators, being later than these times [sc. those of Dion] supposed that the sun himself lost his rays (ἀποβαλεῖν τὰς ἀκτῖνας) for the three hours." These examples, with others given incidentally above, illustrate the temptation which would be felt to get rid of the difficulties arising from the assumed interpretation of ἐκλείποντος.

On the other hand the word ἐκλείπω contains no such intrinsic difficulty as need raise a scruple as to its acceptance now. It might be applied to any striking occultation of the sun, whether by the moon or through any other cause. Indeed the wide and various use of ἐκλείπω in the LXX suggests that, as employed by a Greek-speaking Jew, it might easily preserve its original force, and the sun by a simple figure be said to "fail". Some such sense is implied in the interpretations of the commentators noticed by Maximus, and of the anonymous scholium (p. 69); and probably in the paraphrase of Irenæus.

xxiii 48 *fin.*] + *dicentes Vae nobis quae facta sunt hodie propter peccata nostra ; appropinquavit enim desolatio Hierusalem ger₁*(syr.vt): syr.vt differs by prefixing 'and', substituting 'woe to us' for *hodie*, and omitting the last clause. The Syriac *Doctrina Addaei* (Cureton *Anc. Syr. Doc.* 10), evidently referring to these words, seems to have had the longer text.

xxiii 55 *ai*] + ἄλλα + Western (Gr. [D 29 Eus.*Mar*] Lat.) ; cf. Mt xxvii 61 ; Mc xv 47 : similarly in xxiv 1 after μνῆμα some Mixed (British) Latin MSS add *Maria Magdalena et altera Maria et quaedam cum eis.* Also < *ai* Alexandrian and Syrian

(Gr.Æth.Arm.); incl. ℵAC Eus. 2/3. Text BLPX 1-131 13-69-346 22 33 157 al^p me the syr.vt-vg-hl.

xxiv 3   [τοῦ κυρίου Ἰησοῦ] < Western (Gr. Lat.: partly Syr. Eg.) : < the whole D *a b c ff rhe* Eus. *D.E.*: < κυρίου D 42 *a b e f ff rhe* syr.vt-vg the Eus. *D.E.*; not Eus. *Ps.*

A Western non-interpolation, like that in xxii 19, 20 ; and the first of a series of Western non-interpolations in this chapter, which illustrate and confirm each other : the omission of ἀπὸ τοῦ μνημείου in v. 9, being more doubtful than the rest, is marked with [ ] only.

The combination ὁ κύριος Ἰησοῦς is not found in the genuine text of the Gospels, though perhaps in [Mc] xvi 19.

xxiv 6   [οὐκ ἔστιν ὧδε ἀλλὰ ἠγέρθη.] < Western, D *a b e ff rhe*; not syr.vt Eus. *Ps*; *Mar*: *c* has the probably independent insertion *resurrexit a mortuis*; Marcion (ap. Epiph) ἠγέρθη only, unless Epiph has loosely omitted the rest ; aeth has ἠγέρθη, οὐκ ἔστιν ὧδε, exactly as Mc; C*ger₂ syr.vg omit ἀλλά. Text comes from Mt xxviii 6 ‖ Mc xvi 6, thrown into an antithetic form.

A Western non-interpolation.

xxiv 12 . [Ὁ δὲ Πέτρος … γεγονός.] < Western (Gr. Lat.), D *a b e rhe* Eus. *Can*; not *c ff* syr.vt Eus. *Mar* (distinctly). Omitted likewise at the beginning of one lection (first hand) in syr.hr, and in the harmonistic narrative of *fu*; but probably in both cases by accident. Text from Jo xx 3—10 (except ἀναστάς and θαυμάζων τὸ γεγονός), condensed and simplified, with omission of all that relates to "the other disciple".

A Western non-interpolation.

xxiv 13 ἑξήκοντα] ἕκατον ἑξήκοντα Alexandrian (Gr. Lat.[vg.codd] Syr. [hl. txt *v.* mg] Arm.) ; incl. ℵ, probably Orig and perhaps Cyr.al;

implicitly Eus.*Onom* Hier.*Ep*.108 p. 696; Soz v 21. So "the accurate copies and Origen's confirmation of the truth" according to a scholium in 34 194 (Birch *V.L.* i cvii f.; Burgon in *Guardian* 1873, p. 1085). A fragment ascribed to Cyr.al (Mai *N.P.B.* ii 440), perhaps rightly, appears anonymously in the Cramerian catena (p. 172) in a somewhat fuller form, which contains ἕκατον ἐξήκοντα, though Cramer omits ἕκατον as a blunder. An Alexandrian geographical correction, though not of the type of Γεργεσηνῶν or Βηθαβαρά; evidently arising from identification of this Emmaus with the better known Emmaus which was later called Nicopolis. The identification is distinctly laid down by Eus Hier Soz, though they do not refer to the distance.

xxiv 27 ἀρξάμενος...διερμήνευσεν] + ἦν ἀρξάμενος ἀπὸ Μωυσέως καὶ πάντων τῶν προφητῶν ἑρμηνεύειν + Western (Gr.[D : cf. ℵ*] Lat. : cf. Syr.) with variations (lat.eur *interpretans* but -*are mm*): ℵ* has καὶ διερμηνεύειν, probably a vestige of a form of the Western reading: ἦν ἱρξάμενος and καὶ διερμήνευεν apparently (*e*) syr.vt-vg.

xxiv 32 ἡμῶν καιομένη ἦν] + ἦν ἡμῶν κεκαλυμμένη + Western (Gr. [D]: cf. Lat.) ; probably from 2 Co iii 14 f.: *excaecatum c, optusum rhe*, both implying πεπηρωμένη according to the renderings of πηρόω elsewhere, from Mc vi 52 ; *exterminatum* (= *externatum*) *e*, which is perhaps a third rendering of the same original, and certainly expresses utter bewilderment (ἐκτὸς φρενῶν): *c e rhe* transpose ἦν and ἡμῶν: also βραδεῖα syr.vt the arm, from v. 25 : aeth has an obscure conflate reading. These various corrections attest the difficulty found in καιομένη, its true force not being understood.

xxiv 36 [καὶ λέγει αὐτοῖς Εἰρήνη ὑμῖν]] < Western, D *a b e ff rhe*; not *c* syr.vt Eus.*Mar* expressly. Text from Jo xx 19. After text + ἐγώ εἰμι, μὴ φοβεῖσθε GP cu³ *c f* vg me.codd(non opt) syr.vg-hl-hr (aeth, transposing the clauses) arm Amb Aug; from Jo vi 20.
A Western non-interpolation.

xxiv 39 ψηλαφήσατέ με] < με Western (Gr.[D] Lat. Syr.). Also σάρκα καὶ] < Marcion(Epiph and perhaps Tert) Tert Hil². Apparently a Western reading of limited range. Another Western reading is the substitution of the common classical σάρκας for σάρκα (ℵ*D Iren.lat Adam.1/2); both pp place καὶ σάρκας last.

xxiv 40 [καὶ τοῦτο εἰπὼν ἔδειξεν αὐτοῖς τὰς χεῖρας καὶ τοὺς πόδας.]] < Western, D *a b e ff rhe* syr.vt; not *c* Eus.*Mar*. Text from Jo xx 20, with a natural adaptation.
A Western non-interpolation.

xxiv 42 ἰχθύος ὀπτοῦ μέρος] + + καὶ ἀπὸ μελισσίου κηρίον + Western and (with κηρίον changed to κηρίου) Syrian (Gr. Lat. Syr. [Eg.] Æth. Arm.); incl. Ps.Just.*Res* Cyr.hr² [Ath. *Or. c. Ath.* codd, see below] Epiph.*Haer*.652 Aug 'Vig.'*Varim.* i 56 ; but not D *e* or any Greek uncial better than NX. Text ℵAB DLII *e* me.cod.opt syr.hl.* (Clem) (Orig.*Cels*; *Mt*) (Eus.*Mar*²) Ath. *Or. c. Ar.* iv 35 cod(in Mai *N.P.B.* ii 582) (Cyr. *Lc*; ?? *Jo*). The references in Clem Orig Eus Cyr.*Lc*, though not quotations, are such as to render it highly improbable that the writers would have left out all allusion to these words had they stood in their MSS of Lc. Clement's omission is the more remarkable because he proceeds πρὸς τούτοις οὐδὲ τραγημάτων καὶ κηρίων περιοpατέον τοὺς δειπνοῦντας κατὰ λόγον, language which in its context is decisive. In Montfaucon's edition of Ath the words are present and no variation is noticed: but, as they are wanting in Mai's MS, a corruption of Ath from the current biblical text must be suspected. Epiph. *Haer.* 143 certainly has Jo xxi 9, 13 chiefly if not solely in view, and cannot be cited for omission: elsewhere he clearly has the inserted words. Cyr. *Jo.* 1108 quotes vv. 36—43: but his comment refers only to the fish, the text of the passage is virtually dependent on a single late MS, and the reference in the fragment on Lc omits the honeycomb.

A singular interpolation, evidently from an extraneous source, written or oral.

xxiv 43 *fin.*] + καὶ [λαβὼν] τὰ ἐπίλοιπα ἔδωκεν αὐτοῖς Pre-Syrian (? late Western), KII* 13-346 al[P] and all vv except lat.vt.codd.opt (*a b e ff*) syr.vg me.cod.opt; also Ath Epiph.*Haer.* 143 Aug 'Vig.'

xxiv 46 οὕτως γέγραπται] + καὶ οὕτως ἔδει Syrian (Gr. Lat. Syr.): also οὕτως ἔδει omitting οὕτως γέγραπται καὶ cu[4] arm Eus.*Theoph.* syr. iv 2 (Epiph): also < οὕτως *c e* Cyp. Probably three independent corrections of the (in the sense intended) abrupt phrase οὕτως γέγρα-

πται παθεῖν; though the Syrian reading might be a conflation of text and the second, had the second more substantive attestation: ἔδει comes from the similar v. 26.

xxiv 51 [καὶ ἀνεφέρετο εἰς τὸν οὐρανόν] < Western, אּ*D *a b c ff rhe* Aug. 1/2; not *c* Aug. 1/2 : syr.vt is defective.

A Western non-interpolation. Text was evidently inserted from an assumption that a separation from the disciples at the close of a Gospel must be the Ascension. The Ascension apparently did not lie within the proper scope of the Gospels, as seen in their genuine texts: its true place was at the head of the Acts of the Apostles, as the preparation for the Day of Pentecost, and thus the beginning of the history of the Church.

xxiv 52 [προσκυνήσαντες αὐτὸν] < Western, D *a b e ff rhe* Aug. 1/1: < αὐτὸν cu[1] *c* vg.

A Western non-interpolation. Text is a natural sequel to καὶ ἀνεφέρετο εἰς τὸν οὐρανόν : also cf. Mt xxviii 9, 17.

xxiv 53 εὐλογοῦντες] + αἰνοῦντες + Western, D *a b e ff rhe* vg.codd. For a Syrian conflation see *Introd.* § 146.

ST JOHN

i 4 ἦν] + ἐστίν + Western (Gr. Lat. Syr.); incl. אD and some copies known to Orig.*Jo*; regarded with some favour by Orig himself (iv 72 τάχα οὐκ ἀπιθάνως). A change arising naturally out of the punctuation universally current in the earliest times, ὃ γέγονεν ἐν αὐτῷ ζωὴ ἦν, since the combination of γέγονεν with ἦν has considerable superficial difficulty.

The punctuation in the margin seems to be little if at all older than Cent. IV : Amb.*Ps.*793 speaks of it as the punctuation of 'the Alexandrians and Egyptians'; *i.e.* probably Hesychius, certainly not Clem or Orig, or apparently Ath: it is found in Epiph.*Haer.* 379, 609, 779; *Anc.* 80 B; Did.*Trin.* i 15 p. 19 f.; and the Syrian Fathers. [Yet the punctuation of MSS Versions and Fathers has no textual authority, being only an embodiment of ancient interpretations, not a part of the transmitted text, nor a transmitted record of the punctuation intended by the original writers; and the construction in the margin has high claims to acceptance on internal grounds. H.] A singular modification of this construction is found in Epiph.*Anc.* 80 D and Greg.nys.*Eun.* 348, (443,) who join ἐν αὐτῷ as well as ὃ γέγονεν to the preceding verse.

i 13 οἱ...ἐγεννήθησαν] *qui...natus est.* Western, as a reading of the text possibly Latin only; so *b* Tert (Iren. lat³, verified by context) (Amb) Aug (Sulp); the indirect quotations in Iren Amb Sulp admit of being taken as adaptations only, and the same may be said of a possible allusion in Just.*Dial.*63.

i 18 μονογενὴς θεός] ┤ ὁ μονογενὴς υἱὸς ├ Western and Syrian (Gr. Lat. Syr. [Æth.] Arm.); incl. (Iren. lat. 2/3) Eus(once noticing txt) Eustath Alex.al Ath Greg.naz ppˢᵉʳ. Text ℵ*(omitting ὁ ὤν)BC*L(33)syr.vg-hl.mg (me, apparently) Valentiniani (cited by Iren and Clem) Iren.lat. 1/3 Clem.al Orig (Eus, see above) Epiph (Bas) Did Greg.nys Cyr.al: ὁ is prefixed by ℵᶜ 33 me. The patristic evidence is in some cases uncertain and conflicting. In Cent. IV and even later the phrase μονογενὴς θεός detached from the biblical context was widely used by theologians of opposite schools, as Ath Bas Greg.naz Greg.nys Cyr.al on the one side, Arius and Eunomius on the other; and also by Hil Fulg on the one side, and various obscure Latin Arian writers on the other, though all the Latin biblical texts have *filius.*

The whole attestation (D is defective here) distinctly marks ὁ μονογενὴς υἱός as in the first instance Western; while the evidence of early Greek MSS (B, ℵ, CL) for text is amply varied.

Both readings intrinsically are free from objection. Text, though startling at first, simply combines in a single phrase the two attributes of the Logos marked before (θεός v. 1, μονογενής v. 14): its sense is ‘One who was both θεός and μονογενής’. The substitution of the familiar phrase ὁ μονογενὴς υἱός for the unique μονογενὴς θεός would be obvious, and μονογενής by its own primary meaning directly suggested υἱός. The converse substitution is inexplicable by any ordinary motive likely to affect transcribers. There is no evidence that the reading had any controversial interest in ancient times. And the absence of the article from the more important documents is fatal to the idea that θC̅ was an accidental substitution for Υ̅C̅. The variation has been examined fully in one of *Two Dissertations* by F. J. A. Hort, Cambridge, 1877.

i 28 Βηθανίᾳ] Βηθαβαρὰ probably Alexandrian (Gr. Syr. [Æth.] Arm.); incl. CᵃTᵇ some good cursives syr.vt Orig.*loc*⁵ Eus.*Onom* Epiph Chr: adopted by Orig (and apparently found by him in some copies, iv 140 σχεδὸν ἐν πᾶσι τοῖς ἀντιγράφοις κεῖται Ταῦτα ἐν Βηθανίᾳ ἐγένετο) on geographical grounds. Epiph, who like arm (Lagarde) reads Βηθαβρά, speaks of Βηθανίᾳ as found ‘in other copies’. Chr, doubtless following Orig, gives Βηθαβαρά as the reading of ‘the more accurate copies’. The form varies in the present text of Orig, which has chiefly Βηθαρά (with two cursives), Βαθαρά, or Βηθαραβά (with ℵᵉᵇ syr.hl.mg aeth: cf Jos xv 6, 61; xviii 22). His interpretation οἶκος κατασκευῆς points however to Βηθαβαρά.

i 34 ὁ υἱὸς] ⊣ ὁ ἐκλεκτὸς ⊢ Western
(Gr.[א] Lat.[*e* Amb] Syr.) : D is defective. Some documents (Lat.[eur.]
Syr.) variously combine the two
readings (*electus filius Dei* &c.).

ii 3 ὑστερήσαντος οἴνου] ⊣ οἶνον
οὐκ εἶχον ὅτι συνετελέσθη ὁ οἶνος τοῦ
γάμου· εἶτα ⊢ Western (Gr.[א] Lat.
[Syr.hl.mg] Æth.) : D is defective.
A characteristic paraphrase. In *e*
(and approximately in *rhe*) *per mul-
tam turbam vocitorum* (*-atorum*) is
added.

iii 5 γεννηθῇ] ἀναγεννηθῇ Western
(Gr.[pp] Lat.); incl. Just Hom.Cl
Iren.*Fragm* Eus.*Is* and some later
Fathers (Dr E. Abbot) : D is defective. The Latin renderings are
renatus a b c e ff m sess vg (? Cyp.1/4)
Tert. 1/3 Philast. 1/2 al^mu ; *regenera-
tus* Philast. 1/2 ; *denuo natus* auct.
Rebapt ; *denuo renatus* Ruf Orig.
*Mt.*lat : (text) *natus f* (Tert.2/3)
Cyp. 3 v. 4/4 Faust : *denuo* comes
doubtless from v. 3, where it represents ἄνωθεν in all Latin documents : in vv. 3, 4 *bis*, 7, 8 *renascor*
has always some Latin evidence,
doubtless by assimilation to v. 5 ;
denuo being also found in *e f* in v.
4 (1°).

ibid. τὴν βασιλείαν τοῦ θεοῦ] τὴν
βασιλείαν τῶν οὐρανῶν Western
(Gr.Lat.); incl. א *e m* Just Docetae
(ap.Hipp) Hom.Cl 'Iren.' *Fragm*
Eus.*Is* Tert Orig.*Mt.*lat ; *Rom.*lat.
Ruf.1/3 ; not syr.vt Cyp : D is
defective. Perhaps derived from a
traditional form of the words ; but
also naturally suggested by the same
phrase εἰσέρχομαι εἰς τὴν βασιλείαν
τῶν οὐρανῶν in Mt, where it occurs
five times (εἰσερχ. εἰς τ. β. τοῦ θεοῦ
once only, xix 24), while the combination of ἰδεῖν with τ. β. τῶν οὐρανῶν (v. 3) occurs nowhere. Here
א*M have ἰδεῖν.

iii 6 σάρξ ἐστιν] + ὅτι ἐκ τῆς σαρκὸς ἐγεννήθη Western (Gr.[161*])
Lat. Syr.); incl. *e* Tert; not *m*

Cyp.2/2 Nemes.thub(Conc.Carth.)
Hil.2/2 : D is defective.

ibid. πνεῦμά ἐστιν] + *quia Deus
spiritus est* Western (Lat.Syr.); incl.
e m Tert Nemes Hil.1/2 Ambr(*De
Sp.* iii 11) expressly, not Cyp.2/2
Hil.1/2 : D is defective. In some
documents (Lat. Syr.) the gloss (cf.
iv 24) is enlarged by the addition *et
ex* (*de*) *deo natus est*. In correspondence with the former gloss
161* adds ὅτι ἐκ τοῦ πνεύματός ἐστιν.

iii 8 ἐκ] + ⊣ τοῦ ὕδατος καὶ ⊢ Wes-
tern(Gr.[א] Lat. Syr.): D is defective. From v. 5.

iii 13 τοῦ ἀνθρώπου] + ⊣ ὁ ὢν ἐν
τῷ οὐρανῷ ⊢ Western and Syrian
(Gr. Lat. Syr. [Eg.] Arm.); incl.
A (< ὤν) Hipp Epiph Bas Did²
Orig. *Gen.* lat.Ruf. ; *Rom.* lat. Ruf
(with context). Text אBLT_b 33
me.cod.opt aeth Cyr.*loc.*comm (the
addition in the printed text is evidently due to Aubert, as in many
other cases). No continuous Greek
commentary on this part of Jo earlier
than Chr has survived ; and there
are no quotations including at once
v. 13 and v. 14, doubtless owing to
the want of obvious connexion
between the two verses. But there
are many quotations of v. 13 which
stop short at τ. ἀνθρώπου ; and it is
morally certain that most of them
would have included ὁ ὢν ἐν τῷ
οὐρανῷ, if it had stood in the texts
used by the writers. So Orig.*Prov.*
110Tisch;*Is.*lat Eus.2/2 Adamant
(in Orig. *Opp.* i. 855) Epiph.*Haer.*
487, 911 Greg.naz.*Cled.*87; *Nect.*
168 Did.*Act.* 41 Cramer(= 1657 Mi)
Greg.nys.*Apoll.* 6 Ps. Jul. rom. 119
Lag Cyr.al.13/13 (see P. E. Pusey
on *Incarn. Unig.* p. 128) Hier.*Eph.*
iv 10 Ephr.*Diat.*arm.168, 187, 189.
CD are defective.

The character of the attestation
marks the addition as a Western
gloss, suggested perhaps by i 18 :
it may have been inserted to correct

any misunderstanding arising out of the position of ἀναβέβηκεν, as coming before καταβάς.

iv 1 (†) ὡς...βαπτίζει [ἢ] Ἰωάνης] < ἢ AB*LGΓ cuᵖ Or.Ἰο Epiph. *Haer.*480 Dindorf (the passage is wanting in earlier editions): not אBᵃCD vv.omn Cyr.al.*loc.* For ὁ κύριος the Western text, with all the earlier vv, has ὁ Ἰησοῦς; so אD(Λ) 1-118-209 22 61 81 alᵐᵘ lat.afr-eur-vg syr.vt-(vg)-hl.txt me arm Chr, Λ cuᵖ syr.vg omitting the subsequent Ἰησοῦς: while ὁ κύριος is attested only by lat.it syr.hl.mg aeth and the Syrian Greek text in addition to ABCLTᵦ.

The Western change is doubtless due to the apparent awkwardness of the combination ὁ κύριος... Ἰησοῦς: but the difficulty lies rather in the absence of any perceptible force in the double naming; the most probable explanation being that ὅτι is 'recitative', and that Ἰη-σοῦς...Ἰωάνης are in *oratio recta* as the very words of the report. [It remains no easy matter however to explain either how the verse as it stands can be reasonably understood without ἢ, or how such a mere slip as the loss of Η after ΕΙ should have so much excellent Greek authority, more especially as the absence of ἢ increases the obvious no less than the real difficulty of the verse. The dissent of the versions may easily have a connexion with their prevailing support of the Western reading; that is, ὁ Ἰησοῦς and ἢ may have come in together: the authority for the combination of ὁ κύριος with ἢ consists of BᵃCTᵦ later MSS *f q* syr.hl.mg aeth Nonn Cyr, a group of mainly Syrian complexion. On the whole the text of the verse cannot be accepted as certainly free from doubt. H.]

iv 46, 49 βασιλικὸς] + βασιλίσκος ⊦

Western (Gr. Lat.).

v 1 ἑορτὴ] ἡ ἑορτὴ Alexandrian (Gr. Eg.); incl. אCLΔ 1-118 33 (me the) Cyr.al.*loc.*txt(*s.q.*); not ABD Orig.Ἰο Epiph.*Haer.* p.481 Dind.(μετὰ ταῦτα ἦν ἑορτὴ τῶν Ἰουδαίων, οἶμαι δὲ ὅτι περὶ ἄλλης ἑορτῆς Ἰουδαίων λέγει, ἢ πεντη-κοστῆς ἢ σκηνοπηγιῶν). The insertion of the article, easily made after ΗΝ, seems to have been an attempt to define the chronology. If it were genuine, the reference would be to the Feast of Taber-nacles, emphatically '*the* Feast of the Jews' (see note on vi 4), and not to the Passover. The additions τῶν ἀζύμων and ἡ σκηνοπηγία are found in Λ and 131 respectively.

v 2 ἐπὶ τῇ προβατικῇ κολυμβήθρᾳ] προβατικὴ κολυμβήθρα Western (Gr. Lat. Æth.) incl. Eus Theod.mops (Epiph. *Haer.* p. 481 Dind.): lat.vg. codd syr.vt-vg omit ἐπὶ τῇ προ-βατικῇ, which was strangely misun-derstood by some Latin translators (*in inferiorem partem*).

ibid. Βηθζαθά] (marg.) Βηθσαιδά B *c* vg me(Βηθσ.cod.opt) the(Βηθσ.) syr.hl.txt-mg.gr aeth (Βηθασ.)Tert: Βηθεσδά Syrian (Gr. Lat.[it] Syr. Arm.); incl. Did. Text א 33 (*rhe*); also Βηζαθά L *e* Eus.*Onom;* also Βελζεθά D (*a*), *Betzatha* (-*ata, -eta*) *b ff*vg.codd: hence -ζ -θα אLD 33 lat.vt Eus. Text and margin are but slight modifications of the same name; and perhaps its purest form would be Βηθζαιθά, *the House of the Olive.* Βηθσαιδά may however be right, as it is supported by B and a great variety of vv: a tank hewn in the rock might naturally bear the name *House of Fish.*

v 3 ξηρῶν] + παραλυτικῶν West-ern, D *a b rhe cant* alᵐᵘ. This Western addition was not taken up into any known later text: not so those that follow.

+ ἐκδεχομένων τὴν τοῦ ὕδατος κίνησιν Western and Syrian (Gr. Lat.
Syr. [Eg.] Æth. Arm.); incl. Aᵃ
D, but no better uncial; also Chr.
Text אA*BCᵇL 18 157 314 *q* syr.vt
me.codd.opt(15 at least, see Lightfoot in Scrivener *Introd.*² p. 331 ff.)
the.

+ (v. 4) ἄγγελος δὲ (*v.* γὰρ) Κυρίου
[κατὰ καιρὸν] κατέβαινεν (*v.* ἐλούετο)
ἐν τῇ κολυμβήθρᾳ καὶ ἐταράσσετο (*v.*
ἐτάρασσε) τὸ ὕδωρ· ὁ οὖν πρῶτος ἐμ-
βὰς [μετὰ τὴν ταραχὴν τοῦ ὕδατος]
ὑγιὴς ἐγίνετο οἵῳ (*v.* ᾧ) δήποτ' οὖν
(*v.* δήποτε) κατείχετο νοσήματι. Western and Syrian (Gr. Lat. Syr. [Eg.]
Æth. [Arm.]) incl. AL, but no better uncial; also Chr (??Nonn) Amm,
also Tert (? Ephr) allusively. Text
אBCᵇD 33 157 314 *f q rhe* vg.codd
syr.vt me.codd.opt.(15 at least, but
not bodl.opt) the arm.codd: *cant*
has in its text after v. 4 *hoc in Grecis
exemplaribus non habetur*: Abulfeda
states that 'according to some' this
v. is not by St John (Nestle *Theol.
LZ.* 1878 p. 413). SΛΠ and at
least 17 cursives mark this verse
with asterisks or obeli.

The first Greek Father who shews
any knowledge of either interpolation is Chr. Cyr.al does not comment on either, though both stand
in the text which Aubert has supplied without MS authority at the
head of the section. The Comm.
of Orig is defective here.

The documents which omit ἐκδεχομένων κ.τ.λ. but not ἄγγελος κ.τ.λ.
are AL 18 me.bodl.opt, probably
Alexandrian; those which omit ἄγγελος κ.τ.λ. but not ἐκδεχομένων
κ.τ.λ. are D 33 *f rhe* vg.codd, almost certainly Western: the clearly
Pre-Syrian documents which support both insertions are lat.afr.eur.
It would thus appear that the first
interpolation was ἐκδεχομένων κ.τ.λ.,
easily suggested by v. 7, τὴν κίνησιν
being simply intended to prepare

28

for ἐταράσσετο without reference to
any special cause of the troubling
of the water; and that the rest was
added somewhat later in explanation
of τὴν κίνησιν, perhaps embodying
an early tradition. A late Alexandrian text seems to have adopted
the last interpolation, for the sake
of its interesting detail, but to have
rejected the earlier explanatory gloss
to which it was attached. The Syrian text adopted both.

vi 4 (†) ἦν δὲ ἐγγὺς τὸ πάσχα, ἡ
ἑορτὴ τῶν Ἰουδαίων] < τὸ πάσχα
apparently some Fathers and other
ancient writers, though it stands in
all extant Greek MSS and vv.

[According to Epiph.*Haer.*444
the persons whom he calls *Alogi*
found fault with St John's Gospel
as assigning *two* passovers to the
Ministry while the other Gospels
spoke of one only. Against the
supposition that the Ministry lasted
but a year (see below) Iren. 146
ff. maintains three passovers, the
second being the 'feast' of v 1;
while he is silent as to vi 4, though
he goes on to refer to particulars
furnished by the neighbouring
verses. Orig.*Jo.* 250, whose Comm.
is defective for the whole of cc. v—
vii, in contending that the saying
in iv 35 was uttered at an earlier
time than the winter following the
passover of c. ii, urges that the unnamed feast of v 1 was not likely to
be the passover, giving as a reason
'that shortly afterwards the statement occurs' (μετ' ὀλίγα ἐπιφέρεται
ὅτι) ᾿Ην ἐγγὺς ἡ ἑορτὴ τῶν Ἰουδαίων,
ἡ σκηνοπηγία : as these words now
stand only in vii 2, either he must
have treated vi 4 as referring to the
feast of tabernacles (whether as
containing the name ἡ σκηνοπηγία,
or as containing no name of a feast,
and therefore to be interpreted by
vii 2), or his text must have lacked
vi 4 altogether; nor indeed could

he have failed to appeal to the stronger and more obvious argument furnished by τὸ πάσχα, had he known it in this place. The comment of Cyr.al on vi 1 has the two indirect quotations ἦν ἐγγὺς τὸ πάσχα τῶν Ἰουδαίων, ἐγγὺς εἶναι τὸ πάσχα τῶν Ἰουδαίων, in the printed text, which here rests on two MSS; but what is evidently the same feast he shortly afterwards twice names as τῆς σκηνοπηγίας. This contradiction, pointed out by Mr H. Browne (*Ordo Saeclorum* 87 ff.), disappears in the Latin condensed paraphrase of George of Trebizond (Cent. XV), which has *Et quoniam festus dies* [the common Latin rendering of ἡ ἑορτή] *Judaeorum prope erat, ut paulo post legitur, in quo lex Mosaica omnes undique ut tabernaculorum solemnitatem &c.* (i 151 Bas. 1566), where the first eleven words stand for καὶ ἐπείπερ ἦν ἐγγὺς τὸ πάσχα τῶν Ἰουδαίων, ὡς ὀλίγον ἐν τοῖς ἐφεξῆς εὑρήσομεν. George of Trebizond's paraphrases enjoy no high reputation for fidelity; and he may possibly have adapted the first part of the passage to the second : but it is no less possible that he had access to purer MSS, which had merely ἡ ἑορτὴ τῶν Ἰουδαίων. The only other tenable explanation of the contradiction would be to suppose that Cyr in the second part of his comment made free use of a predecessor's language without observing its discordance with his own. On this supposition, to judge by the manner of writing, the predecessor can hardly have been any other than Origen. The most obvious inference from the language of both passages would be that ἡ σκηνοπηγία was read for τὸ πάσχα: but it is more probable on other grounds that no particular feast was named in the text or texts commented on. In this case the language used would arise naturally

out of the identification suggested by vii 2, supported by the familiar sequence,—Passover (ii 13, 23), Pentecost (v 1), Feast of Tabernacles (vi 4; vii 2): the reference of v 1 to Pentecost is distinctly laid down by Cyr, and is assumed in Origen's argument.

Besides the Alogi, Iren, Orig, and (perhaps) Cyr.al, whose testimony has direct reference to the presence or absence of the name of the passover in vi 4, several writers are shown indirectly to have known nothing of a passover in this place by their reckoning of the interval between the Baptism and the Crucifixion as a year, or but a little more. The idea was manifestly suggested by a misinterpretation of ἐνιαυτὸν Κυρίου δεκτόν in Lc iv 19 (from Is lxi 2): but it could never have been maintained without strange carelessness by any one who read τὸ πάσχα here, since Jo distinctly speaks twice of an earlier passover (ii 13, 23) as well as of the final passover. In Cent. IV Epiph ingeniously attempted to harmonise the single 'acceptable year' of early times with the longer chronology by adding to it a 'year of gainsaying' (*Haer.* 447, 450; cf. p. 481 Dind.): in the original sense however it was certainly conceived to include the Passion, as may be seen by the distinct language of the passages marked below with an asterisk. The writers who assume a single year are *Ptol.ap.Iren.15, 144, 148; Hom. Cl. xvii 19; Clem.*Strom.* i 407; vi 783 Orig.*Princ.*160 gr.lat. (ἐνιαυτὸν γάρ που καὶ μῆνας ὀλίγους ἐδίδαξεν); *Lev.* lat. Ruf.239; *Lc.*lat. Hier. 970; Hipp.*Chron.* A.D. 234 (*Opp.* i 56 Fabr.); Archel.*Dial.*lat. 34; *Philast.106; *Gaud.iii p. 51 f. Gat.; *Aug.*Ep.* cxcix 20; *auct. *Prom.*i 7; v 2; Evagr.*Alterc.* lat. (Migne xx 1176); also apparently

Just. *Apol.* i 46 (γεγεννῆσθαι ... ἐπὶ Κυρηνίου, δεδιδαχέναι δὲ ... ὕστερον χρόνοις ἐπὶ Ποντίου Πιλάτου). The single year is assumed with especial distinctness in the *Expositio de die paschae et mensis* of Julius Hilarianus, written in 397: *uno proinde anno Judaicae genti ad quam venerat praedicavit, in quo anno non solum regnum caelorum advenire praedixit, sed et ut crederent in virtutibus* [= miracles] *manifestum se Dominum ostendit: hoc usque in annum sextum decimum imperium Tiberi Caesaris; in quo jam non ut assolet Judaicae solemnitati agnus ex ovibus, sed ipse pro nobis Dominus, immolatus est Christus:* * * * *eo quippe anno, ut supputationis fides ostendit et ratio ipsa persuadet, passus est idem Dominus Christus luna* xiv, viii *kal. April. feria sexta* (Migne xiii 1114).

More or less distinct traces of the same view occur in several commentaries on Isaiah, known to be partly taken from Origen's lost Comm.; especially on xxxii 10 Eus.482; (Hier.430;); Cyr.al.446; Procop.386 f.: on xxix 1 (ἐνιαυτὸν ἐπὶ ἐνιαυτόν) the evidence (Eus.470 ; Hier.390 ; Cyr.al.408; Procop.356) is confused; but suggests that Orig spoke of 'the acceptable year of the Lord's preaching, and perhaps also a second', and that Eus (followed, as often, by Procop) added 'or even a third'. A more clearly marked change of view in Orig will be noticed further on : the limitation to a single year he doubtless inherited from an earlier time. The arrangement of Tatian's Diatessaron, so far as it can be traced in Ephrem's Commentary, suggests that it was constructed on the basis of a single year (Harnack), but · the evidence is not clear. Ephrem (*Serm. in Nat.* xiii. *Opp. Syr.* ii 432) speaks of Christ as having 'sojourned on earth poor and needy for 30 years': yet cf. *Diat.*166.

A third class of patristic evidence is furnished by a series of writers who directly or indirectly identify the year of the Passion with the 15th (or 16th) of Tiberius, and who would thus be manifestly contradicting the notice of the 15th of Tiberius in Lc iii 1 f. if a passover intervened at this place. The evidence is clearest where 15 (or 16) Tib. is expressly named; as by Clem. *Strom.*i.*l.c.* ; Jul.Afric. (Cent. III) ap.Hier.*in Dan.* ix 24 p. 683 B (in the Greek as preserved by Eus. *D.E.* 389 f. the Passion is apparently implied but not named); Ps.Cyp.*Comp.*20 (A.D. 243); the *usitatior traditio* in Prosp.*Chron.* p. 702 (in some MSS, *quidam* in others); Jul.Hilarianus *Exp.pasch.* (see above); *De mund. dur.* 16 (Migne xiii 1104). The consular year corresponding to 15 Tib. is assigned to the Passion by the Latin writers Tert.*Jud.* 8; Lact. *Inst.* iv 10; *Mort. pers.* 2 ; the Chronogr. Rom. of A.D. 354 (619, 634 Momms.); Sulp.Sev.*Chron.* ii 27 ; Aug.*C.D.* xviii 54. The same year is indicated by the position of the words ΠΑΘΟΣ ΧΥ in the Paschal Canon of Hipp inscribed on his statue (A.D. 222 [H. Browne *l.c.* 75, 474 ff.] or 224 [Salmon in *Hermathena* i 88]). Thus Hipp, like Clem, supplies evidence under both the last heads. It is of course impossible to tell how far the several writers who adopt or assume this date of the Passion were conscious of its connexion with the text of St John, or even (Hilarianus excepted) with the length of the Ministry. Their testimony is therefore quite compatible with the presence of τὸ πάσχα in their copies of the Gospel: what it proves is the wide diffusion of a tradition intrinsically incompatible with this reading.

The Ante-Nicene patristic testi·

monies at variance with this date, or with the reckoning of less than three passovers after the Baptism, are as follows. Melito (or the author of a fragment quoted in his name by Anast.sin from a book not included by Eus in his list) speaks of Christ as shewing His Deity by His signs in the three years (τῇ τριετίᾳ) after the Baptism (*Fragm.* vi p. 416 Otto). Iren, cited above, speaks of three passovers, though v 1 is the only place with which he connects the second. Possibly however he confused v 1 with vi 4: the third alternative, that he interpreted ἐγγύς as meaning 'lately past', can hardly be reconciled with Greek or biblical usage. Orig in two of his latest works (*Cels.* 397 ; *Mt.*lat.859, a very difficult and confused passage) seems to reckon the length of the Ministry at "not so much as three years" (οὐδὲ τρία ἔτη), 'about three years' (*fere annos tres*). A condensed and corrupt fragment of Hipp on Daniel (p. 153 Lag.: cf. Bardenhewer *Hipp. Comm. Dan.* 37) states that Christ 'suffered in the 33rd year' (ἔπαθε δὲ ἔτει τριακοστῷ τρίτῳ): but the discrepance with the Paschal Canon and Chronicle raise a suspicion of some corruption (Lipsius *Pilatus-acten* 23 f.) : indeed the clause as it stands has no apparent bearing on the context. Mr H. Browne (*l. c.* 82 ff.) has produced some evidence which shews that the three years might in early times include a long period between the Resurrection and the Ascension, the words δι' ἡμερῶν τεσσεράκοντα in Act i 3 being interpreted, as they certainly were by Eus. *D. E.* 400 and perhaps by Orig.*Mt. loc.*, and as Greek usage fully permits, to mean "at intervals of 40 days". But Orig.*Cels* refers to Judas Iscariot, and therefore to a period ending with the Passion.

The first extant appeal to St John for the three years (that of Irenæus excepted), and the first reference of the Passion to the later date, are made by Eus.*Chron* (cf. *H.E.* i 10 οὐδ' ὅλως ὁ μεταξὺ παρίσταται τετραετὴς χρόνος), who places the Baptism at 15 Tib. and the Passion at 18 (Arm. 19) Tib., calling as witnesses Phlegon (see below), St John, and Josephus, as though the arrangement specially needed defence: and in this as in other respects his chronology soon became a widely accepted standard. Epiph, who e chronology is peculiarly elaborate and apparently independent of Eus, fixes the Passion at a consular date two years later than 15 Tib. (*Haer.* 448); and as against the Alogi (see above) appeals to the Gospels as recording three passovers. Three passovers are likewise maintained by his contemporary Apollinaris (ap. Hier. *Dan.* 690) on St John's authority ; as they are also by Hier on Is xxix 1 (p. 390: see above).

It is difficult if not impossible to account for the large body of indirect evidence which points to the neglect of τὸ πάσχα here except on the supposition that these words (or the whole verse) were absent from various texts of Cent. II and III. In some few cases a traditional date might hold its ground for a little while beside a text of the Gospels manifestly inconsistent with it : but this consideration affects only a part of the evidence. On the supposition that the words are genuine, they might be omitted by assimilation to v 1. Supposing them however to be not genuine, it is no less easy to explain their insertion by assimilation to ii 13 (καὶ ἐγγὺς ἦν τὸ πάσχα τῶν Ἰουδαίων) and by the gain in explicitness: it is true that no addition of τὸ πάσχα has taken place in v 1 ; but there the absence of ἐγγύς makes the resemblance to ii 13 much slighter. A wide acceptance of τὸ πάσχα, when once it had been inserted, would also be natural. An identification of the darkness of the Crucifixion with a notable eclipse recorded by Phlegon (Cent. II) found favour as confirming the truth of the Gospels against heathen gainsayers : and the date of Phlegon's eclipse was Ol. 202. 4, four (in Eus. *Chron* three) years later than 15 Tib.; so that the acceptance of the identity of the two events could not fail to introduce or favour a lengthened chronology of the Ministry. Their identity was assumed by Origen when he wrote against Celsus (ii 33, 59), though shortly afterwards (*Mt*.lat. 923 : see note on Lc xxiii 45), probably under the influence of Africanus (Lipsius *l.c.* 25), he rejected it. In Eus. *Chron* however it holds the foremost place as evidence for the date of the Passion, St John's supposed testimony to a Ministry of three years after 15 Tib. being referred to in confirmation : and the precedence which Eus thus gives to the supposed testimony of Phlegon illustrates the manner in which the identification of his eclipse with the darkness of the Crucifixion may at an earlier time have affected the text of this passage.

In itself the shorter reading presents no difficulty : "the Feast of the Jews" was a fitting designation of the feast of tabernacles, which was known to the Jews preeminently as "the Feast" (cf. Cheyne on Is xxx 29), and was regarded by them as not only the last but the greatest of the primary series of feasts ; for its representative character see Zech xiv 16 ff. The same is indeed the probable sense of the phrase in vii 2, as otherwise the article is unmeaning. The reservation of the name of the feast till the second

passage might be accounted for by a purpose of associating it with the events of the feast itself (vii 3-14, 37). On the other hand, apart from the debateable ground of chronology, the longer reading is by no means easy. It has at least the appearance of bestowing on the passover a preeminence unknown elsewhere, or else of repeating information already given in ii 13, 23.

The difficulty interposed by the common text in the way of constructing a probable chronology of the Gospels has led G. J. Voss, Mann, and others to suspect the genuineness of τὸ πάσχα, or of the whole verse. The question has been reopened and ably discussed by Mr Henry Browne (*l.c.* 73—94), with especial reference to the patristic evidence ; and his materials (as also those of Lipsius and Dr E. Abbot) have been freely used in this note. The supposition that τὸ πάσχα formed no part of the original text must remain somewhat precarious in the absence of any other apparent corruption of equal magnitude and similarly attested by all known MSS and versions. But as a considerable body of patristic evidence points to the absence of the words in at least some ancient texts, and Internal Evidence is unfavourable to their genuineness, while the chronology of the Gospel history is fundamentally affected by their presence or absence, it has seemed right to express suspicion, and to justify it at some length. H.]

vi 51 καὶ ὁ ἄρτος.....ζωῆς] καὶ ὁ ἄρτος δὲ ὃν ἐγὼ δώσω ὑπὲρ τῆς τοῦ κόσμου ζωῆς ἡ σάρξ μου ἐστίν ℵ *m* Tert, probably Western of limited range : καὶ ὁ ἄρτος δὲ ὃν ἐγὼ δώσω ἡ σάρξ μού ἐστιν ἣν ἐγὼ δώσω ὑπὲρ τῆς τοῦ κόσμου ζωῆς Syrian (Gr. Lat.[it.] Syr. Eg. Arm. Goth.); incl. Clem.codd. Orig.*Orat*² (*s.q.*):

A is defective. Text BCDLT 33 157 al lat.vt-vg syr.vt the aeth Clem. cod.opt Orig.*Jo*² Ath Cyr.al.*loc* ; *Un.Chr.*; *Lc.*syr.667 al² Cyp. The transposition and the addition, which is perhaps due to a conflation of text with the transposition, are obvious attempts to bring out the sense of the passage.

vi 56 ἐν αὐτῷ] + καθὼς ἐν ἐμοὶ ὁ πατὴρ κἀγὼ ἐν τῷ πατρί. ἀμὴν ἀμὴν λέγω ὑμῖν, ἐὰν μὴ λάβητε τὸ σῶμα τοῦ υἱοῦ τοῦ ἀνθρώπου ὡς τὸν ἄρτον τῆς ζωῆς, οὐκ ἔχετε ζωὴν ἐν αὐτῷ. D : *a ff* have a modification of the last sentence (*si acceperit homo corpus......habebit...*). Western of limited range.

vi 59 Καφαρναούμ] + ⊣ σαββάτῳ ⊢ Western of limited range (Gr.[D] Lat.).

vii 39 ἦν πνεῦμα] + δεδομένον lat. eur-vg syr.vg Eus.*Lc* pp^lat, Western.

+ ἅγιον LX unc⁹ cu^pl (cf. syr.hl) (aeth) Or.*Mt.*lat.1/3 Ath Did Chr Thd⸏, Pre-Syrian (? Alexandrian) and Syrian.

+ ἅγιον ἐπ' αὐτοῖς D *f* go : D has τὸ πνεῦμα [τὸ] ἅγιον.

+ ἅγιον δεδομένον B (254) *eq* syr. hr-hl(δεδ.*) epit.Chr (Or.*Mt.*lat. 1/3) : 254 has δοθέν, perhaps from a gloss of Chr.*Jo.*301 A.

Text ℵTKΠ 42 91 lat.vg.codd syr.vt me (the) arm Orig.*Mt.*gr.; *Jo*³; (*Mt.*lat.1/3) Cyr.al.5/5 al auct. *Rebapt.* 14.

The singular distribution of documents is probably due in part to the facility with which either ἅγιον or δεδομένον or both might be introduced in different quarters independently. Text explains all the other readings, and could not have been derived from any one of them.

vii 52 ἐγείρεται.] + (vii 53—viii 11) ⊣ καὶ ἐπορεύθησαν...ἁμάρτανε. ⊢ Western and (with verbal modifications) late Constantinopolitan

(Gr. Lat. [Syr.] [Eg.] Æth.: [cf. Arm.]); incl. D Const.Ap.ii 24 'Nicon'(see below) (Euthym.*Jo* with a reservation) Amb Aug Hier.*Pelag.* ii 17 and later Latin Fathers. On lectionaries see below.

Amb. *Ep.* i 25 speaks of *semper quidem decantata quaestio et celebris absolutio mulieris.* Aug. *Conj.adult.* ii 6 shews knowledge of the difference of text by saying "Some of little faith, or rather enemies of the true faith, I suppose from a fear lest their wives should gain impunity in sin, removed from their MSS the Lord's act of indulgence to the adulteress". He also notices the ridicule directed by some 'sacrilegious pagans' against Christ's writing on the ground (*Faust.* xxii 25); and one of his quotations from his contemporary the Manichean Faustus includes a reference to Christ's 'absolution' of *in injustitia* or *in adulterio deprehensam mulierem* (xxxiii 1). According to Hier. *l.c.* "in the Gospel according to John many MSS, both Greek and Latin, contain an account of an adulterous woman" &c.: at the close he implies that the narrative belonged to Scripture. A Nicon who wrote a Greek tract *On the impious religion of the vile Armenians* (printed by Cotelier *Patr. Apost.* on Const.Ap.*l.c.*), and has been with little probability identified with the Armenian Nicon of Cent. x, accuses the Armenians of rejecting Lc xxii 43 f. and this Section, as being "injurious for most persons to listen to": like much else in the tract, this can be only an attempt to find matter of reproach against a detested church in the difference of its national traditions from Constantinopolitan usage. The *Synopsis Script. Sac.* wrongly ascribed to Ath, a work of uncertain date printed from a single MS, has near this place (c. 50) the words ἐνταῦθα τὰ περὶ τῆς κατηγορηθείσης ἐπὶ μοιχείᾳ: but they can only be an interpolation; for (1) they betray insertion, made carelessly, by standing after the substance of viii 12—20, not of vii 50—52; and (2) ἐνταῦθα suits only a note written at first in the margin, while the author of the Synopsis habitually marks the succession of incidents by the use of εἶτα. Euthymius Zygadenus (Cent. XII) comments on the Section as 'not destitute of use'; but in an apologetic tone, stating that "the accurate copies" either omit or obelise it, and that it appears to be an interpolation (παρέγγραπτα καὶ προσθήκη), as is shown by the absence of any notice of it by Chrys. The evidence of syr.hr is here in effect that of a Greek Constantinopolitan lectionary (see p. 42). It has vii 53—viii 2, instead of viii 12, after vii 23—52 as the close of the Whitsunday lesson, doubtless following a Greek example: the variations of Greek lectionaries as to the beginnings and endings of lections are as yet imperfectly known. In the Menology of syr.hr viii 1, 3—12 is the lection for St Pelagia's day, as in many Greek lectionaries (see below). The Section is found in some Syriac MSS, some Memphitic MSS (not the two best and some others: Lightfoot in Scrivener *Introd.*² 331 ff.; cf. E. B. Pusey *Cat. Bodl. Arab.* ii 564 f.), and some Armenian MSS; but it is evidently a late insertion in all these versions.

Text   ℵ(A)B(C)LTXΔ   MSS known to Hier 22 33 81 131 157 al^mu (besides many MSS which mark the section with asterisks or obeli) *a f q rhe* Latin MSS known to Hier and to Aug syr.vt-vg-hl me.codd.opt the arm go (Orig.*Jo*, see below) (Eus. *H.E.*, see below) (Theod.mops.*Jo*, see below) (Apoll.*Jo*, see below)

Chr.*Jo* Nonn.*Jo* Cyr.al.*Jo* (Amm. *Jo*.Cram. 272 apparently) Thphl.*Jo* (Ps.Ath.-*Syn*, see above). A and C are defective; but the missing leaves cannot have had room for the Section. In L and Δ blank spaces indicate (see pp. 29 f.) that the scribes were familiar with the Section, but did not find it in their exemplars: in Δ the blank space is an afterthought, being preceded by Πάλιν ...λέγων, written and then deleted. Origen's Comm. is defective here, not recommencing till viii 19: but in a recapitulation of vii 40—viii 22 (p. 299) the contents of vii 52 are immediately followed by those of viii 12. One scholium states that the Section was "not mentioned by the divine Fathers who interpreted [the Gospel], that is to say Chr and Cyr, nor yet by Theod.mops and the rest": according to another it was not in "the copies of (used by) Apollinaris". These and other scholia in MSS of the ninth (or tenth) and later centuries attest the presence or absence of the Section in different copies: their varying accounts of the relative number and quality of the copies cannot of course be trusted. The only patristic testimony which any of them cite in favour of the Section is Const.Ap (οἱ ἀπόστολοι πάντες ἐν αἷς ἐξέθεντο διατάξεσιν εἰς οἰκοδομὴν τῆς ἐκκλησίας). No Catenæ as yet examined contain notes on any of the verses. Negative evidence of some weight is supplied by the absence of any allusion to the section in Tertullian's book *De pudicitia* and Cyprian's 55th epistle, which treat largely of the admission of adulterous persons to penitence; nor can it be accidental that Cosmas (in Montf. *Coll. N. P.* ii 248) passes it over in enumerating the chief incidents narrated by St John alone of the evangelists.

Eus. *H. E.* iii 39 16 closes his ac-

count of the work of Papias (Cent. II)
with the words " And he has likewise
set forth another narrative (ἱστορίαν)
concerning a woman who was mali-
ciously accused before the Lord
touching many sins (ἐπὶ πολλαῖς ἁμαρτίαις διαβληθείσης ἐπὶ τοῦ κυρίου),
which is contained in the Gospel
according to the Hebrews ". The
notice is vague, and the language
is probably that of Eus himself : but
it is natural to suppose that the narrative referred to by him was no other
than the Section. The only discrepance lies in the probably exaggera-
tive word πολλαῖς: ἁμαρτίαις is justified by ἁμαρτίᾳ in D in place of
μοιχείᾳ, and by ἑτέραν δέ τινα ἡμαρ-
τηκυῖαν in Const.Ap (cf. in injustitia
in Faustus above) : διαβάλλω almost
always implies malice and frequently
falsehood, but is used of open no
less than secret modes of producing
an unfavourable impression. The
form of expression leaves it doubtful
whether the Gospel according to
the Hebrews was cited by Papias as
his authority or mentioned independently by Eus : no other evidence of use of that Gospel by
Papias occurs in our scanty information respecting him. If the Section
was the narrative referred to by
Eus, his language shews that he
cannot have known it as part of the
canonical Gospels.

The Section stands after Lc xxi 38
(on which see note) in the closely
related MSS 13-69-124-346; after
Jo vii 36 in 225, this transposition with the preceding paragraph
vii 37—52 being probably due to
some such accidental error as the
misplacement of a mark referring to
the Section as written in the upper
or lower margin ; and at the end of
the Gospel in a few cursives (including 1) and in the later Armenian
MSS. In some cases the introductory verses (or parts of them) vii 53

—viii 2 do not accompany the bulk
of the Section.

The Constantinopolitan lection for
the ' Liturgy' on Whitsunday consists of vii 37—52, followed immediately by viii 12; and examination
confirms the *prima facie* inference
that the intervening verses did not
form part of the Constantinopolitan
text when this lection was framed.
If read here as part of the Gospel,
they constitute a distinct narrative,
separating the conversation of vii
45—52 from the discourses that follow, and marking out v. 12 with
especial clearness as the opening
verse. The process involved in overleaping the narrative and fetching
back v. 12 out of its proper context
would be difficult to account for :
whereas, if the Gospel is read without the Section, there is no conspicuously great breach of continuity
in passing from vii 52 to viii 12, and
the advantage of ending the lection
after viii 12 rather than vii 52 is
manifest. The verses thus wanting
do not appear elsewhere among the
Constantinopolitan lections for Sun-
days or ordinary week-days; and
their absence is the more significant
because they are the only distinct
and substantive portion of St John's
Gospel which is not included in
these lections, unless we except the
short passage i 29—34, read on the
very ancient festival of John the
Baptist, and xiii 18—30, replaced by
the parallel account from Mt. Their
presence, or rather in most cases
the presence of viii 3—11 only, in
such Greek lectionaries as contain
them is confined to the Menologium
or system of saints' days, which is
probably for the most part of late
date; and the variety of their position in different MSS implies late
introduction into the Menologium.
They form a lesson sometimes (*e. g.*
in syr. hr) for St Pelagia's day, some-

times for the days of St Theodora (or Theodosia) or St Eudocia or St Mary of Egypt, or, without special appropriation, εἰς μετανοοῦντας καὶ μάλιστα ἐπὶ γυναικῶν or εἰς σχῆμα γυναικός, &c. (Matthaei² i 568 f.; Griesbach² i 479; cf. Scrivener *Introd.*² 81 and in *Dict. of Chr. Ant.* 965). It is worthy of notice that Lc vii 36–50, a lection used on saints' days having the same peculiar character, is not omitted in the ordinary week-day system, being read on Monday of the fourth week of the (Greek) New Year.

Since the Section stands in the text of St John according to the Latin Vulgate, it naturally finds a place in at least two of the Latin lection-systems; in the Roman on the fourth Saturday in Lent, and in the Mozarabic on the fourth Friday in Lent. It is included in the Armenian system as now in use, but only as the last part of a lection (for the fifth Thursday after Easter: see Petermann in Alt *Kirchenjahr* 232) which begins at vii 37, and which, if it ended at vii 52, would be fully as long as the neighbouring Gospel lections; so that it is reasonable to suppose the lection-system to have been in due time adapted to the interpolated text of the Armenian Bible. A Jacobite Syriac lectionary in the Bodleian Library (Cod. Syr. 43: see Payne Smith *Cat.* 143) reads vii 37-52 followed by viii 12-21 on the Eve of Thursday in Holy Week, as M. Neubauer kindly informs us: another in the British Museum (Add. 14,490 f. 113ᵃ) terminates the lection at vii 49 (Dr Wright). The Section is absent from the documents from which Malan and Lagarde (see p. 43) have edited the system in use among the (Jacobite) Copts.

The documentary distribution of the Section may be resumed in a

few words. It is absent from all extant Greek MSS containing any considerable Pre-Syrian element of any kind except the Western D; and from all extant Greek MSS earlier than Cent. VIII with the same exception. In the whole range of Greek patristic literature before Cent. (X or) XII there is but one trace of any knowledge of its existence, the reference to it in the Apostolic Constitutions as an authority for the reception of penitents (associated with the cases of St Matthew, St Peter, St Paul, and the ἁμαρτωλὸς γυνή of Lc vii 37), without however any indication of the book from which it was quoted. This silence is shared by seven out of the eight Greek Commentators whose text at this place is in any way known; while the eighth introduces the Section in language disparaging to its authority. In all the Oriental versions except the Ethiopic (where it may or may not have had a place from the first), including all the Syriac versions except that of the Palestinian Christians in communion with Constantinople, it is found only in inferior MSS. In Latin on the other hand it had comparatively early currency. Its absence from the earliest Latin texts is indeed attested by the emphatic silence of Tert and Cyp, and by the continuity of vii 52 with viii 12 in *rhe* (the non-vulgate element of which is mainly African) and *a*; nor is it found in the 'Italian' MSS *f q*: the obliteration in *b* is of too uncertain origin to be cited, for it begins in v. 44. But the Section was doubtless widely read in the Latin Gospels of Cent. IV, being present even in *e*, as also in *b c ff j* vg and the Latin MSS referred to by Amb Aug and Hier. Thus the first seven centuries supply no tangible evidence for it except in D, Greek

MSS known to Hier, and Const. Ap;—in *e*, the European and Vulgate Latin, and Amb Aug Hier and later Latin Fathers;—and in the Æthiopic, if its known texts may be trusted. It follows that during this period, or at least its first four centuries, the Section was, as far as our information goes, confined to Western texts, except in a single late reference in Const.Ap, which is almost wholly Syrian in its quotations. The Section cannot have been adopted in the Syrian text, as it is wanting not only in the later Syriac versions proper but in the Antiochian Fathers and the older part of the Constantinopolitan lection-system, as well as in seventy or more cursives. At some later time it was evidently introduced into the text and liturgical use of Constantinople. As a Western reading,— and that of comparatively restricted range, being attested by D *e* lat.eur aeth but not (lat.afr) syr.vt or any Greek Ante-Nicene writer,— owing its diffusion in Greek in the Middle Age to an admission which must have taken place after the rise of the eclectic texts of Cent. IV, it has no claim to acceptance on Documentary grounds.

The Transcriptional evidence leads to the same conclusion. Supposing the Section to have been an original part of St John's Gospel, it is impossible to account reasonably for its omission. The hypothesis taken for granted by Aug and Nicon, that the Section was omitted as liable to be understood in a sense too indulgent to adultery, finds no support either in the practice of scribes elsewhere or in Church History. The utmost licence of the boldest transcribers never makes even a remote approach to the excision of a complete narrative from the Gospels; and such rash omissions as do occur

are all but confined to Western texts; while here the authorities for omission include all the early Non-Western texts. Few in ancient times, there is reason to think, would have found the Section a stumbling-block except Montanists and Novatians. In Latin Christendom, if anywhere, would rigour proceed to such an extreme; and it is to three typical Latin Fathers, men certainly not deficient in Latin severity, that we owe the only early testimonies to the Section which are not anonymous, testimonies borne without reserve or misgiving. According to a second hypothesis, which is easier in so far as it postulates no wilful and direct mutilation of the Gospel, the omission was first made in the Constantinopolitan lection-system, assumed to have been the one lection-system of all Greek and Eastern Christendom from the earliest times, and then, owing to a misunderstanding of this purely liturgical proceeding, was reproduced in MSS of St John at a time early enough to affect the multitude of ancient texts from which the Section is now absent. But this view merely shifts the difficulty; for no scribe of the Gospels was likely to omit a large portion of the text of his exemplar because the verse following it was annexed to the verses preceding it in a lection familiar to him. Moreover the whole supposed process implicitly assigns to the Antiochian lection-system an age and extension incompatible with what is known of ancient liturgical reading (see pp. 42 f.). Once more, no theory which appeals to moral or disciplinary prudence as the cause of omission, whether in the biblical text or in liturgical use, is competent to explain why the three preliminary verses (vii 53 ; viii 1, 2), so important as apparently descriptive of the time and place at which all the discourses of c. viii were spoken, should have been omitted with the rest.

On the other hand, while the supposition that the Section is an interpolation derives no positive transcriptional probability from any difficulty or other motive for change in the context, it would be natural enough that an extraneous narrative of a remarkable incident in the Ministry, if it were deemed worthy of being read and perpetuated, should be inserted in the body of the Gospels. The place of insertion might easily be determined by the similarity of the concluding sentence to viii 15, ὑμεῖς κατὰ τὴν σάρκα κρίνετε, ἐγὼ οὐ κρίνω οὐδένα, the incident being prefixed to the discourse at the nearest break (Ewald *Joh. Schr.* i 271): indeed, if Papias used St John's Gospel, he may well have employed the incident as an illustration of viii 15 (Lightfoot *Contemp. Rev.* 1875 ii 847) in accordance with his practice of 'expounding' the written 'oracles of the Lord' by reference to independent traditions of His teaching.

The Intrinsic evidence for and against the Section is furnished partly by its own language and contents, partly by its relation to the context. The argument which has always weighed most in its favour in modern times is its own internal character. The story itself has justly seemed to vouch for its own substantial truth, and the words in which it is clothed to harmonise with those of other Gospel narratives. These considerations are however independent of the question of Johannine authorship: they only suggest that the narrative had its origin within the circle of apostolic tradition, and that it received

its form from some one in whom the spirit of apostolic tradition still breathed. On the other hand, it presents serious differences from the diction of St John's Gospel, which, to say the least, strongly suggest diversity of authorship, though their force and extent have sometimes been exaggerated.

In relation to the preceding context the Section presents no special difficulty, and has no special appropriateness. In relation to the following context there is, as noted above, a resemblance between vv. 11 and 15; and the declaration "I am the light of the world" has been supposed to be called forth by the effect of Christ's words on the conscience of the accusers: but in both cases the resemblances lie on the surface only. On the other hand, if v. 12 is preceded by the Section, the departure of the Scribes and Pharisees, leaving the woman standing alone before Christ (v. 9), agrees ill with αὐτοῖς in v. 12, and οἱ Φαρισαῖοι in v. 13. Still more serious is the disruption in the ordering of incidents and discourses produced by the presence of the Section. If it is absent, "the last day, the great day of the Feast" of Tabernacles is signalised by the twin declarations of Christ respecting Himself as the water of life and the light of the world; answering to the two great symbolic and commemorative acts, of pouring out the water and lighting the golden lamps, which were characteristic of the Feast of Tabernacles; and followed by two corresponding promises, ὁ πιστεύων εἰς ἐμέ κ.τ.λ., ὁ ἀκολουθῶν μοι κ.τ.λ. The true relation between the two passages is indicated by Πάλιν οὖν in v. 12. If however the Section is interposed, the first passage alone falls within the time of the feast, while the second is de-ferred till the day after the conclusion of the feast, and a heterogeneous incident disseuers the one from the other.   Thus Internal Evidence, Intrinsic as well as Transcriptional, confirms the adverse testimony of the documents.

When the whole evidence is taken together, it becomes clear that the Section first came into St John's Gospel as an insertion in a comparatively late Western text, having originally belonged to an extraneous independent source.   That this source was either the Gospel according to the Hebrews or the *Expositions of the Lord's Oracles* of Papias is a conjecture only; but it is a conjecture of high probability. It further appears that the Section was little adopted in texts other than Western till some unknown time between the fourth or fifth and the eighth centuries, when it was received into some influential Constantinopolitan text.   The historical relations between the addition to the biblical text and the introduction of at least viii 3—11 into liturgical use as a lection appropriate to certain secondary saints cannot be exactly determined.   The original institution of the lection seems to presuppose the existence of the interpolated text in the same locality: but the diffusion of the lection probably reacted upon the text of biblical MSS, for instance in the addition of the Section, or the principal part of it, at the end of the Gospels.   These complexities of mediæval Greek tradition are however of no critical importance.   Being found in the bulk of late Greek MSS and in the Latin Vulgate, so considerable a portion of the biblical text as the Section could not but appear in the sixteenth century to have in a manner the sanction of both East and West.

Erasmus shewed by his language how little faith he had in its genuineness; but "was unwilling", he says, "to remove it from its place, because it was now everywhere received, especially among the Latins": and, having been once published in its accustomed place by him, it naturally held its ground as part of the 'Received Text'.

The text of the Section itself varies much in the several documents which contain it.   As in all cases of Western readings adopted with modification in later texts, we have endeavoured to present it in its early or Western form, believing that the Constantinopolitan variations are merely ordinary corruptions of the paraphrastic kind.   We have accordingly given most weight to D, to those of the other Greek MSS which seem to preserve a comparatively early text, and to the Latin MSS and quotations.   So much complexity of variation however exists between these best authorities that we have been obliged to print an unusual number of alternative readings, and are by no means confident that the true text can now be recovered in more than approximate purity.

viii 38 ἃ ἐγω...πατρὸς] ⊣ ἐγὼ ἃ ἑώρακα παρὰ τῷ πατρί μου [ταῦτα] λαλῶ· καὶ ὑμεῖς οὖν ἃ ἑωράκατε παρὰ τῷ πατρὶ ὑμῶν ⊢ Western and, with ὅ twice substituted for ἅ, and ταῦτα omitted, Syrian (Gr. Lat. Syr. Æth.): but aeth omits μου and ὑμῶν.

x 8 ἦλθον πρὸ ἐμοῦ] < πρὸ ἐμοῦ Western and perhaps Syrian (Gr. Lat. Syr. Eg. Goth.); incl. ℵ* Cyr.al Chr Aug(expressly) and scholia: but not D me (Clem) Orig Ephr. *Diat*.arm.200. The omission perhaps seemed to emphasise the sense of ἦλθον; or to be a natural simplification on the assumption that πάντες means 'they all' (τῶν ἀλλοτρίων v. 5: cf. v. 1), as ὅσοι ἐλάλησαν Act iii 24; or to obviate or lessen risk of reference to the prophets.

xi 54 χώραν] + Σαμφουρεὶν D (*Sapfurim d*): perhaps a local tradition, though the name has not been identified with any certainty. Sepphoris is apparently excluded by its geographical position.

xii 28 τὸ ὄνομα] τὸν υἱὸν Alexandrian (Gr. Lat. Syr.[hl.mg] Eg. Æth. Arm.); incl.Or.*Cant.*lat.Ruf.77 Ath Cyr.al(giving both readings).

xii 32 πάντας] ┤πάντα├ Western (Gr. Lat. Syr. Æth.) incl. Aug expressly: D aeth, as also me the, place παντ. after ἑλκύσω. Cf. ii 24 *v.l.*

xii 41 ὅτι] ὅτε Western and Syrian (Gr. Lat. Syr. Æth. Goth.); incl. [Orig.*Rom.*lat. Ruf.codd] Eus. *D.E.*[3] Did.*Tri* [Cyr.al.*Heb.* p. 118 Mai (*s.q.*); *Is.* 102 cod (*s.q.*)]. Text ℵABLMX 1 33 al[3] *e* me the arm Orig.*Rom.*lat.Ruf Epiph Nonn Cyr.al.*Jo.*505; 2*Co.*85 Mai; *Is.* 102 cod.

xiii 31 ἐν αὐτῷ·] + εἰ ὁ θεὸς ἐδοξάσθη ἐν αὐτῷ, Pre-Syrian (?Alexandrian) and Syrian (Gr. Lat. Syr. Eg. [Æth.] Arm. Goth.); incl. *e* me the Orig.*Jo*[3](expressly) Nonn [Cyr.al.*Lc.*syr.716]. Text ℵ*BC*D LXII 1 al[p] *a b c ff q* vg.codd (incl. *rhe**) syr.hl aeth.codd Cyr.*loc*[2] Tert (vdtr) Amb. The clause, which might easily have been added by accidental repetition, or no less easily lost by *homoeoteleuton*, mars the true symmetry of the passage; and the documentary range of the omission excludes the hypothesis of accident.

xvii 7 ἔγνωκαν] ┤ἔγνων├ Western (Gr. [ℵ 'some' according to Chr] Lat. Syr. Eg. Goth.): a few cursives have ἔγνωκα. A natural return to the first person: cf. v. 25.

xvii 11 ἔρχομαι] + · οὐκέτι εἰμὶ ἐν τῷ κόσμῳ, καὶ ἐν τῷ κόσμῳ εἰμὶ Western, D *a* (omitting the first clause of the verse) *c* (first part only) *e* (second part only, inserted before καὶ αὐτοί): Orig.*Mt.*599 (cf. lat) has perhaps a trace of the first part of the same reading.

xvii 21 ἐν ἡμῖν] + ἓν Pre-Syrian (probably Alexandrian) and Syrian (Gr. Lat. Syr. Eg. Æth. Goth.); incl. ℵLX me Clem Orig.*Hos.*439 (from Philocalia); *Jo.* 28 (but see below), (395;) (*Eph.* 110 Cram.); lat. *saepe* Eus.*Marc.*1/3 Ath.(509,)567 codd,(574) Cyr.al (Hil.1/4). Text BC*D *a b c e* the arm Orig.*Mart.* 300;*Jo.*28(cod.Ferr) Eus.*Marc.*2/3 Ath.567codd Cyp.codd.opt Firmil. lat.codd.opt Hil.3/4. The addition comes directly from the first clause of the verse (cf. 11, 22): confusion between these clauses renders several of the patristic quotations ambiguous.

xvii 23 ἠγάπησας] ἠγάπησα Western (Gr. Lat. Syr. Eg. Æth. Arm.). Cf. xv 9.

xviii 1 τῶν Κέδρων] ┤τοῦ Κέδρου├ Western, ℵ*D *a b* (both, as *d, cedri*) *e* (*caedrum*, following *torrentem*) me (with 'tree' prefixed) the aeth: τοῦ Κεδρὼν (?early Syrian) ASΔ cu[1], and apparently *c* lat.it-vg syrr ? arm go Amb Aug; this is the form used by Josephus, except that according to his custom he gives it Greek inflexions; and it occurs 1 Re xv 13 in A. Text, which is also the late Syrian reading, ℵ[c]BCLX unc[10] cu[pl] Orig.*Jo* Chr.*Jo*; this is the reading of LXX in 2 Sam xv 23 1° B cu and 2° A cu, 1 Re ii 37 in N cu[12], 1 Re xv 13 in AB and most MSS, and elsewhere in a few cursives. Also τῶν κένδρων cu[10], τῶν δένδρων 9 Cyr.*loc*.

Text, though not found in any version, is amply attested by Greek MSS. It cannot be a mere error of scribes of the N. T., being already in the LXX. It probably preserves the true etymology of קִדְרוֹן, which seems to be an archaic (? Canaanite) plural of קדר, "the Dark [trees]"; for, though no name from this root is applied to any tree in biblical Hebrew, some tree resembling a cedar was called by a similar name in at least the later language (see exx. in Buxtorf *Lex. Talm.* 1976); and the Greek κέδρος is probably of Phœnician origin. In this as in some other cases נַחַל (φάραγξ, χειμαρροῦς) denoted less the stream than the ravine through which it flowed, the valley of Jehoshaphat (τῷ δὲ ἀρχαίῳ περιβόλῳ σύναπτον [the third wall] εἰς τὴν Κεδρῶνα καλουμένην φάραγγα κατέληγεν Jos. *B. J.* v 4 2 &c.: cf. Grove in *Dict. Bib.* ii 13 f.). Isolated patches of cedar-forest may well have survived from prehistoric times in sheltered spots. Even in the latest days of the Temple 'two cedars' are mentioned as standing on the Mount of Olives (*Taanith* iv 4, cited by J. Lightfoot *Chorog. Dec.* iv 2, and thence Stanley *Sin. and Pal.* 187). Another Κεδρών, a town in the region of Jamnia, was likewise near a χειμαρροῦς (1 Mac xv 39, 41; xvi 5, 6, 9).

xix 4 οὐδεμίαν αἰτίαν εὑρίσκω ἐν αὐτῷ] αἰτίαν οὐχ εὑρίσκω א*: cf. 131*, which likewise omits ἐν αὐτῷ. For οὐδεμίαν the Western reading is οὐχ. There is much variety of order in different documents.

xix 14 ἕκτη] τρίτη אᶜDˢᵘᵖLXΔ cu⁴ Nonn Chron.Pasch(stating this to be the reading of 'the accurate copies' and of the evangelist's autograph preserved at Ephesus). Eus. *Mar*, as cited by Sev, maintains that the numeral Γ (3) was misread by 'the original copyists of the Gospel' as F (6); and the same conjectural explanation of the ap-

parent discrepancy with Mc xv 25 (where see note on the converse corruption) is repeated more briefly in a scholium of Ammonius. Text אAB unc¹¹ cuᵒᵐⁿ vvᵒᵐⁿ Marcus (ap. Iren Hipp) Hipp Eus(see above) Amm(see above) Hesych Cyr.al.*loc* Aug.

xxi 25. According to Tischendorf in א this verse, with the concluding ornament and subscription, is not from the hand of the scribe (A) who wrote the rest of this Gospel, but of another (D) who wrote a small part of the Apocrypha and acted as corrector (διορθωτής) of the N. T., of which he likewise wrote a few scattered entire leaves; the same scribe in fact to whom he with much probability (see *Introduction* § 288) ascribes the writing of the Vatican MS. Tregelles, who examined the MS in Tischendorf's presence, believed the difference in handwriting to be due only to a fresh dip of the pen. At the same time however he disputed the difference of scribes throughout the MS, apparently on insufficient grounds. It seems on the whole probable that the verse and its accompaniments were added by the corrector; but it does not follow that the scribe A intended to finish the Gospel at v. 24, that is, that his exemplar ended there. Some accident of transcription may well have caused the completion to be left to the scribe D, who in like manner, if Tischendorf is not mistaken, yielded up the pen to the scribe A after writing two thirds of the first column of the Apocalypse: for it is not likely that A would have left what he considered to be the end of the Gospel without any indication to mark it as such. He concludes Mt with the ornament, and Lc with the ornament and subscription: the last leaf of Mc, which likewise has the ornament and subscription, is by D.

According to various scholia an unnamed writer stated this verse to be a marginal note of some careful person (τινὸς τῶν φιλοπόνων), which was incorporated by mistake with the text. Abulfaraj (Nestle *Theol. L.Z.* 1878 413) likewise mentions the verse with v 4 as said 'by some' not to have been written by the evangelist. The omission seems however to have been conjectural only, arising out of comparison with v. 24. Verse 25 stands not only in all extant MSS and vv but in a considerable series of Fathers, including Orig Pamph Eus Cyr.al.

Section on the Woman taken in Adultery

See note on [Jo] vii 53—viii 11.

9 (†) ἀπὸ τῶν πρεσβυτέρων] Various evidence makes it probable that πάντες ἀνεχώρησαν originally followed here as an independent clause; it would be naturally altered or omitted as seeming merely to repeat ἐξήρχοντο. D adds ὥστε πάντας ἐξελθεῖν: c *ff* arm add *omnes recesserunt*: for ἐξήρχοντο M 264 substitute πάντες ἀνεχώρησαν: and Nicon's brief paraphrase includes ἀνεχώρησαν ἅπαντες.

10 κατέκρινεν] *lapidavit ff* Amb (often and distinctly): *judicavit e.*

ACTS

ii 9 Ἰουδαίαν] *Armeniam* Tert Aug: (*habitantes in*) *Syria* Hier. Evidently suggested by the collocation of regions.

ii 30 τῆς ὀσφύος αὐτοῦ] + [κατὰ σάρκα] ἀναστῆσαι τὸν χριστὸν [καὶ] Western and (with τό prefixed, and reading ἀναστήσειν) Syrian (Gr. Syr.); incl. Orig.*Ps.* (XV Cord. Gall.) Eus. *Ps*: but not latt Iren.lat Eus.*Ecl.* Perhaps from 2 Sam vii 12.

iv 25 (†) ὁ τοῦ πατρὸς ἡμῶν διὰ πνεύματος ἁγίου στόματος Δαυεὶδ παιδός σου] Western texts (Gr. and most or all vv) in various ways separate διὰ π. ἁ. from στόματος Δ. π. σ., simply inserting διά or καί before στόματος, or reading στόματι, or reading πνεύματι and διὰ στόματος; and further either omit τοῦ πατρὸς ἡμῶν (D syr.vg me) or join it to Δ. π. σ. (latt syr.hl the aeth arm Iren.lat): Hil Aug omit διὰ πνεύματος ἁγίου, which syr.hl arm. codd transfer to the end. The Syrian text (Gr.) omits both τοῦ πατρὸς ἡμῶν and πνεύματος ἁγίου. Text אABE₂ (13) 15 27 29 36 (38) lt 12 Ath. The various Western and Syrian readings are evidently attempts to get rid of the extreme difficulty of text, which doubtless contains a primitive error. [A confusion of lines ending successively with ΔΙΑ ΔΑΔ ΔΙΑ may have brought πνεύματος ἁγίου too high up, and caused the loss of one διά. W.] [If τοῦ πατρός is taken as a corruption of τοῖς πατράσιν, the order of words in text presents no difficulty, David (or the mouth of David) being represented as the mouth of the Holy Spirit. H.]

iv 32 ψυχὴ μία] + καὶ οὐκ ἦν διάκρισις ἐν αὐτοῖς οὐδεμία (χωρισμὸς ἐν αὐτοῖς τις) Western, DE₂ Cyp² Amb Zen; not *g m* Orig.lat.

v 38 ἄφετε αὐτούς] +, μὴ μιάναντες (v. μολύνοντες) τὰς χεῖρας [ὑμῶν] Western, D(E₂) 34; not *g*.

vii 16 ἐν Συχέμ] τοῦ Συχέμ Western and Syrian (Gr. Lat. Æth.): τοῦ ἐν Συχέμ א°AE₂ 27 29 40 *tol* (syr.hl), perhaps conflate. Text א*BC 36 44 69 100 105 al⁵ me the arm.

vii 43 Ῥομφά] Ῥεμφάμ Western, D lat.vg Iren.lat: Ῥεμφά 61 lat.codd arm Orig.*Cels*.cod: Ῥομφάν א* 3 Chr.cod: Ῥαιφάν or Ῥεφάν Alexandrian (Gr. Syr. Eg. Æth.): Ῥεμφάν Syrian (Gr.), incl. Orig.*Cels*.cod. Text א*B 3 lat.vg.cod Orig.*Cels*. cod Chr.cod, as regards Ῥομ-; אBD 61 cupl latt arm Orig.*Cels* Chr Iren.lat, as regards -μφ-; B 61 lat.vg.codd arm Orig.*Cels*, as regards -φά; B Orig.*Cels*.cod throughout. In the LXX of Am v 26 the form used is Ῥαιφάν or Ῥεφάν, which is similar to *Repa* or *Repha*, one of the names of the Egyptian Saturn (Seb).

vii 46 (†) τῷ θεῷ Ἰακώβ] < τῷ οἴκῳ Ἰακώβ א*BDH₂. Text א°ACE₂P₂ cuᵒᵐⁿ vvᵒᵐⁿ Chr. Documentary authority, supported by the improbability that τοῦ θεοῦ and τῷ θεῷ would stand so near each other, and that θεῷ would be altered by scribes, renders it nearly certain that θεῷ is a very ancient correction of οἴκῳ. Yet οἴκῳ can hardly be genuine, and seems to be a primitive error. The common reading θεῷ is that of LXX in Ps cxxxii (cxxxi) 5, (ἕως οὗ εὕρω τόπον τῷ κυρίῳ, σκήνωμα τῷ θεῷ Ἰσραήλ); but it represents the peculiar and rare word אֲבִיר (*Strong One*), rendered δυνάστης in the fundamental passage Gen xlix 24. The true reading may have been some nearer equivalent of the Hebrew than θεός, and the following ΙΑΚѠΒ would facilitate the introduction of ΟΙΚѠ. [Probably the lost word is κυρίῳ, the two clauses of the Psalm being fused together : ΤѠΚѠ might easily be read as ΤѠΟΙΚѠ. H.]

viii 24 *fin.*] + ┤· ὃς πολλὰ κλαίων οὐ διελίμπανεν ├ Western, D* syr.hl. mg ; not *g*.

viii 36 *fin.*] + (v. 37) ┤ εἶπεν δὲ αὐτῷ [ὁ Φίλιππος] Εἰ πιστεύεις ἐξ ὅλης τῆς καρδίας σου [, ἔξεστιν]. ἀποκριθεὶς δὲ εἶπεν Πιστεύω· τὸν υἱὸν τοῦ θεοῦ εἶναι τὸν Ἰησοῦν [Χριστόν]. ├ Western (Gr. Lat. Syr.[hl*] Arm.); incl. E₂, some good cursives, and *g m* Iren. gr.lat Cyp : D is defective : there is much variation in details. This interpolation, which filled up the apparent chasm left by the unanswered question of v. 36 with matter doubtless derived from common Christian practice, stands on the same footing as the other Western amplifications in the Acts. Though not contained in the Greek MS chiefly used by Erasmus (2), and found by him in the margin only of another (4), he inserted it as " having been omitted by the carelessness of scribes": it is absent from the best MSS of the Latin Vulgate, as well as from the Syriac Vulgate and the Egyptian versions; but it soon found its way from the Old Latin into the late text of the Vulgate, with which alone Erasmus was conversant. From his editions it passed into the 'Received Text', though it forms no part of the Syrian text.

29

viii 39 πνεῦμα Κυρίου] πνεῦμα ἅγιον ἐπέπεσεν ἐπὶ τὸν εὐνοῦχον, ἄγγελος δὲ Κυρίου Western (Gr. Lat. Syr.[hl*] Arm.); incl. A (correction by first hand) and apparently Hier Aug; not *g*: D is defective.

x 25 Ὡς...Πέτρον,] Προσεγγίζοντος δὲ τοῦ Πέτρου [εἰς τὴν Καισαρίαν] προδραμὼν εἷς τῶν δούλων διεσάφησεν παραγεγονέναι αὐτόν. ὁ δὲ Κορνήλιος [ἐκπηδήσας καὶ] Western, D *g* syr. hl.mg : *g* omits the bracketed words.

xi 2 Ὅτε...περιτομῆς] Ὁ μὲν οὖν Πέτρος διὰ ἱκανοῦ χρόνου ἠθέλησεν (-σαι) πορευθῆναι εἰς Ἰεροσόλυμα· καὶ προσφωνήσας τοὺς ἀδελφοὺς καὶ ἐπιστηρίξας αὐτοὺς πολὺν λόγον ποιούμενος διὰ τῶν χωρῶν [? δι' αὐτῶν ἐχώρει] διδάσκων αὐτούς· ὃς καὶ κατήντησεν αὐτοῖς [? αὐτοῦ] καὶ ἀπήγγειλεν (-γιλεν) αὐτοῖς τὴν χάριν τοῦ θεοῦ. οἱ δὲ ἐκ περιτομῆς ἀδελφοὶ διεκρίνοντο πρὸς αὐτὸν Western, D (syr. hl) ; not *g*: this corrupt passage is but partially preserved in syr.hl, which marks διδάσκων αὐτούς with a *, and then recommences the verse according to the common text.

xi 20 Ἑλληνιστάς] Ἕλληνας probably Western, Nᶜ AD 112 (Eus) (? Chr). Text BD**E₂H₂L₂P₂ 61 and all cursives but one; also N* εὐαγγελιστάς, which presupposes text. Versions are ambiguous; they express only 'Greeks', but would naturally have found it difficult to find a distinctive rendering for so rare and so peculiar a word as Ἑλληνιστής. It occurs twice elsewhere; vi 1, where in like manner all versions seem to have 'Greeks'; and ix 29, where the versions (except syr. vg, 'Jews who knew Greek') have the same, and A has, as here, Ἕλληνας, D being defective.

The testimony of the best documents in favour of text is strongly confirmed by transcriptional evidence. A familiar word standing in an obvious antithesis was not likely to be exchanged for a word so rare that it is no longer extant, except in a totally different sense, anywhere but in the Acts and two or three late Greek interpretations of the Acts; more especially when the change introduced an apparent difficulty. In the two other places there was less temptation to make the change, as the locality was manifestly Jerusalem, so that a reference to Gentiles would seem to be out of place. Ἕλληνας has *prima facie* Intrinsic evidence in its favour, as being alone in apparent harmony with the context. This is true however only if it be assumed that Ἰουδαῖοι is used in a uniformly exclusive sense throughout the book; whereas it excludes proselytes in ii 10 and (τ. σεβομένοις) xvii 17 (compare xiii 43; xvii 4 [taken with 1]; and the double use of Ἰουδαίων in xiv 1), and may therefore exclude ' Hellenists ' here. Indeed the language of vv. 19, 20 would be appropriate if the 'Hellenists' at Antioch, not being merged in the general body of resident Jews, were specially singled out and addressed (ἐλάλουν καὶ πρὸς τοὺς Ἕ., not as in v. 19, λαλοῦντες...Ἰουδαίοις) by the men of Cyprus and Cyrene. Moreover, if Gentiles in the full sense are the subjects of vv. 20—24, the subsequent conduct and language of St Paul are not easy to explain. In this as in other passages of the Acts the difficulty probably arises from the brevity of the record and the slightness of our knowledge. It is certainly not serious enough to throw doubt on the best attested reading.

xii 25 (†) εἰς Ἰερουσαλήμ] (marg.) ἐξ Ἰερουσαλὴμ A 13 27 29 44 69 110 al^mu syr.vg.hl.txt me the aeth. codd arm Chr.codd: ἀπὸ Ἰερουσαλὴμ DE₂ 15 36 40 68 100 112 180 al^mu g vg Chr.cod (on B see below):

with both readings E₂ cu^mu.bo syr.vg the add εἰς Ἀντιοχίαν (-είαν). Text אBH₂L₂P₂ 61 102 al^mu syr.hl.mg aeth.codd Chr.codd: according to Tischendorf the scribe of B had begun to write ἀπό.

A perplexing variation. Ἐξ and ἀπό are alike free from difficulty. Neither of the two was likely to give rise to the other, still less to εἰς; and the attestation on the whole suggests that ἀπό is Western, ἐξ Alexandrian. On the other hand εἰς Ἰερουσαλήμ, which is best attested and was not likely to be introduced, cannot possibly be right if it is taken with ὑπέστρεψαν (see xi 27 ff.). It makes good sense if taken with πληρώσαντες τὴν διακονίαν. But this is not a natural construction of the words as they stand; and it may be reasonably suspected that the original order was τὴν εἰς Ἰερουσαλὴμ πληρώσαντες διακονίαν. The article is more liable than other words to careless transposition.

xiii 18 ἐτροποφόρησεν] ἐτροφοφόρησεν AC*E₂ 13 68 100 105 al^5 d (ac si nutrix aluit) g (aluit) [e nutrivit] syr.vg-hl.txt me the aeth arm. The word occurs in other Fathers, but without any indication that this verse was the source. Text אBC^a DH₂L₂P₂ 61 al^pm lat.vg (mores... sustinuit) syr.hl.mg(gr) Chr.

Both readings occur in the LXX rendering of Deut i 31, to which passage reference is evidently made here. The original word נָשָׂא, meaning simply to 'bear' ('carry' [so Aq. ἦρεν, Sym. ἐβάστασεν; and cf. Ex xix 4; Is xlvi 3 f.; lxiii 9], or 'endure', 'be patient with'), was much less likely to be rendered by τροφοφορέω (so AFMN cd^pm Cyr. al), to 'nourish', than by τροποφορέω, which in the only two places where it occurs independently of Deut and Acts (Orig treats it as coined by the LXX) means distinctly to 'be patient with' (Cic. *Att.* XIII 29 *In hoc tòn τύφον μου πρὸς θεῶν τροποφόρησον*; Schol. Aristoph. *Ran.* 1432 ἢ μὴ καταδέξασθαι ἢ καταδεξαμένους τροποφορεῖν), and which has the authority of B* [*sic*] cu[10] Orig.*Jer.*248 (expressly). When however the original was forgotten, the immediate context ('bare thee as a man doth bear his son') naturally led to the change of a single letter so as to introduce explicit reference to a nurse or nursing father, though τροφοφορέω means to 'supply nourishment to', not to 'carry as a nurse does'. This plausible corruption of the LXX was doubtless widely current in the apostolic age, and might easily have stood in the text of the LXX followed here. But there can be no reason for questioning the genuineness of the reading of אB 61 (with many good cursives) lat.vg, when it is also the best authenticated reading of the LXX and agrees with the Hebrew, and when it was peculiarly likely to be changed by the influence of the common and corrupt text of the LXX. Both here and in Deut either reading gives an excellent sense.

xiii 32 (†) τοῖς τέκνοις ἡμῶν] τ. τ. αὐτῶν (? Western) *g* the Amb.cod: τ. τ. me : τ. τ. αὐτῶν ἡμῖν Syrian (Gr. Syr. Arm.); incl. 61 : τ. τ. ἡμῖν '76' (Scholz). Text אABC*D lat.vg aeth Hil Amb.codd. Text, which alone has any adequate authority, and of which all or nearly all the readings are manifest corrections, gives only an improbable sense. It can hardly be doubted that ἡμῶν is a primitive corruption of ἡμῖν, τοὺς πατέρας and τοῖς τέκνοις being alike absolute. The suggestion is due to Bornemann, who cites x 41 in illustration. A similar primitive error occurs in He xi 4.

xiii 33 δευτέρῳ] πρώτῳ Western, D *g* Latin MSS known to Bede Orig.*Ps.*(expressly) Hil. According to Orig (followed in looser language by Eus Apoll Euthym Ps. Hier.*Psalt*) Psalms i and ii were joined together in one of the two Hebrew copies which he had seen; as they are in many extant Hebrew MSS. The same arrangement must have passed into some copies of the LXX, for Justin (*Ap.* i 40) transcribes both Psalms continuously as a single prophecy; and Tert Cyp. codd.opt (at least *Test.* i 13, and probably elsewhere) and other African Latin writers cite verses of Ps ii as from Ps i. In other words, the authorities for πρώτῳ here and for the combination of the two Psalms are in each case Western; so that a 'Western' scribe, being probably accustomed to read the two Psalms combined, would be under a temptation to alter δευτέρῳ to πρώτῳ, and not *vice versa.* Accordingly Transcriptional Probability, which *prima facie* supports πρώτῳ, is in reality favourable or unfavourable to both readings alike.

xiii 42 (†) Ἐξιόντων δὲ αὐτῶν παρεκάλουν...ταῦτα] < παρεκάλουν BE₂ (? 81); but B (and ? 81) inserts ἠξίουν after σάββατον; while Chr (Mill), though not *ad l.*, substitutes ἠξίουν for παρεκάλουν. Two late Constantinopolitan glosses, ἐκ τῆς συναγωγῆς τῶν Ἰουδαίων after or for αὐτῶν, and τὰ ἔθνη after παρεκάλουν, are due to a true sense of the obscure and improbable language of the text as it stands. This difficulty and the curious variation as to παρεκάλουν suggest the presence of a primitive corruption, probably in the opening words. [Perhaps Ἀξιούντων should replace Ἐξιόντων, and παρεκάλουν and the stop at the end of the verse be omitted. The language of vv. 42 f. would then be natural if the requests for another discourse on the following sabbath were interrupted by the breaking up of the congregation by the ἀρχισυνάγωγοι (v. 15), *e.g.* for prudential reasons (cf. v. 45). H.]

xiv 2 *fin.*]+ὁ δὲ κύριος ἔδωκεν [ταχὺ] εἰρήνην. Western, DE₂*g dem* codd.lat syr.hl.mg (Cassiod).

xv 2 ἔταξαν...ἐξ αὐτῶν] ἔλεγεν γὰρ ὁ Παῦλος μένειν οὕτως καθὼς ἐπίστευσαν διισχυριζόμενος· οἱ δὲ ἐληλυθότες ἀπὸ Ἰερουσαλὴμ παρήγγειλαν αὐτοῖς τῷ Παύλῳ καὶ Βαρνάβᾳ καί τισιν ἄλλοις ἀναβαίνειν Western, D syr.hl. mg; also *g* '*bodl*' as far as ἐπίστευσαν.

xv 18 γνωστὰ ἀπ' αἰῶνος.] ⊣ γνωστὸν ἀπ' αἰῶνός [ἐστιν] τῷ κυρίῳ τὸ ἔργον αὐτοῦ. ⊢ Western, AD lat.vg syr.hl.mg Iren.lat (the two latter having θεῷ); not *g*: also, by conflation with text, γνωστὰ ἀπ' αἰῶνός ἐστιν τῷ θεῷ [πάντα] τὰ ἔργα αὐτοῦ Syrian (Gr. Lat.[*g*] Syr.). Text ℵBC 61 27 29 36 44 100 180 al⁵ me the arm: ἅ ἐστι γνωστὰ αὐτῷ ἀπ' αἰῶνος cuᵖ (aeth). Since the quotation from Am ix 12 ends at ταῦτα, and the connexion of the concluding words with the rest was not obvious, it was natural to make them the foundation of an independent sentence.

xv 20 *fin.*]+καὶ ὅσα ἂν μὴ θέλωσιν αὐτοῖς γίνεσθαι ἑτέροις μὴ ποιεῖν Western, (D) 27 29 69 110 al⁷ lat. codd the aeth Iren.lat Leg.Alfr; not *g*. Similarly in v. 29 after πορνείας the clause καὶ ὅσα μὴ θέλετε ἑαυτοῖς γίνεσθαι ἑτέρῳ (*v.* ἑτέροις) μὴ ποιεῖτε is added by nearly the same documents, with the addition of syr.hl.* Cyp; not *g* Clem.*Paed* Orig.*Rom.* lat.Ruf Tert.*Pud.* This negative form of the 'golden rule' of Mt vii 12 ‖ Lc vi 31 appears to be quoted separately without indication of the source by Theoph.*Aut.*ii 34; and also in Const.Ap.vii 21 (Πᾶν ὁ μὴ

θέλεις γενέσθαι σοι τοῦτο ἄλλῳ οὐ ποιήσεις), where it is followed by a similar quotation from Tob iv 15 (ὁ σὺ μισεῖς ἄλλῳ οὐ ποιήσεις, a saying likewise attributed to Hillel). In the interpolated recension of Tobit the resemblance to these readings of Acts is closer still. Compare Lamprid. *Alex. Sev.* 51 *Clamabatque saepius quod a quibusdam sive Judaeis sive Christianis audierat et tenebat...*Quod tibi fieri non vis alteri ne feceris.

xv 33 *fin.*]+(v. 34) ⊣ ἔδοξεν δὲ τῷ Σίλᾳ ἐπιμεῖναι αὐτούς (v. αὐτοῦ) [, μόνος δὲ Ἰούδας ἐπορεύθη]. ⊢ Western and, for the first clause, probably Alexandrian (Gr. Lat. Eg. Æth. Arm.) : the second clause D *g* vg.codd. Text ℵABE₂H₂L₂P₂ 61 alᵖᵐ lat.vg syr.vg-hl.txt me.cod Chr. The first clause was inserted by Erasmus, doubtless under the influence of a late text of the Latin Vulgate, though he found it only in the margin of one of the Greek MSS : he supposed it to have been omitted ' by an error of the scribes'.

xvi 12 (†) πρώτη τῆς μερίδος Μακεδονίας] πρώτη μερίδος τῆς M. B: πρώτη μερὶς M. E₂ *dem* arm : κεφαλὴ τῆς M. D syr.vg: πρώτη τῆς M. 105 112 137 al³ syr.hl aeth(vdtr) Chr: πρώτη τῆς μερίδος τῆς M. H₂L₂P₂ cuᵖᵐ. Text ℵACE₂ 61 31 36 40 68 69 180 al⁴ (vv). [None of these readings gives an endurable sense. Μερίς never denotes simply a region, province, or any geographical division : when used of land, as of anything else, it means a portion or share, *i.e.* a part in a relative sense only, not absolutely (μέρος). Secondly, the senses ' of its district ', ' of that district ', would not be expressed naturally by τῆς μ. Thirdly, πρώτη as a title of honour for towns (used absolutely) is apparently confined to Asia. Nor can it mean 'capital', for Philippi was not the capital of its district, but Amphipolis, a much more important place. Nor again can it mean 'first on entering the country'; for πρῶτος unaccompanied by any interpretative phrase never has this local force, and moreover Neapolis would come first on the route in question. Both towns alike were politically in Macedonia, in popular language in Thrace; so that no kind of frontier would lie between them. There is therefore doubtless some primitive corruption. It is not impossible that μερίδος should be read as Πιερίδος (M for ΠΙ), for Philippi belonged to the Pieria of Mount Pangæon, and might well be called "a chief city of Pierian Macedonia": so Steph.Byz. Κρηνίδες, πόλις Πιερίας (codd. Σικελίας), ἃς Φίλιππος μετωνόμασε Φιλίππους: cf. Herod. vii 212; Thuc. ii 99. The name ἡ Πιερὶς Μακεδονία does not seem however to occur elsewhere, and would more naturally be applied to the more famous Pieria in the S. W. of Macedonia. For the present the reading must remain in doubt. H.]

xvi 30 ἔξω]+τοὺς λοιποὺς ἀσφαλισάμενος Western, D syr.hl.* ; not *g* Lucif.

xviii 21 Πάλιν] ⊣ Δεῖ με πάντως τὴν ἑορτὴν τὴν ἐρχομένην ποιῆσαι εἰς Ἱεροσόλυμα· [*et iterum*] ⊢ Western and, slightly modified, Syrian (Gr. Lat. Syr. [Æth.]): the last two words, answering to text, are omitted by D (as also by theb, which is free from the interpolation) but preserved in Latin (*g dem*); πάντως δέ is Syrian. Text ℵABE₂ 13 36 69 105 110 180 al² lat.vg (me the) aeth.cod arm.

xviii 27 βουλομένου...αὐτόν·] ⊣ ἐν δὲ τῇ Ἐφέσῳ ἐπιδημοῦντές τινες Κορίνθιοι καὶ ἀκούσαντες αὐτοῦ παρεκάλουν διελθεῖν σὺν αὐτοῖς εἰς τὴν πατρίδα αὐτῶν· συνκατανεύσαντος δὲ αὐτοῦ οἱ

Ἐφέσιοι ἔγραψαν τοῖς ἐν Κορίνθῳ μαθηταῖς ὅπως ἀποδέξωνται τὸν ἄνδρα· ⊢ Western, D syr.hl.mg.

xix 1,2 Ἐγένετο...εἶπέν τε] ⊣ Θέλοντος δὲ τοῦ Παύλου κατὰ τὴν ἰδίαν βουλὴν πορεύεσθαι εἰς Ἱεροσόλυμα εἶπεν αὐτῷ τὸ πνεῦμα ὑποστρέφειν εἰς τὴν Ἀσίαν· διελθὼν δὲ τὰ ἀνωτερικὰ μέρη ἔρχεται εἰς Ἔφεσον, καὶ εὑρών τινας μαθητὰς εἶπεν ⊢ Western, D syr. hl.mg : the Syrian text (Gr. Syr.) adopts the last five words.

xix 9 Τυράννου]+⊣ ἀπὸ ὥρας ε̄ ἕως δεκάτης ⊢ Western, D 137 syr.hl. mg.

xix 28 θυμοῦ]+ ⊣ δραμόντες εἰς τὸ ἄμφοδον ⊢ Western, D (137) syr.hl. mg.

xix 40 (†) περὶ τῆς σήμερον...ταύτης] < περὶ τῆς 1° Western, D *g* aeth. Also < οὐ Western (? and Alexandrian), DE₂ cu^mu *g* vg me the : text ℵABH₂L₂P₂ cu^pm (61 is defective) *seld* syr aeth arm. Also <περὶ 3° Western and Syrian (Gr. Lat. [? Syr.Eg.]) : text ℵABE₂ cu^14 *d g* (? aeth arm). Οὐ might be easily either added or lost after οὖ; but the plausible omission of οὐ, adopted from the Latin by Erasmus and the 'Received Text', though not found in the Syrian text, escapes the difficulty of construction only by giving a forced sense to αἰτίου...περὶ οὖ. [The difficulty is however too great to allow acquiescence in any of the transmitted texts as free from error. Probably αἴτιοι ὑπάρχοντες should be read for αἰτίου ὑπάρχοντος, with the construction μηδενὸς αἴτιοι ὑπάρχοντες περὶ οὖ οὐ κ.τ.λ. ('although we are guilty of nothing concerning which' &c.). The usage of the N.T. admits this use of μή with a participle, and the interchanges of Ι and Υ, ϵ and Ο, in uncials are of the commonest. H.]

xx 4 αὐτῷ]+⊣ ἀχρὶ τῆς Ἀσίας ⊢ Western and Syrian (Gr. Lat. Syr.

Arm.). Text אB 13 (61 is defective) lat.vg me the aeth.

ibid. 'Ασιανοί] 'Εφέσιοι Western, D the; not *g*: syr.hl.mg combines both readings.

xx 15 τῇ δὲ] ⊣ καὶ μείναντες ἐν Τρωγυλίῳ τῇ ⊢ Western and Syrian (Gr. Lat. Syr. Eg.): many of the later Greek documents have Τρωγυλλίῳ. Text אABCE₂ cu⁸ lat.vg me aeth arm.

xx 18 πῶς...ἐγενόμην] ὡς τριετίαν ἢ καὶ πλεῖον ποταπῶς μεθ' ὑμῶν ἦν παντὸς χρόνου D.

xx 28 (†) θεοῦ...ἰδίου] κυρίου (for θεοῦ) AC*DE₂ 13 15 36* 40 69 95* 110 130 180 al⁶ *g* me the syr.hl.mg arm Iren.lat Ath(probably) Did pp^ser Lucif auct. *Quaest* Hier (? Amb): κυρίου καὶ θεοῦ Constantinopolitan (Gr.): χριστοῦ (? syr.vg) aeth(probably) pp; *Jesu Christi m.* Text אB 68 lt 12 al¹² (61 is defective) lat. vg syr.vg(probably)-hl.txt Epiph Bas (Const. Ap, see below) Th.mops. 1 *Ti.*gr.lat Cyr.al. *Deip* pp^ser (? Amb) pp^lat.ser.

It is impossible to examine here the documentary evidence in detail: much of it is obscure and uncertain. Much has been done towards a rigorous sifting of it by Dr Ezra Abbot in an elaborate article in defence of τ. κυρίου, contributed to the *Bibliotheca Sacra* for 1876, pp. 313 ff., where will also be found an account of the variations of Syriac and Æthiopic MSS on Dr Wright's authority. Unfortunately no certified patristic evidence is extant for the Ante-Nicene period; and the controversial purposes which the passage might naturally serve were not such as would justify inferences from the silence of extant writers. It is probable however that Iren had the same reading as Iren.lat. The documentary evidence for κυρίου is very good and various. On the other hand the combination אB,

further supported by lat.vg, which in Acts exhibits a singularly good text in its Non-Western readings, and by Cyr.al, is a group which by Internal Evidence of Groups deserves all confidence in the absence of strong adverse Transcriptional or Intrinsic evidence.

Transcriptional evidence is in our opinion more favourable than unfavourable to τοῦ θεοῦ: although even in early times, and much more about the fifth century, there were some to whom the immediate association of τ. θεοῦ with what follows would not be repellent and might even be attractive, this was by no means the case with the main body of the Church. The prevalent instinct, as far as we can judge, would always be to change τ. θεοῦ to τ. κυρίου, and not *vice versa:* the fear of sanctioning language that might easily be construed in a 'Monarchian' or, in later times, a 'Monophysite' sense would outweigh any other doctrinal impulse. Some are seen to have avoided the difficulty by giving a special force to τοῦ ἰδίου (see below); and some whose interpretation is unknown probably did the same: but the other interpretation suggested itself so easily that it would naturally act as a motive for the preference of the safer phrase τ. κυρίου. No similar difficulty would be found in the conflate reading (and mediating phrase) τ. κυρίου καὶ θεοῦ, which naturally found favour in the Church of Constantinople, the special depositary of Chalcedonian doctrine. It is doubtless possible that τ. θεοῦ might arise from recollection of the familiar apostolic phrase ἡ ἐκκλησία τ. θεοῦ, if the subsequent language were overlooked: but this is the less probable contingency. The existence of the variant τ. χριστοῦ may be left out of account altogether, as it might with equal facility be a synonym of τ. κυρίου or an independent means of escaping from the difficulty of τ. θεοῦ.

This difficulty must itself be counted as Intrinsic evidence against τ. θεοῦ. On the other hand important Intrinsic evidence in its favour is supplied by the manifest derivation of the peculiar combination of τὴν ἐκκλησίαν with περιεποιήσατο (*adquisivit* latt) from Ps lxxiv 2 (the LXX rendering τῆς συναγωγῆς σου ἧς ἐκτήσω [*congregationis tuae quam adquisisti* Cod.germ] gives nearly the same sense), following on τῷ ποιμνίῳ ('the sheep of Thy pasture' Ps lxxiv 1); and by the consequent probability that the subject of περιεποιήσατο would be the same in both places.

[While however τ. θεοῦ is assuredly genuine, the difficulty suggests a possibility of corruption in the following words. The supposition that by the precise designation τοῦ θεοῦ, standing alone as it does here, with the article and without any adjunct, St Paul (or St Luke) meant Christ is unsupported by any analogies of language. The converse supposition, that, while τοῦ θεοῦ retains its ordinary sense, the passage implicitly contains the purport of the phrase τοῦ αἵματος τοῦ θεοῦ, though illustrated and to a certain extent supported by isolated rhetorical phrases of two or three early writers, is equally at variance with apostolic analogy.

Doubt is moreover thrown on both these interpretations by the remarkable form διὰ τοῦ αἵματος τοῦ ἰδίου (not, as in the Syrian text, διὰ τοῦ ἰδίου αἵματος), which seems to imply some peculiar force lying in the word ἰδίου. On the supposition that the text is incorrupt, such a force would be given by the sense 'through the blood that was His

own', *i.e.* as being His Son's. This conception of the death of Christ as a price paid by the Father is in strict accordance with St Paul's own language elsewhere (Ro v 8; viii 32). It finds repeated expression in the Apostolic Constitutions in language evidently founded on this passage (ii 57 13; 61 4; vii 26 1; viii [11 2;] 12 18; 41 4). All these places contain a prayer addressed to God for His Church (or heritage, or people), ἣν περιεποιήσω τῷ τιμίῳ αἵματι τοῦ χριστοῦ σου (or with some almost identical phrase, always including τιμίῳ from 1 Pe i 19); so that, though MSS differ as to τ. θεοῦ or τ. κυρίου in the only place where either phrase occurs (ii 61 4), the language used throughout presumes τ. θεοῦ on the one hand and an interpretation agreeing with the supposed special force of τοῦ ἰδίου on the other. One of these passages, from the liturgy in Book VIII (12 18 "Ετι δεόμεθά σου, κύριε, καὶ ὑπὲρ τῆς ἁγίας σου ἐκκλησίας τῆς ἀπὸ περάτων ἕως περάτων, ἣν περιεποιήσω τῷ τιμίῳ αἵματι τοῦ χριστοῦ σου,...καὶ ὑπὲρ πάσης ἐπισκοπῆς τῆς ὀρθοτομούσης τὸν λόγον τῆς ἀληθείας) has indirectly made the same interpretation familiar to English ears; being imitated in one of the Ember Collects of 1662 ("who hast purchased to Thyself an universal Church by the precious blood of Thy dear Son").

It is however true that this general sense, if indicated, is not sufficiently expressed in the text as it stands. A suggestion often made, that τ. ἰδίου is equivalent to τ. ἰδίου υἱοῦ, cannot be justified by Greek usage. Since however the text of the Acts is apparently corrupt in several other places, it is by no means impossible that ΥΙΟΥ dropped out after ΤΟΥΙΔΙΟΥ at some very early transcription affecting all existing documents. Its insertion leaves the whole passage free from difficulty of any kind. H.]

xxi 1 Πάταρα] + ἢ καὶ Μύρα ⊢ Western, D (*g*) codd.lat the.

xxi 16 ξενισθῶμεν] + καὶ παραγενόμενοι εἴς τινα κώμην ἐγενόμεθα παρὰ Western, D syr.hl.mg.

ibid. Μνάσωνι] Ἰάσονι ℵ *g dem seld* al me.

xxiii 15 ἀνελεῖν αὐτόν] +, ἐὰν δέῃ καὶ ἀποθανεῖν Western, 137 syr.hl. mg; not *g* (Lucif): D is defective here, and to the end of the book.

xxiii 23 ἑβδομήκοντα] ἑκατὸν Western, 137 syr.hl.mg the aeth.cod: XX (doubtless error for LXX) *g*.

xxiii 24 *fin.*] + ἐφοβήθη γὰρ μήποτε ἁρπάσαντες αὐτὸν οἱ Ἰουδαῖοι ἀποκτένωσι [? -είνωσι], καὶ αὐτὸς μεταξὺ ἔγκλημα ἔχῃ ὡς ἀργύριον εἰληφώς. Western, 137 codd.lat syr.hl.*; not *g*.

xxiii 29 ἔγκλημα] + ἐξήγαγον αὐτὸν μόλις τῇ βίᾳ Western, 137 (*g*) syr.hl.*.

xxiv 6 ἐκρατήσαμεν,] + καὶ κατὰ τὸν ἡμέτερον νόμον ἠθελήσαμεν (*v.* ἐβουλήθημεν) κρῖναι. (v. 7) Παρελθὼν δὲ Λυσίας ὁ χιλίαρχος μετὰ πολλῆς βίας ἐκ τῶν χειρῶν ἡμῶν ἀπήγαγεν, (v. 8) κελεύσας τοὺς κατηγόρους αὐτοῦ ἔρχεσθαι ἐπί (*v.* πρός) σε· Western and (with κρῖναι changed to κρίνειν, and καὶ πρὸς σε ἀπέστειλεν probably inserted after ἀπήγαγεν) Syrian (Gr. Lat. Syr. Æth. [? Arm.]) incl. E₂. Text ℵABH₃L₂P₂ cu^mu lat.vg.codd. opt me the; also, to judge by the space, C, which has lost a leaf here.

xxiv 27 θέλων...δεδεμένον] τὸν δὲ Παῦλον εἴασεν ἐν τηρήσει διὰ Δρούσιλλαν Western, 137 syr.hl.mg; not *g*.

xxv 13 (†) ἀσπασάμενοι] ἀσπασόμενοι (?? Western and) Syrian (Gr. Lat. Syr. Arm.); incl. 61. Text ℵABE₂H₂L₂P₂ 13 31 68 95 102 105

180 al^mu me aeth. [The authority for -άμενοι is absolutely overwhelming, and as a matter of transmission -όμενοι can be only a correction. Yet it is difficult to remain satisfied that there is no prior corruption of some kind. H.]

xxvi 28 (†) ποιῆσαι] γενέσθαι (? Western and) Syrian (Gr. Lat. Syr. [? Æth.] [? Arm.]); incl. E₂. Cyr.hr. Text ℵ(A)B 61 13 17 40 me (? aeth) syr.hl.mg (Cassiod). Both authority and the impossibility of accounting for ποιῆσαι as a correction leave no doubt that γενέσθαι (from v. 29) was introduced to remove a felt difficulty. There must however be some error in text, for ποιῆσαι used epexegetically in the sense of ὥστε ποιῆσαι gives Agrippa's abrupt exclamation a languid and halting form, and the absence of a second με throws doubt on the construction. The difficulty is somewhat lightened by reading ΠΕΙΘΗ for ΠΕΙΘΕΙC with A. [Yet πείθῃ can hardly be equivalent to πέποιθας or to πείθεις σεαυτόν, as the sense requires; more especially since πείθομαι has been used in the sense 'am persuaded', 'believe', just before (v. 26). Possibly ΠΕΠΟΙΘΑC should be read for ΜΕΠΕΙΘΕΙC, for the personal reference expressed by με loses no force by being left to implication, and the changes of letters are inconsiderable: but it is no less possible that the error lies elsewhere. H.]

xxvii 5 διαπλεύσαντες] + ⊣ δι' ἡμερῶν δεκάπεντε ⊢ Western, 112 137 syr.hl.*; not *g*.

xxvii 15 ἐπιδόντες] + τῷ πλέοντι καὶ συστείλαντες τὰ ἱστία Western, 44 112 137 codd.lat syr.hl.*; not *g*.

xxvii 35 ἐσθίειν] + ἐπιδιδοὺς καὶ ἡμῖν Western, 137 the syr.hl.*; not *g*.

xxviii 16 ἐπετράπη τῷ Παύλῳ] ╡ ὁ
ἑκατόνταρχος παρέδωκεν τοὺς δε-
σμίους τῷ στρατοπεδάρχῳ, τῷ δὲ
Παύλῳ ἐπετράπη ├ Western and Syrian (Gr. Lat.[*g*] Syr.[hl.*] Æth.).
Text ℵABI_d 13(vdtr) 40 61 lt 12 lat.
vg syr.vg-hl.txt me arm Chr.

ibid. ἑαυτὸν] + ╡ ἔξω τῆς παρεμ-
βολῆς ├ Western, 137 *g dem* syr. hl.*.

xxviii 28 *fin.*] + (v. 29) καὶ ταῦτα
αὐτοῦ εἰπόντος ἀπῆλθον οἱ Ἰουδαῖοι,
πολλὴν ἔχοντες ἐν ἑαυτοῖς ζήτησιν
(v. συζήτησιν) Western and Syrian
(Gr. Lat. Syr.[hl.*] [Æth.]). Text
ℵABE_2 61 13 40 68 *s* lat.vg syr.
vg-hl.txt me arm aeth.cod.

I PETER

i 7 (†) τὸ δοκίμιον] τὸ δόκιμον 23 69 110 al. [This reading, supported by two of the better cursives (69 110) but by no primary document, is apparently right. Τὸ δοκίμιον is the instrument of trial, not even the process of trial, much less the thing tried; while it is only the thing tried that can be compared, as here, to gold refined in the fire. The neuter adjective might naturally be changed to a substantive, and that the substantive used in the similar passage Ja i 3; and I might easily be read in after M. H.]

iii 21 (†) ὅ] ᾧ cuᵖ; conjectured by Erasmus in the note to his first edition; printed in the Complutensian text (ᾧ ἀντίτυπον νῦν καὶ ἡμᾶς), probably by conjecture; and thence adopted by Beza; < ὅ ℵ* 73 aeth. [The order of the words renders it impossible to take ἀντίτυπον with βάπτισμα, whether in apposition to ὅ or to the sentence; and it is hardly less difficult to take ἀντίτυπον with ὅ, as though it were either ἀντίτυπον ὄν or ἀντιτύπως. Accordingly ὅ seems to be a primitive error for ᾧ, the force of which might be hidden by the interposition of καὶ ὑμᾶς before ἀντίτυπον: this deviation from the more obvious order is justified by the emphasis on καὶ ὑμᾶς. Both by sight and by sound the interchange of letters would be easy. H.]

iii 22 θεοῦ] +*deglutiens mortem ut vitae aeternae haeredes efficeremur* lat.vg.codd ppᵃᵗ; apparently from a Greek original which had the aor. part. καταπιών (cf. I Co xv 54).

iv 14 δόξης]+καὶ δυνάμεως Pre-Syrian (? Western and Alexandrian) (Gr. Lat. Syr. Eg. Æth. Arm.); incl. (ℵ) AP₂ cuᵇᵒ·ᵐᵘ (Ath Did) Cyp. 2/2; with various modifications, as the omission of καὶ τό (cuᵇᵒ vvᵐᵘ Cyp), and the insertion of ὄνομα for or in combination with πνεῦμα (cuᵒᵖᵗ syr.hl Cyp). Text, which is also Syrian, BK₂L₂ cuᵖᵐ (lat.vg syr.vg) Clem Cyr.al.*Un.Chr.*753 ppˢᵉʳ Tert Fulg: < καὶ lat.vg syr.vg.

ibid. fin.]+κατὰ μὲν αὐτοὺς βλασφημεῖται, κατὰ δὲ ὑμᾶς δοξάζεται Western and Syrian (Gr. Lat. Syr. [hl*] Eg.[the] ; incl. Cyp.2/2. It is to be observed that lat.codd Cyp² prefix *quod*, agreeing in Cyp with *nomen*, and this was probably the original form of the reading (cf. v. 16; Ro ii 24; Ja ii 7 : Ap xiii 6; xvi 9), intended as an explanation of the phrase τὸ...ὄνομα ἐφ᾽ ὑμᾶς ἀναπαύεται.

v 2 θεοῦ,]+ἐπισκοποῦντες Pre-Syrian (? Western and Alexandrian) and Syrian (Gr. Lat. Syr. Eg. Æth. Arm.); incl. ℵᶜAP₂ *m q*. Text ℵB 27 29 ppᵍʳ·² Hier 'Vig'.

ibid. ἑκουσίως]+κατὰ θεόν Pre-Syrian (Western and Alexandrian) (Gr. Lat. Syr. Eg. Æth. Arm.); incl. ℵAP₂ cuᵇᵒ·ᵐᵘ (*m*) *q* : in the paraphrastic rendering of *m* it is included in a phrase added at the end of v. 3. Text, which is also Syrian, BK₂L₂ cuᵖᵐ syr.vg 'Vig'.

2 PETER

i 10 σπουδάσατε] +ἵνα διὰ τῶν καλῶν [ὑμῶν] ἔργων and ποιεῖσθε (-ῆσθε) for ποιεῖσθαι Pre-Constantinopolitan, probably Alexandrian, (Gr. Lat. Syr. Eg. Æth. Arm.); incl. ℵA 5 36 68 69 73 110 112 137 alᵖ: *q* is defective from i 4 to the end of the Epistle. Text, which is also Constantinopolitan, BCP₂K₂L₂ cuᵖᵐ ppˢᵉʳ Amb.

iii 10 (†) εὑρεθήσεται] οὐχ εὑρεθήσεται syr.bod[=an obscure Syriac version of the three Catholic Epistles not in the Syrian Canon] theb: κατακαήσεται (? Alexandrian and) Constantinopolitan (Gr. Lat. Syr. Eg. Æth.); incl. AL₂ lat.vg.codd Cyr.al

Aug: ἀφανισθήσονται C: < *m*: < the whole clause (καὶ γῆ...κατακ.) lat.vg ppˢᵉʳ pplat.ser. Text ℵBK₂P₂ 27 29 66** syr.hl.mg arm: cf. syr.bod the. The great difficulty of text has evidently given rise to all these variations (*Introd.* § 365). It is doubtless itself a corruption of ῥυήσεται (ῥεύσεται) or of one of its compounds.

iii 12 (†) τήκεται] τακήσεται C 36 40 100 137 alᵖ: -σονται P₂ Thphl; future lat.vg syr.bod arm pplat. [Τακήσεται, -ονται, are evidently mere corrections: but the sense appears to require a future, and τήκεται might easily be a corruption of the rare τήξεται. H.]

1 JOHN

ii 17 αἰῶνα]+*quomodo* [*et*] *ille manet in aeternum* Western, (the) Cyp²; also, with *Deus* for *ille*, tol Cyp³ Lucif Aug Vict.tun.

v 6 καὶ αἵματος]+καὶ πνεύματος Western and Alexandrian (Gr. Lat. Syr.[hl] Eg.); incl. ℵA cubo·mu Cyr. al¹: +καὶ πνεύματος καὶ αἵματος P₂ cu³ aeth arm: cu³ Cyr.al¹ substitute πνεύματος for αἵματος. Text BK₂L₂ cuᵖᵐ *q* vg syr.vg Cyr.al² ppˢᵉʳ Tert auct.*Rebapt.* 15.

ibid. τὸ πνεῦμα] ¡*Christus* lat.vg (also 34=cod.Montfort., from lat.vg); not *m q*. The reading has apparently no Greek authority, nor that of any version but lat.vg: it is perhaps only a clerical error, X̅P̅S̅ for S̅P̅S̅, though Jo xiv 6 may have helped to give it currency.

v 7 f. τὸ πνεῦμα καὶ τὸ ὕδωρ καὶ τὸ αἷμα] *in terra, spiritus* [*et*] *aqua et sanguis, et hi tres unum sunt in Christo Jesu: et tres sunt qui testimonium dicunt in caelo, Pater Verbum et Spiritus   m tol cav*; also, omitting *in Christo Jesu*, and reading *sicut* [*et*] *tres* for *et tres*, various MSS of vg.lat, with slight variations, as *dant* for *dicunt*. In *q*, which has lost nearly half of each line, *unum...tres* seems to have dropped out by *homoeoteleuton*, leaving the presence or absence of *in Christo Jesu* uncertain; the only other differences from *m* are *et aqua* and (with Cassiod Epiph.*Cant*) *testificantur*. The later MSS of lat.vg transpose the clauses, reading *in caelo, Pater Verbum et Spiritus Sanctus, et hi tres unum sunt: et tres sunt qui testimonium dant in terra, spiritus et aqua et sanguis,* many of them omitting the clause which ends v. 8, *et hi tres unum sunt.* Two late Greek cursives contain the interpolation in forms which are manifestly translations from this latest state of the Latin Vulgate, 162 (about Cent. XV), a Græco-Latin MS, and 34 (Cent. XVI). In fulfilment of a rashly given pledge, Erasmus introduced it into the text of his third edition on the authority of 34, keeping however the genuine καὶ οἱ τρεῖς εἰς τὸ ἕν εἰσιν at the end of v. 8. Various crudities of language were subsequently corrected, partly by the help of the Complutensian text, which was a third independent rendering of the Latin Vulgate into Greek; till at length, by editorial retouching without manuscript authority, the interpolation assumed the form which it bears in the 'Received Text', ἐν τῷ οὐρανῷ, ὁ πατήρ, ὁ λόγος, καὶ τὸ ἅγιον πνεῦμα, καὶ οὗτοι οἱ τρεῖς ἕν εἰσι· καὶ τρεῖς εἰσιν οἱ μαρτυροῦντες ἐν τῇ γῇ. followed by τὸ πνεῦμα καὶ τὸ ὕδωρ καὶ τὸ αἷμα.

There is no evidence for the inserted words in Greek, or in any language but Latin, before Cent. XIV, when they appear in a Greek work written in defence of the Roman communion, with clear marks of translation from the Vulgate. For at least the first four centuries and a half Latin evidence is equally wanting. Tert and Cyp use language which renders it morally certain that they would have quoted these words had they known them; Cyp going so far as to assume a reference to the Trinity in the conclusion of v. 8 (*et iterum de Patre et Filio et Spiritu Sancto scriptum est* Et tres unum sunt), as he elsewhere finds *sacramenta Trinitatis* in other occurrences of the

number three (*Dom.Orat.*34), and being followed in his interpretation more explicitly by Aug, Facundus, and others. But the evidence of Cent. III is not exclusively negative, for the treatise on Rebaptism contemporary with Cyp quotes the whole passage simply thus (15 : cf. 19), *quia tres testimonium perhibent, spiritus et aqua et sanguis, et isti tres unum sunt.* The silence of the controversial writings of Lucif Hil Amb Hier Aug and others carries forward the adverse testimony of the Old Latin through the fourth into the fifth century ; and in 449, shortly before the Council of Chalcedon, Leo supplies positive evidence to the same effect for the Roman text by quoting vv. 4—8 without the inserted words in his epistle to Flavianus (*Ep.* xxviii 5). They are absent from lat.vg according to its oldest MSS *am fu* and many others, as also from the (Vulgate) text of the Gallican (Luxeuil) Lectionary.

The words first occur at earliest in the latter part of Cent. V, that is, about the time of the persecution in N. Africa by the Arian Vandals. They are quoted in part in two of the works attributed on slender grounds to Vigilius of Thapsus (one of which has the whole passage, with the curious variations *in terra, aqua sanguis et caro, et tres in nobis sunt*), and in an argumentative *libellus* found in the MSS of the History of Victor of Vita (written about 484), and professing to be a memorial presented in 483, but now justly suspected of being a different work, inserted afterwards (Halm p. 26, referring also to Papencordt). The conventional date of this obscure and as yet unsifted group of controversial writings rests on little evidence, but it is probably not far from the truth. At all events a quotation of some of the disputed words occurs early in Cent. VI in another North African work, written by Fulgentius of Ruspe; and soon after the middle of Cent. VI they stand paraphrased in the *Complexiones* of Cassiodorius, written in the southern extremity of Italy. A prologue to the Catholic Epistles, falsely professing to be written by Jerome, impugns the fidelity of Latin translators, accusing them especially of having placed in their text the 'three words' *aquae sanguinis et spiritus* only, and omitted *Patris et Filii et Spiritus testimonium*. This extraordinary production is found in the Fulda MS written at Capua in 546,7 (E. Ranke in his ed. p. viii), the biblical text of which is free from the interpolation, as well as in many later MSS, and probably belongs to the Vigilian period and literature. Even after Cent. VI the references to the inserted words are few till Cent. XI.

The two Old Latin MSS in which they are extant have texts of a distinctly late type : they are *q*, of Cent. VI or VII (Ziegler) and *m*, of Cent. VIII or IX (Tregelles, Reifferscheid, Hartel), *m* being in strictness only an arranged collection of quotations from an Old Latin MS. A MS like that which supplied *m* with its text must have contributed the foreign element to the common ancestor of the Toledo and La Cava Vulgate MSS; and it is remarkable that *m* quotes the spurious Ep. of St Paul to the Laodicenes, which is included in both these copies of the Vulgate.

These two interesting MSS likewise illustrate the manner in which the interpolation probably arose. After v. 9 *tol* adds these words, *quem misit salvatorem super terram, et Filius testimonium perhibuit in terra scripturas perficiens : et nos*

testimonium perhibemus quoniam vidimus eum, et annuntiamus vobis ut credatis ; et ideo qui &c. : and in v. 20 after *venit* they both add (with *m*, two London MSS cited by Bentley, and virtually Hil) *et carnem induit nostri causa, et passus est, et resurrexit a mortuis, adsumpsit nos, et dedit* &c. Paraphrastic interpolations like these argue strange laxity of transcription, such as we find elsewhere in the quotations from the Catholic Epistles in *m*; but they do not imply deliberate bad faith : and the interpolation of vv. 7, 8 doubtless seemed to its author merely to place explicitly before future readers an interpretation which he honestly supposed to give the true sense of the passage, as it had been indicated by Cyprian and expounded by Cyprian's successors. This interpretation was the more plausible since the Latin text did not contain the significant εἰς of the original (omitted likewise by Cyr.al and apparently others), which probably was early lost after τρεῖς; and it is no wonder that controversial associations should lead Latin readers to assume such words as *et tres unum sunt* to contain a reference to the Trinity. Even in Greek there are traces of a similar interpretation : one scholiast writes εἷς θεός, μία θεότης in the margin of v. 8; and another first explains the spirit, water, and blood, and then adds ΟΙ ΤΡΕΙΣ δὲ εἶπεν ἀρσενικῶς, ὅτι σύμβολα ταῦτα τῆς τριάδος κ.τ.λ.

The adverse testimony of Greek MSS and of all the oriental versions is supported by the silence of all the Greek Fathers ; and positive evidence is added by Cyr.al, who three times transcribes vv. 7, 8 with the context (*Thes.* 363; *Fid.* 95 ; *Nest.* 143).

The most essential facts as to the history of the reading were well set forth by Simon in 1689 (*Hist. Crit. du texte du N. T.* 203 ff.). The evidence as enlarged by Mill and Wetstein was rigorously examined by Porson (*Letters to Travis*) in 1790; and admirably expounded afresh in a more judicial spirit by Griesbach in his second edition (ii App. 1—25) in 1806. Three new and interesting testimonies on behalf of the inserted words have subsequently come to light, those of *m* in 1832, of *q* in 1875, and of the occurrence of the Pseudo-Hieronymic Prologue in *fu* in 1868. They all however leave

unaffected the limit of date which was indicated by Simon and fixed by Porson.

v 10 (†) τῷ θεῷ] τῷ υἱῷ Λ 5 27 29 66** 112 al bo.p lat.vg syr.hl.mg (the aeth arm) Cyr.al.*Fid.*33codd : *Jesu Christo m* : < *am**.   Text ℵBK₂L₂P₂ cuᵖᵐ *q* syr.vg-hl.txt me Cyr.al.³ᵛ·⁴ ppˢᵉʳ Aug 'Vig'.   None of the datives yield a good sense in this context; and it is probable that ὁ μὴ πιστεύων should stand absolutely, as in Jo iii 18 : cf. Jo vi 47 *v. l.*

2 JOHN

11 πονηροῖς] + *ecce praedixi vobis ut in diem* (v. *die*) *domini* [*nostri Jesu Christi*] *non confundamini*

(v. *ne in diem domini condemnemini*) (*m*) lat.vg.codd.

JUDE

1 (†) ἐν θεῷ πατρὶ ἠγαπημένοις καὶ Ἰησοῦ Χριστῷ τετηρημένοις] τοῖς ἔθνεσιν is prefixed by 27 29 (66**) syr.bod-hl arm: ἡγιασμένοις (for ἠγαπημένοις) Constantinopolitan (Gr.): Ἰ. Χριστοῦ 40 180 al mu Orig. *Mt.*gr ppˢᵉʳ; ἐν Ἰ. Χριστῷ *m* vg.codd syr.bod the aeth Orig.*Mt.*lat Lucif Cassiod: < καὶ...τετηρ. 163 syr.hl. Text ℵAB cuᵖ lat.vg me Aug. [The combination ἐν θεῷ πατρὶ ἠγαπημένοις is without analogy, and admits no natural interpretation. Apparently the ἐν was intended to stand before Ἰησοῦ Χριστῷ (so in part J. Price [Pricæus]). H.]

5 (†) πάντα] πάντας syr.bod: τοῦτο Constantinopolitan (Gr. Eg.[the]). [Possibly πάντας may be right (cf. 1 Jo ii 20 *v.l.*): C would easily be lost before O. H.]

5 (†) Κύριος] Ἰησοῦς AB 6 7 13 29 66** lat.vg me the aeth Did.*Ps*² (expressly: lxv 6; cxxxv 10) Cyr.al. *Thes.*302(expressly) Hier(expressly) (? Cassiod): ὁ θεὸς Cᵃ 68 al² *tol* syr.bod arm Clem Lucif (*Dominus Deus* Clem.*Hyp.*lat.).   Text ℵC*ᵛᵈᵗʳ (syr.hl) and, with ὁ prefixed, Constantinopolitan (Gr. ? Syr.).   The best attested reading Ἰησοῦς can only be a blunder.   It seems probable that the original text had only ὁ, and that OTIO was read as OTIIC and perhaps as OTIKC.

6. δεσμοῖς ἀϊδίοις] + ἁγίων ἀγγέλων (Clem.*Paed*(ἀγρίων ἀγγ. *s.q.*) *m* Lucif (all apparently in connexion with ὑπὸ ζόφον); not Clem.*Hyp.*lat Orig Cyr.al Hier.

22, 23 (†) οὓς μὲν ἐλεᾶτε διακρινομένους σώζετε ἐκ πυρὸς ἁρπάζοντες, οὓς δὲ ἐλεᾶτε ἐν φόβῳ] οὓς μὲν ἐλέγχετε διακρινομένους, οὓς δὲ σώζετε κ.τ.λ. A 5 6 13 27 29 66** alᵖ lat.vg me aeth arm 'Ephr'; also (omitting οὓς δὲ ἐλεᾶτε) C*: as text with οὓς δέ inserted after διακρινομένους א; also (omitting οὓς δὲ ἐλεᾶτε) Cᵃ syr.hl: οὓς μὲν σώζετε ἐκ πυρὸς ἁρπάζοντες, οὓς δὲ [διακρινομένους] ἐλεεῖτε ἐν φόβῳ approximately syr.bod Clem.*Strom*;*Hyp*.lat Hier: οὓς μὲν ἐλεεῖτε διακρινόμενοι, οὓς δὲ ἐν φόβῳ σώζετε ἐκ πυρὸς ἁρπάζοντες Constantinopolitan (Gr.). There are other variations.   Text B. The smooth reading of A &c. has every appearance of being a correction of the difficult double ἐλεᾶτε

of א and B; and the intermediate reading of א is intrinsically improbable, and may easily be due to conflation. The triple division found in both these readings gives no satisfactory sense; and two clauses only are recognised by BC syr.bod-hl Clem.*Strom* ;*Hyp*.lat Hier, as well as by the artificial Constantinopolitan text. The reading of B involves the incongruity that the first οὓς must be taken as a relative, and the first ἐλεᾶτε as indicative. Some primitive error evidently affects the passage. Perhaps the first ἐλεᾶτε, which is not represented in syr.bod Clem Hier, is intrusive, and was inserted mechanically from the second clause.

ROMANS

i 7 ἐν Ῥώμῃ and v. 15 τοῖς ἐν Ῥώμῃ] < G₃ (anon, see below); not D₂ in v. 15 or d (D₂ being defective) in v. 7, or Orig.loc.lat.Ruf(text and comm) Amb Ambst in either place, or Orig.Jo; Num.lat.Ruf Aug in v. 7. The second rendering of τοῖς οὖσιν by g in v. 7 is substantibus, resembling subsistentibus in Eph i 1. A scholium on v. 7 in 47 states that "he [or it] mentions ἐν Ῥώμῃ neither in the exposition nor in the text": the reference is probably to what is called "the old copy" in another scholium in 47 on viii 24, perhaps a late uncial copy with a marginal commentary, like Ξ of the Gospels.

i 32 (†) ποιοῦσιν...συνευδοκοῦσιν] ποιοῦντες ... συνευδοκοῦντες B, and (with οἱ prefixed in both places) lat. vg.codd and apparently 'some' who appealed for the reading to "the ancient copy" according to Isid.pel, also (Clem.rom.) Epiph ('Ephr') Orig.loc.lat.Ruf² Lucif pplat; not Cyp.codd.opt Ambst: the Latins however (with D₂ Bas. 1/2) insert οὐκ ἐνόησαν before ὅτι. This reading is perhaps due to assimilation with οἱ...πράσσοντες: but text seems to involve an anticlimax, and probably contains some corruption. The change from ποιοῦσιν to πράσσουσιν suggests that συνευδοκοῦσιν τοῖς [or συνευδοκοῦσιν only (W.)] may have arisen from συνευδοκοῦντες.

iii 22 εἰς πάντας] + καὶ ἐπὶ πάντας Western and Syrian (Gr. Lat. Syr.); incl. Orig.loc.lat.Ruf(text) Did.Trin. Text ℵ*ABCP₂ 47 67** 137 me aeth arm Clem Orig.Ps; Rom.lat. Ruf³ Did.Ps. Cyr.al² Aug. For text lat.vg.codd.opt Dam substitute ἐπὶ πάντας: and this may be an early

reading which contributed to the common reading by conflation.

iii 26 Ἰησοῦ] < G₃ 52 : + χριστοῦ lat.vg.codd me (syr.vg) Orig.loc.lat. Ruf(text) pplat : Ἰησοῦν D₂L₂ cumu Clem, by an easy clerical error.

iv 12 (†) ἀλλὰ καὶ τοῖς στοιχοῦσιν] [Text implies that the persons intended are distinct from οἱ ἐκ περιτομῆς, whereas the context (v. 11) shews that they are a class of οἱ ἐκ περιτομῆς. Apparently καὶ τοῖς is a corruption of καὶ αὐτοῖς, ΚΑΙΤΟΙΣ for ΚΑΙΑΥΤΟΙΣ, or, as Mr VanSittart suggests, for ΚΑΥΤΟΙΣ. The difficulty was noticed by Beza, who suggested either the transposition of τοῖς and καί or the omission of τοῖς. H.]

iv 19 κατενόησεν] οὐ κατενόησεν Western and Syrian (Gr. Lat. Syr.); incl. Orig.loc.lat.Ruf². Text ℵABC 67** 93 137 lat.vg.codd.opt syr.vg me aeth arm Orig.Gen.lat.Ruf Meth.cod.opt(ap. Epiph) Cyr. hr (v 5) Dam al.

v 6 (†) εἴ γε] ἔτι γὰρ, with ἔτι below, ℵ*ACD₂* 31 137 syr.pl Marcion (ap. Epiph) Dam; without a second ἔτι, Syrian (Gr. [Lat.] ? Arm.): εἰς τί γὰρ Western, D₂ᵇG₃ lat.vg Iren.lat pplat: εἰ γὰρ cu¹ fu* (cf. me) Isid.pel Aug: εἰ γὰρ ἔτι me: εἰ δὲ syr.vg. Text B. [Text gives a more probable sense than any of the other variants: but εἴ περ (cf. 2 Co v 3 v. l.; Ro iii 30; 2 Th i 6) would better explain all the variations, and be equally appropriate. H.]

v 14 τοὺς μὴ ἁμαρτήσαντας] < μὴ MSS known to Orig.loc.(Ruf) to Ambst and perhaps to Aug (see below) 67^{**} al³ (? d^*) "most Latin MSS" known to Aug   the older Latin MSS known to Ambst Orig. $\mathcal{J}o^{1\,v.\,2}$ Orig.*loc*.lat.Ruf(often and expressly) Ambst(expressly, and referring to Tert Victorin and Cyp as having the same: *s. q.*) Sedul(expressly).   Text $\aleph$ABCD₂G₃K₂L₂ "some [Greek] copies" known to Orig.Ruf Greek and Latin MSS known to Ambst and to Aug cu^pl lat.vg syrr me aeth arm Iren.lat [Orig.$\mathcal{J}o^1$ *s. q.*: cf. Griesbach *Opusc.* i 282 ff.] Archel.lat Cyr.hr Ath Cyr.al⁵ pp^mu Pelag Amb Aug Hier.

viii 1 Ἰησοῦ] + μὴ κατὰ σάρκα περιπατοῦσιν Western and Syrian (Gr. Lat. Syr. Goth. [? Arm.]); incl. *m* Victorin. Text $\aleph$*BCD₂ (G₃ by the space) 47 67^{**} al me the aeth arm. cod Orig.*loc*.lat.Ruf Adam Ath Cyr.al Aug.

Also + ἀλλὰ κατὰ πνεῦμα Constantinopolitan (Gr. Syr.[hl]). Text the same documents as above, and also AD₂^a 137 *m* vg syr.vg arm go Bas Chr Victorin Pelag Ambst Hier al.

Both additions are from v. 4.

viii 2 (†) σε] (marg.) με ACD₂ K₂L₂P₂ cu^omn lat.vg syr.hl the arm.codd go Clem Orig.*loc*.lat. Ruf.txt Ath Did⁶ Cyr.al² pp^al Tert.*Res*.cod: ἡμᾶς me aeth Adam. Text $\aleph$BG₃ *m* syr.vg Chr.codd Tert. *Res*.cod ;*Pud*. The distribution of documents, combined with internal evidence, favours the omission of both pronouns, which is supported by some MSS of arm and perhaps by Orig.*loc*.Ruf.com: σε, a very unlikely reading, is probably only an early repetition of –ce.

ix 5. The important variation in the punctuation of this verse belongs to interpretation, and not to textual criticism proper: but a few words on the alternative punctuations adopted

here may not be out of place. The oldest Greek MSS $\aleph$BA, as written by the original scribes, have no punctuation in the passage: C and some good cursives have a full stop after σάρκα. Versions are either ambiguous or imply a comma after σάρκα. This last construction is taken for granted by Iren Tert Cyp Novat, and in the Antiochene epistle to Paul of Samosata. On the other hand this treatment of all the words from καὶ ἐξ ὧν to αἰῶνας as 'a single clause' (μονοκώλως), when put forward by Noetus, was condemned by Hipp; his ground of objection being apparently the combination of ἐπὶ πάντων with θεός as favourable to Patripassianism: referring the concluding words to Christ, he nevertheless makes them a separate sentence having three affirmations,— οὗτος ὁ ὢν ἐπὶ πάντων is θεός, He is become (γεγένηται) θεὸς εὐλογητός He is εἰς τοὺς αἰῶνας (*Noet*. 3, 6). In Rufinus's Latin rendering of Orig.*loc*. the comma after σάρκα is taken for granted: but there is not a trace of Origenian language, and this is one of the places in which Rufinus would not fail to indulge his habit of altering an interpretation which he disapproved on doctrinal grounds. With this questionable exception, there is no evidence to shew what construction was adopted by Orig, or indeed by any Ante-Nicene Alexandrian writer: but it is difficult to impute Origen's silence to accident in the many passages in which quotation would have been natural had he followed the common interpretation. Eusebius is equally silent, probably for the same reason: his repeated use of ὁ ἐπὶ πάντων θεός as a name of the Father points in the same direction, though it is not conclusive. The Apostolic Constitutions and the interpolator of the Ignatian epistles (cf. Melito p. 413 Otto) still more emphatically distinguish ὁ ἐπὶ πάντων θεός from Christ, but do not notice this passage. With these two probable though not certain exceptions, the construction with a comma after σάρκα is found universally in Post-Nicene times in East and West alike. All these particulars however belong merely to the history of ancient interpretations, and have no textual authority.

The punctuation in the margin, [which alone seems adequate to account for the whole of the language employed, more especially when it is considered in relation to the context, (H.)] though it may be understood with more or less difficulty in other ways, is here taken as an expression of the interpretation which implies that special force was intended to be thrown on ἐπὶ πάντων by the interposition of ὤν. This emphatic sense of ἐπὶ πάντων (cf. i 16; ii 9 f.; iii 29 f.; x 12; xi 32, 36) is fully justified if St Paul's purpose is to suggest that the tragic apostasy of the Jews (vv. 2, 3) is itself part of the dispensations of "Him who is God over all", over Jew and Gentile alike, over past present and future alike; so that the ascription of blessing to Him is a homage to His Divine purpose and power of bringing good out of evil in the course of the ages (xi 13—16; 25—36). [Yet the juxta-position of ὁ χριστὸς κατὰ σάρκα and ὁ ὤν κ. τ. λ. seems to make a change of subject improbable. W.]

ix 28 συντέμνων]+ἐν δικαιοσύνῃ, ὅτι λόγον συντετμημένον Western and Syrian (Gr. Lat. Syr. Goth. Arm.); incl. Eus. D.E. 1/2(in part) Orig.loc. lat.Ruf. Text ℵ*AB 23* 47* 67** syr.vg me aeth Eus.Es.; D.E.1/2 Dam Aug. From Is x 22 f. LXX.

xi 6 χάρις.]+εἰ δὲ ἐξ ἔργων οὐ-

κέτι χάρις, ἐπεὶ τὸ ἔργον οὐκέτι ἐστὶν χάρις. B, and (with ἐστὶν added after οὐκέτι and with a second ἔργον for the second χάρις) Syrian (Gr. Syr.); incl. ℵᶜ: part is omitted in some cursives, but probably by homoeoteleuton. Text ℵ*ABCD₂G₃ 47 lat.vg me the (aeth) arm Orig.loc.lat.Ruf (? Cyr.al) Dam pp^lat.

xii 11 κυρίῳ] καιρῷ Western (Gr. Lat.). Perhaps a clerical error only, but probably supported by a sense of the difficulty of the position of so comprehensive a clause as τῷ κυρίῳ δουλεύοντες in the midst of a series of clauses of limited sense.

xii 13 χρείαις] μνείαις Western (Gr. Lat.) ; incl. 'some copies' known to Theod.mops. Probably a clerical error, due to the hasty reading of an ill written MS (ΧΡ being liable to become somewhat like a ligature of Μ with Ν), but yielding a passable sense (cf. He xiii 7). There is no probability in the supposition that it originated in a desire to find a sanction for the practice of commemorations at the tombs of martyrs.

xiii 3 (†) τῷ ἀγαθῷ ἔργῳ] τοῦ ἀγαθοῦ ἔργου lat.vg pp^lat.: τῶν ἀγαθῶν ἔργων Syrian (Gr. Syr. Arm.). [The harshness of the phrase gives probability to a very slight change suggested by Patrick Young, who would read τῷ ἀγαθοεργῷ (so apparently aeth); cf. 1 Ti vi 18: the apparent antithesis to τῷ κακῷ could hardly fail to introduce τῷ ἀγαθῷ. H.]

xiii 8 ὀφείλετε] ὀφείλητε ℵᶜ(ὀφιλ-) B(-ειτε) : ὀφείλοντες ℵ* cu² Orig. Jer (not Orat).

xiv 6 φρονεῖ]+,καὶ ὁ μὴ φρονῶν τὴν ἡμέραν κυρίῳ οὐ φρονεῖ Syrian (Gr. Lat. Syr. Arm.). Suggested by the similar clause at the end of the verse.

xiv 23 fin.] The great doxology (xvi 25—27) is inserted here as well as at the close of the Epistle in AP₂ (? MSS known to Orig, see below) 5 17 al arm.codd. (? Cyr.al), probably Alexandrian; and in this place alone in the Syrian text (Gr. Syr. Goth.); (? incl. Cyr.al :) a vacant space in G₃ apparently attests the scribe's acquaintance with the Syrian text (see p. 29). Its omission here by Erasmus (and the 'Received Text') is due to the influence of the Latin Vulgate. The cause of its insertion here cannot be known with certainty. Possibly, as Bengel has suggested, in an early lection-system it was appended to the latter verses of c.xiv. For this combination there would be a twofold reason : the latter verses of c.xiv form an unsatisfactory close to a lection; and again it would not be strange if xvi 1—25 were passed over in the selection of passages for public reading, while the grandeur of the concluding Doxology might cause it to be specially reserved for reading in combination with another passage, since it was too short to read alone. The Syrian revisers may well have thought it superfluous to retain a passage of this length in both places; and have preferred to keep it here rather than at the end of c.xvi, which had been already provided with a conclusion of a more usual type by the Western transposition of the Benediction from xvi 20. In closing the Epistle without the Doxology they would be supported by the precedent of Western MSS.

In connexion however with the question as to the original insertion of the Doxology after c.xiv it is right to notice a curious feature of the table of Latin capitulations or headings prefixed to the Epistle in many Vulgate MSS. These headings correspond in number, and also substantially in subject, to the *Breves* or paragraphs likewise found in

many MSS of the Latin Vulgate. The last heading but one begins at xiv 15 and may easily cover the rest of c.xiv, with possibly the opening verses of c.xv as far as v. 13, but not more; and then the last heading passes at once to the Doxology (*De mysterio Domini* &c.). It has been naturally inferred that this table of headings, which abounds in language derived from the Old Latin version and implies some Western readings, was drawn up from a MS of the Epistle which lacked cc.xv xvi, but in which nevertheless the Doxology was appended to c.xiv. This textual combination however has no other attestation; and the interpretation must be doubtful while the origin and purpose of the *Breves* and corresponding Capitulations remain unknown. The analogy of the common Greek Capitulations shews how easily the personal or local and as it were temporary portions of an epistle might be excluded from a schedule of chapters or paragraphs. In three epistles the first heading begins expressly μετὰ τὸ προοίμιον, to the exclusion of Ro i 1—17; 1 Co i 1—9; Ga i 1—11: and no trace of anything after xv 21 is perceptible in the last heading for Romans, or after the end of c.xv in the last heading for 1 Corinthians. Thus it would not be surprising that another schedule constructed under similar limitations should include Ro xvi 25—27, and yet pass over xv 14—xvi 23.

The rest of the supposed evidence for the omission of cc.xv xvi, with or without the Doxology, is very slight and intangible. The table of headings in the Fulda MS comes from two sources; the first 23 headings, which extend to xiv 20, being unknown elsewhere, and the remaining 28, which begin at ix 1, being identical with the last 28 of the common table of headings. It is thus possible that the common table was used to eke out the deficiencies of the other table, as by making up the number of headings to the LI of other MSS; and that cc.xv xvi were absent from the MS (of the Epistle) on which the specially Fuldensian headings were founded, since the contents of xiv 14—23 might in some sense be covered by the 23rd heading. It is however at least equally probable that, having begun to copy a local table of headings, the scribe changed his mind in the midst; and, without cancelling what he had written, preferred thenceforward to substitute the common headings, going back to the chief break in the middle of the Epistle, and starting afresh from that point. The Fulda MS has no trace of any other than the common headings to the rest of St Paul's own epistles; and the comparatively rare headings which it prefixes to Hebrews break off likewise in the midst (c.x), the contents of the remainder of the Epistle being left unnoticed.

Tert once (*Adv. Marc.* v 13) refers to xiv 10 as in the close (*clausula*) of the Epistle: but it would be unsafe to infer that his copy ended with c.xiv, since he is speaking in express antithesis to passages standing early in the Epistle (i 16 ff.; ii 2), and he uses the word *clausula* elsewhere (*De fug. in pers.* 6) in a still more comprehensive sense. Again the absence of quotations from cc.xv xvi in Iren Tert and (with one doubtful exception) Cyp is *prima facie* evidence that they were wanting in some Western texts; but, as these chapters contain no passages which any of these writers had specially strong reasons for quoting, and many of their verses are quoted nowhere in patristic literature except in continuous commentaries, this is

not a case in which much weight can be attached to silence.

Lastly, it is usually assumed that we have the direct testimony of Orig to the absence of cc.xv xvi from Marcion's text. But internal evidence is strongly at variance with this interpretation of Rufinus's words, though it is their most obvious meaning according to the form which they assume in the printed editions. The supposed testimony, given not *ad loc.* but on xvi 25, follows immediately on a statement that Marcion (to whom alone Orig refers in either place) "completely removed this passage" (*caput hoc*), xvi 25—27, "from the Epistle". Now it is hardly credible that he would describe the omission of the part and of the whole by the same person in two separate and successive allegations. The natural logic of the passage requires rather that the second sentence should be taken as an explanation of the strong phrase cited above; its purport being that Marcion retained the Doxology neither at the end of the Epistle nor after c.xiv, where, as Orig goes on to mention, it was found in some MSS. As it stands, the text of Ruf will hardly bear this sense; for, though *non solum hoc* may as easily mean 'he not only [did] this [act]' as 'he not only [removed] this [passage]', the act referred to is complete removal from the Epistle, not simply removal from the end of the Epistle. But the apparent contradiction between the required and the expressed sense vanishes by the slight change of *hoc* to *hic*, more especially if with what seems to be the best MS we read *et in eo loco* for *et ab eo loco*. It must also be remembered that we do not possess Origen's own language in full, but merely a loose Latin abridgement. The interpretation here given is at least illustrated by a passage of Hier, cited on xvi 25, in which the omission of xvi 25—27 alone is noticed, Marcionite doctrine being referred to shortly after, and in which Hier is evidently following a longer exposition of Origen. Moreover, if Marcion's list really lacked the whole of these two chapters, the silence of Epiph would be hard to explain: imperfect doubtless as is his list of Marcion's readings, he could hardly have passed over an omission of 60 verses. In his own person he quotes c. xv two or three times.

xv 31 διακονία] δωροφορία Western (Gr. Lat.); incl. B.

xv 32 (†) θεοῦ] κυρίου Ἰησοῦ B, perhaps only a clerical corruption (κ for χ) of Χριστοῦ Ἰησοῦ, Western (Gr. Lat.): Ἰησοῦ Χριστοῦ ℵ* Ambst. Text ℵ°ACD₂°L₂P₂ cuᵒᵐⁿ lat.vg syrr me arm Orig.*loc*.lat.Ruf ppˢᵉʳ Pelag. This singular variety of reading suggests that St Paul wrote only διὰ θελήματος, in an absolute sense: cf. 1 Co xvi 12; Ro ii 18; (Sir xliii 16 [B];) also Ro xii 19. Dr Lightfoot, to whom the suggestion is due, refers likewise to Ign.*Rom*.1; *Eph*.20; *Smyrn*.1 codd. (*On a fresh revision of the English N.T.* 106 f.)

xvi 5 Ἀσίας] Ἀχαίας Syrian (Gr. [?? Lat.] Syr.). From 1 Co xvi 15.

xvi 20 ἡ χάρις...ὑμῶν] < Western (Gr. Lat.) here, being transposed to follow v. 23 and thus to form a close to the Epistle, vv. 25—27 being omitted. In 1 Co xiv the Western text similarly transposes vv. 34 f. and 36—40.

xvi 23 *fin*.] + (v. 24) ἡ χάρις τοῦ κυρίου ἡμῶν Ἰησοῦ Χριστοῦ μετὰ πάντων ὑμῶν· ἀμήν. Western and Syrian (Gr. Lat. Syr. Goth.): < Ἰησοῦ Χριστοῦ G₃: < Χριστοῦ 71. The double Benediction is found under

three conditions. (1) In v. 20 and at the end of the Epistle, but preceded by the Doxology; so P₂ 17 80 syr.vg arm Ambst. (2) In v. 20 and at the end of the Epistle, the Doxology being here omitted; Syrian (Gr. Syr. [? Goth.]). (3) In v. 20 and after v. 23, but followed by the Doxology; so two or three obscure cursives, and the inferior MSS of the Latin Vulgate. This last combination, which rests on hardly any authority, and is due to late conflation, was adopted by Erasmus from the Latin, and is preserved in the 'Received Text'. The single Benediction in xvi 20 (text) is attested by ℵABC 5 137 lat.vg.codd.opt me aeth Orig.*loc*.lat.Ruf; the single Benediction in xvi 23 (Western) by D₂G₃ (? go) Sedul.

xvi 25-27] < G₃ Marcion(ap.Orig. *loc*.lat.Ruf: see on xiv 23). Probably Marcion is also intended in a passage of Hier on Eph iii 5, in which the Montanists are said to appeal to "that which is found [in the epistle] to the Romans in most MSS," reading *Ei autem qui potest*" &c.: Hier goes on immediately to what is evidently a condensation of an argument against Marcionite doctrine, containing likewise allusions to the Doxology; and the exceptions to his general statement about "most MSS" are thus not unlikely to have been Marcionite MSS. The whole passage abounds in matter evidently derived from Orig, and the quotation itself agrees exactly in reading and extent with the form which it repeatedly assumes in Origen's writings (see on v. 26), and nowhere else. Thus this passage and the fuller account in the Comm. on Romans (quoted on xiv 23) explain each other.

Indirectly D₂ and Sedul likewise attest complete omission of the Doxology; for they join in attesting the

Western transposition of the Benediction, the motive of which must have been to place the Benediction at the end of the Epistle. The accession of the Doxology immediately following the Benediction seems therefore to be a later addition to their texts.

These Western authorities, direct and indirect, for the absolute omission of the Doxology receive at least a formal support from the Syrian text (Gr. Syr. Goth.), which omits it in this place but inserts it between cc. xiv and xv. For further particulars see note on xiv 23.

Text אBC(D₂) 'most' MSS known to Hier(*i.e.* Orig) 80 137 al² lat.vg syr.vg me aeth Or.*loc*.lat.Ruf Dam Ambst Pelag (Sedul); besides the documents (cited on xiv 23) which have the Doxology in both places.

xvi 26   προφητικῶν] + καὶ τῆς ἐπιφανείας τοῦ κυρίου ἡμῶν Ἰησοῦ Χριστοῦ Orig.*Princ.*163; *Cels.*(389,) 488; (*Ps.*724;) *Jo.*105, 226, 257; *Rom.*lat.Ruf.672 (perhaps not *loc*); also Hier after Orig in a passage cited in the last note; not Clem Cyr.al. This strangely constant misquotation has probably arisen from an instinctive interpretation of τε as 'both', combined with a recollection of 2 Ti i 10: in all cases the quotation stops at this point, omitting κατ᾽ ἐπιταγήν...ἀμήν.

I CORINTHIANS

v 6   Οὐ καλὸν] Καλὸν ' some MSS, especially Latin,' known to Aug ; also Lucif Ambst; not Hier Sedul. Probably an accidental loss of ΟΥ due to the preceding κυρίου or Χριστοῦ, but accepted as giving an ironical sense.

ibid. ξυμοῖ] δολοῖ Western, D₂* Bas.²codd (? Hesych.*Lex*), *corrumpit* lat.vg pp^lat; not G₃ *m*. The same Western correction occurs in Gal v 9.

vi 20   δοξάσατε δή] + *et portate* (*tollite*) g *m* vg Tert Cyp Lucif pp^lat.mu; not D₂G₃gr Iren.lat. This curious Western reading doubtless represents ἄρατε (with *et* prefixed in translation), an easy corruption of

ἄρά γε (-τε for -γε), which is actually found, prefixed to δοξάσατε (without δή), in Meth: Chr has ἄρατε after δή. Apparently δοξάσατε δή gave rise to various changes, ἄρά γε being one, οὖν another, and omission of δή (א*d me[?? Orig.*loc*] Did.1/3 pp^al) a third.

ibid. σώματι ὑμῶν] + καὶ ἐν τῷ πνεύματι ὑμῶν, ἅτινά ἐστιν τοῦ θεοῦ Syrian (Gr. Syr. Arm.). Another attempt to soften away St Paul's abruptness, and complete his sense.

vii 33 f. Several variations affect the punctuation of these two verses:—

v.33 καί] < Western and Syrian (Gr. Lat.: cf. Syr.); incl. Tert; also,

with δέ after μεμ., syr.vg. Text אAB
D₂*(gr)P₂ 6 17 31 46 67 73 137 al⁸
lat.vg syr.hl me basm aeth arm
Meth Eus Cyr.al pp^al Pelag Hier.
Jov (expressly) Aug. The clearly attested genuineness of this καί leaves
it open whether μεμέρισται is to be
taken with what precedes or with
what follows: if it were spurious,
the latter construction alone would
be possible.

v.34 καί 1°]< Western of limited
range (Gr.[D₂*] Lat. Syr. Eg.
Arm.); incl. Tert; not G₃ *d* vg Meth
(Cyp. 2/2, who however each time
substitutes *Sic* for καί μεμέρισται):
in syr.vg me basm arm the omission
may be only a natural accident of
translation. The adoption of this
comparatively unimportant reading
by Erasmus, and hence in the 'Received Text', must be due either to
a blunder (in his note he cites the
Greek both with and without this
καί) or to the influence of Amb and
Latin MSS known to Hier, referred
to in his long note.

ἡ γυνὴ ἡ ἄγαμος καὶ ἡ παρθένος]
ἡ γυνὴ καὶ ἡ παρθένος ἡ ἄγαμος
Western and Syrian (Gr. Lat. Syr.
Arm.); incl. Meth Tert Cyp:
ἡ γυνὴ ἡ ἄγαμος καὶ ἡ παρθένος ἡ
ἄγαμος (? Alexandrian) אA 17 al
(aeth) Bas.codd Euth.cod Aug²:
ἡ γυνὴ καὶ ἡ παρθένος lat.codd. Text
BP₂ 6 31 46 71 73 137 al² lat.vg me
basm Eus.*D.E.* Amb³ Pelag Hier.
Jov (expressly, apparently on Greek
authority): also virtually Epiph.
*Haer.*98 cod, 523, 710 (<ἡ γυνή);
and indirectly Ps.Ath.*Virg.*2 (<καί
ἡ π.) Dam.*Par* (γαμήσασα for παρθένος).

The variations appear to have
arisen from the difficulty of distinguishing ἡ γ. ἡ ἄγαμος from ἡ παρθένος; and partly also from a reference of μεμέρισται to the two following substantives, causing it to be
interpreted in the ill attested and

improbable sense 'differ from each
other' (διεστήκασιν ἀλλήλων Chr),
instead of 'is distracted'. A stop
after ἡ παρθένος is necessary for the
Syrian reading: with the reading of
אA there may be either two stops,
after γυναικί and παρθένος, or after
μεμέρισται only. The sense given
by these several readings is too
feeble to afford any ground for distrusting the best group of documents. The difficulty would be
lessened if the second ἡ were absent:
and H might easily slip in before Π.
But, since the καί before ἡ γυνή
certainly belongs to the whole clause
down to κυρίου, ἡ ἄγαμος may well
be the more comprehensive term
answering to ὁ ἄγαμος in v. 32, and
ἡ παρθένος the narrower term specially suggested by the question of
the Corinthians (vv. 25, 36 ff.). The
true sense of μεμέρισται, with the
consequent punctuation, was vigorously maintained by Hammond
soon after the reading of A became
known.

viii 6   δι' αὐτοῦ]+καὶ ἐν πνεῦμα
ἅγιον, ἐν ᾧ τὰ πάντα καὶ ἡμεῖς ἐν
αὐτῷ cu⁴ (Greg.Naz) Cyr.al.*Ador*¹
and later pp referring to Greg.naz;
also in some MSS of Bas.*Spir.* p. 4,
but apparently wrongly, the context which *prima facie* confirms the
addition being probably founded
on Ro xi 36 (cf. *Eun.* p. 311; also
p. 315; *Ep.* p. 83): Greg.naz omits
all the three clauses beginning with
καὶ ἡμεῖς. The addition is absent
from the quotations of Iren.lat Orig
Eus Cyr.hr Ath Epiph Apol Did
Cyr.al(except once) al pp^lat: Chr
and others expressly mention the
absence of a clause on the Holy
Spirit.

ix 5   ἀδελφὴν γυναῖκα] γυναῖκας
Western,G₃(?Clem.*Paed*;not *Strom*²)
Tert Hil Helvid Hil (auct. *Sing.cl*;
Sedul; not Aug: ἀδελφὰς γυναῖκας

arm Hier: γυναῖκα ἀδελφὴν lat.vg.
codd: γυναῖκα Ambst.

xi 10 ἐξουσίαν] κάλυμμα (Ptolem
ap. Iren), *velamen harl*** al (Pelag)
Hier Aug Bed: (*velamen et potes-
tatem* Orig.*Cant*.lat.Hier :) not
D₂G₃ lat.vg Valentiniani(ap. Clem)
Tert Ambst. Doubtless only a conjectural gloss. Notwithstanding the
obscurity of the phrases ἐξουσίαν
ἔχειν ἐπὶ τῆς κεφαλῆς and διὰ τοὺς
ἀγγέλους the text does not appear
to be corrupt. Certainly none of
the known emendations of it can
possibly be right; and the intrinsic and obvious difficulty is itself
enough to set aside the suggestion
that the whole verse is an interpolation.

xi 24 Τοῦτο] Λάβετε φάγετε, τοῦτο
Syrian (Gr. Lat. Syr. Goth.): aeth
prefixes Λάβετε only. From the |||
in the Gospels.

ibid. τὸ ὑπὲρ ὑμῶν] + κλώμενον
Western and Syrian (Gr. Lat.
[Ambst] Syr. [Arm.] Goth.), from
ἔκλασεν above, &c. : θρυπτόμενον D₂,
specially used of the breaking of
bread (as διαθρύπτω Lev ii 6; Is
lviii 7): '*given*' me the aeth arm.ed
Euth.cod: *tradetur* (perhaps a very
early corruption of *-itur*, the reading
of at least *harl*) lat.vg. Text ℵ*ABC*
17 67** arm.codd ('Ath.' *Serm.
maj.fid.*29) Cyr.al.*Nest* Cyp.codd.
opt.7/8 (*quod pro vobis est*) Fulg:
the same was doubtless the reading
of syr.vt, which in Lc xxii 19 presents the interpolation from 1 Co in
this form.

xi 29 πίνων] + ἀναξίως Western and
Syrian (Gr. Lat. Syr. Eg. Arm.
Goth.); perhaps incl. Orig.*Jo; Prov*
Cyr.*Jo; Ador*; but all four quotations are free, and partly taken from
v. 27. Text ℵ*ABC* 17 the aeth.
codd. From v. 27.

xii 2 (†) ὅτι ὅτε] < ὅτε Western
G₃.gr K₂^mg cu^p *d nev** syr.vg me,

Ambst; not D₂.gr *g* vg Pelag
'Vig': < ὅτι K₂* 23 37 al² (aeth)
pp Aug; also *cum autem* Orig.*Num.*
lat.Ruf. Both corrections are unsatisfactory in themselves, as well as
ill attested. There is nothing in
this short and detached sentence to
account for a participle where a
finite verb would be naturally expected. Probably ὅτι ὅτε is a primitive error for ὅτι ποτέ (ΤΙ for ΤΙΠ):
cf. Eph ii 11; and also ii 2 f., 13;
v 8; Ro xi 30; Tit iii 3.

xiii 3 καυχήσωμαι] καυθήσομαι
(-σωμαι) Western and Syrian (Gr.
Lat. Syr. [Æth.] Arm. Goth.); incl.
C Greek and Latin MSS known to
Hier Meth Cyr.al⁴ Tert Cyp aeth.
Reb Aphr Ephr. Text ℵAB Greek
MSS known to Hier 17 me the
(aeth.codd) go.mg (? Clem.rom)
(Clem.al) Orig.*loc.* Hier.*Gal.*499,
517 f.; *Is.*688 (in the two latter
places noticing the difference of
reading; in all three probably following Orig) 'Ephr'.

This is distinctly the reading of
memph in both editions, though
mistranslated by Wilkins: Mr A.
W. Tyler (in an elaborate article in
Bibl. Sacr. 1873, p. 502) points out
that Tuke's Grammar p. 107 gives this
reading for both memph and theb.
The Roman text of aeth, perhaps
conflate, contains *ut praemio affi-
ciar.* The coincidence with Clem.
rom. 55 (πολλοὶ βασιλεῖς καὶ ἡγού-
μενοι ... παρέδωκαν ἑαυτοὺς εἰς
θάνατον, ἵνα ῥύσωνται διὰ τοῦ ἑαυτῶν
αἵματος τοὺς πολίτας. ... ἐπιστάμεθα
πολλοὺς ἐν ἡμῖν παραδεδωκότας
ἑαυτοὺς εἰς δεσμὰ ὅπως ἑτέρους
λυτρώσονται. πολλοὶ ἑαυτοὺς παρέδωκαν [so A and apparently syr:
ἐξέδωκαν C] εἰς δουλείαν, καὶ λαβόν-
τες τὰς τιμὰς αὐτῶν ἑτέρους ἐψώμισαν) is not likely to be accidental;
and, if it is not, it implies the absence of καυθ.: besides the heathen

example two cases of παραδοῦναι ἑαυτόν are here noticed, one of exchanging places with prisoners, the other of selling oneself as a slave to obtain the means of feeding the poor (ἐψώμισαν). Clem.al similarly twice omits ἵνα κ. (*Strom.* 867 οὔτε ἀπὸ τῆς αὑτῆς αἰτίας τῷ γνωστικῷ οὔτε καὶ τὸ αὐτὸ προθέμενοι, οὐδ᾽ ἄν τὸ σῶμα ἅπαν ἐπιδιδῶσιν, ἀγάπην γὰρ οὐκ ἔχουσι κατὰ τὸν ἀπόστολον κ.τ.λ.: 614 ἐὰν τὸ σῶμά μου ἐπιδῶ, φησίν, ἀγάπην δὲ μὴ ἔχω κ.τ.λ.), evidently following a text in which παραδῶ was absolute, but substituting ἐπιδῶ which in this sense is a commoner word; and a few lines below the second passage he says ἔστι γὰρ καὶ ὁ λαὸς ὁ τοῖς χείλεσιν ἀγαπῶν, ἔστι καὶ ἄλλος παραδιδοὺς τὸ σῶμα ἵνα καυχήσηται, for so the parallelism to τοῖς χείλεσιν makes it necessary to read, though the only extant MS has καυθήσεται. Similarly the text from which Cramer (p. 252) has printed a scholium of Origen has καυθήσωμαι, but evidently wrongly, for it proceeds ὡς δυνατοῦ ὄντος ψωμίσαι τινὰ τὰ ὑπάρχοντα οὐ διὰ τὴν ἀγάπην ἀλλὰ διὰ τὴν κενοδοξίαν, καὶ ὡς δυνατοῦ ὄντος καὶ μαρτυρῆσαί τινα ἕνεκεν καυχήσεως καὶ δόξης ἧς δοξάζονται ἐν ταῖς ἐκκλησίαις οἱ μάρτυρες.

Text gives an excellent sense, for, as v. 2 refers to a faith towards God which is unaccompanied by love, so v. 3 refers to acts which seem by their very nature to be acts of love to men, but are really done only in ostentation. First the dissolving of the goods in almsgiving is mentioned, then, as a climax, the yielding up of the very body; both alike being done for the sake of glorying, and unaccompanied by love. Three causes probably led to the early corruption of text. First, the familiarity with Christian martyrdoms, which led even writers who retained

the true text (Clem.al Orig Hier, though not Clem.rom) to interpret in this manner the 'yielding up' of the body, would soon suggest martyrdom by fire. Secondly, the words might easily be affected by their similarity to what is said in Dan iii 28 (95 LXX) of Shadrach, Meshach, and Abednego, that παρέδωκαν τὰ σώματα αὐτῶν εἰς ἐμπυρισμόν. Thirdly, the unfamiliar absolute use of παραδίδωμι (cf. Jo xix 30) might cause difficulty, more especially as ἵνα might seem to introduce a description of some special mode of surrender. For the phrase itself cf. Plut.*Demet.*49 f. (p.913 f.) τολμήσαντος δέ τινος εἰπεῖν τι, ὡς Σελεύκῳ χρὴ τὸ σῶμα παραδοῦναι Δημήτριον, ὥρμησε μὲν τὸ ξίφος σπασάμενος ἀνελεῖν ἑαυτόν κ.τ.λ., and again εἰ καὶ πρότερον ἐδόκει τὴν παράδοσιν τοῦ σώματος αἰσχρὰν πεποιῆσθαι κ.τ.λ.

xv 5 δώδεκα] ἕνδεκα Western (Gr. Lat. Syr.[hl. mg] Goth.) ; incl. Eus.*Mar.*2/4 Archel.lat. Evidently a correction made to exclude Judas Iscariot.

xv 47 ὁ δεύτερος ἄνθρωπος] +ὁ κύριος Pre-Syrian and Syrian (Gr. [? Lat.] Syr. Arm. Goth.) ; incl. AD₂ᵇ Marcion(ap. Tert Adamant) [Orig.*Ps.* 559, but in a context that suggests interpolation from the catenæ] [Hipp.cod¹] Bas. *Spir.*40 ed. Garn. Cyr.al.*Jo.*994 ; *Glaph.* 11 ; *Fid.* 92 ; *Schol.*gr.syr. 507 Pusey (=780 Aub.) Maximin(ap. Aug). The text of Cyr.al is a little uncertain, the uncertainty being increased by his constant reference of ὁ δ. ἄ. to Christ; but apparently he knew and used both readings. The testimony of the Gothic (Arian) bishop Maximinus is probably in strictness Greek or Gothic rather than Latin; there is no other Latin authority for ὁ κύριος. Text אBCD₂*G₃ 17 67** lat.vg me aeth arm.codd.mg Orig.

*Jo.*302; *Gen.*lat.Ruf[3]; *Lc.*lat.Ruf;
*Rom.*lat.Ruf Hipp. *Genes.*codd.2/3
Petr.al.*Anim* 'Ath'.*Serm. maj. fid.*
25 Photin(ap.Epiph) Bas. *Spir.* ed.
Erasm. Greg.naz.*Ep.* 87,168(citing
also Apoll) Greg.nys. *Orat.*1*Co.*xv
(p. 1312 Mi) Cyr.al.(*loc;*)*Hab.*397
Pusey; *Un.Chr.*725,771; *Hom.pasch.*
228; *Ap.adv.Orient.*194(and perhaps
elsewhere) al Tert[3] Cyp[5] pp[lat].

xv 51 πάντες οὐ κοιμηθησόμεθα
πάντες δὲ ἀλλαγησόμεθα] + μὲν after
πάντες Pre-Syrian (? Western) and
Syrian (Gr. Lat. Syr. Eg.); incl.
ℵAC*D₂[b(?)]G₃ Greg.nys Cyr.al Tert.
Text BC*D₂* Greek MSS known
to Pelag and to Hier 23* al[1] (syr.
vg) aeth arm Orig. This insertion,
evidently intended to strengthen the
antithesis, is best noticed separately,
though in its origin it may have
been connected with the important
complex variation which follows.
The evidence as to the position of οὐ
claims attention first.

Transposition of οὐ to the second
clause (before πάντες) is attested by
a great mass of ancient authority,
ℵ(? A) CD₂*G₃ 17, with Greek MSS
mentioned by at least six ancient
writers, lat.vg aeth arm, Orig.*Ps.*
552; *Mt.*lat. 872; (?*Is.*lat.Ruf.105)
Adamant.cod Acac Did(both ap.
Hier) Cyr.*loc.*comm.316 Pusey(distinctly); *Jo.*645, all Latin writers
but (apparently) Tert (none however
before Cent. IV), and finally Aphr.
Retention of οὐ as in text (after [or,
loosely, in some quotations before]
the first πάντες) is attested by B and
all the inferior Greek MSS, Greek
MSS mentioned by the same ancient
writers as above, syrr me go,
Orig. *Cels.*589; *Thess.*lat.Hier.692
distinctly (and apparently elsewhere)
Adamant.cod Theod.herac Apoll
(both ap Hier) Greg.nys.*Hom.*103
[Cyr.al. *Hos.* 30: οἱ πάντες δέ makes
the reading doubtful] pp[ser], and apparently Tert. *Res.* 42 by the sense

of the context, despite the MSS, as
Sabatier has pointed out.

A* has ΟΙΠΑΝΤΕΣ...ΟΙΠΑΝΤΕΣΔΕ
[cf. Cyr.al above], the second ΟΙ
being altered (? by the first hand)
into ΟΥ: an early hand has also
superadded ΟΥ after οἱ πάντες μέν,
leaving the text unchanged. G₃ has
likewise (without a Latin rendering)
ΟΥΝ in the same place. These petty
variations are perhaps only relics of
mixture, ΟΥ being easily confounded
with O͞Y and ΟΙ. For πάντες δέ 17
(pp[lat]) have ἀλλὰ πάντες.

Further, the documents which
transpose οὐ fall into two groups.
Ἀναστησόμεθα is read for κοιμηθησόμεθα by D* lat.vg and Latin MSS
mentioned by several ancient writers
(the language of Hier implies that
he knew of no such Greek MSS)
arm.codd.mg. (? Tert) Hil.3/3 pp[lat]
Aphr.: κοιμηθησόμεθα by ℵ(? A)C
G₃ 17, Greek MSS mentioned by
Aug, Latin MSS mentioned by the
same ancient writers, aeth arm, the
Greek patristic evidence, and Hier.
Ἀναστησόμεθα comes from 1 Th iv
16, which has in like manner suggested the Western ἀναστήσονται for
ἐγερθήσονται in v. 52.

It is possible to extract a meaning
from either reading, as may be seen
from the comments of the Fathers,
several of which are quoted at length
by Hier in his *Ep.* 119: but the
reading of text is alone strictly consonant to St Paul's language in the
context and in 1 Thess, and it is
supported by B me Orig (though
perhaps not in all his quotations),
as well as by less considerable authorities. The position of οὐ after
πάντες has probably a corrective
force, 'We all — I say not, shall
sleep, but we shall be changed'.
The other pair of readings is doubt

less Western in origin, like some other readings in St Paul which attained a wide currency in Cent. IV and yet were not adopted in the Syrian text (see *Introd.* § 324 f.). In all probability the transposition

was in the first instance accompanied or preceded by the change to ἀναστησόμεθα, the other form being due to a later (possibly Alexandrian) combination with the original reading.

2 CORINTHIANS

iii 3 (†) πλαξὶν καρδίαις σαρκίναις] καρδίας for καρδίαις (probably Western and) Syrian (Gr. Lat. Syr. Eg. Æth. Arm. Goth.); incl. F₂ (doubtless by assimilation to the annexed lat.vg) [Iren.lat.txt] Orig. *Ps.*(from a single catena); *Rom.*lat. Ruf⁵ [Adamant.txt] Did.*Ps.*ip.272 Cord. Cyr.*loc.* (*s.q.*); *Is.* 504 (*s.q.*). Text ℵABCD₂G₃L₂P₂ cu²⁵ syr.hl Iren.com (? Clem.*Paed.*307) Eus. *Mart* Adamant.com Did.*loc* (Macar.*Hom.*91) Cyr.al.*Fid.*65(Pusey) Euth.cod : Iren.lat and Adamant have καρδίαι σάρκιναι (*corda carnalia*) in the immediate context. The testimonies of Orig Did¹ Cyr.al¹ for καρδίας must also be held doubtful: the change was exceptionally slight and easy for scribes and editors.

Intrinsically the correction is weak and improbable, though superficially easy. Text is possibly right: but the apposition is harsh and strange, and it is not unlikely that the second πλαξίν was a primitive clerical error suggested by the line above, and immediately discovered and cancelled by dots which escaped notice at the next transcription.

iii 17 (†) οὗ δὲ τὸ πνεῦμα Κυρίου, ἐλευθερία] [These words contain no obvious difficulty: yet it may be suspected that Κυρίου is a primitive error for κύριον (Υ for Ν). First, the former clause of the verse does not in sense lead naturally up to this clause, whether the emphasis be laid on πνεῦμα or on Κυρίου (or κυρίου). Secondly, in ἀπὸ κυρίου πνεύματος at the end of v. 18 neither principal word can naturally be taken as a substantive dependent on the other, nor both as substantives in apposition. The simplest construction is to take κυρίου as an adjective ('a Spirit exercising lordship', or, by a paraphrase, 'a Spirit which is Lord'); and apparently the Scriptural source of the remarkable adjectival phrase τὸ κύριον in the (so called) Constantinopolitan Creed (τὸ πνεῦμα τὸ ἅγιον τὸ κύριον τὸ ζωοποιόν) can be only v. 18 construed in this manner, the third in the triad of epithets being likewise virtually found in this chapter (v. 6) as well as elsewhere. This adjectival use of κυρίου in the genitive would however be so liable to be misunderstood, or even overlooked altogether, that St Paul could hardly use it without some further indication of his meaning. If he wrote οὗ δὲ τὸ πνεῦμα κύριον, ἐλευθερία, not only do the two clauses of v. 17 fall into natural sequence, but a clue is given which conducts at once to the true sense of ἀπὸ κυρίου πνεύματος. H.]

vii 8 (†) βλέπω]+γὰρ Pre-Syrian and Syrian (Gr. [Lat.] Syr. Eg. Arm. Goth.); incl. ℵCD₂ᵇG₃: *videns* lat.vg Ambst.cod: *videns enim* lat.vg.codd. Text BD₂*(aeth) Ambst. cod. There can be no doubt that γὰρ was inserted to ease the construction: but the harshness of βλέπω suggests that lat.vg alone has preserved the true reading, βλέπων, ῶ being read as ω. Lachmann makes the same suggestion.

xii 7 (†) διό]<Western and Syrian (Gr. Lat. Syr. Arm. Goth.); incl. Iren.lat Orig.*Num*.lat.Ruf; *Lc*.lat.Hier. Text ℵABG₃ 17 (67, omitting ἵνα) (aeth) Euth.cod.

ἵνα μὴ ὑπεραίρωμαι 2°]<Pre-Syrian (? Western) (Gr. Lat. Æth.); incl. ℵ*AD₂G₃ 17 Iren.lat. Text, which is also Syrian, ℵᶜBK₂L₂P₂ cuᵖˡ syrr me arm go ppᵍᵉʳ Ambst;

also, but beginning at ἐδόθη, and therefore perhaps only by a free transposition, Orig.*Orat*;*Jer* Macar Chr. 1/6 Tert Cyp².

The documentary and transcriptional evidence place the genuineness of διό above doubt: its omission is a characteristic Western attempt to deal with a difficulty by excision; rounded off by the Latins, who place ἵνα μή next to καί; and completed by the omission of the second ἵνα μὴ ὑπεραίρωμαι. A broken construction is not in this context improbable: but the logical force of διό is unfavourable to the supposition that καὶ τῇ ὑπ. τ. ἀποκ. is the beginning of an unfinished sentence. If then there is no corruption, these words must either be connected with v. 6, as in text, or with v. 5 (εἰ μὴ ἐν τ. ἀσθενείαις) after a parenthesis, as by Lachmann. Neither construction however justifies itself on close examination; and in all probability there is a corruption somewhere. In itself the repetition of ἵνα μὴ ὑπεραίρωμαι presents no great difficulty, as was seen by the Syrian revisers; but it may have arisen out of a disarrangement of text.

GALATIANS

ii 5 οἷς οὐδὲ]<Western, D* 'very many Greek and Latin MSS' known to Victorin Latin MSS known to Hier Iren.lat(apparently confirmed by context) Tert Victorin Ambst (all three expressly) Pelᵗg.com; not

G₃ 'certain' [? MSS] known to Victorin 'the Greeks' according to Ambst '[the] Greek MSS' known to Hier lat.vg Marcion(ap. Tert) Amb Aug Hier(expressly) Pelag.txt. The omission may have been caused partly by the preceding broken construction, partly by δέ in v. 4, which might seem to require a sense in some degree adverse to that of v. 3 ('Titus was not compelled to be circumcised, but I did think it right to shew a temporary personal deference'): it thus apparently presupposes the probably erroneous interpretation of οὐδὲ...ἠναγκάσθη as a statement that Titus was not circumcised at all.

ii 12 ἦλθον] ἦλθεν אBD₂*G₃ 73 al¹ (Orig.*Cels* distinctly, ἐλθόντος Ἰακώβου). Text ACD₂ᵇH₃K₂L₂P₂ cuᵖˡ *r* vg syrr me arm go (? Iren. lat. 200) Euth.cod ppˢᵉʳ Victorin Ambst Pelag. It is not easy to decide whether ἦλθεν is an unusually well attested Western reading (see *Introd.* § 303), none of the extant Latin evidence for ἦλθον being early, or a primitive error (Є for O). It cannot in any case be genuine, and is probably due to ὅτε δὲ ἦλθεν (Κηφᾶς) in v. 11.

ii 20 τοῦ υἱοῦ τοῦ θεοῦ] τοῦ θεοῦ καὶ Χριστοῦ Western, BD₂*G₃ Victorin.com : *filii Dei et Christi* (conflate) Victorin.txt Hier.txt.codd(but against context). Txt אACD₂ᵇK₂ L₂P₂ cuᵒᵐⁿ *r* vg syrr me the aeth arm go Clem Adamant Cyr.al.6/6 Euth.cod ppˢᵉʳ Ambst Hier Aug 'Vig' ppˡᵃᵗ.

iii 1 ἐβάσκανεν]+τῇ ἀληθείᾳ μὴ πείθεσθαι probably Syrian (Gr.Lat. Syr. Æth. Arm.); incl. C 'some [Greek] MSS' known to Hier Orig. *Num.*lat.Ruf. From v 7.

iv 7 διὰ θεοῦ] διὰ Χριστοῦ lat. cod** the Hier: διὰ Ἰησοῦ Χριστοῦ cu²: θεοῦ διὰ ['Ιησοῦ] Χριστοῦ (perhaps conflate) Syrian (Gr.Syr.Æth. Goth.); incl. D₂. Text א*ABC* 17 vg.lat me Clem Cyr.al.*Jo*; *Heb.*155(Cram) Bas Did² (all but Clem expressly) ppˡᵃᵗ: also διὰ θεόν G₃ ; '*of God*' aeth arm.

iv 25 τὸ δὲ "Αγαρ] (marg.) τὸ γὰρ אCG₃ *r₃* vg the aeth go Orig. *Cant.*lat.Ruf Epiph Cyr.al.*Glaph.* 75 ; *Zech.*782 cod Dam ppˡᵃᵗ : alsc τὸ δὲ (by loose rendering) lat.vg. codd the (aeth) Ambst.txt : omitted altogether by goth : τὸ γὰρ "Αγαρ (by conflation of text with τὸ γάρ) Syrian (Gr. [? Lat.] Syr.) ; incl. (*d*, omitting Σινά) Cyr.al.*Zech.*cod ; *Glaph.*433(*s.q.*) (?Ambst.com). Text ABD₂* (? 17*) 37 73 80 lt 40 me syr.hl.mg (?Ambst.com).

Both the early readings, which differ only by the presence or absence of ΔЄΔ, are perplexing and hard to interpret ; but there is no need to have recourse to Bentley's violent remedy, and to suppose Σινὰ ὄρος ἐστὶν ἐν τῇ Ἀραβίᾳ to be a marginal gloss, the intrusion of which led to the insertion of δέ after συνστοιχεῖ. [The difficulties which he points out seem however to be fatal to the presence of both "Αγαρ and Σινά in the text, and thus to indicate the marginal reading as alone probable. W.] [On the other hand the unfavourable presumption created by the Western character of the attestation of τὸ γάρ is borne out by the difficulty of accounting for the reference to Arabia with this reading, for it assumes the connexion between Arabia and Hagar to be obvious to the Galatians without explanation. This difficulty vanishes if we keep the reading of text, and take ὄρος as common to subject and predicate (cf. Ro ii 28 f.; iii 29). Hagar and Sinai, St Paul apparently means to say, are connected by literal external fact as well as spiritual relationship: the home of both is in the same land, Arabia ; 'Mount Hagar [in the full sense of 'Hagar', 'Hagar with her children'] is Mount Sinai, in Arabia.' The term 'Mount' (hill-country) is similarly joined in the Old Testament to 'Amalek', 'the Amorites', 'Ephraim', 'Naphtali', &c.: but the closest parallel is 'the Mount of Esau', in Obad 8,9,19,21; Esau being, like Hagar's son, an elder brother rejected in favour of a forefather of the chosen race. The *Hagri* ('Αγραῖοι of Greek writers, 'Αγαρηνοί LXX) are known as inhabitants of northern Arabia from the days of Ps lxxxiii 7 and 1 Chr till quite late times (Gesen. *Thes.* i 365): cf. Epiph. i 9 αἱ φυλαὶ τῶν 'Αγαρηνῶν, τῶν καὶ 'Ισμαηλιτῶν, Σαρακήνων δὲ τανῦν καλουμένων). During St Paul's sojourn in 'Arabia' (i 17) he must often have heard their name; and thus their traditional origin might come to be associated in his mind with the higher memories of the Sinaitic peninsula. The difficulty of text is so patent that, though it might often be disguised by allegorical interpretation, it would, when taken literally, lead naturally to alteration. The difficulty of the marginal reading on the other hand lies below the surface; and it is hardly likely that scribes would be perplexed by the simple statement that 'Sinai is a mountain in Arabia'. H.]

v 1 (†) Τῇ ἐλευθερίᾳ] ᾗ ἐλευθερίᾳ Western (Gr. Lat. Goth.); incl. G₃ r₃ Orig.*Gen.*lat.Ruf;*Cant.*lat.Ruf Tert: + ᾗ, with omission of οὖν after στήκετε, Syrian (Gr. Lat. Syr.). The Western reading was doubtless intended to connect the detached first clause of v 1 definitely with iv 31. In the absence of punctuation however it might be hastily read with στήκετε; the artificial connexion thus created would seem to be confirmed by the apparent antithesis between ἐλευθερίᾳ and ζυγῷ δουλείας, στήκετε and ἐνέχεσθε; and thus the Syrian reading would be suggested, consisting in resolution

of the initial relative and extrusion of οὖν. A third change (Constantinopolitan, Greek only) completed the transformation by inserting οὖν after ἐλευθερίᾳ. Text ℵABC*H₃P₂ 17 73 (me) the (aeth) (Cyr.al. *Glaph.*75; *Thes.*280): me differs only by inserting γάρ after τῇ, while aeth has virtually the same ('*of the free, because Christ set us free: stand ye therefore also, and*') but omits τῇ ἐλευθερίᾳ: Cyr.al² (at least as edited) adds ᾗ after ἐλευθερίᾳ.

The documentary distribution shews that text is certainly the parent of all the other readings, and it will easily account for the existence of them all. The difficult abruptness of text would *prima facie* be removed by the adoption of the ᾗ after τῇ ἐλευθερίᾳ, as having been lost before ἡμᾶς. This simple change however has virtually no authority: the documents which attest it, themselves a Syrian group, simultaneously omit οὖν after στήκετε, the only exception being Cyr.al, and that only in books which have not been critically edited. But even as a conjecture the insertion of ᾗ is improbable, the resulting diction being languid and redundant. [Yet it is difficult to believe that St Paul would either use τῇ ἐλευθερίᾳ in the sense of εἰς τὴν ἐλευθερίαν, or insert an article in such a construction as παραγγελίᾳ παρηγγείλαμεν. It seems more probable that τῇ is a primitive corruption of ἐπ': in early papyrus writing H and N are often not to be distinguished, and the sagitta of ε is sometimes so near the top of the 'arc', not seldom also crossing it, that confusion with a hastily written τ would be easy. It is natural that ἐπ' ἐλευθερίᾳ should recur in v. 13, where the thread of v. 1 is taken up afresh after the digressive appeal of vv. 2—12. H.]

v 8]< οὐκ Western (Gr. Lat.); incl. (apparently Orig. *Princ* ;) Lucif; not G₃ Orig. *Cels*(distinctly) (? Ambst Pelag) Aug.

v 9 ξυμοῖ] δολοῖ Western (Gr. Lat. Goth.); incl. Marcion(ap. Epiph); not G₃. The same Western correction occurs in 1 Co v 6.

EPHESIANS

i 1] <[ἐν Ἐφέσῳ] ℵ*B "the older of the MSS" consulted by Bas 67** (Marcion, see below) Orig.*loc.* (distinctly) Bas (expressly). Orig interprets τοῖς οὖσιν absolutely, in the sense of 1 Co i 28, as he could not have done had he read ἐν Ἐφέσῳ: Bas probably has Orig in mind when he refers for this reading to 'predecessors', from whom however Bas manifestly distinguishes MSS consulted by himself (οὕτω γὰρ καὶ οἱ πρὸ ἡμῶν παραδεδώκασι καὶ ἡμεῖς ἐν τοῖς παλαιοῖς τῶν ἀντιγράφων εὑρήκαμεν). It is doubtless again to Orig that Hier refers when he speaks of 'certain' as interpreting the passage in this manner 'with unnecessary refinement' (*curiosius quam necesse est*):—a remark which shews on the one hand that Hier was not himself acquainted with the reading, and on the other that Orig in his unabridged commentary can have made no reference to any MSS as containing ἐν Ἐφέσῳ, since otherwise Hier could not have treated the question as though it affected interpretation alone. Tert distinctly states that Marcion retained this epistle, but under the title 'To the Laodicenes'. Epiph is silent on this point in his short account of Mar-

cion's readings in the Ep., but after the conclusion of his remarks on all the epistles (374 A πρὸς Φιλιππησίους ι'· οὕτως γὰρ παρὰ τῷ Μαρκίωνι κεῖται ἐσχάτη καὶ δεκάτη) he subjoins a confused notice of a reading of Marcion (Eph iv 5) " from the so called Ep. to the Laodicenes, in harmony with the Ep. to the Ephesians "; so that the unknown source from which he borrowed his information about Marcion's text seems to have contained a misunderstood reference to the title used by Marcion. It is hardly credible that the Epistle should have received this title, either in a text followed by Marcion or at his own hands, if the words ἐν Ἐφέσῳ had been present. It does not follow that ἐν Λαοδικίᾳ replaced it: a change of the address in the body of the Epistle itself would hardly have been passed over in silence; and it seems more likely that the title was supplied from a misapplication of Col iv 16 in the absence of any indication of address in the text of the Epistle.   Text ℵᶜAD₂G₃K₂L₂P₂ later MSS consulted by Bas(see above) cuᵖˡ vvᵒᵐⁿ Cyr.al.*Thes.*280 ppˢᵉʳ ppˡᵃᵗ.

Transcriptional evidence strongly supports the testimony of documents against ἐν Ἐφέσῳ. The early and, except as regards Marcion, universal tradition that the Epistle was addressed to the Ephesians, embodied in the title found in all extant documents, would naturally lead to the insertion of the words in the place that corresponding words hold in other epistles; and on the other hand it is not easy to see how they could come to be omitted, if genuine. Nor again, when St Paul's use of the term οἱ ἅγιοι (*e.g.* 1 Co xvi 1) and his view of πίστις in relation to the new Israel are taken into account, is it in itself improbable that he should write "to the saints who are also faithful (believing) in Christ Jesus". The only real intrinsic difficulty here lies in the resemblance to the phrases used in other epistles to introduce local addresses.

The variation need not however be considered as a simple case of omission or insertion. There is much probability in the suggestion of Beza and Ussher, adopted by many commentators, that this epistle was addressed to more than one church. It is certainly marked by an exceptional generality of language, and its freedom from local and personal allusions places it in strong contrast to the twin Ep. to the Colossians, conveyed by the same messenger. St Paul might naturally take advantage of the mission of Tychicus to write a letter to be read by the various churches which he had founded or strengthened in the region surrounding Ephesus during his long stay, though he might have special reasons for writing separate letters to Colossæ and Laodicea. Apart from any question of the reading in i 1, this is the simplest explanation of the characteristics of the Epistle; but, if it represents the facts truly, it must have a bearing on the reading. An epistle addressed to a plurality of churches might either be written so as to dispense with any local address, or it might have a blank space, to be filled up in each case with a different local address. The former supposition, according to which καὶ πιστοῖς would be continuous with τοῖς ἁγίοις, has been noticed above. In this case ἐν Ἐφέσῳ would be simply an interpolation. On the other view, which is on the whole the more probable of the two, ἐν Ἐφέσῳ would be a legitimate but unavoidably partial supplement to the true text, filling up a chasm which might be perplexing to a reader in later times. Since it is highly probable that the epistle would be communicated to the great mother church first, and then sent on to the lesser churches around, there is sufficient justification both for the title ΠΡΟΣ ΕΦΕ-ΣΙΟΤΣ and for the retention of ἐν Ἐφέσῳ in peculiar type in the text itself. Whether Marcion's title were derived from a copy actually sent to Laodicea or, as seems more likely, was a conjectural alteration of ΠΡΟΣ ΕΦΕΣΙΟΤΣ, Ephesus must have had a better right than any other single city to account itself the recipient of the Epistle.

i 15 καί] + τὴν ἀγάπην Western and Syrian (Gr. Lat. Syr. Eg. ? Arm. Goth.); also + ἀγάπην after ἁγίους 39 80 al[p.bo] (? aeth) Cyr.al.*Jo* (*s.q.*) Euth.cod. Text אּ*ABP₂17 Orig.*loc.* Cyr.al.*Dial.Trin* Hier.*lcc.* (probably after Orig) Aug.*Praed. sanct.* 39 p. 816. From Col i 4. The at first sight difficult reading of text is illustrated by Philem 5; as also by Tit iii 15; Ro i 12; cf. Ga v 6; Eph iii 17. It is remarkably confirmed by the peculiar phrase τὴν καθ' ὑμᾶς, which stands in antithesis to τὴν εἰς πάντας, κ.τ.λ., and which would have little force as a mere substitute for τὴν ὑμῶν : the single phrase of Ga v 6, πίστις δι' ἀγάπης ἐνεργουμένη, harmonises the language of Col, in which love to men stands simply by the side of faith, with the language of Eph, in which the faith which exists within is represented as itself the source of deeds done to men.

iv 19 ἀπηλγηκότες] ἀπηλπικότες (ἀφηλπ.) Western (Gr. Lat. Æth. Arm. Goth.); incl. Orig.*Jer*.lat. Hier; not Clem Orig.*loc*;*Jer*.gr ; *Ps*. The resemblance of ΠΙ to ΓΗ doubtless contributed with the paradox of the sense to suggest the correction.

iv 29 χρείας] πίστεως Western (Gr. Lat. Arm. Goth.); incl. Greg. nys Cyp²; not 'the Greek' according to Hier Clem Orig.*loc*.

v 14 ἐπιφαύσει σοι ὁ χριστός] ἐπιψαύσεις τοῦ χριστοῦ Western (Gr. Lat.); incl. MSS mentioned by Theod.mops.lat by Chr and by Thdt (the two latter probably not independently) Orig.*Jos*.lat. Ruf; *Cant*.lat.Ruf; not G₃ Marcion(ap. Epiph) Naasseni(ap.Hipp) Clem Orig.*loc*.;*Ps*² Hipp.*Ant* Amb Hier 'Vig'. The supposed intermediate reading ἐπιφαύσει σοι ὁ χριστός appears to be due to the transcribers of Chr, though Aug once, at least as edited, and Ambst.cod have

continget te Christus. The two imperatives doubtless suggested that the following future would be in the second person, the required C stood next after ἐπιφαύσει, easily read as ἐπιψαύσει, and then the rest would be altered accordingly.

v 30 τοῦ σώματος αὐτοῦ] + ἐκ τῆς σαρκὸς αὐτοῦ καὶ ἐκ τῶν ὀστέων αὐτοῦ Western and Syrian (Gr. Lat. Syr. Arm.); incl. Iren.gr.lat. Text ℵ*AB 17 67** me aeth Meth (anon.[? Tit.bost]*Lc*.88Cramer) Euthal.cod : also probably Orig.*Cant*. lat.Ruf, who quotes nothing after σώματος αὐτοῦ. From Gen ii 23.

v 31 καὶ προσκολληθήσεται πρὸς τὴν γυναῖκα αὐτοῦ] < (Marcion, see below) Orig.*loc*.expressly (the scholium, though anonymous, is certainly his) Tert(apparently, as well as Marcion) Cyp.*Ep*.52.codd. opt Hier.*loc*(doubtless from Orig). Text ℵABD₂G₃K₂L₂P₂ cuᵒᵐⁿ vvᵒᵐⁿ Orig.*Cels* ;(? *Mt*.gr.lat) Meth Victorin pp^{lat.ser}. A singular reading, which would not be improbable if its attestation were not exclusively patristic : the words might well be inserted from Gen ii 24. They are absent from the quotation as it occurs in the true text of Mc x 7 ; but were there inserted so early and so widely that the only surviving authorities for omission are ℵB lt 48 go.

COLOSSIANS

ii 2 τοῦ θεοῦ, Χριστοῦ] Several independent variations appear here.
(1) τοῦ θεοῦ, ὅ ἐστιν Χριστός Western of limited range, D₂* Aug

'Vig' (?Ephr.*Diat*.arm. p. 3 *Consilium arcanum Dei Christus est, a quo revelata sunt omnia mysteria sapientiae et scientiae*).

31

(2) τοῦ θεοῦ καὶ Χριστοῦ Cyr.al. Thes.

(3) τοῦ θεοῦ D₂ᵇP₂ 37 67** 71 80 116.

(4) τοῦ θεοῦ πατρὸς [τοῦ] χριστοῦ Alexandrian, א*AC 4 lat.vg me.cod the (< τοῦ 2° א*): whence

τοῦ θεοῦ καὶ πατρὸς τοῦ χριστοῦ אᶜ cu² syr.hl.txt : and

τοῦ θεοῦ πατρὸς καὶ τοῦ χριστοῦ Syrian, 47 73 vg.lat.codd syr.vg me.cod Theod.Mops.lat Chr Pelag: and by combination of the last two

τοῦ θεοῦ καὶ πατρὸς καὶ τοῦ χριστοῦ Constantinopolitan, D₂ᶜK₂L₂ cuᵖˡ syr.hl.* Thdt.txt(s.q.) Dam al.

(5) τοῦ θεοῦ ἐν Χριστῷ (17) (aeth) arm Clem² Ambst: 17 adds a second τοῦ before ἐν, and aeth expresses rather περὶ than ἐν.

No account is taken here of the insertion of Ἰησοῦ with Χριστοῦ or Χριστῷ in some secondary documents.

Text B Hil(distinctly) (? Ephr. Diat: see above).

It is at once obvious that all the variations may easily be corrections of text, and that this is unquestionably the origin of all except (5). The reading of B Hil is therefore amply sustained by documentary and transcriptional evidence, notwithstanding the narrow range of its direct attestation. In considering the intrinsic difficulty of the phrase τοῦ μυστηρίου τοῦ θεοῦ, Χριστοῦ it may be safely taken for granted that, as a matter of interpretation, Χριστοῦ must stand in apposition to τοῦ μυστηρίου. [With this construction, the phrase may on the whole be accepted as genuine: it is illustrated by 1 Ti iii 16. W.] [Yet elsewhere in the New Testament (Col i 27 being included) Christ always appears as the subject of the mystery, not as the mystery itself; and in 1 Ti iii 16 τὸ τῆς εὐσεβείας μυστήριον need not be the antece-

dent of ὅς if, as seems likely, ὅς... δόξῃ is a quotation. The apposition too, without even an article before Χριστοῦ, is unusual in form, and so liable to be misunderstood that St Paul is hardly likely to have used it when it was open to him to say ὅ ἐστιν Χριστός (cf. i 24; ii 10). A very slight change of letters will remove the whole difficulty: τοῦ μυστηρίου τοῦ ἐν Χριστῷ harmonises completely with what follows and with other language of St Paul, and differs from text only as ΕΝΧΩ differs from ΘΥΧΥ, while the misreading of ΕΝ would be facilitated by the preceding ΟΥ of τοῦ, and this misreading would inevitably change ΧΥ to ΧΩ. It may be reasonably suspected that τοῦ θεοῦ ἐν Χριστῷ (5, above) is derived from τοῦ ἐν Χριστῷ, either by conflation with text or by a mere repetition of the last two letters of ΤΟΥ as ΘΥ. H.]

ii 18 (†) θέλων ἐν ταπεινοφροσύνῃ] < ἐν א*(not אᵃ). [This phrase contains two apparently insuperable difficulties. First, no reasonable sense can be obtained from θέλων used absolutely: and the combination of θέλων with ἐν ('delighting in'), though common in the LXX, is not merely without precedent but without analogy in St Paul, whose style, except of course in quotations, is singularly free from crude Hebraisms. Secondly, ταπεινοφροσύνη having invariably in the New Testament a good meaning, St Paul was not likely to use it as a term of reproach without at least some preliminary indication of what he had in view. There is apparently some corruption, perhaps θέλων ἐν ταπεινοφροσύνῃ for ἐν ἐθελοταπεινοφροσύνῃ: this last word is employed by Bas; and compounds of ἐθελο- were used freely when St

Paul wrote. Cf. Aug.*Ep.*149 § 27 : Nemo vos convincat volens : *hoc si per verbum graecum diceretur, etiam in latina consuetudine populi sonaret usitatius; sic enim et vulgo dicitur qui divitem affectat* thelodives, *et qui sapientem* thelosapiens, *et cetera hujusmodi. Ergo et hic* thelohumilis, *quod plenius dicitur* thelon humilis, *id est* volens humilis, *quod intellegitur 'volens videri humilis', 'affectans humilitatem'.* * * * *Mirabiliter ibi eum dixit* inflatum mente carnis suae *ubi* thelohumilem *supra dixerat.* H.]

ibid. (†) ἃ ἑόρακεν ἐμβατεύων] + μὴ (? Western of limited range and) Syrian (Gr. Lat. Syr. Arm. Goth.); incl. C(G₃) Ps.Iren.*Fragm. Pfaff.*35[Orig.*Cels.*ed.Ru.(apparently without authority from MSS); *Rom.*lat.Ruf.txt] Ambst.cod Amb: G₃ has οὐχ, which is perhaps the original (? Western) form of the reading. Text ℵ*ABD₂* 17 67** al Greek MSS known to Hier *m* (? Latin) MSS known to Aug me aeth Marcion (ap. Tert) Orig.*Cels*; *Rom.*lat.Ruf.com(*extollunt enim se in his quae videntur et inflati sunt de visibilibus rebus*) Lucif Ambst. cod al. Many MSS (not ℵBCD₂P₂ cuᵐᵘ) have the form ἑώρακεν.

The insertion of the negative glosses over without removing the manifest difficulty of the phrase, and must in any case be rejected on documentary grounds. Dr Lightfoot has with good reason revived a suggestion of Alexander More and

Courcelles that the last word must be taken with the three preceding letters, so as to make κενεμβατεύων : at the same time in place of ἃ ἑώρα[κεν] he suggests ἑώρᾳ or αἰώρᾳ, a word twice used by Philo in similar contexts and appropriate here. On the whole however ἀέρα, conjectured by Dr C. Taylor (*Journ. of Philol.* (1876) xiii 130 ff.), is still more probable : the transitive construction is amply attested for ἐμβατεύω, and presents no difficulty with ἀέρα. ΑΕΡΑΚΕΝΕΜΒΑΤΕΥΩΝ differs from ΑΕΟΡΑΚΕΝΕΜΒΑΤΕΥΩΝ only by the absence of Ε before Ο.

ii 23 (†) [καὶ] ἀφειδίᾳ ......σαρκός] < καὶ B (*d*) *m* Orig.*Rom.*lat.Ruf Hil Ambst Amb Paulin.*Ep.* 50⁴(p. 298 f. Le Brun): Clem omits the previous καί, reading however ταπεινοφροσύνης (if his text is rightly preserved): + *et non* after τινι lat.cod(*gigas*): + *et diligentiam* after πλησμονήν Ambst Amb. [None of the current explanations of οὐκ ἐν τιμῇ...σαρκός appear to be tenable, and the preceding clause is hardly less suspicious. On the other hand no probable emendation has been suggested. This Epistle, and more especially its second chapter, appears to have been ill preserved in ancient times; and it may be that some of the harshnesses which we have left unmarked are really due to primitive corruption. H.]

1 THESSALONIANS

ii 7 νήπιοι] ἤπιοι Syrian (Gr. Syr. Eg. Arm.) ; incl. ℵᶜACᵃ [Clem. *Paed*.109 codd ;*Strom*.319(*s.q.*) Orig. *Mt*.724(*s.q.*) ; 1 *Co*.84 Cram.(*s.q.*)]. Text ℵ*BC*D₂G₃ 5 23 31* 37 137 alᵖ lat.vg me aeth Clem.*Paed*.codd (with context)² Orig.*Mt*.(609 ;)662 (with context, ἐγένετο νήπιος καὶ παραπλήσιος τροφῷ θαλπούσῃ τὸ ἑαυτῆς παιδίον, καὶ λαλούσῃ λόγους ὡς παιδίον διὰ τὸ παιδίον: cf. 659); lat.878; *Is*.lat.116 Cyr.*Thes* ppᶫᵃᵗ·ᵒᵐⁿ. The second ν might be inserted or omitted with equal facility; but the change from the bold image to the tame and facile adjective is characteristic of the difference between St Paul and the Syrian revisers (cf. 1 Co iii 1,2 ; ix 20 ff.). It is not of harshness that St Paul here declares himself innocent, but of flattery and the rhetorical arts by which gain or repute is procured, his adversaries having doubt-less put this malicious interpretation upon his language among the Thessalonians. Further, the phrase ἐν μέσῳ ὑμῶν exactly suits νήπιοι, and would be an unlikely periphrasis for εἰς ὑμᾶς with ἤπιοι: it corresponds to a position of equality, like that which St Paul would assume in making himself a babe among babes, not to the graciousness of a superior speaking or acting as a superior. Compare the use of συννηπιάζω in Iren.284 and Cyr.al.*Jo*.237C, and Aug.*De catech. rud.* 15 *Quomodo enim paratus esset impendi pro animabus eorum si eum pigeret inclinari ad aures eorum?   Hinc ergo* factus est parvulus in medio nostrum tamquam nutrix fovens filios suos. *Num enim delectat, nisi amor invitet, decurtata et mutilata verba immurmurare?*

2 THESSALONIANS

i 10 (†) ἐπιστεύθη] ἐπιστώθη 31 139: *fidem habuit* Ambst. [It seems hopeless to find an intelligible meaning for ἐφ' ὑμᾶς (< *nev*) in connexion with ἐπιστεύθη. Apparently, as conjectured by Markland, ἐπιστεύθη is a primitive corruption of ἐπιστώθη, suggested by the preceding πιστεύσασιν as well as by the familiarity of πιστεύω and its *prima facie* appropriateness to μαρτύριον. The reference is probably to vv. 4,5: the Christian testimony of suffering for the faith had been confirmed and sealed upon the Thessalonians. Cf. 1 Co i 6 καθὼς τὸ μαρτύριον τοῦ χριστοῦ ἐβεβαιώθη ἐν ὑμῖν; also Ps xciii (xcii) 4, 5 θαυμαστὸς ἐν ὑψηλοῖς ὁ κύριος· τὰ μαρτύριά σου ἐπιστώθησαν σφόδρα; and, for an analogous use of πιστοῦσθαι followed by ἐπί with the accusative, 1 Chr xvii 23; 2 Chr i 9. H.]

HEBREWS

ii 9 χάριτι θεοῦ] χωρὶς θεοῦ M₂ MSS known to Orig and (? Greek, ? Latin) to Hier. *Gal* 67** syr.vg.codd Orig.*Jo*³(twice expressly); *Rom*.lat.Ruf² Theod.M ops.*loc.* (expressly) Thdt.*loc*;*Phil* Anastas. abb.*Jud*(Migne lxxxix 1265) Amb³ Fulg 'Vig'. Text אABCD₂K₂L₂P₂ MSS known to Orig and (? Greek, ? Latin) to Hier cuᵖˡ lat.vg syr.hl me aeth arm Eus.*Ps* Ath Chr Cyr. alˢᵃᵉᵖᵉ (Hier.*Gal*) Faustin: some MSS of syr.vg have a strange rendering which must represent χάριτι θεός, doubtless a corruption of text. The reading χωρίς, apparently Western and Syrian, but not Constantinopolitan, was in late times attributed to the Nestorians, probably because it had been stoutly defended by Theod.mops. Transcriptional evidence is in its favour, as it was more likely to be perplexing to transcribers than χάριτι. Intrinsically however it will not bear close examination. To take it (as do Orig and Thdt) as qualifying ὑπὲρ παντός, like ἐκτός in 1 Co xv 27, is against the order of words: and the qualification would be too readily supplied by every reader to be thought to need expression. A better sense may be put upon it by connecting it directly with γεύσηται θανάτου: but both the order of words and the logical force of the clause (ὅπως) shew the true connexion to be with ὑπὲρ παντός; and conversely χάριτι θεοῦ, which would be almost otiose here in relation to γεύσηται θανάτου

alone, has special force as linking ὅπως and ὑπὲρ παντός together. Χωρίς probably arose from a confusion of letters which might easily take place in papyrus writing.

iv 2 (†) μὴ συνκεκερασμένους τῇ πίστει τοῖς ἀκούσασιν] συνκεκερασμένος for -νους probably Western, א (συγκεκραμένος [??31 41] 114 [-μμ-] Cyr.al.*Glaph*.ed(*s. q.*) [Thdt. *loc.* ed¹, against context]) (? *a*) lat.vg.codd syr.vg Lucif: the συγκεκραμένος of the 'Received Text' comes from Erasmus, who can have had only Latin authority for it. Text, which is also virtually Syrian, ABCD₂*M₂ (17) 23 37 71 73 137 al (? Iren. lat, see below), Theod.mop Euth. cod (also συγκεκραμένος Syrian, D₂ᶜK₂L₂P₂ cuᵖˡ Chr Thdt Cyr.al. *Nest* [pl. acc. by sense] al) lat.vg syr.hl me aeth arm: cf. Iren.lat, who has perhaps a reference to this passage in the words '*perseverantes in servitute pristinae* inobedientiae [cf. iii 18], nondum commixti verbo *Dei Patris*', and, '*commixtus verbo Dei*'. Also τοῖς ἀκούσασιν] τῶν ἀκουσάντων D* 31 syr.hl.mg Lucif: τοῖς ἀκουσθεῖσιν 71 Theod.mops Thdt(apparently after Theod.mops); cf.vg.lat *ex iis quae* (*qui* codd.) *audierunt*.

After much hesitation we have marked this very difficult passage as probably containing a primitive corruption. This Epistle contains several traces of very early injury to its text. [The apparent simplicity of συνκεκερασμένος leads to no satisfactory result: it identifies ἐκείνους with τοῖς ἀκούσασιν, which thus becomes a superfluous and at the same time ambiguous repetition; and it obscures the purpose of the clause by expressing the cause of the inoperativeness of the Divine message in a neutral form, which suggests accidental failure in the message rather than culpable luke-warmness in the receivers. Hence, though a pertinent sense may be obtained from the words, they are hardly such words as would have been naturally used for the purpose of conveying this sense. On the other hand συνκεκρᾶσθαι, like ἀνα-κεκρᾶσθαι, is used (1) of close intimacy with another person, sometimes coupled with κοινωνία, and (2) of inward reception of an influence from without. The reading of text thus makes good sense if τοῖς ἀκούσασιν may be interpreted, in accordance with τῶν ἀκουσάντων in ii 3, to mean the original or immediate hearers (in the one case the Apostles, in the other Moses) through whom the Divine word was conveyed to those who were hearers in the second degree; compare οἵτινες ἐλάλησαν ὑμῖν τὸν λόγον τοῦ θεοῦ in xiii 7. It is however difficult to understand why the bare phrase τοῖς ἀκούσασιν should be used to denote the true and faithful hearers in a context which seems to contemplate a 'hearing' unaccompanied by faith (iii 16—19). H.] [The reading συνκεκερασμένος seems to give a fair sense; but on the whole is suspicious. W.] Perhaps the most probable sense would be supplied by a combination of συνκεκερασμένους with the slenderly supported reading τοῖς ἀκουσθεῖσιν (from ii 1), which is possibly genuine. Noesselt's conjecture τοῖς ἀκούσμασιν however, which would give the same sense, has the advantage of

accounting better for τοῖς ἀκούσασιν; and ἀκούσματα, often coupled with θεάματα or ὁράματα, is a common word to denote simply 'things heard'.

vii 1 ὁ συναντήσας] ὃς συναντήσας אABCᵃD₂K₂ 17 al. Text (Syrian) C*L₂P₂cuᵖˡ (?? vvᵒᵐⁿ) ppˢᵉʳ. It seems more likely that ὅς is a primitive reduplication (occ for oc), perhaps suggested by ᾧ in v. 2, and ὁ a right emendation of the Syrian revisers, than that the writer broke off the sentence two lines below without apparent cause.

ix 2 ἄρτων] +καὶ τὸ χρυσοῦν θυ-μιατήριον (with omission of χρυσοῦν and θυμιατήριον καὶ in v. 4) B basm aeth; not Orig.*Ex.*lat.Ruf.162; Cyr. al.*Ador.*338;*Jo.*1070. Doubtless intended as a correction of the apparent misplacement of the golden altar of incense.

x 1 (†) θυσίαις]+αὐτῶν אP₂ (τ. αὐτῶν θυσίαις 37): (*isdem*) *ipsis hos-tiis* lat.vg. Also ἅς] αἷς D₂*H₃L₂ 5 73 96 137 *harl* (*quibus*) ppˢᵉʳ; also ἅς or αἷς *r* vg me basm aeth: < ἅς A 7* 17 47 syrr arm. Text (ἅς) אCD₂ᶜK₂P₂ cuᵖᵐ (vv, see above) ppˢᵉʳ: B is defective from ix 14 to the end of the N.T. Also διηνεκὲς] + αἱ Aᵃ 31 (? syr.hl arm). Also δύνανται] δύναται probably Western, D₂*·ᶜH₃K₂L₂ 5 39 alᵖ *r* vg me basm ppˢᵉʳ Orig.*Ps.*lat.Ruf: the adoption of this reading by Erasmus, and hence in the 'Received Text', is probably due to Latin authority. Text אACD₂ᵇP₂ 17 37 47 67** 73 80 alᵖᵐ syrr arm ppˢᵉʳ.

Structure and sense together suggest that the opening sentence is perhaps interrupted somewhere, to introduce parenthetic illustration, and never completed. This consideration however by no means suffices to clear up the difficulties of reading. If κατ' ἐνιαυτόν and εἰς τὸ διηνεκές are to retain, as might be expected, the sense which they have in neighbouring and cognate passages, they must stand in antithesis to each other, each being placed for emphasis at the head of the following words. [In conformity with this arrangement of words it seems possible to obtain a good sense by adopting the reading δύναται, and placing a comma after ἃς προσφέρουσιν. W.] [The analogies of ix 9; x 11 (the sacrifices) and x 10 (the Levitical priests, answering to the true High Priest) are in favour of δύνανται, the better attested reading. Also προσφέρουσιν seems to crave the virtual predicate afforded by the preceding or the following phrase; and yet εἰς τὸ διηνεκές, if taken with it, loses its proper and antithetic sense. There is excellent authority for omitting ἃς; but the dative ταῖς αὐταῖς θυσίαις can hardly be taken with προσφέρουσιν in the sense 'make offering with the same sacrifices'. It is difficult to think that we have the text quite complete. If it were written thus, καθ' ἣν κατ' ἐνιαυτὸν τὰς αὐτὰς θυσίας προσφέρουσιν, αἳ εἰς τὸ διηνεκὲς οὐδέποτε δύνανται τοὺς προσερχομένους τελειῶσαι, the sentence would run clearly and easily to the point of interruption by ἐπεί, and καθ' ἣν would find confirmation in the similar verse ix 9, where παραβολή answers to σκιάν here. The alterations here supposed would involve no transposition, being in character like the commonest errors of transcription; they would be the loss of ΚΑΘΗΝ before ΚΑΤΕΝ and of ΑΙ before ΕΙ, and the change of ΑC to ΑΙC in three consecutive words. The suggested text may at least indicate the probable tenor of the sentence generally, though in such a case it is impossible to be confident

about details. H.] It is at all events difficult to be satisfied that any one form of the transmitted text is free from error.

xi 4 (†) μαρτυροῦντος ἐπὶ τοῖς δώροις αὐτοῦ τοῦ θεοῦ] μ. ἐ. τ. δ. αὐτοῦ τῷ θεῷ ℵ*AD₂* 17 ? aeth Euthal. cod* : μ. ἐ. τ. δ. αὐτῷ τοῦ θεοῦ Clem. Text ℵᶜD₂ᶜK₂L₂P₂ cuᵖˡ r vg syrr me arm ppˢᵉʳ. The reading of the best MSS is apparently a primitive error, due to mechanical permutation, the true reading being that which Clem alone has preserved. The common text, an easy correction of either of the other readings, gives substantially the true sense.

xi 23 *fin.*]+πίστει (-τι) μέγας γενόμενος Μωυσῆς ἀνεῖλεν (ανιλεν) τὸν Αἰγύπτιον κατανοῶν τὴν ταπείνωσιν (-πινωσιν) τῶν ἀδελφῶν αὐτοῦ D₂* lat.vg.codd (*dolorem* for τὴν ταπείνωσιν latt).

xi 35 (†) ἔλαβον γυναῖκες] ἔ. γυναῖκας ℵ*AD₂* (me). Text ℵᶜD₂ᵇK₂ L₂P₂ cuᵒᵐⁿ (? lat.vg) syrr aeth Cyr.al.*Jul.*189. The reading of the best MSS must be a primitive error, due to the immediate sequence of γυν. on ἔλαβον, and rightly emended in the later text.

xi 37 (†) ἐπειράσθησαν, ἐπρίσθησαν] (marg.) ἐπρίσθησαν, ἐπειράσθησαν AD₂ᶜK₂ cuᵖᵐ (d) vg me arm Orig. *Cels.*codd ;*Jer.*gr ;*Mt.*465;*Jo.*268; *Mt.*848 ppˢᵉʳ Amb (and so probably D₂* in intention, though ἐπιράσθησαν [*sic*] is written twice) : < ἐπειράσθησαν Orig.*Afric.*; *Mt.*218.lat.Hier Eus Acac al : < ἐπρίσθησαν *fu** *ncv** Clem : < both words aeth.cod. Text ℵL₂P₂ 17 39 syr.hl Euthal.cod.

It is difficult to find here a natural interpretation for a word so general in its sense as ἐπειράσθησαν. Possibly it is only a reduplication of ἐπρίσθησαν, as φόνοι of φθόνοι in Ga v 21; πορνείᾳ of πονηρίᾳ in Ro i 29; and ἀσπόνδους of ἀστόργους in

Ro i 31: but it may with at least equal probability be a primitive corruption of some other word. The most probable of the various suggestions that have been made are ἐπρήσθησαν (Gataker) or ἐνεπρήσθησαν (Lücke: it is cited, but with ζῶντες, from a somewhat similar passage of Philo *Flacc.* 20), ΕΝΕΠΡΗ for ΕΠΕΙΡΔ, as the three nearest verbs denote modes of death (ἐπρήσθησαν is actually read for ἐπρίσθησαν, though perhaps only by itacism, in two cursives 110 111 [Rinck]); or again ἐπηρώθησαν (Tanaquil Faber), which is commended by ἐπειρώθησαν, the reading of at least one of Höschel's MSS in Orig. *Cels.* perhaps itself the right form (cf. ἀνάπειρος Lc xiv 13,21 [all the best MSS]; 2 Mac viii 24 [A, the only extant uncial]).

xii 11 (†) μὲν] (marg.) δὲ ℵᶜA D₂ᶜK₂L₂ cuᵖᵐ lat.vg syrr me ppˢᵉʳ Cyr.al.*Hom.pasch.*298 ppˢᵒ : et...

quidem (? καὶ...μὲν ? καὶ...δὲ) *d harl*: *enim* Hier Aug: < D₂* 31 al² arm aeth (Orig.*Mt.*gr.lat Cyr. *Hos.*38 al). Text ℵ*P₂ 17 21 Orig.*Ps.*lat. Ruf auct.*XLII Mans.* [None of the particles are satisfactory, though δέ was sure to be introduced: nor again is the author of this Epistle likely to have put no particle here. Δή is not improbable; but it hardly accounts for μέν. H.]

xiii 21 (†) ποιῶν] (marg.) αὐτῷ ποιῶν ℵ*AC* 17* (ἑαυτῷ Greg.nys i 853=i 1325 Mi): αὐτὸς ποιῶν 71 (*d ipso faciente*). Text ℵᶜCᵇD₂M₂ K₂P₂ cuᵖˡ lat.vg syrr me (? aeth) arm ppˢᵉʳ. The marginal reading is strongly supported by both documentary and transcriptional evidence: but it is impossible to make sense of αὐτῷ, and αὐτῷ has but slender probability. There can be little doubt that αὐτὸς ποιῶν is the true reading.

1 TIMOTHY

i 4 οἰκονομίαν] οἰκοδομὴν Western, D₂* *g m* vg syr.vg-hl.mg go Iren. gr.lat Hil ppˡᵃᵗ·ᵐᵘ; not G₃: οἰκοδομίαν D₂ᶜ 192 Dam.txt; and so Erasmus, and after him Beza and Elz. (though not Estienne), but doubtless only by a conjectural adaptation of οἰκονομίαν to *aedificationem*.

iii 1 πιστὸς] ἀνθρώπινος D₂* *g* (as an alternative) *m* Ambst Sedul; not G₃. A singular correction, perhaps due to an assumption that the

clause belongs to what follows, rightly condemned by Chrys. The same reading, probably transferred from this place, occurs at i 15 in *r* Latin MSS known to Hier Ambst Julian.pel Aug.3/4.

iii 16 *Ὃς* ὁ Western, D₂* *g* vg [Theod.mops.*loc.*lat] Hil Victorin Ambst Julian.pel Aug Fulg 'Vig' al: θεὸς CᶜD₂ᶜK₂L₂P₂ cuᵖᵐ Did. *Trin*(expressly) Greg.nys(expressly) (? Diod.tars.*Rom.*124Cram:

context neutral) Chrys.(? *loc* ;)*Hom. Philog.*t.i p.497; *Jo.*86 Thdt.*loc* ; *Inconf.* 19, 23; *Qu.Gen.*92 [Cyr.al. *Fid.*124, 153 codd; *Expl. Capp.* codd: see below]: supposed allusions in Hipp and others have no characteristics that connect them with this passage. Text אA*C* (see below) G₃ 17 73 181 syr.hl.mg me the go ?Orig.*Rom.*lat.Ruf(*sicut apostolus dicit Quia* [? *Qui*] *manifestatus est in carne* &c.) Epiph Theod.mops.*loc.*lat (by context, text *quod*) ; *Incarn.*988 Migne (ὅς) [=syr.53 Sachau(*quod*)] ; syr.64(*qui*) Euther.lat Cyr.al.*Fid.*6 (=*Inc.Unig.*680); (124, by sense,) 153; *Expl. Capp.* 148; *Schol.*785 (for Cyr.al see especially *Incarn. Unig.* πλανᾶσθε μὴ εἰδότες τὰς γραφὰς μήτε μὴν τὸ μέγα τῆς εὐσεβείας μυστήριον, τοῦτ᾽ ἐστὶ Χριστόν, ὃς ἐφανερώθη κ.τ.λ.). The result of the most careful examinations of A, with the help of the microscope, is to shew that it had originally OC without a transverse stroke, and without a bar above, such as would mark the contraction Θ͞C, though both have been added in comparatively modern times: in C they are also present, and of older date, but certainly due to a corrector, not to the original hand: in א the letters θε are added above the line by the latest of the various correctors of this MS, who is assigned to Cent. XII. Either ὅς or ὅ is attested by syr.vg-hl.txt aeth arm (?Clem. *Hyp.*1015) (?Apollin[ap.Greg.nys]). There is at first sight a similar ambiguity in two of the passages of Theod.mops: but the context points to ὅς. The change of ὅς to θεός was one of the readings unjustly charged against the patriarch Macedonius at the time of his expulsion by Monophysite influence in 510-1 : so Liberat.*Brev*, cited in part in note on Mt xxvii 49 : see also Bentley in

Works iii 366 f.

The Western ὅ is a manifest correction of ὅς, intended to remedy the apparent breach of concord between the relative and τὸ μυστήριον. Thus all the better MSS agree with all the versions against θεός in favour of either ὅς or a reading which presupposes ὅς. There is no trace of θεός till the last third of Cent. IV, as there could not have failed to be if it had been known to Orig Eus Cyr.hr Ath Bas or Greg.naz ; and the limits of patristic attestation mark it as late Syrian, though not accepted in either Syriac version. Did.*Trin* abounds in Syrian readings, and they are not rare with Greg.nys. The language of Theod. mops throws doubt on the uncertified quotation of his predecessor Diod.tars : but Chr, though his Comm. (in its uninterpolated form) is ambiguous, seems in the other two places to have probably θεός, which was unquestionably read by Thdt. From these circumstances, as well as from the virtual universality of its reception in Greek in subsequent times, θεός may be safely classed as a late Antiochian reading.

It may perhaps have had an accidental origin, permutation or confusion of OC and Θ͞C being peculiarly easy : but the change from ὅς to θεός would be facilitated, if it was not caused, by the removal of an apparent solecism, obtained concurrently with the acquisition of increased definiteness for a theological statement; while there is no similar way of accounting for the converse change.

The intrinsic evidence is to the same effect. Θεός is not a word likely to be chosen deliberately to stand at the head of this series of six clauses, though it might seem to harmonise with the first of the six. The documentary evidence however being unambiguous, the only question that can arise is whether ὅς is intrinsically improbable. Its difficulty is solely grammatical, at least on any interpretation which allows the virtual antecedent of ὅς to be Christ. If He might be Himself described as τὸ τῆς εὐσεβείας μυστήριον (see note on Col ii 2), this condition is directly satisfied, and the sentence runs without interruption. But, however this may be, the concurrence of three independent data, ὁμολογουμένως, ὅς, and the form of· the six clauses, suggests that these clauses were a quotation from an early Christian hymn ; and, if so, the proper and original antecedent would doubtless have been found in the preceding context which is not quoted.

iv 3 (†) κωλυόντων γαμεῖν, ἀπέχεσθαι βρώματων] There are, strictly speaking, no various readings in this very difficult passage, though there are several indications that the difficulty was felt in ancient times. No Greek usage will justify or explain this combination of two infinitives, adverse to each other in the tenor of their sense, under the one verb κωλυόντων ; and their juxtaposition without a conjunction in a sentence of this kind is at least strange. Some primitive corruption is doubtless present ; and it is likely to have created both difficulties. Bentley suggests that κελευόντων has fallen out before ἀπέχεσθαι. [A misreading of ἢ ἅπτεσθαι or καὶ γεύεσθαι would be easy, and would account for the missing conjunction. Both

verbs occur in a similar passage, Col ii 21, and are specially used in reference to ceremonial abstinences, *e.g.* Diog. Laert. vi 73 μηδέν τε ἄτοπον εἶναι...ἢ τῶν ζῴων τινὸς γεύσασθαι, μηδ᾽ ἀνόσιον εἶναι τὸ καὶ τῶν ἀνθρωπείων κρεῶν ἅψασθαι : cf. Porph.*Abst.* ii 31. The former correction has the more probable words, but implies the loss of H after N, or its virtual transposition : the latter comes the nearer to the *ductus litterarum.* Neither however implies an improbable amount of change, as may be seen by the juxtapositions

ΕΙΝΗΑΠΤΕ   ΕΙΚΑΙΓΕΥΕ

ΕΙΝΑΠΕΧΕ   ΕΙΝΑΠΕΧΕ. Η.]

v 19 ἐκτὸς...μαρτύρων] < Latin MSS known to Hier ; also apparently Cyp Ambst, who quote no further than παραδέχου ; not D₂ *r* nor (<ἐπὶ) G₃.

vi 7 (†) ὅτι] ἀληθὲς ὅτι Western. D₂* *m sess*¹ go Ambst : *verum* Cyp. 2/2 Paulin² Aug¹ : ἀλλ᾽ (Polyc) Aug ˢᵃᵉᵖᵉ : *haut dubium quia* (*quod*) lat.vg : *haut dubium verum tamen fu* (? al) : δῆλον ὅτι Syrian, אᶜD₂ᵇ·ᶜK₂L₂P₂ cuᵖˡ (syrr) Bas ppˢᵉʳ : '*and*' me aeth : < arm Cyr.*Lc.*350 Mai(gr. syr) ; 167 syr ; 658 syr Orsies (Galland v 45). Text א*AG₃ 17 *r* (? vg.codd) the. Text is manifestly the parent of all the other readings, which are futile attempts to smooth away its difficulty. A primitive corruption must lurk somewhere. [Perhaps ὅτι is no more than an accidental repetition of the last two letters of κόσμον, ΟΝ being read as ΟΤΙ. Η.]

2 TIMOTHY

i 13 (†) ὑποτύπωσιν ἔχε ὑγιαινόν-
των λόγων ὧν παρ' ἐμοῦ ἤκουσας]
[The order, the absence of τήν, and
the use of ἔχε (not κάτεχε, as 1 Co
xi 2 ; xv 2 ; 1 Th v 21) shew that ὑποτύπωσιν has a predicative force ;—
'hold as a pattern', not 'hold the
pattern'. If this be so, what had
been heard from St Paul must have
been what he desired Timothy to
hold as a pattern. But this sense
cannot be obtained from text except
by treating ὧν as put in the genitive
by an unusual and inexplicable attraction. It seems more probable
that ωΝ is a primitive corruption of
ΟΝ after πΑΝΤωΝ, aided by the
unreal semblance of attraction. The
force that would be given to λόγον
in the singular, as implied in ὄν,
is justified by the comprehensive
use of ὁ λόγος in the Pastoral Epistles. H.]

iii 8 Ἰαμβρῆς] Μαμβρῆς Western,
G₃ *d m* vg go Orig.*Mt*.lat² (? Const.
Ap.cod¹ Macar al², not referring to
this place) Cyp pp^{lat. mu}; not D₂.gr.
Orig.*Mt*.lat.916 refers to an apocryphal book, *Jamnes et Mambres
liber*. The names were at all events
largely current in both forms in
Jewish tradition (Buxtorf *Lex. Talm.*
945 ff.), and the Western text probably derived Μαμβρῆς from a Palestinian source. For Ἰαννῆς C*
Euthal.cod have Ἰωάννης, which
agrees with the form יוחני used in
some of the Jewish authorities : but
the coincidence is doubtless accidental, as there is no trace of Ἰωάννης here in Western documents.

iv 10 Γαλατίᾳ] Γαλλίαν apparently Alexandrian, אC 23 31 39 73
80 lat.vg.codd (? Eus.*H. E.*) Epiph.
A natural correction in accordance
with the later usage as regards
Gaul, both Galatia and Gaul having
in St Paul's time been usually if not
always alike called Γαλατία by the
Greeks. The interpretation may be
right. See Dr Lightfoot *Galat.* 3,
31.

iv 19 Ἀκύλαν] +, Λέκτραν τὴν
γυναῖκα αὐτοῦ καὶ Σιμαίαν (Σημ. 109)
καὶ Ζήνωνα τοὺς υἱοὺς αὐτοῦ, 46
109. Probably from an apocryphal
source.

TITUS

iii 10 καὶ δευτέραν νουθεσίαν] *v.
καὶ δύο* D₂*: *v. καὶ δευτέραν* D₂^c:
v. ἢ δευτέρᾳ (*l. -ραν*) G₃: < *καὶ δευτέραν* MSS (? Greek ? Latin) known
to Hier *m* Iren.lat.1/2(not gr)
Pamph.lat.Ruf Tert Cyp Lucif
pp^{lat. mu}; not lat.vg Iren.gr.2/2
(lat.1/2). Hier refers to text as
found *in Latinis codicibus*; but the
context suggests that he meant to
say *Graecis*.

PHILEMON

9 (†) πρεσβύτης] There can be no
doubt that Bentley and others are
right in suggesting that the meaning
here is 'ambassador' (πρεσβευτής:
cf Eph vi 20). Dr Lightfoot *ad l.*
has collected a number of instances
of the omission of ε in at least
single MSS in places where an ambassador is meant; so that here too
it is possible that ΠΡΕϹΒΥΤΗϹ in
this sense (πρεσβυτής) can be main-

tained as the original reading. [But
in the absence of a verb πρεσβύω it
appears safer to attribute the form
to a very early scribe than to St
Paul, who was not likely to choose
the misleading as well as the incorrect form.   A natural misunderstanding of the meaning would
certainly help much to introduce
ΠΡΕϹΒΥΤΗϹ, *i.e.* πρεσβύτης, in place
of ΠΡΕϹΒΕΥΤΗϹ.   H.]

APOCALYPSE

i 5 λύσαντι] λούσαντι (? Alexan-
drian and) Constantinopolitan (Gr.
Lat. Eg. Æth. [Arm.]); incl. *g*: cu[p]
And Areth combine both readings.
Text אAC 1 38 79 al[6] *h* syr arm.
codd And.cod.txt Prim Cassiod.
Due to failure to understand the
Hebraic use of ἐν to denote a price
(v 9: cf. 1 Chr xxi 24), and a natu-
ral misapplication of vii 14.

i 20 (†) αἱ λυχνίαι αἱ ἑπτὰ ἐκκλησίαι εἰσίν] [αἱ] ἑ. λυχνίαι ἑ. ἐκκλησίαι
εἰσίν (some adding ἃς εἶδες) א cu[pm]
And: < ἑπτὰ 7 al *h* Prim: + αἱ
before ἐκκλ. cu[4] arm And[c]. The
second ἑπτά, omitted by lat.vt but
without sufficient Greek authority,

must be an erroneous repetition of
the first, due to a feeling that the
number of the lamps was likely to
be specified as well as of the stars:
it is morally impossible that τῶν
ἑπτὰ ἐκκλησιῶν should be followed
by ἑπτὰ ἐκκλησίαι without the article.

ii 12 (†) τῷ ἀγγέλῳ τῆς] In five
out of the seven addresses prefixed
to the seven epistles in cc. ii iii
there is some good authority for τῷ
ἀγγέλῳ τῷ in place of τῷ ἀγγέλῳ
τῆς.   Prim expressly calls attention
to the peculiarity in his comment on
ii 1: *Dativo hic casu* angelo *posuit,
non genetivo, ac si diceret* Scribe
angelo huic ecclesiae; *ut non tam*

angelum et ecclesiam separatim videatur dixisse quam quis angelus exponere voluisset, unam scilicet faciens angeli ecclesiaeque personam. At ii 1 he makes no change in the translation, having merely the name transposed so as to stand after ἐκκλ. (*angelo ecclesiae Ephesi*), as have Aug at the same place, Orig.*Lc.*lat.Hier at ii 12, vg at iii 1, and *fu* at iii 14: but at ii 18; iii 1, 7 he expresses τῷ in his rendering, *angelo ecclesiae qui est Thyatirae* (*qui est Sardis*; *qui est Philadelphiae*). Another probable indication of the same reading as having caused difficulty is the occasional omission of ἐκκλησίας: the substitution of ἐκλησίαις in ii 12 (91); iii 1 (C); and iii 7 (א*) deserves mention, but is difficult to explain.

The evidence as to the several passages is as follows.

ii 1 τ. ἀ. τῷ AC (36) Prim(expressly): 36, a good cursive, is reported by Alter to have τ. ἀ. τῷ τῆς ᾿Ε. ἐ.

ii 8 τ. ἀ. τῷ A (95); 95, one of the best cursives, has τ. ἀ. ὁ: < ἐκκλησίας (?95) *am**.

ii 12 no evidence.

ii 18 τ. ἀ. τῷ A (Epiph) Prim: τῷ ἀ. τοῖς (?? TOICEN for TWEN) 1 28 31: < τῆς C: < ἐκκλησίας A: Epiph.*Haer*.455, in a passage probably taken mainly from Hipp, has once τ. ἀ. τῆς ἐκκλησίας τῷ ἐν Θ., once τ. ἀ. τῷ τῆς ἐν Θ. ἐκκλησίας.

iii 1 τ. ἀ. τῷ (? syr) Prim : < ἐκκλησίας syr.

iii 7 τ. ἀ. τῷ Prim.

iii 14 < ἐκκλησίας 95.

The evidence here points to τῷ as the true reading throughout, for it is incredible that the several addresses should differ from each other in form in this word alone. The small amount of the evidence is not surprising in the Apocalypse, the

representatives of the most ancient texts being very few. The temptation to alter τῷ to τῆς would be strongly felt ; and intrinsically **τῷ** receives a singular corroboration from the form of the title given in numerous inscriptions to the high officials of the new imperial ('Augustan') worship, at this time popular and dominant in Asia Minor. Their style, as set forth in numerous inscriptions, was ἀρχιερεὺς τῆς Ἀσίας ναοῦ τοῦ (sometimes ναῶν τῶν) ἐν Ἐφέσῳ (Κυζίκῳ, Περγάμῳ &c.), ναοῦ (-ῶν) being always left without a preceding article, as is ἐκκλησίας with the reading τῷ. These personal representatives of the tyrannical 'Babylonian' power and hierarchy (cf. cc. xiii, xvii, xviii) might well suggest a pointed contrast to the obscure heads of the persecuted little Christian communities in the same cities.

We have accordingly ventured to give τῷ a place in the text where it is supported by Greek MS authority (AC, A, A), and to mark the other four passages as containing a primitive error.

ii 13 (†) ἐν ταῖς ἡμέραις Ἀντίπας, ὁ μάρτυς μου, ὁ πιστός [μου], ὃς ἀπεκτάνθη] variously altered, the chief change being the insertion of [ἐν] αἷς after ἡμέραις, a few further omitting ὕς. Text is attested by (א*) AC lat.vg me (Prim) Haymo. If however Ἀντίπας is genuine, it must be taken as indeclinable; for the apposition of the nom. ὁ μάρτυς to a preceding genitive is in accordance with the usage of this book, while a nom. Ἀντίπας after ταῖς ἡμέραις would be unprecedented and inexplicable. It seems not unlikely that Ἀντίπα should be read, as Lachmann suggests, C being easily taken up from the following O. The corruption may however lie deeper; though little stress can be laid on the curious itacism ΔΝΤΕΙΠΔC in ℵ*A cu⁸, read also as the verb ἀντεῖπας by syr me.

iii 1, 7, 14   See on ii 12.

iv 4   θρόνοι] (marg.) θρόνους ℵA 34 35 87 And.cod (anon.lat) : C is defective, versions mostly neutral. Text B₂P₂cuᵖˡ And.codd Areth Hier. *Dan*.668. Standing between ἱρις and πρεσβυτέρους, θρόνους was as likely to be altered as θρόνοι, and it is well attested. There is indeed apparently no authority for reading εἴκοσι τέσσαρες as εἴκοσι τέσσαρας : but the analogy of what is found in other places (see Notes on Orthography, p. 150) suggests that τέσσαρες was sometimes used as an accusative, so that it might be consistently combined with θρόνους.

viii 13   ἀετοῦ] ἀγγέλου P₂ 1 7 28 36 47 79 al arm And Victorin; and so Erasmus (after 1) and the 'Received Text' : 13 Prim (not *g*) have the conflation ἀγγέλου ὡς ἀετοῦ.

ix 10   (†) ἔχουσιν οὐρὰς ὁμοίας σκορπίοις] (marg.) ἔ. οὐ. ὁμοίοις σκ. ℵA 14 : C is defective. Text B₂P₂ cuᵖˡ *g* vg (? vv) Prim. Neither reading is probable : apparently we should read ὅμοια, as an adverb (so perhaps me aeth) ; it would easily suffer assimilation to οὐρὰs on the one side and σκορπίοις on the other. A different adverbial use of ὅμοιον (as though it were οἶον) occurs i 13; xiv 14.

xi 3   (†) περιβεβλημένους σάκκους] περιβεβλημένοι σάκκους ℵᶜC cuᵖˡ lat. vg Hipp³ And Areth Prim ppˡᵃᵗ. Text ℵ*AB₂P₂ 4 7 28 48 79 96. The authority for text shews that it must be the source of the other reading, which is quite easy. The accusative may perhaps be due to the virtually transitive sense (cf. v. 18; iv 4; vii 9; xiv 14), as though

e.g. θήσω τοὺς δύο μάρτυράς μου had been written. But it is likewise possible that -νους is an assimilative corruption of -νοις (so apparently *g*, *amictis ciliciis*), which, though itself difficult, would be explicable on the probable supposition that προφητεύσουσιν represents or includes προφητεῦσαι following δώσω κ.τ.λ.

xiii 10   (†) ἀποκτενεῖ] (marg.) ἀποκτείνει ℵ 28 (35) 79 (95) And.cod *g* (syr me) : ἀποκτανθῆναι A : < cu²⁰. Text CB₂P₂ cuᵖˡ vg Iren.lat And. codd Areth Prim. The reading of A gives the right sense; for the former clause, as well as Jer xv 2, on which both clauses are founded, shews that not requital but fulfilment of a Divine appointment is intended. But the same sense would be given more vividly, and in a form better answering to the prophetic terseness of εἴ τις εἰς αἰχμαλωσίαν, by ἀποκτείνειν (or ἀποκτεῖναι), which would account naturally for all the existing readings.

xiii 15   (†) αὐτῇ] αὐτῷ ℵB₂P₂ᵃ cuᵒᵐⁿ Hipp And Areth. Text ACP₂*⁽ᵛⁱᵈ⁾. Versions ambiguous. It is impossible either to account for text as a corruption of αὐτῷ, or to interpret it as it stands. [Perhaps αὐτῷ and αὐτῇ are alike interpolations. W.] [Or there may be a reference to the earth, mentioned five times in the four preceding verses, and distinguished from the dwellers on the earth in v. 12 (cf. v. 4) : the conception of a spirit of the earth as given to the image of the beast agrees with the obvious characteristics of heathen oracles. But the obscurity of the expression, as it stands, suggests that τῇ γῇ may have been lost after αὐτῇ, or have given place to it. H.]

xiii 16   (†) δῶσιν] (marg.) δώσει 1 (cf. ℵᶜ δωσι); δώσῃ Hipp², this being also the reading of Erasmus (by conjectural correction of 1) and

the 'Received Text': *ut det iis*
anon.lat: δώσωσιν, -ουσιν, cu^mu And[1]
al: *dari* (Iren.lat): λάβωσι (< αὐτοῖς and followed by τὸ χ. αὐτοῦ) 26
95 (Victorin): *habere* vg Prim. Text
א*ACB₂P₂ cu^mu *g* (*ut dent sibi in-
vicem*) And². It seems probable that
the true reading was δώσει, and that
an itacistic transcription of it as
δωσι caused the tense to be misunderstood; when the insertion of
ν would naturally follow, ΔωCI for
ΔωCI. The singular construction,
which is intrinsically justified by
xiii 13, would render the misinterpretation inevitable.

xiii 18 ἑξακόσιοι ἑξήκοντα ἕξ]
ἑξακόσιοι δέκα ἕξ C 11 'some' according to Iren (who speaks of
text as found "in all the good and
ancient copies", "and attested by
those who had themselves seen John
face to face") Tich. Text אAB₂P₂
cu^pl vv^omn Iren(as above) Orig(expressly) And Prim.

xiv 20 χιλίων ἑξακοσίων] χιλίων
διακοσίων א* 26: *mille sexaginta*
lat.vg.cod: *mille quingentis g*: ἑξακοσίων α:π*; χιλίων ἑξακοσίων ἕξ
And[1] (whence αχϛ´ 79).

xv 6 λίθον] λίνον P₂ cu^pl vg.codd
(*lino*) syr arm And Areth Tich
(*lino*); also λινοῦν B₂ cu⁵ (? *g lin-
theamen*) (? Orig.*Jer.*192), λίνους
א cod.lat known to Haymo me
Prim (*lintea*): < aeth. Text AC
'some MSS' known to Andr 38^mᵍ
48 50 90 lat.vg.codd.opt(*lapide*).
The bold image expressed by this
well attested reading is justified by
Ez xxviii 13, παντα λίθον χρῆστον
ἐνδέδεσαι, σάρδιον καὶ τοπάζιον κ.τ.λ.,
where ἐνδέδυσαι is a various reading
(cu³ Thdt Cyr.al Tert Hier[both
indutus]): cf. Chrys 1 *Ti.* 682 ἐν
λαμπρῷ τῷ σχήματι προῄει· εἴτε
ὁπλίζεσθαι ἔδει, χρυσῷ καὶ λίθοις
τιμίοις ὁπλιζόμενος ἐξῄει· εἴτε ἐν
εἰρήνῃ, ἀλουργίδα περικείμενος. On

the other hand λίνον, as distinguished from λινοῦν (used in the LXX),
never denotes a fabric or garment
made of flax except according to
Etym.Magn. and possibly in Æsch.
Suppl. 121; but always flax, whether
in its rough state or spun into cord,
or a net, or a sail. In the Apocalypse λίνον does not occur elsewhere, while fine linen is five times
mentioned under the definite name
βύσσινον.

xviii 12 (†) μαργαριτῶν] (marg.)
μαργαρίτας CP₂: μαργαρίταις A
fu al: plural syr me Prim: μαργαρί-
του B₂ cu^pl lat.vg aeth arm Hipp
Andr. Text א 35 87 95 (?*g* Prim).
Text is suspicious as failing to
account for the other readings.
The marginal reading is doubly suspicious because in the only documents which attest it, themselves of
little authority when standing alone,
it is but the last of a series of accusatives, γόμον χρυσοῦν καὶ ἀργυροῦν
καὶ λίθους τιμίους: moreover, as its
sense is not generic, its position as
a solitary accusative among genitives is unaccountable. The reading of A makes no sense, but may
conceal some unusual form, such as
μαργαρίδος (-OC, -EC, -αις) from
μαργαρίς, which is used by Philos-
tratus and others.

xix 13 (†) ῥεραντισμένον] βεβαμ-
μένον AB₂ cu^pl And² Areth: ἐρραμ-
μένον (Orig.*Jo.*1/2.ed): περιρεραμμένον א*: περιρεραντισμένον א°. Text
P₂ 36 Orig.*Jo.*1/2. cod; also (ἐρραν-
τισμένον) 32 35 87 95 Hipp Orig.
*Jo.*1/2 And[1]. The versions are somewhat ambiguous: but all the Latins
(including Cyp² Iren.lat Hier Prim)
have *sparsam*, *aspersam*, or *consper-
sam* (*-sum*, *-sa*, *-so*), all of which
renderings point to ῥαίνω or ῥαντίζω,
or one of their compounds, rather
than to βάπτω. A word denoting
sprinkling seems also to agree best

with the context, and with biblical symbolism generally : see especially Is lxiii 3, where ἐρραντίσθη, or according to some MSS ἐρράνθη, is used by Aquila and Symmachus. All the variations are easily accounted for if the form used was ῥεραμμένον (on which see Notes on Orthography, p. 170) from ῥαίνω. In Mc vii 4 authority is in like manner divided between ῥαντίσωνται and βαπτίσωνται.

II. NOTES ON ORTHOGRAPHY

WITH ORTHOGRAPHICAL ALTERNATIVE READINGS

The principles which have been followed as to the orthography adopted in this edition have been explained in the Introduction (§§ 393—405). Often however the decision in favour of one spelling as against another is more or less precarious; so that a wrong impression would be produced if those spellings which, though not preferred, are also not rejected were left unrecorded. While therefore alternative readings of an orthographical character have been excluded from the margin of the text (*Introd.* § 403), it is fitting that they should have a place in the Appendix.

What spellings are sufficiently probable to deserve inclusion among alternative readings, is often difficult to determine. Although many deviations from classical orthography are amply attested, many others, which appear to be equally genuine, are found in one, two, or three MSS only, and that often with an irregularity which suggests that all our MSS have to a greater or less extent suffered from the effacement of unclassical forms of words.

It is no less true on the other hand that a tendency in the opposite direction is discernible in Western MSS : the orthography of common life, which to a certain extent was used by all the writers of the New Testament, though in unequal degrees, would naturally be introduced more freely in texts affected by an instinct of popular adaptation (*Introd.* § 176). For these reasons the limits of orthographical alternative readings can be only approximately fixed; and readings not marked as alternative have sometimes been cited in the accompanying notes.

The accompanying notes are not intended to form a complete or systematic account of the orthography of the New Testament. Their chief purpose is to elucidate the alternative readings (marked ALT.), and to indicate the prevalence or the exceptional occurrence of particular spellings. Local references are given but sparingly, as it is presumed that Bruder's Concordance will be in the hands of any one who is likely to read this part of the Appendix: but the distribution of spellings among the books or the writers of the New Testament is often marked by abbreviated names, usually accompanied by numerals indicating the number of times of occurrence. Sometimes the proportional occurrence of one form as compared with others is expressed by a fractional notation : thus at p. 168 l. 14 the abbreviation 'Mc.4/4 Jo.1/3' denotes that δοῖ occurs in St Mark four times, and that there are but these four opportunities for its occurrence; and that it occurs in St John once, whereas there are three opportunities for it, so that δῷ remains in two places. Occasionally, as under 'Breathings', the total number of places in which a form occurs in each principal MS has been given. Some few of the notes refer to points of orthography as to which no doubt has been entertained and therefore no alternative readings have been given; but for the most part only where they illustrate doubtful points, which without some such accessory elucidation might appear to have a more accidental and irregular character than really belongs to them, or where they required notice for some special reason : on such well-known forms as λήμψομαι it would have been beside our purpose to comment.

Illustrative evidence from the Septuagint and other extraneous sources has often been added, but only to a limited extent. The MSS of the New Testament, in their genuine and their corrupt spellings alike, furnish important materials for the history of the variations of the Greek language, and have not yet received due attention from philologers. It was sufficient however for our purpose to let it be clearly seen by a series of illustrative examples that the orthography of these MSS is no isolated phenomenon. Many additional particulars of various kinds are brought together in the Grammars of the New Testament by Winer and A. Buttmann, in Dr Moulton's additions to his translation of Winer, and in scattered statements in Tischendorf's editions. Considerable details of language will be found in all the larger general grammars, especially the elder Buttmann's still invaluable work, with Lobeck's additions, in Lobeck's own various treatises, in Didot's Stephanus, in the writings of Curtius and other living representatives of scientific etymology, and (for one large class of forms) in Dr Veitch's *Greek Verbs Irregular and Defective*. But numerous facts still remain to be gathered from such sources as the Greek versions of the Old Testament, the Apocrypha proper, the Testaments of the Twelve Patriarchs and the Apocryphal literature generally, the writings of the Fathers of the second century and of such later Fathers as Cyril of Jerusalem and Epiphanius, who was virtually a Palestinian writer, the lexicon of Hesychius, and not least from inscriptions.

CONTENTS

I. LETTERS

BREATHINGS

On some unusual aspirated forms found in good MSS of the N. T. and LXX, as also in inscriptions, see *Introd.* § 408. Ἐφ' ἐλπίδι, accepted Ro 8 20, has some primary authority (ℵ². A¹. B¹. C¹. D⁴. D₂¹. G₃⁵) 8/9 times, besides ἀφελπίζοντες 1/1. Καθ' ἰδίαν (ℵ¹. B⁸. D³. Δ¹) occurs 9/16 times, the phrase forming virtually a single adverb : where the ἰδίαν is strictly adjectival (κατὰ ἰδίαν πρόθεσιν 2 Ti 1 9), there is no elision. Another form noticed with these two by Curtius *Gr. Etym.*⁵ 687 f., ἔτος, is unknown to the N.T., κατ' ἔτος being the reading of all MSS in Lc 2 41. The occasional aspiration of εἶδον (and compounds),

accepted Phi 2 23 and (marg.) Act 2 7, is found 6/12 times in good MSS (ℵ². A². B³. D³. Δ¹. E₂². D₂¹. G₃¹. 61¹ of Acts. 17¹ of Paul &c.), and stands on the same footing as these forms, being evidently due to the digamma. Οὐχ ὀλίγος, which good MSS (ℵ⁴. A³. B¹. D¹) exhibit 6/8 times in Acts, has no lost digamma to justify it, but may nevertheless have been in use in the apostolic age : it occurs in good MSS of LXX 2/2, Job 10 20 (B); Is 10 7 (ℵA); but κατ' ὀλίγον ℵABC in Sap 12 2, just as in the N. T. ἐπ' ὀλίγα Mt². These four unusual forms, of which the first two are specially well supported by extraneous evidence, stand alone in the N. T. in the amount and quality of their attestation. Peculiarities of aspiration, more or less constant, are common enough in the late MSS which have breathings, and especially in many cursives: but in the better uncials the consonantal changes that indicate them are so very slightly and irregularly attested that they can hardly be more than casual clerical errors. The transposed aspirate of ἐφιορκ. (Curtius *Gr. Verb.*[2] ii 109; *Gr. Etym.*[5] 517) is probably Western only (Mt[1] ℵ, 1 Ti[1] D₂P₂). The singular but amply attested ἐπίσταται (αἰφνίδιος αὐτοῖς ἐ. ὄλεθρος) of 1 Th 5 3 (so also Sap 6 9 in B) is difficult to explain except as due to a confusion with the other verb (ἐπί-σταμαι): aspiration is universal in the other 14 examples of compounds of ἱστ. with a preposition capable of shewing aspiration, except once in D₂ and also in the unique and doubtful form ἀποκατιστάνει, on which see below, p. 168.

Of breathings as to which the best uncials are indirectly as well as directly neutral two peculiar examples need special notice, ὀμείρομαι and ὕσσωπος. In favour of ὁμ., printed here on Lobeck's authority, is the absence of breathing in the MS of Photius (Cambridge, Trin. Coll. B x 1), ὁμείρειν ὁμοῦ ἡρμόσθαι | ὁμείρονται ἐπιθυμοῦσι (wrongly transcribed and edited by Porson), where the assumed derivation from ὁμοῦ has apparently withheld the scribe from copying a smooth breathing: in both 1 Th 2 8 (where see Matthaei[1]) and Job 3 21 cursives differ. In ὕσσωπος we have simply followed custom: but the smooth breathing is supported by the Hebrew; even the English Bible had *Isope* and *ysope* till the Genevan revisions of 1557—60, as German usage virtually has still. Both εἰλικρινής (-ία) and εἰλικρινής

have good ancient authority: the smooth breathing, suggested by the (very late) compound ἀπειλικρινέω, is perhaps only Attic: a similar doubt affects ἀλοάω, notwithstanding the compounds ἀπαλοάω, καταλοάω. For ἅλωσις see Herodian. i 539; ii 108 Lenz. On the breathings of proper names see *Introd.* § 411 f.

The question as to the admission of the form αὑτοῦ in the New Testament is complicated by the frequent difficulty of deciding between ἑαυτοῦ and αὐτοῦ on documentary grounds; and the difficulty is the greater because this is a point in which, as in the interchange of ἡμεῖς and ὑμεῖς, B shews less than its usual superiority in purity of text. The extent to which simple personal pronouns are replaced by strong reflexive forms is variable in all Greek literature, being partly dependent on individual taste: but in the New Testament reflexive pronouns are certainly employed with unusual parsimony. Moreover οὐκ and the prepositions capable of indicating aspiration in elision of the final vowel hardly ever exhibit an aspirate before αὐτ., and that only in single MSS. For these reasons it is safest to adopt the smooth breathing wherever it can be used without absolute harshness, that is, wherever the reference to the subject of the sentence is comparatively mediate and indirect.

There are places however where documentary evidence shews αὐτ. to be certainly or probably the true reading, while yet the reflexiveness is so direct that a refusal to admit the rough breathing introduces language completely at variance with all Greek usage without the constraint of any direct evidence, and solely on the strength of partial analogies. In the face of such examples as αὐτὸς δὲ Ἰησοῦς οὐκ ἐπίστενεν αυτὸν αὑτοῖς (Jo 2 24), or St Luke's account of the reconciliation of Herod and Pilate, προϋπῆρχον γὰρ ἐν ἔχθρᾳ ὄντες πρὸς αυτούς (23 12), it is not easy to justify the unwavering enforcement of the smooth breathing. Accordingly, after some hesitation, we have abstained from following recent editors in their total exclusion of the form αὑτοῦ. In all the places in which αυτ. is preceded by a hard consonant it is either not reflexive or too indirectly reflexive to make the smooth breathing difficult; so that they afford but weak grounds of inference for the present purpose: and the analogy of the reflexive use of ἐγώ ἡμεῖς σύ ὑμεῖς, which is restricted almost without exception to cases of indirect reflexiveness (A. Buttmann *Gramm.* 96 f.), is in favour of a similar restriction in the reflexive use of αὑτός, in its oblique cases as weak a pronoun. An additional reason for not banishing the aspirated form is the existence of passages where αυτ. can be taken either reflexively or not, a difference of interpretation being involved in the ambiguity: thus in 1 Jo 5 10 alternative interpretations are expressed by the alternative breathings; and in such places as 1 Jo 5 18; Eph 1 5, 10; Col 1 20; 2 15 the smooth breathing is intended to exclude a reflexive sense. The aspirated form has been introduced nearly twenty times, and likewise stands as an alternative to ἑαυτ. for a few places enumerated under the next head. As between αὐτ. and αὑτ., alternative readings are not needed.

ALT. ἀφελπίζοντες Lc 6 35; ἐφ᾽ ἐλπίδι Act 2 26; Ro 4 18; 5 2; 1 Co 9 10 *bis*; Tit 1 2; καθ᾽ ἐλπίδα Tit 3 7. καθ᾽ ἰδίαν Mt 14 23; 17 1, 19; 20 17; 24 3; Mc 4 34; 6

31; 9 28; 13 3. ἐφεῖδεν Lc 1 25; ἔφιδε Act 4 29; οὐχ ἴδ.ντες 1 Pe 1 8; οὐχ εἶδον Ga 1 19. οὐχ ὀλίγ. Act 12 18; 14 28; 17 4; 19 23, 24; 27 20. ὁμειρόμενοι 1 Th 2 8. ὑσσώπῳ (-ου) Jo 19 29; He 9 19. εἰλικρινεῖς (-ῆ, -ίας, -ίᾳ) 2 Pe 3 1; 1 Co 5 8; 2 Co 1 12; 2 17; Phi 1 10. ἀλοῶντα (-ῶν) 1 Co 9 9, 10; 1 Ti 5 18.

CRASIS, CONTRACTION, AND SYNCOPE

Καί often coalesces with ἐγώ (and its oblique cases), ἐκεῖ, ἐκεῖθεν, ἐκεῖνος, and ἄν; but there are many exceptions, and especially where there is distinct coordination of ἐγώ with another pronoun or a substantive. There is much division of evidence.

Once, where τὸ ὄνομα has the sense of ὀνόματι, it becomes τοὔνομα in almost all MSS (Mt 27 57 τοὔνομα Ἰωσήφ). The contracted form ταὐτά has no good authority except in Lc: as Paul[3] has τὰ αὐτά, the accentuation ταὐτὰ οὐ λέγει in 1 Co 9 8 is improbable.

Τετραάρχης (-αρχέω) has good authority, א‍ (or once אᵃ) and me 7/7, and also C⁶. Z¹. Δ¹; but it is nowhere found in B, and may possibly be Alexandrian.

Νεομηνίας (Col¹) is the rarer and less classical form; but may perhaps be Western. Ἀγαθουργῶν stands without variation Act¹, ἀγαθοεργεῖν 1 Ti¹ [cf. note on Ro 13 3]. Ἐλεινός Ap¹ (best MSS); but 1 Co¹ in G₃ only.

Νοσσούς (from LXX), νοσσία, νοσσίαν are certain, 2/3 without variation: ἀλλοτριεπίσκοπος 1/1 codd. opt: ταμεῖον always, Mt² Lc².

Somewhat different is the ἡμίωρον (not -ώριον) of Ap¹ (best MSS). Ἔσθω, a twin rather than a syncopated form of ἐσθίω, occurs Mc¹ and probably Mc¹ Lc⁴, mostly in the participle; elsewhere twice in D and D₂ only. On πεῖν see below.

ALT. κἀγώ (-γώ) Lc 2 48; Act 26 29; καὶ ἐγώ Mt 26 15; Lc 19 23; καὶ ἐμοὶ Jo 17 6; κἀμοὶ Ga 2 8; κἄν Jo 8 16; καὶ ἐὰν 1 Co 13 2 *bis*, 3 *bis*; Ga 1 8; καὶ ἐκεῖ Mt 28 10; κἀκεῖ Mc 1 38; Καὶ ἐκεῖθεν Mc 9 30: κἀκεῖνος Jo 19 35.

ταῦτα Lc 6 23, 26; 17 30.

τετράρχης (-ου) Mt 14 1; Lc 3 19; 9 7; Act 13 1; τετραρχοῦντος Lc 3 1 *bis*.

νουμηνίας Col 2 16.

ἐσθίων Lc 7 33, 34; ἐσθίοντες Lc 10 7; ἐσθίητε Lc 22 30; κατεσθίοντες Mc 12 40. σαρδιόνυξ Ap 21 20.

ἑαυτ. Mt 6 34; Lc 12 17, 21; 24 12; Jo 19 17; Ro 1 27; 2 Co 3 5 (2°); Ap 8 6: also 2 Th 2 6 (-οῦ).

αὑτ. Lc 10 29; 23 2; Act 10 17; 12 11; 28 16; 2 Pe 2 1 (-οῖς); Ap 2 20.

ELISION

Elision takes place habitually and without variation before pronouns and particles; also before nouns in combinations of frequent occurrence, as ἀπ' ἀρχῆς, κατ' οἶκον. In other cases there is much diversity, and occasional variation.

In ἀλλά elision takes place usually before articles, pronouns, and particles, but with many exceptions and much variation. The passage Ro 6 14—8 32 is remarkable as having consecutively (with a single exception 7 15 ἀλλ' ὅ) 9 non-elisions attested by 3 or more primary MSS: in the six following cases (to 10 16) there is no evidence for any non-elision. Before nouns and verbs non-elision is habitual, and there are few cases without variation. Elision is commonest before words (of all kinds) beginning with ε,

rarest before those that begin with α.

Δέ is never elided except in ὅς δ' ἄν, once or perhaps twice in τὸ δ' αὐτό (not Phi 2 18), and perhaps in ἥνικα δ' ἄν 2 Co 3 16 (see margin); οὐδ' occurs a few times.

ALT. ἀπὸ ἄνωθεν Mt 27 51; Mc 15 38. διὰ ἀκροβυστίας Ro 4 11; διὰ ἀπιστίαν He 3 19; διὰ ἀπείθειαν 4 6. ἐπ' ἔθνος Mt 24 7; ἐπὶ ἔθνος Mc 13 8; Lc 21 10; ἐπ' οἶκον Lc 11 17; ἐφ' υἱῷ Lc 12 53; ἐπὶ ἵπποις Ap 19 14. καθ' εἷς Mc 14 19; κατ' ἀκρίβειαν Act 22 3. μετὰ ὅρκου Mt 14 7: μετ' υ. μεθ' ὁρκωμοσίας He 7 21; μετὰ εὐχαριστίας Phi 4 6. ὑπ' ἀνθρώπων 1 Pe 2 4; ὑπ' αὐτῆς 3 Jo 12; ὑπὸ ἁμαρτίαν Ro 3 9; ὑφ' ἁμαρτίαν Ga 3 22.

ἀλλ' Mt 9 12; 17 12; 18 22; Mc 1 45; 3 29; Jo 3 16; 7 10; Act 15 20; 1 Pe 2 25; 1 Jo 3 18; Ro 1 21; 4 20; 5 14; 1 Co 9 27; 15 35; 2 Co 1 9; 3 14; 10 18; 12 14 (ἀλλ' οἱ); Eph 2 19; 4 29; 5 24: Phi 2 17; 3 7; 1 Th 2 7; 2 Th 2 12; Philem 16; Ap 2 14. ἀλλὰ Mt 16 17; Mc 2 17; 7 19, 25; 12 14, 25; Lc 8 16; 22 53; Jo 3 8; 7 28; 8 12; 9 9; 10 8; 13 10; 16 2, 20; Ja 2 18; 1 Pe 3 14; 1 Jo 4 18; 5 6, 18; 3 Jo 13; Ro 2 29 (ἀλλὰ ἐκ); 1 Co 2 4, 5; 4 14; 14 17; 2 Co 2 17; 5 4; 13 8: Ga 3 12, 16; Col 3 22; 1 Th 1 8; 4 7; 2 Th 3 8; Ap 10 9; 20 6.

τὸ δ' αὐτὸ 1 Co 12 4. οὐδὲ ἐάν Lc 16 31; οὐδ' ἡ He 9 18.

MOVEABLE FINAL LETTERS

In dealing with final ν and the final ς of οὕτως before consonants we have been led by the limitations of the evidence to adopt a mechanical rule. In the best uncials, as well as in not a few later MSS, these letters are inserted in a large majority of cases, after ἐστί and εἰσί almost always: but sometimes, especially in datives plural, and in the third person plural of the present or future active of long verbs, their omission is well attested. The traces of omission in MSS other than the four early Bibles אABC are however too scattered to be often useful; and again they are much more abundant in א and B than in A or C. We have failed to detect any clear uniformities connecting differences of attestation with differences of the following consonant or other circumstances of collocation. On the whole it has seemed best to trust here those MSS which we have found worthiest of trust where there are better means of verification; and even, in a matter of so little moment, to be satisfied with collecting the evidence of the four great MSS, except where loss of leaves or diversity of reading materially diminished its amount, and thus made it desirable to obtain accessory evidence elsewhere. Our general practice has been to accept any omission of ν or s vouched for by either א or B supported by one or both of the two other MSS; while in a few cases of defective or anomalous evidence we have been guided partly by analogy, partly by other comparately good uncial authority. The alternative omissions of ν or s here given are chiefly on the authority of א or B: the alternative insertions are chiefly given for places where the whole evidence is specially scanty. It is worth notice that δυσί and δυσίν before consonants are each well attested three times.

ALT. Mt 4 6 ἀροῦσί; 5 15 πᾶσι; 6 5 φανῶσι; 6 16 ἀφανίζουσι, φανῶσι, ἀπέχουσι; 12 10 σάββασι; 12 36 ἀποδώσουσι; 13 5 εἶχε; 13 49 ἀφο-

ριοῦσι; 15 2 παραβαίνουσι; 15 32 προσμένουσί; 18 28 ἔπνιγε; 19 22 ἀπῆλθε; 20 17 παρέλαβε; 21 26 ἔχουσι; 22 21 λέγουσι; 22 34 ἐφίμωσε; 24 11 πλανήσουσι; 24 14, 47 πᾶσι; 26 51 ἀπέσπασε; 27 3 ἀρχιερεῦσι. Mc 1 34 ἤφιε; 2 19 ἔχουσι; 2 23; 3 2 σάββασι; 3 14 ὦσι; 4 5 εἶχε; 4 12 ἴδωσι; 4 16 ἀκούωσι; 4 17 ἔχουσι; 4 20 ἀκούουσι; 5 14 ἐστι; 5 15 θεωροῦσι; 6 17 ἐκράτησε; 6 45 ἠνάγκασε; 7 2 ἐσθίουσι; 7 25 εἶχε; 7 30 εὗρε; 7 34 ἐστέναξε, ἐστι; 8 2 προσμένουσί, ἔχουσι; 9 18 ἐκβάλωσι; 10 33 ἀρχιερεῦσι; 12 42 ἐστι; 14 3 ἦλθε; 14 47 ἔπαισε; 15 10 ἐγίνωσκε. Lc 2 37 δεήσεσι; 2 38 πᾶσι; 4 11 ἀροῦσί; 4 33 ἀνέκραξε; 6 9 ἔξεστι; 8 45 συνέχουσί; 9 27 ἴδωσι; 9 43 εἶπε; 9 56 marg. ἦλθε; 10 34 κατέδησε; 10 39 ἤκουε; 11 1 ἐδίδαξε; 12 23 ἐστι; 13 12 προσεφώνησε; 14 21 εἶπε; 14 33 πᾶσι; 15 7 ἔχουσι; 15 13 διεσκόρπισε; 19 43 περικυκλώσουσί; 20 34 γαμοῦσι; 20 36 εἰσι θεοῦ; 20 41 λέγουσι; 20 47 κατεσθίουσι; 22 50 ἀφεῖλε; 22 61 ἐνέβλεψε; 23 8 ἤλπιζε; 23 15 ἀνέπεμψε; 24 9, 21 πᾶσι. Jo 2 10 μεθυσθῶσι; 3 32 ἤκουσε; 3 34 δίδωσι; 4 27 εἶπε; 4 39 Εἶπε; 4 47 ἤμελλε; 5 25 ἀκούσουσι; 6 6 ἔμελλε; 6 15 ποιήσωσι, ἀνεχώρησε; 6 19 θεωροῦσι; 6 45 ἐστι; 6 46 ἑώρακέ; 7 37 ἔκραξε; 8 29 ἀφῆκέ; 9 30 ἠνοιξέ; 10 4 οἴδασι; 10 12 ἀφίησι; 12 14 ἐστι; 12 40 νοήσωσι, στραφῶσι; 13 16 ἐστι; 15 21 οἴδασι; 16 17, 18 ἐστι; 17 13 ἔχωσι; 17 24 θεωρῶσι; 18 4 ἐξῆλθε; 18 10 ἔπαισε; 18 16 εἰσήγαγε; 18 19 ἠρώτησε; 18 22 ἔδωκε; 18 26 ἀπέκοψε; 18 33 ἐφώνησε; 19 4 ἐξῆλθε; 19 21 εἶπε; 19 35 μεμαρτύρηκε; 19 40 ἐστί; 20 4 ἦλθε; 20 20 ἔδειξε; 20 22 ἐνεφύσησε. Act 2 24 ἀνέστησε; 4 16 πᾶσι; 5 19 ἤνοιξεν; 7 25 δίδωσι; 8 38 ἐκέλευσε; 9 26 ἐπείραξε; 9 40 ἤνοιξε; 10 10 ἤθελε; 11 15 ἐπέπεσε; 12 9 ἐστι; 12 14 ἤνοιξε; 12 16 ἐπέμεㅤε; 12 23 ἔδωκε; 16 17 ἔκραξε;

19 17 Ἕλλησι; 19 38 ἔχουσι; 19 41 ἀπέλυσε; 20 21 Ἕλλησι; 20 38 μέλλουσι; 23 2 ἐπέταξε; 23 14 ἀρχιερεῦσι; 23 18 ἤγαγε; 23 21 ἐνεδρεύουσι; 24 27 κατέλιπεν; 25 23 ἄνδρασι; 26 25 φησί; 27 3 ἐπέτρεψε; 28 7 ὑπῆρχε. Ja 1 6 ἔοικε; 1 11 ἐξήρανε. 1 Pe 4 5 ἀποδώσουσι. 2 Pe 1 9 ἐστι. 1 Jo 2 11 οἶδε; 5 16 ἁμαρτάνουσι. Ro 1 5, 7 πᾶσι; 1 27 ἄρσεσι; 2 7 ζητοῦσι; 1 Co 1 2 πᾶσι; 3 13 ἐστι; 7 29 ἐστί; 9 22 πᾶσι; 14 23 λαλῶσι; 14 35 ἐστι. 2 Co 1 1 πᾶσι; 12 12 τέρασι; 12 14 γονεῦσι. Ga 2 14 ὀρθοποδοῦσι; 3 10 πᾶσι; 5 24 παθήμασι. Eph 1 22 ἔδωκε; 1 23; 3 18 πᾶσι. Phi 1 1 πᾶσι. Col 1 6 ἐστι. 1 Th 5 27 πᾶσι. 2 Th 1 4, 10 πᾶσι. He 1 14 εἰσι; 2 1 ἀκουσθεῖσι; 2 4 τέρασι; 8 6 τέτυχε; 8 13 πεπαλαίωκε; 9 5 ἔστι; 11 7 κατέκρινε. 1 Ti 1 4 παρέχουσιν; 1 20 παιδευθῶσιν; 6 3 ὑγιαίνουσιν; 6 9 βυθίζουσιν. 2 Ti 2 10 τύχωσι; 4 8 πᾶσι. Ap 6 5 ἤνοιξεν; 7 10 κράζουσιν; 8 9 ἀπέθανεν; 9 4 ἔχουσιν; 10 5 ᾖρε; 12 16 κατέπιε; 13 6 ἤνοιξεν; 17 16 μισήσουσιν; 19 17 πᾶσιν; 20 8 τέσσαρσιν; 21 8 φονεῦσιν, πᾶσιν.

οὗτω Mc 7 18; Ja 2 12; Ro 11 26; 1 Co 7 17; Phi 4 1.

Εἴκοσι precedes a vowel 1/1 (Act) in all good MSS; elsewhere it precedes consonants. Πέρυσι 2/2 precedes consonants (2 Co).

Ἄχρι usually precedes vowels (14-16 times), Ga 3 19 ἄχρις ἄν or οὗ being the only certain exception: μέχρι preceding a vowel is certain only Lc 16 16, μέχρις 2–3 times. All good MSS have ἄντικρυς Χίου Act 20 15.

ALT. ἄχρις οὗ Ro 11 25; ἄχρι οὗ He 3 13; μέχρι αἵματος He 12 4.

SINGLE AND DOUBLE CONSONANTS

Ἔνατος, ἐνενήκοντα, ἐνεός, γένημα in the literal or figurative sense of " product of the earth " (but γεννήματα ἐχιδνῶν), ἐκχύννω, συνχύννω, βαλλάντιον, κράβαττος (ℵ 10/11 has the strange form κράβακτος), μαμωνᾶς, ῥάκος, μασάομαι are all certain. Παρησία (-ιάζομαι) is too uncertain for text and is unattested 27/40 times, but stands in different places in ℵBCDLXD₂G₃: ἀραβών seems to be only Western. Πυρός (cf. Steph.-Didot vi 2275 D, 2284 A) for πυρρός has some good authority Ap², πυράζω less Mt².

ALT. παρησίᾳ (-ιάς, -ιαζόμενος, -ιαζόμενοι, -ιάζεσθαι) Mc 8 32; Jo 7 13; 10 24; 11 14, 54; 16 25; 18 20; Act 2 29; 9 28; 14 3; 18 26; Eph 6 19; ἐπαρησιασάμεθα 1 Th 2 2. πυρός Ap 6 4; 12 3.

CHANGES OF CONSONANTS

Σφυρίς (so ℵ².A¹.B¹.C¹.D⁴, cf. Steph.-Didot vii 634 B, 1639 B; Curtius *Gr. Et.*⁵ 503) for σπυρίς is probably right. Ζμύρνα Ap² (ℵ lat.vg) is probably Western (Latin) only, though it held its ground on the coins of Smyrna till Trajan's reign, when it was displaced by Σμύρνα (Waddington *Voy. arch.* 894): ζμάραγδος (-ἀγδινος) has no Greek attestation, ζμύρνα (-ίζω) very little (Mt¹ D, Jo¹ σζμ. [sic] ℵ), ζβεννύω proportionally (3/8) less (Mt² D, Paul¹ BD₂G₃, ἄζβεστον Mc¹ N); all evidently Western. The following words have no exceptional character. Πράσσω (and compounds) always: κρεῖσσον Paul³, κρεῖττον Paul¹, certainly; κρείττων (-ονος, -ονα, -οσιν, κρεῖττον) He¹¹ (κρείσσονα He¹ doubtful); κρεῖττον 1 Pe¹ (2 Pe¹ doubt-

ful) : ἐλαττόω³, ἐλαττονέω¹ (from
LXX), but ἐλάσσων³, ἐλάττων², all
almost without variation: ἧσσον
Paul² and ἡσσώθητε Paul¹, but ἥττημα Paul² and ἥττωνται (ἥττηται)
2 Pe² : ἐξεπλήσσετο (-οντο, ἐκπλήσ-
σεσθαι) always (11), but Act¹ doubtful (-όμενος). θαρσέω³, Gospels Acts,
all imperative ; θαρρέω⁶, 2 Co He,
none imperative : ἄρσην except perhaps Paul 4/4. Μαστός Lc² and
probably Ap¹: μασθός in each place
seems to be Western. Ἄρκου Ap¹,
not ἄρκτου. Σάρδιον Ap², nowhere
σάρδινος or ∹ον. More peculiar is
σφυδρά Act¹, not σφυρά. (Θησαυρός
in D 2/14 is of course of Latin
origin.) Ὄρνιξ Lc¹ (not Mt¹) for
ὄρνις is perhaps only Western (אD).
Φόβηθρον (so also Is 19 17 B) and
φόβητρον are both well attested 1/1:
on twin forms in -θρον and -τρον see
Lobeck in P. Buttmann *G.G.*² ii
413 f., cited by Dr Moulton.

ALT. σπυρίδας (-ων, -ι) Mt 15
37; 16 10; Mc 8 8, 20; Act 9 25.
Ζμύρναν (-η) Ap 1 11; 2 8. ἐκπλησ-
σόμενος Act 13 12. κρεῖσσον 2 Pet
2 21; κρείττονα He 10 34. ἄρρενες
bis and ἄρρεσιν Ro 1 27; ἄρρεν Ga
3 28. μαζοῖς Ap 1 13. ὄρνιξ Lc 13
34. φόβητρα Lc 21 11.

ASSIMILATION OF THE FINAL ν OF σύν ἐν ETC. IN COMPOSITION

The best MSS usually concur in
retaining συν and ἐν unchanged before π, ψ, β, φ, κ, γ, χ, ξ, σ, λ, μ;
but in some words assimilation is
constant according to all or at least
all primary MSS ; while in a comparatively small number of cases
authority is divided. Speaking
generally, assimilation is the rule in
compounds of ἐν, retention of ν in
those of σύν ; and further, as might
be expected, assimilation is most
frequent where the original force of

the preposition is somewhat lost in
the current sense of the compound
word. In the Catholic Epp., among
which 1 and 2 Peter supply nearly
all the examples of compounds of
σύν or ἐν, authority preponderates
for assimilation to an unusual extent, with but two clear exceptions:
but this may be partly due to the
paucity of extant uncials. The N.
T. contains no compounds of σύν or
ἐν in which the following letter is ξ
or ρ.

The certain and constant forms
are συνπάσχω, συνπαθέω, συνπαρα-
γίνομαι, συνπαρακαλέω, συνπαραλαμ-
βάνω, συνπάρειμι, συνπεριλαμβάνω,
συνπνίγω, συνπολίτης, συνπορεύομαι ;
but συμπόσια. σύνψυχος. συνβασι-
λεύω, συνβιβάζω ; but συμβαίνω, σύμ-
βουλος, συμβουλεύω, συμβούλιον. σύν-
φημι; but συμφέρω, σύμφορος, συμ-
φυλέτης, σύμφυτος, σύμφωνος, ἀσύμ-
φωνος, συμφωνέω, συμφώνησις, συμ-
φωνία. συνκάθημαι, συνκαθίζω, συν-
κακοπαθέω, συνκακουχοῦμαι, συνκάμ-
πτω, συνκαταβαίνω, συνκατατίθημι,
συνκαταψηφίζω, συνκεκερασμένος, συν-
κλείω, συνκληρονόμος, συνκοινωνός,
συνκοινωνέω, Ἀσύνκριτος. συγγενής
(-εύς, -ίς), συγγένεια. συνχρῶμαι; but
σύγχυσις. συνζῶ, συνζητέω, συνζήτη-
σις, συνζητητής. σύνσωμος, συνσταυ-
ρόω, συνστενάζω, συνστοιχέω, συνστρα-
τιώτης ; but συστατικός, συστρέφω, συ-
στροφή. συνλαλέω, συνλυπούμαι ; but
συλλαμβάνω (15/16 : not in the sense
'help' (-νου) Phi 4 3), συλλέγω. συν-
μαθητής, συνμαρτυρέω, συνμέτοχος,
συνμιμητής. ἐμπαίζω, ἐμπαιγμονή,
ἐμπαιγμός, ἐμπαίκτης, ἐμπιπλάω,
ἐμπίπτω, ἐμπλέκω, ἐμπλοκή, ἔμπορος,
ἐμπορία (-ίον), ἐμπορεύομαι, ἔμπροσθεν,
ἐμπτύω ; but ἐνπεριπατέω. ἐμβαίνω,
ἐμβατεύω, ἐμβάλλω, παρεμβάλλω,
παρεμβολή, ἐμβλέπω, ἐμβάπτω. ἐμ-
φανής, ἐμφανίζω, ἔμφοβος, ἔμφυτος.
ἐγκαλέω, ἔγκλημα, ἀνέγκλητος, ἐγ-
καταλείπω (except perhaps in Acts),
ἐγκρατής, ἐγκράτεια, ἐγκρατεύομαι ;

but ἐνκαίνια, ἐνκαινίζω, ἐνκατοικέω, ἐνκαιχῶμαι, ἐνκεντρίζω, ἐνκρίνω. ἐνγράφω. ἐλλογάω. ἐμμαίνομαι, ἐμμένω. All other compounds of σύν and ἐν are included in the list of alternative readings.

Ἐμμέσῳ is found in good MSS wherever ἐν μέσῳ occurs, but never in ℵ, B, D, or D₂; it is apparently Alexandrian: other occasional modifications of ἐν (as Jo 2 11 ἐγ Κανά AF) are ill attested: the converse ἔνπροσθεν is exclusively Western.

Other examples of non-assimilation are παλινγενεσία, πανπληθεί, Κενχρεαί, the last two being however doubtful.

ALT. συνπαθεῖς 1 Pe 3 8; συνπληροῦσθαι Lc 9 51; συμπρεσβύτερος 1 Pe 5 1. συμβαλ. Lc 2 19; 14 31. συμφυεῖσαι Lc 8 7. συγκαλ. Lc 9 1; 15 6, 9; συγκατάθεσις 2 Co 6 16; συνκεκαλυμμένον Lc 12 2; συγκεχυμένη Act 19 32; συγκριν. 2 Co 10 12 *bis*; συγκύπτουσα Lc 13 11; συνκυρίαν Lc 10 31. συγγνώμην 1 Co 7 6. συγχάρητέ Lc 15 6, 9; συγχαίρει 1 Co 13 6; συγχύνveται Act 21 31. σύζυγε (Σύ.) Phi 4 3. σύνσημον Mc 14 44. συσχηματιζόμενοι 1 Pe 1 14. συμμερίζονται 1 Co 9 13; συνμορφ. Ro 8 29; Phi 3 10, 21. ἐμπνέων Act 9 1. ἐνβριμώμενος Jo 11 38. ἐγκαθέτους Lc 20 20; ἐγκακ. 2 Co 4 1, 16; Ga 6 9; Eph 3 13; 2 Th 3 13; ἐγκαταλείψεις Act 2 27; ἐνκατελείφθη Act 2 31; ἐνκομβώσασθε 1 Pe 5 5; ἐγκοπὴν 1 Co 9 12; ἐνκόπτεσθαι 1 Pe 3 7; ἐγκύψ Lc 2 5. ἐνχρῖσαι Ap 3 18.

παμπληθεί Lc 23 18. Κεγχρεαῖς Act 18 18.

CHANGES OF VOWELS

A AND E

The substitution of ε for α is well attested in several words. In τέσ-

σαρες and its compounds it is absolutely confined to forms which have α in the third syllable (τέσσερα, τεσσεράκοντα, τεσσερακονταετής,) and is thus apparently due to dissimilation. For τέσσερας however there is no evidence: but τέσσαρες has some good authority as an accus. 7/8 times, Ap 4 4 (2°) being the only exception: for the peculiarity of the reading in Ap 4 4 (1°) see note on the passage. In the LXX likewise τέσσαρες has usually some good authority as an accus., τέσσερας never.

The tenses of καθαρίζω which have an augment or reduplication (aor. act. and pass., and perf. mid.), and no others (nor καθαρισμός), change the second α to ε in 8/8 places in some good MSS (never in ℵ): but the evidence is variable and indecisive.

A small number of the best uncials (ℵ⁷.B⁶.A⁴.C².T¹) 8/8 times have ἐραυνάω, ἐξεραυνάω, ἀνεξεραύνητος, which are doubtless right. More doubtful are ἐγγαρεύω (ℵ². B¹) 2/2, χλιερός 1/1 : μιαρός is not a word of the N.T., and ὕελος (Ap²) and ὑέλινος (Ap³) are found only in cursives. Ἀμφιάζω and ἀμφιέζω 1/1 have both good authority. The interchange of α and ε affects also some proper names.

ALT. τέσσαρες Jo 11 17; Act 27 29; Ap 7 1 *ter*; 9 14. ἐκαθαρίσθη Mt 8 3; Mc 1 42; ἐκαθερίσθη (-ησαν) Lc 4 27; 17 14, 17; ἐκαθέρισεν Act 10 15; 11 9; κεκαθερισμένους He 10 2. ἐγγαρεύσει Mt 5 41; ἐγγαρεύουσιν Mc 15 21. χλιερός Ap 3 16. ἀμφιέξει Lc 12 28.

E AND AI

The substitution of ε for αι is merely the shortening of an identical sound, and stands virtually on the same footing as the late στύλος for στῦλος and κρίμα for κρῖμα. In the N.T. it must certainly be accepted for φελόνης 1/1, and almost certainly for κερέα 2/2 and κρεπάλη 1/1: even for ἐξέφνης and ἐφνίδιος authority is usually (5/7) preponderant: λέλαπος 2 Pe 2 17 (NAC) is made very doubtful by the certainty of λαῖλαψ 2/2 (Mt Lc).

All uncials, strange to say, have ῥεδῶν, not ῥαιδῶν, Ap 18 13 (*redarum g am, raedarum fu*). All early uncials but A have συκομορέα, not -ραία.

Ἐπανάγκαις or ἐπ' ἀνάγκαις (Act[1]) is perhaps Alexandrian only ; but it has good attestation.

The compound form ἀνάγαιον, found in Mc[1] Lc[1] in most MSS, including the best, may be noticed here : ἀνάγεον, ἀνώγεον (so Erasmus and the 'Received Text' but not the Syrian text), ἀνώγαιον, and ἀνώγεων have all only trifling authority.

ALT. κεραία (-αν) Mt 5 18; Lc 16 17. κραιπάλη Lc 21 34. ἐξαίφνης Mc 13 36; Lc 2 13; 9 39; Act 9 3; ἐξέφνης Act 22 6; αἰφνίδιος Lc 21 34; ἐφνίδιος 1 Th 5 3. ἐπ' ἀνάγκαις Act 15 28.

E AND EI

Eι becomes ε (before ω) in the verb ἠχρεώθησαν 1/1 (from LXX); but ἀχρεῖον ἀχρεῖοι stand without variation. Πλέον is certain 3/21 times, and is found occasionally elsewhere in one or two MSS, πλεῖον 18/21, πλείων πλείονος &c. always.

E AND I

The natural interchange of ι after a liquid with ε is exemplified in ἀλεεῖς, the reading of the best MSS 5/5: the peculiarity of ε before εις finds a parallel in Δεκελεεῖς (so four inscriptions) and similar forms cited by Lobeck *Paralip.* 27. Νηφάλιος

(3/3) alone is well attested, and the best evidence is decisive for λεγιών 4/4.

H AND EI

Authority is decisive for ἀνάπειρος against ἀνάπηρος 2/2 : it is found also 2 Mac 8 24 (A, see note on He 11 37), and it is stigmatised as incorrect by Phrynichus : the cognate ἄπειρος is the reading of the principal MSS in Herod. i 32. The εἰ μήν of He 6 14 (from LXX) is proved by abundant evidence in the LXX to be no mere itacism, and is distinctly recognised in *E. M.* 416 50 : its difference from ἦ μήν however is not strictly orthographical.

H AND I

Σιρικός (not σηρικός) Ap.1/1 (so a Neapolitan inscription, *C.I.G.* 5834, σιρικοποιός), and γυμνιτεύω Paul 1/1, in all the better uncials. The once popular substitution of κάμιλος (a form noticed by Suidas and a scholiast on Aristophanes) for κάμηλος in Mt 19 24; Lc 18 25 occurs in a few late MSS only : the sense 'cable', which it was intended to subserve, is at least as old as Cyr.al (on Lc, Greek and Syriac), who attributes it to κάμηλος, stating that " it is the custom of those well versed in navigation to call the thicker cables 'camels'"; but it is certainly wrong.

H AND A

Of 'Doric' forms ὀδαγέω occurs only in single MSS (B 1/8, D 3/7); ῥάσσω for ῥήσσω (=ἀράσσω, not ῥήγνυμι) Mc 9 18 (in D 81), ῥήξωσιν Mt 7 6 (all; D being defective) and ἔρρηξεν Lc 9 42 (all). On the other hand the marginal reading προσαχεῖν (B, =*resonare g*) is strongly commended by internal evidence in Act 27 27 (where the other readings are προσάγειν [-αγα-

γεῖν], προάγειν [-αγαγεῖν], προσεγ-
γίζειν, *apparere*), as expressive of
the roar of the surf from which
alone the nearness of land could be
inferred in the dark night: compare
the converse κυμάτων αἰγιαλοῖς
προσηχούντων Themist. *Or.* p. 32.

I AND Y

ALT. βήριλλος Ap 21 20.

I AND OI

Στιβάδας is much better attested
than στοιβάδας Mc 11 8.

I AND O

The best MSS have ὁμειρόμενοι
for ἱμειρόμενοι 1 Th 2 8 (as Job 3 21
codd.; Ps 62 2 Sym.; ὑπερομείρεσθαι
Iren.60): on the breathing see
above, p. 144.

E AND O

The better uncials vary, as they
do in the LXX, between ὀλεθρεύω
(-ευτής, ἐξολεθρεύω) and the curious
form ὀλοθρεύω, which seems to have
prevailed in late times, and is
adopted in the Syrian text and in
the ordinary editions of the LXX.
In Act 3 23 alone the evidence for
the form with e is decisive; elsewhere it is much weaker.

ALT. ὀλεθρευτοῦ 1 Co 10 10;
ὀλεθρεύων He 11 28.

A AND O

The best MSS have πατρολῴαις
καὶ μητρολῴαις 1 Ti 1 9: for extraneous evidence see L. Dindorf in
Steph.-Didot v 1023 C. Μεσανύ-
κτιον (cf. μέσαβον, μεσαώριον) is not
without authority in 2/4 places;
and βατταλογέω (cf. βατταρίζω) must
probably be read for βαττολογέω,
which seems to be due to wrong
etymology.

ALT. μεσανυκτίου Mc 13 35;
Lc 11 5; βαττολογήσητε Mt 6 7.

O AND Ω

Συκομορέα, not -μωρέα (and not
-ραία), is much the best attested
form, and agrees with συκόμορον:
so also χρεοφιλέτης (not χρεωφ-), on
which see Herodianus(Chœrob.) ii
606; πρόϊμος, but πρωινός, both
with the best MSS of the LXX;
and perhaps Στοϊκός; and on the
other hand ἐνδώμησις (as δώμησις
Hesych., and δώμημα the Venice
MS of Eus. *H. E.* x 4 43: cf. Lob.
Phryn. 587 f.). Ἱερωσύνη and the
three other (later) forms in -ωσύνη
specified by ancient grammarians,
ἀγαθωσύνη, ἁγιωσύνη, μεγαλωσύνη,
all having a short vowel in the previous syllable (P. Buttmann *G. G.*[2]
ii 420; Lobeck *Prol. Path.* 238 f.),
are read by the best as well as most
late MSS in the N. T., the forms
in -οσύνη having little but Western
authority.

ALT. Στοϊκῶν Act 17 18.

OY AND Y

The evidence for κολλούριον as
against κολλύριον preponderates, but
not greatly: both forms are well
attested elsewhere.

ALT. κολλύριον Ap 3 18.

I AND EI

Confusions between ι and ει due
to mere itacism in the MSS of the
New Testament are certainly numerous; but genuine peculiarities
of original orthography abound
likewise: there are also many
ambiguous cases.   Two principal
causes introduced extensive departures from the classical usage of
ι and ει in the popular Greek in
which the New Testament is to a

certain extent written; the tendency to shorten many long sounds, exhibited especially in words of many syllables, and the widely spread habit of using ει to denote the long sound of ι in such words and forms as still retained the long sound. This use of ει to denote long ι (*e.g.* in τειμάω) is widely spread in inscriptions of good character. The writers of the N. T. appear to have employed it much more sparingly, but still to a considerable extent. Thus the very slender attestation of ἡμεῖν and ὑμεῖν, for which there is ancient grammatical authority (Lachmann i p. xl), marks them as due to scribes alone. But the evidence for γείνομαι and γεινώσκω (and their compounds) is so considerable that they would probably have been admitted to the text but for an unwillingness to introduce words of frequent occurrence into a manual edition in an entirely unfamiliar guise. The forms containing γειν. must therefore be regarded as alternative readings everywhere except in 1 Pet 5 3 (γινόμενοι); Ap 3 2 (γίνου); 1 3 (ἀναγινώσκων): in all other places there is at least some, and often much, early uncial authority for γειν.; though it should be mentioned that 8/91 times for γείνομαι and compounds, and 29/108 times for γεινώσκω and compounds (chiefly in Acts and Epp. Cath.), the only attesting document is B, which has little authority on behalf of ει as against ι.

Of rare words κειρίαις Jo 11 44 and σειροῖς 2 Pe 2 4 are certain, and πιθοῖς 1 Co 2 4 hardly less. The only exact parallel to this last singular word is φιδός, written φειδός by some, but distinctly said by Herodianus(Chœrob.) ii 598 Lenz to have ι: compare Lobeck *Rhem.* 279, who cites φυγός from φεύγω. All early uncials, and some others,

have εἰδέα Mt 28 3, a form well attested in late literature (compare Field *Hex.* Dan i 14). It may be suspected that εἶρις (for ἶρις) lurks in the strange ιερεις of אֵ*A 79 al¹ ('priests' aeth arm) and ιρεις of אᶜB₂ in Ap 4 3, and ιρεις of A (ιρης C, θριξ א) in Ap 10 1: but no direct authority can be cited. For λειτουργός and its derivatives the best attested reading on the whole is λιτουργ. in St Paul and Hebrews (but 1 14 א only): in Lc.1/1 it is fairly well attested, while in Act. 1/1 it stands in E₂ alone. This spelling is well supported by inscriptions and other evidence (compare Steph.-Didot), though probably due in the first instance to a confusion; and indeed the use of these words in St Paul and Hebrews suggests that associations derived from the sense of λιτή may have become attached to them. On the whole it has seemed best to place λιτουργ. on the same footing as γείνομαι and γεινώσκω.

The shortening of ει to ι takes place in some abstract substantives in -εία from verbs in -εύω (-εύομαι); ἀλαζονία, ἀρεσκία, ἐθελοθρησκία (but θρησκεία), εἰδωλολατρία (but λατρεία), ἐριθία, ἑρμηνία, ἱερατία, κολακία, κυβία, μαγία, μεθοδία, ὀφθαλμοδουλία (but δουλία at least doubtful), πραγματία, φαρμακία; doubtful cases being ἁγνία, παιδία, πολιτία, πορία (in the same sense as πορεία), πτωχία, στρατία (not to be confounded with στρατιά: compare Krüger on Thuc. i 3 4; Stallbaum on Plat. *Phaedr.* 260 B): but there is no sufficient evidence adverse to the ordinary forms in other cases, as θεραπεία, μοιχεία, νηστεία, περισσεία, πορνεία, πρεσβεία, προφητεία, φυτεία, and also μνεία, χρεία. To these may be added the geographical names Ἀτταλία, Καισαρία, Λαοδικία, Φιλαδελφία, and probably Σαμαρία,

Σελευκία (but 'Αντιοχεία). A similar change takes place in a very few proparoxytones, ἀναιδία, εἱλικρινία, ἐπιεικία, κακοηθία, κακοπαθία, πραϋπαθία, and also ὠφελία (a form which has abundant classical authority); doubtful cases being ἀκριβία, ἀπειθία (in Hebrews, not doubtful elsewhere), ἐκτενία: but ἀλήθεια, ἀσέβεια, and many others, are fully attested, as are also ἀπώλεια, βοήθεια, συντέλεια. Conversely there is some good evidence for εὐτραπέλεια (supported by the considerable classical authority for δυστραπέλεια); and somewhat more for ἐπάρχεια (ἐπάρχειος): but κολωνεία is confined to late MSS. On duplicate forms in -ία and -εια see *E. M.* 462 (= Herodian. ii 453); also P. Buttmann *G. G.*² ii 417. Substantives that in the best MSS have -ιον for -ειον are δάνιον (see δανίζω below) and εἰδώλιον: also στοιχίον and still more πανδόχιον are too well attested to be rejected altogether, but μνημεῖον and σημεῖον are above doubt.

Adjectives that in the best MSS have -ιος for -ειος are αἴγιος (so apparently in LXX 4/4), 'Επικούριος, and perhaps ''Αριος (Πάγος), ἄστιος (cf. Hesych.), ἐπιτήδιος, and μεγάλια, μεγαλιότης (but βασίλειος, γυναικεῖος). Adjectives that in the best MSS have -ινός for -εινός are ὀρινός, σκοτινός, φωτινός. There is a clear predomination of authority for τάχειον (Jo² He²: see Boeckh on *C. I. G.* 3422), but βέλτιον and κάλλιον are above doubt.

Of substantives in -είτης for -ίτης τραπεζείτης is the only example among appellatives (the attempt of grammarians to assign different spellings to different senses being doubtless, as often, successful for the literary language only), μεσίτης (-ιτεύω), πολίτης with its derivatives, and τεχνίτης, as also μαργαρίτης, being above doubt. Of proper names of like form Λευείτης (with Λευειτικός) has good though not abundant evidence, and is justified by the amply attested Λευεί, Λευείς; 'Ελαμείτης (-είτις) and Νινευείτης are likewise morally certain; Σαμαρείτης, adopted by the Syrian text, and Σαμαρίτης (-ῖτις) vary in relative authority in different places, -είτης being on the whole better attested in Jo Act than in Mt Lc; but there is no reason to change 'Αρεοπαγίτης or Νικολαΐτης, or again Τραχωνῖτις. All good uncials support πανοικεί against πανοικί: cf. P. Buttmann *G. G.*² ii 453 f.

The forms δανίζω, δάνιον, δανιστής are alone well supported; so אABC in the LXX with hardly an exception, and various non-biblical evidence. Χρεοφιλέτης 2/2 must certainly be read: but tabulation of evidence confirms ὀφείλω, προσοφείλω, ὀφειλή, ὀφείλημα, ὀφειλέτης, notwithstanding the occasional attestation of -ιλ- by a greater or less number of good MSS. The authority for ἀλίφω, ἐξαλίφω, considerable in Mc 16 1, is not on the whole satisfactory: but we have accepted ἐξαλιφθῆναι Act 3 19, in which אBC concur, and which has the support of some recognised forms. Similarly it is enough to mention here the not unimportant attestation of ἀπιθής (-ία, -έω); ἀποδεδιγμένος, δίγμα, ὑπόδιγμα, [παρα]διγματίζω; ἀδιάλιπτος, ἀνέκλιπτος: it is on the whole safest to refer these and other still more irregularly attested spellings to mere itacism. Authority is amply sufficient however for καταλέλιμμαι, λίμμα, κατάλιμμα (compare Field *Hex.* Lev 18 6), which follow the ancient rule against the retention of a diphthong before a double consonant (Herodian. ii 270: cf. Lobeck *Paralip.* 36 f.): the express reference to κρείσσων as an exception (*ibid.*) is borne out by the

scantiness of the evidence for κρίσ-
σων in the N. T. A curious problem is presented by the constancy
with which the better MSS (אD₂
excepted, which have -λιπ- likewise
in He 10 25, where it is clearly
wrong) have forms in -ειπον (-ειπεν)
for the indicative of compounds of
λείπω in places of the Pastoral
Epistles (cf. Lc 7 45; 10 40) where
the aorist would be the most natural
tense (2 Ti 4 10, 13, 16, 20; Tit
1 5: cf. 3 13).

Of Hebrew names having a Greek
termination in -ιας or -είας three have
on the whole sufficient authority for
-είας (3/33 times however B alone,
Mc 6 15; Jo 1 21; Ja 5 17), 'Ηλείας,
'Ιωσείας, and 'Οζείας; while almost
all the evidence supports, 'Ανανίας,
Βαραχίας, 'Εξεκίας (less exclusively
than the rest), Ζαχαρίας, 'Ιερεμίας,
'Ιεχονίας, Μαθθίας, Ματταθίας, Οὐ-
ρίας. The inscription on the statue
of Hippolytus (see below, p. 159)
contains 'Εξεκίας *bis* and 'Ιωσείας.
The Greek transcripts of all Hebrew
names ending in ‑ֹ‑ take -εί, 'Αδδεί,
'Αρνεί, 'Εσλεί, 'Ηλεί, Μελχεί, Νηρεί;
as also of the Hebrew appellatives
ῥαββεί, ῥαββουνεί, ‑ ἠλεί ⊢ (but ἐλωί),
σαβαχθανεί: analogous forms are
'Αχείμ, 'Ελιακείμ, 'Ιωρείμ, (Νεφθαλείμ
in Mt,) Σαλείμ, 'Αδμείν, Βενιαμείν,
Σεμεείν, Χοραζείν (but 'Εφραίμ, Ναίν,
and in Ap, if the best evidence
may be trusted, Νεφθαλίμ), as also
Χερουβείν; and again Δανείδ, Κείς,
and Λευείς. The penultimate and
earlier syllables of names take ει for
the same Hebrew vowel, not only
in 'Ιάειρος, Θυάτειρα, Σάπφειρα, but
in 'Ιερειχώ, and probably in 'Ελεισα-
βέτ, and (on slighter evidence) Τα-
βειθά and ταλειθά: but ι stands
for ‑ֹ‑ in other names, as 'Αμινα-
δάβ, Μελχισεδέκ, Σινά, Σιών. Of

proper names of other origin the
form Πειλᾶτος has sufficient authority (2/55 however B alone, Mt 27
2; Act 4 27); and Εἰκόνιον, though
probably due in the first instance to
erroneous etymology, has good attestation, and is supported by extraneous evidence, including that of
coins.

ALT. λιτουργ. Lc 1 23; Act 13
2; Ro 13 6; 15 16, 27; 2 Co 9 12;
Phi 2 17, 25, 30; He 1 7, 14; 8 2,
6; 9 21; 10 11.

ἀγνείᾳ 1 Ti 4 12; 5 2; ἀκριβίαν
Act 22 3; ἀπειθίαν (-ίας) He 4 6,
11; δουλίας (-ίαν) Ro 8 15, 21; Ga
4 24; 5 1; He 2 15; ἐκτενίᾳ Act
26 7; ἐπαρχίας Act 23 34; ἐπαρχίᾳ
(margin ἐπαρχίῳ) 25 1; εὐτραπέλεια
Eph 5 4; παιδία (-ίαν, -ίας, -ίᾳ)
Eph 6 4; 2 Ti 3 16; He 12 5, 7, 8,
11; πολιτίαν (-ίας) Act 22 28; Eph
2 12; πορίαν (-ίαις) Lc 13 22; Ja 1
11; πτωχία (-ίαν, -ίᾳ) 2 Co 8 [? 2,] 9;
Λρ 2 9; στρατίας (-ίαν) 2 Co 10 4;
1 Ti 1 18. Σαμάρεια (-άρειαν, -αρείας,
-αρείᾳ) Jo 4 4, 5, 7; Act 1 8; 8 1,
5, 9, 14; 9 31; 15 3; Σελευκείαν
Act 13 4. πανδόχιον Lc 10 34;
στοιχία Ga 4 3, 9; Col 2 8, 20; He
5 12; 2 Pe 3 [no evidence 10,] 12.

Ἄριον ('Αρίου) Act 17 19, 22;
ἄστιος (-ον) Act 7 20; He 11 23;
ἐπιτήδια Ja 2 16; μεγάλια Act 2 11;
μεγαλιότητι (-τα, -τος) Lc 9 43; Act
19 27; 2 Pe 1 16. Σαμαρίτης (-ῖται,
-ίταις) Lc 10 33; 17 16; Jo 4 9, 40;
8 48; -ιτῶν Mt 10 5; Lc 9 52; Jo
4 39; Act 8 25; -ῖτις, -ίτιδος, Jo
4 9.

Νεφθαλείμ Ap 7 6; 'Ελισάβετ Lc
1 5, 7, 13, 24, 36, 40, 41 *bis*, 57;
Ταβιθά Act 9 36, 40; ταλιθά Mc 5
41; Εἰκόνιον (-ονίου, -ονίῳ) Act 13
51; 14 1, 19, 21; 16 2; 2 Ti 3 11.

II. NOUNS

DECLENSIONS I II

Substantives in -ρα form the gen. and dat. in -ρης, -ρῃ, in the best MSS, with the dissent however of B in Act.3/5; they are μάχαιρα, πλήμμυρα, πρῷρα, σπεῖρα, Σάπφειρα: so also συνειδυίης Act 5 2. The genitive of Λύδδα, indeclinable in acc. Act[2], is Λύδδας in the best MSS (Act[1]): all MSS have Μάρθας (Jo[1]).

Δίψῃ for δίψει 1/1 (B and cursives) need not be an itacism.

On forms in -ια -εια, -ινός -εινός, and the like, see pp. 153 ff.

Γομόρρων is attested by the best MSS Mt[1]: Γομόρρας, which stands almost without variation 2 Pe[1], is the only gen. of the LXX, Γόμορρα being as constantly the accusative.

Λύστρα takes without variation the acc. -αν (Act[3]) and the dat. -οις (Act[2] Paul[1]); and similarly Θυάτειραν, which is well attested, may be right Ap[1], though Θυατείροις stands above doubt Act[1] Ap[2].

Σαλαμίνη, a well attested substitute for Σαλαμῖνι, is perhaps only Alexandrian: Justin and Orosius have the Latin acc. *Salaminam*.

The variations between Μαρία and the indeclinable Μαριάμ are singularly intricate and perplexing, except as regards the gen., which is always -ίας, virtually without variation, and without difference of the persons intended. The Virgin is always (and usually without important variation) Μαριάμ (nom.voc. acc. dat.), except twice in a few of the best MSS, Mt 1 20 (acc.) and Lc 2 19 (nom.). The sister of Martha is also probably always Μαριάμ (nom.[6] acc.[4]), though the attestation curiously dwindles down to B 1 33, B 33, B 1, and 33 in Jo 12 3; 11 2; Lc 10 42; Jo 11 20 respectively. Mary of Clopas on the other hand is always Μαρία (nom.[8]), as is (acc.[1]) St Paul's helper (Ro 16 6). The difficulties arising from gradation of evidence reach their climax in the case of M. Magdalene. She is certainly Μαριάμ Mt 27 61, and perhaps 27 56; 28 1 (all nom.); almost certainly the same Mc 15 40; but not 15 47; 16 1 (all nom.), nor apparently (dat.[1]) in the Longer Conclusion, 16 9; Μαρία again Lc (nom.[2]); and apparently the first 3 places of Jo, 19 25; 20 1, 11 (all nom.): but a clear accession of good evidence certifies Μαριάμ for the peculiar and emphatic vocative of 20 16, where the Hebrew form is specially appropriate; and it is naturally repeated immediately afterwards in the nom. of 20 18.

The variations in good MSS between the forms belonging to ἑκατοντάρχης and -όνταρχος are not wholly irregular. In Mt[3] the nom. sing. is almost certainly -χος (nqt so א*, א* cu[1], אD Orig[1]), there is no acc., and the dat. sing.[1] is -χῃ: in Lc[2] (some good MSS being adverse) and Act[6] the nom. sing. is -χης, and the dat. sing. (Act[3]) and acc. pl. (Act[1]) in like manner -χῃ and -χας respectively, the acc. sing. alone (Act[1]) being of the second declension. Χιλίαρχος stands without variation, as do ἐθνάρχης sing., πατριάρχης, πολιτάρχης, and τετραάρχης (τετράρχης).

The genitives of proper names in -ας pure end in -ου, except Ἠλεία once, Lc 1 17 (not 4 25).

Στάδια Jo. 1/1 for σταδίους (Lc. 1/1 Ap. 1/1 marg.) seems to be only Western.

For σάββασιν, the usual dat. of σάββατα, B twice has σαββάτοις.

Ὀστοῦν, which stands Jo¹ (from LXX), has the uncontracted forms ὀστέα Lc¹ (in most MSS, including the best) and ὀστέων Mt¹ He¹. The uncontracted forms of adjectives in -οῦς are almost confined to ℵ, and that in Ap⁴: but AC have χρυσέων Ap¹. The best MSS have acc. χρυσᾶν Ap¹: but nom. χρυσῆ stands He¹.

Some adjectives usually of three terminations are of two in the N.T., κόσμιος 1 Ti¹, οὐράνιος Lc¹ Act¹, ὅσιος 1 Ti¹; μάταιος is of three 1 Pe¹ 1 Co¹, of two Ja¹ Tit¹; ἕτοιμος of three Mt¹, of two 1 Pe¹ 2 Co¹; αἰώνιος is of three 2 Th.1/1 He. 1/4, of two 52/54 times, though single MSS (chiefly B) have αἰωνίαν Mc 10 30; Act 13 48; 2 Pe 1 11; 1 Jo 2 25.

As λιμός is feminine 2/3 times (Lc¹ Act¹), some doubt rests on the masc. Lc¹, though 13–69 alone support the fem.; and the doubt may be fitly expressed here.

Δανιήλου (Mt¹ D) and Γαμαλιήλου (Act¹ B) may safely be rejected.

The acc. of Ἀπολλώς is Ἀπολλῶν Paul², Ἀπολλώ Act¹, but with some evidence for -λών, which would easily be changed in MSS, ΛΩ becoming ΛΩ. In all good MSS the acc. of Κῶς is Κῶ Act¹.

ALT. πρῴρας Act 27 30; σπείρας Act 10 1; Σαπφείρᾳ Act 5 1. δίψῃ 2 Co 11 27. Θυάτειραν Ap 1 11.

33

Σαλαμίνῃ Act 13 5. ἑκατοντάρχης Mt 8 5, 8; 27 54. σαββάτοις Mt 12 1, 12. χρυσέων Ap 2 1. λιμὸς μεγάλη Lc 4 25. Ἀπολλὼν Act 19 1.

DECLENSION III

The best MSS have κλεῖδας Mt. 1/1, and all but D κλεῖδα Lc.1/1: but κλεῖς¹ (acc.) and κλεῖν² stand in Ap. Ἔρεις in Paul.5/6 has considerable attestation, and has often been naturally taken as a plural; but all MSS have ἔριδες 1 Co 1 11: we have with hesitation allowed ἔρεις (with ζῆλοι, the attestation of which is a perplexing element of the evidence) in Ga 5 20, though it is probably at once an itacistic error for ἔρις, and an assimilation to neighbouring plurals (as in 2 Co 12 20, and still more certainly 1 Ti 6 4: cf. 1 Co 3 3): similarly it stands for ἔριν Tit 3 9. The plural of νῆστις is νήστεις Mt¹ Mc¹: νῆστις, apparently recognised by some ancient grammarians (C. F. A. Fritzsche *Mc.* 796 f.), is found in no early MS but ℵ, which cannot be trusted for ι as against ει. For the substantive χάριν (without var. 40 times, incl. Act⁵) χαρίτα is well attested Act.1/7 and sufficiently Jud¹, and found in A in Act.1/7.

The uncontracted gen. pl. πηχέων, common in LXX, is attested only by A Cyr in Jo¹ and ℵ in Ap¹.

A final ν is often appended to accusatives sing. in α or η (ῇ) in one or more good MSS. The irregularity and apparent capriciousness however of its occurrence, the usual insufficiency of the amount of evidence for it, and its extreme rarity in B have induced us to regard these forms as due to transcribers, even where the evidence is less slender than usual, as in the case of χεῖραν

Jo 20 25, συγγενὴν Ro 16 11, ἀσφα-
λῆν He 6 19.

For συγγενής (which stands Jo¹;
συγγενῆ [-νὴν ABD*] Ro¹) Lc¹ has
the fem. συγγενίς, and Mc¹ Lc¹
probably the dat. pl. συγγενεῦσι (as
1 Mac 10 89) from συγγενεύς.

As an acc. ἅλα is fully attested
1/1, Mc 9 50 (3°): as a nom. it
always occurs as a v. l. in one or
more good MSS; so also Lev 2 13
(1°) in ABG cu⁸.

The variations in the inflexions
of ἥμισυς in MSS are curious. In
Ap³ ἥμισυ each time has the v. l.
ἡμίσου (Aᵃ, ℵA, ℵ* : cf. Is 44 16 B),
which likewise is one of the variants for ἡμίσους Mc¹. In Lc 19 8
MSS clearly certify τὰ ἡμίσια (L alone
has -σεια), apparently from a form
ἡμίσιος, against τὰ ἥμισυ and still
more against τὰ ἡμίση: this peculiar
form occurs in an inscription from
Selinus in Cilicia (C. I. G. 4428),
τὴν δὲ [ἡμι]σίαν (the restoration is
certified by the context); cf. Hesych. Ἡμιτιεύς· ἡμισευτής. Ἡμίτιον·
τετράχουν. The evidence is decisive for βαθέως Lc¹, and sufficient
for πραέως 1 Pe¹.

It is convenient to place here as
alternative readings a few nominatives (without ὁ) used as vocatives,
and differing only in the length of a
vowel: θυγάτηρ Mc¹ Lc¹ Jo¹, πάτηρ
Jo³, ἄφρων Lc¹ 1 Co¹ (cf. υἱός Mt¹⁻⁵)
claim a place in the text: βασι-
λεύς (B) Act 26 13, 27 may apparently be neglected.

A few substantives in -ος, usually
of the second declension, are wholly
(ἔλεος, σκότος) or in part of the third
in the N.T.: πλοῦτος in nom. and
acc. is 8/10 times of the third in St
Paul, but of the second in other
cases and other writers; ζῆλος 2/7
times of the third (acc. dat.) in St
Paul, and perhaps 1/5 (gen., as good
MSS in LXX) in other writers:
conversely there is but little au-

thority for θάμβου 1/1. Whether
ἤχους in Lc 21 25 (ἐν ἀπορίᾳ ἤχους
θαλάσσης) comes from ἦχος or from
ἠχώ is doubtful: ἦχος is apparently
an acc. in Jer 28 (51) 16 (ℵAB),
and Iren.68 according to Epiph has
the dat. ἤχει (but Hipp ἤχῳ); but
there is no other evidence for ἦχος
in the third declension (τοῦ ἤχους in
1 Reg 18 41 is merely a Complutensian conjecture), and ἠχώ might
well be used in an equally general
sense, as Job 4 13 and apparently
Philo Mut. nom. 9 f. (i 588 f.):
the same uncertainty recurs in Ps 77
(76) 17; (?) 65 (64) 7; Sir 47 9; and
in one text of Jer. l. c.

The best MSS (in Mt 1 6 nearly
all MSS, for the acc.) in the Gospels
(Mt³ Lc² Jo¹) have Σολομῶνος, implying Σολομών (or Σολόμων : see
Chandler Gr. Acc. 650, 661) in the
nom.: in Act.1/2 Σολομῶντος is as
decisively attested (implying Σολο-
μῶν in the nom.), while in Act.1/2
authority is divided: in Mt 1 6 ℵ*
1-209 have the indeclinable acc.
-μών, which is of frequent occurrence in the LXX.

Since St Luke makes Ἐλαιῶνος
the gen. of Ἐλαιών in Act 1 12, it
may be reasonably inferred that the
Ἐλαιων of Lc 19 29; 21 37 is not
an indeclinable in agreement with
the accus. τό, but the gen. of ἐλαία
("the Mount that is called [the
Mount] of Olives"); as is also
suggested by the shortly subsequent
use of τὸ Ὄρος τῶν Ἐλαιῶν (as Mt
Mc) in each case: the accent must
therefore be Ἐλαιῶν.

The dat. of Μωυσῆς is everywhere (Mt¹ Mc² Lc¹ Jo² Ro¹ 2 Ti¹)
Μωυσεῖ except Act 7 44, where -σῇ
may come from the LXX : the evidence is decisive except 7/9 times.
The acc. is Μωυσέα Lc¹, Μωυσῆν Act²
1 Co¹ He¹, all without var. Ἰωάνει
is sufficiently attested as the dat. of
Ἰωάνης Mt¹ Lc², and probably Ap¹,

but is unattested Act[1] (see Μωυσεῖ above).

The gen. of Ἰωσῆς is Ἰωσῆ in Mt 27 56, if Ἰωσήφ is not the true reading; in Mc. 3/3 it is Ἰωσῆτος.

The name of the king Manasseh is in Mt acc. Μανασσῆ, followed by nom. -σῆς: but אᵇB may be right in having -σῆ in both places, *i.e.* indeclinable (so 2 Chr 32 33 A*B), as is the name of the tribe in Ap (so Gen 48 5 AB, &c.).

ALT. χάριτα Act 25 9. συγγενέσιν Mc 6 4; Lc 2 44. ἅλα Mt 5 13 *bis*; Mc 9 50 *bis* (1° 2°); Lc 14 34 *bis*. θυγάτηρ Mt 9 22; πάτηρ Jo 12 28; 17 5, 11. ζῆλους Act 5 17. ἤχους Lc 21 25. Σολομῶνος Act 5 12. Μωυσῆ Mc 9 4; Ro 9 15. Ἰωάνῃ Ap 1 1. Μανασσῆ Mt 1 10 (2°).

FORMS OF PROPER NAMES INDEPENDENT OF INFLEXION

Few of the numerous variations in the form of proper names require to be mentioned here. The cases in which decision is difficult are not many.

Ἰωάνης stands for Ἰωάννης almost always (121/130) in B (in א only in parts written by the scribe of B, namely Mt 16 14; 17 1, 13; Lc 1 13; Ap 1 1, 4, and perhaps 9; and the correction of Jo 21 15, where א* omits) and frequently in D: no MS has it Act 4 6; 13 5; Ap 22 8; but this is doubtless accidental. No difference of evidence can be clearly traced with regard to the several persons who bear the name. Ἰωάνης occurs in Christian inscriptions from Seleucia (*C. I. G.* 9237, for a native of Alabanda), Bithynia (8869), Athens (9307), and Rome (9640). It is likewise the form used in the list of writings inscribed on

the base of the Roman statue of Hippolytus, accompanied by a paschal canon which must have been framed in 222 or shortly after (see p. 79); and the inscription itself, notwithstanding the doubts raised (not on palæographical grounds) by Kirchhoff (*C. I. G.* 8613), who is inclined to refer it to the latter part of Cent. IV, belongs assuredly to the same generation as the canon. The absence of Latin attestation and the range of inscriptions render it improbable that Ἰωάνης is due to Western scribes: but it would be hardly safe to reject Ἰωάννης altogether. Ἰωάνα (Lc[2]) is open to a similar doubt, especially in Lc 24 10. Ἰωανάν Lc. 1/1 is amply assured.

Μαθθαῖος is sufficiently attested; and also, somewhat less, Μαθθάν, Μαθθάτ (-άθ), Μαθθίας (compare Μαθθᾶς in two Palmyrene inscriptions, *C.I.G.* 4479, 4502; Γίθθων, in Palestine, Eus. *H.E.* ii 13 3 cod. Ven.); but Ἀφφία and Σάφφειρα appear to be Western only.

Ἐλισαῖος (Lc[1]) and conversely Βαρσαββᾶς (Act[2]) are alone well attested; Ἐλισσαῖος and Βαρσαβᾶς being Syrian. Φύγελος is the right form (2 Ti[1]), not Φύγελλος; as also Τρωγύλιον, not Τρωγύλλιον, in the Western interpolation of Act 20 15.

For Βεελζεβούλ אB substitute Βεεζεβούλ Mt. 3/3 Lc. 3/3, B Mc. 1/1; and there is no sufficient reason for discarding this form of an obscure name (see Weiss *Mt.Ev. u. s. Luc. Par.* 271, 275: cf. *Mc.Ev. u. s. Syn.Par.* 126 f.), unknown except from the N.T.: but the form with λ, analogous to the Heb. *Baalzebub* (LXX Βααλμυιάν) of 2 Reg 1 2, 3, 6, demands recognition. In the N.T. *Beelzebub* has no Greek authority; and *Belial* for Βελίαρ (Βελιάβ, Βελίαν Western) is exclusively Latin.

Ἀπελλής for Ἀπολλώς (Act[2], not Paul[8]) is Alexandrian. Νεεμάν (Lc[1]) is a late, apparently Syrian, corruption of Ναιμάν (so also the better MSS of LXX).

There is everywhere much variation between documents in the spelling of the name *Nazareth*; but the evidence when tabulated presents little ambiguity. Ναζαρά is used at the outset of the Ministry in Mt.1/3 (4 13) and Lc.1/5 (4 16); Ναζαρέθ in Mt.1/3 (21 11), the only later place in the Gospels where the name occurs, and in Act.1/1 ; and Ναζαρέτ certainly or probably in all other places, Mt.1/3, Mc.1/1, Lc.4/5, Jo.2/2 : Ναζαράθ, found 8/11 times in Δ, has little other attestation.

Between Ἱερουσαλήμ and Ἱεροσόλυμα there is usually no variation, though each form is wrongly introduced a few times : Act 15 4 ; 20 16 are the only places where it would be possible to hesitate about decision. Ἱεροσόλυμα is used in Mt always except once in the voc., in Mc and Jo always, sometimes in Lc (a seventh), Acts (roughly two fifths), and St Paul (3/10); Ἱερουσαλήμ in Mt 23 37, the remainder of Lc Act Paul, and He[1] Ap[3].

Καπερναούμ is everywhere a distinctively Syrian corruption of Καφαρναούμ; and Μαγδαλά (Mt 15 39) is a Syrian modification of Μαγδαλάν, an apparently Alexandrian corruption of Μαγαδάν.

Some other local names vary in termination between -ά and -άν. Mt[1](acc.) Jo[1](nom. with *v.l.* Γολγόθ) have Γολγοθά, Mc[1](acc.) in the best MSS -άν. Lc[2](acc. voc.) Jo[2] (gen.) have Βηθσαιδά, Mt[1](voc.) Mc[2] (acc.) -άν. Βηθανιά as an acc. is sufficiently attested Lc 19 29, and stands in B Mt[1] Mc.1/2, but elsewhere is virtually unattested.

Δελματία 1/1 (which has good extraneous authority) and Πατέρα 1/1 are probably Alexandrian but possibly genuine. Σελαθιήλ is perhaps only Western.

The true form of several geographical names in Acts is preserved in only a few documents, chiefly B and versions. Thus Καῦδα replaces Κλαύδην (Syrian, a modification of the Alexandrian reading Κλαῦδα) in 27 16 (see Ewald *ad loc.* p. 292) : both forms were current. Μελιτήνην replaces Μελίτη (preceding ἡ νῆσος) in 28 1 (either of the groups of letters ΗΝΗΗΝΗ and ΗΗΝΗ might be corrupted into the other with equal facility) : it is worth notice that all the MSS of Ptolemy (ed. Wilberg ii 15) have the longer form as the name of the island on the Dalmatian coast. Ἀδραμυντηνῷ (πλοίῳ) replaces Ἀδραμυττηνῷ (27 2). Sometimes the variations are more complicated. Μύρρα (27 5) suffers but slight change as Μύρα in the Syrian text, but becomes Σμύρναν in the Western, and Λύστραν in the Alexandrian. Λασέα (27 8), which by a lengthening of the sound of ε becomes Λασαία in the Syrian text, and also Λασσαία, suffers change in other texts through a confusion of the written character of the same letter with σ (Ϲ C), being read as Ἄλασσα, Θάλασσς, and Λαΐσσα.

ALT. Μαθθαθίου Lc 3 25; Μαθθάθ Lc 3 24, 29. Ἐσρώμ Lc 3 33; Ναθάν Lc 3 31; Καινάν Lc 3 37. Ἰωβήδ Lc 3 32. Ἄχαζ Mt 1 9. Ἰωάννης (-ην, -ου, -ει, -η) passim ; Ἰωάννα Lc 8 3; 24 10. Βεελζεβούλ Mt 10 25; 12 24, 27; Mc 3 22; Lc 11 15, 18, 19; Γεννησαρὲθ Mc 6 53; Ναζαρὲθ (-έθ) Lc 2 4, 39, 51. Ἀχελδαμάχ Act 1 19. Βηθανιά (-ιὰ) Mt 21 17; Mc 11 1. Δελματίαν 2 Ti 4 10; Πάτερα Act 21 1 ; Σελαθιήλ (-ὴλ) Mt 1 12 *bis*.

III. VERBS

'Εργάζομαι, προσεργάζομαι, and not improbably (Paul[4]) κατεργάζομαι have η- for their augment (see Curtius *Gr. Verb.*[2] i 128), but not in the perfect (Jo[1] 1 Pe[1]): this form is well attested elsewhere. Conversely, all good authority is in favour of εἰλκω-μένος Lc[1], for which there is other evidence.

All early MSS read διερμήνευσεν Lc 24 27, and διεγείρετο Jo[1] is probably right: but διήγειραν Lc[1] and διήρχ.[6] διῆλθ.[6] are almost exclusively attested.

The augment ω- for ο- is often neglected by some of the inferior uncials; but the short vowel almost always (even in ὁμοιώθημεν Ro 9 29 [LXX] and ἀφομοιωμένος He 7 3) lacks sufficient authority, the only certain instance being προορώμην Act 2 25 (from LXX, with the best MSS of LXX): there is however good evidence for ἀνορθώθη Lc[1], which likewise occurs twice or more in LXX.

MSS differ much as to the pf. of ὁράω: ἑώρακα is certain in the Gospels, and probable in St John's Epp., where however B has uniformly ἑο-; while in St Paul's Epp. (3 places) the balance is in favour of ἑόρακα.

The usual augment is retained by all MSS in παρῳχημέναις and by almost all MSS in ἐνοικέω, κατοικέω,

παροικέω, κατοικίζω, μετοικίζω; but neglected in several and perhaps in nearly all places (imperf., aor., and perf.) of οἰκοδομέω (and ἐποικοδομέω), the only certain exceptions being according to known evidence being Mt 21 33; Lc 4 29: see Curtius *Gr. Verb.*[2] ii 166. All good MSS but א* have ἐπαισχύνθη 2 Ti 1 16: but κατῃσχύνοντο Lc[1] κατῃσχύνθην 2 Co[1] stand without variation.

The augments of ἀνοίγω and διανοίγω exhibit much intricate variation. The 'aor. 1' act. is certainly ἤνοιξα in Act.4/4 Ap.10/10 (with διήνοιξα Lc.1/1 Act.1/1); and probably or possibly in 5/6 places of Jo 9, but not in the first (v. 14), where and where alone ἀνέῳξα is well attested, ἠνέῳξα being also twice (vv. 17, 32) well attested. For the 'aor. 1' pass. ἠνεῴχθην is certain Jo.1/1, and divides the better evidence with ἀνεῴχθην Mt.3/3 Ap.2/2 and with ἠνοίχθην Act.1/1, while διηνοίχθην is sufficiently attested Lc[1], and Lc[1] almost without var. has ἀνεῳχθῆναι: Mc[1] Act[1] Ap[2] have the 'aor. 2' ἠνοίγην. For the perf. mid. Act[1] has διηνοι-γμένος, Act[2] Paul[2] ἀνεῳγμένος, while all three forms must be regarded as possible Act[1], and with one doubtful exception ἠνεῳγμένος stands Ap[5]. Jo[1] Paul[2] have the strong or 'second' perfect ἀνέῳγα.

The augmented tenses of εὐαγγελίζομαι are always of the form εὐηγ.: in εὐαρεστέω He[1] the evidence is evenly divided; in LXX the augment appears to be never absent. On εὐοδῶται see below, p. 172.

Εὐδοκέω has εὐδ. everywhere in the Gospels, though ηὐδ. is sometimes well supported: in the Epistles the evidence strangely fluctuates. The evidence for ηὐλογ. in the aor. is less slight than in the perf. and imperf., but yet insufficient. Εὐφραίνομαι Acts[2] (ηὐφ. from LXX), εὐκαιρέω (ηὐκ. Act, εὐκ. Mc), and εὐχαριστέω (ηὐχ. Ro, εὐχ. Act), the last with some uncertainty as to ηὐχ., exhibit divided pairs of readings. Εὐπορούμαι and εὐφορέω, each in a single passage, have no augment. So also εὐθυδρομέω.

In εὑρίσκω the good evidence for ηὑρ., in no case quite conclusive, is confined to the imperfect. But in εὔχομαι and προσεύχομαι, aor. and imperf. alike, the forms with ην are commonly and perhaps universally employed. Εὐνουχίζω Mt[2] has no augment.

There is no sufficient evidence for a double augment in ἀνέχομαι: ἀνεσχόμην Act[1] and ἀνειχόμην 2 Co[1] (and marg. 2 Co[1]) are the forms used.

The aorists of ἀποκαθίστημι have always (Mt[1] Mc[2] Lc[1]) a double syllabic augment (twice with the dissent of B): but ἀντικατέστητε He[1] is almost certain. Προφητεύω invariably takes a single augment at the beginning.

Of the verbs in which ἠ- may replace the ordinary syllabic augment δύναμαι has always (8 times) ἠ- in the aor. (ἠδυνήθην, ἠδυνάσθην); with little variation: in the imperf. there is more irregularity, the 3 pl. being ἠδύναντο (Mc[1] Lc[1] Jo[1]), the 2 pl. ἐδύνασθε (1 Co[1]); while as to the sing. authority fluctuates between ἐδ. and ἠδ. in the Gospels, and is generally favourable to ἐδ. elsewhere (Act[1] Ap.4/5). Μέλλω has sometimes ἐμ., sometimes ἠμ., and that within the same books. These variations of form do not appear to depend on the preceding word. Βούλομαι takes only the ordinary syllabic augment.

Ὠθέω (ἀπώσατο Act[2] Ro[2]; ἐξῶσεν Act 7 45, where ἐξέωσεν is an Alexandrian correction) and ὠνοῦμαι (Act[1]) do not take a syllabic augment. Not only κατέαξαν Jo[2] but κατεαγῶσιν Jo[1] and (from LXX) κατεάξω Mt[1] stand without var.: see Veitch *I.D.V.* 356; Cobet *N. T. Praef.* lxxix.

The pluperfect of ἵσταμαι (and so παρίσταμαι) is not εἱστήκειν but ἱστήκειν. The evidence varies in the 14 places; and in Jo 1 35; 7 37; and still more Lc 23 49, it preponderates for εἱστήκειν: but tabulation renders it morally certain that ἱστήκειν is nowhere a mere itacism; more especially since even the habitual addiction of B to ει for ι has not prevented it from supporting ἱστήκει 5 times, and once (Lc 23 10) the ε of the first hand appears to have been deliberately cancelled by the original corrector. This form is also at least of frequent occurrence in the LXX.

Between εἶδον (ἐπεῖδον[1]) and ἴδον the better MSS vary greatly and irregularly, but with complete gradation. Tabulation is however decisive for εἶδον in the Gospels (even Jo 1 39), Acts, and Epistles; and the larger proportion of places where the balance favours ἴδον in the Apocalypse is probably due only to the paucity of MSS, though it has appeared safest to mark the possible alternative.

Ἀφέθησαν Ro[1] (from LXX) and ἀνέθη Act[1] stand in all good MSS.

ALT. κατηργάσατο Ro 7 8; 15 18; 2 Co 7 11; κατηργάσθη 2 Co 12 12.

διηγείρετο Jo 6 18.

ἀνορθώθη Lc 13 13. ἑοράκαμεν
I Jo I 1, 2, 3; ἑόρακεν 3 6; 4 20 *bis*;
3 Jo 11; ἑόρακα I Co 9 1; ἑώρακαν
(-εν) Col 2 1, 18.

οἰκοδόμησεν Mt 7 24, 26; Mc 12
1; Lc 7 5; οἰκοδόμουν Lc 17 28;
ᾠκοδόμησεν Act 7 47.

ἠνέῳξεν Jo 9 14; ἤνοιξέν Jo 9 17,
32; ἀνεῴχθησαν Mt 3 16; 9 30;
ἠνεῴχθησαν Mt 27 52; ἠνοίχθησαν
Act 16 26; ἠνεῴχθησαν, -ῴχθη, Ap
20 12; ἠνοιγμένων v. ἠνεῳγμένων
Act 9 8; ἀνεῳγμένην Ap 3 8.

εὐηρεστηκέναι He 11 5.

εὐδόκησαν (-σεν) Ro 15 26, 27;
1 Co 10 5; εὐδοκήσαμεν 1 Th 3 1;
εὐδοκοῦμεν 1 Th 2 8; ηὐδόκησα (-σεν,
-σας) 2 Pe 1 17; 1 Co 1 21; Ga 1
15; Col 1 19; He 10 6, 8. εὐχαρί-
στησαν Ro 1 21.

εὕρισκον Mc 14 55; Lc 19 48;
Act 7 11; εὑρίσκετο He 11 5
(LXX); προσεύξαντο (-ατο) Act 8
15; 20 36; εὔχοντο Act 27 29.

ἀντεκατέστητε He 12 4.

ἐδύνατο Lc 19 3; ἠδύνατο Mc 6 5;
Lc 1 22; Jo 11 37; Ap 5 3. ἔμελ-
λεν (-ον) Lc 9 31; He 11 8; Ap 10
4; ἤμελλον (-εν) Jo 7 39; 11 51;
Act 21 27.

ἴδον (-ες, -εν) Ap passim, especially 6 8, 9; 8 2; 14 14; 15 1; 19
19.

SINGLE AND DOUBLE Ρ

In most cases verbs beginning
with ρ do not double the ρ after the
initial ἐ of the augmented tenses,
and the compounds of these verbs
do not double the ρ after either the
augment ε or the final vowel of a
preposition or ἀ privative. Usually
the evidence for the single ρ is overwhelming; in a few places it is
scanty in amount but good. All
MSS however have ἔρρηξεν Lc 9 42,
and διαρρήξαντες Act 14 14 (not-

withstanding περιρήξαντες, διαρήσ-
σων, and the like); and διέρηξεν
Mt 26 65 διαρήξας Mc 14 63 rest on
single (good) MSS. Probably ρρ is in
all these cases due to the scribes. Ἐρρέθη or ἐρρήθη (-ησαν) stands everywhere without variation. Of adjectives formed from these verbs
ἄραφος and ἀναντίρητος are probably
the right forms: but all MSS have
ἄρρητος 2 Co 12 4. Of perfects we
have ἐριμμένοι[1] and possibly ἔριπται[1]: but ἐρριζωμένοι (Eph 3 18;
Col 2 7) and ἔρρωσθε (Act 15 29)
stand without variation. All the
early MSS have the reduplicated
ῥεραντισμένοι Heb 10 22, and the
same form (probably a correction
for the lost ῥεραμμένον, see note)
stands in our text of Ap 19 13,
similar forms being among the rival
variants : D alone has ῥεριμμένοι Mt
9 36. We have followed Lachmann
(cf. P. Buttmann *G.G.*[2] i 28; Kühner *G.G.*[2] i 217, 508) in using the
smooth breathing for ρερ-: the limitation to Ῥᾶρος and its derivatives
(Herodian. i 546 20 ff., 12 22 16 f.,
402 13) is apparently arbitrary.

ALT. διέρρηξεν Mt 26 65; διαρ-
ρηξας Mc 14 63; ἐρρύσατο 2 Pe 2 7;
2 Co 1 10; Col 1 13; 2 Ti 3 11;
ἐρρύσθην 2 Ti 4 17. ἄρραφος Jo 19
23; ἀναντιρρήτως (-ων) Act 10 29;
19 36. ἔριπται Lc 17 2.

FUTURES OF VERBS IN -ΙΖΩ

The 3 pl. act. of the future of
verbs in -ίζω takes the 'Attic' form
-ιοῦσι except perhaps in γνωρίζω
1/1; such also are the only 2 pl.
mid. κομιεῖσθε[1], and one 1 sing. act.
παροργιῶ (LXX) against two in -σω.
The 3 sing. act. is habitually in
-σει: but καθαριεῖ He[1] and διακα-
θαριεῖ Mt[1] are unquestionably right;
and there are three or four doubtful

cases. The other forms are θερίσο-μεν², χαρίσεται¹, and once if not twice κομίσεται.

ALT. γνωριοῦσιν Col 4 9. ἀφο-ριεῖ Mt 25 32; ἐγγιεῖ Ja 4 8; φωτιεῖ Ap 22 5; χρονιεῖ He 10 37. κο-μιεῖται Col 3 25.

TERMINATIONS OF AORISTS AND PERFECTS

The N. T. contains various ex-amples of strong or 'second' aorists having the termination of weak or 'first' aorists; not only εἶπα, ἤνεγ-κα, ἔπεσα (see P. Buttmann *G.G.*² 164 f., 313 f., 277 ff.; Veitch *I.D.V.* 232 ff., 666 ff., 540 f.), which have a recognised place in the classical language, and are apparently as old as εἶπον κ.τ.λ., but other forms which may possibly be due only to late assimilation. On both classes, if indeed they are distinct, see Cur-tius *Gr. Verb.*² ii 306—312.

Forms belonging to εἶπα stand without var. in those persons of the imperative which contain τ (εἴ-πατε, εἰπάτω, -τωσαν), while εἰπόν (this is not the 'Attic' accentuation, but we have followed C. F. A. Fritzsche [*Mc.* 515 ff.] and Lach-mann) is sufficiently attested to claim a place in the text in about half the places, the exceptions being chiefly before consonants. In the indicative ἀπειπάμεθα stands with-out var. 2 Co 4 2, and προείπαμεν is amply attested 1 Th 4 6, these two being the only places of any 1 pl.; while εἶπα itself is rare: εἶπας stands without var. Mt² Lc¹, εἶπες being the best attested form in Jo¹ and probably Mc¹: for the 3 pl., which is confined to the historical books, εἶπαν has good evidence everywhere in Acts and (with fewer places) Mc, in most places of Mt Lc,

and in Jo. 3/4. The participles εἴπας, εἴπασα are rare : the forms in -αντος, -αντες, -αντα have no suffi-cient authority anywhere.

The indicatives ἤνεγκα, ἠνέγκαμεν, -έγκατε, ἤνεγκαν are exclusively at-tested ; as also the imperative ἐνέγ-κατε. In Mt¹ προσένεγκον is also probably right, but it stands alone : in Mc 1 44 ‖ Lc 5 14 προσένεγκε and in Mc 14 36 ‖ Lc 22 42 παρέ-νεγκε are certainly the true read-ings, and the rival forms in -αι, though supported by good MSS in the last two places, may be safely neglected. The infinitive is always in -εῖν except 1 Pe 2 5, where ἀνε-νέγκαι stands equally without varia-tion.

The indicatives ἔπεσα, ἔπεσαν (and compounds), and (Ga¹) ἐξεπέ-σατε are everywhere overwhelmingly attested. But the balance of evi-dence is decidedly against the im-perative πέσατε (Lc¹ Ap¹); and this fact sustains the similar preponder-ance for the active 'aor. 2' ἀνάπεσε as against a (supposed) middle 'aor. 1' ἀνάπεσαι in Lc 14 10; 17 7.

The imperatives ἔλθατε, ἐλθάτω (and compounds) are everywhere amply attested, though B five times dissents. The other forms of the 'aor. 1' occur but irregularly : they are ἦλθαν and ἦλθαμεν with their compounds, and once probably ἀπῆλ-θα.

The indicatives εἶδαν and εἴδαμεν must certainly be accepted in a few places, perhaps in more. For εἴ-δατε the evidence is less satisfactory : εἶδα (or ἶδα) is fairly probable Ap². In the imperative, infinitive, and participle the 'aor. 2' forms alone are found.

Ἀνεῦραν and εὕραμεν are suffi-ciently attested each in one place, and may well be right elsewhere : εὑράμενος is still better attested He¹. But εὗρον sing., εὑρεῖν, and εὑρών with its cases are found without exception.

The indicatives ἀνεῖλαν¹, ἀνείλατε¹, ἐξειλάμην¹, εἵλατο¹, ἀνείλατο¹, ἐξείλατο² are abundantly attested, and no others are found elsewhere. The other moods belong exclusively to the 'aor. 2'.

In other verbs the occurrence of forms containing α instead of the aor. 2 is rare even in single MSS; ἔβαλαν¹ and ἐπέβαλαν² alone being entitled to a provisional place in the text. For ἐξέβαλαν¹ (Mc 12 8), ἔλαβαν (Jo 1 12), ἐλάβατε (1 Jo 2 27), ἐλάβαμεν (Lc 5 5), ἔπιαν (1 Co 10 4), ἀπέθαναν (Mt 8 32; Lc 20 31; Jo 8 53), γενάμενος (see P. Buttmann *G.G.*² ii 136) and ἀπογενάμενος (a few places), and others, the evidence at present known is insufficient.

On the whole the imper. ἐκχέετε Ap 16 1 (only the later MSS have ἐκχέατε) may be better referred to an otherwise virtually unknown 'aor. 2' (ἐξέχεον 2 Mac 1 8 cu²) than to the pres., notwithstanding the use of ἐξέχεαν in v. 6. The seven responsive acts denoted by the in itself ambiguous ἐξέχεεν of vv. 2, 3, 4, 8, 10, 12, 17 would naturally be expressed by an aor., and thus they seem to point back to an aor. in the previous command. To the 'aor. 2' should probably be likewise referred συνέχεον (-αν C cuᵖ·ᵇᵒ) Act 21 27, though here the context favours both tenses alike: elsewhere in Acts the pres. and imperf. are συνχύννεται (21 31) and συνέχυννεν (9 22).

Even the imperfect sometimes has forms containing α, as in the LXX and elsewhere. There is sufficient evidence for at least εἶχαν (Mc 8 7) and παρεῖχαν (Act 28 2).

The curious termination -οσαν for aorists and imperfects (see Maittaire-Sturz *Dial.* 298 f.; P. Buttmann *G.G.*² i 346) is exhibited by εἴ-χοσαν Jo 15 22, 24, and (from LXX) ἐδολιοῦσαν Ro 3 13: παρελάβοσαν, which is excellently attested 2 Th 3 6, is rendered somewhat suspicious by the comparative correctness of St Paul's language elsewhere, and by the facility with which it might originate in an ocular confusion with -οσιν (παράδοσιν) in the corresponding place of the line above. In a few other places forms in -οσαν have some Western attestation.

ALT. εἰπὲ Mt 4 3; 22 17; 24 3; Lc 10 40; Jo 10 24. εἶπα Mt 28 7; Act 11 8; 22 10, 19; He 3 10. εἴπας Mc 12 32. εἶπον (pl.) Mc 16 8; Lc 6 2; Jo 4 52; 6 60; Act 2 37 (-όν). εἴπας Act 7 27; 20 36; Ja 2 11.

προσένεγκε Mt 8 4.

ἦλθον (pl.) Mt 7 25, 27; 14 34; Mc 1 29; 3 8; Lc 1 59; 6 17; 8 35; 23 33; 24 23; Jo 3 26; 12 9; Act 14 24; 28 23. ἀπῆλθον (pl.) Mt 8 32; Mc 12 12; Lc 24 24 (-όν); ἀπῆλθαν Jo 11 46. εἰσῆλθαν (pl.) Act 16 40. ἐξῆλθον (pl.) Jo 21 3; Act 16 40; 2 Jo 7; Ap 15 6. προσῆλθον (pl.) Mt 9 28; 19 3; 21 23; Jo 12 21. συνῆλθον (pl.) Act 10 23. ἤλθαμεν Mt 25 39. ἤλθομεν Act 21 8. εἰσήλθομεν Act 28 16. κατήλθομεν Act 27 5. ἀπῆλθον (sing.) Ap 10 9.

εἶδον Mc 6 33; 9 14; Act 6 15; 28 4. εἴδομεν Mt 25 38; Mc 2 12; 9 38 (-έν); Lc 5 26 (Εἴδ-); 9 49 (-έν). εἴδατε Lc 7 22; Jo 6 26. εἶδα Ap 17 3, 6.

εὗρον Lc 8 35. εὗραν Mt 22 10; Act 5 10; 13 6. εὕραμεν Act 5 23 *bis*. All pl.

ἔβαλαν Mt 13 48; Ap 18 19. ἔβαλον Act 16 37. ἐξέβαλαν Mt 21 39; Mc 12 8. ἐπέβαλον Mc 14 46; Act 21 27. ἐξεβάλαμεν Mt 7 22. All pl.

εἶχαν Lc 4 40. εἶχον Ap 9 8, 9. εἴχομεν 2 Jo 5. εἴχατε Jo 9 41. προσεῖχαν Act 8 10. All pl.

There are a few well attested examples of the curious substitution of -αν for -ασι in the 3 pl. of perfects (see Curtius *Gr. Verb.*[2] ii 187), a peculiarity called Alexandrian by Sextus Empiricus (*Adv. Gramm.* 213), but certainly of wider range. They are ἔγνωκαν Jo[1], εἴρηκαν Ap[1] (but εἰρήκασιν Act[1]), εἰσελήλυθαν Ja[1] (but ἐξεληλύθασιν 1 Jo[1]), ἀπέσταλκαν Act[1], γέγοναν Ro[1] Ap[1] (but γεγόνασιν 1 Jo[1]), ἑώρακαν Lc[1] Col[1] (but ἑωράκασιν Jo[1]), τετήρηκαν Jo[1]. The evidence for -ες -ετε in place of -ας -ατε in perfects, and in aorists ending in -κα, is much scantier. These last forms have a better claim to acceptance in the Apocalypse than elsewhere: but they are nowhere free from doubt.

ALT. ἑώρακες Jo 8 57. ἐλήλυθες Act 21 22. πέπτωκας Ap 2 5. εἴληφας Ap 11 17. κεκοπίακας Ap 2 3. ἀφῆκας Ap 2 4. ἔδωκές Jo 17 7, 8. ἀφήκετε Mt 23 23.

FORMS OF CONTRACT VERBS

There is a remarkable consent of the best MSS for ἠρώτουν Mt 15 23. This substitution of -εω for άω occurs here and there elsewhere in one or two good MSS in the same and other verbs, as νικάω, σιωπάω, καταγελάω; but hardly ever has any probability. Κοπιοῦσιν Mt 6 28 has better authority (B 33), but may be due to accidental coincidence in assimilation to the preceding αὐξάνουσιν and the following νήθουσιν. Conversely ἐλεάω[4] and ἐλλογάω[2] are sufficiently attested, except each in one place (the difference of attestation in Ro 9 16 and 18 is singular): the former word has good authority 5/5 times in LXX (not Apocr[2]). Ἐμβριμῶμαι and ·οῦμαι are

both well attested. The best MSS have ἡσσώθητε 2 Co 12 13 after the analogy of ἐλασσόω (the verb is known in its Ionic form ἐσσόω from Herodotus); 2 Pe[2] has ἥττηται, ἡττῶνται, Paul[2] ἥττημα. A form αἰτιόομαι, otherwise unknown except through αἰτίωσις cited from Eustathius, seems to be implied in the abundantly attested αἰτιώματα of Act 25 7 (Ro[1] has προῃτιασάμεθα): αἰτίωμα finds a curious parallel in *oroma* (ὅραμα), 'vision', in the *Pass. Perp. et Felic.* 7, 10.

In 1 Co 11 6, where no MSS have ξυρεῖσθαι, we have followed our predecessors in printing ξυρᾶσθαι: but the combination with κείρασθαι justifies Heinrici in preferring ξύρασθαι, an aor. cited by Dr Veitch from Plutarch and 'Lucian'.

Ἐξουθενέω is the only tolerably attested form 9/11 times (Lc Act Paul), though ἐξουθενόω or ἐξουδενόω or both have some slight evidence 5/9 times. But Mc.1/1 -ωθῇ, though less probable than -ηθῇ, is too well attested to be rejected: the consonant is certainly δ.

The contracted ἐδεῖτο is better attested than ἐδέετο Lc[1] (see P. Buttmann *G. G.*[2] ii 150 f.; Schäfer *Greg. Cor.* 431 f.), though not free from doubt: πλέειν Act 27 2 is supported by two good cursives only (112 137), and ἀποπλεῖν Act[1] ἐξέπλει Act[1] stand without var.: L Chr[1] alone have πνέει Jo[1]. On ἐκχέετε and συνέχεον see above, p. 165.

In Paul[3] and Ap[2] ἐρρέθη (-ησαν) alone is well attested: in Mt[6] ἐρρήθη is throughout supported by BD, and is perhaps right.

On the inf. -οῦν of verbs in -όω see *Introd.* § 413. The evidence is small, but of good quality. Apparently the only exception, and that probably due only to accidental defect of evidence, is πληροῦν Lc 9 31 (πληροῖν lt 59).

[The occurrence of ζηλοῦτε (Ga 4 17) and φυσιοῦσθε (1 Co 4 6) after ἵνα is noticed below, p. 171. In two other cases the context gives reason to suspect that forms of verbs in -όω apparently belonging to the pres. indic. ought perhaps to be referred to the pres. conj.:—ἤ παραζηλοῦμεν (*aemulemur g am*) τὸν κύριον; μὴ ἰσχυρότεροι αὐτοῦ ἐσμέν; 1 Co 10 22; μὴ νοοῦντες μήτε ἃ λέγουσιν μήτε περὶ τίνων διαβεβαιοῦνται 1 Ti 1 7 (cf. Ro 8 26). On the other hand the N. T. contains no distinctive form of the pres. conj. of verbs in -όω, unless it be εὐοδῶται 1 Co 16 2, noticed below (p. 172) as more probably a perf., whether indic. or conjunctive. Thus on the whole the evidence points to an identity of the pres. indic. and pres. conj. forms of verbs in -όω in the N. T. H.]

For the 3 pl. aor. 1 opt. the best evidence favours ποιήσαιεν Lc 6 11, ψηλαφήσειαν Act 17 27; while -ειεν is a well attested Alexandrian correction in both places.

ALT. ἠρώτουν Mc 4 10; κοπιοῦσιν Mt 6 28; νικοῦντι (-τας) Ap 2 7, 17; 15 2; ἐλεᾷ Ro 9 18; ἐνεβριμοῦντο (-μούμενος) Mc **14** 5; Jo 11 38. ἐλλογεῖται Ro 5 13. ἐξουδενωθῇ Mc 9 12.

ἐδέετο Lc 8 38. ἐρρήθη Mt 5 21, 27, 31, 33, 38, 43.

FORMS OF VERBS IN -MI

Ἀφίημι and συνίημι sometimes have forms that presuppose ἀφίω and συνίω. They are ἀφίομεν Lc¹, ἀφίουσιν Ap¹, ἀφίονται Jo¹ marg. (but ἀφίενται Mt² Mc²), συνίουσιν Mt¹ (but συνιᾶσιν 2 Co¹), and συνίων Ro¹ from LXX without var. (but συνιείς Mt¹, συνιέντος Mt¹). The evidence for

these forms is ample in the places cited, though elsewhere they appear merely as Western readings. That they do not belong to contract verbs is proved by ἀφίονται and ἤφιεν. But ἀφεῖς (2 sing. pres. ind.) of Ap 2 20 is best explained by the supposition that ἀφέω existed by the side of ἀφίω, and must thus be accented ἀφεῖς; and this analogy accounts for συνειτε (pres. ind. from συνέω, not aor. from συνίημι), the reading of B in Mc¹. Compare P. Buttmann *G.G.*² i 523.

Δίδωμι (with its compounds), as often elsewhere, has the 'contract' imperfect ἐδίδου: it has also ἐδίδουν pl. Mc¹ Act², but the best MSS read -οσαν Jo¹ Act¹. The verb διδόω implied in the contract imperfect is also seen in the 1 sing. pres. ind. διδῶ Ap 3 9, which follows the analogy of ἀφεῖς, and probably in the neuter participle ἀποδιδοῦν Ap 22 2 (text): the masculine participle παραδιδῶν is a *v.l.* of **N*** Mt 26 46, and of D Mc 14 42; Jo 18 2; 21 20. In Sap 12 19 διδοῖς (2 sing. pres. ind.) is the reading of AB cu². Τίθημι likewise has not only (with its compounds) the usual 'contract' imperfect sing. ἐτίθει², but also the pl. ἐτίθουν Act², though the best MSS have -εσαν Mc¹ Act¹. Here too a contract present existed in the late language, and possibly in the N.T., for it is found in Mc in good cursives (15 17 περιτιθοῦσιν in 13-69-124-346; 10 16 τιθῶν in the same together with 1-28), though not in uncials: τιθῶ (indic.) occurs in Hermas *Vis.* i 1 3; ii 1 2. On these forms generally see P. Buttmann *G. G.*² i 500; *Matthiae G. G.*³ i 482 f.; Kühner *G.G.*² i 644 f.; Lobeck *Phryn.* 244. The uncontracted δίδω of modern Greek cannot be recognised in the termination -ετο of the imperfect, found in the best MSS of the N. T. (διεδίδετο Act¹ παρεδίδετο

1 Co[1]), as in the LXX generally; for it belongs no less to the aor. 2 mid. (ἐξέδετο Mt[1] Mc[1] Lc[1], ἀπέδετο He[1]), and the change in the vowels is here probably euphonic: yet δίδεις (*v.l.* δίδῃς) occurs in the 'Apocalypse of Moses' (Seth) c. 19 p. 10 Tisch. The almost certain reading ἐξεκρέμετο 1/1 seems on the other hand to be derived from a form κρέμομαι, of which there are other traces (P. Buttmann *G. G.*[2] i 518 f.; ii 224 f.).

In Mc. 4/4 Jo. 1/3 according to the best MSS the 3 sing. aor. conj. of δίδωμι (with its compounds) is δοῖ, which likewise is sometimes found (as also ἀποδοῖς 1/2) in Western MSS only (Lc[1] Jo[1] Paul[2]): the 3 sing. pres. conj. occurs but once (1 Co 15 24), and there παραδιδοῖ (BG₃) may safely be treated as Western only: the mood is certainly always the conjunctive (see Dr Moulton in Winer *G. N. T.* 360), not the optative. A similar monosyllabic 3 sing. aor. conj. in -οῖ according to the best MSS is γνοῖ Mc[2] Lc[1] (but γνῷ Jo[3], ἐπιγνῷ Act[1]).

A more perplexing form is δωῇ as used Eph 1 17 (text); 2 Ti 2 25 (also as a *v. l.* in inferior MSS Jo 15 16; Eph 3 16). Elsewhere (2 Th 3 16; 2 Ti 1 16, 18) it is distinctly an optative, δῴη; but in both places, and especially in Eph (cf. 3 16), the sense points to a conjunctive: yet its use for two different moods in the same epistle would be strange, and the evidence of a conjunctive form δώῃ (except in epic poets) is not satisfactory (Nu 11 29: cf. Lobeck *Phryn.* 346).

Δύναμαι has in 2 sing. δύνῃ Mc. 2/3 Lc. 1/3 Ap. 1/1 (but δύνασαι Mt. 3/3 Lc. 2/3 Jo. 1/1; 1 Co. 1/1), a 'tragic' form revived or retained in later Greek (see Lobeck *Phryn.* 359 f.). The ample attestation in these four places throws doubt on δύνῃ Mc[1], δύνομαι Mt[1], δυνόμεθα Mc[1] Act[1], and

δυνόμενος (-νομένου Mt[1] Act[1]); all in B only (cf. δυνόμεθα Is 28 **20** B; ἠδύνοντο Is 59 15 ℵ*).

The aor. imper. of the compounds of βαίνω takes the 'contract' form; καταβάτω Mt[2] Mc[2] Lc[1] and ἀνάβατε Ap[1], in all or nearly all MSS; and also μετάβα Mt[1] (best MSS only) and ἀνάβα Ap[1] (but μετάβηθι Jo[1], κατάβηθι Mt[1] Lc[1] Jo[1] Act[1]). The similar 'contract' intransitive aor. of ἵστημι (and its compounds) is confined to 2 sing., ἀνάστα Eph 5 14; Act 12 7 and, with the alternative ἀναστάς, 9 11 (the same *v. l.* recurs 10 13, 20; 11 7): but elsewhere στῆθι[3], ἐπίστηθι[1]; as also στῆτε[2], ἀντίστητε[2], ἀπόστητε[2], ἀποστήτω[1].

There is much variation in MSS as to the present active of compounds of ἵστημι, which often stands in rivalry with ἱστάνω and a contract form ἱστάω. Συνίστημι Ro[1] and συνίστησι Ro[2] 2 Co[2], all without var., alone exemplify the ordinary type. Except in 2 Co[1] the contract forms ἱστάω, ἐξιστάω, καθιστάω, μεθιστάω, συνιστάω may all be safely rejected. We have uniformly printed forms of the ἱστάνω type, for which there is always excellent evidence, though the balance of authority can hardly be said to be in its favour in 1 Co 13 2; 2 Co 3 1. In Mc 9 12 we have printed ἀποκατιστάνει, the reading of B, but with hesitation: it may be either the parent of the two diverging forms or a mixture of them: ἀποκαταστένει, the reading of ℵ*D (cf. the *vv. ll.* ἀποκαταστάνεις Act 1 6; κατα-στάνοντες Act 17 15; both in D), is illustrated by the Cretan στανύω (*C. I. G.* 2556).

Variations between the forms of verbs in -νμι and -ύω are rare, and doubt is confined to 2/3 active infinitives. The few other forms in -ύω, in addition to those of ὀμνύω (Mc[1] perhaps excepted), are 3/3 imperfects, ἀπόλλυε Ro¹, ἀπολλύεις Jo¹, δεικνύειν Mt¹, δεικνύοντος Ap¹; to which may be added Ἀπολλύων Ap¹.

ALT. συνεῖτε Mc 8 17. ἀποδιδέτω 1 Co 7 3. ἐξεκρέματο Lc 19 48. δύνῃ Mc 1 40; δύνομαι Mt 26 53; δυνόμεθα Mc 10 39; Act 4 20; δυνόμενος Mt 19 12; δυνομένου Act 27 15.

ἀποκαταστάνει v. ἀποκαθιστάνει Mc 9 12; μεθιστάναι 1 Co 13 2; συνιστάντες 2 Co 6 4; συνιστᾶν 2 Co 3 1.

δεικνύναι Mt 16 21; ὀμνύειν Mc 14 71.

MISCELLANEOUS FORMS OF VERBS

The rare act. ἀγαλλιάω occurs Lc¹ (1 47) Ap¹ and perhaps 1 Pe. 1/3, ἀγαλλιάομαι elsewhere.

The aor. of δύναμαι is ἠδυνάσθην Mc.1/2 (אB), and perhaps Mt.1/2; not Mt.1/2 Mc.1/2 Lc¹ Act¹ 1 Co¹ Eph¹ He¹.

For ἔζων as the 1 sing. imperf. of ζάω B has ἔζην Ro¹, perhaps rightly: ἐζῆτε occurs Col 3 7, but no other person of the imperfect.

Ἥκασιν as a perfect of ἥκω in Mc 8 3 is merely a Western paraphrase of εἰσίν after μακρόθεν, corrected in turn to ἥκουσιν in the Syrian text: it is common (with ἥκαμεν) in the LXX. Στήκω, a verb analogous to ἥκω, exhibits στήκετε after ὅταν Mc¹ and ἐάν 1 Th¹ with much better authority than -ετε (or -εσθε) elsewhere obtains as against -ητε (or -ησθε) after these or similar particles, as though the form στήκητε were purposely avoided: Chrys. *Eph.* 170 c uses ἕως ἂν στήκωμεν; the best MSS have στήκοντες Mc 3 31 (στήκον being also a Western variant for the difficult ἑστηκότα of

Mc 13 14), and B στήκειν 1 Reg 8 11.

The use of the pres. conj. of διώκω, likewise a verb in -κω, is also uncertain: διώκομεν is the best attested reading Ro 14 19, where any indicative sense is difficult to maintain; and ἵνα … μὴ διώκονται has much good authority (though not אBD₂) Ga 6 12: in Mt 10 23 however, the only remaining instance of a pres. conj. in form or sense, there is no satisfactory evidence for ὅταν … διώκουσιν.

Ἐθαυμάσθην, a true passive 2 Th¹, is found in a middle sense in a few of the best MSS Ap 13 3, and so θαυμασθήσομαι 17 8 (AP₂). For illustrative evidence see Veitch *I. D. V.* 305 f.

The perf. part. of ἵσταμαι is commonly ἑστώς, occasionally ἑστηκώς.

The variations of ἀποκτείνω and ἀποκτέννω are somewhat difficult. Ἀποκτέννω must certainly be read Ap 6 11 (ἀποκτείνωσιν 9 5, 15 is an aor.), and perhaps everywhere else: it is supported by all MSS but B in Mt 10 28 ‖ Lc 12 4; 2 Co 3 6 (in these three passages it might properly stand in the text); while -είνω has the better evidence in Mt 23 37, and still more in the ‖ Lc 13 34. In Mc 12 5 ἀποκτέννυντες, the reading of B and two or more lectionaries, indirectly supported by other unique variants (ἀποκτίννυντες, ἀποκτείννυντες, ἀποκτιννοῦντες, ἀποκτενοῦντες), is probably right: the MSS of Plutarch *Mor.* 1064 c have ἀποκτέννυσιν (Wyttenbach *Ind.*); ἀποκτέννυσθαι has been substituted for Petau's conjectural (Attic) ἀποκτίννυσθαι by W. Dindorf in Epiph. i 430 D on undivided manuscript authority; and other evidence is given by L. Dindorf in Steph.-Didot ii 1506; iv 2031 A. Compare Curtius *Gr. Verb.*² i 170.

Λείπω (with its compounds) has

the 'aor. 1' once (Act¹) καταλείψαντας (but καταλιπόντες Act¹): there is some good authority Mc¹ for καταλείψῃ (so doubtless must be read the variants καταλίψῃ, καταλείψει), and it may be right.

The best MSS have διορυχθῆναι Lc¹, but διορυγῆναι is as well attested Mt¹. Analogous forms are ψυγήσεται Mt¹; ἡρπάγη, ἁρπαγέντα, 2 Co², ἁρπαγησόμεθα 1 Th¹ (but ἡρπάσθη Ap¹ in the best MSS); ἐκρύβη Lc¹ Jo² He¹, κρυβῆναι Mt¹ 1 Ti¹, περιέκρυβεν Lc¹ (these eleven virtually without var.); ἠνοίγησαν Mc¹, ἠνοίγη Act¹ (these two in the best MSS only: also Lc 24 31 in א*(D)) Ap², ἀνοιγήσεται Mt¹ᵛ·² Lc¹ᵛ·², besides other forms of ἀνοίγω mentioned above, p. 161.

Ἀναπαήσονται Ap.1/2 (אAC) and ἐπαναπαήσεται Lc¹ (אB) are sufficiently attested (but ἀναπαύσονται Ap¹, παύσῃ Act¹, παύσονται 1 Co¹). Analogous forms are κατεκάη Ap³, κατακαήσεται 1 Co¹ (but κατακαυθήσεται Ap¹); παραρυῶμεν He¹ (but ῥεύσουσιν Jo¹); and παρεισεδύησαν (B) Jud¹ (διεκδυῆναι is cited from Hippocrates); and the comparatively common φυέν Lc², συνφυεῖσαι Lc¹.

The singular form ἀκαταπάστους (AB) of 2 Pe 2 14 might be explained as equivalent to the ἀκαταπαύστους of the common texts on the strength of ἀναπαήσονται (also ἐπάην, ἀνεπάην, cited by Veitch I. D. V. 516) ; of ἀναπάεσθε, the reading of D in Mc 14 41; and of a Roman epitaph (C.I.G. 6595) with the words ὧδε ἀναπάεται: compare ἀναπαμός=ἀνάπαυσις in a glossary quoted by Ducange p. 70. The same sense might be obtained from another dialectic modification of παύω preserved in two glosses of Hesychius, ἀμπάζονται· ἀναπαύονται and ἀμπάξαι· παῦσαι. Λάκωνες. But the better sense 'insatiable' is pro

vided by an altogether different verb πάσασθαι (from πατέομαι). After pointing out that in Homer this word means no more than 'to taste', Athenæus adds in contrast (i 43 p. 24 A) Οἱ δὲ νεώτεροι καὶ ἐπὶ τοῦ πληρωθῆναι τιθέασι τὸ πάσασθαι; abridged in a Fragm. Lex. Gr. (in Hermann De em. p. 323) with κορεσθῆναι substituted for πληρωθῆναι. Ἀκατάπαστος is therefore exactly similar to ἄπαστος (ἀπαστία, ἀπαστί).

Πεῖν (καταπεῖν) as the aor. 2 inf. of πίνω occurs everywhere but Mt 20 22 among the variants, and has much good evidence Jo.3/3 1 Co. 2/2. It is often found in MSS of the LXX; and its actual use is shown by an epigram (A.P. xi 140, Lucillus), and by the unfavourable notice of Ps.Herodianus (in Hermann De em. 317). The testimony of MSS is in favour of πειν (A¹. C³.D⁶. L². Tb². D₂². G₃¹, besides B⁸) as against πιν (A¹. C¹. L¹. D₂¹. G₃¹, besides א⁸).

Ῥεραμμένον (περιρεραμμένον א*), from ῥαίνω, suggested in the note on Ap 19 13 as the one reading which will account for the several variants, is a word containing two peculiar elements, for each of which independently there is some little extraneous evidence. Lobeck cites the reduplicated form καταρεραϲμένος from two places of Galen; and the termination -αμμένος, more commonly -ασμένος or -αμένος, occurs in 2 MSS of Athenæus (iv 18, p. 140, from Persæus), ἄλφιτα ἐλαίῳ ἐρραμμένα. See Veitch I. D. V. 571; Kühner G. G.² i. 508, 901.

The fut. and aor. of στηρίζω are in the better MSS ἐστήρισεν Lc¹ (and perhaps ἐπεστήρισαν Act¹), στήρισον Lc¹ Ap¹ (and perhaps στηρίσει 2 Th¹), but not fut. 1 Pe¹, aor. Ja¹ Paul⁴. Analogous forms are σαλπίσω 1 Co¹, ἐσάλπισα Mt¹ Ap⁸, σαλπιστής Ap¹.

The existence of ἐστρέφθην for-

bids the total rejection of -εμμένος
Mt¹ (Z) Act¹ (B): in Lc¹ Act¹ Phi¹
there is no variation.

The best MSS have λελουσμένος
He¹; but this form has very little
authority Jo¹.

Τήξομαι as a fut. of τήκω (see note
on 2 Pe 3 12, where τήξεται is suggested by one of us as a correction
of τήκεται) is cited from Hippocrates by Veitch *I. D. V.* 632, who
likewise cites τήξαιο and τηξάμενος
from Nicander.

Τέτυχε is probably the perf. of
τυγχάνω He¹: but B as well as the
Syrian text has τέτευχε, τετύχηκε
being apparently Alexandrian.

Of the twin forms σκοτίζω σκοτόω
the N. T. has ἐσκοτωμένος Eph¹
Ap¹, and probably once (Ap¹) ἐσκο-
τώθη; but elsewhere (Mt¹ Mc¹ Ro²
Ap¹) ἐσκοτίσθη and σκοτισθήσομαι.
Similarly B has once ἐκαυματώθη
(-ίσθη Mc¹ Ap¹, καυματίσαι Ap¹).
Ζηλόω is replaced in the best MSS
by the rare ζηλεύω Ap 3 19, κυκλόω
by the rare κυκλεύω Ap 20 9, the
rare ἀποδεκατόω (without var. Mt¹
Lc¹ He¹) by the rarer ἀποδεκατεύω
(ℵ*B) Lc 18 12; and again the
unmeaning ἐκεφαλαίωσαν of Mc 12
4 by the otherwise unknown but
intelligible ἐκεφαλίωσαν.

ALT. ἀγαλλιᾶσθε 1 Pe 1 8.
ἠδυνάσθησαν Mt 17 16. ἔξην Ro
7 9. ἑστώτων Mc 9 1; παρεστώτων
Mc 15 35. ἀποκτεννόντων Mt 10
28; Lc 12 4; ἀποκτέννοντες Mc 12
5; ἀποκτέννουσα Mt 23 37; Lc 13
34; ἀποκτέννει 2 Co 3 6; Ap 13 10
(marg.). καταλείψῃ Mc 12 19. διορυγῆναι Mt 24 43. διηνοίγησαν Lc
24 31. πεῖν Mt 27 34 *bis*; Mc 10
38; καταπεῖν 1 Pe 5 8; πιεῖν Act 23
12, 21. ἐπεστήρισαν Act 15 32;
στηρίσει 2 Th 3 3. διεστρεμμένη Mt
17 17; κατεστρεμμένα Act 15 16.

ἐσκοτίσθη Ap 9 2. ἐκαυματώθη
Mt 13 6.

Substitutions of the indicative in
dependent clauses in which the
conjunctive would normally be employed belong properly to Syntax:
but it is convenient to treat alternative readings coming under this
head as in a manner orthographical.
Although variations are numerous,
doubtful cases are comparatively
few, the aberrant forms having usually but little evidence, and that
for the most part probably due to
itacistic accident.

The tense of the indic. which
thus replaces the conj. is almost
always the future. The only forms
belonging to the present indic. (or
simulating it) that have appeared to
claim a place in the text are the
following:—(*a*) ἵνα γινώσκομεν 1 Jo
5 20 (cf. the alt. reading ἵνα γινώσκουσι Jo 17 3), where there seems
to be a pregnant sense (cf. 3 1);—
(*b*) ἐὰν οἴδαμεν 1 Jo 5 15 (all good
MSS), probably due to the tense;—
(*c*) ὅταν στήκετε Mc 11 25; ἐὰν...
στήκετε 1 Th 3 8;- and (*d*) ἵνα...
ζηλοῦτε Ga 4 17; ἵνα μὴ φυσιοῦσθε
1 Co 4 6 (in both cases all MSS but
a few unimportant cursives). The
third and fourth classes probably
owe their existence to special characteristics of στήκω (see p. 169) and
of verbs in -όω: but it is doubtful
(see p. 167) whether the fourth class
properly belongs to the indicative.
On ἵνα...μὴ διώκονται (alt. reading)
see p. 169.

The last of a series of verbs following ἵνα is oftener found in the
future than verbs with which ἵνα
stands in a more immediate relation. In these cases the distance of
ἵνα might affect writers, no less than
transcribers. The expression of

final result is a natural close to the expression of intermediate purpose.

Except in six places, the fut. indic. has no considerable support after relatives with ἄν or ἐάν, though it is often found in some MSS (chiefly late uncials), evidently by itacistic error. In the six places the evidence is large and good, though not conclusive except Mc 8 35 (2°). The case of ὅτι ἐὰν εὐοδῶται 1 Co 16 2 (text) is peculiar. The context [supported by considerations derived from the form itself: see p. 166 H.] suggests that the tense is probably the perfect; and the absence of augment creates no difficulty, for in the LXX (also Sap[1]; not 1 Mac. 4/4) the best MSS have εὐοδ. in the 13 places (the N.T. offers none such, having only the fut. and pres.) in which an augment could exist. It is less easy to decide whether εὐοδῶται is here a perf. indic. (cf. ἐὰν οἴδαμεν above) or one of the very rare perf. mid. conjunctives, on which see Curtius *Gr.Verb.*[2] ii 247 f.; Kühner *G.G.*[2] i 565 f.

The supposed future conjunctive may be safely dismissed as regards the N.T. on comparison of the only places where it has any good evidence (δώσῃ Jo 17 2; Ap 8 3: see also καυθήσωμαι for καυθήσομαι, itself a corruption of καυχήσωμαι, 1 Co 13 3), the best evidence being unfavourable to it: in Lc 13 28 ὄψησθε, if right, as it seems to be, is an aorist (see Veitch *I.D.V.* 496).

ALT.   ὅπως... θανατώσουσιν Mt 26 59. ὅπως ἂν δικαιωθῇς...καὶ νικήσῃς Ro 3 4 (LXX). ἵνα λάβῃ...καὶ ἐξαναστήσει Mc 12 19 ‖ Lc 20 28; ἵνα σταυρώσουσιν Mc 15 20; ἵνα... ...βλέπουσιν Lc 11 33; (see also marg. Lc 22 30;) ἵνα μὴ διψῶ μηδὲ διέρχομαι Jo 4 15; ἵνα... θαυμάζετε Jo 5 20; (see also marg. Jo 15 8;) ἵνα γινώσκουσι Jo 17 3 (cf. 1 Jo 5 20); ἵνα...ἐπισκιάσῃ Act 5 15; ἵνα ξυρήσωνται Act 21 24; ἵνα ἀφῇ... καὶ καθαρίσει 1 Jo 1 9; ἵνα...ἔχομεν 1 Jo 4 17; ἵνα...μὴ διώκονται Ga 6 12; ἵνα...κάμψῃ...καὶ ...ἐξομολογήσεται Phi 2 11 (LXX); ἵνα σωφρονίζουσι Tit 2 4; ἵνα ἀναπαύσωνται Ap 6 11; ἵνα μὴ ἀδικήσωσιν Ap 9 4; ἵνα...τρέφουσιν Ap 12 6; (see also marg. Ap 13 15, 17;) ἵνα ...μετρήσει Ap 21 15. μὴ...ταπεινώσει 2 Co 12 21. μήποτε συνῶσιν καὶ ἐπιστρέψουσιν (followed by καὶ ἰάσομαι) Act 28 27 (LXX). ἐὰν... συμφωνήσουσιν Mt 18 19; ἐὰν... στήκητε 1 Th 3 8. ὅταν στήκητε Mc 11 25; see also marg. Lc 13 28.

ὃς ἂν ὁμολογήσῃ Lc 12 8; ὃς δ᾽ ἂν ἀπολέσῃ Lc 17 33; ᾧ ἂν δουλεύσωσιν Act 7 7 (LXX). ὅσα ἂν λαλήσει Act 3 22 (LXX); ὅσοι ἐὰν μὴ προσκυνήσουσιν Ap 13 15.

IV. PARTICLES

Variations between ἄν and ἐάν are very numerous, and the distributions of evidence peculiarly irregular and perplexing. Predominantly ἄν is found after consonants, and ἐάν after vowels; but there are many exceptions.

Of ἕνεκεν ἕνεκα εἵνεκεν, between which there is often variation, ἕνεκεν is the commonest, and is almost always one of the variants. Εἶτεν (see Steph.-Didot iii 346 A; 1471 C) replaces εἶτα in Mc. 2/4 in the best MSS.

34

ALT. ἄν Mt 7 12; 14 7; 16 19 *bis*, 25 (1°); 18 5, 18 *bis*; 20 4; 23 3; Mc 3 28; 8 35 (1°); 9 18; 14 9, 14; Lc 7 23; 9 57; 17 33 (1°); Jo 15 7 (2°); Act 2 21 (LXX); Ja 4 4; 1 Jo 4 15; 5 15 (2°); 1 Co 16 2, 3; Ga 5 17; 6 7; Col 3 17; Ap 3 19; 11 6; 13 15. ἐάν Mt 10 42; 11 6; 20 26, 27; 21 22; Mc 6 56 (1°); 9 41; Lc 4 6; 9 5, 24 (1°), 48 *bis*; 10 22, 35; 13 25; Jo 11 22; 15 16; Act 3 23; 7 3, 7; 1 Jo 3 22.

ἕνεκα Mt 5 10, 11; 19 29; Mc 13 9; ἕνεκεν Act 28 20.

μόγις Lc 9 39.

III. QUOTATIONS FROM THE OLD TESTAMENT

The following is a list of the passages and phrases which are marked by uncial type in the text as taken from the Old Testament (see *Introduction* § 416), together with references to the places from which they are derived. Many of the quotations are composite, being formed from two or more definite passages, or from one passage modified by the introduction of a phrase found in one or more other definite passages. Sometimes also it is difficult to tell from which of several similar passages a phrase was taken, if indeed it was taken from one more than another. In all these cases we have given a plurality of references. On the other hand we have abstained from multiplying references for the purposes of illustration; and have therefore passed over such passages of the Old Testament as neither had an equal claim to notice with the passages actually referred to, nor contributed any supplementary and otherwise unrepresented element to the language of the quotations in the New Testament. But in all these points, no less than in the selection of passages and words for marking by uncial type, it has not been found possible to draw and maintain a clear line of distinction.

The numeration of chapters and verses is that of the ordinary English editions. It has not seemed worth while to add the numeration current in Hebrew editions except in the few cases in which it differs by more than a verse or two. The same principle has been followed as to the numeration used in editions of the LXX; for instance, that of the Psalms or of chapters in Jeremiah has been given in brackets throughout: but petty differences in the reckoning of the verses have been neglected. Where a quotation, or a substantive element of a quotation, agrees with the Massoretic text but not with the LXX as represented by any of its better documents, we have added 'Heb.' or 'Chald.' to the numerals, and in the converse case 'LXX'. But we have seldom attempted to mark the limitation in mixed cases (as Mt xxiv 7), or in cases where the difference of texts amounts to no more than a slight modification of the one by the other.

We are much indebted to Dr Moulton for a careful and thorough revision of the list. It was unfortunately too late to make use of his suggestions in the text itself: but we have thought it best to incorporate at once with the list such additions as we should now for any reason desire to make. References to passages that are thus left for the present without uncials in the text are marked with asterisks. In Mt x 6, Lc xxiv 5, and 1 Ti v 5 the uncials may be treated as errors.

ST MATTHEW

i	23	Is vii 14
ii	6	Mic v 2
	15	Hos xi 1
	18	Jer xxxi (xxxviii) 15
iii	3	Is xl 3
iv	4	Deut viii 3
	6	Ps xci (xc) 11 f.
	7	Deut vi 16
	10	Deut vi 13
	15 f.	Is ix 1 f.
v	3 f.	Is lxi 1 f. (*)
	5	Ps xxxvii (xxxvi) 11
	8	Ps xxiv (xxiii) 4 *
	21	Ex xx 13; Deut v 17
	27	Ex xx 14; Deut v 18
	31	Deut xxiv 1 (3)
	33	Num xxx 2; Deut xxiii 21
	34 f.	Is lxvi 1
	35	Ps xlviii (xlvii) 2
	38	Ex xxi 24; Lev xxiv 20; Deut xix 21
	43	Lev xix 18
	48	Deut xviii 13
vi	6	Is xxvi 20; 2 Reg iv 33
vii	22	Jer xxvii 15 (xxxiv 12); xiv 14
	23	Ps vi 8
viii	4	Lev xiii 49
	11	Mal i 11; Is lix 19

viii	17	Is liii 4
ix	13	Hos vi 6
	36	Num xxvii 17; Ez xxxiv 5
x	35 f.	Mic vii 6
xi	5	Is lxi 1
	10	Mal iii 1
	23	Is xiv 13, 15
	29	Jer vi 16 Heb.
xii	4	1 Sam xxi 6
	7	Hos vi 6
	18 ff.	Is xlii 1-4; xli 9
	40	Jon i 17 (ii 1)
xiii	14 f.	Is vi 9 f.
	32	Dan iv 12, 21 Chald.
	35	Ps lxxviii (lxxvii) 2
	41	Zeph i 3 Heb.
	43	Dan xii 3
xv	4	Ex xx 12; Deut v 16
	—	Ex xxi 17
	8 f.	Is xxix 13
xvi	27	Ps lxii (lxi) 12; Prov xxiv 12
xvii	11	Mal iv 5 f. (iii 23 f.)
xviii	16	Deut xix 15
xix	4	Gen i 27
	5	Gen ii 24
	7	Deut xxiv 1 (3)
	18	Ex xx 13-16; Deut v 17-20
	19	Ex xx 12; Deut v 16
	—	Lev xix 18
	26	Gen xviii 14; Job xlii 2; Zech viii 6 LXX
xxi	5	Is lxii 11
	—	Zech ix 9
	9	Ps cxviii (cxvii) 25 f. (*)
	13	Is lvi 7
	—	Jer vii 11
	15	Ps cxviii (cxvii) 5 *
	16	Ps viii 2
	33	Is v 1 f.
	42	Ps cxviii (cxvii) 22 f.
xxii	24	Deut xxv 5; Gen xxxviii 8
	32	Ex iii 6
	37	Deut vi 5
	39	Lev xix 18
	44	Ps cx (cix) 1
xxiii	38	Jer xxii 5; xii 7

xxiii	39	Ps cxviii (cxvii) 26	ix 12	Mal iv 5 f. (iii 23 f.)
xxiv	6	Dan ii 28	48	Is lxvi 24
	7	Is xix 2	x 4	Deut xxiv 1 (3)
	10	Dan xi 41 LXX	6	Gen i 27
	15	Dan ix 17; xii 11	7 f.	Gen ii 24
	21	Dan xii 1	19	Ex xx 13-16 ; Deut v
	24	Deut xiii 1		17-20
	29	Is xiii 10	—	Ex xx 12 ; Deut v 16
	—	Is xxxiv 4	27	Gen xviii 14 ; Job xlii 2 ;
	30	Zech xii 12		Zech viii 6 LXX
	—	Dan vii 13	xi 9 f.	Ps cxviii (cxvii) 25 f. (*)
	31	Is xxvii 13	17	Is lvi 7
	—	Zech ii 6 ; Deut xxx 4	—	Jer vii 11
	38	Gen vii 7	xii 1	Is v 1 f.
xxv	31	Zech xiv 5	10 f.	Ps cxviii (cxvii) 22 f.
	46	Dan xii 2	19	Deut xxv 5 ; Gen xxxviii
xxvi	15	Zech xi 12		8
	28	Ex xxiv 8 ; Zech ix 11	26	Ex iii 6
	31	Zech xiii 7	29 f.	Deut vi 4 f. (two texts of
	38	Ps xlii (xli) 5		LXX)
	64	Dan vii 13 ; Ps cx (cix)	31	Lev xix 18
		1 ff.	32	Deut vi 4
xxvii	9 f.	Zech xi 13	—	Deut iv 35
	34	Ps lxix (lxviii) 21	33	Deut vi 5
	35	Ps xxii (xxi) 18	—	Lev xix 18
	39	Ps xxii (xxi) 7 ; cix	—	1 Sam xv 22
		(cviii) 25	36	Ps cx (cix) 1
	43	Ps xxii (xxi) 8	xiii 7	Dan ii 28
	45	Ps xxii (xxi) 1	8	Is xix 2
	48	Ps lxix (lxviii) 21	12	Mic vii 6
			14	Dan ix 27; xii 11
			19	Dan xii 1
			22	Deut xiii 1
		ST MARK	24	Is xiii 10
			25	Is xxxiv 4
			26	Dan vii 13
i	2	Mal iii 1	27	Zech ii 6 ; Deut xxx 4
	3	Is xl 3	xiv 18	Ps xli (xl) 9
	44	Lev xiii 49	24	Ex xxiv 8 ; Zech ix 11
ii	26	1 Sam xxi 6	27	Zech xiii 7
iv	12	Is vi 9 f.	34	Ps xlii (xli) 5
	29	Joel iii (iv) 13	62	Dan vii 13 ; Ps cx (cix)
	32	Dan iv 12, 21 Chald. ;		1 ff.
		Ez xvii 23	xv 24	Ps xxii (xxi) 18
vi	34	Num xxvii 17 ; Ez xxxiv	29	Ps xxii (xxi) 7 ; cix (cviii)
		5		25
vii	6 f.	Is xxix 13	34	Ps xxii (xxi) 1
	10	Ex xx 12 ; Deut v 16	36	Ps lxix (lxviii) 21
	—	Ex xxi 17	xvi 19	2 Reg ii 11
viii	18	Jer v 21 ; Ez xii 2	—	Ps cx (cix) 1

ST LUKE

xxiii 49	Ps lxxxviii (lxxxvii) 8		iii 25	Gen xxii 18
	xxxviii (xxxvii) 11		iv 11	Ps cxviii (cxvii) 22
xxiv 5	Is viii 19		24	Ex xx 11 ; Ps cxlvi (cxlv) 6
			25 ff.	Ps ii 1 f.
			v 30	Deut xxi 22 f.
	ST JOHN		vii 2	Ps xxix (xxviii) 3
			3	Gen xii 1 ; xlviii 4
i 23	Is xl 3		5	Deut ii 5
52	Gen xxviii 12		—	Gen xvii 8; xlviii 4 ; Deut xxxii 49
ii 17	Ps lxix (lxviii) 9			
vi 31	Ex xvi 4, 15 ; Ps lxxviii (lxxvii) 24		6 f.	Gen xv 13 f.; Ex ii 22
			7	Ex iii 12
45	Is liv 13		8	Gen xvii 10 f.
vii 42	Ps lxxxix (lxxxviii) 3 f.		—	Gen xxi 4
—	Mic v 2		9	Gen xxxvii 11
x 16	Ez xxxvii 24; xxxiv 23		—	Gen xlv 4
34	Ps lxxxii (lxxxi) 6		—	Gen xxxix 2 f., 21
xii 13	Ps cxviii (cxvii) 25 f. (*)		10	Gen xxxix 21
15	Zech ix 9		—	Gen xli 40 f., 43, 46 ; Ps cv (civ) 21
27	Ps vi 3 ; xlii (xli) 6			
38	Is liii 1		11	Gen xli 54 f.
40	Is vi 10		—	Gen xlii 5
xiii 18	Ps xli (xl) 9		12	Gen xlii 2
xv 25	Ps xxxv (xxxiv) 19; lxix (lxviii) 4		13	Gen xlv 1
			14 f.	Deut x 22
xvi 22	Is lxvi 14		15	Ex i 6
xix 24	Ps xxii (xxi) 18		16	Jos xxiv 32
28 f.	Ps lxix (lxviii) 21		—	Gen l 13
36	Ex xii 46; Num ix 12; Ps xxxiv (xxxiii) 20		17 f.	Ex i 7 f.
			19	Ex i 9 ff.
37	Zech xii 10		—	Ex i 18
			20	Ex ii 2
			21	Ex ii 5
			—	Ex ii 10
	ACTS		23	Ex ii 11
			24	Ex ii 12
i 20	Ps lxix (lxviii) 25		27 f.	Ex ii 13 f.
—	Ps cix (cviii) 8		29	Ex ii 15, 22
ii 17-21	Joel ii 28-32 (iii 1-5)		30	Ex iii 1 f.
25-28	Ps xvi (xv) 8-11		32	Ex iii 6
30	Ps cxxxii (cxxxi) 11		33	Ex iii 7
31	Ps xvi (xv) 10		—	Ex iii 5
34 f.	Ps cx (cix) 1		34	Ex iii 7 f., 10; ii 24
39	Is lvii 19		35	Ex ii 14
—	Joel ii 32 (iii 5)		36	Ex vii 3; Num xiv 33
iii 13	Ex iii 6		37	Deut xviii 15, 18
—	Is lii 13 *		39	Num xiv 3 f.
22 f.	Deut xviii 15 f., 18 f.		40	Ex xxxii 1, 23
23	Lev xxiii 29		41	Ex xxxii 4, 6

<table>
<tr><td>\ii 42</td><td>Jer vii 18 LXX; xix 13</td></tr>
<tr><td>42 f.</td><td>Am v 25 ff.</td></tr>
<tr><td>44</td><td>Ex xxv 1, 40</td></tr>
<tr><td>45</td><td>Gen xvii 8; xlviii 4; Deut xxxii 49</td></tr>
<tr><td>46</td><td>Ps cxxxii (cxxxi) 5</td></tr>
<tr><td>47</td><td>1 Reg vi 1, 2 (6)</td></tr>
<tr><td>49 f.</td><td>Is lxvi 1 f.</td></tr>
<tr><td>51</td><td>Ex xxxiii 3, 5</td></tr>
<tr><td>—</td><td>Jer ix 26; vi 10</td></tr>
<tr><td>—</td><td>Num xxvii 14; Is lxiii 10</td></tr>
<tr><td>viii 21</td><td>Ps lxxviii (lxxvii) 37</td></tr>
<tr><td>23</td><td>Is lviii 6</td></tr>
<tr><td>32 f.</td><td>Is liii 7 f.</td></tr>
<tr><td>x 34</td><td>Deut x 17</td></tr>
<tr><td>36</td><td>Ps cvii (cvi) 20; cxlvii 18</td></tr>
<tr><td>—</td><td>Is lii 7; Nah i 15 (ii 1)</td></tr>
<tr><td>38</td><td>Is lxi 1</td></tr>
<tr><td>39</td><td>Deut xxi 22 f.</td></tr>
<tr><td>xiii 10</td><td>Hos xiv 9</td></tr>
<tr><td>17</td><td>Ex vi 1, 6 *</td></tr>
<tr><td>18</td><td>Deut i 31</td></tr>
<tr><td>19</td><td>Deut vii 1</td></tr>
<tr><td>—</td><td>Jos xiv 1</td></tr>
<tr><td>22</td><td>Ps lxxxix (lxxxviii) 20</td></tr>
<tr><td>—</td><td>1 Sam xiii 14</td></tr>
<tr><td>26</td><td>Ps cvii (cvi) 20</td></tr>
<tr><td>33</td><td>Ps ii 7</td></tr>
<tr><td>34</td><td>Is lv 3</td></tr>
<tr><td>34 f.</td><td>Ps xvi (xv) 10</td></tr>
<tr><td>36</td><td>1 Reg ii 10; Jud ii 10</td></tr>
<tr><td>41</td><td>Hab i 5</td></tr>
<tr><td>47</td><td>Is xlix 6</td></tr>
<tr><td>xiv 15</td><td>Ex xx 11; Ps cxlvi (cxlv) 6</td></tr>
<tr><td>xv 16</td><td>Jer xii 15</td></tr>
<tr><td>16 f.</td><td>Am ix 11 f.</td></tr>
<tr><td>18</td><td>Is xlv 21</td></tr>
<tr><td>xvii 24 f.</td><td>Is xlii 5</td></tr>
<tr><td>31</td><td>Ps ix 8; xcvi (xcv) 13; xcviii (xcvii) 9</td></tr>
<tr><td>xviii 9 f.</td><td>Is xliii 5; Jer i 8</td></tr>
<tr><td>xx 28</td><td>Ps lxxiv (lxxiii) 2</td></tr>
<tr><td>32</td><td>Deut xxxiii 3 f.</td></tr>
<tr><td>xxi 26</td><td>Num vi 5</td></tr>
<tr><td>xxiii 5</td><td>Ex xxii 28</td></tr>
<tr><td>xxvi 16 f.</td><td>Ez ii 1, 3</td></tr>
<tr><td>17</td><td>Jer i 7 f.; 1 Chr xvi 35</td></tr>
<tr><td>18</td><td>Is xlii 7, 16</td></tr>
<tr><td>xxviii 26 f.</td><td>Is vi 9 f.</td></tr>
<tr><td>28</td><td>Ps lxvii (lxvi) 2</td></tr>
</table>

ST JAMES

<table>
<tr><td>i 10 f.</td><td>Is xl 6 f.</td></tr>
<tr><td>12</td><td>Dan xii 12 *</td></tr>
<tr><td>ii 8</td><td>Lev xix 18</td></tr>
<tr><td>11</td><td>Ex xx 13 f.; Deut v 17 f.</td></tr>
<tr><td>21</td><td>Gen xxii 2, 9</td></tr>
<tr><td>23</td><td>Gen xv 6</td></tr>
<tr><td>—</td><td>Is xli 8 Heb.; 2 Chr xx 7 Heb.</td></tr>
<tr><td>iii 9</td><td>Gen i 26</td></tr>
<tr><td>iv 6</td><td>Prov iii 34</td></tr>
<tr><td>v 3</td><td>Prov xvi 27</td></tr>
<tr><td>4</td><td>Deut xxiv 15, 17; Mal iii 5</td></tr>
<tr><td>—</td><td>Is v 9</td></tr>
<tr><td>5</td><td>Jer xii 3</td></tr>
<tr><td>6</td><td>Hos i 6; Prov iii 34</td></tr>
<tr><td>7</td><td>Deut xi 14; Jer v 24; Joel ii 23; Zech x 1</td></tr>
<tr><td>11</td><td>Dan xii 12 *</td></tr>
<tr><td>—</td><td>Ps ciii (cii) 8; cxi (cx) 4 *</td></tr>
<tr><td>20</td><td>Prov x 12 Heb.</td></tr>
</table>

1 PETER

<table>
<tr><td>i 16</td><td>Lev xi 44; xix 2; xx 7</td></tr>
<tr><td>17</td><td>Jer iii 19</td></tr>
<tr><td>18</td><td>Is lii 3</td></tr>
<tr><td>23</td><td>Dan vi 26</td></tr>
<tr><td>24 f.</td><td>Is xl 6-8</td></tr>
<tr><td>ii 3</td><td>Ps xxxiv (xxxiii) 8</td></tr>
<tr><td>4</td><td>Ps cxviii (cxvii) 22</td></tr>
<tr><td>4, 6</td><td>Is xxviii 16</td></tr>
<tr><td>7</td><td>Ps cxviii (cxvii) 22</td></tr>
<tr><td>8</td><td>Is viii 14 f.</td></tr>
<tr><td>9</td><td>Is xliii 20 f.</td></tr>
<tr><td>—</td><td>Ex xix 5 f.; xxiii 22 LXX</td></tr>
<tr><td>10</td><td>Hos i 6, 8 f.; ii 1 (3), 23 (25)</td></tr>
<tr><td>11</td><td>Ps xxxix (xxxviii) 12</td></tr>
<tr><td>12</td><td>Is x 3</td></tr>
<tr><td>17</td><td>Prov xxiv 21</td></tr>
<tr><td>22</td><td>Is liii 9</td></tr>
<tr><td>24</td><td>Is liii 12</td></tr>
<tr><td>24 f.</td><td>Is liii 5 f.</td></tr>
<tr><td>iii 6</td><td>Gen xviii 12</td></tr>
</table>

iii	6	Prov iii 25	iv 3	Gen xv 6
	10 ff.	Ps xxxiv (xxxiii) 12·16	7 f.	Ps xxxii (xxxi) 1 f.
	14 f.	Is viii 12 f.	9	Gen xv 6
	22	Ps cx (cix) 1	11	Gen xvii 11
iv	8	Prov x 12 Heb.	17 f.	Gen xvii 5
	14	Ps lxxxix (lxxxviii) 50 f.	18	Gen xv 5
	—	Is xi 2	22 f.	Gen xv 6
	17	Ez ix 6	25	Is liii 12 LXX
	18	Prov xi 31	v 5	Ps xxii (xxi) 5
v	5	Prov iii 34	vii 7	Ex xx 14, 17; Deut v
	7	Ps lv (liv) 22		18, 21
			viii 33 f.	Is l 8 f.
			34	Ps cx (cix) 1 *
		2 PETER	36	Ps xliv (xliii) 22
			ix 7	Gen xxi 12
ii	2	Is liii 5 *	9	Gen xviii 10
	22	Prov xxvi 11	12	Gen xxv 23
iii	8	Ps xc (lxxxix) 4	13	Mal i 2 f.
	12	Is xxxiv 4	15	Ex xxxiii 19
	13	Is lxv 17; lxvi 22	17	Ex ix 16
			18	Ex vii 3; ix 12; xiv 4, 17
			20	Is xxix 16; xlv 9
			21	Jer xviii 6; Is xxix 16;
		JUDE		xlv 9
			22	Jer l (xxvii) 25; Is xiii
	9	Dan xii 1		5 Heb.
	—	Zech iii 2	—	Is liv 16
	12	Ez xxxiv 8	25	Hos ii 23
	14	Deut xxxiii 2; Zech xiv 5	26 f.	Hos i 10 (ii 1)
	23	Zech iii 2 ff.	27 f.	Is x 22 f.
			29	Is i 9
			32 f.	Is viii 14
			33	Is xxviii 16
		ROMANS	x 5	Lev xviii 5
			6-9	Deut xxx 12 ff.
i	17	Hab ii 4	11	Is xxviii 16
	23	Ps cvi (cv) 20	13	Joel ii 32 (iii 5)
ii	6	Ps lxii (lxi) 12; Prov	15	Is lii 7 Heb.
		xxiv 12	16	Is liii 1
	24	Is lii 5	18	Ps xix (xviii) 4
iii	4	Ps cxvi 11 (cxv 2)	19	Deut xxxii 21
	—	Ps li (l) 4	20 f.	Is lxv 1 f.
	10 ff.	Ps xiv (xiii) 1 ff.	xi 1 f.	Ps xciv (xciii) 14; 1 Sam
	13	Ps v 9		xii 22
	—	Ps cxl (cxxxix) 3	3	1 Reg xix 10
	14	Ps x 7 (ix 28)	4	1 Reg xix 18
	15 ff.	Is lix 7 f.	8	Is xxix 10; Deut xxix 4
	18	Ps xxxvi (xxxv) 1	9 f.	Ps lxix (lxviii) 22 f.; Ps
	20	Ps cxliii (cxlii) 2		xxxv (xxxiv) 8
			11	Deut xxxii 21

EPHESIANS

i 18   Deut xxxiii f.
  20   Ps cx (cix) 1
  22   Ps viii 6
ii 13 f., 17 Is lvii 19; lii 7
  20   Is xxviii 16
iv 8 f. Ps lxviii (lxvii) 18
  25   Zech viii 16
  26   Ps iv 4
v 2   Ps xl (xxxix) 6
  —   Ez xx 41
  18   Prov xxiii 31 LXX
  31   Gen ii 24
vi 2 f. Ex xx 12; Deut v 16
  4   Prov iii 11; Is l 5
  —   Prov ii 2 LXX, 5
  14   Is xi 5
  —   Is lix 17
  15   Is lii 7
  —   Is xl 3, 9
  17   Is lix 17
  —   Is xi 4; xlix 2; li 16;
       Hos vi 5

PHILIPPIANS

i 19   Job xiii 16
ii 10 f. Is xlv 23
  15   Deut xxxii 5
  16   Is xlix 4; lxv 23
iv 3   Ps lxix (lxviii) 28 *
  18   Ez xx 41

COLOSSIANS

ii 3   Is xlv 3; Prov ii 3 f.
  22   Is xxix 13
iii 1   Ps cx (cix) 1
  10   Gen i 27

1 THESSALONIANS

ii 4   Jer xi 20
  16   Gen xv 16

iv 5   Jer x 25; Ps lxxix
      (lxxviii) 6
  6   Ps xciv (xciii) 1
  8   Ez xxxvii 14
v 8   Is lix 17
  22   Job i 1; ii 3

2 THESSALONIANS

i 8   Is lxvi 14 f.
  —   Jer x 25; Ps lxxix
      (lxxviii) 6
  9 f. Is ii 10 f., 19, 21
  10   Ps lxxxix (lxxxviii) 7;
      lxviii (lxvii) 35 LXX;
      Is xlix 3
  12   Is lxvi 5
ii 4   Dan xi 36 f.
  —   Ez xxviii 2
  8   Is xi 4; Job iv 9
  13   Deut xxxiii 12

HEBREWS

i 3   Ps cx (cix) 1
  5   Ps ii 7
  —   2 Sam vii 14
  6   Deut xxxii 43 LXX; Ps
      xcvii (xcvi) 7
  7   Ps civ (ciii) 4
  8 f. Ps xlv (xliv) 6 f.
  10 ff. Ps cii (ci) 25 ff.
  13   Ps cx (cix) 1
ii 6 ff. Ps viii 4 ff.
  11 f. Ps xxii (xxi) 22
  13 f. Is viii 17 f.
  16   Is xli 8 f. *
  17   Ps xxii (xxi) 22
iii 2, 5 f. Num xii 7
  7-11, 13, } Ps xcv (xciv) 7-11
  15-19   }
  17   Num xiv 29
iv 1, 3 Ps xcv (xciv) 11
  3 f. Gen ii 2
  5 f. Ps xcv (xciv) 11
  7   Ps xcv (xciv) 7 f.

iv 10   Gen ii 2
   10 f.   Ps xcv (xciv) 11
v 5   Ps ii 7
   6   Ps cx (cix) 4
   9   Is xlv 17 *
   10   Ps cx (cix) 4
vi 7   Gen i 11 f.
   8   Gen iii 17 f.
   13 f.   Gen xxii 16 f.
   19   Lev xvi 2, 12
   20   Ps cx (cix) 4
vii 1 f.   Gen xiv 17 ff.
   3   Gen xiv 18; Ps cx (cix) 4
   4, 6 ff., 10 Gen xiv 17 ff.
   11, 15, 17,⎫
   21, 24, 28 ⎬ Ps cx (cix) 4
   28   Ps ii 7
viii 1   Ps cx (cix) 1
   2   Num xxiv 6
   5   Ex xxv 40
   8-13 Jer xxxi (xxxviii) 31-34
ix 20   Ex xxiv 8
   28   Is liii 12
x 5-10 Ps xl (xxxix) 6-8
   12 f.   Ps cx (cix) 1
   16 f.   Jer xxxi (xxxviii) 33 f.
   21   Zech vi 11 ff.; Num
       xii 7 (*)
   27   Is xxvi 11 LXX
   28   Deut xvii 6
   29   Ex xxiv 8
   30   Deut xxxii 35 f.
   37   Is xxvi 20 *
   37 f.   Hab ii 3 f.
xi 4   Gen iv 4
   5 f.   Gen v 24
   8   Gen xii 1
   9   Gen xxiii 4
   12   Gen xxii 17; xxxii 12
   13   1 Chr xxix 15; Ps xxxix
       (xxxviii) 12; Gen xxiii
       4
   17   Gen xxii 1 f., 6
   18   Gen xxi 12
   21   Gen xlvii 31
   23   Ex ii 2
   24   Ex ii 11
   26   Ps lxxxix (lxxxviii) 50 f.;
       lxix (lxviii) 9
   28   Ex xii 21 ff.

xii 2   Ps cx (cix) 1
   3   Num xvi 38 (xvii 3)
   5-8   Prov iii 11 f.
   12   Is xxxv 3 Heb.
   13   Prov iv 26 LXX
   14   Ps xxxiv (xxxiii) 14
   15   Deut xxix 18 LXX
   16   Gen xxv 33
   18 f.   Deut iv 11 f.
   19   Ex xix 16
   —   Deut v 23, 25 f.
   20   Ex xix 12 f.
   21   Deut ix 19
   26 f.   Hag ii 6
   29   Deut iv 24
xiii 5   Deut xxxi 6, 8; Jos i 5
   6   Ps cxviii (cxvii) 6
   11, 13 Lev xvi 27
   15   Ps l (xlix) 14; Lev vii
       12 (2); 2 Chr xxix 31
   —   Is lvii 19 Heb.; Hos
       xiv 2
   20   Is lxiii 11
   —   Zech ix 11
   —   Is lv 3; Ez xxxvii 26

1 TIMOTHY

v 18   Deut xxv 4
   19   Deut xix 15

2 TIMOTHY

ii 19   Num xvi 5
   —   Is xxvi 13
iv 14   Ps lxii (lxi) 12; Prov
       xxiv 12
   17   Ps xxii (xxi) 21

TITUS

ii 14   Ps cxxx (cxxix) 8 *
   —   Ez xxxvii 23
   —   Deut xiv 2

APOCALYPSE

i 1	Dan ii 28
4	Ex iii 14; Is xli 4
—	Ps lxxxix (lxxxviii) 37
—	Ps lxxxix (lxxxviii) 27
—	Ps cxxx (cxxix) 8; Is xl 2
6	Ex xix 6
7	Dan vii 13
—	Zech xii 10, 12, 14
8	Ex iii 14; Is xli 4
—	Am iv 13 LXX
13	Dan vii 13; Ez i 26; viii 2
—	Ez ix 2 f. LXX, 11 LXX
—	Dan x 5 Chald.
14	Dan vii 9
14 f.	Dan x 6
15	Ez i 24; xliii 2 Heb.
16	Jud v 31
17	Dan x 12, 19
—	Is xliv 6 Heb.; xlviii 12 Heb.
19	Is xlviii 6 ; Dan ii 29 Chald.
20	Dan ii 29 *
ii 7	Gen ii 9; iii 22; Ez xxxi 8
8	Is xliv 6 Heb.; xlviii 12 Heb.
10	Dan i 12, 14
14	Num xxxi 16
—	Num xxv 1 f.
17	Ps lxxviii (lxxvii) 24 *
—	Is lxii 2; lxv 15
18	Dan x 6
20	Nu xxv 1 f.
23	Jer xvii 10; Ps vii 9; lxii (lxi) 12
26 f.	Ps ii 8 f.
iii 5	Ex xxxii 33 ; Ps lxix (lxviii) 28
7	Is xxii 22
9	Is xlv 14; xlix 23; lx 14 Heb.; lxvi 23
—	Is xliii 4
12	Ez xlviii 35
—	Is lxii 2; lxv 15
14	Ps lxxxix (lxxxviii) 37

iii 14	Prov viii 22
17	Hos xii 8
19	Prov iii 12 (two texts of LXX)
iv 1	Ex xix 16, 24
—	Dan ii 29
2	Is vi 1; Ps xlvii (xlvi) 8
3	Ez i 26 ff.
5	Ez i 13
—	Ex xix 16 (Heb. + LXX)
6	Ez i 5, 18, 22, 26; x 1
—	Is vi 1 f.
7	Ez i 10; x 14
8	Is vi 2 f.
—	Ez i 18; x 12
—	Am iv 13 LXX
—	Ex iii 14; Is xli 4
9 f.	Is vi 1; Ps xlvii (xlvi) 8
—	Dan iv 34; vi 26; xii 7
v 1	Is vi 1; Ps xlvii (xlvi) 8
—	Ez ii 9 f.
—	Is xxix 11
5	Gen xlix 9
— —	Is xi 10
6	Is liii 7
—	Zech iv 10
7	Is vi 1; Ps xlvii (xlvi) 8
8	Ps cxli (cxl) 2
9	Ps cxliv (cxliii) 9
10	Ex xix 6
11	Dan vii 10
12	Is liii 7
13	Is vi 1; Ps xlvii (xlvi) 8
vi 2, 4 f.	Zech i 8; vi 2 f., 6
8	Hos xiii 14
—	Ez xxxiii 27; xiv 21; v 12
—	Ez xxix 5; xxxiv 28
10	Zech i 12
—	Deut xxxii 43; 2 Reg ix 7
—	Hos iv 1
12	Joel ii 31
13 f.	Is xxxiv 4; xiii 10
15	Ps xlviii (xlvii) 4 LXX; ii 2; Is xxiv 21; xxxiv 12
—	Jer iv 29; Is ii 10
16	Hos x 8
—	Is vi 1; Ps xlvii (xlvi) 8
17	Joel ii 11; Zeph i 14 f., 18
—	Mal iii 2